Preparing for
Career Success

Preparing for
Career Success

Jerry Ryan

Career Education Consultant
Akron, Ohio

Roberta Ryan

Career Education Consultant
Akron, Ohio

WEST PUBLISHING COMPANY

MINNEAPOLIS / ST. PAUL   NEW YORK   SAN FRANCISCO   LOS ANGELES

Copyedit: Judith Mara Riotto
Proofreading: Jennifer Miller, Jill Thomas
Index: Maggie Jarpey
Composition: American Composition & Graphics, Inc.
Cover image: Profiles West, Comstock, and PhotoEdit
Interior photography: PhotoEdit, Dana White Productions,
David Hanover Photography—*Complete photo credits listed after index*

WEST'S COMMITMENT TO THE ENVIRONMENT

In 1906, West Publishing Company began recycling materials left over from the production of books. This began a tradition of efficient and responsible use of resources. Today, 100% of our legal bound volumes are printed on acid-free, recycled paper consisting of 50% new paper pulp and 50% paper that has undergone de-inking process. We also use vegetable-based inks to print all of our books. West also recycles nearly 27,700,000 pounds of scrap paper annually—the equivalent of 229,300 trees. Since the 1960s, West has devised ways to capture and recycle waste inks, solvents, oils, and vapors created in the printing process. We also recycle plastics of all kinds, wood, glass, corrugated cardboard, and batteries, and have eliminated the use of polystyrene book packaging. We at West are proud of the longevity and the scope of our commitment to the environment.

West pocket parts and advance sheets are printed on recyclable paper and can be collected and recycled with newspapers. Staples do not have to be removed. Bound volumes can be recycled after the cover has been removed.

Production, Prepress, Printing and Binding by West Publishing Company.

TEXT IS PRINTED ON 10% POST CONSUMER RECYCLED PAPER

British Library Cataloguing-in-Publication Data. A catalogue record for this book is available from the British Library.

Library of Congress Cataloging–in–Publication Data

Ryan, Jerry
        Preparing for career success / Jerry Ryan, Roberta Ryan.
              p.   cm.
        Includes index.
ISBN 0-314-04883-9 (hc : alk. paper) Teacher's Annotated Edition (0-314-04884-7)
        1. Vocational guidance. 2. Career development. 3. Job hunting.
4. High school graduates -- Employment. I. Ryan, Roberta. 1921 -
II. Title.
HF5381 . R796   1996   95-37416
650 . 14--dc20   CIP

Dedication

To our family

To our parents for nurturing us during the first stages of life and their continuous love and encouragement

To our daughters, Bonnie and Linda, for giving us a sense of purpose, returning our love, and becoming our reliable, understanding, and supportive friends as well as daughters

To our sons-in-law for the love and commitment they provide to our extended family

To our grandchildren for helping us remember the joy of laughter and play, the magic of dreams, and the importance of preparing for career success.

Jerry and Roberta

Contents in Brief

Introduction   1

Unit 1 Getting Ready for the World of Work   4

Chapter 1   Life's Many Tasks   5
Chapter 2   Knowing Yourself: Interests and Aptitudes   21
Chapter 3   Knowing Yourself: Values and Goals   44
Chapter 4   Problem Solving: Making Choices   59
Chapter 5   Looking Ahead: Education and Training   72

Unit 2 Job Search and Job Success   98

Chapter 6   Expressing Yourself: Effective Communication   99
Chapter 7   The Job Search   129
Chapter 8   Applying and Interviewing for a Job   150
Chapter 9   Job Success Is Your Responsibility   177
Chapter 10 Making Progress on the Job   195
Chapter 11 Roles, Rights, and Responsibilities   228
Chapter 12 Career Change and Growth   260

Unit 3 Understanding the World of Work   280

Chapter 13 A Changing Workplace   281
Chapter 14 Economics and Work   306
Chapter 15 Entrepreneurs and Small Business Ownership   333
Chapter 16 Researching and Understanding Career Information   356

Unit 4 Living on Your Own   373

Chapter 17 Managing Your Income   374
Chapter 18 Being a Consumer: So Many Choices   401
Chapter 19 Health: You Can't Work without It!   433
Chapter 20 Work and the Family   450
Chapter 21 Civic Responsibility: You Make a Difference   471
Chapter 22 Your Life and Your Career   484
Glossary   495
Index   505

Table of Contents

Introduction   1
Unit 1

Getting Ready
for the World of Work   4

CHAPTER 1 **Life's Many Tasks**   5

Section 1 **Choosing a Career**   6
Section 2 **Work: What Is It, and Why Do People Do It?**   12
Section 3 **Developing Your Career Skills**   17
          Chapter 1 Review   20

CHAPTER 2 **Knowing Yourself:**
Interests and Aptitudes   21

Section 1 **Who Am I?**   22
Section 2 **Personality**   26
Section 3 **Identifying Interests**   31
Section 4 **Working With Data,**
          People, and Things   33
Section 5 **Identifying Aptitudes**   36
Section 6 **Leisure Time**   40
          Chapter 2 Review   43

CHAPTER 3 **Knowing Yourself:**
Values and Goals 44

Section 1 **Clarifying Values** 45
Section 2 **Defining Goals** 49
Section 3 **Attitudes** 52
Section 4 **Planning a Lifestyle** 56
Chapter 3 Review 58

CHAPTER 4 **Problem Solving:**
Making Choices 59

Section 1 **The Process of Decision Making** 61
Section 2 **Knowing Yourself and Career Decisions** 64
Section 3 **Decisions and Goals for Today and Tomorrow** 69
Chapter 4 Review 71

CHAPTER 5 **Looking Ahead:**
Education and Training 72

Section 1 **Education and Training Are Important** 74
Section 2 **High School Is Important Preparation** 77
Section 3 **Apprenticeship Programs** 82
Section 4 **Vocational Training Opportunities** 85
Section 5 **On-the-Job Training, Civilian and Military** 89
Section 6 **Community Colleges, Colleges,**
 and Universities 92
Chapter 5 Review 97

Unit 2

Job Search and Job Success

98

CHAPTER 6 **Expressing Yourself: Effective Communication**   99

Section 1 **The Magic of Language: Understanding**   101
Section 2 **Speaking, Listening, and Responding**   104
Section 3 **The Written Word**   110
Section 4 **Interpersonal Relationships**   117
Section 5 **Conflict Resolution**   123
Chapter 6 Review   128

CHAPTER 7 **The Job Search**   129

Section 1 **Planning Your Job Search**   130
Section 2 **Finding Job Leads**   132
Section 3 **Your Personal Data Sheet and Résumé**   141
Section 4 **Write a Successful Cover Letter**   145
Chapter 7 Review   149

CHAPTER 8 **Applying and Interviewing for a Job** **150**

Section 1 **Job Application Forms** **151**
Section 2 **Preemployment Tests** **156**
Section 3 **Making a Good Impression** **159**
Section 4 **Successful Job Interviews** **162**
Section 5 **Part-time Jobs** **170**
Section 6 **Full-time Jobs** **173**
Chapter 8 Review 176

CHAPTER 9 **Job Success Is Your Responsibility** **177**

Section 1 **Attitude Makes a Difference** **178**
Section 2 **Beginning a New Job** **181**
Section 3 **Laying the Groundwork for Career Success** **186**
Chapter 9 Review 194

CHAPTER 10 **Making Progress on the Job** **195**

Section 1 **Conforming to the Organization** **196**
Section 2 **Being Supervised** **198**
Section 3 **Getting Along with Co-Workers** **205**
Section 4 **Career Advancement Through Promotion** **210**
Section 5 **Labor Unions** **215**
Section 6 **Health and Safety in the Workplace** **219**
Chapter 10 Review 227

CHAPTER 11 Roles, Rights, and Responsibilities 228

Section 1	Employers Evaluate Performance	229
Section 2	The Matter of Ethics	234
Section 3	Federal Rules and Regulations	239
Section 4	Fringe Benefits	247
Section 5	The Work Schedule	253
Section 6	Organizational Training and Education	256
	Chapter 11 Review	259

CHAPTER 12 Career Change and Growth 260

Section 1	Career Success	261
Section 2	Changing Jobs	268
Section 3	Losing Your Job	271
	Chapter 12 Review	279

Unit 3

Understanding the World of Work 280

CHAPTER 13 A Changing Workplace 281

Section 1	The Changing Role of Women	283
Section 2	Issues in a Changing Workplace	288
Section 3	Changing Opportunities	294
Section 4	Preparing for a Changing World of Work	300
	Chapter 13 Review	305

CHAPTER 14 Economics and Work 306

Section 1 **Production and Service Systems** 309
Section 2 **Producing for Consumers** 313
Section 3 **Our Monetary System** 317
Section 4 **Good Times and Bad Times** 319
Section 5 **Technology and Change** 322
Section 6 **A Global Economy** 327
Chapter 14 Review 332

CHAPTER 15 Entrepreneurs and Small Business Ownership 333

Section 1 **The American Dream: Your Own Business** 334
Section 2 **Different Forms of Business Ownership** 340
Section 3 **Planning for Success** 343
Section 4 **Financing a Business** 347
Section 5 **Piles of Paperwork** 350
Chapter 15 Review 355

CHAPTER 16 Researching and Understanding Career Information 356

Section 1 **Reading and Research** 358
Section 2 **Listen and Observe** 362
Section 3 **The Real Thing** 365
Section 4 **Classifying Occupational Information** 368
Chapter 16 Review 372

Unit 4

Living on Your Own 373

CHAPTER 17 Managing Your Income 374

Section 1	Your Paycheck	375
Section 2	Bank Services	379
Section 3	Borrowing and Credit	385
Section 4	Money Management and Budgets	393
	Chapter 17 Review	400

CHAPTER 18 Being a Consumer: So Many Choices 401

Section 1	Necessities and Frills	403
Section 2	Advertisements and the Media: Wanting It All	408
Section 3	Finding a Place to Live	410
Section 4	Consumers Have Rights	417
Section 5	Purchasing Your First Automobile	423
Section 6	Insurance Protection	429
	Chapter 18 Review	432

CHAPTER 19 Health: You Can't Work Without It! 433

Section 1	A Sound Mind in a Sound Body	434
Section 2	Medical Care and Health Insurance	440
Section 3	Substance Abuse	445
	Chapter 19 Review	449

Chapter 20 **Work and the Family** **450**

Section 1 **Dating and Courtship** **451**
Section 2 **Marriage** **452**
Section 3 **Parenting and Work** **458**
Section 4 **Raising Children** **463**
Section 5 **Divorce** **467**
Chapter 20 Review 470

Chapter 21 **Civic Responsibility:**
You Make a Difference **471**

Section 1 **Your Civic Responsibility** **472**
Section 2 **Solving Social Problems** **476**
Chapter 21 Review 483

Chapter 22 **Your Life and Your Career** **484**

Section 1 **The Stages of Life** **485**
Section 2 **Your Career Philosophy** **491**
Chapter 22 Review 494

Solving The Problem

Who Gets the Promotion?   11
Year-round School?   53
A Dead End on "the Easy Road"   76
It Pays to Listen   105
Selecting the Best Approach   158
Where Does Tiffany Belong?   189
Being Pleasant Is Important   201
A Healthy Choice?   222
Fair Choices or Discrimination?   241
Who Pays the Bills?   245
Made in America?   299
Investment Creates Jobs   311
Changes in the Auto Industry   329
Eric Faces Reality   369
Difficult Budget Decisions   397
What's a Fair Share?   455

BUILDING SELF-ESTEEM

Encouragement Makes a Difference   30

Time Well Spent   42

Role Models Are Important   47

Education — A Family Value   55

Success Increases Confidence   87

Jessie Feels Capable   115

Confidence Wins   164

A Feeling of Pride   212

Challenging Work?   264

Persistence Pays Off   274

What's the Message?   287

What's Your Worth?   290

Who Is Robert?   489

PLANNING MAKES A DIFFERENCE

Is Experience Always the Best Teacher?	9
Education and Training are Important	36
Keep Your Eye on the Goal	51
Each Job Is a Learning Experience	70
It Pays to Network	134
A Flexible Plan	254
Will Carrie Hit the Target?	344
Everyday Tasks Are Important	357
Antonio's Savings Plan	381
Rita Shops for a Loan	390
Robert Discovers Comparison Shopping	404
Jackie Plans for Good Health	441
Glen's Plan for Career Success	493

Being Responsible

A Story with Two Endings	24
Small Lies — Big Problems	153
All Work Is Important	184
Unethical, Criminal, or Acceptable?	238
Financial Responsibility Is Important	388
Alan's Honest Mistake?	418

Acknowledgements

The authors appreciate the contributions of the numerous individuals listed. They are especially grateful to Lynda Kessler and Mario Rodriguez of West Educational Publishing for the creativity and organization they added to the text and supplemental materials. The suggestions, contributions, and decisions of our editor, Robert Cassel, have shaped the final content and organization of the entire project. His patience, confidence, and editorial wisdom are greatly appreciated.

Reviewers

In addition, we would like to acknowledge the invaluable contributions of several other individuals who participated in the reviewing of this text:

Dennis Ballard
Naperville High School
Naperville, IL

Alton W. Barnes
Southern High School
Durham, NC

Christopher Black
Bingham High School
S. Jordan, UT

Marguerite Bolerjack
Joliet Central High School
Joliet, IL

Cathy Dickey
Napa High School
Napa, CA

Carol Fogel
Westlake High School
Westlake Village, CA

Ray Fortner
Mt. Pleasant High School
Mt. Pleasant, TX

Johnette Harper
Duncan High School
Duncan, OK

Sondra G. Harroff
Jefferson High School
Louisville, KY

Arlene J. Inglis
Morristown High School
Morristown, NJ

Mildred Landers
Whitesboro High School
Whitesboro, TX

Carol A. Lobi
Chantilly High School
Chantilly, VA

Carol Metzler
Skyline Development Center
Dallas, TX

Kathleen Morris
Caesar Rodney High School
Camden, DE

Juanita Motley
Fairfax High School
Fairfax, VA

Michael J. Nacinovich
Carl Hayden High School
Phoenix, AZ

Gordon Nicholson
West High School
Manchester, NH

Janice M. Pettite
Greece Arcadia High School
Rochester, NY

Daphne Richmond
Mountainburg High School
Mountainburg, AR

Donald R. Shaffner
Granite City Senior High
School Granite City, IL

Jill Simpson
Bethel Park High School
Pittsburgh, PA

Shirley T. Washington
Peach County High School
Fort Valley, GA

Gena Wright
Gosnell High School
Gosnell, AR

Introduction

Are you looking forward to being independent and making your own decisions? Are you concerned about getting a good job when you complete your education and training? If you answered yes to these questions, then *Preparing for Career Success* was written with you in mind.

Acquiring additional education and training will increase your number of occupational choices. As you move from the world of education to the world of work, a few of your high school classmates will decide to drop out and become full-time workers. Others will join the work force after graduation, but most will continue their education and training beyond high school. Which group will you join?

Higher-paying jobs are becoming more complex and technical. High school students, parents, educators, and employers are becoming concerned about the education and training of the nation's future work force. In response to these concerns, many high schools are offering career guidance courses. Some are limited to a few weeks or a semester; others last an entire school year.

If your career course will last only a semester or less, your class will probably not be able to cover the wide range of material in *Preparing for Career Success*. Whether you have a few weeks or an entire year to explore the information in your textbook, the following overview will help you identify which sections deal with your most important career concerns. In addition, you may wish to do independent work in certain chapters.

Unit 1: Getting Ready for the World of Work

Self-understanding is the foundation of a wise career choice. Unit 1 helps you explore your personal characteristics and shows how your major interests, aptitudes, and values relate to various occupations.

A worker's career success frequently depends on attitude. Numerous activities will help you examine your attitude toward education, work, and people. Becoming aware of how you react to people and situations and how people react to you is an important step in your career preparation.

Have you ever examined your role as a student, a son or daughter, a brother or sister, or a friend? An examination of your present roles will help you develop a plan to achieve the adult roles and goals you seek.

You will learn a process for making everyday decisions. You can also use this process to make career decisions.

Next, you will explore several education and training options. This will help you determine the level and amount of education and training you will need for the career path you are considering.

Unit 2: Job Search and Job Success

Effective communication skills are the key to getting and keeping a job. Information in this section will help you improve your interpersonal skills and resolve conflicts.

You will discover ways to find and follow up on job leads. Knowing how to use a personal data sheet and how to compose an effective cover letter and résumé will give you an edge over many job seekers.

After you locate a job opening, you will need to be familiar with job application forms, preemployment tests, and interview techniques.

What are the roles, rights, and responsibilities of workers and employers? What should you do if you become aware of illegal or unethical behavior in the workplace? Learning about specific federal rules and regulations will help you answer these questions.

Once you have been hired, what can you do to be successful on your new job? What will your employer expect from you? How will you be eval-uated? Getting along with co-workers and adjusting to your new boss will require special skills.

You will probably have several jobs during your lifetime. If you know how to adjust to changing job situations, every job on your career path will be an exciting challenge.

Unit 3: Understanding the World of Work

During the first day of your career course, new stores and businesses will open in all parts of the nation, thousands of people will interview for jobs, and numerous families will move to new homes and schools because of career changes. Other stores and businesses will close, and these workers will be forced to seek new jobs. Much of your career success will depend on how well you understand the *changing* world of work.

In most families, the parents are employed. How can you be a responsible parent and a responsible employee at the same time? The issues covered in this section include

- The changing role of women
- The child-care needs of working parents
- Changing opportunities in the world of work
- Job mobility

Career success is only possible if you have a career opportunity. Our economy determines the number and type of jobs available. Learning about supply and demand, goods and services, the profit motive, and our monetary system may not seem very exciting or important. However, these are the forces that influence good times and bad times for workers. How will goods and services produced by workers in other nations affect your career success? What is our government's role in protecting your career opportunities? These questions will be answered in this unit.

Perhaps you have dreamed of owning your own business. If so, you will be interested in this unit. Do you know the characteristics of successful business owners? What form of business will you own? What are the advantages and disadvantages of being self-employed? You will learn how to develop a business plan, check out the competition, determine what price to charge, find a location, and get additional information about starting your own business.

Once you decide on a tentative career path, you will want to learn as much as possible about the occupations that interest you. You will discover several sources of career information. The numerous activities in this unit will help you read and research, listen and observe, and make a plan for acquiring real work experience in the career areas you are considering.

Unit 4: Living on Your Own

Deciding which occupation you would like and getting the necessary education and training is only a part of life. When you begin living on your own, you will need to know as much as possible about finding a home, managing your income, using bank services, borrowing and credit, and maintaining budgets.

Salespeople will be eager to get your paycheck. Television commercials will try to convince you that the only way to be lovable, beautiful, or successful is to buy the product advertised. Learning the difference between necessities and frills and understanding your legal rights as a consumer will help you make mature financial decisions.

Good physical and mental health are necessary for career success. You will learn how nutrition, fitness, safety, and medical care are related to your career. The problem of substance abuse in the workplace will also be explored.

Family issues and how they relate to the world of work may be the most important issues covered in this text. How have men and women changed their views concerning work and marriage? How do the issues of pregnancy, parenthood, child care, workplace flexibility, family leave, and divorce affect careers?

Political and social problems will influence your career opportunities. As a responsible citizen and a worker, you will need to be informed about issues concerning the environment, educational reform, poverty, population growth, and the rights of minorities.

You will learn that your career is more than a job. It is what life is all about. It is understanding children, senior citizens, and yourself; living in a family; being a responsible citizen and worker; caring for the world you live in; and enjoying the rewards of your work. When you understand this, you will be prepared for career success.

A Handbook Of Occupational Clusters

A handbook describing thirteen occupational clusters (groupings) is available with this textbook. The thirteen clusters follow a system used by the U.S. Department of Labor. You will have an opportunity to compare your personal characteristics to the characteristics of successful workers in each occupational cluster. In addition, you will learn

- Where the workers are employed
- Where you can obtain additional information
- What education and training you will need
- How specific high school subjects will help prepare you for employment.

Unit One

Getting Ready for the World of Work

CHAPTERS

1   LIFE'S MANY TASKS
2   KNOWING YOURSELF: INTERESTS AND APTITUDES
3   KNOWING YOURSELF: VALUES AND GOALS
4   PROBLEM SOLVING: MAKING CHOICES
5   LOOKING AHEAD: EDUCATION AND TRAINING

CHAPTER 1

Life's Many Tasks

Learning Objectives

After completing this chapter, you should be prepared to:

- list specific personal characteristics related to the identity stage of development
- appreciate the opinions of others but accept full responsibility for your decisions
- describe how a worker's paycheck, job security, human relationships, and work tasks contribute to his or her level of job satisfaction
- identify nine steps in a career plan and describe how each step relates to your life goals

Enrich Your Vocabulary

In reading this chapter and doing the exercises you will learn the following important terms:

career	equal pay
submissive	human relationships
aggressive	self-concept
assertive	underemployed
drudgery	variety
absolute earnings	delay gratification
relative earnings	

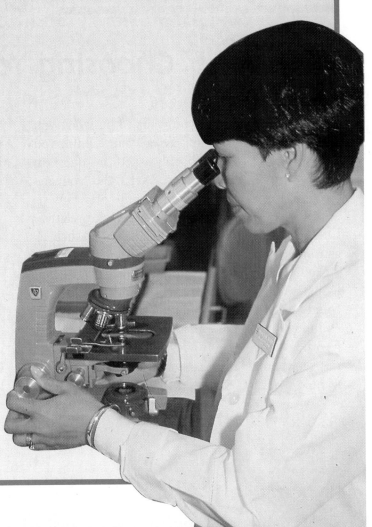

As a small child, you depended on and admired certain adults. These adults handled life's many tasks for you. They provided you with food, clothing, and shelter, and they influenced your opinion about yourself. When you made a mistake or found yourself in trouble, these adults protected you because you were a child.

As you grew older, the adults in your life probably took less and less responsibility for your behavior and decisions. The responsibility for making decisions and living with the consequences of those decisions has probably increased as you've become more mature.

As you move into adulthood, you will face important decisions and responsibilities. To handle them effectively, you will need a great deal of information—information about yourself and about the world around you. You will also need many skills, including skills for decision making, planning, and communication. The list goes on and on.

A key part of adulthood—a part that will have a major impact on all the other parts of your adult life—is your career. Your **career** (the paid and unpaid work you do during your lifetime) will determine:

- how much money you have to spend
- whom you interact with every day
- how much free time you have
- how you feel about your activities and accomplishments

This chapter, like all the chapters in *Preparing for Career Success*, contains information that will help you make the important career decisions you will soon face. This chapter also helps you develop several skills you will need to be successful and happy. After completing this chapter, you will be off to a fast start in your search for career and life success.

Section 1

Choosing Your Career

What do you want to be when you grow up? As a young child, you were probably asked this question many times. What did you answer? Many children give the name of a famous entertainer, a sports figure, or a favorite relative. Others name a "glamorous" occupation, such as astronaut, police officer, or fire fighter.

Young children like to pretend, and they enjoy living in a fantasy world. As a small child, you could be anything you imagined. The fantasies of childhood were like a magic carpet that took you to other lands, let you talk to the animals in stories, and provided whatever exciting career you wanted that day.

As you grow older, the world of fantasy gives way to the real world. As a teenager, you are looking through the window of reality and examining your personal interests, values, resources, and opportunities. Selecting your future career path is no longer a childhood fantasy. Suddenly, it is a responsibility with many tough choices. In the real world, you will need to make some compromises.

It is important to realize that you can be in control as you prepare for career success. Whether you take control or allow others to make your decisions for you, the future will arrive, and you will have a career. Your career will determine your lifestyle and your level of satisfaction with that lifestyle.

▲ *During the teenage years, it is important to consider more than one occupation. What occupations have you considered?*

The Identity Stage

As a child develops into a teenager, the question "Who am I?" arises more and more frequently. Many people answer this question by their early twenties. Others find the answer much later in life, and a few never find a satisfactory answer. The question "Who am I?" or "Who will I be?" must be answered in terms of numerous adult roles:

1. What career role will I have?
2. Will I have a role as a wife or husband?
3. Will I be a parent? If so, what kind of parent will I be?
4. How will my gender affect and be affected by the adult roles I am seeking?

It is common for teenagers to seek out experiences in which they can try out adult roles. Like actors on a stage, they experiment with different life roles. Having these experiences enables young people to discover their unique identities. Can you think of adult roles you have tried? Did you discover that they should be part of your life as an adult, or did you decide that they were not for you?

Four methods used by teenagers to try out adult work roles are:

1. Volunteer work
2. Part-time employment
3. Career exploration ("hands-on" activities at a worksite)
4. Career shadowing (observing a worker's normal routine at a worksite).

▲ *Managing time is as important as managing money. Are you making wise use of your time?*

During the identity stage, good time management becomes an important factor. School schedules require you to complete certain long-range tasks. You might have to integrate a part-time work schedule with your school schedule. In addition, your family might expect you to assume more responsibility at home. When you were a child at play, you could frequently ignore time. Now, hours, days, weeks, and years have become the ruler by which your life's accomplishments are measured.

During the identity stage, young people realize that they will soon be responsible for obtaining their own food, clothing, and shelter as well as the "good things" that they desire. Paying for these items will no longer be their parents' responsibility. At this point in life, young adults can no longer afford a lack of self-confidence. They must have strong feelings of competence and a healthy level

of self-esteem as they prepare for career success in the adult world.

For many teens, the identity stage is a time to leave the self-centered, small world of "me" and join the larger world of "we." It is a time for being true to a personal set of values and being loyal to self, friends, and causes. In the world of "we," adults join together to accomplish productive work tasks.

Planning Your Career

What will your life be like when you are twenty-two years old? Will you be working a job or going to school? Will you be responsible for children?

What will life be like when you are thirty? Will you own a business or work for someone else? Will you drive a new car or own your own home?

It is important for you to take time to plan your future career. Think about how you will support yourself after high school or college. Think about the occupation you are preparing for and the lifestyle you want

You may decide to work in one career area for life, but you will probably have several different jobs. Some people change to totally different career areas during their working life. For example, someone might leave a job in chemical research to become a high school teacher. The worker has not only changed jobs, but has also moved from the broad career area of science and technology to the broad career area of education. Whether you stay in one career, change jobs several times, or totally change your career path, your decisions will be based on a combination of personal choices and available opportunities.

C AREER TIP

When planning for a career, consider what skills you have or will have to offer an employer and what you expect in return.

PLANNING MAKES A DIFFERENCE

Is Experience Always the Best Teacher?

Ted Johnson knew that he wanted to be a bricklayer since he was in the eighth grade. His Uncle Fred is a bricklayer, and together they built a brick barbecue for Ted's grandparents.

After Ted graduated from high school, he entered a bricklayer's apprenticeship program. He hated that first winter. He had to work when his fingers were so cold he could hardly feel them. Summer wasn't much better. Working in the hot summer sun was a lot different from going to the beach or driving around in his car.

Ted felt trapped. He had never considered an occupation other than bricklayer. Ted quit the apprenticeship program and decided that the best way to select a job was to get more experience. Ted has been employed on six different jobs in the last two years.

Stacey Adams began reading about occupations when she was in the ninth grade. The school counselor gave Stacey's class a career interest inventory, explained where to find career information, and suggested ways to use it. The school librarian demonstrated the use of a computerized career information system that contained information about occupations, training programs, and colleges.

Using her knowledge about herself and about possible occupations, Stacey narrowed her choices to the very broad area of construction work. Then she completed a two-year carpentry course at Midway High.

Following her sixteenth birthday, Stacey applied to several small construction companies for employment. She was hired for a summer job doing cleanup work at a construction site. Stacey took every opportunity to ask different construction workers about their job tasks and responsibilities. Stacey also asked how she could get training for that type of work.

Stacey is currently taking a one-year course in construction technology at a local technical college. She is not certain whether she wants to work as a plumber or an electrician. Stacey plans to make her choice when she graduates and then enter an apprenticeship program.

Critical Thinking

1. How would you describe Ted's career plan? How did career planning affect his career success? Give examples to support your opinion.
2. How would you describe Stacey's career plan? How did career planning affect her career success? Give examples to support your opinion.

Can you imagine an NFL football team showing up for the Super Bowl without a game plan? If you are a football fan, you know that the team would lose. Making a career plan won't guarantee your future success any more than making a game plan ensures a football team of winning. However, not making a career plan will probably put your career success in the loss column, and you will have to live with the disappointment. Developing a career plan now will help you achieve a higher level of success later in life.

Your career plan should include the following steps:

1. List your personal and career interests, natural abilities, job skills, academic achievements, and values.
2. Establish short- and long-term goals. It is important to establish dates for reaching your

goals and to identify a method for evaluating your progress.

3. Locate and use occupational information.

4. Identify broad career areas that are related to your interests, talents, and important values.

5. Choose as many occupations as possible within your broad areas of career interest. Make certain that your selections are expected to offer future growth and stability and will provide experiences leading to higher-paying, more desirable occupations.

6. Narrow down your occupational choices to a few.

7. Develop a plan to acquire the education and training you will need to enter the occupations you have selected.

8. Learn job-seeking and job-keeping skills.

9. Decide what sacrifices you are willing to make to fulfill your career plan.

▲ *It is important to have a workable plan before you jump into a career.*

Each chapter of *Preparing for Career Success* contains information to help you develop your unique career plan.

It isn't necessary to leap off of a tall bridge to understand what will happen when you hit the water below. Unless you are using a bungee cord, the outcome of this experiment could result in a personal catastrophe. Similarly, it isn't necessary to make poor career decisions to understand the personal and economic catastrophes they can cause in your life.

Thinking for Yourself

Have you ever had doubts about your ability to make a wise career choice? Should you ask your friends or family what career to select? Choosing a specific occupation is very difficult because there are so many parts to the career puzzle. It is important to get as much information as possible about each piece.

Selecting a satisfactory career path is your responsibility. Wise decision makers ask others for their opinions and carefully consider the advice they receive. However, each individual must accept responsibility for the outcomes of his or her actions and should always make the final decision. If you make a poor career selection, you are the person who will study school subjects you dislike, pay for the education and training that doesn't prepare you for the future, and go to work every day to a job that provides very little satisfaction.

Submissive, Aggressive, or Assertive?

How do you behave with a group of friends? Do you go where they decide and do what they wish even when you disagree? If so, you are probably a submissive person. Submissive people frequently have problems with everyday life situations because of their failure to communicate

Solving The Problem

Who Gets the Promotion?

Jessie Young is a supervisor for the Mid-State Machinery Corporation. He is reviewing the employment files of three workers to determine who will be offered a promotion. All three have good attendance, four years of experience assembling specialized machinery, and all of the necessary technical skills.

The promotion will involve machine installation for customers. It will require a strong knowledge of machinery, the ability to diagnose and solve problems with newly installed machines, and good communication skills. The person selected must be an independent thinker. Help Jessie decide by reviewing the characteristics of the three workers being considered.

Sue: Everyone in the plant considers Sue to be a very nice person. Sue was planning to go to college when she graduated from high school, but she decided to stay home, work, and help her parents with their living expenses. When any subject related to career success comes up, Sue talks about her plan to go to college—someday. During manufacturing team meetings, Sue always goes along with whatever the team wants to do. She doesn't like to rock the boat.

Tony: Most people think Tony is a little hard to take, but even those who dislike him personally agree that he knows more about manufacturing, installing, and troubleshooting machinery than anyone else in the plant. Tony always seems to notice when someone else is having a problem with a machine. He immediately drops what he is doing and gets involved in the other person's situation. His usual opening line:

"Why don't you try doing it the right way for a change?" Tony gets on people's nerves, but he's usually right. It isn't wise to give Tony suggestions, though, because he will probably do it the opposite way.

Ashley: Ashley always tries to do a good job and doesn't get upset about things she can't control. If Ashley doesn't understand something, she asks someone for advice. She doesn't proceed with a job until she is confident that she is doing it correctly. She has even asked Tony for advice, although she considers him to be a self-centered jerk. Ashley takes pride in assembling quality machines. She tries to get along with everyone and is usually willing to compromise. However, when Ashley decides to do something a certain way, that's the way she does it.

Critical Thinking

1. Which worker is best in situations that require independent thinking? Give examples to support your position.
2. If you were Jessie, which of the three workers would you select for the promotion? Why? How would you explain to the other workers why they were not selected?

their beliefs honestly. Their submissive behaviors cause them to lose confidence and self-respect. *Apologetic*, *indifferent*, *passive*, and *yielding* are good words to describe people who behave in a **submissive** manner.

On the other hand, perhaps you refuse to listen to other points of view, argue until you get your way, and tend to become verbally or physically abusive when others disagree with you. If so, you would be considered an aggressive person. Aggressive people try to dominate others. They think for themselves but block out all other points of view. They send the message, "We'll do it my way, or we won't do it." *Unfriendly, insulting, domineering, relentless,* and *quarrelsome* are good words to describe people who behave in an **aggressive** manner.

A third type of behavior is assertiveness. Assertive people think for themselves without becoming angry or aggressive. They can express their feelings and values openly and honestly. Assertive people respect the rights of others, including the right to disagree. They may go along with group decisions even when they disagree, but they never compromise when strong values about right and wrong are at stake. *Persistent, understanding,* and *cooperative* are good words to describe people who behave in an **assertive** manner.

It isn't always easy to express a feeling or an idea that you value highly. Some people or some situations can make you feel awkward or put you on the defensive. You may want to behave in an assertive manner but end up being submissive or losing your cool and being aggressive. Has this ever happened to you? Did you think for yourself in this particular situation?

Submissive, aggressive, and assertive behaviors take place in the world of work every day. They affect a worker's performance evaluations, raises, promotions, and future recommendations.

Section 1 — GET INVOLVED

Answer the following on a separate sheet of paper, and be prepared to discuss your responses in class.

1. List the three people whom you admire and respect the most, in the order of their importance to you. They may be people you know well or people you have learned about from books or television. Have any of these people influenced your thinking about what career you should consider? Explain.

2. Have you done anything to discover more information about yourself, about occupations, or about the education and training needed for certain careers? If so, what have you done? If not, what could you do?

3. What decisions have you made using independent thinking skills? What decisions have you let others make for you?

4. Think of a situation in which you behaved in a passive or aggressive manner. If you could do it over again, what assertive behavior would you use?

Section 2

Work: What Is It, and Why Do People Do It?

Before you choose a career, you should have a good concept of what work is and why people do it. People have many reasons for working. Which of the following reasons are most important to you?

1. "I have no choice. I must work."
2. "I work to pay for my food, shelter, and clothing."

▲ *Some people enjoy training birds or animals. What type of work would you enjoy?*

> Choose a job you love, and you will never have to work a day in your life.
>
> **Confucius**

for your career is an important part of preparing for career success.

Tim Watson is taking a career-planning class at Central High School. His assignment is to write a few paragraphs defining the word *work*. It seemed like an easy assignment before he started writing. The more Tim read about work, however, the more complicated the definition of the word became. Tim decided to interview several workers and ask them for their ideas about work. The following list contains their responses:

1. "Work is the way you get the things that are important to you."
2. "Work is the only way you can survive in today's world."
3. "You only get as much out of your work as you put into it."
4. "Work is doing what someone else wants and getting paid for it."
5. "Being a volunteer or just doing something to help someone can be hard work, and you don't get paid in money. It makes you feel good."
6. "People respect a person who does good work."
7. "I feel good inside when I know I've done a good job."

3. "I work to buy the 'good things' of life—things I want but don't need."
4. "I work to provide my family with an acceptable lifestyle."
5. "I work to feel productive, to make use of my skills and talents, and to gain rewards."

The most mature response is number 5. It implies a desire to be a productive member of society. This response also demonstrates a knowledge of personal interests and how they relate to the work activities of certain occupations. In addition, it considers the personal and financial rewards of the occupation.

The least mature response is number 1. It implies a lack of personal control in the process of selecting a satisfying career. Taking responsibility

Tim suddenly realized that people were using their own words to tell him all of the things he had been reading about work. He decided that work involves all of the parts of a person—physical, social, and psychological. A worker's attitudes, abilities, interests, values, personal satisfaction, and problems go to work with him or her every day. Whether the work involves tools, people, or information, working indoors or out, or

CAREER TIP

Your effectiveness on the job will depend to a great degree on the match between yourself, the job task, and the workplace.

working alone or with others, the worker is involved as a total person.

Tim decided that there's more to work than a paycheck. After all, some people hate their jobs but want the paycheck. The word **drudgery** (dull and tedious labor) seems to describe their jobs better than the word *work*. They regard their work as being uninteresting and disagreeable rather than interesting and enjoyable. Other people volunteer to work for no pay, and they find their work to be interesting and rewarding. Tim concluded that work can be paid or nonpaid but that if it isn't valued by the worker, it isn't work. It's drudgery.

Tim was eager to attend his career-planning class the next day. He was really beginning to understand the meaning of work. The teacher presented a lot of new information, and Tim took careful notes. He wanted to build the following ideas into his report.

The Paycheck

Although work can be paid or unpaid, the paycheck is an important part of most work. First of all, people must have money to pay for their food, clothing, and shelter. Whether you eat macaroni or steak for dinner, buy your clothes at a discount house or have them tailored, or live in public housing or a mansion, your lifestyle is determined by the size of your paycheck.

Your level of absolute earnings will determine how well you live. **Absolute earnings** refers to the amount of goods and services you can buy with your income. **Relative earnings** refers to the amount of goods and services you can buy with

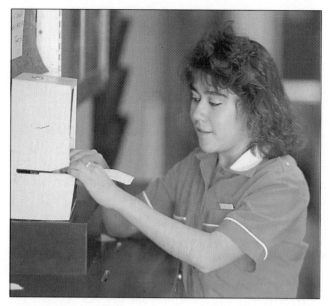

▲ *A satisfying career is more than punching a time clock and receiving a paycheck.*

your income compared with what your neighbors can buy with theirs. Your absolute earnings must be sufficient to maintain an adequate standard of living. However, your relative earnings are an important factor in determining your attitude toward your work and your job satisfaction.

Regardless of their age, sex, or race, people expect to be paid as much as their co-workers in the same occupation. **Equal pay** gives them a sense of personal worth and causes them to feel valued by their employer. People also expect to be paid as much as the employer can afford and as much as might be earned elsewhere.

Job Security

Job security is an important part of work for most people. Job security means that workers can be confident that their jobs will always be available to them. They know that they will have an income and that they need not worry about layoffs.

Job security is one reason many workers seek seniority with one employer. Others work in an occupation that is minimally affected by seasonal

C A R E E R T I P

High pay is effective in attracting workers to new jobs, but it is less effective in holding them on the job.

or periodic ups and downs in business. For some, job security is achieved through hard work and thrift. In today's rapidly changing world of work, job security increasingly depends on a worker's ability to adapt to new situations and to continually update employment skills.

That evening, Tim phoned his aunt Janet to discuss his report on work. Janet is a human relations specialist for a large corporation. She invited Tim to stop by her office the next day.

When Tim arrived at Janet's office, he showed her his report and asked if she could think of any additional information about work. Janet read the report and told Tim that it contained excellent information. In fact, she wanted a copy of the final draft for her office. Janet suggested that Tim might add some additional information about human relationships and work. She provided the following information.

Human Relationships

Human relationships are the personal connections people develop with others through their thoughts and behaviors. Human relationships are a very important work value for some people. The communication skills of reading, writing, speaking, and listening are involved in most successful human relationships. In the workplace, human relationships exist between workers and their coworkers, superiors, subordinates, and customers. To establish and maintain effective two-way communication, all workers need the following:

- Recognition from other workers that they are different in some ways but are still understood and accepted
- A feeling of being important and appreciated
- A certain amount of independence to accomplish their job tasks (this could involve setting the pace of the work, being free from close supervision, or being able to openly express opinions about the work)
- Knowledge that evaluations and rewards are based on fair, clearly understood standards

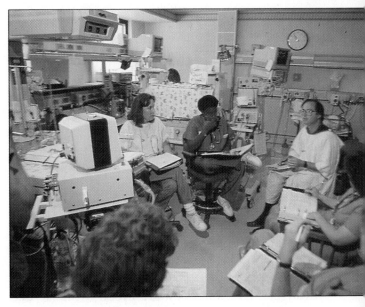

▲ *Solving complex problems requires group thinking. What are you doing to develop your reading, writing, speaking, and listening skills?*

- Knowledge that loyalty will be rewarded

Although most workers must be able to communicate and get along with others, being highly skilled in human relationships is especially important for managers, personnel specialists, salespeople, teachers, and psychologists. What other occupations can you think of that require a high level of human relations skill?

Tim thanked his Aunt Janet for the information and promised her a copy of his finished report. That evening, Tim reviewed all of the material he had collected on work and sat down at his computer to write the last section of the report. He wanted to include a little more information about the work tasks that people perform. He planned to end the report with a summary of the factors that provide job satisfaction to workers and the importance of making wise career choices.

The Work Task

The opportunity for self-expression exists in the performance of a work task if the task provides the worker with outlets for his or her abilities and interests. In other words, the work task and the work situation create a job role that is in keeping with the worker's **self-concept** (how people view their own skills, interests, and competence level).

For some workers, having a variety of work tasks is directly related to job satisfaction. For others, it is unimportant. **Variety** entails a periodic change in the task, the pace, or the location of the work. The physical conditions in which the work task is performed, the way the job tasks are organized, and the availability of equipment and materials all contribute to a worker's job satisfaction.

As he wrote his ideas on paper, Tim wondered why some people seem very satisfied with their work while others consider their jobs to be drudgery. He interviewed several workers and asked them to list the rewards they received from their jobs. Tim used their answers to demonstrate the wide range of job satisfaction, from the highest level to the lowest. See Figure 1.1 for Tim's list. Of the job rewards listed in the figure, which three would be most important to you? Which would be least important?

Tim decided to pay a visit to his school counselor to ask some questions about career decision making. Mr. Rotunda gave him a lot of ideas and let Tim borrow some workbooks from his office. Equipped with new information, Tim concluded his report with a discussion about the importance of career decisions.

Career Decisions Are Important

Work makes an important contribution to workers' self-esteem and causes them to behave in positive or negative ways. Job success usually provides workers with a sense of personal identity, enjoyment, and a feeling of competence. On the other hand, failure on the job may cause feelings of role confusion, anger, depression, and incompetence. How would you feel if you were **underemployed** (overqualified for the job)?

Levels of Job Satisfaction	Rewards of the Job
High	• Paycheck satisfies realistic lifestyle desires • High level of skill provides security and job choices • Job provides prestige at work, home, and in the community • Co-workers are cooperative and supportive • Management has a high regard for the worker's performance • Work is interesting and requires the worker's full ability • Work tasks are valued by the worker
Average	• Paycheck covers more than basic necessities • Seniority and job skills provide some security • Job provides respect at work, at home, and from peers • Co-workers are usually pleasant • Supervisor usually approves of worker's performance • Work is usually interesting • Tasks sometimes require full use of worker's skills
Low	• Paycheck covers basic food, shelter, and clothing • Security depends on the economy and approval of supervisor • Job is considered menial by others • Most co-workers are unpleasant or unconcerned • Supervisor is demanding and lacks understanding • Work is boring and repetitious

▲ *Figure 1.1 Tim's list of Levels of Job Satisfaction.*

CAREER TIP

Choose an occupation you will enjoy. Otherwise, the financial rewards or fame you receive will not be enough to make you happy.

Your work will affect the total pattern of your life—the place where you live, your personal relationships, the schedule you live by, your leisure activities, and your economic security.

There is more than one job that will satisfy each worker, and there is certainly more than one worker capable of satisfying each job. Take time to consider many possible careers, develop a plan, and prepare for your life's work with enthusiasm.

Section 2 GET INVOLVED

Answer the following on a separate sheet of paper, and be prepared to discuss your answers in class.

1. List six characteristics of work. Which characteristic is most important to you? Which is least important?
2. If you won a million dollars and could do anything you wanted with your time, what would you do?

Would the activity you select be work? Why or why not?

3. List ten ways that our society would be different if nobody worked. What useful purpose does work serve?
4. Make a list of the feelings a person might have from being unemployed. From being underemployed.

Section 3

Developing Your Career Skills

Once you decide on a promising career area, you should begin preparing to acquire the necessary skills. For some occupations, a high school education is sufficient, though many occupations require a college degree. Other occupations require the completion of specialized course work or training. The difficulty, time, and cost of qualifying for an occupation vary widely and must be considered in your career planning. Depending on the occupation you select, preparation to begin work may last a few weeks, several months, or many years.

How many years do you plan to work? How much money will you earn during your working life? Some students in your graduating class will decide to increase their job skills before entering the world of work. Others will go directly into the job market. Those who enter the job market directly from high school will make less money during their working years.

If you begin a full-time job at age twenty and retire at age sixty, you will spend forty years earning money. Acquiring additional vocational or technical training, joining apprenticeship programs, and going on to college increase the amount of money you will earn during your working years. Participation in education and training programs requires the maturity necessary to **delay gratification** (postpone the acquisition of certain things or the participation in certain activities). Examine the information in Figure 1.2 before making your education or training decision.

Many states have instituted competency tests for basic high school subjects as a requirement for receiving a high school diploma. It is a well-known fact that the basic skills of reading, writing, and mathematics are related to success on the job. Consider these examples:

Situation 1. Of the companies that responded to a survey about basic skills in the work force,

- 30 percent reported that secretaries were having difficulty reading at the level required by the job,
- 50 percent reported that managers and supervisors were unable to write paragraphs that were free of grammatical errors,
- 50 percent reported that skilled and semiskilled employees, including bookkeepers, were unable to use decimals and fractions in math problems.

Situation 2. One employee in a major manufacturing company didn't know how to read a ruler and mismeasured several yards of steel sheet metal. Almost seven hundred dollars' worth of material was wasted in one morning.

This company had just invested heavily in equipment to regulate inventories and production

Figure 1.2 REQUIRED TRAINING AND AVERAGE EARNINGS FOR SELECT OCCUPATIONS

Occupation	Training Required	Median Annual Earnings 1992	Forty Years of Earnings Based on Annual Income
Fast Food Worker	less than high school	$ 9,734	$ 389,360
Kitchen Helper, Restaurant	less than high school	$11,440	$ 457,600
Retail Sales Worker	high school	$16,770	$ 670,800
General Office Clerk	1 or 2 years associate college certificate or degree	$18,500	$ 740,000
Electrician	high school and a 4 or 5 year apprenticeship	$28,600	$1,144,000
Firefighter	2 or 4 year college degree	$33,072	$1,322,880
Registered Nurse	2 to 4 years nursing school diploma or college degree	$34,421	$1,376,840
Engineer	4 or 5 year college degree	$52,500	$2,100,000

*Training requirements are for average (median) classification
Source: U.S. Dept. of Labor

▲ *Employers assign the most important and highest-paying jobs to their best-qualified workers. What job skills will you be able to offer your first full-time employer?*

schedules. Unfortunately, the workers were unable to enter numbers accurately, which literally destroyed inventory records and resulted in production orders for the wrong products. It cost the company more than a million dollars to correct the errors, which wiped out the savings projected as a result of the new automation.

These employees did not have the occupational skills needed to perform their work accurately. If you were the employer, what would you do? If you were an employee, what would you expect the employer to do?

Section 3 GET INVOLVED

Answer the following on a separate sheet of paper, and be prepared to discuss your responses in class.

1. In situation 1, the difficulty was with reading and writing skills. If all of these employees are fired for incompetence, how can the employer ensure that new employees will perform the work more accurately? Is there a better solution to the problem than firing the employees? Explain your answer.

2. In situation 2, assume that employees who regulated inventories and scheduled production were adequately skilled for their jobs when they were hired. Whose responsibility is it to ensure that employees' skills are upgraded when job skill requirements change? Why?

3. Is your skill level in basic academic courses good enough for employment in the career field you are considering? List some examples to prove your point.

CHAPTER 1 REVIEW

ENRICH YOUR VOCABULARY

On a separate sheet of paper, number from 1 to 13, and complete the following activity. (Do not write in your textbook.) Match each statement below with the most appropriate term from the "Enrich Your Vocabulary" list at the beginning of the chapter by writing that term next to the correct statement.

1. The amount of goods or services you can buy with your income
2. The personal connections people develop with others through their thoughts and behaviors
3. Overqualified for the job performed
4. Apologetic, indifferent, passive, and yielding
5. Unfriendly, insulting, domineering, relentless, and quarrelsome
6. The amount of goods or services you can buy with your income compared with what your neighbors can buy with theirs
7. How people view their own skills, interests, and competence level
8. Persistent, understanding, and cooperative
9. Postpone the acquisition of certain things or the participation in certain activities
10. Periodic change
11. The paid and unpaid work you do during your lifetime
12. Dull and tedious labor
13. To be paid as much as a co-worker in the same occupation

CHECK YOUR KNOWLEDGE

On a separate sheet of paper, complete the following activity. (Do not write in your textbook.)

1. Why are many childhood thoughts about a career considered to be fantasy?
2. The identity stage comes just before adulthood. Why are independence, good time management, close relationships, a commitment to a cause, and a sense of "we" such important preparation for being an effective adult?
3. List five steps that your career plan should include.
4. If you make a poor career selection because you followed someone else's advice, who is to blame?
5. Would you prefer to be supervised by someone who is submissive, aggressive, or assertive? Explain your answer.
6. Providing one definition for the word *work* was difficult for Tim because he discovered that the word means different things to different people. What four main ideas did Tim use in his report to define the meaning of work?
7. List four of the ways that work affects the total pattern of your life.

DEVELOP SCANS COMPETENCIES

Government experts say that successful workers can productively use Resources, Interpersonal skills, Information, Systems, and Technology. This activity will give you practice in developing Information skills.

Develop a survey to find out what people feel is important about their jobs. Use the "Rewards of the Job" listed in Figure 1.1 on page 16 for your survey. List each reward and then list a number scale after each reward. For example, Paycheck satisfies realistic lifestyle desires

Not Important				Very Important
1	2	3	4	5

People should circle the number that indicates how important that item is to them. Have at least 10 people respond to your survey.

After 10 people have completed the survey, total the numbers circled for each item on the survey. For example, if in response to the item "Paycheck satisfies realistic lifestyle desires", 4 people marked 3, 5 people marked 5, and 1 person marked 2, the total for that item would be 39.

After you have totaled the points for each item on the survey, rank the items in order from the one with the highest total to the one with the lowest total.

Those items with the highest totals are more important to people than items with lower totals. How did your results compare with the results listed in Figure 1.1? Were they very similar, or were they very different?

CHAPTER 2

Knowing Yourself: Interests and Aptitudes

Learning Objectives

After completing this chapter, you should be prepared to:

● describe how your environment, heredity, culture, and life experiences have influenced your interests and career goals

● define the personality components of character, temperament, ability, and interests

● explain the relationship between Worker Trait Groups and specific occupations

● explain the effect self-concept has on self-esteem

● identify your preferences for work involving data, people, or things

● give examples of the relationship between your leisure-time activities, personality, and tentative career roles

Enrich Your Vocabulary

In reading this chapter and doing the exercises you will learn the following important terms:

environment	reference groups
heredity	self-esteem
culture	interest surveys
life experiences	aptitude
personality	ASVAB (Armed Services
character	Vocational Aptitude Battery)
temperament	GATB (General
ability	Aptitude Test Battery)
interests	working with data
personality trait	working with people
traits	working with things
Worker Trait Groups	leisure time
self	avocation
social self	

Have you ever heard someone say that she feels "personally fulfilled"? Perhaps you have heard another person say that he doesn't get a "feeling of fulfillment" from his job. What do people mean when they talk about feeling fulfilled?

Your sense of personal fulfillment can be influenced by three things: (1) the extent to which your daily tasks and relationships are interesting; (2) whether you have opportunities to use your skills and abilities to their full potential; and (3) the amount of harmony you enjoy between your personality and the other parts of your daily life.

You will soon enter a long-term career role. The career you select can enhance your sense of fulfillment. This can be accomplished through self-expression, the respect of people who are important to you, and personal feelings of self-worth.

The only person who can make correct career choices for you is *you*. Getting to know yourself better is the first step. Begin by looking at all of your personal characteristics, and discover your uniqueness as a person. The following chapters will help you see yourself in new ways and will help you consider career options you may not have considered before. As you study these chapters, ask yourself the following questions:

1. What strengths or weaknesses do I have for doing and learning certain things?
2. Why do I prefer some activities more than others?
3. Which of my viewpoints are most important to me?
4. How do my personal beliefs and characteristics fit into the world of work?
5. What specific actions can I take to reach my career goals?

Section 1

Who Am I?

As a child, you went forth each day and were impressed by the world around you. The home where you lived, the neighborhood where you played, the major events you experienced, and the people you came in contact with all became a part of you—and you became a part of them.

Environment

From the day you were born you have been influenced by your **environment** (surroundings) and in turn your environment has been influenced by you. The lessons you learned from your childhood environment affected your present values

> There was a child went forth every day,
> And the first object he look'd upon,
> that object he became,
> And that object became part of him for the day or a certain part of the day,
> Or for many years or stretching cycles of years.
>
> **Walt Whitman (1819–1892)**

and interests. They also affected your attitudes towards people, school, and work.

▲ *How has the school you attend influenced your feelings about education?*

▲ *What have you learned from the students you associate with?*

It is important to discover the positive and negative ways your environment has impressed you. Think for a minute about your present neighborhood and its influence on your daily life. Has the neighborhood influenced the way you think about work and workers? If so, how?

Heredity

Did you ever wish you would inherit a million dollars from a rich relative? Most of us would like that, but it's not something to count on. Instead, you can count on inheriting all the traits and characteristics that make up your physical features, intelligence, reflexes, and temperament. These are part of your **heredity** (the transmission of physical or mental characteristics from parent to offspring).

The next time you look into a mirror, try to identify your physical characteristics that are also recognizable in your close relatives. Do you "take after" one family member more than others? If so, how?

You have probably inherited certain talents for music, athletics, writing, leadership, art, mathematics, or working with tools. Can you think of occupations where your special talents would be useful? If so, how?

Culture

The **culture** (way of life in the society in which you live) also influences your attitude toward education and training. How has the accepted way of life in your community influenced the way you spend your time? Your hopes for the future? Your sense of right and wrong? Your career interests?

Behaviors that are acceptable by a certain employer or social group of people, might be rejected by a different employer or different social group. Can you think of a time when you were in a cultural situation that was different from your own and you were embarrassed by your behavior or the behavior of another person?

As a small child, you probably learned that girls and boys were expected to behave in certain ways.

A Story with Two Endings

Lowanda Anderson lived with her mother, grandmother, and younger brother Daniel. They rented a third floor apartment in the central part of a very large city. The neighborhood was littered with trash and endless graffiti provided a means of art expression as well as gang communication. Landlords neglected repairs, and criminals conducted business in the streets. Many families relied on public assistance for food and shelter. Most of the employed people had minimum wage jobs.

Lowanda's grandmother rode the bus several miles each day to a large office building where she was employed as a cleaning lady. Unable to obtain day care for her children, Lowanda's mother stayed home to care for the family.

There was a positive side to Lowanda's environment. Although the family was poor, the apartment was neat and clean. The food was plain, but Lowanda's family rarely went to bed hungry. The family attended church every Sunday.

Lowanda was taught to live by the golden rule and to have hope for a better future. Most evenings, Lowanda's mother would read stories to the children. She would help them with their homework assignments and tell them about life beyond the neighborhood.

Lowanda is presently a student at City College. She also does volunteer work in a tutorial program at her former elementary school and hopes to become a teacher in the inner city.

Lowanda's brother Daniel is serving a six month jail sentence for stealing cars. Unable to find a job when he graduated from high school, Daniel joined a street gang and became involved in crime to acquire money.

Critical Thinking

1. How have Lowanda's environment, heredity, culture, and life experiences influenced her interests and career goals? How has Lowanda influenced her environment?
2. How have Daniel's environment, heredity, culture, and life experiences influenced his interests and career goals? How has Daniel influenced his environment?
3. Why do you suppose Lowanda and Daniel turned out so different?

You also learned acceptable table manners, language, personal hygiene, and what was expected of you in certain social situations. Now that you are a teenager, what is your standard of acceptable dress and behavior for school, church, or going to the mall? What level of education are you expected to complete? Are you expected to pursue a particular career because of your gender? How have you reacted to these cultural expectations?

Life Experiences

In addition to your environment, heredity, and culture, your **life experiences** have been different

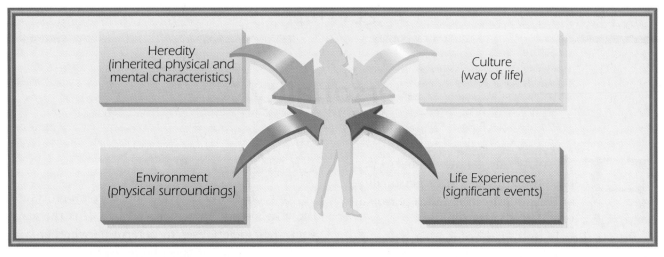

▲ *Figure 2.1 Factors that influence your development.*

than those of other people. These experiences cause you to feel confident or fearful as you prepare for a career, develop friendships, or enter into a lifelong relationship. What positive or negative influence would you expect each of the following life experiences to have on a child's development?

1. The parents abuse alcohol or drugs.
2. The child participates in a statewide musical festival.
3. The child watches a loved one die a violent death.
4. The child enjoys a family vacation.
5. The child is abused at home.
6. The child wins free tickets to a major event for

having good grades.

What life experiences have influenced you? How have they affected your attitudes and decisions?

Exploring your past experiences will increase your understanding of your career interests, ambitions, values, and skills. Self-understanding will help you to gain more control over your life as you prepare for career success. The adult person you become will be a mixture of your environment, heredity, culture, and significant life experiences. Figure 2.1 demonstrates how these important factors overlap each other as they influence your development.

Section 1 GET INVOLVED

Answer the following on a separate sheet of paper and be prepared to discuss your answers in class.

1. In your classroom, what cultural groups are represented? African American? Latin? Asian? American Indian? Euro American? Do members of these groups stick together or mingle freely with other cultural groups? Can you think of a situation where you have been re-

jected or accepted by other people because of your cultural background?

2. List three of your important childhood memories. Examples could include memories of family, school, places, friends, or major events. How did the events you have remembered influence you to become the person you are?

Personality

How many times have you heard people say, "He has a nice personality," or "She doesn't have much personality"? What do they mean?

Personality is the relationship that exists between all of a person's psychological parts. These parts are internal (within the person) and cannot be observed easily by others. These inner parts are referred to as the *self*.

Personality determines the unique way that each person influences and responds to his or her surroundings, to new situations, and to other people. Most psychologists believe that personality is formed early in childhood. They also believe that major changes from early patterns of behavior are rare. However, gradual changes take place within all of us every day. Just as the wind slowly changes the face of a desert, gradual shifts in personal attitudes and beliefs change the way a maturing person adjusts to personal, interpersonal, and social situations.

Four terms are frequently used to describe the parts of personality: *character, temperament, ability,* and *interests*.

Career Tip

Don't confuse pleasant or rude attitudes and behaviors with personality. Keep in mind that everyone has a personality and that certain personality characteristics are related to specific occupations.

Character

Your **character** is your sense of morality and the ethical code by which you live. It is the yardstick that society uses to determine whether your personal conduct is acceptable. Behaviors and beliefs that demonstrate honesty, fairness, and trustworthiness are usually expected in social and work situations. How would you describe the behaviors and beliefs you find acceptable in the character of your friends? What behaviors and beliefs would you expect from co-workers and managers in the world of work?

Temperament

Temperament refers to the way you usually act, feel, and think in certain situations. How well you will be able to meet the demands of certain jobs will be influenced by your temperament. For example, one worker might enjoy a variety of duties, whereas another might prefer repeating the same tasks, with few changes in the daily routine. Can you think of jobs that would be satisfying or frustrating for workers with each of these temperaments? Some job situations require different worker temperaments, for example:

- Following detailed instructions, with little independent decision making
- Working in isolation from others
- Influencing other people
- Working under stressful conditions (deadlines and quotas)
- Using personal judgment or valid information to make decisions
- Interpreting ideas, feelings, or facts

- Setting standards to achieve goals

Which of these job situations match your temperament? Which don't?

Ability

Ability refers to how well you perform specific work tasks. It also refers to the potential you have to master a work skill. Perhaps you have been told that you have the ability to do well in auto mechanics. However, you will not be able to land a job as an auto mechanic until you acquire the skills to do the job well.

Interests

Your **interests** are the preferences you have for specific topics or activities. Some examples of career interests are social, musical, outdoor, mechanical, scientific, mathematical, literary, clerical, persuasive, and artistic interests. Notice that some words, such as *mechanical*, are listed under both interests and abilities. It is possible to have high interest but low ability in a certain area, and vice versa.

Examining Your Personality

Take a moment to form an image of yourself. Start by closing your eyes and forming a mental description of your physical characteristics. If you gave this description of yourself to a stranger over the telephone, would he or she be able to find you in a room full of people?

In writing, describe your interests, abilities, temperament, and character. Your list reflects your perception of yourself. Next, have a friend or close relative read your description and then agree with it or make any changes they wish. This is that person's perception of your personality.

Physical characteristics like appearance, physical strength or weakness, and general health may affect certain personality characteristics, such as temperament and ability. You are the total of all of your physical and psychological characteristics; these cannot be separated.

A **personality trait** is any personality characteristic that can be measured. The measurement of personality traits enables psychologists, counselors, social workers, and other helping profes-

▲ *Using your abilities and skills successfully will give you feelings of joy and satisfaction and will motivate you to achieve at higher levels.*

▲ *Do you ever think about your physical and psychological characteristics?*

sionals to make mathematical comparisons between individuals. Personality traits change very little, and the results of accurate testing are useful over a long period of time.

Worker Trait Groups

So far in this chapter you have been learning about the **traits** (characteristics) that cause people to be similar to and different from other people. Jobs also have certain traits that cause them to be similar to and different from other jobs.

In a book called the *Dictionary of Occupational Titles (DOT)*, the U.S. Department of Labor has arranged more than 20,000 jobs into families (categories) of occupations. These families are called **Worker Trait Groups**. Several specific traits are described for each occupation in a Worker Trait Group. These include physical demands, aptitudes, temperaments, environmental conditions, training time, general education development, and specific vocational preparation. To work successfully in a particular occupation, the worker must be able to perform at the level designated for each worker trait necessary to that particular occupation.

Figure 2.2 provides an example of one physical worker trait: lifting. In addition to lifting, there are numerous physical traits, including carrying, pushing, pulling, climbing, balancing, stooping, kneeling, crouching, crawling, reaching, handling, feeling, talking, hearing, and seeing. Each of these worker traits can be performed at a variety of levels. The worker must possess physical capacities at least in an amount equal to the physical demands of the job.

Name one specific occupation that you have considered for your future. What level of the worker trait "lifting" would be required to perform the necessary tasks of that occupation? Before selecting an occupation for life, you would be wise to compare your interests, abilities, temperament, and character with the worker traits of the occupation.

> This above all—to thine own self be true;
> and it must follow, as the night the day,
> Thou canst not then be false to any man.
>
> **William Shakespeare**

Self-Concept

Self-concept can be thought of as your attitude toward your personality. **Self** is that part of your experience that you regard as essentially you. It includes your inner thoughts, feelings, aspirations, fears, and fantasies. It is your perception (image) of what you were in the past, are in the present, and might become in the future. It is learned from your experiences and interactions with other people. The image you have developed about yourself includes these components:

1. Your physical and material self. This is made up of your physical body and the material possessions you own.

2. Your psychological self. This includes your inner thoughts and ideas, your feelings of self-worth, and your personal motivation to seek particular goals.

3. Your emotional self. This means the way you think and deal with your emotions when you are experiencing a situation. Experiences can have a positive or negative effect on a person's self-concept. For example, a frightening past experience may cause one person to fear water and refuse to learn to swim. Another person may decide to become a doctor because of a serious illness in childhood and a strong desire to help others in a similar situation.

4. Your social self . This is your involvement with other people and your view of what they think about you. Self-acceptance and self-respect are the result of being accepted and respected by

Figure 2.2 LIFTING DEMANDS OF DIFFERENT TYPES OF WORK

Type of Work	Lifting Demands
Sedentary work	Lifting ten pounds maximum. Although a sedentary job is defined as one that involves sitting, a certain amount of walking and standing is often necessary.
Light work	Lifting twenty pounds maximum, with frequent lifting and/or carrying of objects weighing up to ten pounds. May involve a degree of pushing and pulling of arm and/or leg controls.
Medium work	Lifting fifty pounds maximum, with frequent lifting and/or carrying of objects weighing up to twenty-five pounds.
Heavy work	Lifting one hundred pounds maximum, with frequent lifting and/or carrying of objects weighing fifty pounds or more.
Very heavy work	Lifting objects in excess of one hundred pounds, with frequent lifting and/or carrying of objects weighing fifty pounds or more.

others. On the other hand, being blamed, rejected, and belittled by others could lower your feelings of self-worth.

5. Your ideal self. This includes how you would like other people to think of you and react to you, tasks you would like to perform, and the social and career roles you would like to have.

Your self-concept provides you with an image of the type of occupations you should pursue. Unfortunately, a person's self-concept is not always accurate. One person might have a poor self-concept, consider himself to be inadequate, and eliminate from consideration careers that he is capable of achieving. Another person might overestimate her abilities and strive for a career goal that is beyond reach. It is important to obtain an accurate understanding of your aptitudes, abilities, interests, and values and then acquire the skills and self-confidence you need to identify realistic career goals.

A young person's self-concept is shaped in large part by those around him or her. With encouragement from family, friends, and teachers, a young person can develop a positive self-concept. When this encouragement is missing, a negative self-concept might be the result. Consider the situation of Rhonda Benson and her twin brother, Roger, on the next page.

When people are members of a group, they feel similar to other members and strive to be like

CAREER TIP

Be certain that your self-image is accurate. An individual seeks a career that is consistent with his or her self-image.

BUILDING SELF-ESTEEM

Encouragement Makes a Difference

Rhonda enjoys her roles as student, basketball player, Sunday school teacher, and daughter. She feels as though she is a unique and capable person in each of her life roles. The people closest to Rhonda—her teachers, basketball coach and teammates, the members of her church, and her parents—have all provided encouragement and made her feel successful. Rhonda is exploring possible careers in teaching, nursing, and social work. She likes helping people and sees herself as being successful in life situations involving others.

Roger, on the other hand, gets passing grades but has never really enjoyed school. He hasn't been very involved with activities at school or at church. Roger's main source of enjoyment is his street bike. He likes to put on his bike clothes and ride. He spends hours repairing or adjusting his bike, only to have his parents tell him he would be more successful if he spent the same amount of time on his schoolwork. Roger sometimes feels as though the whole world thinks he's a failure. Even Rhonda doesn't seem to understand him anymore. Roger plans to graduate in June and then travel all over the country on his bike. When he gets tired of riding and seeing things, Roger thinks he might go to college.

Critical Thinking

1. People constantly measure their ideal self against their actual self. When their perceptions of who they ought to be are similar to who they actually are, then they have a positive, mature self-concept. Like most people, Rhonda and Roger have a strong desire to be unique. Is Rhonda's self-concept positive and mature? Is Roger's? How do you account for any differences?

2. Parents and other family members create a large part of our world. Young people measure their personal success and failure according to the judgments of that world. Labels like *hard working* or *lazy*, *bright* or *dumb*, *friendly* or *mean*, *pretty* or *unattractive* are attached to a young person's self-concept by the family and other social environments, such as school. Make a list of labels for Rhonda, Roger, and a child you love.

3. Many of the standards that people set for ideal behavior are learned as members of **reference groups**. Examples of reference groups include your family, classes at school, and clubs or organizations you have joined. Can you think of other reference groups to which you belong? Comparing yourself to other members of these groups affects your beliefs and values. What reference groups do Rhonda and Roger belong to? How do the standards of each reference group affect Rhonda? How do they affect Roger?

them. They compare themselves to the standards of other group members. The beliefs and feelings and the self-image that grow out of these comparisons have a strong effect on the individual's career choices.

Self-Esteem

Everyone makes a judgment about his or her level of competence and adequacy as a person. This personal evaluation is called **self-esteem**. It is not always an accurate evaluation, but it is always viewed by the individual as being accurate. Self-esteem has a strong effect on how the individual perceives relationships with other people and situations such as school or work.

A person with a high level of self-esteem feels competent, of value to society, in control of most life events, important to other people, and useful. On the other hand, a person with a low level of self-esteem feels incompetent, of little value to society, controlled by most life events, unimportant, and without purpose. Most people have areas of high and low self-esteem.

Strengthening your self-concept and raising your level of self-esteem is an important step in preparing for personal and career success. Exploring and understanding yourself and accepting the person you are will help you establish realistic career goals, make desired changes, and fulfill career objectives.

Section 2 GET INVOLVED

Answer the following on a separate sheet of paper, and be prepared to discuss your responses in class.

1. Do you present the same image to everyone, or do you present a different image to your teachers, friends, and family? Describe the image you present to each.

2. Describe an experience that affected you in a positive way and one that affected you in a negative way. Perhaps it was a grade you received or something that was said to you about the way you look, talk, or act.

3. Which of the following best describes the image you project at school, at home, and with friends? Explain your answer by giving an example of when you project this image.

A leader	Idealistic	Self-confident
A loner	Reliable	Critical
A follower	Cooperative	Compassionate

Section 3

Identifying Interests

Sometimes people get so involved in what they *have* to do that they forget what they *want* to do. If you first discover what your personal interests are, then you will be in a position to choose an interesting career.

Personal interests are those inner feelings that cause you to *want* to know something or *want* to perform a certain activity. If you were driving to a distant city, you would probably begin by identifying all of the possible routes and then selecting the one you prefer. If the route you select enables you to see things you like and do things you enjoy, it satisfies your interests.

Think for a moment about a school activity that you enjoy. Now, think about an activity that you do only because it is required. Have you ever noticed that when an activity arouses and holds your interest, you are less likely to quit and more likely to succeed?

We sometimes participate in activities that we don't enjoy in order to obtain something we want. The goal could be a certain grade, another person's approval, education or training for a certain occupation, or a job promotion. It is sometimes necessary to delay gratification and perform activities we don't particularly enjoy in order to obtain

CAREER TIP

Find an interesting route to your career goal, and you will enjoy the journey as much as the destination.

a goal. Can you think of an activity you presently do or plan to do in the future that is not very interesting but has a payoff that will make it worthwhile?

Some people develop such a high interest in a certain activity that they become restless and bored when they are away from it. Have you ever started to read a book, watch a program on TV, build or repair something, or discuss a situation with another person and suddenly realized that several hours had passed without your noticing? What is the interest that kept you involved? mechanical things? information? people?

A specific interest may be related to many occupations. As an example, mechanical interest is related to the occupations of mechanic, mechanical engineer, appliance repairperson, broadcast technician, vocational teacher, aircraft mechanic, and machinist, to name only a few. What occupations can you think of that would be related to the following interests?

- Helping other people
- The outdoors
- Science and mathematics

CAREER TIP

Interests change very little between the ages of twenty-five and fifty-five. They change much more between the ages of fifteen and twenty-five.

- Leading, persuading, and convincing other people

How are the occupations you selected related to these interests? Tests used to measure interests are frequently known as career or occupational **interest surveys**. They match your interests with the work activities or situations experienced in certain occupations. They also compare your interests with those of people who are successful and satisfied in certain occupations. There are no correct or incorrect responses to statements in an interest survey. Instead, you choose among numerous activities and situations, expressing your preference for one over another.

▲ *When Chris was a teenager, he enjoyed cooking at home. He never dreamed that he would become a highly skilled chef. What is your dream?*

Section 4

Working with Data, People, and Things

If you could have the "perfect" job, what percentage of your time would you spend **working with data** (verbal or numerical information), **working with people**, and **working with things** (tools, instruments or machines)?

A preference for working with data, people, or things is another method used to relate personal interests to various occupations. It is an effective method to use because every occupation requires workers to spend some of their time performing tasks in each of these three categories.

Once again, think of an occupation you are considering for your future career. As you read the following descriptions, take into account how

much of your time would be spent working with data, people, or things in that occupation. Is this consistent with your interest in the three categories of work?

- **Data:** This category of job tasks includes everything related to using, identifying, or organizing information and knowledge. Numbers and words are the tools of the person who works with data.

- **People:** This category includes everything related to human relations. It includes all work situations that provide opportunities to lead, persuade, help, teach, or counsel others.

- **Things:** This category includes everything re-

▲ *Taking orders and serving meals in a friendly and orderly manner are essential people skills for a waiter or waitress. (What level of data, people, and things involvement do you prefer?)*

lated to the design, use, or repair of machines, tools, and instruments.

Each of the three categories may require the worker to use a complex level of responsibility and judgment or may be performed at a much less complicated level. For example, the occupations of waiter and physician are highly involved with people. However, the waiter works at the level of taking instructions, helping, serving, and speaking, whereas the physician must have higher-level skills in mentoring (serving as a trusted adviser), instructing, and persuading. Physicians must also work at a very high skill level with data and things.

The *Dictionary of Occupational Titles* establishes levels of involvement with data, people, and things that are required for many occupations. Each occupation in the *DOT* has a nine-digit code. The second group of three digits (000.456.000) tells you the occupation's level of involvement with data, people, and things. The level of involvement is designated by numbers, with 0 representing the highest level of involvement and 6, 7, or 8 representing the lowest level of involvement. Figure 2.3 lists the categories for the various levels of involvement.

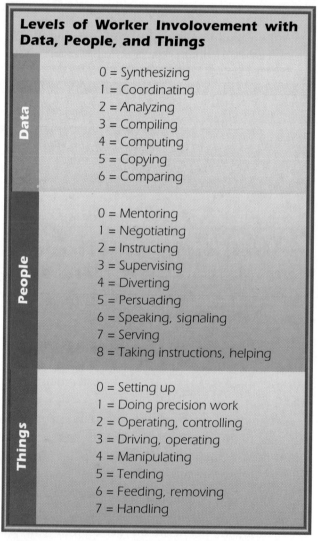

Levels of Worker Involvement with Data, People, and Things

Data	
	0 = Synthesizing
	1 = Coordinating
	2 = Analyzing
	3 = Compiling
	4 = Computing
	5 = Copying
	6 = Comparing

People	
	0 = Mentoring
	1 = Negotiating
	2 = Instructing
	3 = Supervising
	4 = Diverting
	5 = Persuading
	6 = Speaking, signaling
	7 = Serving
	8 = Taking instructions, helping

Things	
	0 = Setting up
	1 = Doing precision work
	2 = Operating, controlling
	3 = Driving, operating
	4 = Manipulating
	5 = Tending
	6 = Feeding, removing
	7 = Handling

▲ *Figure 2.3 Levels of Worker Involvement with Data, People, and Things.*

CAREER TIP

It is not unusual for people to delay the education and training they need to develop their aptitudes to a higher level of achievement. Many workers reenter some type of schooling several years after high school.

In most occupations, workers perform job tasks related to all three of the data, people, and things categories. When considering a future occupation, it is important to know the level of involvement required in each of the three categories. Figure 2.4 shows the level of involvement for six occupations.

Figure 2.4 WORKER INVOLVEMENT WITH DATA, PEOPLE, AND THINGS FOR SIX SAMPLE OCCUPATIONS

Occupation	DOT Code	Data	People	Things
Mechanic	620.261-010	2 = Analyzing	6 = Speaking, signaling	1 = Doing precision work
Typist	203.362-010	3 = Compiling	6 = Speaking, signaling	2 = Operating, controlling
Counselor	045.107-010	1 = Coordinating	0 = Mentoring	7 = Handling
Cashier, bagger	211.452-018	4 = Computing	5 = Persuading	2 = Operating, controlling
Firefighter	373.364-010	3 = Compiling	6 = Speaking, signaling	4 = Manipulating
Registered nurse	075.264-010	2 = Analyzing	6 = Speaking, signaling	4 = Manipulating

Section 4 GET INVOLVED

Answer the following on a separate sheet of paper, and be prepared to discuss your response in class.

1. Once again, think of a specific occupation that you are considering. What levels of involvement (refer to Figure 2.3) would be required in the data, people, and things categories? Are these levels of involvement consistent with your present skills? What level of education or training would be required to achieve job skills at the required levels of involvement? Where could you acquire the necessary training?

Identifying Aptitudes

Have you ever overheard a teacher tell a student, "You are not working up to your potential"? An **aptitude** is a person's potential for success in performing a certain activity. This potential may be for acquiring certain knowledge or skills with education or training.

Perhaps you have an aptitude for performing arithmetic operations quickly and accurately. If so, you have the potential to be a successful bookkeeper. However, you would need special education and training to develop your arithmetic skills and turn your aptitude for arithmetic into a bookkeeping career.

Regardless of your aptitude, you may not have an interest in becoming a bookkeeper. Aptitudes are only one part of the career-choice puzzle. Your aptitude for arithmetic could be used in several

PLANNING MAKES A DIFFERENCE

Education and Training are Important

Alan Henderson is a senior at King High School. Alan has planned to attend college, study engineering, and design airplanes since he was in the eighth grade. That was the year his class took a field trip to a local aerospace manufacturing company.

Last week, Alan received the results of an aptitude test from his counselor. He scored very high in numerical aptitude and average in general learning ability. Review Alan's recent mathematics grades.

Although Alan achieves high in arithmetic, he finds higher forms of math to be very difficult. His four-year high school grade point average (for all subjects) is 2.55.

When colleges began returning Alan's applications, it became obvious that he wouldn't be accepted to an engineering program because of his low achievement in higher forms of math. He feels very discouraged. Alan's counselor wants him to review his college plan and consider earning a two-year associate degree in engineering. Alan is a dedicated student, and his chance of success would be very good.

Grade	Course	Semester 1	Semester 2	Final
8	General Mathematics	A	A	A
9	Introduction to Algebra	B	B	B
10	Algebra I	B	C	C+
11	Algebra II	C	C	C
12	Geometry	C	D	C–

Critical Thinking

1. Are Alan's aptitude results in agreement with his grades in school? Review the aptitude descriptions in Figure 2.5 on page 37 before you answer.

2. Should Alan consider a two-year associate degree program? Why or why not?

▲ *School counselors are trained to administer and interpret aptitude tests.*

occupations. Can you think of another occupation that would require this aptitude?

You probably possess one or more aptitudes that haven't been developed to a high level of skill. Figure 2.5 provides a description of eleven aptitudes that the U.S. Department of Labor uses in the *Dictionary of Occupational Titles*. Read the descriptions, and decide whether your potential for each aptitude is high, average, or low. Different occupations require higher or lower degrees of

Figure 2.5 APTITUDES

Aptitude	Description
General Learning Ability, Intelligence	Ability to understand instructions and underlying principles. Ability to reason and make judgments. Closely related to doing well in school. A physician requires a high degree of this aptitude, a registered nurse requires less, and an electrocardiogram technician requires even less.
Verbal	Ability to understand the meaning of words and the ideas associated with them and to use them effectively. Ability to comprehend language, to understand relationships between words, and to understand meanings of whole sentences and paragraphs. Ability to present information or ideas clearly. An editor requires a high degree of this aptitude, a teacher requires less, and a salesperson requires even less.
Numerical	Ability to perform arithmetic operations quickly and accurately. A mechanical engineer requires a high degree of this aptitude, a bookkeeper requires less, and a salesclerk requires even less.
Spatial	Ability to comprehend forms in space and to understand relationships of plane and solid objects. Ability to visualize objects of two or three dimensions and to think visually of geometric forms. A dentist requires a high degree of this aptitude, a machinist requires less, and a carpenter requires even less.

Figure 2.5 CONTINUED

Aptitude	Description
Form Perception	Ability to perceive pertinent details in objects or in pictorial or graphic material. Ability to make visual comparisons and discriminations and to see slight differences in shapes and shading of figures and widths and lengths of lines. A drafter requires a high degree of this aptitude, a paperhanger requires less, and a furniture assembler requires even less.
Clerical Perception	Ability to perceive pertinent detail in verbal or tabular material. To observe differences in copy, to proofread written works and numbers, and to avoid perceptual errors in arithmetic computation. A proofreader requires a high degree of this aptitude, a general office clerk requires less, and a cashier requires even less.
Motor Coordination	Ability to coordinate eyes and hands or fingers rapidly and accurately in making precise movements with speed. Ability to make a movement response accurately and quickly. A word-processing operator requires a high degree of this aptitude, a machine tool operator requires less, and a butcher requires even less.
Finger Dexterity	Ability to move the fingers and manipulate small objects with the fingers rapidly and accurately. A surgeon requires a high degree of this aptitude, an automobile mechanic requires less, and a cosmetologist requires even less.
Manual Dexterity	Ability to move the hands easily and skillfully and to work with the hands in a placing and turning motion. An airplane engine specialist requires a high degree of this aptitude, a diesel mechanic requires less, and an upholsterer requires even less.
Eye-Hand Coordination	Ability to move the hand and foot coordinately with each other in accordance with visual stimuli. A baseball player requires a high degree of this aptitude, a truck driver requires less, and a forklift operator requires even less.
Color Discrimination	Ability to perceive or recognize similarities or differences in colors or in shades or other values of the same color. Ability to identify a particular color, to recognize harmonious or contrasting color combinations, and to match colors accurately. An interior designer requires a high degree of this aptitude, a textile designer requires less, and a floral designer requires even less.

certain aptitudes. Which aptitudes have you developed the most? The least?

Every person possesses a unique set of aptitudes. Infants are born with the potential for certain kinds of learning, and they begin to use their aptitudes right away. As they grow older, their interests and values help them establish goals. To achieve their goals, they must use their aptitudes to learn specific skills.

Are you a fast runner or a graceful dancer? Can you use your hands and fingers to work with small objects quickly and efficiently? Can you see differences in sizes and shapes quicker than other people? If so, you owe these skills and abilities to your natural aptitudes.

Do you need glasses, a hearing aid, special medication, or a special device to help you perform physical tasks? How does this affect your aptitudes?

An efficient way to discover your potential strengths is to take an aptitude test. Ask your high school counselor if this type of testing is available at your school. Your counselor may have access to the **Armed Services Vocational Aptitude Battery (ASVAB)** or the **General Aptitude Test Battery (GATB)**. The ASVAB is a group of twelve tests that measure your aptitudes in five broad career fields. The GATB suggests job clusters for which you have strong aptitudes. Most aptitude tests suggest specific careers and programs of study to explore.

CAREER TIP

A self-appraisal of your aptitudes as well as your interests, values, and goals will prepare you to make realistic career decisions.

Aptitude tests are best used in conjunction with other personal data, such as interests, values, school grades, personality traits, and vocational preferences. Upon completion of your aptitude test, ask your high school counselor to review all of the personal data, academic information, and test results in your permanent records. Ask your counselor to explain the relationship of this information to your aptitude test results.

Once you have identified your strong aptitudes, it is important to use your potential and learn specific career skills.

When you develop an aptitude to its full potential, it will give you a sense of personal pride. When you begin using that aptitude to perform meaningful work, you will feel a sense of satisfaction. This cycle of pride and satisfaction is the cornerstone of career success.

Section 5 GET INVOLVED

Answer the following on a separate sheet of paper, and be prepared to discuss your responses in class.

1. List three occupations you have considered for your future career. For each occupation on your list, identify two or more aptitudes, and tell how they would be used in that particular occupation. Rate yourself high, average, or low for the aptitudes on your list. Which occupation is best suited to your aptitude strengths? Which is least suited?

2. Can you think of something you have repeatedly tried to do but cannot do very well, no matter how hard you try? Maturity and practice help to overcome some limitations, for example when learning to ride a bike or to read. Sometimes, however, limitations are caused by physical handicaps we are born with or that occur because of an accident or illness.

List the aptitudes that you read about in this chapter. Next to each aptitude list any physical disabilities you can think of that would have a negative effect on a person's ability to use that aptitude in the world of work.

Leisure Time

Leisure time is time free from your everyday job responsibilities. During leisure time you may rest, be involved in recreation (fun and games), or pursue an **avocation** (a constructive activity that provides you with personal satisfaction).

Leisure time had little or no meaning to most of our nineteenth-century ancestors. Although most people lived and worked on farms, a move-

▲ *The amount of time American workers have for leisure is increasing. What recreational or avocational activities do you enjoy?*

ment had started to factory jobs in the cities. Typically, the husband worked six days a week and at least ten hours a day. The wife stayed home with several children and had no electrical household appliances to assist with cooking, cleaning, laundry, child rearing, and home maintenance. Both parents frequently worked to the point of exhaustion. When leisure time was available, it was usually spent resting.

By the early 1900s, most Americans lived and worked in cities. The labor movement (workers organizing unions) was well under way. Higher wages, shorter working hours, and new labor-saving devices increased the amount of leisure time that was available to many working Americans. The nation's rapidly increasing standard of living resulted in the growth of recreation activities, such as amusement parks, professional sports, swimming and boating, vaudeville (live theater), and motion pictures.

According to the U.S. census of 1990, the amount of time that Americans have available for leisure activities has changed dramatically. In 1990, the average workweek for a full-time worker was 37.5 hours, with most employers providing paid vacations as well as flexible schedules, three- and four-day workweeks, and several legislated three-day holiday weekends. These policies have allowed time for workers to become involved in avocational as well as recreational activities.

Age and geographic location have an obvious effect on leisure. What is appropriate or even possible at one age may not be appropriate or possible at another. At what age did you learn to ride a tricycle? a bicycle? drive a car? How many people over 50 have you noticed riding skateboards? Although people change their leisure-time activities as they grow older, past or present skills and experience will influence their future selections.

People also develop recreational interests based on the geography of the region. For example, lake country lends itself to fishing, coastal regions to beach activities, and the mountains to hiking and skiing.

As a student, you probably spend some of your leisure time on volunteer service, hobbies, part-time jobs, or involvement in organizations. All of these leisure-time pursuits are good ways to identify possible interests in certain career areas as well as to develop employment skills. Figure 2.6 shows the relationship between some common leisure-time activities, the personality characteristics associated with those activities, and related occupations.

▲ *What leisure-time activity would you expect Tony and Alice to enjoy when they are fifty?*

Figure 2.6 RELATING LEISURE ACTIVITIES TO WORK

Leisure Activity	Personality Characteristics of Participant	Related Occupations
Being a club officer	Enjoys leading and persuading people	Politician, manager, supervisor
Collecting stamps or coins	Has good organizational skills; likes structured activities	Accountant, bookkeeper, bank teller
Doing science projects	Likes working with information; enjoys solving problems	Chemist, oceanographer, astronomer
Teaching Sunday school, baby-sitting	Likes helping people; enjoys children	Teacher, day-care worker, social worker
Making posters, working on sets for school plays	Likes creating things; likes using drawing skills; enjoys beautifying the environment	Designer, architect, commercial artist
Rebuilding cars, repairing bicycles	Enjoys using tools and machines; likes analyzing mechanical problems	Mechanic, machinist, engineer
Hunting, fishing, raising plants	Likes being outdoors; enjoys learning about nature	Fish and game warden, forester, farm operator

BUILDING SELF-ESTEEM

Time Well Spent

James Millard is 36 years old, married, and has three children. The family participates in numerous recreational activities. James enjoys working with people in leading, persuading, and helping ways. He also likes to work with data. On the job, James enjoys the feeling of discovery when he learns how a new machine works, what causes people to be successful, or how he can change a process to make the work more efficient.

Although James is very happy with his job, marriage, and recreational activities, something seems to be missing in his life. He feels that he should be making a more important contribution to the welfare of other people. He strongly believes that the world would be a better place if children were given more love, understanding, and direction for their lives.

James has recently begun coaching in a children's softball league and teaching Sunday school. Both of these avocations require him to fulfill scheduled responsibilities. They also place him in a role where he can provide love and understanding to young people, counsel them in times of trouble, and influence the direction of their lives. These avocations reward James with a sense of self-worth and personal accomplishment.

Critical Thinking

1. If, instead of coaching and teaching Sunday school, James had selected leisure-time activities at the rest or recreation level, would they have increased his feelings of personal worth? Why or why not?
2. Interview a family member or friend who is presently employed full-time. List each of this person's leisure-time activities, how much time he or she spends on each, and whether the activity is at the level of avocation, recreation, or rest.

Section 6 GET INVOLVED

Answer the following on a separate sheet of paper, and be prepared to discuss your responses in class.

1. List the leisure-time activities you have been involved in during the past month. Are these activities more often
   a. involved with data, people, or things?
   b. done alone or with others?
   c. done outdoors or indoors?

2. What is one leisure activity you would like to try that isn't on your list?

3. Name two occupations that are related to your list of leisure activities, and tell how they are related.

CHAPTER 2 REVIEW

ENRICH YOUR VOCABULARY

On a separate sheet of paper, number from 1 to 25, and complete the following activity. (Do not write in your textbook.) Match each statement below with the most appropriate term from the "Enrich Your Vocabulary" list at the beginning of the chapter by writing that term next to the correct statement.

1. The sense of morality and the ethical code by which a person lives
2. The judgment you make about your level of competence and adequacy
3. A person's potential for success in performing a certain activity
4. General Aptitude Test Battery
5. A category of job tasks that involves the use of machines, tools, and instruments
6. The relationship that exists between all of a person's psychological parts
7. The way a person usually acts, feels, and thinks in certain situations
8. Preferences a person has for specific topics or activities
9. Characteristics
10. A personality characteristic that can be measured
11. Armed Services Vocational Aptitude Battery
12. A category of job tasks that includes everything related to human relations
13. Job categories that include physical demands, aptitudes, temperaments, environmental conditions, training time, and vocational preparation
14. The part of your experience that you consider to be you
15. Time that is free from normal occupational responsibilities
16. A constructive leisure-time activity that provides personal satisfaction
17. Your involvement with other people and your view of what they think about you
18. Groups that set behavior standards
19. How well you perform specific work tasks
20. Tests used to measure interests
21. A category of job tasks that involves the use of words and numbers
22. Your surroundings
23. The process of transmitting physical or mental characteristics from parent to child
24. The way of life in the society in which you live
25. Experiences that cause you to be confident or fearful as you prepare for a career

CHECK YOUR KNOWLEDGE

On a separate sheet of paper, complete the following activity. (Do not write in your textbook.)

1. What are the four major influences discussed in this chapter that shape the physical, psychological, and social characteristics of an individual?
2. Name three of the four terms used to describe the parts of personality.
3. What are five of the specific traits described in each Worker Trait Group?
4. List three of the components of self.
5. List three reference groups. Give an example of how each group might influence the beliefs of its members.
6. What can an individual do to reach a higher level of self-esteem?
7. What comparisons do career interest surveys make? Will interests match more than one occupation?
8. List six of the aptitudes described in the chapter.
9. Would a mechanic have a higher level of involvement with people and things, data and people, or things and data?
10. What are the three levels of leisure-time activities?
11. Would a person who enjoys collecting stamps be more likely to enjoy the occupation of bookkeeper or social worker? Why?

DEVELOP SCANS COMPETENCIES

Government experts say that successful workers can productively use Resources, Interpersonal skills, Information, Systems, and Technology. This activity will give you practice in developing Interpersonal skills.

Work with someone who knows you well to determine whether he/she sees you as you see yourself. (Make sure you work with a person you can trust and who will help rather than hurt you.)

Use the five "self" components listed in Section 2 under the head "Self-Concept." Discuss with your partner how you see yourself in these areas and how he/she sees you in each of these areas.

Knowing Yourself: Values and Goals

Learning Objectives

After completing this chapter, you should be prepared to:

- explain the relationship between your personal values, goals, attitude, career choices, and lifestyle options
- describe your unique set of values and relate them to lifestyle and job satisfaction
- set realistic short-term and long-term career goals
- recognize your positive and negative attitudes toward yourself, others, and work

Enrich Your Vocabulary

In reading this chapter and doing the exercises you will learn the following important terms:

values	time line
nonmaterialistic	attitude
social environment	components
tentative	contradictory
goal	prejudice
materialistic	preconceived beliefs
tangible	self-fulfilling prophesy
realistic	lifestyle

In the first two chapters of this text, you learned how differences in interests and aptitudes affect a worker's personal satisfaction with career choices. In this chapter, self-understanding will focus on values, goals, attitudes, and lifestyle choices.

Sorting and prioritizing your unique combination of values and goals should provide a better understanding of the factors that motivate you to be successful. You may discover potential talents and career choices that you had never considered. Self-understanding will help you set realistic goals, maintain a positive attitude, and begin making important decisions about your personal journey to career success.

Section 1

Clarifying Values

How much importance do you place on owning a new car? How much time, work, and money are you willing to invest in a home entertainment center? Why is donating money to a certain charity important to you? Examining your **values** (cherished ideas and beliefs) will help you answer these questions. Understanding your values will help you determine the importance you place on particular material things, people, ideas, or situations.

Your values are not necessarily right or wrong. However, as long as you consider them to be true, you will use them to guide the direction of your life. Think about one of your strongest beliefs about people or ideas. Use the following questions to determine if your belief is strong enough to be considered a value.

1. Do I have strong feelings about this belief?
2. Have I carefully considered this belief and selected it to be an important personal value, without pressure from other people?
3. Do I cherish the belief I have selected?
4. Do I behave in such a way that other people are aware of my belief?

If you answered "yes" to three or four of these questions, your belief is a strong value. If you answered "no" to three or four questions, your belief isn't very strong and should not be considered a personal value. If you had two "yes" answers and two "no" answers, you might wish to reevaluate your belief. If you decide the belief is important, use the criteria in the four questions to strengthen your belief.

▲ It is important to clarify your values before you make important career decisions. Is working out-of-doors important to you?

People with well-defined values also have high levels of self-understanding and self-esteem. In addition, they are better prepared to make realistic career plans.

People frequently express their values to others by making a statement. Some of the most famous "values statements" in history were made by the Continental Congress on July 4, 1776. In a document called the Declaration of Independence, the members of the Continental Congress notified their king of a willingness to sacrifice their lives and fortunes to support their cherished beliefs. (See Figure 3.1.)

Your values are more than how you see extremes of right and wrong, good and bad, or true and false. They are a driving force behind your willingness or reluctance to make commitments, accept changes, strive for high achievement, or develop new skills. Your values have already influenced the way you feel, think, and behave in your social life. In the future, they will influence the decisions you make about your career and lifestyle.

People should make decisions based on their values and their interpretation of the available facts. Sometimes, though, people decide which facts to use on the basis of their personal values, rather than on the accuracy of the facts.

Figure 3.1 VALUES IN THE DECLARATION OF INDEPENDENCE	
Value	**Values Statement**
Equality	All men are created equal.
Freedom	All men have the right to life, liberty, and the pursuit of happiness.
Democracy	The just powers of government must come from the consent of the governed.

▲ The Declaration of Independence contains some of the most famous "values statements" in history. Are these "statements" as important today as they were on July 4, 1776?

BUILDING SELF-ESTEEM

Role Models Are Important

Reggie Swanson's parents are alcohol abusers. They sometimes argue loudly and even fight. Each morning during his childhood, Reggie had to select his clothes, fix something to eat, and walk to school alone. Reggie was ashamed of his parents and avoided lasting friendships. His grades were usually very low, and his parents didn't seem to care.

When Reggie was eleven, he started taking liquor from his parents' bottles while they were asleep. He replaced it with water, and they never knew the difference. In the seventh grade, he was suspended from school for ten days for being drunk during a school assembly program.

When Reggie was in the eighth grade, he became friends with Jack Anderson. Jack's parents make Reggie feel like one of the family. Reggie frequently eats meals and spends the night at Jack's house. The Andersons even took him along on their vacation last summer. Jack's parents don't approve of drinking, and neither does Jack. Reggie has decided to quit drinking because he respects the Andersons and wants them to respect him.

Jack's parents have encouraged Reggie to acquire a good education. Reggie's grades have improved, and he has decided to attend the vocational high school next year. He wants to study diesel engine repair.

Critical Thinking

1. In Reggie's case, expanding his **social environment** (the people he frequently comes in contact with) helped him discover new values and improve the quality of his life. Can you imagine a situation in which expanding a young person's social environment and experiences could have a *negative* effect on the quality of his or her life? Describe the situation.

2. Who is responsible for the values a child accepts? Is it the child's parents? friends? school? church? the government? the child? Be prepared to explain your answer in class.

3. Nonmaterialistic values are ones that have no monetary worth. What nonmaterialistic value(s) were expressed by Jack's parents? by Reggie?

Some people take their values for granted, without identifying or understanding them. Taking time to clarify your values will give you a more accurate understanding of yourself.

Values are learned from close social relationships, largely from early childhood home situations. Children constantly observe the choices made by parents, teachers, and other important adults. They are quick to understand the values being expressed by adult behaviors. Children mimic the behavior of the adults around them, and they frequently accept the adults' values.

As children grow older and are exposed to a larger number of people and experiences, they may change the importance they place on certain values.

Work Values

Work adds a sense of purpose to a person's values. An occupation that is related to your values will increase your likelihood of career success, financial rewards, and personal satisfaction. It is wise to choose an occupation that will reward your personal values and allow you to live your values every day.

Determine the values that are important to you and relate them to **tentative** (trial) occupations. Do you place a high value on adding beauty to the world, protecting the environment, helping humanity, or discovering new ways of doing things? What values would your ideal occupation allow

▲ *Choose an occupation that will reward your personal values. Would you enjoy teaching small children? Do you enjoy arts and crafts?*

you to express? Here is a list of values you should consider:

- **Security**–Is it important for you to have a steady job during recessions? Are you willing to trade a higher paycheck for more security?
- **Knowledge**–Is it important for you to learn why certain events occur or how a certain device operates? Would you enjoy working with information?
- **Family relationships**–Would you relocate for a career opportunity if it meant being far away from family members or close friends?
- **Independence**–Is it important for you to determine your methods of working and your work schedule? Would you give up security to own a business?
- **Money**–Is it important for you to earn a great deal of money? Could you be satisfied with an average or somewhat above average income?
- **Religion**–Would you accept a job if the employer's product, service, or philosophy conflicted in any way with your religious beliefs?
- **Creativity**–Would you like to design new prod-

ucts or use new ideas? Is music, art, or literature important to you?

- **Leadership**–Would you like to plan work tasks for others? Do you enjoy making decisions, controlling a situation, and persuading others?
- **Work environment**–Is it important for you to work outdoors, in an office or factory, to have air conditioning, or work in a quiet setting?
- **Social relationships**–Is it important for you to work with people you like? Would you enjoy social relationships with some of your co-workers? On the other hand, would you prefer working alone?
- **Involvement with things**–Is it important for you to use tools, machines, or instruments to perform your work?

As you begin to consider more values in your career choice, fewer occupations will satisfy all of them. Review the following examples:

Relating Work Values to Occupations

Values Considered	Related Occupations
• Working outdoors	Forester, bricklayer, bulldozer operator
• Working outdoors • Working with your hands	Bricklayer, bulldozer operator
• Working outdoors • Working with your hands • Working with machines	Bulldozer operator
• Working outdoors • Working with your hands • Working with machines • Working with people	[None of the three occupations satisfy all four of these work values.]

Section 1 GET INVOLVED

Answer the following on a separate sheet of paper, and be prepared to discuss your responses in class.

1. Rank the following with the item that has been most influential in forming your values as 1 and the item that has been least influential as 6. Be prepared to discuss your reasons in class.
   a. Family   b. School   c. Church
   d. Government   e. Media   f. Friends
2. If you knew the world would end in two days, what would you do during that time? What does your answer tell you about your values? What do you cherish?
3. If you won a five-million-dollar lottery, how would you spend the money? List the values expressed in your answer.
4. Cut out several help-wanted ads in the classified section of your Sunday newspaper. Based on the message in each ad, what work values do the different employers expect?

Section 2

Defining Goals

At one point in Thomas Edison's career, he had spent more than forty thousand dollars in fruitless experiments on the incandescent lamp (the forerunner of today's electric light bulb), but he did not give up. Finally, on October 21, 1879, Edison succeeded in making the lamp work for more than forty hours. By the year 1928, the great American inventor owned the rights to 1,033 inventions. During his lifetime, Edison achieved thousands of career goals.

A **goal** is an aim or objective. In a football game, the goal is clear. It is marked with a crisp white line. Each team's objective is to carry the football across the opposing team's goal line. There is a difference between short-term and long-term goals. In football, the short-term goal may be to move the ball ten yards on four plays. The long-term goal is to make more touchdowns than the other team.

The game of life is similar. Successful players have several goals; some are short-term goals, and others are long-term goals. However, the players in the game of life are responsible for choosing the location of their own goal line and determining the type of goals they are trying to achieve.

A **materialistic** goal (one that has monetary worth) would be the ownership of a **tangible** item (anything you can touch), such as a new coat, a bike, a computer, an automobile, or a house. A

> I never did anything worth doing by accident, nor did any of my inventions come by accident; they came by work.
>
> **Thomas Alva Edison (1847–1931)**

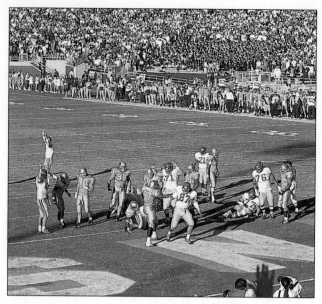

▲ *Determine the goal, then work to achieve it. What is your long-term career goal? What short-term goals must you reach first?*

nonmaterialistic goal—such as helping less fortunate people, cleaning up the natural environment, or getting a good education—provides inner satisfaction.

Establishing a goal gives you a feeling of confidence. Achieving the goal gives you a sense of accomplishment and raises your self-esteem. On the other hand, people without goals often lack confidence, have no sense of accomplishment, and have a lower level of self-esteem.

Most people will tell you that they want to improve their personal relationships, learn new skills, purchase a new car, or advance their career. However, many lack the plan and sense of commitment they need to achieve these goals. They substitute

CAREER TIP

Values give shape to your goals, and goals are the cornerstone of a successful career plan.

delays, excuses, and postponements for deadlines. They prefer a flexible schedule, free from specific responsibilities, rather than a disciplined schedule aimed at a specific accomplishment.

Every plan contains specific goals. Learning to set **realistic** (obtainable) goals is an important part of planning for career success; it puts you in charge of the direction your career takes.

Goals are an important part of every successful life plan. They are like the route numbers on a road map. Can you imagine trying to drive across the country without having route numbers on your map or signs along the highways? Use the following guidelines to make a list of goals for your life plan.

1. Set your own goals. Listen and learn from other people, but set goals that are important to *you*.

2. Base your goals on your important values. Otherwise, you will not consider them worthy enough to act on.

3. Make sure that the meaning of each goal is clear. Write your goals on a sheet of paper, or keep them in a small notebook.

4. Separate your general goals into easy-to-understand parts.

5. Be certain that each goal has a clear objective. This will help you measure your success in achieving it.

6. Make sure that each goal is possible. Consider any factors that could prevent you from achieving it.

7. Determine the amount of time and energy you are willing to invest in achieving each goal.

8. Develop a plan of action for reaching each goal. Be prepared to do what is necessary to make your plan succeed. Include a specific time to begin, as well as a time to reach each goal.

9. Review your written goals frequently.

Get into the habit of setting and achieving short-term goals. Be sure to have a **time line**

PLANNING MAKES A DIFFERENCE

Keep Your Eye on the Goal

Alice DePrato is ranked eighth in the senior class at Jefferson High School. She works part-time at a dry cleaner, pays for all of her clothes, and is saving money to attend a junior college in the fall. When Alice was in the ninth grade, she set three goals:

- To help her mother with the family expenses
- To save money for education after high school
- To rank among the top ten students in her graduating class

Alice never lost sight of her three goals. She knew in the ninth grade that her daily actions were contributing to their achievement. Now that she is about to accomplish her goals, Alice feels very proud of her-self. Her employer has offered her a full-time job as assistant manager when she graduates. Although the job offer gave Alice a great sense of confidence, her goal is still to graduate from a junior college.

Critical Thinking

1. Does Alice take life as it comes, or does she make things happen? Be prepared to explain in class the reasons for your answer.
2. How are you and Alice alike? How are you different?

(schedule) for the completion of each goal. Some short-term goals you might wish to consider are improving your school attendance or tardiness, obtaining a part-time job, cleaning or improving a part of your home, or establishing a friendship with a certain person.

After you acquire some experience setting and achieving short-term goals, begin working on long-term, more challenging, goals. These might include acquiring and saving money for additional education or training, earning a scholarship, being accepted for an apprenticeship program, or purchasing an automobile.

Career Goals

Once you have a clear understanding of your values, interests, and aptitudes, it will be time to set career goals and make plans to achieve them. Be certain that your long-term career goals are related to your values and personal interests. This will increase your likelihood of achieving career satisfaction.

For every long-term career goal you achieve, you will need several short-term goals. Accomplishing short-term goals will help you realize that you can achieve long-term goals. Success will motivate you to achieve more success.

You will probably discover that some of the day-to-day tasks required to accomplish your goals are not very interesting. Sometimes, the only satisfaction to be found in completing a short-term goal is knowing that the long-term goal is one step closer. Every successful worker performs

> Employment is nature's physician, and is essential to human happiness.
>
> *Galen*

some tasks they dislike.

It is easy to become frustrated when you fail to reach a goal. Failure can cause feelings of anger and incompetence and can cause you to blame others. A wiser response to failure is to take a little time to cool off, determine the reasons for the failure, and make a new plan. When striving for goals, the old saying, "Winners never quit, and quitters never win," is a good philosophy to follow.

Section 2 GET INVOLVED

Answer the following on a separate sheet of paper. Be prepared to discuss your responses in class.

1. What are three materialistic goals you would like to achieve in the next year? The next ten years? What is your plan to reach each of these goals? Be sure to include the necessary short-term goals in your plan.
2. What are three nonmaterialistic goals you would like to achieve in the next year? the next ten years? Of the goals you have listed, which goal do you consider to be most important? Why?
3. What tentative career goals have you set? What are you presently accomplishing in school that will help you achieve your tentative career goals? How will your school accomplishments help?

Section 3

Attitudes

An **attitude** is the way you think about things and act toward others. Attitudes are revealed through your positive or negative responses to another person's thoughts, feelings, and beliefs. They are demonstrated by your favorable or unfavorable reactions to life situations.

An attitude may be as simple as your evaluation of a certain breakfast cereal or as complex as your beliefs about free speech or gender equality. In either case, your attitude is an evaluation for or against a certain position.

There is an old saying, "The apple doesn't fall far from the tree." Your attitudes were learned from your family and friends, newspapers and magazines, TV, and personal experiences. Your family has probably had the greatest influence.

▲ *Showing an interest in assigned tasks demonstrates a positive working attitude. Do you demonstrate a positive working attitude when you are assigned a task at home or school?*

Solving The Problem

Year-round School?

Rachael Scheck is a sophomore at Westfield High School. She hopes to be accepted into a Tech Prep program for her junior and senior years. The Westfield Board of Education is considering a plan for year-round school. Figure 3.2 below is a diagram of Rachael's attitude toward the plan. The diagram includes the positive and negative components of her attitude.

Rachael has a weak positive attitude toward year-round school. After considering the positive and negative components of her attitude, Rachael would like to try the idea of year-round school.

Critical Thinking

1. What positive or negative attitude components do you have toward year-round school? Is your overall attitude positive or negative? Is it a strong or weak attitude?

2. Your attitudes are expressions of your personal values. They are based on your cherished beliefs. Which one of the following subjects arouses the strongest positive attitude in you? Which arouses the strongest negative attitude? Identify a strong personal value that is related to each of your choices.

Wealthy people	Working-class people
Alcohol	Employment
Marriage	School
Government	Recreation
Drugs	Children

> If you don't know where you're going, you will probably end up somewhere else.
>
> **Laurence Johnston Peter**

Your attitudes are a combination of negative and positive **components** (parts), and they are valuative (express worth). Your attitudes will cause you to behave in a certain way toward the person, thing, or situation you are evaluating. When your positive feelings and emotions are stronger than your negative feelings and emotions, you have a positive attitude. When the reverse is true, your attitude is negative.

A strong attitude is weighted heavily in one direction. What strong positive or negative attitude do you have toward a certain person, thing, or situation? A weak attitude is slightly weighted in

Positive Components

- There will be several vacations during the year.
- Students will be better prepared for college and work.
- The plan will reduce loss of learning during long summer vacations.
- Exams will cover less material.

Negative Components

- Students won't be able to work summer jobs.
- The building is hot in the summer and will need air-conditioning
- Families will have a shorter period for taking summer vacations
- Students will have to study for more exams

▲ *Figure 3.2 Diagram of Rachael's attitude toward year-round school proposal.*

CAREER TIP

The attitude you have toward yourself influences your attitudes toward other people and toward work.

favor of its positive or negative component. Can you think of a certain person, thing, or situation that causes you to have a slightly positive or slightly negative attitude?

Attitudes toward people whose gender, skin color, language, religion, or customs are similar to or different than our own frequently bring out strong feelings and emotions leading to extreme positive or negative attitudes. A stereotype is a strong attitude that resists change in spite of **contradictory** (showing an opposite point of view) information. A **prejudice** is an attitude that refuses to change regardless of new contradictory information or experiences.

Your attitudes are probably similar to those of your closest associates (family or friends). If your attitudes were different from theirs, you would be faced with continual criticism and correction. Re-

member the old saying, "Birds of a feather flock together."

Do you take time to question the accuracy of your personal beliefs and feelings before you take certain actions? Are you open to the fact that other people and situations change? If you can answer "yes" to these questions, you have probably reduced the role of prejudice and stereotypes in your personal relationships.

It is important to evaluate all new information that you receive. Have you ever listened to a speaker and wondered if he really knew what he was talking about? If the subject is unfamiliar to you, it would be a good idea to find out the speaker's qualifications. Is he an expert in the topic? Does he belong to a group with a special interest? Can the facts being presented be verified? Perhaps you can obtain a book by another expert to check the facts. Speakers present their opinions. Check the facts before forming yours.

Have you ever been in a conversation where a certain topic came up and you knew your opinion immediately? Perhaps your **preconceived beliefs** (opinions formed beforehand) were so strong that they blocked out any information that didn't agree with your personal position. If your preconceived

▲ *Attitudes are influenced by those we know, like, and trust.*

BUILDING SELF-ESTEEM

Education—A Family Value

Benita Russell is an African American teenager who lives in a large city. She is an honors student at Kennedy High School. Benita's parents have always stressed the relationship between education, better-paying jobs, and a more desirable lifestyle. Family encouragement and success in school have helped Benita understand herself and develop a high level of self-esteem.

Last summer, Benita attended a two-week workshop sponsored by a community program called IN-ROADS. The INROADS workshop gave her an opportunity to discuss several career areas with African American professionals. In addition, the program helped Benita explore her personal career interests and educational options. Figure 3.3 below shows the components of Benita's attitude (beliefs, feelings, and actions) toward education.

Critical Thinking

1. Many students who attend schools in large cities have negative attitudes toward education. Why are their attitudes different from Benita's?

2. In no more than three sentences, describe Benita's attitude toward education. When you finish, describe your own attitude toward education.

---

attitude insists that anything connected with a certain situation, thing, or person is absolutely right or wrong or that you can't accomplish a certain educational or occupational goal, then it will indeed become fact. This is called a **self-fulfilling prophesy**.

Can you think of a time when you

- refused to fly in an airplane?
- stayed awake all night because the weather was bad?
- were a guest at a meal and refused to eat the food?
- had a teacher or employer you couldn't tolerate?

What was your strongest attitude in that situation? Try to determine the cause of your attitude, the purpose it served, and the effect it had on your life. What influenced your attitude most: emotions or facts? If the source of an attitude is a single personal experience, make certain your information is accurate and not too generalized.

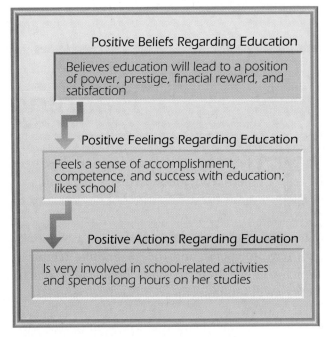

▲ *Figure 3.3 Benita's attitudes toward education.*

A Working Attitude

Your attitude toward work is as important as your job performance. You demonstrate a positive work attitude to your employer when you show an interest in your assigned tasks, perform work beyond the required limits, and display approved behaviors on the job.

Your attitude affects your feelings about the future and, as a result, influences your career choices. If family and friends appreciate and encourage your aptitudes, skills, and accomplishments, you will be motivated toward future achievement and career success. On the other hand, if family and friends criticize your aptitudes and skills, overlook your accomplishments, and emphasize your failures, you will feel that future achievement and career success are unobtainable goals. You will become discouraged.

Many times, a person is motivated toward career success by the encouragement of one particular person. Who has encouraged you? Who has discouraged you? Whom have you encouraged?

Section 3   GET INVOLVED

Answer the following on a separate sheet of paper, and be prepared to discuss your responses in class.

1. Identify three strong opinions that you have about a person, situation, or thing. Where did you learn these opinions? Have you ever had different opinions about these topics? If so, what caused you to change your mind?

2. What influenced the formation of your attitudes most? Was it personal experience, other people, or your emotions? Provide an example.

3. Describe a situation in which the media (TV, magazines, newspapers) influenced you to believe in something or someone. Do you still feel the same? Why or why not?

Section 4

Planning a Lifestyle

The occupation you select and the career path you follow will fix the limits of your lifestyle options. The demands of your occupation will determine your daily and yearly schedules, the amount of money you have to spend, and the geographic region in which you live. In turn, your schedule and your finances will set limits on your lifestyle options.

It is up to you to select your future **lifestyle** (the way you live). Use the information you have learned about yourself thus far to relate your per-

> Genius is one percent inspiration and ninety-nine percent perspiration.
>
> **Thomas Alva Edison**

sonal values, interests, aptitudes, and experiences to your lifestyle choices. Review the following lifestyle options in terms of your personal characteristics.

Lifestyle Options

- What region of the country do I prefer? North, East, West, South, Midwest?
- What geographic environment do I prefer? Mountains, coastal regions, forested areas, river areas, lake regions, farmland?
- What size community would I like to live in? City, suburb, small town, rural area?
- Which type of climate is best for me? Dry or rainy? Long cold winters or warm winters? (Be sure to consider special health problems in your decision.)
- What type of home do I prefer? Modest or luxurious? House, apartment, condominium, highrise? Do I want to rent or own? Be sure to include the distance to your place of employment, the method of transportation you will use, and the daily travel time in your decision.
- What social surroundings do I prefer? Living close to family and friends? Single or married? Children? Being mobile and making new friends to obtain career advancements, or staying in the same social environment at the expense of career advancements?

Your future lifestyle will be a compromise between the lifestyle options you select and the requirements and rewards of your future occupation. For each occupation you consider, de-

▲ *The rewards and requirements of your future occupation will affect your lifestyle options. How important is it for you to live close to your family?*

termine how many of your lifestyle options would be satisfied. Which options are your top priorities? Which options would you be willing to trade for career advancement?

Learning to make lifestyle adjustments and adapting to new and sometimes unwanted situations are necessary elements of every successful career. However, it is important to accept and be satisfied with each lifestyle compromise you make.

Section 4 GET INVOLVED

Answer the following on a separate sheet of paper, and be prepared to discuss your responses in class.

1. Which of your preferred lifestyle options do you presently enjoy? Which of your preferred options are missing from your present lifestyle?
2. Among the occupations you are considering, which is most likely to provide you with your desired lifestyle? Why? Which is least likely? Why?
3. Locate a copy of the *Occupational Outlook Handbook* in your school or public library. Find the description of an occupation you are presently considering. What are the average earnings? What are the hours of work? What is the job outlook? What education or training will be required? How do these factors relate to your preferred lifestyle goals?

CHAPTER 3 REVIEW

ENRICH YOUR VOCABULARY

On a separate sheet of paper, number from 1 to 16, and complete the following activity. (Do not write in your textbook.) Match each statement below with the most appropriate term from the "Enrich Your Vocabulary" list at the beginning of the chapter by writing that term next to the correct statement.

1. The way a person thinks about things and acts toward others
2. An aim or objective
3. The way you live
4. Having monetary worth
5. Having no monetary worth
6. People you frequently come in contact with
7. Opinions formed beforehand
8. An attitude that refuses to change regardless of new contradictory information or experiences
9. Obtainable
10. Important beliefs you consider to be true and use to guide the direction of your life
11. A strong preconceived idea that becomes fact
12. Showing an opposite point of view
13. Trial
14. Parts
15. Anything you can touch
16. Schedule

CHECK YOUR KNOWLEDGE

On a separate sheet of paper, complete the following activity. (Do not write in your textbook.)

1. Values are not necessarily right or wrong, but they guide the direction of your life. What three values mentioned in this chapter were expressed in the Declaration of Independence?
2. Personal values explain a person's willingness or reluctance to make commitments, accept changes, strive for high achievement, or develop new skills. How does clarifying your values help you make plans that are more likely to be successful?
3. People choose a certain type of work because it rewards their personal values and allows them to live their values daily. Which of the following occupations is most closely related to a high value of working outdoors?
   a. Bricklayer
   b. Teacher
   c. Computer programmer
4. Most values are nonmaterialistic. Name six non-materialistic values.
5. Establishing a goal gives you a sense of direction. It is part of making a plan. Name six of the guidelines given in this chapter for developing a list of goals for your life plan.
6. Attitudes are revealed by positive or negative responses to another person's values. Where are values learned?
7. Attitudes toward people of different racial or ethnic backgrounds frequently evoke strong feelings and emotions. When does an attitude become a prejudice?
8. The occupation you select will limit your lifestyle options. What are two ways an occupation influences your lifestyle?

DEVELOP SCANS COMPETENCIES

Government experts say that successful workers can productively use Resources, Interpersonal skills, Information, Systems, and Technology. This activity will give you practice in developing Information and Interpersonal skills.

Choose three careers to research. During your research, identify the values necessary for a worker to be successful in that career. Your list might include: has knowledge, enjoys precision work, works under pressure, works at a fast pace, works with others, enjoys contact with the public, works alone, has creative abilities, enjoys change and variety, is physically able to do the work, is trustworthy, is punctual, etc.

After making your own list, talk with people who work in each of the careers you researched. Ask if there are any values they would add to the list.

When you have a completed list of values, make a chart (see example) that shows which values are required in which careers. Notice the similarities and differences.

	Career 1	Career 2	Career 3
enjoys change	√	√	
works alone	√		
is punctual	√	√	√

Problem Solving: Making Choices

Learning Objectives

After completing this chapter, you should be prepared to:

- discuss how decisions are made from a continual selection of choices with more than one solution
- apply the rational style of decision making, and increase your satisfaction with personal and career decisions
- identify three satisfactory decisions that were influenced by your personal orientation
- explain why satisfactory decisions depend on self-knowledge, reliable information, and clear thinking

Enrich Your Vocabulary

In reading this chapter and doing the exercises you will learn the following important terms:

problem solving
consequences
authority style of
  decision making
intuitive style of
  decision making
fatalistic style of
  decision making
impulsive style of
  decision making
rational style of
  decision making
personal
  characteristics
work environments
personal orientation

environmental
  orientation
mechanical
  orientation
spatial perception
scientific orientation
creative orientation
introspective ability
sociable orientation
empathizing
conciliating
persuasive
  orientation
structured
  orientation

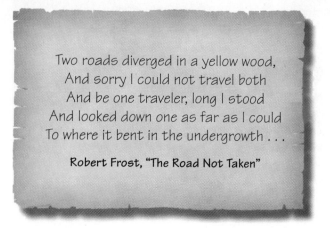

Two roads diverged in a yellow wood,
And sorry I could not travel both
And be one traveler, long I stood
And looked down one as far as I could
To where it bent in the undergrowth . . .

Robert Frost, "The Road Not Taken"

Like the traveler in Robert Frost's poem, you will arrive at points along the road of life where you must choose between two options. The choices you make will have different outcomes for your career, friendships, future lifestyle, and even selection of a spouse. You may wish to travel both roads, but reality will dictate that you make a choice.

Everyday, you face situations in which you must make choices. **Problem solving** (often called decision making) is the process used to make decisions when you select from two or more possible choices. Skill in the decision-making process provides you with a sense of control in achieving daily and long-term goals and increases the likelihood of satisfaction with your personal decisions.

What clothes will you wear to school? Will you go to the basketball game this evening or stay home and finish your schoolwork? Will you look for a part-time job? Will you offer to help a friend who's in trouble, or will you mind your own business? The decisions you make in situations like these and your satisfaction with the outcomes (results) of those decisions are influenced by your personal values and your knowledge of the facts.

Making satisfactory choices will become easier as you learn to anticipate how well the decisions you are considering meet your personal needs. The ability to anticipate the possible outcomes of a choice depends on your knowledge of yourself and the facts, and on your ability to think clearly.

When a person acts on a decision, there are always **consequences** (resulting advantages and disadvantages). Can you think of a situation in which someone made a decision that resulted in a pleas-

▲ *Successful workers are also successful problem solvers. What problems will you need to solve in your future career?*

ant consequence for you? An unpleasant consequence? Can you think of a situation in which a decision you made had a pleasant or unpleasant consequence for another person?

The freedom to make choices is accompanied by the need to be responsible for the consequences of those choices. As a responsible adult, it is very important to have an effective process for making decisions. In the world of work, an organization's ability to achieve its strategic objectives frequently depends on the problem-solving skills of its work force.

Section 1

The Process of Decision Making

What's your problem? Schoolwork? Your best friend? Trouble at home? Your job? It is especially difficult to face problems and make decisions when there are many choices. The element of risk is always involved. You cannot be absolutely certain that the choice you make is best for the situation. Understanding yourself and all of the facts concerning the situation will help you to make realistic, acceptable decisions.

When you were a small child, you had little or no control over life situations. Adults made decisions for you, and your only role in decision making was to obey. This is sometimes called the **authority style of decision making**. Some adults never outgrow this style and continue to rely on a spouse, parent, or other person to make decisions for them. The authority style of decision making places you in a dependent position.

Most adults rely on authorities to make legal or medical decisions. How is this different from a small child's decision-making situation? How is it the same? How can a person be certain that an authority is making the right decision?

Sean Ward is a self-employed sales representative. He buys used furniture at auctions and resells it. When Sean has a decision to make, he usually follows his "gut-level" feelings. Sean's philosophy of decision making is to make the choice that feels best and seems like the right thing to do. This method is sometimes called the **intuitive style of decision making**. Intuitive decision making is based on personal feelings and values rather than facts. Intuitive hunches could be nothing more than wishful thinking. Can you think of a situation in which intuitive decision making would be effective? Where would it be ineffective?

Some people believe that whatever will be, will be, and it doesn't make any difference what a person decides. Believing that whatever you decide will happen anyway is known as the **fatalistic style of decision making**. Do you know anyone who uses this approach to decision making?

Vanessa Payne rarely considers the consequences of her decisions. She doesn't like to think ahead. She uses an **impulsive style of decision making**. Last week, she bought a new car. Vanessa liked her old car and really didn't plan to buy a new one for two more years. When she saw the new car in the dealer's showroom, however, she got very excited about it and bought it. Now Vanessa is concerned about her monthly payments and may need to take a second job. Did you ever make an impulsive decision? How did it work out? Would you recommend this style of decision making?

A **rational style of decision making** considers the feelings and values of the decision maker as well as the facts concerning the situation. It requires the decision maker to be logical and thoughtful and to plan. Rational decisions balance the demands of a situation against the pros and cons of the alternatives. They take into account the feelings and opinions of experts and of people close to the decision maker.

It would be a waste of time and energy to use the rational decision-making process to select lunch in the school cafeteria, to buy a newspaper, or to determine which day you will bathe your pet. On the other hand, whether to go steady, buy a new car, or enter a certain occupation are all complex decisions that require a higher-level method of decision making. Rational decision making will be more satisfactory in solving complex life situations than the other approaches mentioned.

The Rational Decision-Making Process

The rational decision-making process involves seven steps. Here's how it's done.

1. **Recognize that you need to make a decision.**

   Have you ever been frustrated, anxious, or uncomfortable with a life situation? Your feel

▲ *Buying a car requires a high level of decision-making skill. Which car do you want? Which one do you need? Which car can you afford?*

ings could have been coming from a conflict that was taking place between you and another person or between two people who were important to you. You will be faced with these situations in the world of work, just as you are in your personal life. You may have to choose between two or more job offers or decide on the purchase of an expensive item such as an automobile or a house. In each of these cases, you begin to realize a need for change. You become aware that you need to make a decision.

2. **Identify the problem to be solved.**

   What is preventing you from reaching your goal? How does this situation make you feel? What is the cause of the problem? Why does this concern you? Who else is involved? What is preventing you from making a decision? Take time to consider these questions, and then write or state the answers to the "who, what, when, where, why, and how" of the situation.

3. **Analyze all of your alternatives.**

   Gather as much information as possible about the problem and each alternative for reaching an acceptable solution. Facts found in newspapers, magazines, books, and research articles; advice from others; and personal experience are all good sources of information. Make certain that your information is accurate and complete.

   Make a list of your present alternatives, and try to find several new ones. Develop a "what-if" solution using each alternative. What are the satisfactory and unsatisfactory results of each alternative? List the consequences of each alternative in terms of time, cost, usefulness, and effect on other people. Eliminate the least acceptable alternatives, and then determine which of the remaining ones are most practical and attainable.

The possibility of risk and failure can create feelings of confusion, conflict, or anxiety. Can you think of a situation in which you took a chance by selecting one choice over another? How did you feel about the risk you were taking? Exploring and evaluating the alternatives when making a decision lessens negative feelings and gives you more confidence in the likelihood of a positive solution.

As an example, there is information available for more than 20,000 occupations. When exploring the requirements and commitments for several occupations, you might feel anxious about the risks involved and the possibility of failure. However, by identifying the risks, advantages, and disadvantages of a particular occupation before making a decision to pursue it, you greatly reduce the probability of failure and increase the probability of career success.

4. **Be satisfied with your choices.**

Check each alternative solution against your personal attitudes, values, and culture. (Check your notes for the information that you learned about yourself in Chapters 2 and 3.) How personally desirable or undesirable do you find each alternative? Throw out the solutions that conflict most with your personal characteristics, and consider those that are most similar to your attitudes, values, and culture.

Remove from consideration any solutions that you lack the skill or information to accomplish. Avoid the temptation to pursue alternatives with high expectations for unrealistic goals.

5. **Make the decision.**

Review each acceptable alternative in terms of how it will affect you and the other people who are involved. Be certain that other people are satisfied with the solution. Rank the alternatives from most acceptable to least acceptable. It is important that you select one

▲ *Rank your alternatives from most acceptable to least acceptable and then select one.*

alternative at this point. No decision can be pursued to its most successful conclusion if the decision maker is emotionally divided and spending energy trying to make other alternatives workable. Choosing one alternative means eliminating others, at least temporarily and perhaps permanently.

All decisions involve a risk of failure. Successful decision makers have the courage to look at each decision honestly, reevaluate their decisions, and alter or abandon them if necessary. However, wise decision makers don't surrender to the pressure of personal conflicts, financial difficulty, being considered unpopular, or fear of failure.

6. **Implement the decision.**

A decision isn't a decision until something happens. Do you know someone who talks a lot about the things that he or she is going to do, but rarely follows through? Take action to see that the alternative you have selected is carried to a successful conclusion. Perhaps your decision is to enter a training program in the fall, purchase a new car next spring, or raise your grades in a certain course. Whatever the situation, you will need to be firm, disciplined, and persistent in the course of action you follow.

7. **Evaluate the decision.**

Implementing a decision could mean practicing new behaviors, following different procedures, or altering the life patterns of people who are involved. Situations change, mistakes can be made, revisions may be needed, and certain parts of the plan may have to be delayed. It is important to evaluate all of the factors involved in a decision.

A successful decision maker remains flexible and open to the process of change. If the evaluation of a decision reveals that it's a failure, new information indicates a better solution, and the goal is still appropriate, a new alternative will be considered.

One of the most important things to remember when evaluating a decision is that changes will keep occurring in your social, physical, and economic environment. Your goals, beliefs, attitudes, values, and skills may be affected. Today's successful decision could be unacceptable tomorrow because of ever-changing factors.

Section 1 — GET INVOLVED

Use the seven steps of the rational decision-making process to complete the following. Be prepared to discuss your responses in class.

1. Using step 1, identify a situation in your life that will require a decision on your part. What feelings do you have about this situation?
2. Using step 2, clearly define the problem of doing your homework assignments for the next two weeks.
3. Using step 3, make a list of at least three risks you will be taking if you choose to wait until after graduation from high school to make a tentative career decision.
4. Using step 4, describe a past decision that satisfied you. What factors gave you satisfaction? Describe a decision that you were not satisfied with. What factors caused you to be dissatisfied?
5. Using step 5, describe a situation in which you selected from two or more alternatives before making a decision. What factors influenced your choice?
6. Using step 6, list the decisions you have made and acted on today, this week, and this year.
7. Using step 7, consider a major decision you have made. How did it change your behavior, the procedures you followed, or the day-to-day pattern of your life?

Section 2

Knowing Yourself and Career Decisions

What occupational roles will you have in the world of work? What career decisions should you make to ensure satisfaction and success? Not being certain of the answers to these questions bothers most high school and college students.

The choice of an occupation begins when you identify **personal characteristics** (qualities that make an individual unique) and match them to

▲ *Do you enjoy the natural environment? Would you like to work outdoors?*

▲ *People with a strong mechanical orientation develop their physical and mechanical skills more fully than their verbal communication skills.*

related occupations and **work environments** (work settings). When this happens, career decisions tend to be both satisfying and meaningful.

You have a **personal orientation** (unique individual direction), which is the combination of your abilities, interests, aptitudes, and overall personality. This unique personal orientation makes you different from everyone else. It is this uniqueness that directs you toward the occupational roles and work environments that are most likely to provide personal satisfaction.

In general, personal characteristics can be divided into seven broad orientations. Most people can identify two or more orientations that include several of their personal characteristics and one or more orientations that are very different from their personal characteristics.

CAREER TIP

As you make decisions, keep as many future options open as possible.

The following are descriptions of the seven orientations people have toward work. Which ones are most like you? Which are least like you?

The Environmental Orientation

People with a strong **environmental orientation** tend to be frank, open, and natural. They are doers rather than talkers.

They like physical activity in the outdoor environment. They frequently enjoy fishing, camping, hiking, skiing, bicycle riding, backpacking, and other outdoor activities.

They are frequently skilled in working with their hands. They are practical problem solvers and are able to use self-control in tense situations. People with this orientation tend to be more physical than verbal, and their physical skills are often developed to a higher level than their human relations, leadership, or verbal skills. In many ways, they are like people with a mechanical orientation.

▲ *Ideas, words, and symbols are the tools of a chemist. Do you enjoy working with information? Have you considered a scientific career?*

▲ *Creative aptitudes in music, writing, and sketching can be developed into career skills.*

The Mechanical Orientation

People with a strong **mechanical orientation** tend to prefer work involving machines, tools, and logic (reasoning, common sense) to work involving constant verbal communication. They are usually practical and physical in their approach to problem solving.

These people frequently enjoy working on bikes or cars, building things, making repairs, and being active participants in sports activities. They frequently demonstrate skills requiring practical thinking, working with hand tools, and good **spatial perception** (recognizing forms in space and the relationships of plane and solid objects).

People with a strong mechanical orientation often develop their physical and mechanical skills more fully than their human relations and verbal communication skills.

The Scientific Orientation

People who have a strong **scientific orientation** frequently use their intellect (mind, mental power) more than their social or physical skills to solve problems. Ideas, words, and symbols are the tools of scientifically oriented people.

They enjoy working with their thoughts and speculating about possible solutions to problems. They frequently enjoy playing chess, building models, reading mysteries, and using computers.

People with a strong scientific orientation usually prefer working with information to working with people. They occasionally prefer working alone to being in social situations or leadership roles. They enjoy intellectual activities.

The Creative Orientation

People who have a strong **creative orientation** frequently react to social, school, and work situations by using their feelings, imaginations, and intuition (instincts, hunches). They may solve problems by nontraditional methods using unique ideas. In making decisions, they may rely on feelings and emotions more than practical information and facts.

Creative people frequently enjoy reading fiction, playing musical instruments, singing, writing, sketching, painting, theater, and photography.

People with this orientation frequently have good spatial perception, good eye-hand coordination, musical skills, writing skills, and **introspective ability** (skill to examine one's thoughts and feelings).

People with a strong creative orientation tend to dislike rigid rules of behavior, highly structured assignments, and other conventional social and economic values.

The Sociable Orientation

People with a strong **sociable orientation** are usually helpful to others. They focus their caring nature on the poor, sick, aged, and young and those who need help or counseling.

When solving problems, they rely more on their personal concern and emotion than on their intellectual ability. They discuss situations with other people and try to make decisions that others will accept.

Sociable people frequently enjoy attending parties, writing letters to friends, having conversations, and visiting with family and friends.

People with a strong sociable orientation frequently display skills in speaking, teaching, **empathizing** (sharing another's thoughts and feelings), listening, and **conciliating** (bringing others together, pacifying, winning over).

The Persuasive Orientation

Those who have a strong **persuasive orientation** enjoy involvement with people more than information or things. They like using their powers of persuasion in sales and leadership roles. They frequently place a high value on power and money.

When solving problems, they rely heavily on a small group of trusted associates for accurate information. They tend to make sensible decisions based on the facts provided and the goal they are trying to achieve.

These people usually enjoy being class or club officers, speaking to groups, dressing well, and talking with important people. People with this

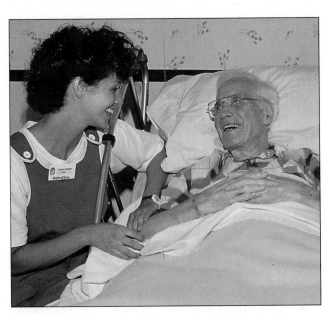

▲ *Which sociable characteristics are similar to your characteristics? Would you enjoy this caregiver's job?*

▲ *Retail sales and management is a growing career field. What other occupations would satisfy a person with a strong persuasive orientation?*

The Structured Orientation

People with a strong **structured orientation** tend to select educational and career goals that are approved by society. They solve problems using traditional, proven methods.

These people are usually well-groomed, appropriately dressed, and self-disciplined. They frequently enjoy collecting coins or stamps, participating in church activities and club meetings, and keeping a diary.

Structurally oriented people are frequently skilled in coding, classifying, and computing information; retaining and following instructions; self-control; and maintaining a system or process.

They usually dislike subjects or work tasks that require imagination and adjustment to changing situations. They appreciate clearly defined tasks.

Your career choice may be the most important decision you will ever make because of the effect it will have on your other major life decisions. Some people hesitate to make career choices because they fear that a poor choice will keep them from succeeding in other areas of their life. It is important to remember that if you are not satisfied with one career choice, you can make another one. In fact, most people have several jobs and make numerous important career decisions before they settle on one career path.

The more you know about occupations and your personal characteristics, the easier it will be to make satisfying career decisions.

▲ *Coding, classifying, and computing information is very structured work. Are you good at following directions and carrying out details?*

orientation have strong personal relations, persuasion, verbal communication, organization (structuring, arranging), and leadership skills.

Persuasive people frequently lack scientific skills and interests and tend to avoid activities that require information gathering and repeated observations. Confining activities restrict their adventurous spirit.

Section 2 GET INVOLVED

Answer the following on a separate sheet of paper, and be prepared to discuss your responses in class.

1. Which two orientations are most like you? Describe the similarities. How is your decision-making style similar to or different from the style of people who have these two orientations?

2. Which two orientations are least like you? Describe the differences. How is your decision-making style similar to or different from the style of people who have these two orientations?

Section

3

Decisions and Goals for Today and Tomorrow

People make numerous decisions every day without thinking about the decision-making process. For most people, solving everyday problems is almost automatic. Think about your day up to this point. When you were awakened by the alarm clock this morning, you recognized that a decision had to be made. You had to decide whether to ignore the alarm or get out of bed. Obviously, you chose to get up. You made other decisions this morning: you selected clothes to wear, decided whether to bathe, made at least one decision concerning breakfast, and chose to come to school.

Our daily lives are a continual selection of choices with countless possibilities. Some decisions are less complex than others. We may already have the information needed to make these decisions, or it may be as handy as the *Yellow Pages*. Still, each decision has alternative solutions with different possible effects on our daily lives. Decisions on this level include getting the car repaired, buying groceries, or going on a date.

Some decisions have consequences with a greater, long-term impact on our lives. Decisions on this level include taking a position on drugs or alcohol; planning a lifestyle; selecting a marriage partner; or making a career choice.

As you get older and gain career experience, your skill level will increase and your career aspirations (hopes, goals) will change. Social and economic conditions and events, such as wars, inflation, immigration, and natural disasters, might also affect your career opportunities. Do you know anyone who has had to change career plans due to circumstances such as these? Making career decisions in response to expected and unexpected changes will be a lifelong process.

Although you may have several jobs during your career, it is important to take certain steps toward a future occupational goal while you are still a student. If you change your occupational goal later, simply repeat the process. Like Dwayne Richards (see feature on next page), you may make occupational changes based on personal career maturity and available opportunities. The following steps will help you reach each of your occupational goals.

1. Decide on a specific occupation as a tentative goal.

2. Gather as much information as possible about the tentative occupation. Be sure to include the day-to-day nature of the occupational role, working conditions, employment opportunities, potential earnings, and necessary education and training.

3. Explore the occupation by interviewing a person employed in that occupation, visiting a

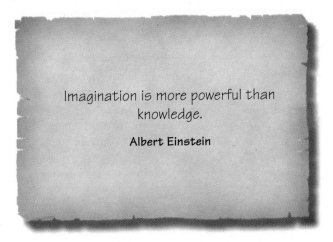

Imagination is more powerful than knowledge.

Albert Einstein

PLANNING MAKES A DIFFERENCE

Each Job Is a Learning Experience

Dwayne Richards graduated from high school last June. Within two weeks, he had a job interview at a car dealership. During his interview, Dwayne demonstrated a pleasant, positive attitude. In addition, the owner of the agency was impressed with Dwayne's excellent high school attendance record.

Ten days later, Dwayne began his first full-time job at the car agency. In the beginning, Dwayne performed custodial work and sometimes cleaned new cars. He occasionally took early-morning customers to their jobs while the agency worked on their cars. Six months later, Dwayne was promoted to cashier in the service department.

Dwayne has learned a lot about several jobs since he began working in the service department. One job in particular that fascinates him involves using a computer to maintain an inventory of several thousand parts and to identify the exact location of each part. Dwayne plans to attend night school to obtain the computer and business skills needed for an inventory-control job.

Critical Thinking

1. If Dwayne follows his plan, do you think this will be his last major career decision? Explain your answer.
2. How are Dwayne's immediate behaviors related to his longer-term career goals? How are your immediate behaviors related to your longer-term career goals?

work site to observe the occupation, taking related course work in school, accepting related part-time employment, or doing volunteer work at a related work site.

4. Decide whether to pursue entry into the occupation or to establish a new tentative occupa-

tional goal. Be certain to consider personal, educational, and financial barriers to your goal.

5. Take specific steps to acquire the necessary skills.

6. Seek employment in the occupation. See Unit 2 of this text, "Job Search and Job Success."

Section 3 GET INVOLVED

Answer the following on a separate sheet of paper, and be prepared to discuss your responses in class.

2. What economic conditions in your community have helped or hindered your career opportunities during the past year? What about national

economic conditions? Ask an adult friend this question, and be prepared to discuss your findings in class.

3. Name three changes during the past ten years that have occurred in a career you have been considering.

CHAPTER 4 REVIEW

ENRICH YOUR VOCABULARY

On a separate sheet of paper, number from 1 to 21, and complete the following activity. (Do not write in your textbook.) Match each statement below with the most appropriate term from the "Enrich Your Vocabulary" list at the beginning of the chapter by writing that term next to the correct statement.

1. A style of decision making in which decisions are made for you
2. Results
3. A personal orientation in which people frequently react to social, school, and work situations by using their feelings, imagination, and emotions
4. The process you use to make decisions
5. A style of decision making in which you believe that whatever you decide will happen anyway
6. A style of decision making in which you rarely consider the consequences of your decision
7. A style of decision making based more on personal feelings than on facts
8. A personal orientation in which people tend to be frank, open, and natural
9. A style of decision making that requires logic, thoughtfulness, and planning and considers your feelings and values as well
10. A personal orientation in which people frequently use their intellect more than their social or physi-

cal skills to solve problems
11. The qualities that make an individual unique
12. Bringing together, pacifying
13. Work settings
14. Sharing in another's thoughts and emotions
15. A unique individual direction
16. A personal orientation in which people frequently develop physical and mechanical skills more than their human relations and verbal communication
17. Recognizing forms in space and the relationships of plane and solid objects
18. Skill to examine one's thoughts and feelings
19. A personal orientation in which people focus their caring nature on the poor, sick, and aged
20. A personal orientation in which people have strong personal relations, persuasive, verbal communication, organizational, and leadership skills
21. A personal orientation in which people are frequently skilled in coding, classifying

CHECK YOUR KNOWLEDGE

On a separate sheet of paper, complete the following activity. (Do not write in your textbook.)

1. On what three things does your ability to anticipate the possible outcome of a choice depend?
2. What are the five styles of decision making discussed in this chapter?
3. What are the seven steps in the rational decision-making process?
4. One of the most important things to remember when evaluating a decision is the changing nature of the social, physical, and economic environments and your goals, beliefs, attitudes, values, and skills. Why are these things important?
5. People solve everyday problems almost automati-

cally. Does this mean there are no alternatives to everyday problems? Explain your answer.
6. What four areas of self make each person unique?
7. Personal characteristics are divided into seven broad orientations in this chapter. What are they?
8. Selecting a career may be the most important decision you will make. Why is a career choice so important?
9. Social and economic conditions make learning to adapt an important part of today's lifestyle. What steps will help you reach future occupational goals if you change your present goal?

DEVELOP SCANS COMPETENCIES

Government experts say that successful workers can productively use Resources, Interpersonal skills, Information, Systems, and Technology. This activity will give you practice in developing Systems skills.

Choose a career in which you have an interest. Use the rational decision-making process to determine the steps you would follow to become employed in this career. Draw a diagram similar to the one shown, which specifically details each step.

Recognize need → Identify problem → Analyze alternatives → Be satisfied → Make decision → Implement decision → Evaluate decision

Looking Ahead: Education and Training

Learning Objectives

After completing this chapter, you should be prepared to:

- state why education and training will be continuous throughout your career
- explain why education and training must be included in career planning
- discuss the relationship between proficiency in specific school subjects and tentative occupational choices
- state the relationship between levels of education and levels of employment in specific career fields
- evaluate the requirements and advantages of different types of educational institutions and training programs

Enrich Your Vocabulary

In reading this chapter and doing the exercises you will learn the following important terms:

adapt
postsecondary
employment
  structure
apprenticeship
guilds
journey worker
proprietary school
technical school
GED
accredited
correspondence
  courses

Job Corps
Tech Prep programs
on-the-job training
  (OJT)
competencies
open-admissions
  policy
baccalaureate degree
university
preprofessional
  programs

As you begin to narrow your career choices to a few specific occupations, you should make plans to obtain the specific education and training you'll need to enter those occupations. Throughout your working years, education and training will play a key role in your career success. Each career move will involve specific education and training requirements.

Several employment trends have emerged in recent years that will be important to you in planning your career:

1. The highest-paying jobs with the best chance for career growth will go to the workers who have the most education and training.
2. Job opportunities for highly trained and educated workers are increasing, and job opportunities for the unskilled are decreasing.
3. More workers than ever before are obtaining education and training after high school graduation.
4. Today, fewer low-skilled workers are needed in the U.S. work force than in the past, but an increasing number of middle- and upper-level workers are needed to develop and sell new products.
5. Workers will require lifelong education and training if they are to **adapt** (fit into) to the changing world of work.
6. Some form of **postsecondary** (after high school) education and training will be required for 75 percent of all job classifications during and beyond the 1990s.

Some years ago, manufacturing was a growing source of employment for U.S. workers. Job opportunities were available that offered workers with less than a high school education the possibility of promotion to higher-paying jobs. However, manufacturing employment peaked at twenty-one million jobs in 1979. By 1990, almost two million manufacturing jobs were lost. The U.S. work force is expected to lose another 600,000 manufacturing jobs by the year 2005. How old will you be in 2005? Will there be a manufacturing job for you if you do not graduate from high school?

▲ *Some form of postsecondary education and training will be required for 75 percent of all job classifications during and beyond the 1990's. Are you taking the courses you will need to enter the occupation of your choice?*

Education and Training Are Important

Global competition for worldwide markets, new technologies, and political forces have influenced the **employment structure** (types of jobs available). Jobs are now more likely than ever to require postsecondary education and training (Figure 5.1).

▲ *There are 312,000 packaging and filling machine operators and tenders in the U.S. labor force. This low-skilled, declining occupation requires a high school education.*

Occupation	Percent
Paralegals	85%
Medical assistants	74%
Radiologic technologists and technicians	70%
Physical and corrective therapy assistants	64%
Data processing equipment repairers	60%
EEG technologists	57%
Occupational therapy assistants and aides	55%
Surgical technologists	55%
Medical records technicians	54%
Nuclear medical technologists	53%
Respiratory therapists	52%
Electromedical and biomedical equipment repairers	51%
Legal secretaries	47%
Registered nurses	45%
Licensed practical nurses	42%
Restaurant cooks	42%
Producers, directors, actors, and entertainers	41%
Dental hygienists	41%
Dancers and choreographers	38%
Dispensing opticians	37%

▲ *Figure 5.1 Fastest growing occupations requiring some postsecondary education, projected 1990 to 2005. Notice that many of the occupations listed are in the career area of health services.*

Graduating from high school without specific job preparation (vocational training) or preparation for further education (college-preparatory education) increases your likelihood of being unemployed. Employers are no longer interested in the graduate who "just barely made it." Although projections indicate that jobs will be available for those without training beyond high school, the prospects for high-paying jobs will be better for those who have postsecondary education and training.

Dropping out of high school reduces employment opportunities even more. High school dropouts are more likely to obtain jobs that are low paying, offer little chance for advancement, and are projected to be declining or growing very slowly. The risk of unemployment is also higher for high school dropouts (Figure 5.2).

When an economic recession takes place, high school dropouts are usually the first workers to be laid off. As an example, 400,000 students dropped out of high school between October 1990 and October 1991. During the recession of 1992, more than 40 percent of these dropouts were unemployed.

It is important that you begin now to identify and develop education and training skills that are marketable in the world of work. The best employment opportunities increasingly depend on education and training preparation.

High schools, postsecondary educational institutions, and colleges consistently expand their offerings to better prepare students for the increasing education and training demands of growing occupations. You can acquire employment skills through formal and informal instruction in programs as short as a few months or as long as several years. The type and length of education or training you select will determine the range of your occupational qualifications.

Is high school a rewarding part of your life, or do you just want to get it over with? What level of accomplishment will you reach with your high school education?

- Dropout?
- A diploma with minimum passing grades?
- Specific entry-level vocational skills?
- Acceptance by a two-year college program?
- Acceptance by a four-year college program?

Some type of education and training will be required for any occupation you select. Your present thoughts and attitudes about education and training will affect your future career success. Many students decide to work and be independent for a period of time after high school graduation before continuing their education and training. Unfortunately, increased personal and financial responsibilities frequently prevent them from rising above the unskilled-worker classification.

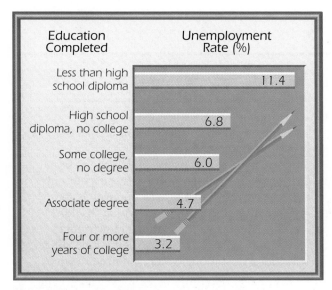

▲ *Figure 5.2 Schooling Versus the Rate of Unemployment.*

Solving The Problem

A Dead End on "The Easy Road"

Bennie Lee liked high school most of the time, but he didn't like to study. Bennie took the "easy road" when it came to mathematics, science, and English courses, but he always passed with a grade of C or D. Bennie felt that young people should enjoy life and that there would be plenty of time to be serious and work hard when he was older.

Bennie's counselor encouraged him to enter a vocational program in the eleventh grade. Bennie looked at several vocational programs but decided he would rather stay in the general course of study. He had a good part-time job and could see no problem in obtaining a better job after he got his diploma.

As a senior, Bennie discovered he was eligible to obtain financial assistance for college. However, the colleges he applied to would not accept him because of his low grades, his lack of college preparatory courses, and his score of 12 on the ACT.

After Bennie graduated, he bought a four-year-old car. The payments took most of his paycheck, and he continued living at home. He checked out a private vocational school but found that even with financial aid he wouldn't be able to make the payments on his car, pay off the other debts he had acquired, and have enough left to live on even if he stayed at home.

Bennie lost his job last month. He is out of money, the finance company repossessed (took back) his car, and he is waiting for his first unemployment check.

Critical Thinking

1. Why is Bennie having so many problems while many of his friends are experiencing career success?
2. What advice would you give Bennie? What future do you see for him?

Section 1 GET INVOLVED

Answer the following on a separate sheet of paper, and be prepared to discuss your responses in class.

1. Name two occupations that you are presently considering. What education and training skills will you need for each occupation? What high school subjects will be important in preparing for each occupation?
2. Make a list of all of the education and training choices available in your high school. For what further education and training will your high school education prepare you?
3. Many American companies insist that they can't fill job openings because they can't find qualified, skilled, motivated workers. What does this statement mean to you?
4. Study Figure 5.1 on page 74. Which *one* occupation would you select if these were your only career choices? What satisfaction would you receive from this occupation? What wouldn't you like about this occupation? How would this choice fit your personal orientation? What education or training would you need to enter this occupation?

Section

2

High School Is Important Preparation

Taking advantage of your high school education and training opportunities will help you learn important employment skills and will increase your employment options.

If you strive for high achievement in high school, the likelihood of connecting your education and training to employment opportunities will increase. Basic academic school subjects are the starting point for career preparation.

Employers frequently contact a job seeker's high school to obtain information concerning past grades and attendance. Employers understand that success in school is an indicator of success on the job. Students who have acquired a good understanding of basic high school subjects almost always are easier to train than those who have done poorly. Today's employers place a premium

CAREER TIP

The failure to develop basic skills in reading, writing, mathematics, science, and social studies will limit your career choices and your future earnings.

on skills in reading, math, communication, and problem solving.

In one survey of 360 members of the National Association of Manufacturers, almost two-thirds stated that their job applicants lacked the general skills or the motivation to be productive employees (Figure 5.3). What problems could workers' deficiencies in math and reading skills cause in a manufacturing plant?

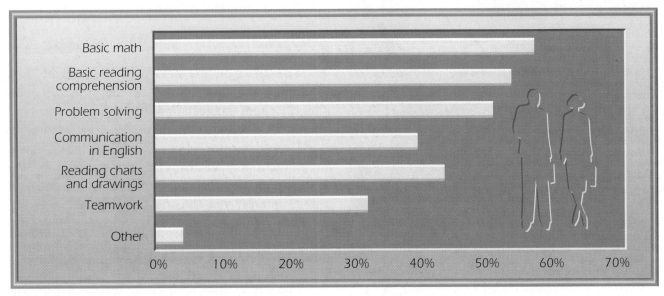

▲ *Figure 5.3 Educational Deficiencies in Present Employee Population.*

An increasing number of employers are testing job seekers to determine their proficiency in basic high school skills. In addition to basic subject skills, a typical employment test measures a job seeker's personal habits, such as self-discipline, reliability, perseverance, acceptance of responsibility, and respect for the rights of others. Teamwork requires highly developed listening skills and an understanding of specific, job-related vocabulary.

Courses

Why did you choose the course of study you are now pursuing in high school? Which courses are preparing you for postsecondary education and training? Which provide you with specific vocational skills? Which prepare you for your intended career? What is the connection between your values and interests, the occupations you are considering, and the subjects you are studying? If you are not satisfied with your answers to these questions, you should discuss possible changes with your parents, teachers, and high school counselor.

More than 1600 high schools and community colleges are working together to provide a new type of occupational training called **Tech Prep**. The education and training begins in high school and ends with an apprenticeship certificate or graduation from a community college program. Tech Prep programs are offered in engineering technology, applied science, mechanical arts and trades, agriculture, health, business, marketing and many other technical career areas.

High schools and community colleges work together to develop the Tech Prep course of study. During the last two years of high school, Tech Prep effectively blends academic and vocational education. Course sequences include mathematics, science, communications, and a "priority occupation" specialty area. Tech Prep students are expected to graduate from high school prepared both for further training (such as an apprenticeship or community college program) and for work.

Education—Who's Using It?

The chart on the next page (See Figure 5.4) demonstrates the strong relationship between high school subjects and certain occupations. Keep in mind that mathematics, English usage, and reading comprehension are needed at some level in all occupations. Which of the subjects listed interest you the most? Which of the occupations interest you the most? Which subjects are needed for the occupations you are considering?

Effective Learning Skills

The key to unlocking future success is *knowing how to learn*. Equipped with this skill, you can

▲ *Tech Prep programs help students turn vocational interests into occupational skills. Does your school offer Tech Prep courses of study?*

Figure 5.4 RELATED HIGH SCHOOL SUBJECTS AND OCCUPATIONS

Foreign Language	Biology	Physics	Chemistry
Customs examiner	Dental Assistant	Electrician	Pharmacist
Missionary	Landscape worker	Civil engineer	Ceramic engineer
Salesperson	Veterinarian	Astronomer	Assayer
Flight attendant	Rancher	Architect	Chemical salesperson
Travel agent	Game warden	Meteorologist	Laboratory technician
Social worker	Park ranger	Physical chemist	Photographer
Immigration worker	Nursery worker	Electrical engineer	Metallurgist
Foreign correspondent	Dietitian	Electronics technician	Chemical engineer
Teacher	Biologist	Physicist	Oceanographer

Physical Education	Business Education	Health Education	English
Lifeguard	Accounting clerk	Chiropractor	Librarian
Dancer	Buyer	Dental assistant	Lawyer
Umpire	Stenographer	Practical nurse	Author
Coach	Legal secretary	Dentist	Proofreader
Professional athlete	Word-processing operator	Surgical technician	Stenographer
Recreation worker	File clerk	EKG technician	Secretary
Swimming instructor	Office manager	Registered nurse	Advertising manager
Sportswriter	Typist	Respiratory therapist	Reporter
	Executive secretary	Physician	Editor

Social Studies	Mathematics	Art	Industrial Arts
Urban planner	Machinist	Fashion designer	Electrician
Psychologist	Actuary	Architect	Locksmith
Social worker	Bank cashier	Cartographer	Plumber
Political scientist	Accounting clerk	Graphic artist	Sheet-metal worker
Court clerk	Engineer	Photographer	Drafter
Counselor	Scientist	Industrial designer	Automobile mechanic
Politician	Electrician	Fine artist	Bricklayer
Lawyer	Carpenter	Landscape architect	Carpenter
Firefighter	Electronic technician	Engineer	Machinist

achieve competency in school subjects and work-place skills.

Successful students think positively, act positively, and study positively. Unsuccessful students have a million reasons why they can't learn. Twelve of the most popular excuses for poor performance—the "dirty dozen"—are listed below. Do you recognize yourself in any of these excuses?

1. *"My teachers are boring."*

   Don't expect all teachers to be exciting. They are teachers in the real world, not performers on TV. Quit complaining and add something to the class. Ask questions, bring new information to class, and act interested.

2. *"I can't concentrate."*

   This attitude accomplishes nothing. Read aloud when you are alone, and answer questions when you are in class. These techniques will help you get your mind back on your schoolwork. If you are distracted from the lesson, by hunger or a personal problem for example, make an effort to solve the problem.

3. *"I don't understand what I'm reading."*

   Read each section you are studying more than once. First, scan all of the material. Look at all of the illustrations, and read the introductory statements, the first and last sentences of each paragraph, and all words in bold print. Consider all of the questions at the end of each section. Read all of the material a second time. Whenever you see a statement in bold print, turn the statement into a question. On a separate sheet of paper, make a list of the points you consider to be important. If you are studying at home, recite what you have learned after each passage you read. Follow this process several times until you feel confident that you understand the material.

4. *"I'm too busy to study."*

   Some students work part-time, take care of brothers and sisters, are responsible for housekeeping tasks, and still get good grades. School should be an important priority, and it is up to you to build a schedule that gives

▲ *Employers evaluate performance. Do you give 100 percent of your effort to your studies? Do you stick with your schoolwork until you succeed? Would an employer consider you a good worker?*

you as much study time as you need. You may have to exchange a certain amount of fun time for study time, but don't worry. People always find time to do the things they want to do.

5. *"I'll never use this stuff anyway."*

You're probably right if you plan to be unemployed. Employers are not interested in workers who lack basic education skills. If you plan to enter the world of work, achieve promotions, and improve your lifestyle, you will need to know "this stuff."

6. *"I can't study without a friend."*

Sorry, but this isn't true. Keep your study area quiet. The stereo, TV, phone, friends, and other distractions will not help you get better grades. It's OK to have a friend tutor you on occasion or ask you questions for review, but normally you should study alone.

7. *"I didn't know it was due today."*

Knowing when assignments are due is your responsibility. Don't write your homework assignments on little scraps of paper. They will probably end up in the wastebasket. Invest in a two-pocket folder and a notebook for each of your subjects. Keep your finished assignments and returned papers in the pockets and your class notes and homework assignments in the notebook.

8. *"Tests freak me out."*

Even the best students in class get a little uptight before a test. Being concerned about something important is normal. You can reduce your anxiety by being well-prepared for the test. Before the test, try to guess what questions the teacher will ask, review your notes, scan the headings in your textbook, and look up information that isn't clear to you.

When you enter the room on test day, listen carefully for any instructions or other information the teacher offers the class. When you receive your test, read the directions carefully. Review the entire test before you

start. Always read an important question more than once before you begin to answer. Respond to the questions asked, and don't provide information that is not part of the test. Think your answers through before you put them on paper. If you finish early, take the extra time to check for possible mistakes or to add new information.

Keep all of the tests that are returned to you. They make great study sheets for future tests. Be sure to learn the correct answers for questions that you miss. Be assured, you will see some of these questions on future tests.

9. *"I don't even know where to begin to study."*

If you use this excuse, you're trying to avoid a situation you don't like. Start each study session with your most difficult assignment because you will be more alert early in the evening. You might want to schedule a break to watch a favorite TV program or, better yet, to do something physical. Make certain that you discipline yourself to return to your study area after the break.

10. *"My memory is terrible."*

The more you memorize, the more you will be able to memorize. Marathon runners start off by running short distances and gradually increase their workout. Visit your school or public library, and get a book on memorizing. Look for specific methods that will help you increase your memory power.

11. *"I don't need to study because I learn it all in class."*

If you are getting low grades, this is a poor excuse. You probably need a reason to learn. Remember that education isn't something you can obtain a few weeks before you begin your working career. The extent (amount) of your education will be the major determinant of your future occupation, earnings, and lifestyle. Ask your teacher or counselor how the subject you are studying will help you reach your career goal.

12. *"Sometimes I'm so depressed about school, I wish I were dead."*

Problems with family or friends, alcohol, drugs, and lack of self-esteem make many adults and teenagers feel this way. It is important to seek help from a parent, counselor, church leader, or social agency when you have problems that are so upsetting. Your school counselor will either help you or direct you to someone who can. If you accept the responsibility to solve your depression first, you will be able to improve your study habits and grades.

Section 2 GET INVOLVED

Answer the following on a separate sheet of paper, and be prepared to discuss your responses in class.

1. Keep a daily log describing your study skills and habits over the course of two weeks. Include a description of your learning strengths, weaknesses, fears, and goals. Describe where, how, and when (the actual hours) you study. Describe the learning strategies that work best for you, and evaluate your learning progress for the two-week period.

2. Make a list of reasons why schools should or should not have minimum proficiency tests in basic skill subjects like English, mathematics, science, and social studies. Be prepared to defend your reasons in class.

3. If you were an employer, what opinion would you form about yourself after reviewing your high school transcript? Can you improve an employer's opinion of you? If so, how?

Section 3

Apprenticeship Programs

Benjamin Franklin was an apprentice printer under his older brother. From this beginning, he became the wealthiest man in the New World.

Apprenticeship is a relationship between an employer and an employee during which the beginning worker, or apprentice, learns a trade. Apprentices train for occupations that require a wide range of skills and knowledge as well as maturity and independence of judgment. Apprenticeship programs combine daily, supervised, on-the-job work experience with technical classroom instruction.

Apprenticeship is a centuries-old method of on-the-job training under the watchful eye of a master. The twelfth-century **guilds** (unions of craftsmen) of England were widespread in the skilled trades associated with construction, printing, shoemaking, and tailoring. Guilds developed the practice of indenturing (writing a legal contract for service) young men to master craftsmen. (Women were not permitted to join guilds.) During the period of indenture, often seven years in length, the young apprentice worked for the master craftsman. In return, the master craftsman provided food and lodging, usually in his own home, and taught the apprentice the skills of the craft. Upon successful completion of his indenture, the apprentice was accepted by the guild as a journeyman, or independent craftsman. Eventually, he could become a master craftsman and indenture an apprentice of his own.

Today's apprenticeship programs usually require about four years of training but may range from one to six years. The apprentice receives wages during this learning period. A beginning apprentice earns about half the pay of a skilled craftsperson, with periodic raises throughout the apprenticeship.

In addition to on-the-job work experience, an apprentice receives classroom instruction from skilled craftspeople and specialists in related occupations. Trade manuals and other educational materials are required reading. Classes cover techniques of the trade, theory, and safety precautions.

An apprentice is supervised on the job by an experienced worker who is known as a journey worker. The **journey worker** is a certified, experienced, skilled craftsperson who has successfully completed an apprenticeship. Under the journey worker's guidance, the apprentice gradually learns the skills of the trade and performs the work under less and less supervision.

Apprenticeship programs are sponsored and operated by employers or employer associations or by management and labor on a voluntary basis. The sponsors plan, administer, and pay for the program. The government's role is to provide support services to these program sponsors.

Almost all programs require applicants to have a high school diploma or its equivalent. In some cases, college graduates are sought. All apprentices must be proficient in reading, writing, and mathematics. Courses in shop math, algebra, geometry, drafting, physics, and other subjects re-

▲ *An apprentice is paid to learn a trade while under the watchful eye of a journey worker. All apprentices must be proficient in reading, writing, and mathematics. Do you have the academic skills necessary to enter an apprenticeship program?*

lated to the technical and mechanical trades are also highly recommended.

Once the application is approved, the Joint Apprenticeship Committee or another administrative body representing the sponsor will interview each applicant. Once accepted, the applicant must wait for a place in the program. The length of the wait depends on the number of qualified applicants and the number of apprenticeship openings.

When an apprentice is accepted into a program, he or she and the sponsor sign an apprenticeship agreement. The apprentice agrees to perform the work faithfully and to complete the related course of study. The sponsor agrees to make every effort to keep the apprentice employed and to comply with the standards established for the program.

Upon successful completion of a registered program, the apprentice receives a certificate of completion from the U.S. Department of Labor or from a federally approved state apprenticeship agency. What similarities do you see between the twelfth-century guilds and today's apprenticeship programs?

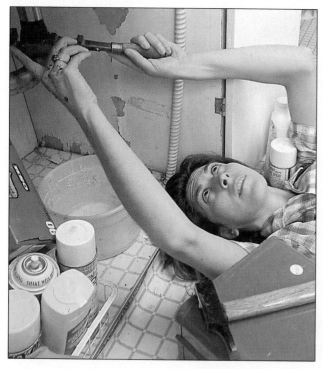

▲ *The earning potential and skills required in apprenticeship programs is the same for men and women.*

Figure 5.5 20 Largest Apprenticeship Programs

Occupation	Number of Apprentices
Electrician	37,033
Carpenter	27,206
Plumber	12,965
Pipe fitter	11,772
Sheet-metal worker	11,061
Electrician, maintenance	6,892
Machinist	6,456
Tool-and-die maker	5,548
Roofer	5,539
Firefighter	5,281
Bricklayer (construction)	5,058
Cook (hotel and restaurant)	5,007
Structural-steel worker	4,464
Painter	4,349
Operating engineer	3,779
Correction officer	3,636
Maintenance mechanic	3,445
Electronics mechanic	3,310
Automobile mechanic	3,024
Millwright	2,797

Although more than 830 occupations may be entered through apprenticeship programs, more than 80 percent of all apprentices are trained in the 20 occupations shown in Figure 5.5. Notice that apprenticeship programs now train workers for public service occupations like firefighting, law enforcement, and emergency medical care.

Section 4

Vocational Training Opportunities

More than 60 percent of today's high school graduates enter some form of educational program after high school. Many of these graduates enter vocational training offered by proprietary and technical schools. A **proprietary school** is privately owned and is operated for profit. A **technical school** focuses on training students in fields related to engineering and the physical sciences.

There are approximately 7,400 proprietary vocational schools and 1,900 technical vocational schools in the United States. These small, single-purpose schools may be independent institutions or may operate as part of traditional high schools or colleges. Their major purpose is to send graduates into the job market with skills.

Tuition for proprietary and technical vocational schools ranges from a few hundred to several thousand dollars. Individual schools will provide information concerning financial aid upon request. Courses are usually offered five days a week (evenings may be an option), and programs are usually completed in less than two years. Courses of study seldom include traditional academic subjects, and course credit can't be transferred to most

GETTING MORE INFORMATION

For more information on private vocational schools, write to

Accrediting Commission
National Association of Trade and
Technical Schools
2251 Wisconsin Ave., N.W.
Washington, DC 20007

Request *The Handbook of Accredited Private Trade and Technical Schools.*

▲ *Have you considered enrolling in a vocational or technical school program?*

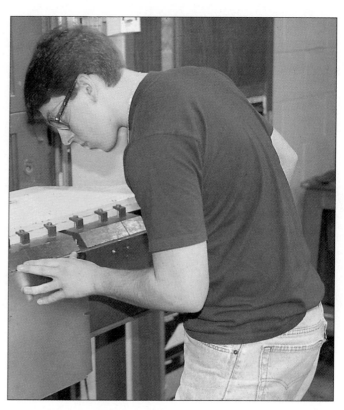

▲ *The major purpose of vocational and technical schools is to prepare students with marketable job skills related to engineering and the physical sciences.*

colleges. Most schools emphasize small classes and offer job-placement assistance after graduation. A high school diploma or general equivalency diploma **(GED)** is usually required for admission.

Guidelines for Selecting a Proprietary or Technical Vocational School

It is important to be very selective in choosing a vocational school because of the wide range of quality and the high cost of tuition. Use the following guidelines to help make a satisfactory choice.

1. Write or visit several schools offering training in your chosen occupation, and ask for their catalog. Compare each school's course offerings, hours of instruction, costs, and job-placement assistance.

2. Carefully read all of the terms of your enrollment application or contract before you sign it. Don't be pressured into signing an application or contract that you don't understand.

3. Telephone your local Consumer Protection Office or Better Business Bureau before you enroll. Also, check to see whether local employers or government agencies offer similar training at no cost. For example, most airlines conduct their own training programs for flight attendants.

4. Check with workers employed in the occupation to be certain that skills being taught by the school are currently being used in the workplace.

5. If using tools, machines, or instruments is part of the training, find out whether the school has enough equipment to enable every

BUILDING SELF-ESTEEM

Success Increases Confidence

Laura Warder graduated from Eisenhower High School last June. Laura's parents didn't think they would ever see her walk across the stage—and neither did Laura. She experienced several personal problems during tenth grade. She even ran away from home for two months.

Laura was placed in an occupational work-experience program when she returned to school. Laura's teacher, Mr. Gary, helped her find a job and made regular visits to her employer to be certain that everything was OK. Laura took mathematics, English, geography, and a special work-experience class during the morning. She had an early release from school in order to go to her job during the afternoon.

Obtaining job-seeking and job-holding skills, learning how to get along better with others, and developing confidence in herself were all part of Laura's educational program. In addition to teaching Laura's English and work-adjustment classes, Mr. Gary was always there for Laura as a counselor and friend. Being in the work-experience program gave Laura a chance to redirect her life, save some money, and make plans for her future.

Laura returned to the regular school program during her senior year and maintained a B average. Although she missed her chance to take a vocational program in high school, Laura decided to continue her education in a postsecondary vocational program and to train for a career in cosmetology. Even though she is no longer in his class, Mr. Gary arranged for Laura to visit the Touch of Beauty Vocational School. Laura is excited about her plans to attend school in the fall. It's hard for her to imagine that she will begin her career in another year. Laura told Mr. Gary that she wants him to be her first customer and that he will get a great hairstyle at no cost.

Critical Thinking

1. Did Laura have a high level of self-esteem during the tenth grade? What evidence can you show to support your opinion?
2. How would you account for Laura's high level of self-esteem during her senior year?

---

student to practice using it. Is the equipment up-to-date? Is there an extra charge for using the equipment?

6. How many recent students graduated? How many found jobs in their field? Did the school help them find jobs, and how long did it take? If possible, discuss the school's program with current and past students.

7. Will the program improve your math, reading, and thinking skills? Will it teach you how to continue learning after graduation?

8. Does the program include on-the-job training? Do teachers work with business and industry on a regular basis to update their skills and information?

9. Will you have to take out a loan to pay for the program? Who will pay back the loan if the school doesn't deliver on its promises?

10. Find out whether the school is licensed by your state's postsecondary school licensing bureau.

11. Check on whether the school is **accredited** (has met certain minimum standards for its program of study, staff, and facilities) by an accrediting agency recognized by the U.S. Department of Education. A nonaccredited

school may be as reputable as an accredited one. Applying for accreditation is voluntary, and the school must be in operation for five years before it can apply.

Correspondence Schools

Home study offers an opportunity to those who are unable to attend regular classes at a vocational school or college. Home study makes it possible for students to study at their own pace and on their own schedule, avoiding conflicts with existing job or family responsibilities. Some **correspondence courses** (home study) may be offered in combination with television classes on educational channels.

The home study school provides materials for study. Instructors correct, grade, and comment on the examination material, which the students mail back to the school as they complete the lessons. Corrected assignments are returned, and this written exchange establishes a personalized student-teacher relationship.

The most popular correspondence courses are business, high school equivalency, electronics, midlevel engineering technician training, other technical and trade courses, and art. These courses generally require one year to complete. Correspondence schools are accredited or evaluated through three major organizations (see "Getting More Information" on this page).

Government Job-Training Programs

Qualified young people may participate in a variety of government-provided training programs while they are in or out of school. These programs are usually limited to applicants from low-income families. Some are residence programs, in which classes are held at public training centers. Other programs provide funds and counseling services to participants and arrange for them to enroll in schools or to work in firms.

The **Job Corps** is a federally administered employment and training program that serves severely disadvantaged young people aged sixteen through twenty-one. Enrollees receive food, housing, education, vocational training, medical care, counseling, and other support. The program prepares them for stable employment and entrance into vocational or technical schools, junior colleges, or other education and training programs.

Enrollees in Job Corps Centers receive a living allowance, part of which is paid when the pro-

GETTING MORE INFORMATION

For more information about correspondence schools, home study courses, and school credibility, write to

National Home Study Council
1601 18th St., N.W.
Washington, DC 20009

National University Extension
Association
1 DuPont Circle
Washington, DC 20036

U.S. Office of Education
Adult Education Section
Washington, DC 20202

gram is satisfactorily completed. Enrollees may stay in the Job Corps for up to two years, although the average length of stay is about eight months.

Job Corps training is provided in occupations such as auto repair, carpentry, painting, masonry, nursing and other health-care occupations, word processing, business and clerical skills, welding, and heavy equipment operation.

Section 4: GET INVOLVED

Answer the following on a separate sheet of paper, and be prepared to discuss your response in class.

1. Write or phone the admissions office of a proprietary or technical school in your community.

Find out all you can about the school using the guidelines presented earlier in this section. Report your findings to the class.

Section 5

On-the-Job Training, Civilian and Military

On-the-job training (OJT) refers to a wide range of education and training provided by employers for their employees. It ranges from brief periods of job instruction for low-skilled jobs to extensive classroom instruction resulting in advanced certificates or licenses.

Civilian On-the-Job Training

Civilian OJT Training is provided through the following:

- Seminars and institutes conducted at the work site
- Separate education and training facilities that are operated by the organization (McDonald's Hamburger University for merchandising and retail sales training and the Xerox Learning Center are examples)

▲ Once tasks are learned through on-the-job training, workers are assigned jobs. Do you know anyone who has had OJT?

- Approximately twenty accredited corporate-owned colleges that grant degrees
- Satellite universities, such as the National Technological University, that beam course work by satellite to corporate classrooms around the country
- Numerous cooperative learning programs sponsored by employers and presented at local universities or community colleges

Although OJT programs may involve some classroom instruction, most on-the-job learning involves supervised work experience. OJT usually

▲ *Attending a private military school requires self discipline and dedication. What advantages would this type of education offer? What disadvantages?*

prepares younger workers to perform job tasks that can be learned in a brief demonstration period and that require minimal general education. Once the tasks are learned, the workers are assigned to the jobs for which they were hired.

Advances in the technical requirements for entry-level jobs and the increasing lack of academic proficiency among high school graduates have caused employers to dramatically increase OJT for younger workers. Employers are finding it increasingly necessary to bridge the widening gap between knowledge learned in high school and knowledge needed on the job.

New employees frequently learn to perform complex work tasks by observing and assisting skilled workers. In some cases, employers rotate new employees through a series of job experiences so they will know the overall operations of the organization. This generally helps new employees perform more effectively when assigned to a specific job.

Military On-the-Job Training

Each branch of the armed services provides training through on-the-job assignment, specialized schools, or a combination of both. Upon completion of basic training, an enlisted person may be given a duty assignment or sent to a school for specialized training.

The education and training taught in the special technical schools provide the military services with a skilled work force. The quality of training available in military schools usually equals or exceeds the training that can be acquired in similar civilian schools.

Many military occupations have some relationship to civilian occupations. However, the degree to which training can be transferred from military to civilian work will vary. Figure 5.6 lists several occupations that can be entered with military education and training. Numerous job skills learned in these particular occupations can be transferred

Mechanical and Craft	Electronics and Electrical	Business and Clerical	Health, Social, and Technology
Aircraft mechanic	Aircraft electrician	Accounting specialist	Air traffic controller
Automobile body repairer	Electronic instrument repairer	Administrative support specialist	Cardiopulmonary and EKG technician
Cargo specialist	Flight engineer	Payroll specialist	Computer operator
Dispatcher	Powerhouse mechanic	Shipping/receiving specilist	Computer programmer
Machinist	Precision instrument repairer	Personnel specialist	Data-entry specialist
Heating and cooling mechanic			Dental specialist
Airplane pilot			Environmental health specialist
			Fuel/chemical laboratory technician
			Intelligence specialist
			Nurse
			Physician
			Nursing technician
			Quartermaster

▲ *Figure 5.6 Civilian Occupations with Military Training Available.*

to civilian occupations.

Military personnel are encouraged to study voluntarily while off duty. Each military service contracts with colleges and universities to operate correspondence schools. In addition, the United States Armed Forces Institute provides correspondence courses to enlistees in all branches of the armed forces.

Most military installations have tuition-assistance programs for military personnel who wish to take courses during off-duty hours. These may be correspondence courses or degree programs offered by local colleges or universities.

Each branch of the armed forces provides opportunities for full-time study to a limited number of exceptional applicants. Military personnel accepted into these highly competitive programs receive full pay, tuition, and related allowances. In return, applicants must agree to serve an additional amount of time in the service.

Section 5 GET INVOLVED

Answer the following on a separate sheet of paper, and be prepared to discuss your response in class.

1. Contact the human resources department of a large employer in your community. Find out what positions can be learned with OJT. Report your findings to the class.

2. Imagine that you are an employment counselor hired to help discharged military personnel find employment in the civilian sector. What businesses or industries would you contact to find employment for the following discharged veterans?

Name of Veteran	Military Experience
Janet T. Brown	Accounting specialist
Ronald J. Adams	Heating and cooling mechanic
Frederick K. Zeller	Electronic instrument repairer

Community Colleges, Colleges, and Universities

Do you plan to enroll in a college after you graduate from high school? If so, which type of college program will prepare you for the career path you have selected?

One- and Two-Year Community Colleges

A major share of postsecondary education is provided by public and private colleges that award associate degrees after two years of full-time study. Many of these colleges also offer shorter-term certificate and diploma programs in specific career areas. Accreditation of these schools rests primarily with state or regional agencies.

Community colleges offer specialized programs of education and training to fill the needs of businesses and industries, health organizations, and public service groups. They teach up-to-date employment **competencies** (qualifications) to students preparing to enter the work force, workers who have been laid off, and employed workers who want to upgrade their job skills.

Most public two-year colleges have an **open-admissions policy**, meaning that they grant admission to all applicants without regard to grade point average, test scores, or class rank. However, they require students to take diagnostic placement tests after admission. Approximately half of all two-year college students enter directly from high school. Others become employed after high school and later enroll as part- or full-time students. These programs are well-suited for students who want to further their education after

high school but do not want to pursue a four-year degree. A wide variety of schedule options are offered, and more than half of the students are enrolled on a part-time basis.

Community colleges generally provide a four-part program that includes the following:

- A two-year university program for students who plan to transfer to a four-year college or university to complete a specific four-year program
- A technical program to prepare students to enter employment upon completion of the two-year curriculum
- A variety of short courses to retrain local workers or upgrade their job skills

▲ *One- and two-year community colleges offer a wide variety of programs for many students who want to further their education after high school. Have you explored the offerings at one of these colleges?*

GETTING MORE INFORMATION

At your school or public library, request the most recent publication of any of the following:

- *Lovejoy's College Guide*, published by Simon & Schuster
- *Peterson's Annual Guide to Undergraduate Study* (four-year college edition), published by Peterson's Guides
- *Peterson's Competitive Colleges*, published by Peterson's Guides
- *Comparative Guide to American Colleges*, published by HarperCollins
- *The College Handbook*, published by College Board Publications
- *Barron's Profiles of American Colleges*, published by Barron's Educational Series
- *The College Planning/Search Book*, published by the American College Testing Program

- Adult education programs, consisting of formal or informal courses

Four-Year Colleges and Universities

In 1636, Harvard became the first college established in the American colonies. By the time of the American Revolution, the colonies had established nine colleges, and all but one were founded by religious organizations. Today, there are more than 3,300 accredited colleges, community colleges, and universities in the United States. They enroll more than twelve million students at both the undergraduate and graduate levels.

More than two thousand offer four years of full-time study leading to the **baccalaureate degree**. This degree, sometimes called a bachelor's degree or an undergraduate degree, is a four-year degree in a specific subject. Many colleges offer two-year programs from which a student can transfer into a baccalaureate degree program. Four-year colleges and universities vary considerably in their policies on enrollment and attendance, their curriculum offerings, and their graduation requirements.

A **university** is the largest type of institution of higher learning. It is composed of several undergraduate colleges and graduate schools for advanced study. Figure 5.7 lists the colleges within a typical large university.

College of Agriculture	College of Social Work	College of Law
College of Business	Agricultural Technical Institute	College of Nursing
College of Consumer and Family Studies	Colleges of the Arts and Sciences	College of Pharmacy
College of Medicine	College of Engineering	College of Veterinary Medicine
College of Optometry	College of Education	College of Dentistry

▲ *Figure 5.7 Colleges within the Ohio State University.*

Universities usually include a liberal arts college and several other specialized colleges. Each college has its own specific admissions requirements, which must be met by every student seeking to earn a degree in that college. In addition, the university establishes certain requirements that every undergraduate student must meet.

State universities are supported by public funding and are usually less expensive than private universities. State universities may charge increased tuition fees and have higher entrance requirements for out-of-state students.

Liberal arts colleges offer Bachelor of Arts degree programs that combine a broad four-year education in the arts, humanities, social sciences, and sciences with a major in a subject or area such as government and political science, mathematics, or biology. A large proportion of liberal arts colleges are small private colleges with less than five thousand students.

Specialized colleges and schools offer Bachelor of Science degree programs that focus more on preparation for a specific career and less on a broad liberal arts education. Examples of these programs are engineering, education, business, agriculture, and home economics.

Graduate Schools

A student may be eligible for graduate studies after completion of a four-year baccalaureate degree. Graduate studies usually lead to a master's degree, which requires one or two years of advanced study in a specific subject, or a doctoral degree, which requires three or four years of advanced study in a specific subject. To obtain a graduate degree, a student must meet the requirements established by the college or school awarding the degree.

Many occupations require a graduate degree. Here are some examples: economist, education administrator, historian, librarian, political scientist, psychologist, school counselor, sociologist, and urban planner.

Professional Schools

Professional schools prepare students for specific professions, such as lawyer, dentist, veterinarian, and physician. To obtain a professional degree, a student must meet the minimum requirements established by the college or professional school offering the degree.

▲ *Curriculum offerings and admissions requirements vary widely at the college and university level. Will you be one of the more than 12 million students that enroll in one of the schools?*

Many colleges or universities offer courses of study that satisfy the admissions requirements for a specific professional school as part of the baccalaureate degree. These programs are known as **preprofessional programs**.

Specialized Colleges and Schools

Specialized colleges and schools prepare students for specific occupations, such as minister, artist, nurse, optometrist, and chiropractor. These colleges and schools are similar to professional schools in that they often provide training in only one field. However, they seldom require a baccalaureate degree as a condition of enrollment. Training usually takes three to five years.

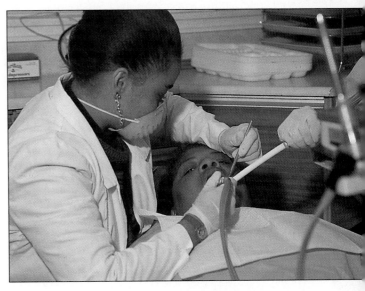

▲ *To qualify for licensure, a dental hygienist must graduate from an accredited dental hygiene school and pass both a written and a clinical examination.*

Section 6 GET INVOLVED

1. Ask your school librarian for one of the publications listed in "Getting More Information" on page 93, and use it to answer the following. Be prepared to discuss your responses in class.

   a. Locate a two-year or four-year college in your state and one other state that interests you.

   b. Select one program of study that you would consider pursuing.

   c. What is the college tuition for this program in the college located in your state? At the college in the other state?

   d. What is the cost of living on campus at the college in your state? At the college in the other state?

   e. What are the entrance requirements for each school?

   f. What career opportunities would be available to you when you completed the program?

2. Most professional schools permit an applicant to pursue a baccalaureate degree of his or her choosing but require that certain courses be included. In addition, the student must pass an admissions test to be considered for acceptance. Use one of the publications listed in the Getting More Information on page 93 to find the following information:

   - The requirements for entering the professions of law and medicine at your largest state university
   - The tuition for a law or medical student for one year
   - The various professional programs that are offered at your largest state university
   - The specialized colleges in your state that prepare students for the occupations of minister, nurse, and chiropractor

IMPORTANT FACTS

The Backbone of the American Work Force

The Secretary of Labor's Commission on Achieving Necessary Skills (SCANS) reports that 70 percent of young people in the United States do not complete college, yet they make up the backbone of the U.S. work force. The SCANS report gets to the heart of what students should know to prepare for work. Students need the three R's (reading, writing, and arithmetic), but they need much more. They need reasoning skills, computation skills, and communication skills. They need to know how to approach technology confidently and how to interpret the data generated by today's technology. They need to know how to work as a team member, how their jobs relate to those of other workers, how to coach fellow workers, and how to work with people from culturally diverse backgrounds.

Source: Labor Relations Today, U.S. Department of Labor.

Education and Training—Who Will Pay the Bill?

Cost is a major reason why companies, unions, and community agencies become training partners. For example, AT&T and the Communications Workers of America created the Alliance for Employee Growth and Development to assist workers in making the transition to new careers. The Big Three auto manufacturers have training and skills upgrade agreements with the United Auto Workers.

Germany is a model for this type of training cooperation. A dense network of industry associations allows German firms to pool both the costs and benefits of worker training.

Source: Labor Relations Today, U.S. Department of Labor.

No Education and Training, No Skills, No Job

During October 1991, the jobless rate was 25.3 percent for the 860,000 high school graduates of 1991 who didn't continue their education and training. Unemployment topped 40 percent for 1990–91 dropouts. For all 15.7 million sixteen- to twenty-four-year-olds not in school that October, those who had gone to college had the lowest unemployment rate: 8.3 percent.

Source: U.S. Department of Labor.

Can't Read, Can't Write, Can't Spell—Can't Get a Job

According to employers who responded to the Employability Skills Survey, 60 percent of the young people who applied for jobs with their companies were rejected because of deficiencies in the application/interview process. Young applicants were particularly weak in legible writing, spelling, and English usage. In addition, they often failed to express an interest in or knowledge of the position and the company.

Source: Building a Quality Work Force, U.S. Departments of Commerce, Education, and Labor.

United States Spends Less and Gets Less

A newly hired Japanese auto worker receives more than three hundred hours of training in the first six months of work. In contrast, new American workers receive less than fifty hours of training.

The United States ranks ninth among industrialized nations in the percentage of gross national product spent on worker training. For example, Sweden spends 1.7 percent; Ireland, 1.4 percent; Italy, 0.8 percent, and the United States, 0.2 percent.

Source: U.S. Office for Economic Cooperation and Development.

CHAPTER 5 REVIEW

ENRICH YOUR VOCABULARY

On a separate sheet of paper, number from 1 to 19, and complete the following activity. (Do not write in your textbook.) Match each statement below with the most appropriate term from the "Enrich Your Vocabulary" list at the beginning of the chapter by writing that term next to the correct statement.

1. General equivalency diploma
2. After high school
3. Fit into
4. Unions of craftsmen
5. Qualifications
6. A certified, experienced, skilled craftsperson who has successfully completed an apprenticeship
7. Types of jobs available
8. Relationship between an employer and an employee during which the worker learns a trade
9. A school privately owned and operated for profit
10. Home study
11. Has met certain minimum standards for its program of study, staff, and facilities
12. Occupational training programs developed jointly by high schools and community colleges
13. A federally administered employment and training program that serves severely disadvantaged young people
14. Intended to train students in fields related to engineering and the physical sciences
15. A wide range of education and training provided by employers for their employees
16. The largest type of institution of higher learning, composed of several undergraduate colleges and graduate schools for advanced study
17. A four-year degree that is sometimes called a bachelor's degree or undergraduate degree
18. A course of study that satisfies the admissions requirements for a specific professional school as part of the baccalaureate degree
19. A policy of granting admission to all applicants without regard to grade point average, test scores, or class rank

CHECK YOUR KNOWLEDGE

On a separate sheet of paper, complete the following activity. (Do not write in your textbook.)

1. Occupations that require more education and training have been growing faster than those that require less education and training. What is the underlying message in this statement?
2. What is the unemployment rate shown in Figure 5.2 for students with less than twelve years of schooling?
3. All high school subjects provide specific training for certain occupations.
   a. List three high school courses.
   b. Name an occupation that is closely related to each course.
   c. Name a specific skill learned in each course that is used in the related occupation.
4. Why are grades used as a basis for evaluating a job applicant?
5. What percentage of all job classifications require postsecondary education and training?
6. Approximately how many occupations can be entered through apprenticeship programs?
7. Why is it that those with a high school diploma are not likely to receive on-the-job training beyond basic job requirements? As a worker's general level of education increases, why does the opportunity for more advanced levels of OJT also increase?
8. What needs have community, junior, and technical colleges filled in training and retraining workers?
9. What graduate certificates and degrees can be earned in graduate school?

DEVELOP SCANS COMPETENCIES

Government experts say that successful workers can productively use Resources, Interpersonal skills, Information, Systems, and Technology. This activity will give you practice in developing Information skills.

Develop a chart that compares information from a number of post-high school educational facilities. Contact any universities, colleges, community colleges, vocational training institutes, and apprenticeship programs in your area. Find the following information for each facility: courses of study offered; end result—degree, certificate, etc.; time investment required; financial investment required.

Unit Two
Job Search and Success

CHAPTERS

6 EXPRESSING YOURSELF: EFFECTIVE COMMUNICATION
7 THE JOB SEARCH
8 APPLYING AND INTERVIEWING FOR A JOB
9 ROLES, RIGHTS, AND RESPONSIBILITIES
10 JOB SUCCESS IS YOUR RESPONSIBILITY
11 MAKING PROGRESS ON THE JOB
12 CAREER CHANGE AND GROWTH

Expressing Yourself: Effective Communication

Learning Objectives

After completing this chapter, you should be prepared to:

- give examples of the importance of the spoken and written word in the world of work
- identify and use at least six listening skills
- describe several characteristics of a group
- identify several forms of leadership and describe situations in which each is appropriately used
- list at least three strategies for resolving conflicts

Enrich Your Vocabulary

In reading this chapter and doing the exercises you will learn the following important terms:

communication	paraphrasing
recognition vocabulary	memorandum
	business letter
active vocabulary	monitor
context	facilitate
nonverbal communication	conflict
	negotiation
inflection	compromise
feedback	arbitrator
empathy	withdrawal

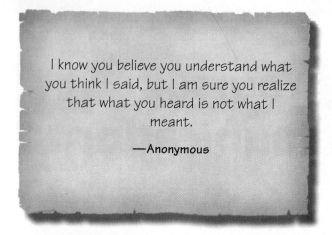

I know you believe you understand what you think I said, but I am sure you realize that what you heard is not what I meant.

—Anonymous

Communication is sending and receiving messages—and understanding and being understood. It is the exchange of thoughts, ideas, and beliefs between two or more individuals. To communicate a message, the sender's thought or idea is translated into words that the listener, reader, or viewer interprets and to which he or she reacts. When all goes well, there is understanding between the sender and the receiver. Effective communication requires the communicators to interpret the same things in the same way.

Consider a communication taking place at the Thrifty Buy Discount Store. The store manager, Mrs. Roberts, realizes that she will need someone on the day shift to work overtime during the evening rush. She directs her message to a clerk, Kenneth Johnson.

Mrs. Roberts: How would you like to work over?

Kenneth Johnson: I could probably use the extra cash.

The diagram below describes the understanding of the sender, Mrs. Roberts, and the receiver, Kenneth, regarding Mrs. Roberts' question. It also describes the understanding of the sender, Kenneth, and the receiver, Mrs. Roberts, regarding Kenneth's answer.

Without further communication, Kenneth will probably go home at quitting time. When Mrs. Roberts discovers that he hasn't worked overtime, she will be very angry. Whether you are the sender of a message or on the receiving end, it is important that you continue the communication until it becomes obvious that both parties have an accurate understanding. Given Kenneth's response, Mrs. Roberts might say, "Does that mean I can count on you to work over this evening?"

As individuals, we are unique, and this uniqueness can affect what we say, how we say it, and how others receive it. In the communication between Mrs. Roberts and Kenneth, the message sent and the message received are vastly different and could cause serious problems between the communicators unless they communicate further.

Communication involves a knowledge of words, beliefs, attitudes, and values. You can in-

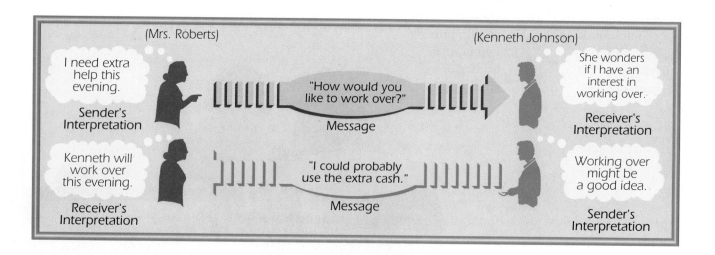

(Mrs. Roberts)   (Kenneth Johnson)

I need extra help this evening.

Sender's Interpretation

"How would you like to work over?"

Message

She wonders if I have an interest in working over.

Receiver's Interpretation

Kenneth will work over this evening.

Receiver's Interpretation

"I could probably use the extra cash."

Message

Working over might be a good idea.

Sender's Interpretation

crease understanding and reduce misunderstanding considerably by using common terms of reference, recognizing that unique qualities exist, and being as specific as possible.

As a high school student, you have studied grammar, spelling, vocabulary, composition, speech, and reading. These are all critical tools for effective communication. Without these tools, communicating in the world of work would be impossible. If you learn communication skills in high school, you will avoid frequent embarrassment and job limitations after you are employed.

Workers spend most of their job time using some form of communication. They communicate with customers and with one another about procedures and problems. Communication is an integral part of every industry and business in the United States. It is central to the smooth operation of an organization. Vocational research indicates that only job knowledge ranks above communication skills as a factor in career success.

For the average worker, the time spent communicating can be divided as follows:

- Writing, 8.4 percent
- Reading, 13.6 percent
- Speaking, 23.0 percent
- Listening, 55.0 percent

These methods of communication may not be specifically required for all careers. However, writing, reading, speaking, and listening play some part in almost every job.

Section 1

The Magic of Language: Understanding

Your skill at expressing your thoughts and understanding the expressed thoughts of others is directly related to your knowledge of words, their meaning, and their usage. The relationship between a word and what it refers to is a mental one. A word has no real meaning of its own apart from the uses people give it.

The effective use of the English language in written and oral communication is very important for success in the workplace. Today, English is the most commonly used language in the international world of work. It is the native language of more than 300 million people and is the most widely used second language in the world. (Standard Chinese is spoken by more people, but its importance is geographically limited.)

Principal Varieties of English

Using modern English to communicate effectively in the workplace requires a knowledge of the different varieties of usage and traditions of

CAREER TIP

Good reading, writing, and verbal communication skills and the ability to work effectively with people are important in all occupations.

▲ *Informal English is spoken more often than written. It includes words related to a particular occupation, slang, and other everyday words. General English is both written and spoken. It is used in talks to general audiences, conversations, and most business letters. Formal English is more often written than spoken. It is used to write formal essays, literature, scientific or professional articles, and college term papers.*

style, especially the informal, general, and formal styles.

Your use of English sends a message about you to other people. Your language skills and the style of English you use are a large part of the message you send. It is your responsibility to be perceived in a positive way. Informal, general, and formal English blend together to make up what is known as standard English. Which form of the English language do you use most frequently? Most people use the informal, general, and formal varieties of English. What percentage of your verbal com-munication time is spent using each? What percentage of your written communication time is spent using each?

Improving Your Vocabulary

Your recognition vocabulary contains the words you understand when you read them or hear them spoken. One expert estimates that there are twenty-four thousand words in the recognition vocabulary of the average child enter-ing the first grade. This number is thought to in-

It is important to recognize your personal style of communication and to understand the style of other workers.

crease by five thousand words per year. If you are average, your recognition vocabulary will include at least eighty thousand words by the time you leave high school.

Your **active vocabulary** contains the words you use in your speech or writing. It is estimated to be somewhere between 25 and 33 percent the size of your recognition vocabulary. This means that you probably use somewhere between twenty and thirty thousand words in your active vocabulary. Does this seem high or low to you?

Having an adequate vocabulary is an important part of career success and personal satisfaction, but how do you determine what an adequate vocabulary is? One way is to consider the difficulty you have expressing yourself to others in school, at work, and in social situations. If you have ever been in a situation in which you said, "I know what I mean, but I can't put it into words," you probably need to increase your vocabulary in that area of your life. The most natural way to do this is to learn new information.

Learning new information is often a part of everyday life. Think about the time you learned to ride a bike or drive a car. You probably learned the meaning of several new terms during this experience, such as *right of way* and *transmission*. New vocabulary words come from every life experience, including jobs, sports, books, school subjects, and conversations with other people. Consider how many words you might add to your vocabulary by pursuing a new interest in computers, sailing, cooking, skiing, chemistry, or history.

If your choice of words is limited, your communication skills will also be limited. Increasing your understanding of words will improve your

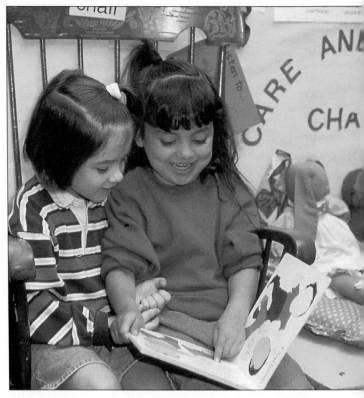

▲ *It is estimated that the average child entering first grade can recognize 24 thousand words. Are you satisfied with the number of words in your active vocabulary?*

communication effectiveness. Methods frequently used for learning and recognizing the meanings of new words include using the word in a sentence and using the dictionary as a reference.

You can usually tell the meaning of a word by analyzing the whole statement in which the word is used. Consider the following examples:

- The pilot took a vacation during the fall.
- The pilot frantically pulled back on the controls during the fall.

The statement or situation in which the word *fall* is used is knows as its **context**.

It is usually safer to begin using new words in your writing rather than in conversation because it is easier to check and revise your written words. As you work to improve your vocabulary, choose new words for their usefulness, not their impressiveness. After all, the goal of increasing your vocabulary is to improve your communication skills.

Section 1
GET INVOLVED

Answer the following on a separate sheet of paper, and be prepared to discuss your responses in class.

1. Among the many languages that Americans use in their daily lives are Spanish, Chinese, and Japanese, but the predominant language is English. Should all U.S. students be required to study more than one language, as they are in Canada? Why or why not?

2. Use a standard unabridged dictionary to look up the word *career*. What part of speech is it? What is its derivation? Identify its meanings, synonyms, and antonyms.

Section 2

Speaking, Listening, and Responding

Speaking, listening, reading, and writing are related, overlapping skills. The failure to master any one skill is likely to affect the others. How would an employer rate your speaking, listening and responding skills?

Speaking

Most communication between people is accomplished the same way today as it was two thousand years ago: It is spoken. Through conversation, discussion, and debate, the spoken word continues to be used more often than any other form of communication. Children learn to communicate their needs and desires to parents and siblings at a very early age by speaking. Remember, the average student comes to the first grade with a vocabulary of more than twenty thousand words.

Correct or incorrect usage of language is a habit. Frequently, we know better when we use incorrect language, but we don't always pay attention to the correctness of what we are saying. As an example, listen to Nel Brunson's job interview at the W.J. Hardware Store.

Owner: What would you say to a customer who asks for a brand of paint we don't stock?

Nel: Well, I think you oughta show 'em what we got and tell 'em how good it works. Ours is prob'ly better anyhow.

▲ *Describing hardware products accurately requires precise, easy-to-understand language.*

Solving The Problem

It Pays To Listen

Angela Dawson works on an automobile assembly line, where she is a very competent worker. She normally speaks with a soft voice and pleasant tone. Last week she began noticing occasional minor defects in the auto body parts passing her workstation.

Brent Johnson is Angela's supervisor. Brent normally speaks with a firm, authoritarian voice. He is conducting a "quality circle" meeting with the fourteen workers who report to him. Let's listen to part of the meeting.

Brent: I have a letter from the plant manager praising the quality of the body parts being assembled on our line. Let me read it to you.

Angela places her hand over her eyes and shakes her head back and forth while Brent reads the letter. Brent is busy reading to the workers and doesn't notice their nonverbal reactions.

Brent (looking around the group): What are your feelings about the quality level of our products?

Angela (quietly): I've been noticing lately that—

Betty (loudly): I think we're doing a great job. The company should share more of the profit with us.

When other workers begin supporting Betty's point of view, Angela shakes her head back and forth and sits quietly. Brent changes the subject to the financial difficulty the company has faced due to competition from foreign car makers.

A year later, several thousand new cars, with body parts assembled by Brent's team, developed rust marks

on the defective area that Angela had noticed. Angela's inability to communicate her message to the rest of her team and the team's inability to recognize her attempt to communicate were costly mistakes for all concerned.

Critical Thinking

1. Could Brent have prevented this situation? If so, how?
2. What could Angela have done to communicate her views?
3. What value did Angela's team place on her ideas?
4. What would you have done in Angela's place?

Stop the interview right here! If you were the owner of the store, would you have a problem with Ned's communication? If so, why? Would you correct Ned or simply ignore his incorrect speech and not hire him?

Some words are vague, and their usage increases the possibility of communication errors. Vague words are open to personal interpretation and miscommunication. Consider the following conversation between two eleventh-grade students attending Amity High School.

Margo: I saw you at the game Saturday. Your new girlfriend is cool. Her dress was outrageous.

Jerome: Thanks, Margo. A couple of the guys thought you were pretty cool yourself.

The words *cool*, *outrageous*, and *couple* are very general and fail to convey an exact meaning. Vague words of this type are more likely to be used in conversation than in writing. Using vague words to provide important job instructions could have disastrous results.

Workers have different styles of verbal communication (speaking) and **nonverbal communication** (facial expressions and body posturing). In the workplace, effective oral communication skill requires an understanding of the

▲ *Using facial expressions, hand movements, and maintaining eye contact help Anna to express the meaning of her thoughts through sign language.*

▲ *Symbols are frequently used to communicate safety requirements for drivers and pedestrians. What messages are being sent by these signs?*

meaning of voice **inflection** (a change in tone or pitch) and **body language** (thoughts or feelings communicated by posturing of the body).

Employees who lack proficiency in oral communication and listening skills cost employers millions of dollars each year in lost productivity and errors. Contributing to quality circle meetings, resolving conflicts, and providing meaningful **feedback** (a reaction or response to what is said) all require effective oral communication and listening skills.

Nonverbal Communication

It is often said that actions speak louder than words. When we speak to someone and when someone speaks to us, we send and receive both verbal and nonverbal messages. Sometimes, we convey our meaning without using words at all. We express our meaning by gestures, facial expressions, and voice inflections. The reactions of others to our trustworthiness, expertise, or likableness rely not only on what is said, but also on how it is said.

The message you send with your voice may depend on your voice inflection. How would the following speakers use different inflections?

Situation: A football game.
Message: "He's running for a touchdown."

Speaker 1: An excited student from the runner's school.

Speaker 2: A discouraged player on the other team.

Speaker 3: A student who can't believe the runner could make the team much less run for a touchdown.

Expressions like smiling when happy and crying or looking dejected when sad are almost universal. Most of us respond favorably to a person with an attractive and spontaneous smile, and we respond unfavorably to someone whose smile seems forced or phony.

Body language must be interpreted as it relates to different situations. To become more aware of body language, observe those around you. Try to analyze the nonverbal behaviors you observe. Do you interpret a person standing with his arms crossed as cold and unreceptive? How about someone with clenched hands and crossed legs? Are these gestures of suspicion? Do hands on hips indicate readiness? Does it seem like a person is really interested in what you are saying when she leans forward and looks in your eyes when talking with you? What about when someone leans back and ignores your eyes? Most of us use these and many more nonverbal signs to reinforce the meaning of the spoken word.

Listening

Don't assume that everything you say or everything you hear is clearly understood. In the role of listener, you are continually exposed to various kinds of listening, all requiring your attention. In the workplace, it is important to listen for content, long-term meaning, and emotional meaning and to follow directions.

When listening to a speaker, always pay particular attention to words like *never, always, all, none, everyone,* and *no one.* These words assume 100 percent exactness. Listen with doubt to a speaker who forgets that information can be incorrect and subject to revision. Listen with distrust to someone who states opinions as though they were facts.

Good listening demands alert and active participation and is developed through training and practice. You receive messages based on your personal expectations and feelings. You must be careful not to read unintended ideas into the message you hear. Your interpretation of a verbal message depends on your interpretation of the words spoken, on the speaker's body language, and sometimes on your previous relationship with the speaker.

Effective communication exists when the receiver interprets the sender's message in the same way as the sender intended it. Miscommunication occurs when the message sent does not accurately describe the speaker's intention. Continuous checking is required to ensure accurate understanding. One technique for checking the speaker's meaning is to rephrase the speaker's statement in your own words and then ask, "Is that what you meant?"

Many barriers can block effective listening. These include interrupting, not paying attention, having a closed mind, daydreaming, reacting emotionally to what is said, putting down the speaker, and being argumentative. Annoyances can also block effective listening. These include the ring of a telephone, conversations going on around you, the way you feel, and being seated where it is difficult to hear the speaker.

Responding

Have you ever been told, "I might as well be talking to a brick wall!" If so, you were probably not responding in a way that showed that you understood what was being said. A person who is speaking expects feedback from the listener to show that what he or she is saying is understood. Learning to respond effectively is an important part of the communication process.

Most listening and speaking occurs in social conversation, which can be both the easiest and yet the most difficult way to communicate with others. In social conversation, we switch from the role of listener to that of speaker over and over. Active participation from both the speaker and the listener is required at all times. Observe how Janet and Fred continually reverse roles in Figure 6.1 on the next page.

Have you ever been in a conversation in which both participants took the role of speaker or listener at the same time? What effect did this have on the communication?

In one-to-one verbal communication, you can follow the effects that your words have on the other person by carefully observing his or her body language and verbal responses. The ability to

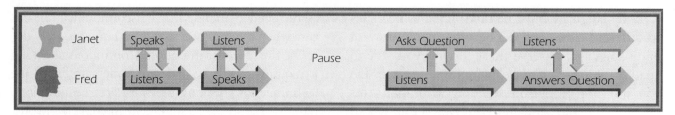

▲ *Figure 6.1 Roles for Effective Conversation.*

understand another person's feelings and motives is called **empathy**.

Paraphrasing is one technique used by a listener to convey interest to the speaker. It requires repeating the speaker's ideas or thoughts in your own words. Examine Figure 6.2.

In summary, effective listeners try to use these techniques:

1. Keep an open mind about the speaker's thoughts.
2. Listen quietly and show interest.
3. Maintain eye contact without staring.
4. Use attentive body language (usually by bending slightly forward).
5. Paraphrase when it is appropriate.
6. Listen carefully to the speaker before deciding on a response.

7. Ask questions only when certain that the speaker has finished.

A Communication Lifeline

The telephone is often the communication lifeline of a business. It is a means to speak, listen, and respond. The telephone is used to communicate or exchange information with customers and prospects, suppliers, colleagues, branch offices, and sales staff. In fact, just about everywhere in the world, the telephone supports business growth. By providing regular communication, it multiplies the effectiveness of face-to-face contact.

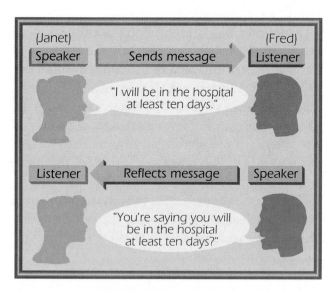

▲ *Figure 6.2 Paraphrasing.*

▲ *Using good telephone manners projects a positive image of your organization to the listener.*

When making telephone calls:
- Always identify yourself and the company you represent. With a business associate you call frequently, drop the name of your company but still identify yourself by name, no matter how many times a day you speak to one another.
- Always make your own phone calls. Having a secretary make your calls is showy and outdated. He or she probably has better things to do.
- Be sure you know the name and title of the person you are calling. People like to be called by their name and title.

When receiving telephone calls:
- Identify yourself by name, company, and department.

Good policy for all telephone calls:
- Speak into the phone with a clear, normal voice. A loud telephone voice may disturb others in your office as well as the listener.
- Be courteous and alert and respond in a positive manner, even when the circumstances are trying.
- Don't talk too long. In business, time is money, so don't waste it.
- Make notes before and during an important call.
- Remember that the words umm, uh-huh, and ah, are not standard English.

▲ *Figure 6.3 Good Telephone Manners for the World of Work.*

Every employee in a company who has telephone contact with customers or potential customers is in a position to contribute to the company's sales effort. On the other hand, they are also in a position to hurt sales and damage the company's image. Successful employers provide telephone communication training for employees in order to

- Get the maximum sales potential from each customer contact
- Assess the satisfaction level of existing customers
- Handle angry callers and resolve customer conflicts
- Improve the company's image and make good impressions
- Manage more than one call at a time effectively

Every time you speak on the telephone, it can make or break a sale and affect the public image of your company. Your phone communication can also cause a task to be completed efficiently or can disrupt progress within the organization. Telephone skills that enable you to communicate effectively, solve problems quickly, and reflect a positive image will make you a successful employee in a successful organization. Study the guidelines in Figure 6.3 to improve your telephone manners.

▲ *Facsimile (FAX) machines transmit and receive, over telephone lines, any image that is on paper.*

The telephone is also the link with facsimile (FAX) machines. Facsimile machines transmit and receive, over regular telephone lines, virtually any image that is on paper. FAX machines are easy to use and a quick way to transmit and receive information. They enable users to transmit communication to anywhere in the world within seconds.

FAX technology combines imaging technology and telephone technology. An add-on-circuit board (known as a FAX card), used in an expansion slot of a personal computer, enables a PC to function as a sending or receiving fax terminal. These FAX cards enable the computer to transfer images (data, text, drawings, signatures, photographs) into electronic signals. The signals are transmitted over telephone lines or by satellite to a compatible receiving facsimile machine. Within seconds, the page is reproduced as an exact copy or "facsimile."

In the past few years, the use of fax machines has skyrocketed and become part of the workplace automation revolution. For small and large businesses alike, they are almost indispensible. The importance of understandable written and verbal communication will increase as the world continues to get smaller through advances in telecommunications technology.

Section 2   GET INVOLVED

Answer the following on a separate sheet of paper, and be prepared to discuss your responses in class.

1. Observe the body language of close friends as they talk to one another. What are they doing with their arms, legs, hands, and feet as they talk? What do their nonverbal behaviors seem to mean?
2. What is your personal style of communicating?
3. Imagine that you suddenly become deaf. How would you learn? Would you be able to follow through with your present career plans? Would it change your personality? If yes, how? How would you communicate with your friends? Your family?
4. How do you rate as a listener? Ask two friends and two family members how they would rate you as an effective listener on a scale of 1 to 10, with 10 being outstanding and 1 being very poor. What can they suggest to improve your communication with them?

Section 3

The Written Word

Writing is a very important job skill. It is still the most often used method of communicating policies, procedures, and concepts in the workplace. In many work relationships, communication is conducted almost entirely by the written word. Effective workplace writing relies on these five factors:

- Carefully sorting out the facts (analysis)
- Figuring out the general idea (conceptualization)

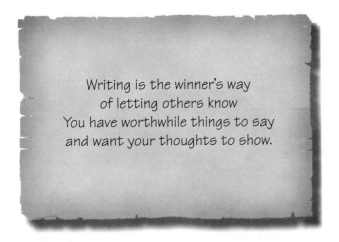

*Writing is the winner's way
of letting others know
You have worthwhile things to say
and want your thoughts to show.*

- Combining all of the parts to develop written material (synthesis)
- Eliminating unnecessary words and ideas (distillation of information)
- Making your point in a short, clear statement (succinct articulation)

Words should be picked carefully in written communication. Remember, there is no voice or body language to convey your meaning. Consequently, it is a good idea to test whether your written words are understood by reading what you have written as a stranger might. If the meaning is so clear that it can be understood without hearing it said, you have done a good job.

Spelling

Correct spelling is essential for successful communication in the world of work. However, most workers do make occasional spelling mistakes. The English alphabet of twenty-six letters can produce more than forty sounds. This makes the spelling of words very difficult. Three of the letters, c, q, and x, duplicate the work of other letters. This leaves it up to the other twenty-three letters alone or in combinations to represent all of the sounds. Examples include *sh*, *ea*, and *th*.

The vowels (*a, e, i, o, u*) create the most spelling problems. Consider the different vowel sounds created by the letter *a* in the words *lap*, *far*, *fare*, *was*, *lay*, and *many*.

Six Tips to Improve Your Spelling. Study these guidelines to improve your spelling.

1. Pronounce words accurately. Surprise, not suprise.
2. Visualize the word before you spell it.
3. Use difficult words in a sentence. This will help you remember them.
4. Learn to spell words correctly as soon as you hear or read them.
5. Practice spelling words that are hard to keep separate, such as *there* and *their* or *peace* and *piece*.
6. Keep a dictionary handy, and use it when you have doubts about the spelling of a word.

Proofreading

The average worker could greatly improve in the use of correct grammar, sentence and paragraph construction, and punctuation. This requires simply a commitment to proofreading and correcting.

▲ *Writing is a valuable job skill. Do you enjoy writing letters to family or friends?*

CAREER TIP

Take pride in everything you write. Train yourself to proofread your work and correct all mistakes so that your writing meets the expectations of even the most discriminating employers.

Use the following techniques for proofreading and refining written materials:

1. Read the final copy for logic, meaning, clarity, and interest.

2. Read it again for good sentence structure and punctuation.

3. Check for typographical errors, misspellings, precise word choice, agreement of subjects and verbs, correct tense of verbs, and agreement of pronouns and their antecedents.

4. Compare the final copy to the final draft. Have someone read aloud the final draft as you check the final copy, or lay the two copies side by side and follow both copies with your index fingers as you compare them word by word.

Business Writing

The writing of business letters, memorandums, and reports is not confined to the workplace. You have had to write reports in proper English since elementary school, and practically everyone must occasionally write a business letter or memorandum. A **memorandum** is a note used to aid the memory. It is often an informal communication about office matters sent among the staff of a company.

Business Memorandums. Business memorandums are used for intraoffice (within one office) communication. Many organizations provide printed forms for memorandums, but it is also acceptable to type them on plain paper. Today, these documents are usually titled "Memo" rather than

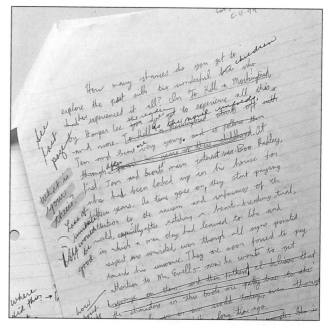

▲ *Many workers are expected to write business letters, memorandums and reports. Will an employer be satisfied with your writing skills?*

the formal word "Memorandum." This reflects the informality of the correspondence.

Keep the following suggestions in mind when writing memos:

1. The current trend is to type the memo in block style, with the copy typed flush left and ragged right.

2. Memorandums are informal. Never use titles like Mr., Mrs., Miss, or Ms. However, occupational titles like manager, supervisor, or custodian are permissible.

3. Triple-space between the subject line and the body of the memo.

4. Decide on the main purpose of the memo, and subordinate every fact or idea to this main purpose. Make certain that you show how these facts or ideas are related to the central theme. Reject any material that is unnecessary for the reader's understanding of the central idea.

5. Do not use a salutation or closing.

Examine the memo reproduced in Figure 6.4 on the next page.

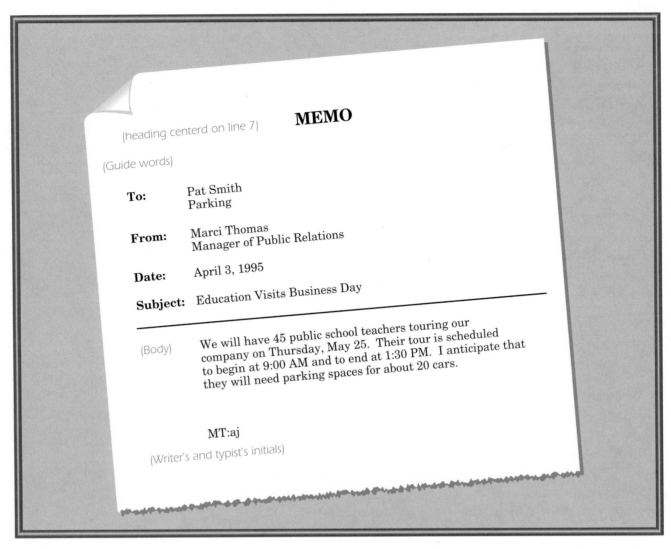

▲ *Figure 6.4 Sample Memo.*

Business Letters. A large and important part of business is transacted through the exchange of business letters. A **business letter** is a written document sent to someone outside an organization. It is usually formal in appearance, style, and tone. Some of the most common types of business letters are application, order, inquiry, reply, recommendation, introduction, claim, adjustment, acknowledgment, appreciation, collection, congratulation, and sales letters. Business letters may communicate good news or bad news to the reader. They are not written for reasons of friendship.

The form and appearance of business letters are very important. Most businesspeople follow these guidelines when preparing business letters:

1. Center the letter on the page, and frame it with adequate margins.

2. Separate the various parts of the letter from one another with extra spacing: two lines between the return address and the inside address, between the inside address and the salutation, between the salutation and the body, and between the body and the complimentary close.

3. Take care when writing the opening sentence. It sets the stage for the entire message.

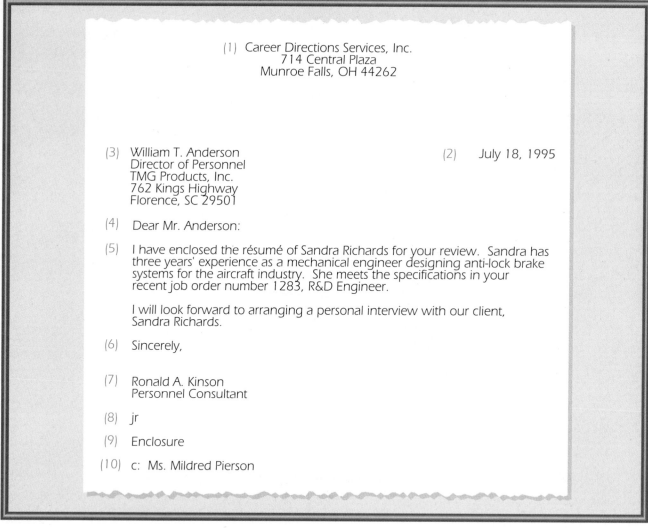

(1) Career Directions Services, Inc.
714 Central Plaza
Munroe Falls, OH 44262

(3) William T. Anderson   (2)   July 18, 1995
Director of Personnel
TMG Products, Inc.
762 Kings Highway
Florence, SC 29501

(4) Dear Mr. Anderson:

(5) I have enclosed the résumé of Sandra Richards for your review. Sandra has
three years' experience as a mechanical engineer designing anti-lock brake
systems for the aircraft industry. She meets the specifications in your
recent job order number 1283, R&D Engineer.

I will look forward to arranging a personal interview with our client,
Sandra Richards.

(6) Sincerely,

(7) Ronald A. Kinson
Personnel Consultant

(8) jr

(9) Enclosure

(10) c: Ms. Mildred Pierson

▲ *Figure 6.5 Sample Business Letter.*

4. Type the letter on company stationery.

The business letter shown in Figure 6.5 has ten main parts:

1. Return address
2. Date
3. Inside address
4. Salutation
5. Body of the letter
6. Complimentary close
7. Signature
8. Reference initials
9. Enclosure notation
10. Copies notation

Reading

The average employee spends one and a half to two hours per workday reading forms, charts, graphs, manuals, computer terminals, memos, letters, reports, signs, and bulletin boards. These reading tasks require the successful worker to

• **Monitor** (check for accuracy) his or her own understanding of the reading task

BUILDING SELF-ESTEEM

Jessie Feels Capable

Jessie Maxwell is a machine operator for the Twin City Manufacturing Corporation. Last month, Jessie's nephew invited her to speak to his sixth-grade class as part of Career Day. Jessie was scheduled to work the day shift that week, so she needed to obtain permission from her employer to be absent for two hours. Although it caused her to lose two hours of pay, Jessie was very pleased to speak to the class. Jessie is proud of her job and welcomed the chance to encourage young people.

Jessie brought her protective glasses, gloves, and safety shoes to show the students. Then she explained the typical work tasks she performs during her shift.

The students were surprised when Jessie told them that she was very shy in elementary school. She explained that being a poor reader caused her to have problems in other subjects. She was often embarrassed by her poor reading ability and hated going to school.

Then Jessie told the class about Mrs. Willis, her seventh-grade teacher. Mrs. Willis understood Jessie's problem and made arrangements for her to receive help from a reading specialist. Mrs. Willis encouraged Jessie and avoided giving her assignments that would embarrass her in front of the other students. By the end of the seventh grade, Jessie could read at the grade level. She was proud of her accomplishment, felt confident that she could reach a higher level of reading skill, and began to enjoy going to school.

Jessie explained to her nephew's class how she uses reading skills to follow directions, note details, and organize the order of events that are essential to the efficient and safe operation of a machine. Jessie demonstrated how she evaluates written information and makes comparisons. The students were very interested in the operating manual that Jessie passed around the class. They didn't realize the importance of recognizing the relationship between the main points in an operating manual and the small details.

Jessie concluded her visit by giving each student the following list of reading skills:

- Find the main ideas.
- Summarize and organize material.
- Evaluate what you read.
- Understand the general idea, and make conclusions.
- Understand the meaning of phrases, sentences, and paragraphs.
- Identify important details.
- Read to answer questions.
- Read to follow directions.
- Read to predict outcomes.
- Be able to read graphs, tables, and drawings.

Critical Thinking

1. Jessie explained how her level of self-esteem was raised by improving her reading skills. Can you think of a situation in which your level of self-esteem was raised or lowered because of your reading skills?

2. Name an occupation that you are considering. Describe how you would use five of the reading skills on Jessie's list in the occupation you are considering.

- Summarize information (identify the main parts of the topic)
- Be analytical (examine the separate parts of the topic)

How would you rate your ability to read? Excellent? Average? Below average?

Reading is a complex process requiring many skills in order to understand and interpret ideas

▲ *The average worker spends one and a half to two hours per workday using his or her reading skills. How much time do you spend each day using your reading skills?*

CAREER TIP

If you feel you are lacking in the reading skills you need to succeed in life, talk with your teacher or counselor about ways to improve or get help.

symbolized in writing. Reading the sports page of the daily newspaper for pleasure and reading the operator's manual for a complex machine do not require the same level of reading skill or concentration.

Skimming. Skimming is a method used to get a quick, general impression of printed material. Although it only provides a shallow understanding of written information, skimming can help you use your reading time efficiently. Take time now to evaluate your skimming and reading comprehension skills.

1. Skim through Chapter 7 of this book by reading the first sentence in each paragraph. (If the first sentence doesn't make sense, try the last sentence.)
2. What are the main ideas of the chapter?
3. How long did it take you to skim the chapter?
4. Answer the "Check Your Knowledge" questions, and grade yourself.
5. Read the same material in depth for facts and details when your teacher assigns it.
6. Answer the "Check Your Knowledge" questions again, and grade yourself.
7. How much did your comprehension improve when you read for facts and details?
8. If you were not being tested, would skimming have provided you with enough information for a general understanding of the chapter?

There are many times when skimming material will provide all that is necessary for you to understand what you need from printed material. Newspapers and magazines are good examples.

Section 3 — GET INVOLVED

Complete the following on a separate sheet of paper. Be prepared to discuss your findings in class.

1. Using the format shown in Figure 6.5, write a business letter to the public relations department of an organization you think you would like to work for in the future. Ask for information about the company's products or services. If you do not know the address of the company, ask your school or public librarian for help in locating the correct address.

Section 4

Interpersonal Relationships

Successful interpersonal relationships are built on mutual trust, acceptance, empathy, and understanding. These four building blocks are necessary when two or more people seek common values, attitudes, and interests through personal communication.

Each of us needs to have a close relationship with someone in order to feel secure and comfortable. We need to trust and be trusted, accept and be accepted, empathize and be empathized with, and understand and be understood in that relationship. Think of a close relationship you have with someone. In what ways have you and that special person expressed or demonstrated these qualities to each other? Did the importance you place on this relationship occur quickly, or did the relationship take a long time to become special? Why?

The ability to relate well with others is a characteristic of successful people in all walks of life. It is a part of the "fitting in" process at work, school, home, or play. Relating well with others doesn't require having a close personal relationship with everyone. It does require communicating effectively with the other group members and earning their respect and acceptance.

Acceptance into a group makes people feel worthy. When you were growing up, you probably belonged to a school club, a youth organization like Scouts, or an informal group of kids in your neighborhood. You probably didn't think about the building blocks of relationships at the time, but they were a part of being a member of the group. Can you remember a situation in which you wanted to fit in, but didn't—in which you wanted to be accepted, but weren't? Did it make you wonder if you would ever be accepted? Did you have doubts about your self-worth?

> People fail to get along because they fear each other. They fear each other because they don't know each other. They don't know each other because they have not properly communicated with each other.
>
> Martin Luther King, Jr.

▲ *Developing your interpersonal skills and learning to work in groups is valuable preparation for your future career.*

Developing Interpersonal Skills

Did you ever get along well with everyone in a group but one person? As you have learned so far in this chapter, effective communication is important in all interpersonal aspects of life. Unpleasant relationships are frequently caused by poor communication.

Interpersonal relationships are built on the understanding that grows between two or more people. Each of us tends to like people whose behavior satisfies or rewards us in some way, someone with whom we have similarities. We tend to dislike people who are very different from us.

CAREER TIP

Unpleasant relationships in the workplace are frequently caused by poor communication.

Brian Westfall has just transferred to a new school. Brian was a B student at his former school. He wants to play on the baseball team, and he is rebuilding a 1966 Ford Mustang. Brian quickly became friends with Alan Benson, who is a member of the school baseball team and also likes to work on cars. Alan frequently receives detentions and occasional suspensions from school for misbehavior in class. Alan barely passes most of his courses, but he always maintains passing grades during the baseball season. What common interests caused Brian and Alan to become friends? What effect could this relationship have on Alan? On Brian?

Mutual trust occurs when two people become convinced that the other person is reliable and honest. It takes several experiences with the other person over a period of time to develop trust. Think about a person you trust, perhaps a friend, relative, or teacher. What experiences convinced you that this person is trustworthy? How much time did this take?

Take a moment to consider the relationship that developed between Brian Westfall and Alan Benson. Alan placed a high value on his new friendship with Brian. He wanted Brian's respect and approval. Both boys reported to the baseball team tryouts together. Brian quickly learned to respect Alan's ability as a second baseman. However, he secretly wished that Alan's attitude toward schoolwork was as enthusiastic as his attitude toward baseball and cars.

For example, Alan frequently asked Brian for homework assignments to copy. Brian realized that their teachers knew what was going on. Will Alan and Brian build a feeling of mutual trust in their relationship? Why or why not? If you were Brian, what would you say to Alan? How do you think Alan would respond?

Belonging to a Group

Whether it is a family, clique, school class, social club, athletic team, church, musical group,

CAREER TIP

Say "Good morning" or another appropriate greeting to a co-worker you don't know very well. A handshake and personal introduction is a good way to learn another person's name. The next time you meet, make a point of greeting your co-worker by name.

employee union, political party, work team, or professional association, you will be a member of various groups throughout your life.

A group is made up of a number of people interacting with a common purpose in mind. Some groups have many rules and are highly organized; others are informal and have very few rules and little organization. However, all groups have some form of organization, rules for establishing leadership, and expectations regarding member behavior.

Effective groups have an atmosphere of equality among members. Each member has a sense of belonging, importance, and purpose. Members usu-

▲ *The Chamber of Commerce in your community is an organized group of employers and business leaders. What makes a group successful?*

ally know one another on a first-name basis. Depending on the situation, leadership is frequently shared by different members of the group. Every member is a leader, and every member is a follower. Members are sensitive to the roles that other members perform and how they relate to their own particular role in the group.

Group meetings are related to the needs of members. Problems are expressed, alternatives are discussed, and solutions are arrived at through joint effort. Groups are more effective when tasks are divided among the members. Members are more likely to follow the established rules of the group and to identify with the group's goal when they are personally involved in the process of group communication and problem solving.

Changes in the behavior of an individual frequently reflect membership in a particular group. Groups can exert considerable pressure on individual members to conform. Can you think of a group you belong to that expects you to behave in a certain way? Do you do anything to please the group that you don't think is right?

As you will learn in Chapter 10, groups called workplace teams are organized so that appropriate talents and skills can be directed through group effort to accomplish important tasks and achieve goals. When the group achieves its goals, the members are more cohesive, feel more secure about their jobs, communicate more openly, and work more cooperatively.

Successful team members are aware of the skills that fellow members have, and they understand how those skills can be applied to resolve problems and make improvements. Each member of a successful work team must be able to use interpersonal and negotiation skills. Verbal feedback must be provided and received. Each individual must be able to recognize and cope with the unique personalities of other team members. Differences between team members must be recognized as strengths to be added to group knowledge and skill rather than points of difference taking away from group harmony.

Tips for Effective Group Relationships.

1. Treat others with respect.
2. Be willing to listen attentively.
3. Stick to the task.
4. Don't dominate the group.
5. Think before you speak.
6. Don't be afraid to speak up.
7. Avoid making cynical remarks.
8. Apologize if you offend someone.
9. Recognize and correct your mistakes.
10. Take the initiative to participate.
11. Provide feedback to other speakers.
12. Don't prejudge other people.
13. Keep an open mind.
14. Don't be a know-it-all.
15. Cooperate with others.
16. Be open to suggestions.
17. Make suggestions to the group.
18. Evaluate all suggestions sincerely.
19. Criticize in a constructive way.
20. Tolerate differences in others.
21. Speak for yourself (say "I believe . . .").
22. Allow speakers time to pause and think.

Which four tips do you practice most often? Which four tips do you practice the least?

Leadership

"How did she ever get elected to Congress?" "He should be in jail instead of being the mayor!" "Why does a big corporation pay an idiot like him three million bucks a year to lose their money and our jobs?" If phrases like these sound familiar, it's because you have probably been listening to them and reading them all of your life. Remarks like these are sometimes justified. Most of the time, however, they are based on a lack of accurate information.

The way group members speak and write, their life experiences, and the overall purposes of the group determine the way group members relate to each other and the type of leader they will accept.

▲ *The Speaker of The House of Representatives encourages active communication among the other members. Who encourages you to communicate with others?*

A feeling of mutual dependence emerges between members of the group and the leader. The relationship between those who lead and those who follow can range from very rigid control to anything goes. Each group has its own style.

Democratic Groups. In a democratic group, leadership relies on the active participation of members in the decision-making process. Group members are encouraged to have active communication with their leaders. The United States Congress is an example of a group that uses the democratic style of leadership. Would a democratic group function better if the rank-and-file members were unskilled and poorly educated or highly skilled and well-educated? Why?

Closed Groups. In a group with a closed system of leadership, group members are not permitted (or are at least discouraged from) active communication with the leaders. Street gangs and military governments are examples of groups with closed leadership. Would a closed system of leadership function better if the rank-and-file members were unskilled and poorly educated or highly skilled and well-educated? Why?

Leaders of both democratic and closed groups are seen as having more influence than other members of the group. Successful leaders have the ability to persuade group members to accept their ideas, opinions, and orders. In addition, they have the power to delegate authority, motivate, and control their followers. Their credibility is measured by the success or failure of group tasks and goals.

In a favorable situation, the leader enjoys good relations with other group members, the task on which the group works is successful, and the leader's power in the group is strengthened. In an unfavorable situation, the leader's relationship with other group members is poor, the task on which the group works is unsuccessful, and the leader's power in the group is weakened.

A group member may be a leader in one situation and not in another. All groups are not alike. The size of the group and its purpose are important determinants of the type and style of leadership needed. As an example, the larger the group, the more leadership it requires. Most often, leadership in an organization falls into one of two types: shared leadership or controlled leadership.

Shared Leadership.

In the shared leadership style, the leader's activities and those of the group members provide mutual satisfaction. The leader stops being a leader the moment the followers stop following. Shared leadership requires a greater ability to persuade and a greater knowledge of the job than do other leadership approaches. Group participation is encouraged. Discussion and informal planning by the whole group usually precede any important group action. Having a stake in the project motivates members to make their best contribution. The leader works as a member of the group with special responsibilities for keeping the group on the right track. Individuals are encouraged to use their ingenuity (skill to think out new ideas), and they quickly discover that their contributions are welcomed and appreciated.

A group using shared leadership is usually cooperative and demonstrates high morale. Although the leader must **facilitate** (encourage) group performance, influential and involved members feel confident, secure, and useful.

Controlled Leadership.

In the controlled, or forced, leadership style, the leader uses means under his or her control to satisfy the needs of the group. The leader maintains a separate status, initiating and directing activities of the group rather than participating in them. The alternative to following this type of leader is to be punished.

Military organizations and some privately owned businesses rely on forced leadership. Fear of punishment is used to maintain discipline and obedience. The leader directs with a firm hand, and the group carries out the orders (policies) but has no voice in formulating or changing them.

Those who work under a controlled type of leadership frequently develop hostile feelings toward the organization. They have no voice in running the organization, and they tend to feel a lack of responsibility for the quality of the product or service being manufactured or provided. The work will probably proceed smoothly as long as the leader is able to exert firm control. When a leader is removed from power, the group usually develops a sense of powerlessness and fails unless a new, powerful leader emerges quickly.

Throughout history, many important military battles were lost due to the death of a leader. One reason for the success enjoyed by American military forces in modern times is the high degree of training and leadership ability among lower-ranking officers and noncommissioned officers. When a leader is killed or wounded, another trained person quickly steps into the leadership role.

Paternalism (managing like a father) is a form of controlled leadership in which the leader hopes to gain the gratitude and loyalty of the group. Although many group needs are met, control and power remain with the leader.

Interpersonal relationships develop between leaders and group members in all styles of leader-

▲ *Who is the leader in this office scene? Why do you think he or she is the leader?*

ship. All leaders must assign tasks, come up with new ideas, seek information, give information, clarify situations, and make certain that tasks are carried out. All successful leaders:

1. Influence other people. When they speak, others listen.
2. Enlist the support and cooperation of other people.
3. Communicate in a way that is clearly understood.
4. Seem fair, accessible, and honest.
5. Listen to other points of view without making judgments.
6. Accept future uncertainty without panic or unnecessary stress.
7. Interact with others to share responsibilities.
8. Set an example that inspires confidence in others.
9. Behave in a manner appropriate to the situation.

Section 4 GET INVOLVED

Answer the following on a separate sheet of paper, and be prepared to discuss your responses in class.

1. When your class has a discussion,
   - Who usually gives their opinion?
   - Who usually asks others what they think?
   - Who usually takes over or performs on their own?
2. If you were a leader, which leadership style would you prefer to use? Why?
3. Reread "Tips for Effective Group Relationships" on page 120.

a. Spend twenty minutes observing the actions of a family member or a classmate in a group situation with four or more participants.
b. On a separate sheet of paper, record the tips you observe this person using and the number of times he or she uses each of the tips.
c. Which tips did your subject practice the most? Which did he or she practice the least?

Section 5

Conflict Resolution

A **conflict** is a clash or struggle that sometimes occurs when individuals or groups have different points of view. These collisions can be at the spiritual (religious), intellectual, emotional, or physical level. Some conflicts are organized; others are not. Some are short-term (lasting a few days); others last for years.

A failure to resolve the conflict by communication may lead to physical violence and long-term unresolved feelings of anger.

In all phases of social interaction, there are periods of disagreement. How often have you said, "Every time I try to talk with him, we get into an argument." Whether it is between parents and children, siblings, friends, or co-workers, unkind words are said, feelings are hurt, and disagreements arise. Responding to these situations by ex-pressing anger or showing irritation creates the possibility of conflict. Either of these emotions can prevent you from saying what you really feel.

Each person involved in a conflict has personal biases, priorities, expertise, and interests. These affect the points of agreement and create outright opposition on many issues. What do you do when there is a difference of opinion or an open conflict among your family or friends? How do you feel?

Workers depend on one another to get their jobs done. When joint decisions are made, workers are expected to interact by offering ideas to the group and expressing opinions. However, new ideas, insights, and differing opinions sometimes cause friction instead of cooperation. When friction develops into conflict, strategic plans may be interrupted, and productivity lowered. Effective communication must be used to resolve the conflict.

Negotiation

Negotiation (bargaining by persuasion rather than argument) is one method frequently used to resolve conflicts. Negotiation can be used to resolve disputes between two or more individuals or groups.

When nations, labor unions, or individuals negotiate, they engage in a mutual trading of offers and concessions in an attempt to reach a formal agreement concerning issues of common concern. The sides have conflicting interests but share a desire for a reasonable settlement of their differences. Negotiation is not successful until a solution is acceptable to both sides.

Successful negotiators begin by focusing on points of agreement to build a sense of together-

▲ *Teammates and good friends have occasional disagreements. How do you solve personal conflicts?*

Figure 6.6 NEGOTIATION VERSUS ARGUMENT

Negotiation	Argument
Focus is on the issues. Personal feelings and personalities are left out.	Personal feelings and emotions are frequently included.
Focus is on important interests.	Focus is on fixed positions.
Strives to propose options for mutual gain.	Strives to win a point of view.
Insists on objective information.	Presents information supporting one side of the dispute.
Relies on each participant having good interpersonal skills.	Relies on verbal domination without considering the other viewpoint.
Depends on each side openly expressing all their beliefs.	Expects the other side to accept a new set of beliefs.
Focus is on points of agreement.	Focus is on points of difference.

ness. After points of agreement are established, major differences are identified. Unlike arguers, negotiators don't expect to win all of their points (Figure 6.6).

Have you ever been involved in a lengthy discussion that turned into an argument and heard someone say, "What are we arguing about anyway? We're all saying the same things in different ways. We're arguing over nothing." Try using negotiation techniques to resolve your day-to-day personal conflicts. It is easiest to solve a minor disagreement before it grows into a major conflict.

In most situations, whether personal or work related, disagreements focus on the facts of a situ-

CAREER TIP

Persuasion is not accomplished by argument, insulting remarks, or making the other person look foolish. If you are seeking a friendly agreement, be pleasant, respectful, and tolerant of differences.

▲ *This organization's management team and labor union representatives have concluded a successful contract negotiation. Can you determine which side won? How?*

ation and do not revolve around personality conflicts. Personal communication provides the opportunity to establish and increase cooperation while resolving a conflict. However, the effect of communication depends on the nature of the conflict and what is being communicated. Different opinions must be identified and revealed totally, and negative as well as positive feelings must be accepted. Once this is done, the conflict can be examined, discussed, and studied, and a compromise can be reached.

It is important for participants in a negotiation to be confident, open, and honest. Sometimes, people agree in a negotiation because they are intimidated (feel threatened) by others, because they don't want to hurt another person's feelings, or simply because they want a quick end to a bad situation. Have you ever felt like this? Did you act with confidence, openness, and honesty? Did you live up to the agreement after you realized that it was not consistent with your real beliefs?

Win or Lose

During a conflict, each side has choices. The following are types of choices you will face as you try to manage conflicts.

1. *"You can't lose."*   Either choice is to your advantage. However, one choice may be more of an advantage than the other.

2. *"You can't win."*   Either choice is to your disadvantage. However, one choice may be less of a disadvantage than the other.

3. *"You could win or lose."*   One choice is clearly to your advantage, and the other is clearly to your disadvantage.

Think of a time when you were faced with one of these three situations. If you had it to do over again, would you make the same choice?

▲ *President Clinton served as an arbitrator to help the government of Israel and the Palestinian Liberation Organization (PLO) achieve a major compromise concerning self rule.*

A strategy is a skillful plan used to manage a situation. Professional athletes use several strategies. They practice for years to develop the skills they need to make their strategies work during a game. Studying and practicing the following strategies will help you develop the necessary skills for resolving conflicts.

Compromise

In a **compromise**, each side gives up some of its demands and meets the other side halfway. Compromise is an important part of negotiation. It can be as simple as two children deciding to take turns or as complex as two nations deciding where to place their border.

Third-Party Assistance

A third person, respected by both sides, is asked to join the discussion and give an opinion. Students frequently ask a teacher to enter a dispute and give an opinion. Business owners and employee groups frequently solve labor disputes by using a third-party expert called an **arbitrator**.

"I" and "You" Statements

The words *I* and *you* can mean the difference between resolving a problem and making it worse. Imagine that Fred is waiting at a red light and Carl drives into the back of his car. Neither Fred nor Carl are hurt, but both cars have a lot of damage. The two men get out of their cars and walk toward each other.

The "I statement" approach.

Fred: I was scared to death when I saw you in my rearview mirror. I'm glad to get out of this alive. I just bought this car last month.

How do you think Carl will respond to these "I" statements?

The "you statement" approach.

Fred: You drove right into my new car. You could have killed us both.

How do you think Carl will respond to these "you" statements?

When an "I" statement is made, the person making the statement expresses ownership of a problem and ownership of his or her feelings. When a "you" statement is made, the person making the statement blames the other person. The speaker takes no responsibility for the problem or for his or her feelings.

Withdrawal

Withdrawal means to pull away from a volatile situation and to give the other person time to cool off before attempting to resolve the conflict. This strategy is not a cop-out. It should not be confused with surrendering and letting others take advantage of you. Have you ever experienced a conflict in which good friends or family members were so angry that they lost their temper? An "I" statement followed by withdrawal would be an appropriate response to this situation. Try using the following example: "I would like some time to think this through. I feel it would be best if we discussed this later. I hope you feel the same."

Apologizing

Apologizing isn't necessarily a way of saying, "You're right, and I'm wrong." It may mean, "I know your feelings are hurt and you're angry, and I'm sorry about that." It can be a very effective way to stop a conflict before it gets out of hand. Try the following:

- "I feel bad about this whole situation."
- "I'm sorry. I really didn't want this to happen."
- "I regret this, and I hope we can put it behind us."

Section 5   GET INVOLVED

Answer the following on a separate sheet of paper, and be prepared to discuss your responses in class.

1. Do you always have to win in a conflict? Give an example of a conflict you were involved in that supports your answer.

2. Imagine that none of your family or friends could disagree with you and you couldn't disagree with them. How would this improve your life? How would this cause problems for you?

3. We usually behave toward others in a manner that is similar to their past treatment of us. Can you think of a situation in which this was true for you and you behaved in a positive way? In a negative way?

4. What effect do emotions have on quarrels between friends? On disputes between parents and children? On disputes between labor and management?

.I M P O R T A N T F A C T S

Listening

Studies show that people spend about 80 percent of their waking hours communicating. At least 45 percent of that time is spent listening. In schools, students spend 60 to 70 percent of their classroom time listening. In business, listening has often been cited as being the most critical managerial skill.

Listening habits are not the result of formal training. Listening is the communication skill used the most but taught the least. Consider the following:

Skill	Order in which Skill Learned	Percentage of Time Skill Is Used	Amount of Classroom Time Spent Teaching the Skill
Listening	1st	45%	4th (least)
Speaking	2nd	30%	3rd
Reading	3rd	16%	2nd
Writing	4th	9%	1st (most)

Most people are inefficient listeners. Tests have shown that immediately after listening to a ten-minute oral presentation, the average listener has heard, understood, properly evaluated, and retained only about 50 percent of what was said. Within 48 hours, that drops off to a 25 percent level of effectiveness. In other words, we usually comprehend and retain less than a quarter of what is said.

Every business day, letters must be retyped, appointments rescheduled, and shipments reshipped. Ideas are distorted by as much as 80 percent as they travel through the chain of command in the world of work. With more than 100 million workers in America, a simple ten-dollar listening mistake by each of them would cost a billion dollars.

Good listening can be taught.

Source: Your Personal Listening Profile Publisher; UNISYS Corporation

Reading in the Workplace

Profound changes in the structure of the workplace and the nature of jobs make reading, writing, and other communication skills vital to the performance of jobs, even at the entry level. Research conducted at Indiana University revealed that 70 percent of the reading material in a national cross section of jobs is written between the ninth- and twelfth-grade level of difficulty. (15 percent is even higher.)

It is likely that job and social requirements for literacy will increase even more in the years ahead. The fact that massive numbers of present and future workers have only minimal or marginal proficiency in the basic skills presents a major problem for U.S. competitiveness in the international world or work.

High-Tech Communication

Videoconferencing allows employers to use television equipment to link together all employees involved in a project. Participants located hundreds or even thousands of miles away have two-way verbal and visual communication. Videoconferencing is effective for staff meetings, chalkboard presentations, and roundtable discussions. It costs from five hundred to as high as three thousand dollars an hour. This is still cheaper than sending dozens of employees to a meeting for several days in another city or another country.

CHAPTER 6 REVIEW

ENRICH YOUR VOCABULARY

On a separate sheet of paper, number from 1 to 18, and complete the following activity. (Do not write in your textbook.) Match each statement below with the most appropriate term from the "Enrich Your Vocabulary" list at the beginning of the chapter by writing that term next to the correct statement.

1. Understanding another person's feelings and motives
2. Third party to solve disputes
3. An informal communication
4. The statement or situation in which a word is used
5. To encourage group performance
6. An agreement in which each side gives up some of its demands
7. Bargaining by persuasion rather than argument
8. Pulling away from a volatile situation
9. A written document sent outside an organization
10. Meaning expressed by facial expressions and body posturing
11. Words you understand when you read them
12. A clash or struggle
13. A reaction or response to what is said
14. A change in tone or pitch
15. Words you use in your speech
16. Repeating the speaker's ideas or thoughts in your own words
17. Sending and receiving messages and understanding and being understood
18. Check for accuracy

CHECK YOUR KNOWLEDGE

On a separate sheet of paper, complete the following activity. (Do not write in your textbook.)

1. Effective communication in the workplace requires a knowledge of three styles of English. What are these three styles? When, where, and how, are each of the three typically used?
2. When we communicate with other people, we send and receive verbal and nonverbal messages. Describe the two skills that are essential for effective oral communication in the workplace.
3. Good listening demands alert and active participation and is developed through training and practice. List some of the barriers and annoyances that can block effective listening.
4. The average employee spends one and a half to two hours per workday reading. Describe three skills needed to be a successful reader in the workplace.
5. Group meetings are related to the needs of the members. Name three major reasons why groups meet in the workplace?
6. List four of the characteristics of a leader.
7. Negotiation is one method frequently used to resolve conflicts in the world of work. List the seven major differences between negotiation and argument.

DEVELOP SCANS COMPETENCIES

Government experts say that successful workers can productively use Resources, Interpersonal skills, Information, Systems, and Technology. This activity will give you practice in developing System skills.

Study the diagram below. Use this format to diagram three conversations you were involved in today.

Be sure to identify the sender and the receiver. Briefly explain the message and the feedback.

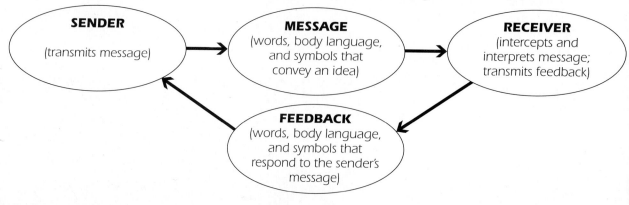

SENDER
(transmits message)

MESSAGE
(words, body language, and symbols that convey an idea)

RECEIVER
(intercepts and interprets message; transmits feedback)

FEEDBACK
(words, body language, and symbols that respond to the sender's message)

The Job Search

Learning Objectives

After completing this chapter, you should be prepared to:

- plan a successful job search
- obtain job leads by using six different methods
- keep track and follow-up on job leads
- prepare a personal data sheet and résumé
- write a successful cover letter

Enrich Your Vocabulary

In reading this chapter and doing the exercises you will learn the following important terms:

job search	job fair
job market	personal data sheet
job applicant	résumé
job lead	chronological résumé
networking	functional résumé
job jargon	references
employment service	cover letter
initial screening	

More than 123 million workers in the U.S. work force compete for approximately 120 million jobs. This is a growing work force that will increase to more than 141 million by the year 2000. At some point, you will be a worker seeking one of these jobs.

Once you decide to seek a job, you will need to develop and implement a **job search** (the process of seeking employment). More than good luck or knowing the "right people" will be necessary. Planning and persistence are almost always required in a successful job search.

As you begin organizing your job search, treat it as you would an important, paying job. Commit your time and energy to being successful. Once your job search is planned, begin making the plan work.

Section 1

Planning Your Job Search

Before you begin your job search, take time to think about yourself. Make certain that you can answer the following questions:

1. What type of work interests me?
2. What skills can I offer an employer?
3. What rewards do I expect from the job?
4. Who can help me make contacts with possible employers?
5. How can I convince an employer that hiring me would benefit the organization?

▲ *Help-wanted ads are a good source of information about local and regional employment opportunities.*

When you think of the word *market*, you probably have thoughts about stores and where they are located, buying and selling goods, and prices. Think of the job market in the same way. **Job market** refers to the type and number of jobs available. Ask yourself the following questions as you get ready for your job search:

1. What businesses, industries, or agencies are hiring (buying) new workers with my job skills?
2. Where are these potential employers located?
3. What wages and benefits (prices) will they offer for my skills?
4. How can I become a job applicant with the employers I choose? (A **job applicant** is a person who applies for employment with a specific company.) How will I sell my skills to these employers?

Workers frequently move to other cities or states when faced with local factory closings or limited opportunities for career growth. This requires knowledge of local and national job markets. As you read the information in Figure 7.1, imagine that you are conducting a nationwide job

Figure 7.1 THE U.S. JOB MARKET

Selected Goods-producing Industries		Selected Service-producing Industries	
Type of Industry		**Type of Industry**	
Mining	604,000	Transportation and public utilities	5,716,000
Oil and gas extraction	343,000	Transportation	3,540,000
Construction	4,660,000	Trucking and warehousing	1,643,000
General building contractors	1,088,000	Transportation by air	738,000
Manufacturing	17,763,000	Communications and public utilities	2,176,000
Production workers	12,172,000	Wholesale trade	6,140,000
Durable goods	10,520,000	Retail trade	19,928,000
Production workers	6,780,000	General merchandise stores	2,328,000
Lumber and wood products	703,000	Food stores	3,222,000
Furniture and fixtures	487,000	Automotive dealers and service	
Stone, clay, and glass products	517,000	stations	2,085,000
Primary metal industries	677,000	Apparel and accessory stores	1,135,000
Blast furnaces and steel products	238,000	Eating and drinking places	6,968,000
Fabricated metal products	1,324,000	Finance, insurance, and real estate	6,667,000
Machinery, except electrical	1,895,000	Finance	3,266,000
Electrical and electronic		Depository institutions	738,000
equipment	1,514,000	Insurance	2,114,000
Transportation equipment	1,712,000	Real estate	1,287,000
Motor vehicles and equipment	875,000	Services	30,706,000
Aircraft and parts	500,000	Business services	5,966,000
Instruments and related products	860,000	Hotels and other lodging places	1,590,000
Miscellaneous manufacturing	363,000	Personal services	1,109,000
Nondurable goods	7,711,000	Personal supply services	2,154,000
Production workers	5,392,000	Auto repair and parking	970,000
Food and kindred products	1,640,000	Health services	9,023,000
Tobacco products	44,000	Hospitals	3,818,000
Textile mill products	663,000	Legal services	931,000
Apparel and other textile		Educational services	1,767,000
products	952,000	Social services	2,106,000
Paper and allied products	678,000	Membership organizations	1,968,000
Printing and publishing	1,506,000	Engineering and management	
Chemical and allied products	1,062,000	services	2,532,000
Petroleum and coal products	152,000	Government	18,948,000
Rubber and miscellaneous		Federal	2,901,000
plastics products	898,000	State	4,497,000
Leather and leather products	116,000	Local	11,550,000
		Agriculture	3,077,000
Total	86,409,000	Total	172,000,000

(*Source:* U.S. Department of Labor Statistics.)

search for yourself. Each industry listed is composed of several thousand corporations, subsidiaries (companies that have more than half their stock owned or controlled by another company), and other businesses employing millions of workers.

Section 1 GET INVOLVED

Analyze the information presented in Figure 7.1. Answer the following on a separate sheet of paper, and be prepared to discuss your responses in class.

1. Of the 123 million workers in the United States, what is the percentage of workers currently employed in durable goods manufacturing? What percentage work in service-producing industries?

2. What do you think has brought about the recent growth in services? If this trend continues, what employment opportunities would a young worker be wise to pursue in manufacturing? In service-producing industries?

3. In terms of employment, what are the three leading service industries? What are the three leading durable goods industries?

Section 2

Finding Job Leads

Wanting a job isn't enough. You must find employers and convince them to hire you. This is where job leads come into the picture. A **job lead** is information about an organization that is hiring new employees and the name of the person who is responsible for hiring.

The U.S. Department of Labor ranks the following as the most successful methods for a job search:

- Applying directly to the employer
- Networking
- Responding to help-wanted ads
- Using schools and job fairs for placement services
- Contacting professional and trade organizations

CAREER TIP

Some employers keep a file of potential job candidates so that as openings occur, they can fill a job vacancy without paying for advertising or using an employment agency.

- Using the State Bureau of Employment Services

The sooner you become skilled at using these six proven methods, the sooner you will find the type of employment you are seeking.

Applying Directly to the Employer

The yellow pages section of the telephone book is a very useful source of employers to contact for your job search. It does not tell you who is presently hiring, but it is a source of *who* hires. Organization names, addresses, and telephone numbers are listed under the service they offer or the product they produce.

Take time to prepare yourself before using the telephone to make your initial contact with an employer. Consider the type of job you are seeking and then select appropriate organizations to call. Record the name of these organizations on a sheet of paper, and include the phone number and name of the person (if known) to call. As you make the calls, write down the following information:

- Any openings for the type of job you are seeking
- When or if you are to call back
- When or if an interview is set up

Keep the information on a sheet of paper or make job lead cards for each organization. (Look

▲ *Local customers frequently become the best employees of retail merchants. Should this girl apply for the job now?*

ahead to Figure 7.4 on page 140 for a sample job lead card.) Have your personal data sheet handy in case you have the opportunity to discuss your qualifications over the telephone. (Personal data sheets are discussed later in this chapter.)

Your first contact will probably be with a receptionist. Introduce yourself and request the name and title of the person who is responsible for hiring new employees. Make certain that you have the correct pronunciation of that person's name. Ask to speak with him or her. If the person responsible for hiring is unavailable, ask for an appropriate time to call back.

Once you make contact with the person responsible for hiring, again introduce yourself and explain why you are calling. Inquire about the procedures for getting a job with the organization. In some organizations, you may be able to schedule an appointment for an interview over the telephone. If you cannot schedule an interview, ask that an employment application be sent to you, and ask permission to submit a résumé to the organization. Whatever the outcome of the conversation, always be courteous.

Many job openings in retail trade (see Figure 7.1 on page 131) are obtained by direct contact. The owner or manager of the retail business is usually responsible for hiring new employees. Retail merchants know that local customers frequently become their best employees. If you are seeking a job in one of the retail trades, walk into the business appropriately dressed and with your personal data sheet or résumé in hand. Ask to speak with the manager or owner. If the manager has a secretary, introduce yourself and ask to speak with the manager, or schedule an appointment for an interview. You may have to fill out a job application before being granted an interview.

Networking

Networking involves using personal contacts to find a job. Teachers, parents, students, friends, neighbors, local merchants, and members of the church or clubs you belong to are examples of per-

PLANNING MAKES A DIFFERENCE

It Pays to Network

Samantha Wilson is a good example of a successful networker. She recently graduated from Middletown High School, where she had taken a general education program. She had a part-time job at a local grocery store during her senior year.

Samantha didn't want to continue bagging groceries and stocking shelves for the rest of her life. She sat down one evening and took an inventory of her employment skills and her career interests. She really enjoyed driving and frequently drove her dad's pickup truck. She had an excellent safety record and wondered if someone might hire her to drive a small truck or van for their business.

Samantha made a list of acquaintances who might know of a possible job opening. She called seventeen people in the next three days to tell them of her interest and to enlist their help in looking for a driving job. She also checked the help-wanted ads every day.

Three weeks passed, and during that time, Samantha visited twenty-four different businesses to seek a driving job. Then her big break came. The manager of the store where Samantha worked part-time mentioned Samantha to her brother, who operated an auto parts store. Mrs. Greene told her brother that Samantha had an excellent attendance record and was one of the best workers in her store.

Networking paid off, and Samantha is now a successful driver for South Shore Auto Parts, Inc.

Critical Thinking

1. If Samantha asked seventeen friends and relatives to help with her job search, and each of them told five people about Samantha, and each of them told two people, how many people would be networking to help Samantha?
2. What specific job-search techniques did Samantha use?

sonal contacts you have right now. As you gain work experience, you will develop other valuable contacts for networking your particular job skills.

Using people you know to obtain job leads can be very successful. In fact, personal contacts help millions of individuals get jobs each year. In many cases, your contacts can offer you suggestions, direct leads, or referrals to other people. Clearly, this is a good approach for making your skills and availability for work known to as many people as possible.

The thought of asking personal contacts for help in seeking employment is embarrassing to some people. In fact, however, most people are flattered when asked for help in such an important matter.

Responding to Help-Wanted Ads

The Sunday edition of most major newspapers carries advertisements about job openings from organizations and employment agencies. The job descriptions are generally broad and request that candidates interested in the advertised position respond by calling or sending a résumé to the address that is listed.

In most newspapers, the job openings are arranged alphabetically by job title in the classified section of the newspaper. Most job advertisements include the following:
• Job title
• A brief description of the job

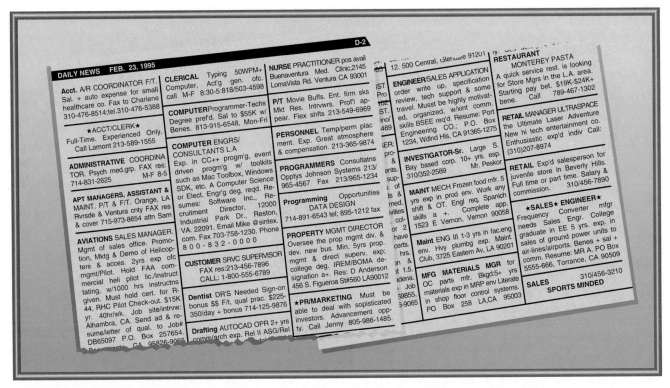

DAILY NEWS   FEB. 23, 1995   D-2

Acct. A/R COORDINATOR F/T. Sal. + auto expense for small healthcare co. Fax to Charlene 310-476-8514;tel.310-476-5388

★ACCT/CLERK★ Full-Time. Experienced Only. Call Lamont 213-589-1555

ADMINISTRATIVE COORDINA TOR. Psych med.grp. Mess: M-F 8-5 714-831-2625

APT MANAGERS, ASSISTANT & MAINT. P/T & F/T. Orange, LA Rvrsde & Ventura cnty FAX res & cover 715-973-8654 attn Sam

AVIATIONS SALES MANAGER. Mgmt of sales office. Promotion, Mktg & Demo of Helicopters & acces. 2yrs exp ofc mgmt/Pilot. Hold FAA commercial heli pilot lic./Instruct tating, w/1000 hrs instructns given. Must hold cert. for R-44, RHC Pilot Check-out. $15K yr. 40hr/wk. Job site/intrvw: Alhambra, CA. Send ad & resume/letter of qual. to Job# DB65097 P.O. Box 257654.

CLERICAL Typing 50WPM+ Computer, Act'g gen. ofc. call M-F 8:30-5:818/503-4598

COMPUTERProgrammer-Techs Degree pref'd. Sal to $55K w/ Benes. 813-915-6548, Mon-Fri

COMPUTER ENGRS/ CONSULTANTS L.A Exp. in CC++ progm'g, event driven progm'g w/ toolkits such as Mac Toolbox, Windows SDK, etc. A Computer Science or Elect. Engr'g deg. reqd. Resumes: Software Inc., cruitment Director, 12000 Industrial Park Dr., Reston, VA. 22091. Email Mike @sintex. com. Fax 703-758-1230. Phone 800-832-0000

CUSTOMER SRVC SUPERVISOR FAX res:213-456-7896 CALL: 1-800-555-6789

Dentist DR'S Needed Sign-on bonus $$ F/t, qual prac. $225-350/day + bonus 714-125-9876

Drafting AUTOCAD OPR 2+ yrs comm/arch exp. Rel II ASG/Rel

NURSE PRACTITIONER pos avail Buenaventura Med. Clinic.2145 LomaVista Rd. Ventura CA 93001

P/T Movie Buffs. Ent. firm sks Mkt Res. Intrvwrs. Prof'l appear. Flex shfts 213-549-6969

PERSONNEL Temp/perm plac ment. Exp. Great atmosphere & compensation. 213-365-9874

PROGRAMMERS Consultatns Opptys Johnson Systems 213/ 965-4567 Fax 213/965-1234

Programming Opportunities DATA DESIGN 714-891-6543 tel; 895-1212 fax

PROPERTY MGMT DIRECTOR Oversee the prop mgmt div. & dev. new bus. Min. 5yrs prop. mgmt & direct superv. exp; college deg. IREM/BOMA designation a+. Res: D Anderson 456 S. Figueroa St#560 LA90012

★PR/MARKETING Must be able to deal with sopisticated investors. Advancement opp-ty. Call Jenny 805-986-1485.

12. 500 Central, Glendale 91201

ENGINEER/SALES APPLICATION order write up, specification review, tech support & some travel. Musst be highly motivat ed, organized, w/xint comm. skills BSEE req'd. Resume: Port Engineering CO., P.O. Box 1234, Wdlnd Hls, CA 91365-1275

INVESTIGATOR-Sr. Large S. Bay based corp. 10+ yrs. esp. 310/352-2589   Mr. Peskor

MAINT MECH Frozen food mfr. 5 yrs exp in prod env. Work any shift & OT. Engl req, Spanish skills a +. Complete app. 1523 E Vernon, Vernon 90058

Maint ENG III 1-3 yrs in fac.eng env. Hvy plumbg exp. Maint. Club, 3725 Eastern Av, LA 90201

MFG MATERIALS MGR for OC parts mfr. Bkgd:5+ yrs materials exp in MRP env Literate in shop floor control systems. PO Box 258 LA,CA 95003

RESTAURANT MONTEREY PASTA A quick service rest. is looking for Store Mgrs in the L.A. area. Starting pay bet. $19K-$24K+ bene.   Call   789-467-1302

RETAIL MANAGER ULTRASPACE the Ultimate Laser Adventure New hi tech entertainment co. Enthusiastic exp'd indiv Call: (310)207-8974

RETAIL Exp'd salesperson for juvenile store in Beverly Hills. Full time or part time. Salary & commission.   310/456-7890

★SALES★ ENGINEER★ Frequency Converter mfgr needs Sales Engr. College graduate in EE 5 yrs. exp. in sales of ground power units to air-lines/airports. Benes + sal + comm. Resume: MR A. PO Box 5555-666, Torrance, CA 90509

SALES   310/456-3210 SPORTS MINDED

▲ *Figure 7.2 Sample Job Advertisements.*

- Required qualifications
- A short statement about the organization
- The name and address of the organization
- How and with whom to make contact in the organization

Job advertisements may be confusing and may leave much unsaid (Figure 7.2). Job advertisers use abbreviations in their ads to get as much information as possible in a limited amount of space. These abbreviations are frequently referred to as **job jargon**. Figure 7.3 contains a list of job jargon found in many newspaper advertisements. Familiarity with these frequently used abbreviations will help you conduct a successful job search.

Employers receive anywhere from twenty to one thousand résumés or letters of response for each classified ad they place. This high number of responses for each job results in keen competition among job seekers.

Using Placement Services at Schools

Any service that helps a job seeker find employment is called an **employment service**. Assistance with your job search may be as close as your high school. Your school may have a bulletin board where jobs with area employers are posted. Frequently, these listings cover part-time, summer, and temporary jobs. Local employers sometimes contact school counselors and vocational teachers to tell them about job openings. Workstudy teachers are also in frequent contact with employers and are a good source of jobs related to their particular area of vocational training. Ask your counselor to help you locate these resources in your school.

High schools, technical schools, and colleges occasionally arrange **job fairs**. Several potential employers are invited to one meeting place in the

Abbreviation	Meaning	Abbreviation	Meaning	Abbreviation	Meaning
Amer	American	Hrly	Hourly	Pls	Please
Ans	Answer, reply	Hskpr	Housekeeper	Proc	Processing
Appt	Appointment	Immed	Immediate;	Refs	References
Asst	Assistant		immediately	Ref req	References required
Attr	Attractive	Ind	Industry	Rel	Reliable
Bldg	Building	Info	Information	Req; Req'd	Required or requested
Bus	Business	Lic	License	Sal	Salary (a set amount
Clk	Clerk	Lt	Light		paid)
Co	Company	Mang	Manager	Sal open	Salary open (is flexible)
Comm	Commission	Maint	Maintenance	Sat	Saturday
Dept	Department	Mech	Mechanic;	Sm	Small
Dr	Drive		mechanical	Spec	Specialist
Drv Lic	Driver's license	M-F	Monday through	Sr	Senior
Elect	Electrical		Friday	Temp	Temporary
EOE	Equal opportunity	Mgr	Manager	Trans	Transportation
	employment	Mo	Month	Trk	Truck
Eve	Evening, night	Natl	National	Typ	Typing
Execl	Excellent	Nec	Necessary	Vac	Vacation
Exper; Ex	Experience	Opptys	Opportunities	Wk	Week; work
Fax	Facsimile machine	Opr	Operator	Wkdys	Weekdays
	number	Prod	Production	Wkly	Weekly
Flex	Flexible	P/T	Part-time	Xllent	Excellent
F/T	Full-time	Pt time	Part-time jobs	Yr	Year
Gd sal	Good salary	Perm	Permanent	Yrly	Yearly
Gen	General	Per mo	Per month	$$	Dollars; money
Hr	Hour	Per wk	Per week		

▲ *Figure 7.3 Abbreviations Used in Job Advertisements.*

▲ *Job fairs are a good way to learn about several job openings at one time and place.*

school. Tables are set up where each employer can distribute information describing the organization and briefly discuss career opportunities with interested job seekers. If your school has a job fair, the principal or counselor will announce the dates and times that you can attend.

Job fairs are a good way to learn about several possible places of employment at one time. They provide an opportunity to meet several employers and to obtain job application forms. Note that interviews at job fairs are usually not lengthy and rarely lead to on-the-spot job offers.

Contacting Professional and Trade Organizations

Labor unions, professional and trade organizations, and groups for the physically challenged often receive and post openings for positions. These groups provide employment assistance to individuals who are associated with their particular organization. Many publish trade journals or magazines that include listings of job openings and other career information of interest to their members.

Professional and trade organizations conduct local meetings and sponsor state or national conventions for their members. Job fairs are frequently included on the agenda of large meetings and conventions. Speakers from local professional and trade organizations are frequently available to speak to students about their profession. If you are interested, ask your counselor to help you make the appropriate contact.

Using the State Bureau of Employment Services

The U.S. Employment Service (USES) operates more than two thousand local offices in partnership with state employment services to provide free testing, counseling, and job place-

GETTING MORE INFORMATION

Your school or public librarian may be able to help you select a trade or professional journal in an area of your interest. These journals contain considerable information about current happenings in their career fields. Here are some suggestions for finding out about openings in particular fields:

- Chemistry: Read the *Journal of the American Chemical Society*, published by the American Chemical Society, 1155 16th St., N.W., Washington, DC 20036.

- Paper industry: Read the *Tappi Journal*. Published by the Technical Association of the Pulp and Paper Industry, Inc., P.O. Box 105113, Atlanta, GA 30348.

- Carpentry trades: Contact local carpentry contractors, or the Associated Builders, and Contractors, Inc., Associated General Contractors, United Brotherhood of Carpenters and Joiners of America, or National Association of Home Builders. Look in your phone book for local branches of these organizations.

- Music: Contact the American Federation of Musicians, 1501 Broadway, New York, NY 10036.

- Jobs for women in accounting, banking, and sales, with a special focus on engineering and technology: Read *Career Woman* magazine, 44 Broadway, Greenlawn, NY 11740.

- Special opportunities for African Americans, Hispanics, Native Americans, and Asian Americans in engineering: Read the publication *Equal Opportunity*, 44 Broadway, Greenlawn, NY 11740.

▲ *There are several thousand privately owned employment services in the United States.*

ment. These state-operated employment services, called *Job Service* in most states, form a national network of public employment offices that follow federal guidelines.

The USES offices counseled 33 million people in job-seeking skills and filled 126 million jobs during its first 50 years. Through the USES network, job seekers have access to job banks, which contain computerized listings of job vacancies in their particular geographic area. This enables them to match their skills to the available jobs.

The Job Service also channels applicants into various training programs through screening and referral services. Summer youth programs provide summer jobs in city, county, and state government agencies for low-income youth. Students, school dropouts, or graduates entering the labor market who are between sixteen and twenty-one years of age are eligible. In addition, the Job Corps, which has more than one hundred centers throughout the United States, helps young people learn skills or obtain education.

Job Service offices are listed in the telephone directory under "State Government." They do not charge for their services. They receive job listings from employers and match potential candidates to these openings. Many of these state agencies have employment counselors that specifically assist young people in entering the job market.

To register for employment services, fill out a Bureau of Employment Job Services application at your local Job Service office. You will be asked to list your skills, training, and work history and to identify one or two specific types of jobs for which you would qualify. All applications are filed in the "job-match" system by occupation, so you need to be specific when identifying the types of jobs you are seeking. The application form you complete will be kept and sent to employers seeking someone with your credentials. When there is an interest from an employer, you will be contacted, and an interview will be arranged.

Notify your local Job Service staff if you change your address or phone number, and keep in touch. Your application will remain in the "actively seeking work" files for sixty days from the last date on which you contacted the bureau. Unanticipated openings may occur at any time.

What skills, training, and work experience would you list on a Bureau of Employment Job Services application? What specific types of jobs are you qualified to do?

Using Private Employment Agencies

There are several thousand privately owned employment services in the United States. These private employment services or agencies find jobs for about 4 percent of all unemployed workers entering the job market and for about 15 percent of all employed workers who are making job changes.

Although these agencies are in business to make money, they can also be very helpful. They operate on a commission basis, and the fee depends on a successful match. Always find out the exact cost and who is responsible for paying the fee before using the service. Fees may be paid by the employer, the applicant, or both.

CAREER TIP

Before you sign on with an employment agency, remember to read the contract to determine who is responsible for the fee.

Some employment agencies are generalists and recruit candidates for all types of jobs. However, most agencies specialize in a particular type of occupation, such as clerical, engineering, or sales. When you contact an agency, they will tell you whether or not they specialize.

Employers submit job descriptions detailing their requirements to employment agencies. Agency personnel check their files for individuals who are qualified to fill the opening. If they have no one in their files, they may advertise the position in the newspaper.

If you contact an employment agency, you will probably have an initial screening interview. The purpose of the initial screening is to eliminate job seekers who are obviously unsuited for the job opening. If your qualifications match an opening, the agency will arrange an interview for you with the employer. If no match is found, the information about you is placed in the agency's files until a more appropriate opening arises. When working with an employment agency, call periodically to see whether an opening has occurred.

If you are asked to sign an employment contract or another agreement with an agency, ask to take the document home to read thoroughly before signing. Let the placement counselor know that as a matter of policy you want to be certain that you understand the agreement and that you will either return it in person or mail it back promptly.

Temporary services are another type of private employment agency. These services have grown

▲ *Private employment services charge the employer, applicant, or both for their services. Would you be willing to pay a fee to get a job you want?*

▲ *Nine out of ten companies use temporary help. What temporary services are available in your community?*

rapidly in the last fifteen years. The idea behind temporary employment services is to "rent" employees for a short or limited amount of time, thus the term *temporary*. The temporary service acts as the employer and hires the temporary worker. The organization where the temporary worker is assigned pays the temporary service, which in turn pays the temporary worker. Many permanent employees start out as "temps."

Keeping Track of and Following Up on Job Leads

A job search usually requires communication with numerous potential employers. It may take twenty-five job leads to generate one interview, and five interviews to get one job offer. In terms of sheer numbers, it is a difficult but important task to remember whom you talked with and contacted over the period of your job search.

Purchase a small notebook or use three-by-five-inch cards to organize your job leads. A card file is easiest to retrieve information from because you can arrange the cards in alphabetical order. If you are using a notebook, you will probably arrange the job leads sequentially by date of initial

```
                              Date of contact:  2/6/95
Company name: Tasty Beef Incorporated
Company address: 349 Industrial Parkway
                 Kansas City, KS 66110
Company phone number: (913) 000-0000
Job lead source: Sunday classified ad, Kansas City News
Position: Packer
Company business: Meat Processing
Person to contact for hiring: Ms. Danielle Santos
Title of contact: Personnel Administrator
Results of contact: 2/6/95 Ms. Santos's Secretary said to
     send a short résumé and Ms. Santos would contact
     me if there was any interest.
     2/9/95 Called Ms. Santos.  She was reviewing
     résumés.  She pulled my résumé out and said
     she wasn't sure I met the qualifications.
     2/17/95  I had an initial interview.
Other information: _____
```

▲ *Figure 7.4 Sample Job Lead Card.*

contact. In either case, the information you record will be the same. The information that you should record on your job lead cards, in your notebook, or on your computer is shown in Figure 7.4. This information will help you maintain an orderly record and appraisal of job prospects.

Following through on leads may mean getting a job offer long after you thought there was no hope. Remember that it takes an average of six to eight weeks for an employer to fill a position.

Section 2 GET INVOLVED

Answer the following on a separate sheet of paper, and be prepared to discuss your responses in class.

1. Using the yellow pages of your telephone book, do the following:
   a. Select and develop a list of appropriate employers for whom you would be qualified to work following high school graduation.
   b. List four questions you would ask the receptionist if you called.
   c. What personal information about you will interest the employer?
2. Learn to network by thinking of a job you are qualified to perform.
   a. Ask two relatives, two friends, and a teacher for suggestions on finding an employer who might hire you.
   b. Ask these people if they have friends or relatives who work for these employers. Make a list of friends and relatives they mention.
3. Read the help-wanted ads in the Sunday edition of your local or regional newspaper. Clip out four employment opportunities you would be interested in pursuing, and bring them to class for discussion.

Section
3

Your Personal Data Sheet and Résumé

Maria waited patiently for her turn to speak with the receptionist. The Great Value Discount Store had advertised for two part-time stock clerks in the morning paper. The working hours would be perfect for her senior year at Edison High School. Maria hoped that the three men and two women ahead of her would not be hired before she had a chance.

Finally, it was Maria's turn. She introduced herself and explained why she was seeking the part-time stock clerk position. She could tell that the receptionist liked her attitude because she gave her a job application and asked her to bring it back as soon as possible.

The application had a lot of questions on it, but Maria had come prepared with a personal data

> "A fair day's wages for a fair day's work": it is as just a demand as governed men ever made of governing. It is the everlasting right of man.
>
> **Thomas Carlyle**

sheet. In twenty minutes, she had completed the application. She checked it over to make certain that her spelling was correct and that her writing was neat. Then she returned it to the receptionist. Maria left the store knowing that she had moved ahead of the five people who took their applications home with them.

Being prepared to provide potential employers with information about yourself, as Maria was, will help you make a positive first impression. Before you begin your job search, review your skills, experiences, and employment objectives and then develop a thorough personal data sheet and a well-written résumé.

Prepare a Personal Data Sheet

A **personal data sheet** lists accurate information about you that employers will ask for when you fill out a job application or are interviewed for a job. The data sheet contains a wide range of information, including your Social Security number,

▲ *Accurate, concise information in the personal data sheet will help you complete job applications and write an effective résumé. Have you organized the information you will need to write an effective résumé?*

1. Personal Information
   Your full name: _____ Social Security number: _____
   Address (number and street): _____ State: _____ Zip: _____
   Phone number: _____ Date available for employment: _____
   Date of birth: _____ Marital Status: Single ☐ Married ☐
   Height _____ Weight: _____ lbs. Citizenship status: _____
   Name and phone numbers of people to contact in an emergency:
   Name: _____ Address: _____ Phone number: _____ Relationship: _____
   Name: _____ Address: _____ Phone number: _____ Relationship: _____
   Name: _____ Address: _____ Phone number: _____ Relationship: _____

2. Educational Background
   Name of high school: _____
   School address; _____ City: _____ State: _____ Zip: _____
   School phone number: (_____)_____
   Present status of student: Part-time ☐   Full-time ☐   Graduated ☐
   Grade point average: _____ Class rank: _____
   Dates of Attendance: From (month and year): _____ To (month and year): _____
   Course of Study: General _____ Vocational _____ College preparatory _____
   Extracurricular Activities (clubs, sports) _____
   Awards or honors: _____
   Favorite subjects: _____

3. Part-time or Full-time Work Experience
   Name of company: _____ Dates employed: _____
   Your position _____
   Your responsibilities: _____
   Wages or salary: Start _____ Last _____
   Reason for leaving _____

4. Volunteer Work
   Name of organizaition: _____
   Why you choose to volunteer for this organization: _____
   Your responsibilities: _____

5. Your Future Educational Goals _____

6. Your Present Career/Job Goal _____

7. References
   (Complete name, address, job title, and phone number)
   Reference 1: Name _____ Address _____ Job title _____
                Phone number _____ Relationship _____
   Reference 2: Name _____ Address _____ Job title _____
                Phone number _____ Relationship _____
   Reference 3: Name _____ Address _____ Job title _____
                Phone number _____ Relationship _____

8. Major Qualifications for a Position
   (Skills you have such as typing or operating equipment)

   _____

9. Leisure-Time Activities and Hobbies: _____

▲ *Figure 7.5 Sample Personal Data Sheet.*

the addresses and phone numbers of friends or past employers who will give you a recommendation, and the number of days you were absent from school last year.

The personal data sheet is written for your use only. You will not give it to an employer. It will help as you fill out job applications and prepare for job interviews. Just as identifying and keeping track of job leads will help you find possible jobs, your personal data sheet and résumé will help you get the job you want after you find it. Study the personal data sheet outline in Figure 7.5.

Name: Include your first, middle, and last names.

Address: Give the address at which you can most readily be contacted by mail.

Phone number: Give the number for a phone or answering machine that will always be answered during normal business hours.

Career objective: Write a brief statement that describes the type of work you want to do. This should be a realistic objective based on your career goals and employment skills.

Education: Give the name and location of your high school and the date when you graduated or expect to graduate. Include your class rank, grade point average, and any awards or honors you earned.

Activities and work experience: Stress your skills and accomplishments. Account for important school, volunteer, and work activities. Begin with your most recent experience, and work backward. Include dates, job titles if employed, the name of your employer's business, and a full description of all jobs held. Always write in the first person.

Personal information: Include hobbies, social skills, extracurricular activities, and date of birth.

Date available for employment: State the earliest date you will be available. If you are a student seeking part-time employment, specify the hours and days of the week that you are available.

References: References are people who have agreed to provide an employer with a written or verbal statement about your character or ability. Identify at least three references. Ask teachers, counselors, principals, previous part-time or full-time employers, or professional people who know you personally or have met you through school activities. Request their permission before citing them as references. Make certain that you have their names spelled correctly, and include their job titles, mailing addresses, and phone numbers. The names and contact information of references need not be included on your résumé. A statement such as "References are available on request" will do. You don't want your references contacted unless the employer is sincerely interested in hiring you.

▲ *Figure 7.6 Chronological Résumé Outline.*

Compose an Effective Résumé

A **résumé** is a written summary of a job seeker's employment objectives, work experience, education and training, proven skills, and certain personal information. Your résumé is a written portrait of who you are. Its content and appearance are very important. Your résumé may create the first impression the interviewer has of you.

In the last decade, it has become common for employers to request a résumé from job seekers. Years ago, many employers hired workers without much investigation. Competition among compa-nies, the cost of hiring unqualified employees, laws that protect employees from unfair labor practices, and lengthy lawsuits have made it necessary for employers to screen and thoroughly investigate potential employees before putting them on the payroll.

Some employers do not require a résumé from first-time job seekers, though many do. If you need to submit a résumé, the employer will probably ask for it before scheduling you for an interview. This procedure enables the employer to read several résumés and narrow down the number of job candidates to interview. When reading résumés, employers read only as far as their interest

Résumé
of
Lamar T. Grant

40 North High St.   (614) 000-0000
Mount Vernon, Ohio 43050

Career Objective
Employment using my word-processing skills. Opportunity for long-term career
growth and advancement.

Education
High school diploma. Majored in Cooperative Office Education. GPA 3.14
Knox County Joint Vocational School, Mount Vernon, Ohio. June 7, 1991

- Treasurer of senior class. ▪ Second place state competition in word processing.

Activities and Work Experience
September 14, 1990 - present
Anderson Printing, Inc., Mount Vernon, Ohio.
Employed as a part-time word processor during my senior year of high school
and presently working 20 hours per week. Using Apple Macintosh computers with
Microsoft Word and Pagemaker software.

September 1989-Present
First Baptist Church, Mount Vernon, Ohio.
Work as a volunteer to type the weekly church bulletin.

May 1989-June 1991
Knox County Joint Vocational School, Mount Vernon, Ohio.
Student helper for the school newspaper. Word processing final copy using
Apple II computer with PFS Write software.

Personal Information
Date of birth: August 7, 1971
Health: Excellent
Marital status: Single
Hobbies: Hiking, singing in church choir, collecting old coins
Willing to relocate for good employment opportunity.

Date Available for Employment
Available for immediate employment.   Present employer can replace me with a
COE student from Knox County JVS on short notice.

References
Excellent references available on request.

▲ *Figure 7.7 Sample Chronological Résumé.*

is maintained. Therefore, it is worth your time and effort to prepare an interesting, well-written résumé.

Because your résumé may determine whether or not you will be interviewed, it is best to prepare it before you begin your job search. This will give you time to do a thorough job. Then, when an employer asks for it, you'll be ready.

The two most accepted résumé styles are chronological and functional. The **chronological résumé** lists the jobs you have held in chronological order. It begins with your most recent experience and works backward. The focus is on work history and other pertinent information, such as education. The chronological résumé is best for people who have a steady school or work record that shows continuous growth. It is the easiest style to write, and most hiring managers prefer it.

The **functional résumé** deemphasizes dates and jobs held in order to highlight qualifications, skills, and accomplishments. This style of résumé is generally written by people with lengthy work experiences, those who may be short on experience, and others who have held a variety of jobs. The functional résumé groups qualifications by functions, such as repairing, organizing, managing, and selling. Dates are usually not given. This format allows job seekers to exclude experiences that do not relate to the kind of work they want to do.

The chronological résumé is outlined in Figure 7.6 (see page 143). Read it carefully. Figure 7.7 shows a chronological résumé written by Lamar Grant. Notice that Lamar's résumé

- Is one neatly typed page in length
- Focuses on accomplishments and qualifications
- Is composed with clear, precise, and logical statements
- Is well organized and free of errors

Section 3 — GET INVOLVED

Answer the following on a separate sheet of paper, and be prepared to discuss your responses in class.

1. Use the outline in Figure 7.5 to develop your own personal data sheet.
2. If an employer could read your personal data sheet, what do you think he or she might expect from you on the job? Explain the reasons for your answer.
3. In the sample chronological résumé, what words does Lamar use to describe his career objective?
4. What skills can Lamar offer an employer?
5. List Lamar's positive personal characteristics.
6. What three questions would you ask Lamar if you were an employer?
7. Using your personal data sheet and the outline for a chronological résumé, write a résumé for yourself.

Section 4

Write a Successful Cover Letter

The purpose of a **cover letter** is to introduce yourself to a specific employer regarding your interest in a specific job opening. A cover letter should accompany each résumé you send to an employer. It begins with a statement telling the prospective employer why you are writing and why he or she should read your résumé. A successful cover letter creates enough interest in your résumé to produce an interview.

When you send a cover letter in response to an advertisement, always respond to the requirements stated in the ad by relating them to your personal career skills and goals.

▲ *Each résumé you send to an employer should include a cover letter that expresses your interest in a specific job opening. What is the most difficult task in writing a cover letter?*

A cover letter should
• Be one page in length
• Always be written for a specific employer and position
• Be individually typed and free of errors
• Have single-spaced paragraphs and double spacing between paragraphs
• Be addressed to a specific person

CAREER TIP

Do not waste valuable space in the cover letter by claiming that you are sincere, dedicated, or 100 percent honest unless you can prove your statement. Most employers do not take these statements seriously.

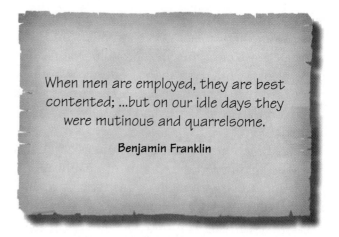

When men are employed, they are best contented; ...but on our idle days they were mutinous and quarrelsome.

Benjamin Franklin

• Express interest in the position (paragraph 1)
• Indicate that you know something about the organization
• Include a list or statement of your qualifications that relate to the job (paragraph 2)
• Include only statements that you can support in an interview
• End with a request for an interview and a statement about your desire to work for the organization (paragraph 3)
• Include your name, address, and phone number so you can be contacted
• Include an attachment of the job advertisement if you are responding to a job advertised in the classified section of the newspaper
• Be duplicated for your records (you may forget whether or not you have responded to a particular advertisement or sent a résumé to a specific organization)
• Be signed in ink, preferably blue, so it won't look photocopied

Lamar Grant used the cover letter shown in Figure 7.8 for an ad he read in the *Columbus Dispatch*. He attached a copy of the ad and his résumé before he mailed the letter.

Write a new cover letter for each résumé you send to an employer, and have someone proofread the cover letter and résumé before you mail them. Remember, this may be the only chance you have to make a good impression.

Your address ———————————————————————{ 40 North High St.
                                                                    Mount Vernon, OH 43050

Date ——————————————————————————————{ August 14, 1995

Direct your letter to
a particular person. —————————————————————— Barbara J. Eiber
                                                                    Data Processing Manager
                                                                    DATATRONICS, Inc.
                                                                    2312 Broad St.
                                                                    Columbus, OH 43219

Greeting ——————————————————————————{ Dear Ms. Eiber:

Paragraph 1:
Express your ——————————————————————— Please consider me for the position of Word
interest in the position.   Processor advertised in the *Columbus Dispatch* on
                                                                    Sunday, August 13. A review of my résumé will
                                                                    demonstrate that I am skilled and experienced.

                                                                    The following list of my skills and experiences
                                                                    match with those listed in your ad:
Paragraph 2: Include a   • One year as a word processor with Anderson Printing,
statement or listing of ——————————————   Mount Vernon, OH.
your qualifications for   • Experienced with Microsoft Word software.
this particular job.   • Two years of word processing training,
                                                                      Knox County Joint Vocational School.

                                                                    DATATRONICS is widely recognized as a rapidly
                                                                    expanding organization, and I would welcome the
                                                                    opportunity to be a contributing staff member.
Paragraph 3: State your   Thank you for taking the time to review my enclosed
desire to work for the ——————————————   résumé, I will look forward to interviewing with you in
employer, and ask for an   the near future. My home telephone number is
interview.   (614) 000-0000.

Salutation ——————————————————————{ Sincerely,

Your signature ——————————————————{ *Lamar T. Grant*

Your name typed ——————————————————{ Lamar T. Grant

Enclosure that will be ——————————————{ Enclosure: Résumé
found in the envelope.

▲ *Figure 7.8 Sample Cover Letter.*

Section 4 GET INVOLVED

1. Select one of the ads in Figure 7.2, and write a cover letter responding to it. Have a friend or teacher check your cover letter for content, appearance, grammar, and format.

IMPORTANT FACTS

The Job Hunt Trail

Steps in the path to employment.

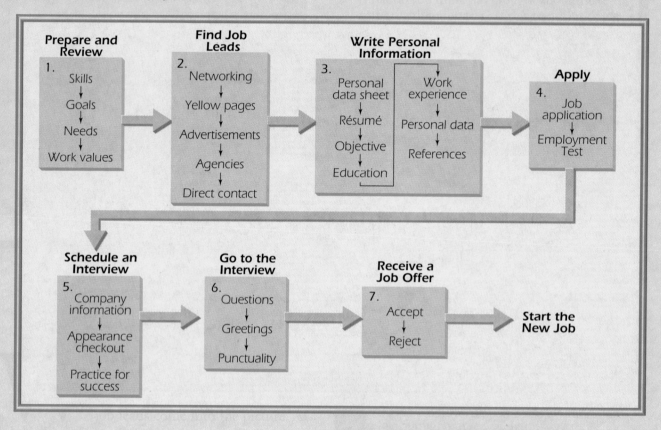

Prepare and Review
1.
Skills
↓
Goals
↓
Needs
↓
Work values

Find Job Leads
2.
Networking
↓
Yellow pages
↓
Advertisements
↓
Agencies
↓
Direct contact

Write Personal Information
3.
Personal data sheet
↓
Résumé
↓
Objective
↓
Education

Work experience
↓
Personal data
↓
References

Apply
4.
Job application
↓
Employment Test

Schedule an Interview
5.
Company information
↓
Appearance checkout
↓
Practice for success

Go to the Interview
6.
Questions
↓
Greetings
↓
Punctuality

Receive a Job Offer
7.
Accept
↓
Reject

Start the New Job

New Hires

- Nationwide, only 50 percent of all newly hired employees last more than six months.
- The U.S. Department of Labor estimates that a bad hiring decision costs a company one-third of the new hire's annual salary.
- Some estimates say that the cost of replacing an employee is five hundred to seven hundred times the hourly rate for that job.

Finding the Right Employee Takes Time

18 percent of all job openings are filled in less than four weeks

34 percent take four to six weeks

25 percent take five to eight weeks

17 percent take eight to twelve weeks

6 percent take more than twelve weeks

On the average, it takes six to eight weeks to fill a position.

Source: Employment Management Association, 1989.

CHAPTER 7 REVIEW

ENRICH YOUR VOCABULARY

On a separate sheet of paper, number from 1 to 15, and complete the following activity. (Do not write in your textbook.) Match each statement below with the most appropriate term from the "Enrich Your Vocabulary" list at the beginning of the chapter by writing that term next to the correct statement.

1. A summary of a job seeker's work experience, education and training, and proven skills
2. Information about an organization that is hiring
3. People who recommend you to an employer
4. The process of seeking employment
5. A person applying for employment with a specific company
6. Using personal contacts to find a job
7. The type and number of jobs available
8. Abbreviations used in newspaper job advertisements
9. A preliminary interview to eliminate unqualified candidates
10. A good way to meet several potential employers at one time
11. Any service that helps a job seeker find employment
12. Lists accurate information about you that is important to employers
13. Lists jobs you have held in chronological order, beginning with the most recent
14. Groups qualifications by functions
15. A letter of introduction to a specific employer regarding your interest in a specific job opening

CHECK YOUR KNOWLEDGE

On a separate sheet of paper, complete the following activity. (Do not write in your textbook.)

1. Approximately how many jobs are there in the United States at the present time?
2. What are the three leading durable goods industries in the United States?
3. What job search method does the U.S. Department of Labor rank as the most successful?
4. List three services that are available from the State Bureau of Employment Services.
5. How many job interviews are usually required to obtain a job offer?
6. What is the average length of time it takes an employer to fill a job opening?
7. In what type of industry do most Americans earn their living?
8. Is it wise to submit a job application to an employer who isn't hiring at the present time? Why or why not?

DEVELOP SCANS COMPETENCIES

Government experts say that successful workers can productively use Resources, Interpersonal skills, Information, Systems, and Technology. This activity will give you practice in developing Information and System skills.

It is important to be systematic and organized when searching for a job. Being organized not only helps you, but it impresses prospective employers and could be the difference between getting or not getting a job.

There are a number of hints listed in this chapter that will help you stay organized during your job search. You may want to review these hints. Then compare the two flow charts for finding a job shown at the right and the opposite page. Use the best aspects of both charts to develop your own flow chart. Making your flow chart as specific as possible. Then write a paragraph explaining how your flow chart improves upon the two examples.

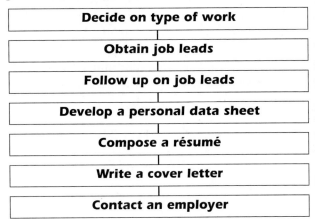

Decide on type of work

Obtain job leads

Follow up on job leads

Develop a personal data sheet

Compose a résumé

Write a cover letter

Contact an employer

Applying and Interviewing for a Job

Learning Objectives

After completing this chapter, you should be prepared to:

- complete an acceptable job application form
- describe preemployment tests and explain why employers use them
- locate several sources of information about companies and other organizations
- present yourself well in a job interview, follow up with the interviewer, and evaluate your performance
- list the advantages and disadvantages of volunteer, part-time, and full-time work

Enrich Your Vocabulary

In reading this chapter and doing the exercises you will learn the following important terms:

job application form
work permit
Fair Labor
  Standards Act
health certificate
employment
  eligibility
  verification form
background check
bond
felony
preemployment test
valid

civil service
  examination
initiative
job interview
personnel
  department
fair employment
  program
job offer
temporary service
minimum wage
volunteer work
full-time job

Finding your first full-time job is a major step in your preparation for career success. The experience and training you acquire will determine whether your second full-time job is a move up or down the career ladder. Before you begin searching for your first full-time job, you need answers to several questions:

1. What personal documents will employers require?

2. What preemployment tests am I likely to encounter?

3. How can I obtain information about major employers?

4. How can I improve my job interviewing skills?

5. What are my legal rights as a job seeker?

Once you have planned your job search, developed a personal data sheet, and written a résumé, the next step will be to pursue job leads and prepare for interviews with potential employers. Once an employer has expressed an interest in hiring you, it's important to follow through with any additional information that is requested and to be punctual for your job interview. Finally, you will need to be mentally prepared for job offers and rejections. The information in this chapter will help you prepare for each part of your job search.

Section 1

Job Application Forms

A **job application form** is generally used by employers to screen out unqualified applicants before job interviews are conducted. Your application form creates an impression of you with the person who selects interview candidates. In most hiring situations, several qualified applicants apply for the same job. A neat, accurate application will

CAREER TIP

When you apply for a job, be sure to have your personal data sheet (see Chapter 7) with you. It contains the information that is requested on most job application forms.

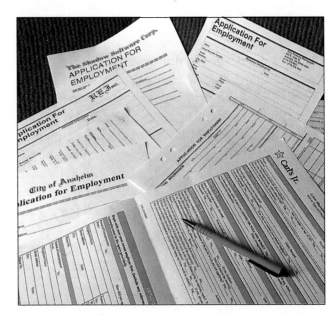

▲ Be sure to read all employment applications carefully before filling out all the questions.

Personal Information	Employment Desired
• Name • Home address • Home phone number • Social Security number • Date of birth	State the specific job for which you are applying.
Education Most employers will request a copy of your high school transcript.	**Previous Employment** List all full-time, part-time, and volunteer work experience. Include the name, address, and phone number of each former employer.
References List individuals who will say positive things about you. Include the name, address, and phone number of each reference.	**Hobbies and Personal Interests** Hobbies and personal interests tell an employer a lot about your personality,

▲ *Figure 8.1 Basic Information Requested on a Job Application Form.*

help you join the group being interviewed for the job opening.

Job application forms are factual in content. Very little space is devoted to your personal motivation or past accomplishments. Instead, a restricted amount of space is usually provided for personal information, job skills, work experience, and education. If a résumé isn't required, your job application form will be the potential employer's major source of information about you. Figure 8.1 lists the basic information that is usually requested on a job application form.

If you are hired, your employer will keep your application form on file for the duration of your employment. A job application form becomes a legal document when you sign and date it. Your responses must be honest. If you misrepresent yourself in any statement and it comes to your employer's attention later on, it can be considered a breach of trust and is grounds for dismissal.

Documents Needed for Employment

An employer must review certain documents before you are legally permitted to begin work. When you begin a job search, make sure you have the following documents in your possession.

Social Security Card. The number on your social security card is used for your tax and retirement records and as a way for numerous agencies and organizations to identify you.

Birth Certificate. Your birth certificate is proof of your age and place of birth. To obtain a copy of your birth certificate, contact the Department of Health, Division of Vital Statistics, in the county where you were born.

Work Permit. Employees under eighteen years of age must have a **work permit** for most nonfarm jobs. Your school counselor or principal can help you get the application. You will not be able to obtain the work permit until you are hired, though, because the employer must complete some of the information on the application. Laws concerning work permits are part of the **Fair Labor Standards Act**. This important federal legislation protects all workers. It includes laws concerning work permits that regulate the employment of minors (anyone under eighteen years of age). In addition, state laws also regulate the employment of minors.

Federal law states that fourteen- and fifteen-year-old minors may not be employed

• During school hours, except for students enrolled in work-experience and career-exploration programs

• Before 7 A.M. or after 7 P.M., except from June 1 through Labor Day (when minors may work until 9 P.M.)

• More than three hours per day on school days

• More than eighteen hours per week when school is in session

Being Responsible

Small Lies—Big Problems

When Russell Wakefield answered the following question on his job application form, he didn't tell the truth: "Are you now dependent on or a user of any addictive or hallucinogenic drug other than for medical treatment under the supervision of a doctor?" That was fourteen months ago.

A cough broke the silence in the back of the courtroom as the judge looked down from her bench and pronounced Russell's sentence. "Russell Wakefield, you are sentenced to spend the next six months in the county jail and to pay your former employer, Tri-City Delivery, $7,200 for damage to the truck you were driving. In addition, you will pay the United Utility Company $1,800 for damage to their utility pole and electrical wires. Because you were driving under the influence of alcohol, you will lose your chauffeur's license in this state for a period of one year."

Russell didn't know how he would pay the damages. Tri-City Delivery had fired him, and it seemed doubtful that another company would hire him. The $700 Russell had saved after high school graduation was a source of personal pride to him. Now it was gone. Russell felt angry, foolish, and humiliated. How would he ever face his parents or friends?

Again, the gray eyes of the judge looked down from the bench as she announced to everyone in the courtroom, "Because this is your first such offense, the court suspends the six months in jail. However, you will be placed on probation for a period of one year. During your probation, you must attend weekly counseling sessions sponsored by this court."

Critical Thinking

1. Before a new employer hires Russell, they will probably ask on the job application form or during the job interview about his use of drugs or alcohol. If Russell elects to cover up his past and a new employer discovers the truth, he could be fired. The truth might not come out for several years. If you were Russell, how would you handle this situation? How might your solution help his career? How might it hurt his career?

- More than eight hours per day on nonschool days
- More than forty hours per week when school isn't in session.

Fourteen- and fifteen-year-old minors are permitted by federal law to work in the following occupations, among others

- Office and clerical work (including the operation of office machines)

- Cashiering, sales, art work, window trimming, price marking, packing, and stocking shelves
- Bagging and carrying out customer orders; delivery work by foot, bicycle, or public transportation
- Dispensing gasoline and oil and washing and polishing cars (may not use pits, racks, or lifting devices or inflate tires with removable retaining rings)

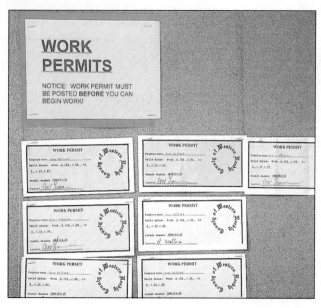

▲ *The Fair Labor Standards Act requires employees under eighteen years of age to obtain a work permit.*

The following occupations are among those prohibited to fourteen- and fifteen-year-old minors

- Any manufacturing, mining, or processing occupation
- Operating or tending hoisting apparatuses or power-driven machinery
- Work requiring the use of ladders or scaffolds
- Cooking, working with food slicers or grinders, and working in food coolers or freezers
- Loading goods to and from trucks, railroad cars, or conveyers

The Fair Labor Standards Act requires a minimum age of eighteen for any nonagricultural occupations declared to be particularly hazardous for sixteen- and seventeen-year-olds or detrimental to their health and well-being.

Health Certificate. Certain jobs require a **health certificate**. This document may certify that you don't have a specific infectious disease or that you are free of certain drugs. Your employer will know whether or not you need this kind of documentation. If you do, your family doctor or the local health department can help you obtain the proper health certificate.

Employment Eligibility Verification Form (Form I-9). Employers are required to verify a worker's eligibility to be employed in the United States. They do this by completing an **employment eligibility verification form** (Form I-9). Upon request, employers must present Form I-9 for inspection to officials of the Immigration and Naturalization Service or the Department of Labor. An employer who fails to produce the form within the time specified by the regulation or who improperly completes or retains the form may be found to be in violation of the law and may face a monetary penalty. Application forms for the required government documents include complete instructions.

Completing a Job Application Form

Employers expect you to be neat and thorough when you fill out a job application form. Use the following guidelines:

1. Follow the instructions. Employers know that an applicant who doesn't follow directions on the job application form isn't likely to follow directions on the job.

2. Read the entire application form before you begin, and write something in every blank space. If a question doesn't apply to you, write "N/A" (not applicable), or draw a line through the blank. Completing all of the blanks will demonstrate your thoroughness.

3. Print is usually easier to read than longhand. Ink is usually preferred to pencil. However, if you use ink and make a mistake, it is unlikely that you will be able to correct it without ruining the neat appearance of the application form.

4. When writing your last name first, use a comma after your last name. For example: Jones, Roberta.

5. If possible, find out in advance what jobs are available. Emphasize your qualifications for

▲ *Carl asked the secretary for permission to take the job application form home and write a few paragraphs about his qualifications for the job opening.*

one specific job. Some employers take a dim view of applicants who apply for "just any job" or who write "will take anything."

6. Some employers may schedule an interview with you before they ask you to complete a job application form. In this case, ask for a copy of the form before the interview. This will give you enough time to consider your answers and to type in the requested information. If you are not satisfied with the first application you complete, request another from the office worker who is helping you. Keep in mind, though, that some employers frown on applicants who make mistakes and require additional forms.

7. Your "expected pay" may be requested on the application form. If so, it is best to state that you will accept the standard rate for the position or that your pay is negotiable. The salary or hourly rate may be fixed, but pay is usually open for discussion. If possible, wait until you are offered a job before discussing pay. Asking for too much money will eliminate you from consideration. On the other hand, willingness to accept an uncompetitive, low

wage will not gain an employer's respect or advance your career.

8. If permitted, take the application form home with you. Then, take time to prepare a few paragraphs about your skills and qualifications for the present job opening or other jobs in the organization. If you have a résumé, attach a copy of it to the application before returning it. This will ensure that your best qualifications are stated.

9. If the application form asks for the name of a person to notify in case of emergency, list the name of your closest relative or a best friend living in the area. Include that person's home and work telephone numbers.

10. Be honest about the information you provide. Employers usually conduct a **background check** (an investigation to verify your former employers, schools attended, and personal references).

11. Some job application forms request a list of your memberships in social or civic clubs and organizations. Some employers consider this as an indication of how well you get along with other people.

12. Employers favor applicants who have reliable transportation. If you own or have access to a reliable car or can rely on public transportation, emphasize that fact.

13. Most job application forms ask if you have ever been convicted of law violations. In addition, many employers run a routine police check before hiring a new employee. This is very important if you must be bonded. A **bond** is a type of insurance that pays financial losses if an employee fails to perform his or her duty or is guilty of theft. The law requires you to admit to felony convictions. (A **felony** is a serious crime.) However, you are not required to acknowledge violations for which you were arrested but not convicted. Traffic violations, other than felonies, need not be disclosed.

14. Job application forms usually ask if you are willing to undergo a physical examination. Tests for chemical dependency are frequently included in the physical. Lost production, poor job performance, and safety violations caused by workers' substance abuse are very costly to employers.

15. Some employers want to know how many days of school or work you missed during the past twelve months. Missing seven or more days usually indicates an unreliable worker.

16. When you submit your job application to the employer, ask what the procedures are for finding out the status of your job application. Persistence indicates your interest in the job and may result in a job offer. Don't be a nuisance, but do follow up on your application by calling or writing the employer.

Section 1 — GET INVOLVED

Answer the following on a separate sheet of paper, and be prepared to discuss your responses in class.

1. Practice filling out job application forms before you begin a job search. Your school librarian, counselor, or the owner of a local business may be able to provide you with a blank form. Fill out the application with the same care and thoroughness you would use if you were submitting it to an employer.

2. When you are finished filling out the form, use the following criteria to evaluate your work:
   - Is my typing or printing neat and easy to read?
   - Are all of the words spelled correctly?
   - Is all of the information accurate?
   - Does the finished application make me look like a good job candidate?

Section 2

Preemployment Tests

Just as your counselors and teachers have given you tests to determine how well you can perform in a particular school subject, employers may test you to determine how well you can perform in a specific area of work. Some employers use a **preemployment test** to help them screen for the most skilled potential employees. The use of preemployment tests is

▲ *Some people argue that preemployment tests are the only fair way to determine a job applicant's qualifications and others consider them to be discriminatory. What is your opinion?*

growing rapidly. In 1990, employers used ten times more preemployment tests than in 1985. Why do you suppose this is?

Many employers consider testing to be the most objective and unbiased method for screening potential workers. Personal feelings do not influence the selection of employees when this approach is used. For most employers, preemployment testing is only one of the methods used to select new employees. Most employers know that attitude, experience, education, training, and appearance are all important to job success.

The use of preemployment tests is very controversial. Some people argue that it is the only **valid** (true and supported by facts) means an employer can use to assess the skill level, honesty, personality style, attitude, or communication ability of job applicants. Others argue that preemployment tests are discriminatory and eliminate job applicants without totally understanding them.

A **civil service examination** is a preemployment test developed by the federal government for specific government jobs. Do you know someone who works for the government? Most government workers qualified for their jobs by achieving a certain score on a civil service examination.

The Civil Service Commission administers civil service tests and announces job openings. These announcements are posted in government office buildings, at Civil Service Career Information and Testing Centers, and at local offices of the Bureau of Employment Services. Each civil service examination is specifically designed for a particular job classification.

Basic Types of Tests

An employer may give you a preemployment test before or during a job interview. The test may require you to answer questions, solve problems, perform certain tasks, or a combination of all three. Some tests are timed; others allow as much time as you need. Employers commonly use four types of preemployment tests:

1. **Aptitude tests** predict success in some occupation or course of training. For example, there are tests of musical aptitude, math aptitude, and engineering aptitude.
2. **Intelligence tests** measure the intellectual abilities used for all types of thinking. Examples include memory and communication skills.
3. **Proficiency tests** measure a person's ability to perform some particular task. Some examples are troubleshooting engine problems, operating a word processor, reading, and playing a musical instrument.
4. **Psychological tests** are used to measure your interests, attitudes, honesty, and personality traits.

Taking a Preemployment Test

The following tips will help you achieve your best possible score on a preemployment test:

1. Make certain that you are well rested and relaxed on the day of the test.

Solving The Problem

Selecting the Best Approach

The timer sounded, and Mrs. Greene told Helen to stop. Helen Clark was the sixth employment candidate to complete the word-processing skill test that day.

Helen asked Mrs. Greene if she would be permitted to repeat the test if her score was not satisfactory. Mrs. Greene explained that company policy would not permit job applicants to repeat the test.

Helen was certain that she hadn't performed at her best. She explained to Mrs. Greene the difficulty she experienced with timed tests in high school. Despite her anxiety with timed tests, Helen's teacher recommended her as a highly skilled, very thorough word-processing operator.

As Helen left the office, she thanked Mrs. Greene for giving her the test and considering her for a word-processing job.

Critical Thinking

1. Helen's test results were average. Two other applicants scored higher. However, Mrs. Greene felt that Helen would be a pleasant, sincere, and thorough worker. If you were Mrs. Greene, would you schedule Helen for an interview with the manager? Explain your reasons.

2. Could Mrs. Greene's decision affect her own future career? If so, how? If not, why not?

2. Arrive at the test site a few minutes early.

3. Before the test, ask the test administrator what is expected of you. Some tests do not allow the examiner to answer questions after testing has begun.

4. Find out if you will be penalized for giving a wrong answer. If so, skip questions that you aren't sure you can answer correctly.

5. If the test has a time limit, skip difficult questions that might slow you down. If time allows, go back to the difficult questions after you finish.

When the test is over, ask the test administrator when you will be notified of the results. If you do well on the preemployment test, you will probably be invited to an interview.

Section 2 GET INVOLVED

Answer the following on a separate sheet of paper and be prepared to discuss your answers in class.

1. Should job applicants be permitted to retake employment tests? Explain your answer.

2. Which type of employment test is most important for job success? Explain your answer.

Section 3

Making a Good Impression

It is important to be well informed about the company and the job before the interview. The more you know the better. Your overall appearance as well as your verbal and non-verbal behaviors send a message of the importance you place on getting the job. Put your best foot forward. Let the employer know this opportunity is important. In fact, a positive first impression influences the rest of the interview. The first impression an employer has of you may be the difference between being hired or not being hired.

Become Informed about the Company

Before you attend a job interview, learn all you can about the potential employer's business operations. Being well informed about the employer's purpose and operations will help you make a good impression. It demonstrates to the interviewer your interest in the company and the importance you place on the job. It also shows your personal **initiative** (readiness and ability to take the first steps in any undertaking) and your responsibility for getting things done. Advance preparation for a job interview could result in a long and satisfying career. Figure 8.2 lists several common sources of information about potential employers.

If information about a specific employer is not easily available, investigate the operations of similar companies or the industry as a whole. For example, you may not be able to find out how a particular insurance agency operates, but information on the types of insurance and services that insurance companies provide is readily available in your public library.

Figure 8.2 SOURCES OF INFORMATION ABOUT COMPANIES AND OTHER ORGANIZATIONS

Source of Information	Means of Contact
Employees who currently work for the organization	Networking
Annual reports of finances, products, and services	Public library and stockbrokers
Brochures published by the organization	The organization's public relations office
Advertisements for their products or services	Newspapers and magazines
The Better Business Bureau	Telephone
Friends or relatives	Networking
The organization itself	Your contact at the organization
Business periodicals and reference books	Public library
The local chamber of commerce	Telephone

▲ *Edmond has a job interview at the Crest Manufacturing Company tomorrow morning. In order to be well informed and make a good impression, he is reading about Crest's business operations and the occupation of assembler.*

Look and Behave Your Best

Many factors contribute to your overall image, and you have control over most of them. When you enter an office to apply for a job or to be interviewed, what type of personal image do you project? Are you

- Self-confident or insecure?
- Concerned or indifferent?
- Cooperative or arrogant?

First impressions are not easily changed. Before you begin to speak, your appearance and actions will influence the opinion being formed by the office worker or interviewer.

CAREER TIP

You never get a second chance to make a good first impression.

For example, good posture indicates self-confidence. Walking with a springy step indicates an upbeat and energetic person. On the other hand, slumping when you walk, letting your head hang down, and crossing your hands sends a message of low self-esteem and insecurity. A tightly closed mouth and stiff jaw indicates anger or frustration, but having a twinkle in your eye and a smile on your face indicates a pleasant, cooperative nature. Your walking and standing posture changes as situations change. At different times, you have probably projected all of these messages.

Employers want to hire interested, enthusiastic workers. They are also concerned about the image their employees present to customers, clients, and the public. During your job interview, the employer will try to determine how well you match the organization's image. For example, if you are hired, will you fit in and be accepted by your co-workers? Will your appearance help or harm the organization?

Take Responsibility for Your Appearance

T-shirts, sweats, jeans, and running shoes may be appropriate dress for school, but not for a job interview. If you don't have appropriate clothes for an interview, consider buying an outfit with money you earned from a part-time job or gift money you receive for graduation.

Your personal appearance is your responsibility. The following guidelines are especially important for a job interview, but you should also follow them after you are hired.

1. Be freshly showered or bathed, and use a modest amount of deodorant.
2. Have clean teeth, and use a modest amount of mouthwash.
3. Make sure your fingernails are clean and neatly trimmed. "Fashion nails" are an indication that you don't intend to work with your hands.
4. Your hair should be clean, neat, and trimmed.

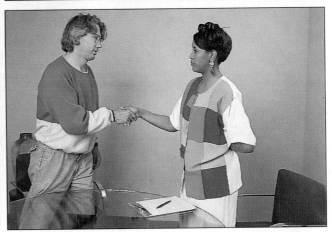

▲ *Compare the appearance of the job applicants in the four job interview scenes to the interviewing guidelines and tips described in this section. Which examples of appearance are appropriate? Which examples are inappropriate?*

5. Your clothes should be clean, well pressed, and well fitting.
6. Your shoes should be cleaned and polished.

Tips for females: Hemlines that are just below the knee and blouses that are conservative or tailored are appropriate. Short skirts and shorts should be saved for other events. Hosiery that is neutral in color is always correct, as are medium-heel, closed-toe shoes. Select simple jewelry, and use a modest amount of cosmetics and cologne. Use conservative nail polish and eye shadow.

Tips for males: If you wear a suit or sport jacket, select one that is conservative in style and color. Make certain that your slacks are long enough to cover the top of well-polished, dark-colored shoes. Under no circumstances should you wear earrings or distracting neck chains.

When you attend a job interview, it's a good rule of thumb to be well groomed, to be neatly attired, and to project an image of success. Trying to make a good impression on the interviewer may seem phony to you, but to the interviewer, the appearance you project in the job interview is the same appearance you will project to co-workers, customers, clients, and the public. When you display a satisfactory personal appearance, many employers will regard it as a sign of your having a positive attitude and a willingness to follow rules. If you don't know what's appropriate, dress conservatively but a little better than you will be expected to dress for the job. Avoid wearing trendy fashions.

Section 3 — GET INVOLVED

Answer the following on a separate sheet of paper, and be prepared to discuss your response in class.

1. Select a major employer. Use the information sources listed in Figure 8.2 on page 159 to learn as much as possible about the organization's product or service, annual sales, and number of employees. Report the information to your class.

2. Interview a white-collar worker and a blue-collar worker. Ask each to list the necessary clothing and to describe the personal appearance expected for a person with his or her job. How do the clothing requirements and personal appearance expectations relate to the employee's job tasks? Be specific.

Section 4

Successful Job Interviews

The **job interview** is an opportunity to present yourself personally to the employer. Not everyone who applies for a job is granted an interview. Only 25 percent of all applicants are interviewed. All of the effort you put into your job search is in preparation for this important meeting. How effectively you present yourself will probably determine whether or not you are offered a job.

In large organizations, interviewers are well trained and work in the **personnel department**. This department is usually responsible for recruiting and hiring new employees, for administering employee benefit programs, and for employee relations. Most initial interviews are conducted by personnel assistants or personnel administrators. Additional interviews are usually conducted by department managers. In smaller organizations, the owner or manager usually conducts the interviews.

Whether you are interviewing for a job with a neighborhood pizza parlor or a worldwide corporation, the interviewer will evaluate your suitability for the job opening by considering

- Your job skills and whether or not you take pride in your work
- Your willingness to follow company rules
- Your ability to work with others
- Your sincerity, honesty, and attitude

When you arrive for your job interview, be businesslike and friendly with everyone you meet. After you leave, the interviewer will probably ask the receptionist or secretary for his or her impression of you. Introduce yourself in a friendly, relaxed manner, and offer a firm handshake. Remember that your nonverbal actions, such as posture and facial expressions, send messages to the interviewer about your attitude and self-confidence. Use your body language to make a good impression.

Once introductions are made, let the interviewer guide the conversation. He or she will explain the responsibilities of the job, company benefits,

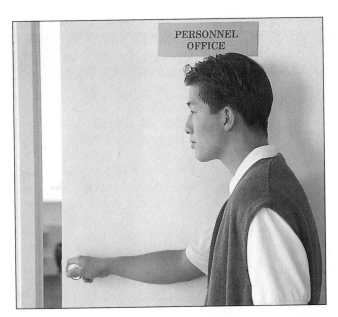

▲ *Stephen Chen is interviewing with a local car rental agency for the position of rental clerk. He is arriving ten minutes early for the interview.*

▲ *While Stephen is waiting to be called into the interviewer's office, he is double-checking the information and papers he will need for the interview.*

and vacation policies. Later, if a job is offered to you, the interviewer will negotiate an acceptable wage or salary with you. The interviewer is also the person who will notify you when a hiring decision has been made, will answer your questions about the job or benefits, and will address any other concerns you have regarding the opening.

You can expect the interviewer to be knowledgeable about the job opening and about the characteristics that the employer is seeking in a job applicant. Most interviewers will try to put you at ease and will treat you in a very professional and friendly manner.

During the interview, you will probably be asked several questions about your background and your interest in the job. While the interviewer is talking with you, he or she will be making judgments about your character, personality, and skills. The entire conversation will probably last between thirty minutes and an hour. This is not a long time to communicate your interests and abilities.

The interviewer will signal the end of the interview by standing up, shaking hands, and making a concluding statement. Thank the inter-

viewer for his or her time and consideration in meeting with you. Restate your interest in the job, and ask when you can expect to be contacted.

Preparing for an Interview

Gather all of the information and papers you will need for your interview and place them in a folder or briefcase. This will prevent you from dropping or losing them. Include your résumé, personal data sheet, recommendations from teachers and previous employers, school grades, Social Security number, birth certificate, and a work permit application. This will demonstrate to the interviewer that you are organized and prepared. Both of these qualities are important on the job. If you are permitted to complete a job application before the interview, make certain that it is neat and accurate before turning it over to the interviewer.

Call the interviewer's secretary the day before the interview to confirm the appointment. Don't trust your memory. Make a note of the date, time, address, name of the interviewer, and directions.

BUILDING SELF-ESTEEM

Confidence Wins

Mr. Waters called his secretary on the intercom and told him to send Roberta Castile in for the interview. He had more than twenty years of experience as a personnel administrator for the International News Publishing Company. Mr. Waters wondered how many job applicants he had interviewed over the years.

Roberta was applying for a position as a copy editor. A brief review of Roberta's résumé told him that she had a college education, three years' work experience as a high school English teacher, and two years' summer experience editing articles for a small newspaper.

Roberta walked into the room with a confident stride and a pleasant smile. After a firm handshake and a personal introduction, Mr. Waters asked Roberta why she wanted to work for his company. It was easy for Roberta to explain what she liked about the publishing business and to describe the skills she could bring to the job. Roberta had given a great

deal of thought to this career change, and she was confident that it was the right thing to do.

Roberta told Mr. Waters how she enjoyed working with people on writing projects. She especially liked to organize and coordinate materials, make them more understandable, and work with people in the art department to develop interesting graphs and pictures.

When Mr. Waters concluded the interview by standing up and extending his hand, Roberta responded with a firm handshake and thanked him for the interview.

Critical Thinking

1. On a separate sheet of paper, list the reasons you would or wouldn't hire Roberta for the job of copy editor.

2. Roberta displayed a high level of self-esteem during the interview. List the behaviors that demonstrated her confidence to the interviewer. Next, place a check mark beside each behavior on your list that you would display in an interview as well as Roberta did. Circle each behavior that you would not display as well as Roberta and that you would like to improve.

Carry this information with you on the day of the interview.

Interviewing Tactics

Read the following interviewing tactics carefully. They will increase your chances for a successful job interview.

1. Always be on time—preferably a little early. If you are not familiar with the organization's location, make a trial run a few days before the interview.

2. Know what skills are required to do the job.

3. Go to the interview alone. This demonstrates your independence and maturity.

4. Listen to each question carefully. If you don't understand a question, ask for clarification before you answer.

5. Take time to think about the question before responding.

6. When you answer questions, make positive, brief, but complete statements. Be prepared to expand on your answers when asked.

7. Show an enthusiastic interest in the job and a sincere desire to learn.

8. Relax. You don't have to be perfect. Being nervous is normal.

9. Keep your personal problems out of the conversation.

10. Be sincere, and give honest answers. Never argue with the interviewer.

11. Use proper English and avoid slang. Speak clearly.

12. Don't interrupt! If you want to ask a question or make a statement, wait for an appropriate opening in the conversation.

13. Look directly at the interviewer's eyes and listen carefully.

14. Always thank the interviewer for his or her time. Thank the secretary and the receptionist if you get a chance. Their opinions may count.

Interviewing Practice

During an interview, you have a limited amount of time to convince the interviewer why you should be hired. In most job interviews, your success will be determined by how well you communicate your answers to specific questions. The interview is the time for you to elaborate on the information in your résumé or job application form.

Don't attempt to memorize your part for an interview, but do anticipate certain questions and be prepared. Practice answering the frequently asked interview questions listed in Figure 8.3 on the next page. Practicing with your family or friends will help you build self-confidence and will reduce your level of anxiety. Being well prepared for an interview is very similar to being well prepared for a test at school. When you understand the material, you do well.

Your Rights in an Interview

Employment application forms and preemployment interviews have traditionally been used

▲ *Being well prepared for the job interview helped Stephen Chen to relax and convey his feeling of confidence to the interviewer. When you are well prepared for a school assignment, are you more relaxed and confident?*

by employers to eliminate unsuitable or unqualified job applicants from consideration at an early stage of the hiring process. Unfortunately, some employers have also used them to deny or restrict employment opportunities for women and minorities.

The Equal Employment Opportunity Law, a part of the Civil Rights Act of 1964, was designed to remedy this problem. The law prevents employers from asking questions and considering factors that would disproportionately screen out members of minority groups or members of one sex. Questions and factors that are not valid predictors of successful job performance or that cannot be justified by "business necessity" are forbidden.

In other words, certain questions are unlawful for an employer to ask unless they reflect bona fide job requirements. If these unlawful questions are asked, the interviewer is in violation of your equal employment opportunity (EEO) rights. You

- Why should I hire you?
- How many times were you tardy from school last year?
- What are your strengths?
- Why do you want to work for our company?
- Tell me something about yourself.
- What type of position are you most interested in?
- Why did you leave your last job?
- How do you feel about working overtime?
- Did you drop out of school? Why or why not?
- How much money do you expect to earn by the age of twenty-five?
- Do you prefer working with others or by yourself?
- Have you ever had difficulty getting along with fellow students, school faculty, or co-workers?
- Can you work under pressure?
- Are you underqualified for this job?
- Do you plan to get married soon?
- I see you have never done this type of work before.

- How many days of school did you miss last year?
- What are your weaknesses?
- Are you seeking temporary or permanent work?
- Tell me some of your life history.
- Why do you think you would like this particular type of work?
- How do you presently support yourself.
- What courses did you like best in school? What courses did you like least?
- What is the present source of your spending money?
- Can you take instructions without becoming upset?
- What has your relationship been with people who have a different background than yours?
- What are your long-term career goals?
- Are your overqualified for this job?
- What kind of salary do you expect?
- I've already interviewed ten people for this job, and four of them are well qualified. Why should I hire you?
- What makes you think you can do the job?

▲ *Figure 8.3 Questions Frequently Asked during a Job Interview.*

may choose to answer the question or to tell the interviewer that you see no relationship between the question and the job requirements. As an example, see Figure 8.3. Do you think an employer should be able to ask the question, "Do you plan to get married soon?"

Questions that are not needed to judge an applicant's competence or qualification for the job are a violation of the EEO laws. In general, these laws make it illegal to discriminate against job applicants because of their race, religion, sex, national origin, disability, age, or ancestry. However, an employer may be required or permitted to request such information because of involvement in a legitimate affirmative-action program or because the company is under order from a state, federal, or local fair employment practices agency.

Involvement in an affirmative-action program or a **fair employment program** may require employers to hire minorities, women, or the physical-

ly challenged. In such cases, the employer has the right to request information to help identify employment candidates from the desired group.

Interview Follow-up

After the interview, write the interviewer a brief letter expressing your appreciation. Use the format illustrated in Figure 8.4 on the next page. If you are still interested in the job, emphasize your interest and restate your background qualifications that match the job requirements. In closing, let the interviewer know that you look forward to hearing the decision soon.

If you haven't been contacted within two weeks, call the interviewer and politely inquire as to when the company plans to make a hiring decision and when you will be notified. This is also a good time to restate your qualifications and interest in the job.

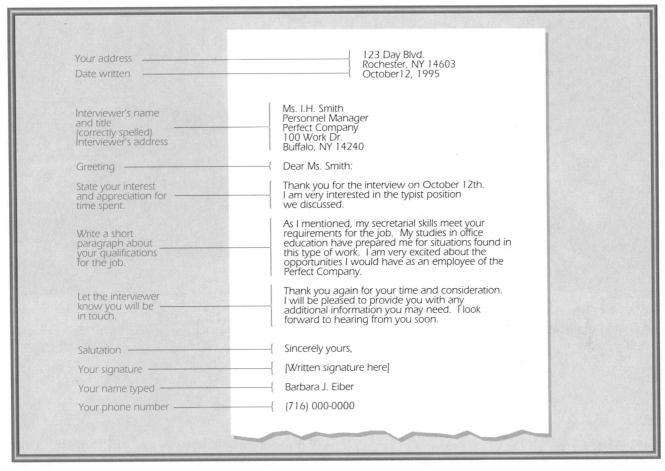

Your address	123 Day Blvd. Rochester, NY 14603
Date written	October12, 1995
Interviewer's name and title (correctly spelled) Interviewer's address	Ms. I.H. Smith Personnel Manager Perfect Company 100 Work Dr. Buffalo, NY 14240
Greeting	Dear Ms. Smith:
State your interest and appreciation for time spent.	Thank you for the interview on October 12th. I am very interested in the typist position we discussed.
Write a short paragraph about your qualifications for the job.	As I mentioned, my secretarial skills meet your requirements for the job. My studies in office education have prepared me for situations found in this type of work. I am very excited about the opportunities I would have as an employee of the Perfect Company.
Let the interviewer know you will be in touch.	Thank you again for your time and consideration. I will be pleased to provide you with any additional information you may need. I look forward to hearing from you soon.
Salutation	Sincerely yours,
Your signature	[Written signature here]
Your name typed	Barbara J. Eiber
Your phone number	(716) 000-0000

▲ *Figure 8.4 Thank You Letter for an Interview.*

If you are not interested in the job, it is still good business manners to write a letter expressing your appreciation for time spent and to inform the interviewer that you no longer wish to be considered as a candidate. In addition, you may wish to express your interest in being considered for other positions that are more related to your background and career interests.

Interview Evaluation

Keep a written record of all of your job interviews. Include the date, time, place, interviewer's name, and a copy of your thank you letter. Learn as much as possible from each job interview. Begin by:

- Evaluating the interviewer's reaction to what you said
- Considering any additional information you might have stated
- Reviewing any statements you wish you hadn't made

CAREER TIP

Remember the old saying, "Don't count your chickens until they hatch"? Keep your job search active until you accept a job offer and you are actually hired.

▲ *Stephen Chen keeps a record of each job interview on his family's home computer. What method could you use to record information about job interviews?*

▲ *After being turned down on nine previous job interviews, Stephen received a job offer for the position of rental clerk. How would you feel if you had been turned down for nine jobs in one month?*

Also consider these points:

- What did you emphasize that seemed to interest the interviewer?
- How well did you present your qualifications?
- Did you talk too much or too little?
- Did you learn everything about the job that you wanted to know?
- Did you project a positive attitude?
- Was your appearance appropriate for the position?
- What improvement can you make for the next interview?

The Job Offer

You will probably have several job interviews before you are hired. It isn't unusual to be turned down up to sixteen times before receiving a suitable job offer. Learning to accept rejection is one of the important lessons you can learn from the job-seeking process.

After reviewing your interview, what grade will you give yourself? Excellent, good, or needs improvement? What grade will you give the person who interviewed you?

After each job interview, be optimistic and plan on receiving a **job offer** (a specific offer of employment). Most job offers are made within two weeks after the interview. They are usually extended over the telephone by the person who interviewed you. If you accept the offer, a congratulatory letter, welcoming you to the organization, will usually follow. This letter should include details of the salary or wage agreement, job benefits, and a request for any information the employer will need before you can begin the job.

Occasionally, a job offer is made during the interview and the applicant is asked to make an immediate decision. It is a good idea to plan ahead for this possibility. If you are certain that you want the job, you will be prepared to accept the offer. However, you will probably want time to think about information you have learned during the interview.

If you don't wish to make an immediate decision, ask the interviewer if you might think about it overnight and phone the next day with your decision. If the interviewer still insists on an immediate decision, take a few minutes to determine your answers to the following questions about three major areas of the job being considered:

1. **Job Tasks**

   a. Are you prepared to handle the responsibilities of the job?

   b. Will the employer provide training to help you learn the specific job?

   c. Are the employer's work rules too strict or too lax?

2. **Work Setting**

   a. Did you have a chance to tour the company to observe and meet other workers? If not, could the interviewer or another person take you on a tour before you make your decision?

   b. Do the people who will be your co-workers seem to get along with one another? Do you think you will fit in with them? How do the managers seem to get along with the workers?

   c. Will you have any transportation problems getting to this job? Does the work setting seem safe to you?

3. **Financial Needs**

   a. Did the interviewer specify the wage or salary range of the job? If so, is it similar to the pay range you observed in newspaper ads for similar jobs? What future pay increases can you expect?

   b. What employee benefits are included with this job? Are the costs of employee benefits paid by the employer or shared with the employee? If shared, what is your cost?

Think carefully about the advantages and disadvantages of working for a certain employer before you accept or reject a job offer. Decide whether or not you will earn enough to maintain your present lifestyle and whether or not your pay will increase as you increase your job skills. Will the job being offered provide an opportunity for you to learn valuable job skills? This could compensate for lower wages. Whatever your criteria for accepting or rejecting a job offer, be realistic about your ability to perform the job and your worth to the employer.

Section 4 GET INVOLVED

Answer the following on a separate sheet of paper, and be prepared to discuss your responses in class.

1. Select ten interview questions from Figure 8.3 on page 166, and write them on sheet of paper. For each question you select,

   - Write the answer you would give in an actual interview
   - Write the reason you believe an interviewer would ask the question

2. Imagine that you have interviewed with Marsella Kent, Personnel Manager of the Ultimate Corporation, for a specific job. Use a job title you are considering for your future career. Using the format shown in Figure 8.4 on page 167, type a thank you letter to Ms. Kent.

Section
5

Part-Time Jobs

Your first job will probably be a part-time, temporary, or summer job. It will provide you with an opportunity to learn about the challenges and rewards of work, to explore possible careers, and to earn money. You may be required to work a few hours each day, several days each week, or an occasional full shift. In any case, working a part-time job will provide you with money for clothing, graduation expenses, or savings toward your education and training after high school.

Employers usually hire part-time and temporary workers during vacation periods, when someone is sick, or when additional help is needed for a specific project. Most part-time jobs are for clerical and secretarial positions. However, employers are increasing their use of part-time workers for general labor, accounting, technical, and management work.

Many part-time workers are hired through a **temporary service**. These services "rent" temporary employees (temps) to companies for short and limited amounts of time. The temporary service is the temp's employer. The organization where the temp is assigned pays the temporary service, which in turn pays the temp. Many permanent employees start out as temps.

If you accept a part-time or temporary job while you're still in school, it will be important to reorganize your time to meet the demands of school and the job. You will need to decide whether or not working a part-time job will lower your grades or will prevent you from graduating.

Where are the part-time, temporary, and summer jobs in your area? Using the information in Figure 8.5 as a guideline, make a list of specific local employers.

The Employers	The Jobs
Local government agencies	Summer youth employment
New stores or businesses	Clerking, cleaning, stocking
Temporary-help firms	Clerical work
Restaurants	Waiter, busser, kitchen work
Fast-food restaurants	Counter and kitchen work
Day-care centers	Teacher's helper
Summer camps and resorts	Kitchen work, lifeguard, counselor
Food stores	Stock clerk, cashier, bagger
Automobile service station	Attendant, cashier
Movie theaters	Cashier, usher, concession clerk
Retail stores	Sales or stock clerk, janitor
Farms	Fruit or vegetable picker
Construction companies	Helper, cleanup person
Manufacturing companies	Helper, shipping or receiving clerk, janitor
Amusement parks	Cashier, guide, performer, helper

▲ *Figure 8.5 Where the Jobs Are.*

Each year, the number of young people in the labor force expands sharply from April to July. This is due to the large number of students and recent graduates who enter the labor force in search of temporary or permanent jobs.

The vast majority of young workers are employed in private-sector nonagricultural jobs. Nearly 60 percent of them work in the retail trade and service industries. The prosperity of these industries is of critical importance for the summer job prospects of young workers.

The Minimum Wage Law

Do all jobs for teenagers pay minimum wage? No, some pay less. Basic wage standards are set by the federal government's Fair Labor Standards Act (FLSA). In March of 1995, the **minimum wage** (the lowest wage an employer may pay for certain types of work) was $4.25 per hour. The employees who are covered by FLSA include

▲ *Laurie will be on her school vacation for the next twelve weeks. She is applying for the position of lifeguard at a local hotel. Can you think of other seasonal jobs for students?*

▲ *Kenneth is working for a national chain of pizza parlors. They are required to pay him no less than the minimum wage. Labor shortages are forcing many employers to pay more than minimum wage.*

- Employees engaged in interstate commerce or in the production of goods for interstate commerce, regardless of the employer's annual volume of business
- Employees who work for enterprises that have an annual gross volume of sales or business of more than $500,000
- Employees of hospitals, residential facilities that care for those who are physically or mentally ill, disabled, or aged, schools for children who are mentally or physically disabled or gifted, preschools, elementary and secondary schools, and institutions of higher education, regardless of the annual volume of business
- Employees of public agencies

Certain full-time students, student learners, apprentices, and workers with disabilities may be paid less than the minimum wage under special certificates issued by the Department of Labor. Employers of certain amusement and recreational places of business, certain retail or service businesses, and baby-sitters are also exempt from minimum-wage laws.

The FLSA contains a training wage provision. A training wage of $3.60 per hour or 85 percent of the applicable minimum wage, whichever is greater, may be paid to most employees under twenty years of age for up to ninety days under certain conditions. Individuals may be employed at this training wage for a second ninety-day period by a different employer if certain additional requirements are met. No individual may be employed at the training wage, in any number of jobs, for more than a total of 180 days. Employers may not displace regular employees to hire those eligible for the training wage.

Volunteer Work

Not all work is paid work. You can learn a lot about the responsibilities and rewards of paid work by volunteering in an organization. **Volunteer work** (a contribution of free labor, usually to a nonprofit organization) gives you a chance to observe various workers and to learn new skills. It can also help you clarify your career interests and build your self-confidence. Volunteer work can be included in a résumé and treated as work experience on a job application form. Volunteer work occasionally leads to paid employment.

Hospitals	Symphony orchestra groups
Museums	Zoos
YMCA or YWCA	American Cancer Society
Regional food banks	
Amateur theatre groups	Churches
Government housing authorities	American Red Cross
Special Olympics	Nursing home
Libraries	Public parks
United Way	Salvation Army
Urban league	Animal shelters
School	Women's networks
	Mobile meals programs (Meals on Wheels)

▲ *Figure 8.6 Where the Volunteer Jobs Are.*

Before you decide to work as a volunteer, study the requirements of the volunteer job. How do they match the personal characteristics you identified in Chapters 2 and 3? Before you make a commitment, interview with several organizations that depend on volunteers.

Where are the volunteer jobs in your area? Using the information in Figure 8.6 as a starting point, list a few local agencies that use volunteer help. Ask your school counselor if your community has a volunteer center.

Section 5 GET INVOLVED

Answer the following on a separate sheet of paper, and be prepared to discuss your responses in class.

1. Each year, thousands of students and adults accept part-time employment. Describe the advantages and disadvantages of part-time employment for each of the following:

   - A woman who is a homemaker, has a husband who works full-time, and has a son who will be in college next year
   - A high school senior who plans to join the armed forces after graduation
   - The owner of a restaurant where most of the business occurs during a two-hour lunch period and a four-hour dinner period

Section

6

Full-Time Jobs

Imagine being hired for your first **full-time job**. This will probably be your first opportunity to assume the responsibilities of an independent adult. Perhaps you will rent an apartment or buy a car. On the other hand, you may decide to stay at home and help with family finances. Whatever the situation, a full-time job requires a major commitment of your time and labor.

When you begin a new job, you'll know the amount of your wages and fringe benefits and what the job site is like. You'll probably know less about advancement opportunities, the personality of your supervisor and co-workers, and the satisfaction you'll receive from performing the job.

Some workers accept a job they dislike because they don't have the education or training for a job they would like. Others need to earn a living and can't wait for the ideal job to come along. If you're fortunate enough to receive more than one job

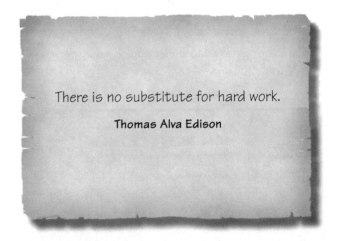

> There is no substitute for hard work.
>
> Thomas Alva Edison

offer, the likelihood of meeting your interests, using your skills, and obtaining your career goals will be increased. In any case, once you accept your first full-time job, work at it as though it were your lifetime career choice.

Some experts believe that most people of your generation will make six or more major job changes during their working lives. If this is true, success or failure on your first job could determine your future jobs, including

- Your career progress
- What work tasks you will be performing
- The skill level of your co-workers
- The type of employer you will have
- How much will you earn

Your decision to stay with one employer will be determined by the opportunities you create. What you presently consider to be job satisfaction and success will change as you increase your job skills. You may decide to acquire additional education or training to enter a higher level of your present occupation or to help you enter a different occupation. As you have been learning, today's economy

▲ *Remember Stephen Chen? He plans to be the office supervisor within two years. Do you have a plan?*

and technology are changing rapidly. As changes in your skills, technology, and the economy occur, you will need to reexamine your job skills in terms of the current job market.

Unlike in your grandparents' time, few of today's workers remain on one job, working for the same employer, for most of their careers. In fact, most first-time job seekers change jobs within two years. Reasons for changing jobs include

- More money available elsewhere

- An unfair boss

- An unsatisfying job
- Being transferred to another city or state

Automation has changed the jobs of many workers, resulting in the growth of service occupations and a rapid decline in the number of manufacturing jobs. Many jobs have completely disappeared. Throughout your working years, improved technology and the efficiency it brings will continually change the job market.

Section 6 GET INVOLVED

Answer the following on a separate sheet of paper, and be prepared to discuss your responses in class.

1. Review the following list of entry level jobs. Divide a sheet of paper into three columns titled *Entry-level Job*, *Higher Paying Job*, and *Education or Training*. For each entry-level job list a higher paying job that could be obtained as a result of more experience and a good work record. Next, list the education and training that would be required to acquire the higher paying job. (This information can be found in the Occupational Outlook Handbook in your school library). For example a Lubrication worker could move up to a higher paying job such as automotive mechanic after attending a technical school. Now fill out your sheet for *Fast-food worker, Typist, Hotel desk clerk,* and *Hospital attendant.*

2. Review "Defining Goals" in Chapter 3.

   a. List the goals that were most important to you.
   b. Which of these goals do you expect to satisfy on your first full-time job?
   c. What career steps will you take to reach your highest goals?

IMPORTANT FACTS

Using the "W" Questions

During a job interview, always listen for the "W" questions. One technique interviewers use in getting the information they seek is to ask the following questions:

- **Who** influenced you to look for this type of work?
- **What** were the highlights of your high school years?
- **When** will you expect a promotion?
- **Where** did you learn the skills that are required to do this job?
- **Why** are you interested in working for us?

Nine out of Ten Companies Use Temporary Help

Where are temporaries used? The following are the most common positions:

Clerical,	79.9 percent
Secretarial,	65.0 percent
Warehousing and shipping,	29.9 percent
Accounting,	22.4 percent
Technical,	12.9 percent
General labor and maintenance,	5.8 percent
Production,	3.1 percent
Other,	1.7 percent

Employers give these reasons for hiring temporary help:

Vacation relief,	56.4 percent
Overload relief,	51.8 percent
Special projects,	50.0 percent
Sickness,	32.5 percent
Seasonal need,	28.6 percent
Interim periods,	28.2 percent
Expansion,	6.4 percent
Leave of absence,	1.8 percent

Videotaped Interviews

Many companies have discovered that they can use videotaping to conduct cost-effective preliminary interviews. These companies may use professional media services or in-house resources to conduct structured interviews with job candidates. The employer is able to see and hear many job candidates before inviting a few back for costly and time-consuming selection interviews.

A Summer Job: What's in It for You?

The POINT Is Fun

- Live Away from Home
- Ride Roller Coaster For FREE
- Make Friends
- Play on the Beach
- Become an Expert People-Watcher

The POINT Is Jobs

- Gain Valuable Job Experience
- Enjoy Unique Resort Atmosphere
- Make Money
- Explore College Credit Opportunities
- Live in Convenient, Low-Cost Housing

CEDAR POINT
AMUSEMENT PARK ▼ SANDUSKY, OHIO

The Most Common Reasons for Worker Absence

Accident off the job	Military obligation
Transportation problem	Medical appointment
Leave of absence	Personal problem
Discipline	Lateness
Excused absence	Honor being bestowed
Family illness	Temporary suspension
Holiday	Death in the family
Jury duty	Weather
Birthday	Vacation
Unexcused absence	Layoff

CHAPTER 8 REVIEW

ENRICH YOUR VOCABULARY

On a separate sheet of paper, number from 1 to 20, and complete the following activity. (Do not write in your textbook.) Match each statement below with the most appropriate term from the "Enrich Your Vocabulary" list at the beginning of the chapter by writing that term next to the correct statement.

1. A statement containing information that employers require before hiring new employees
2. A law that protects all workers, including minors
3. A document stating that you don't have an infectious disease or that you're free of certain drugs
4. A document stating that a person is eligible to work in the United States
5. A type of insurance that pays financial losses if an employee fails to perform his or her duty or is guilty of theft
6. A serious crime
7. A preemployment test for government jobs
8. True and supported by facts
9. Readiness and ability to take the first steps in any undertaking
10. The department that is responsible for recruiting and hiring new employees
11. A program in which employers actively seek to hire minorities
12. An employer's formal proposal of employment
13. A job that provides you with an opportunity to assume adult responsibilities
14. A contribution of free labor
15. An agency that "rents" employees to employers
16. A document that is necessary for employees under eighteen in most nonfarm jobs
17. An investigation of a job applicant's former employers, schools, and references
18. A test to determine how well an applicant is likely to perform in a certain area of work
19. An opportunity to personally present yourself to an employer
20. The lowest wage an employer may pay for certain types of work

CHECK YOUR KNOWLEDGE

On a separate sheet of paper, complete the following activity. (Do not write in your textbook.)

1. List four kinds of information requested on most job applications.
2. When do job applications become legal documents?
3. How can you prove your date of birth to an employer?
4. At what age do you no longer need a work permit?
5. List five occupations permitted for fourteen- and fifteen-year-olds.
6. List three types for preemployment tests.
7. Name five resources that you can use to find information about a company or an organization.
8. How much time does a job interview usually take?
9. What determines the success of most job interviews?
10. What act of Congress contains the Equal Employment Opportunity Law?
11. Why do some companies like to use temporary help?
12. Approximately how many job changes will most people of your generation make during their working lives?
13. What sector of the job market has had the greatest decline as a result of automation?

DEVELOP SCANS COMPETENCIES

Government experts say that successful workers can productively use Resources, Interpersonal skills, Information, Systems, and Technology. This activity will give you practice in developing Technology.

Choose 4-5 careers in which you have an interest. These could be part-time jobs you will look for in the near future, or they could be jobs that will require more education on your part.

Make a list of the technology you will need to be familiar with to be successful in each of these jobs. The technology might include using different types of equipment such as soft drink dispensers, cash registers, movie equipment, adding machines, calculators, typewriters, or computers.

List technology with which you are already familiar. How can this knowledge help in your search for a job?

Chapter 9

Job Success Is Your Responsibility

Learning Objectives

After completing this chapter, you should be prepared to:

- explain the relationship between your attitude, future job satisfaction, and career success
- describe the procedures for beginning a new job and list several of the employer's expectations
- describe a suitable appearance for a job and explain the importance of being present and punctual
- explain the purpose of a company's policies and procedures

Enrich Your Vocabulary

In reading this chapter and doing the exercises you will learn the following important terms:

positive attitude
negative attitude
competence
interdependence
etiquette
stress
job orientation
full potential
probationary period
manuals

success
orientation period
morale
personal appearance
image consultants
legitimate absence
scheduled breaks
policies and
    procedures

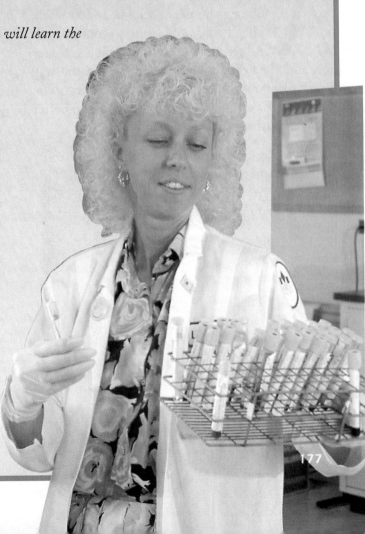

Congratulations, you're hired! From a list of several applicants, the employer has selected you for the job. This selection demonstrates your ability to be successful. Your new job will provide you with opportunities for continuing success.

If you're like most new employees, you don't know anyone at your new job, and you're feeling a little bit nervous about starting. Perhaps you're concerned about having the skills to do the job. Maybe you have doubts about your ability to fulfill the supervisor's assignments. Maybe you wish you didn't have to begin at all. If any of these statements are true, don't panic. Your feelings are normal.

Did you ever enter a new school? Think back to your first few days at the new school or even the first few days of this school year. In many ways, the first few days of a new job are very similar. When you began school, you had a pretty good idea of what it was going to be like. You had new students and teachers to meet and new school rules to obey. You were probably excited, yet uneasy, about the new experience. After a few weeks, you probably adjusted to your new situation and felt comfortable. Like school, it may take several weeks to become adjusted and comfortable with a new job.

^{Section}

1

Attitude Makes a Difference

Attitudes affect the way people get along at home, at school, and at work. The attitude you bring to your job will influence your feelings of job satisfaction and your career success. Attitude is the way you think about things and act toward others. The effort you make to do a good job will be no better than your attitude allows.

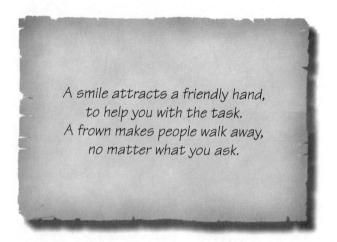

A smile attracts a friendly hand,
to help you with the task.
A frown makes people walk away,
no matter what you ask.

In fact, many employers believe that the most important factor in job success is a positive attitude. They know that the quality and quantity of an employee's work performance is related to his or her attitude. Employee attitudes are linked to the bottom-line profit. Companies with a dedicated work force enjoy better business performance. In these companies, there is a good feeling among employees.

If you view a new job as an opportunity, a chance to learn new things, and act interested and enthusiastic about the experience, you are expressing a **positive attitude**. You also demonstrate a positive attitude when you are courteous, cooperative, and considerate with your co-workers and superiors. People with a positive attitude

• view the world as a friendly place
• are accepting of others
• take responsibility for their decisions
• are honest in expressing their thoughts and feelings

▲ *Maria views her job as an opportunity. She is interested and enthusiastic about her work. Elena views her job as a responsibility that must be fulfilled. She frequently complains, is critical, and has careless work habits. Are your attitudes toward schoolwork, home responsibilities, and paid employment more like Maria's or Elena's?*

- have the ability to control their feelings
- are open to suggestions for improvement and accept constructive criticism without getting angry

As you begin your new job, guard against a **negative attitude**, one in which you look on the job as drudgery or as a responsibility that must be fulfilled. People with a negative attitude

- frequently complain and use sarcasm

GETTING MORE INFORMATION

Ask employers about the importance they place on positive attitudes and good communication skills. Use your phone book to contact and schedule an interview with a recruiter at an employment agency, a job consultant at the state employment service, or the owner of a small business.

- are critical and blame others for their problems
- have careless work habits
- are indifferent to the needs of other people

How Attitudes Are Formed

Many attitudes are learned in early childhood. People who are important to a child, such as parents, siblings, relatives, and friends, teach attitudes by what they say and do. The child accepts the feelings, values, and preferences of these important people as the correct and proper way to act and feel.

The mass media, such as newspapers, radio, and television, influence attitudes and opinions. People tend to read newspapers and listen to speeches that agree with their own attitudes and opinions. They usually avoid exposing themselves to information and opinions that disagree with their own point of view. When exposed to information and opinions that disagree with their own, they like to talk about the matter with others who agree with them. As an example, many adults believe that certain types of music should be banned from television and radio. Do you agree? Do you disagree? If you were expressing your own attitude

▲ *Learning to appreciate work begins at home. Are you a responsible member of your family?*

and opinion toward this issue, would you talk it over with a friend who agrees with your view or with a friend who disagrees and offers opposing information?

Attitudes toward work and personal responsibility start at home. Suppose that a child is expected to help with household work, such as washing dishes, taking out the trash, mowing the yard, or cleaning the basement. The child is learning to be a responsible member of the family. She will notice an increased acceptance and appreciation from other family members. Being appreciated

and accepted causes the child to value productive work. A feeling of **competence** (being capable) grows within her. In later years, she will use the work values learned as a child to acquire acceptance and appreciation from employers and co-workers as well as from family and friends.

Suppose that another child is raised in a home where he is discouraged from taking responsibility as a member of the family. He might be told to stay out of the way when household work is being done. This child learns to depend on others instead of being independent, grows into an adult who lacks self-confidence in his ability to work, and places little value on being a productive worker.

After you learn to be independent, your next step is to become a member of society at the highest level, **interdependence**. Interdependence occurs when you depend on a group, and the group depends on you. It is the highest level of human relations at the personal level or in the world of work.

Interdependent people are not independent in the sense of doing everything "their way," nor are they totally dependent in the sense of being helpless. Instead, they are contributing members of a family of relatives and friends at the personal level and are part of a team of workers in the world of work and in society. Think of situations in which you acted in a dependent way, an independent way, and an interdependent way.

Section 1 GET INVOLVED

Answer the following on a separate sheet of paper, and be prepared to discuss your responses in class.

1. Name three family members or close friends that you feel express a positive attitude toward work or school.

2. Select one word from the following list that best describes each of the three people you selected. Tell how each person expresses this positive characteristic in his or her attitude toward school or work.

- Confidence
- Cheerfulness
- Responsibility
- Acceptance of others
- Courtesy
- Open-mindedness
- Patience
- Flexibility
- Helpfulness

3. Briefly describe a situation in which you displayed one or more positive characteristics in your attitude. Which characteristics did you display?

Beginning a New Job

Beginning a new job is both exciting and scary. It's one thing to read about and prepare for a career, but it's quite another to actually do the job. On a new job, you must learn the particular duties and responsibilities you were hired to perform, and your performance must meet your employer's expectations. You must also learn the protocol of the organization. *Protocol* is another word for the rules of diplomatic **etiquette** (manners). You have already learned how to be diplomatic at school; now you must learn the protocol of the working world.

As a beginning employee, you will be expected to learn a lot during your first days and weeks on the job. Your new job will probably place unusual demands on your emotions. Some of this emotional pressure might be self-imposed, but a certain amount is unavoidable.

Building new relationships, adjusting to the unexpected, and making an extra effort to create a favorable impression can certainly contribute to emotional **stress** (tension). As you learn new information, new procedures, and the names of your co-workers, the stress will diminish. Remember that as a new employee, you are not expected to know everything.

You will probably be told to report to the personnel office on your first day. This could be a large department in a big corporation or simply the boss's desk in a small business. A personnel worker or the boss will help you complete the necessary paperwork, including payroll and hospitalization forms. Bring your personal data sheet (see Chapter 7) with you, and the task of filling in personal information will be easier.

Once you have completed the necessary paperwork, the remainder of your first day will probably be spent on **job orientation**. Job-orientation programs are meetings and activities to acquaint you with the employer's purpose and organization. Depending on the organization's size, your job orientation may take an hour or several days. During this time, you will learn about your employer's

▲ *Calvin will begin his new job tomorrow. Do you think he will get along with Mr. Garcia? Why?*

CAREER TIP

During the first few days of a new job, many introductions are made. It is important to learn the names of your supervisors and co-workers and to pronounce them correctly.

organization of management, the services provided or products manufactured, and the company's rules and regulations.

You can expect to be formally introduced to your boss and co-workers. One of these people will probably work closely with you until you can perform your assigned tasks on your own.

If you apply extra concentration on your work performance during the first few days and weeks of a new job, you will win the respect of your supervisor. It is also very important to use this time to build good relationships with co-workers. Getting along well with others will help you enjoy your work, and your supervisor will appreciate your cooperative attitude.

▲ *Does this employer provide a safe work environment?*

What You Can Expect as a New Employee

Most employers realize that helping a new employee make full use of his or her skills improves the productivity and quality of the entire organization. For this reason alone, most employers want you to reach your **full potential** (highest level of productivity).

As a new employee, this is what you can expect:

- You will be paid for your time. When you accepted the job, you and your employer agreed on the hours to be worked and the wages or salary to be earned.
- The employer will provide a safe work environment. Employers are required by law to maintain certain safety standards established by the government.
- The employer will provide you with equipment and supplies to perform your job. Certain mechanics and other skilled workers may be required to provide the tools designated in their employment agreement.
- You will have a probationary period of one to three months. A **probationary period** is a specific period of time in which you are expected to prove your ability to perform the job. During this time, you will probably receive training and assistance from supervisors and co-workers.

▲ *What steps are you taking today to reach your full potential in your future career?*

Failure to perform the job to the employer's satisfaction will be cause for terminating your employment at the end of the probationary period.

• You will receive some job training, on-the-job coaching, or other help that the employer normally provides for that specific job. This may include special courses away from the actual work site, special orientation meetings, self-study, correspondence school courses, college credit courses, and programs to earn special certificates or licenses. Training **manuals** are frequently provided during training sessions. These handbooks detail the use or repair of equipment or describe procedures to follow on the job. You may be placed in a training program that moves you from one job to another until a final job assignment is made.

• You will make mistakes. Should you damage equipment or offend a customer, report the mistake as soon as possible. Covering up a mistake can result in serious consequences later. Asking questions ahead of time will help you avoid making mistakes or violating job rules. If possible, look for the answer you are seeking in manuals or brochures that have already been provided. Once you ask for help, listen carefully.

• You will be evaluated. Formal evaluations do not usually occur during the early weeks of a new job. However, informal evaluations will be made by your immediate supervisor.

• Discipline methods will vary. Some companies maintain high levels of discipline that may be unfamiliar to new employees. For example, manufacturing firms, where safety is a key concern, maintain discipline standards that are more restrictive than those of service firms, such as retail stores.

• You will probably dislike some of your assignments. Take the bad with the good. It's all part of the job. You're not being realistic if you think you will enjoy all of your work assignments.

• You will have assigned responsibilities. A specific job description, detailing the duties, pur-

▲ *As a new employee, Terry expects to dislike some of her assignments, but she realizes that it's all part of the job. Terry's supervisor is demanding, but fair.*

pose, equipment, and demands of your job, should be explained to you. Knowledge of the various tasks, the work load, and the pace of your work will give you a chance to prove your potential and to demonstrate your willingness to do a good job.

• You will be supervised. Your immediate supervisor may be lenient or demanding. In either case, try to build a good working relationship with him or her. Resist the temptation to challenge your supervisor.

What Your Employer Will Expect of You

Employers know that doing the job isn't enough to build a successful organization. During your time on the job, your employer will expect you to

• Be conscientious in meeting performance expectations. Spend additional time, when neces-

All Work Is Important

It was 2:45 in the afternoon when John Strand entered the door of the Golden Candle. Although he had been hired as a busser only three months ago, John already had a dream of owning his own restaurant. John didn't begin work until 3:00, but he liked to arrive early and have some time to get ready for his shift.

John's job was considered by some to be of the lowest level, but he had already learned that it was very important. As soon as customers finished dining, John quickly and thoroughly cleaned and reset the table. During busy dinner hours, tables that are unused and waiting to be cleaned mean lost dollars. On the other hand, seating customers at a table that is not properly cleaned can anger them and cause lost business.

Mrs. Crimaldi, the owner and manager, asked John to step into her office before his shift started. She told him that she was very pleased with his attendance, the efficiency with which he handled his work tasks, and the attitude he displayed toward customers and other employees. She needed a person to train under the head chef and offered John the job. The new job would pay more, and it would provide him with an opportunity to learn the various operations of a restaurant kitchen.

John was very happy when he went home that evening. He knew that he was one step closer to his dream of owning his own restaurant.

Critical Thinking

1. Would John be better off if he found a higher-paying job, saved his money, and then opened his own restaurant? List the reasons supporting your opinion.

sary, to accomplish assigned work tasks at a high standard.

- Be responsible and use care in handling tools and equipment. If equipment breaks while you are using it, report the damage. When you complete a task, leave your work area and equipment in good condition.

- Use effective written and oral communications. Think before you speak. Then speak clearly, and listen carefully.

- Be enthusiastic and express a positive attitude toward your work.

- Be cooperative with supervisors, co-workers, and customers. Establish and maintain respectful and honest interpersonal relationships. Help co-workers, but follow the supervisor's instructions.

- Demonstrate an interest in learning. Determine the skills required for your new job, then evaluate your skills in terms of the company's requirements. If you lack certain skills, take the responsibility for acquiring them. Observe the methods of successful co-workers, and copy them.

- Be loyal. When asked, keep certain information about the organization confidential. Follow company rules and procedures. If you violate a standard procedure, apologize to those whom you have offended. Learn all you can about your employer's business.

- Perform a full day's work. If you must leave your workstation for something other than a regular break or lunch, let others know where you can be reached. Look for additional tasks as you complete those assigned to you.

- Be emotionally stable and respond to stress in an appropriate manner.

- Be reliable by consistently arriving at work on time and attending all expected functions. Being punctual and involved and having good attendance lets management know that you're conscientious and dependable.

- Be pleasant in appearance and personal hygiene. For career success, you must comply with the dress code and maintain acceptable levels of personal cleanliness and grooming.

- Separate your business and personal life. Your lifestyle outside the company is your business, but when you bring personal concerns to work, it becomes your employer's business. Personal

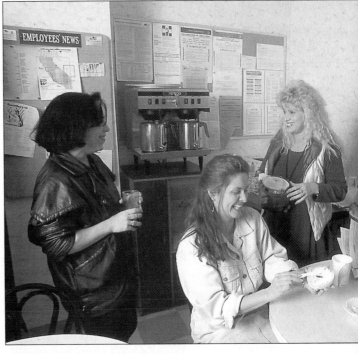

▲ *Don't abuse the time period allotted for scheduled breaks. Successful workers give a full day's work for a full day's pay.*

telephone calls should be reserved for emergencies. Keep them to a minimum.

These expectations may be difficult to get used to at first. As you read each one, which do you expect to have the most difficulty in meeting? Which will be easiest?

Section 2 GET INVOLVED

Answer the following on a separate sheet of paper, and be prepared to discuss your responses in class.

1. Compare being a student to being an employee. For example, an employee is rewarded for time and effort spent on the job with wages or salary. A student is awarded for time and effort spent in school with grades.

    a. What is done to provide a student with a safe work environment?

    b. What equipment and supplies does a school provide students?

    c. When may a student be given a probationary period?

    d. What methods of discipline are used with students?

    e. Who supervises students?

2. Are the expectations of employers different from those of your teachers? Explain your answer.

Laying the Groundwork for Career Success

What is success? It can mean different things to different people, but basically **success** is a favorable result or a hoped-for ending. Success results when someone fulfills a wish, a need, or a desire. Motivation to succeed is frequently based on the need to survive, to gain social approval, or to obtain self-respect. Several motives usually operate at once. Personal values are major motives causing people to strive for career success. Look again at the work values discussed in Chapter 3. Which four work values are most important to you?

Successful people know their values and have learned to listen to them. They depend on their values when they make career decisions. Another word for the values that help us make decisions is *conscience*. Your definition of career success may involve several factors:

- Promotion to a position with greater responsibility
- An increase in pay
- Job security
- Recognition of your accomplishments
- Personal satisfaction of knowing you are competent

For some, success means fame and fortune. You will need to determine what success means to you before you can strive to achieve it.

Successful workers balance their personal activities with their work. How you choose to live your

▲ *Renee places a high value on job security, family relationships, religion, and a comfortable work environment. Which work values are important to you?*

life outside the organization is your decision. However, personal lifestyle activities sometimes intrude on job responsibilities and hamper career success. How might you solve the possible career problems in each of the following situations?

Lifestyle Activity	Possible Effect on Job
A busy social life on weekends	Coming to work tired on Monday
A very emotional love relationship	Mind is on personal concerns
Alcohol or drug abuse	Job performance is impaired
Personal business appointments	Leaving work early
Being in debt for your lifestyle	Not dressing appropriately

The first few weeks and months on a new job make up an **orientation period**. This is a time to learn what is expected of you, to establish your credibility, and to begin building your performance record. During the orientation period, you will become more aware of your strengths and weaknesses. It is a good time to learn new skills. You will probably encounter certain job tasks that you perform well and others that cause you difficulty. Your supervisor will closely watch your job performance.

Employers want to maintain high **morale** (level of enthusiasm) in the workplace. Carry out your duties and responsibilities with sincerity and enthusiasm. When you complete a work assignment, ask your supervisor for another task. This will help you learn more about the job. It will also

CAREER TIP

When you begin a new job, use formal names in addressing others until granted permission to use first names. Even then, be slow in using first names, and revert to formal names when you are involved in important or formal business situations.

demonstrate to your supervisor that your morale is good and that you want a more important role in the organization. Like a successful student, a successful worker isn't satisfied with completing the minimum requirements.

Once you have been hired, your supervisor and your closest co-workers will have considerable influence on your career success. The supervisor will explain the overall job objectives and your specific role. If you do not have a clear understanding of what is expected, ask questions. Show courtesy and respect for the expertise of your supervisor and your co-workers. This will help you build good working relationships.

Organizational Survival and Success Factors

Many studies have been carried out to identify why some people have more career success than others. One study included more than 660 managers of Fortune-500 firms. Their rankings of success and organizational survival factors were based on their personal background, experience, and knowledge. Figure 9.1 shows the order of importance they placed on eleven personal qualities or conditions that influence career success.

Personal Appearance

There is much to be said for "looking the part" in terms of success in a company. Chapter 8 describes the importance of making a good **personal appearance** during the job interview. In Figure 9.1 on the next page, appearance ranked eighth out of eleven success factors. This demonstrates that employers consider personal appearance to be just as important after you get the job as when you interview for the job. Dress codes and personal appearance expectations are different from one organization to another. Some employers establish dress codes for their workers, and others expect employees to follow standards of good taste or to adhere to the norm in the organization. In any case, promotion and acceptance in

1. Performance record
2. Personality
3. Communication skills
4. Technical skills and ability to stay up to date with skills
5. Human relations skills
6. Significant work experience and assignments
7. Ability to stay cool under pressure
8. Personal appearance
9. Ability to make tough business decisions
10. Health and energy level
11. Ability to judge people

▲ *Figure 9.1 Personal Qualities and Conditions That Influence Career Success.*

an organization tend to increase when workers have an acceptable appearance.

As you begin a new job, view yourself as others might view you. Your appearance is a form of nonverbal communication. It reveals your self-image, personal pride, and self-confidence. Maintain a good sitting and standing posture, and develop a businesslike image.

Dress in a suitable manner. Your appearance should be in keeping with your position and the

public image of the organization. Personal appearance codes differ from one employer to another and for different jobs within each organization. What would be considered suitable clothing for

- A female or male secretary in a large office?
- A female or male clerk in a large discount store?
- A female or male machine operator in a factory?
- A female or male home appliance repairperson?

Image consultants (people who help others project a desired image) generally recommend the following as acceptable grooming standards:

- Conservative style and color (men and women)
- Short, neat hairstyle (men and women)
- Not too much jewelry (men and women)
- Pressed clothes, polished shoes, and clean nails (men and women)
- Manicured nails with discretion as to color (women)

The employees of International Business Machines (IBM) and Apple Computer have presented different images for many years. As the world's largest computer company, IBM expected employees to dress with conservative dignity.

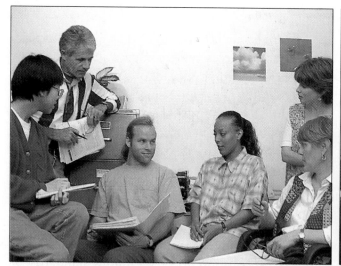

▲ *Which group of workers is writing a million dollar advertising campaign for a large corporation? Why do you think so? Which group of workers is responsible for making customer loans at a small bank? Why do you think so?*

Solving The Problem

Where Does Tiffany Belong?

Tiffany Fenton carefully moved through the lunchroom, balancing her tray, avoiding other workers with one eye and looking for Jeff Lange with the other. Lunch was the one part of her new job at CompuData that she felt comfortable with. Jeff had graduated from Wilson High last year, and he knew his way around the company. Tiffany wanted all the advice she could get to help her be successful on the new job. It seemed strange that last week she was an important senior at Wilson, and now she was a nobody at CompuData.

"Over here Tiff!" Jeff called to her. "How's everything in the bookkeeping department today?"

"Not very good, Jeff," she replied. "Reynolds has been picking on me all morning. Sometimes I feel like running his tie through the printer. This morning, he started out being upset about my new outfit and ended up angry because I broke a nail. In the first place, these are not shorts. That shows you how little Reynolds knows about fashion! In the second place, I'm the one who can't use the word processor with a sore finger, not him. What can I do to please the man?"

"For openers, he's not down on you Tiff," Jeff said. "He told me that you have become more accurate on the spreadsheet program in one week than some of the bookkeepers have in one year. Reynolds is OK. He's been here a long time, and he's playing the corporate game. If his manager should walk in and see you dressed in . . . high fashion and not working on the books because your nails are . . . very fashion-

able, he would come down on Reynolds like a ton of bricks.

"We're all people Tiffany," Jeff continued, "and we all want to belong. A year ago, I decided to belong at CompuData. Maybe that's not what you want. If it is, then you have to get in the mainstream. Watch Jan Morris and other successful workers in your department. Look at the clothes they wear and how they behave on the job. If that's the identity you want, then go for it. If not, don't blame Reynolds. He knows what he wants."

The next day, Mr. Reynolds called Tiffany into his office. He started the discussion by telling Tiffany that her job was very important to the success of his department and that he was very pleased with the level of her computer skills. Then he asked Tiffany if she really wanted to work at CompuData, and if so, how could he help her fit in?

Critical Thinking

1. Work with another class member to role-play the end of the conversation between Mr. Reynolds and Tiffany. Your classmates will have different endings to present.

Apple, the underdog competitor, began in the owner's garage. Apple's free-thinking, less inhibited approach to developing, manufacturing, and selling computers is symbolized by the casual but appropriate dress of its employees.

IBM recently announced that its employees will shed their dark suits, white shirts, and striped ties for a more relaxed dress code. Informal dress

codes and casual Fridays in offices nationwide are becoming a trademark of the 90s world of work.

Fashion changes. Dress standards of ten years ago have changed, and what is acceptable now may be outdated next season. Before you start a new job, take an inventory of your wardrobe. Begin by placing all of your appropriate work clothes in one area of the closet. Mix and match items that may be suitable for your new job. Make a list of any additional clothing you will need. Decide how much you can afford to budget for new clothes, and make a tentative list of what you will buy with that amount.

Is it more important to be accepted by your employer as "who you are" or to conform to the expected personal appearance and dress code?

Being There: Attendance

Is your presence at work so important you can't afford to miss a day? When is a family crisis more important than a job? Don't you deserve a day off if you're a conscientious worker and you haven't been absent for months? What are legitimate reasons for being absent from work?

Since you were in the first grade, you have probably been told about the importance of being present and on time for school. Have you ever received a certificate for perfect attendance or for never being tardy? Were there times when you missed school because of sickness or family situations? If so, you probably had to make up the schoolwork you missed. Did you depend on others to help you catch up? The lessons you have already learned about the importance of attendance and punctuality are a big part of preparing for career success.

On the job, your supervisor and co-workers will depend on you. Your absence could affect other workers' ability to proceed with their jobs. If you are assigned to a task and you're absent, other workers may be required to perform more than their share of the work in order to get the job done. If you work as part of a team, work may slow down or stop if you are absent.

A **legitimate absence** occurs when an employee must miss work for a reason that is acceptable to the employer. In cases of legitimate absence, employers have procedures for employees to follow. In most organizations, you will be expected to notify your supervisor or co-workers as soon as possible. You may be instructed to telephone the workplace before starting time on a day when you will be absent to explain the situation. If you know in advance that you must miss work on a particular day, it is a good practice to let your supervisor or someone in charge know as far ahead of time as possible. If you become ill late in your shift, notify your supervisor that you will probably be absent the next day.

Sometimes it is necessary to take time off for a doctor's appointment or for necessary personal business. Always try to make these appointments outside of your scheduled working hours. If this is impossible, notify your employer in advance and obtain permission to be away from work.

Being There: Punctuality

Employers insist on punctuality for many of the same reasons that they expect regular attendance. Employers with specific business hours need to have workers at those times to answer the telephones, service customers, and carry out the work of the organization. Your employer will expect you to be ready to work at starting time, stay until quitting time, and take no more than the allotted time for lunch and other scheduled breaks.

Scheduled breaks are rest periods that employers provide so employees can take time out from the workday to relax, have refreshments, handle personal needs, or socialize with co-workers. These breaks usually last ten or fifteen minutes. In some work operations, another employee will perform your job during your scheduled breaks.

CAREER TIP

Employers view irregular attendance, habitual lateness, and frequent abuse of policies regarding lunch periods and scheduled breaks as reasons for dismissal.

▲ *Employers expect workers to be on time and have good attendance.*

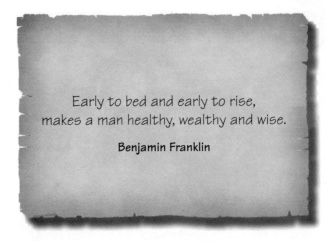

Early to bed and early to rise, makes a man healthy, wealthy and wise.

Benjamin Franklin

Although most of us would agree with Benjamin Franklin (see top of next column), getting to work on time isn't easy for some people. For them, it seems easier to roll over, get some extra Zs, and be a few minutes late to work. Unfortunately, most employers expect workers to arrive on the job promptly and be ready to work as scheduled. If getting started in the morning is not easy for you, prepare for your job the night before. Practice the following suggestions, and make a commitment to be on time.

1. Get enough sleep. Plan your activities so you are home in time for a full eight hours of sleep—no late TV or parties on work nights.

2. Buy a clock radio that has an alarm or an alarm clock that has a light plus an alarm. Place your alarm where you will be forced to walk across the room to turn it off.

3. Before you go to bed, decide what you will wear to work the next day. Lay your clothing out, and make certain that everything is clean, pressed, and ready to wear. Place shoes and accessories, such as jewelry, next to your outfit.

4. If you drive to work, leave your car keys on the night stand along with your wallet or purse. If you use public transportation, have the correct change laid out so it's ready to go in the morning.

5. Set all but the refrigerated parts of your breakfast on the table the night before. If you want coffee in the morning, prepare the pot and have it ready to turn on.

6. Skip the newspaper until evening, read it at lunch, or read it on your way to work if you use public transportation.

7. Time yourself. For several days, write down the amount of time it takes you to complete each of the tasks listed.

Policies and Procedures

All employers have a unique (one-of-a-kind) set of rules known as **policies and procedures**. They are established to serve the organization's unique needs, purpose, and management system. Usually, a considerable amount of time is spent developing and testing different procedures. If you expect to receive the rewards of working for an employer, you should also expect to follow the organization's policies and procedures.

As you become familiar with the day-to-day operations of your employer, the organization's policies and procedures can provide you with a sense of order and eliminate many confusing situ-

▲ *Successful workers follow their employer's policies and procedures. Successful students follow their school's policies and procedures.*

ations. In addition, they can provide employee protection. For example, a company that manufactures hazardous chemicals would expect employees to follow a long list of safety policies and procedures. A different company, such as the owner of a chain of retail stores, would be more concerned with policies and procedures that focus on customer relations.

Much of your job success will depend on how well you follow the policies and procedures of your employer. Learning and adjusting to your employer's methods are an important part of establishing yourself as a member of the organization. It is best to follow policies and procedures even when you don't understand why. The failure to follow established rules could result in the termination of your employment.

Many employers give their employees policies and procedures manuals when they begin working. If you did not receive one, your supervisor or a co-worker may be able to inform you about the organization's policies and procedures. Manuals concerning absence, punctuality, evaluation, grievances, use of equipment and tools, safety, rest periods, and theft are usually available.

Section 3   GET INVOLVED

Answer the following on a separate sheet of paper, and be prepared to discuss your responses in class.

1. Five of the top ten career success determinants in Figure 9.1 on page 188 are personal qualities and are not related to job skills or education and training levels. Evaluate yourself in terms of items 2, 5, 7, 8, and 10. What personal improvements could you make in these areas?

2. Numerous studies indicate the relationship between school attendance and attendance on the job. How much emphasis should employers put on school attendance and tardy records when making hiring decisions? Why?

3. Here are some reasons people offer for being late to their jobs:

   - Anxiety about work
   - Conflicts with co-workers
   - Job boredom
   - Dislike of getting up early
   - Conflicts with the boss
   - Transportation problems

   Which of these reasons would be most likely to result in your being late for work? Explain your answer.

4. Other than family emergencies, what are two legitimate reasons for being late to work? Explain your answer.

5. Ask a family member or friend who is employed about their employers' policies and procedures regarding absence, punctuality, evaluation, grievances, use of equipment and tools, and safety. Report your findings to the class.

IMPORTANT FACTS

Facts That Concern Employers

- Personality conflicts cause bad morale, reduced production, and lower-quality products or services.
- Training new employees costs money and productivity. Will new workers stay, or are they looking for greener pastures?
- Personal responsibilities and interests can interfere with job performance.
- Employee absence or tardiness causes work slowdowns and costs money.
- Employee theft of property and secrets costs employers millions of dollars each year.

Comparing School and Work

School Facts	Work Facts
You are required by law to attend school.	You may enter or leave employment by choice.
Public schools must accept all students who wish to attend.	Employers hire only the workers they want.
Teachers must continue to teach students with poor attendance.	Supervisors may fire workers with poor attendance.
Teachers evaluate students on the quality of their work.	Employers evaluate employees on the quality of their work.
Teachers continue to help students who perform poorly.	Employers terminate workers who perform poorly.
Students are rewarded with skill development, knowledge, and personal satisfaction.	Workers are rewarded with paychecks, promotions, and personal satisfaction.
Education is most successful when students and teachers respect and trust each other.	Employment is most successful when workers and employers respect and trust each other.
Students receive a long summer vacation, Christmas vacation, and spring break.	Workers receive a week or two of vacation after a full year of work.
School problems are solved by the student and and the teacher. A counselor, principal, or parent may help.	Work problems are solved by the worker and employer. A union representative may help.

The Most Common Reasons for Worker Absence

Accident on the job	Personal illness	Leaving work early
Accident off the job	Jury duty	Honor being bestowed
Transportation problem	Birthday	Temporary suspension
Leave of absence	Unexcused absence	Death in the family
Discipline	Military obligation	Weather
Excused absence	Medical appointment	Vacation
Family illness	Personal problem	Layoff

CHAPTER 9 REVIEW

ENRICH YOUR VOCABULARY

On a separate sheet of paper, number from 1 to 18, and complete the following activity. (Do not write in your textbook.) Match each statement below with the most appropriate term from the "Enrich Your Vocabulary" list at the beginning of the chapter by writing that term next to the correct statement.

1. Depending or relying on one another
2. Manners
3. A favorable result or a hoped-for ending
4. People who help others to project a desired image
5. Handbooks
6. Getting acquainted with a new job and the employer's organization
7. Expressing interest and enthusiasm
8. Complaining and using sarcasm
9. A period of time in which you are expected to learn the job
10. Tension
11. Highest level of productivity
12. The first few weeks and months on a new job
13. The way you look to others
14. Missing work for an acceptable reason
15. Rest periods that employers provide
16. Rules and regulations
17. Being capable
18. Level of enthusiasm

CHECK YOUR KNOWLEDGE

On a separate sheet of paper, complete the following activity. (Do not write in your textbook.)

1. What do many employers believe is the most important factor in job success?
2. List three ways that people demonstrate a positive attitude.
3. List three ways that people demonstrate a negative attitude.
4. Why do employers want employees to be successful?
5. List five things that employees can expect from their employers.
6. List five things that employers expect from their employees.
7. What is the first-ranked determinant of career success in Figure 9.1?
8. Which determinant of career success can only be earned through education?
9. Give one reason why attendance and punctuality are very important on the job.

DEVELOP SCANS COMPETENCIES

Government experts say that successful workers can productively use Resources, Interpersonal skills, Information, Systems, and Technology. This activity will give you practice in developing Information skills.

Employers often use forms with items similar to these to appraise their employees' performance. Rate your school performance on the items listed and analyze the information to determine where you might need to improve your performance.

Quality of Work	☐ Very high quality	☐ Work sometimes superior but usually accurate	☐ A careful worker, small amount needs to be redone	☐ Work frequently below acceptable quality	☐ Work often almost worthless
Cooperation	☐ Always congenial and cooperative	☐ Cooperates well	☐ Usually courteous and cooperative	☐ Does only what is specifically requested	☐ Unfriendly and uncooperative
Attendance and Punctuality	☐ Routine usually exceeds normal	☐ Excellent	☐ Normally dependable	☐ Needs close supervision in this area	☐ Unreliable

Making Progress on the Job

Learning Objectives

After completing this chapter, you should be prepared to:

- explain the relationship between job progress and conforming to an organization's written and unwritten rules
- compare the team-oriented and control-oriented management styles and describe the responsibilities of each
- identify several positive and negative effects that interpersonal relationships can have on management and co-workers
- discuss several factors that cause workers to be promoted
- discuss the major causes of job-related accidents and describe the procedures for reducing on-the-job health and safety hazards
- identify six major goals of early labor unions and evaluate the positive and negative aspects of union membership

Enrich Your Vocabulary

In reading this chapter and doing the exercises you will learn the following important terms:

entry level
corporate culture
staff
subordinate
superior
team adviser
quality circle
co-workers
work ethic
career advancement

line of progression
mentor
seniority
time management
labor unions
NLRB
collective bargaining
grievances
OSHA

Unless you have previous experience, your first job will probably be at the **entry level** (the lowest level of experience for the job). If you are like most people, you will have many ups and downs as you develop the skills and experience required to meet your new job responsibilities. Fortunately, you can expect to become more confident and productive as you learn the job.

When you seek a promotion with more responsibility and higher pay, keep these things in mind:

1. You will need to demonstrate to your employer that you have mastered your present assignment.

2. You will need to demonstrate your ability to get along with managers and co-workers.

3. You will need to understand and conform to the organization's philosophy and management structure.

4. You will need to understand the requirements of the next highest job level in the organization.

Section 1

Conforming to the Organization

Schools, businesses, government agencies, labor unions, and professional associations are created for the purpose of exchanging goods, services, or money for mutual benefit. All of them have a management arrangement (system of organization) within which they operate to meet specific goals or purposes (Figure 10.1).

Since elementary school, you have been conforming to the management organization of a school system. The school system you currently attend has an organizational structure similar to that of a private business. It is structured to meet the educational goals of the community or group it serves.

▲ *Figure 10.1 Business Organization.*

▲ *What is acceptable in one work setting may not be acceptable in another. Which of these three scenes is most related to your thoughts, feelings, manners, and sense of good taste?*

Corporate Culture

The thoughts, feelings, manners, and sense of good taste each business or organization develops is referred to as its corporate culture. The corporate culture is established by its management. It serves as the guideline for personal behavior and job performance for the entire organization. As a new employee, your job progress will depend in large part on your ability to fit into the corporate culture.

When you begin a job, observe other employees and learn the obvious and not-so-obvious signs of individual conformity. What is acceptable in one work setting may not be acceptable in another. For example, in one office your supervisor may encourage you to decorate your work area with pictures, posters, or other items that show you have a personal space in the organization. In another office, a strict policy regarding decor may be followed, and this kind of individuality may not be permitted. How is student individuality encouraged in your school? How is it discouraged?

In the early weeks of a new job, learn all you can about the overall operations of the organization. Learn how it is organized (structured) and who reports to whom in the system of management. To help you learn, keep a notepad and write down the names of people you meet, along with their positions, titles, and functions. Use this notepad as a reference when you want to clarify something you were told, obtain additional information, or remember a specific person's name. Understanding the structure of the organization will help you understand your position within it.

Public expectations influence certain stereotypes of conformity. What is your image of a large bank? Do you think of it as well organized and managed by people who dress in conservative business suits? Have you ever seen clutter in a bank? Do bank employees seem to conform to clearly defined rules about their appearance and conduct with customers? Think about the function of a bank. Does the conformity give you a sense of confidence in their ability to handle your money safely and accurately? Would you want to put your money in a bank that was not well organized? If employees wore jeans and T-shirts, would you question their commitment to being careful with your money? Would you think they were too laid-back and casual to be precise and accurate? Would you feel the same about other large companies? What image does your school project?

Section 1 GET INVOLVED

Answer the following on a separate sheet of paper, and be prepared to discuss your responses in class.

1. Invite the school principal to your class to explain how your school system is organized.
2. Use your local telephone book to locate a local corporate office. Invite an employee to speak with your class about the corporation's culture.
3. What concerns do you have about fitting in at a new job?
4. What signs of conformity would you expect to see in a factory? Why?

Section 2

Being Supervised

The person who will direct your work has a position of management responsibility in the organization. Whether this person is called a manager, supervisor, or foreman, he or she will be important to your success, satisfaction, and progress on the job.

Assigning employees and deciding what each person will do in a specific position is a management function known as *staffing*. As a new employee, you will become a member of your supervisor's **staff** (a group of employees who work for and with someone in charge). As a member of the supervisor's staff, you will also be known as a **subordinate**. This term refers to an employee who follows someone else's orders. The person who gives the orders is known as the subordinate's **superior**.

Regardless of the size of the organization, the supervisor or manager is responsible for getting the best possible performance from his or her staff. As both a member of a staff and a subordinate, you will be assigned specific job duties and responsibilities by your supervisor. Once the assignments are made, the supervisor will provide any special directions that you need. Your supervisor is a part of the first-line management (Figure 10.2).

> It's easier to do a job right than to explain why you didn't.
>
> **Martin Van Buren, Eighth president of the United States**

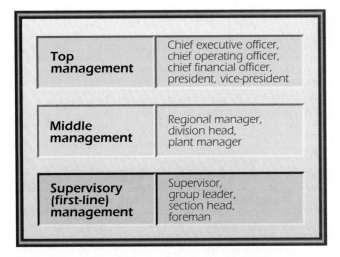

▲ *Figure 10.2 The Three Layers of Management.*

▲ *In a control-oriented corporate culture, your supervisor will determine your work schedule, and inform you about work procedures (including the quality of the product or service provided).*

Control-Oriented Management

Many organizations have a control-oriented system of management. In this corporate culture, the job of first-line managers (supervisors) is to

- Instruct workers to carry out the policies and procedures established by top- and middle-level management
- Generally manage a budget, make work schedules, assign staff to specific work tasks, provide instruction, and maintain worker discipline
- Evaluate the work of subordinates (judge their work performance in terms of their job description)
- Recommend good performers for wage increases, promotions, and special awards
- Deal with poor performers by outlining expectations, counseling them in proper methods, issuing warnings, and recommending their discipline, transfer, or dismissal to middle management
- Orient new employees to departmental procedures and take responsibility for job training
- Evaluate the strengths and weaknesses of new staff members before making a specific assignment

- Ensure that workers, equipment, and materials are used properly and efficiently
- Teach employees safe work practices and enforce safety rules and regulations
- In organizations covered by union contracts, know the provisions of labor-management contracts and run the department according to these agreements

Team-Oriented Management

In the past two decades, many American employers have been moving away from the traditional control-oriented management system to a more team-oriented management approach. This approach has been linked to higher productivity, improved product quality, and increased worker satisfaction. In the team-oriented management system, employees at all levels share responsibilities. This system encourages interdependence in workers. In contrast, the control-oriented management system creates a dependent or independent work force. Figure 10.3 lists other differences between control-oriented and team-oriented management.

Control-Oriented Management	Team-Oriented Management
Job Design	
Individual responsibility is limited to performing a single job	Individual responsibility is extended to upgrading group performance
Dilutes necessary worker skills, fragments work tasks, and separates doing from thinking	Enhances worker skills, emphasizes the whole task, and combines doing with thinking
Accountability is focused on the individual	Accountability is focused on the team
Definition of job duties is fixed	Definition of job duties is flexible, depending on changing conditions
Performance Expectations	
Measured standards define minimum performance, and stability is seen as desirable	Emphasis is placed on higher "stretch" objectives, which tend to be dynamic (not stable) and geared to a changing marketplace
Management Organization, Systems, and Style	
Structure tends to be layered, with top-down controls	Structure tends to be flat, with mutual-influence systems
Coordination and control are based on rules and procedures	Coordination and control are based on shared goals, values, and traditions
Management decisions are based on individual privilege and positional authority	Management decisions are based on problem solving, current information, and expertise
Status symbols are distributed to reinforce the image of the hierarchy	Status symbols are minimized to deemphasize the image of the hierarchy
Compensation Policies	
Individual pay is linked to job evaluation	Individual pay is linked to mastery of skill
Variable-pay systems are used to provide individual incentive and achievement	Variable-pay systems are used to create equity and reinforce group achievement
Employment Assurances	
Employees are regarded as variable costs necessary to do business	Training and keeping the existing work force is a high priority
Employees expect occasional layoffs	A commitment is made to avoid layoffs or assist in reemployment
Employee Voice Policies	
Employee participation is allowed on a narrow range of issues	Employee participation is encouraged on a wide range of issues
Related risks are emphasized	Related benefits are emphasized
Communication methods include an open-door policy, attitude surveys, grievance procedures, and collective bargaining	Communication methods include new group concepts of corporate governance
Business informaiton is shared on a strictly defined "need-to-know" basis	Business information is shared widely
Labor-Management Relations	
Adversarial labor relations	Mutuality in labor relations
Emphasis is on interest conflict	Emphasis is on joint planning and problem solving
Communication is on a narrow agenda	Communication is on a broad agenda
Unions, management, and workers maintain clearly defined roles	Unions, management, and workers redefine their respective roles

▲ *Figure 10.3 Differences in Work–Force Management Strategies.*

Solving The Problem

Being Pleasant Is Important

Connie Lee is very pleased with her new job in the secretarial pool of the training department. After three days on the job, it seems as though her supervisor, Mr. Darrow, approves of her skills. Now he has another assignment for her. "Connie," he says, "type this material for me exactly as it is. Don't change a thing. I'll need it early this afternoon." He drops the handwritten pages in her "in" box and returns to his office.

Connie reviews the material and notices that it has several spelling errors and some very poor grammar. It takes her about an hour longer than she had expected to type the material because of the corrections that are necessary. However, she completes the job on time and has it ready for Mr. Darrow when he returns. He takes a few minutes to read it before saying, "Good job, Connie! I really appreciate the way you handle things."

"Thanks!" Connie replies. "I would have finished much sooner, but half the words were spelled wrong. I haven't seen such poor grammar since the eighth grade."

Mr. Darrow immediately turns around and walks rapidly back to his office.

Critical Thinking

1. What Connie said was true, but was it wise?
2. Should Connie have made the corrections without first discussing the problem with Mr. Darrow? Why do you feel this way?
3. What impression did Connie give Mr. Darrow when she criticized the spelling and grammar in the original material?
4. If you were Connie, how would you have handled this situation?

In the team management system, the supervisor's title is **team adviser** or team consultant. The team adviser's responsibilities include many of those previously listed for supervisors, but focus on

- facilitating (motivating and encouraging) workers rather than directing (telling) them
- ensuring that resources are available so the team can produce quality work on time
- developing the employees into a team and providing leadership in problem solving
- representing the team in the organization

Quality Circles

Quality circle is a team-oriented management style that is currently widely used in the United States. The idea of building quality circles started in the United States but was rejected by traditional control-oriented American business leaders.

Following World War II, Japanese business leaders were quick to embrace this American idea. They used it as a philosophy (system of beliefs and attitudes) to rebuild their industries. When the high quality of Japanese products began to cause a loss of sales for American business and a loss of American jobs, many American business leaders took a second look at quality circles and the team-oriented style of management.

A **quality circle** is composed of employees from the same department who work as a group to identify and solve quality problems with the product they manufacture or the service they provide. The rank-and-file work force is often the group most qualified to solve work-related problems involving quality. American companies like

▲ *In a team-oriented corporate culture, a group of workers from the same department identifies and solves quality problems with the product they manufacture or the service they provide.*

Honeywell, Corning Glass, Chrysler, Northrop, and Lockheed have found that their use of quality circles has increased production, raised quality levels, reduced costs, and increased worker satisfaction.

Getting More Information

For additional information concerning management and supervision, write to:
American Management Association
135 West 50th St.
New York, NY 10020.

When You Have a Problem

If you do not fully understand what your supervisor expects of you or if you have a problem you want to discuss, use proper business etiquette and request a meeting with your supervisor. Follow these guidelines:

1. Do not request a meeting when you are angry. Wait until you have calmed down, even if it takes a day or two.

2. Ask your supervisor or his or her secretary when it would be convenient for a meeting.

3. Handle the problem in private, and do not discuss your meeting with your co-workers.

4. Arrive on time for your scheduled appointment. When you enter the supervisor's office, remain standing until offered a seat.

5. Be prepared to state the problem as you see it. Maintain a positive attitude in your presentation and during the entire meeting. Your cool head will attract respect from your superiors in the organization.

6. Respect the chain of command by accepting the outcome of the meeting. Do not go over your supervisor's head unless you are prepared to live with the possible consequences. End the meeting with a handshake and a positive comment.

Handling Criticism

Did you ever thank someone for criticizing you? Probably not. Criticism makes people feel angry, embarrassed, anxious, and guilty. All of these deflate the ego and lower self-esteem. Criticism seems like a form of rejection. It makes adults feel like unloved children who just got caught with their hands in the cookie jar. Criticism from a supervisor for unsatisfactory work performance does not make your relationship with that person any easier, but it is a part of learning and making progress on a job.

How do you react to criticism? Were you ever scolded for crossing the street without looking both ways? Were you ever punished for not getting along with a brother or sister? Did you ever miss recess because you did not do satisfactory school work? How did you feel in these situations? Were you angry? How did you react? Did you retaliate with similar criticism, or did you become silent and withdrawn? Did you take it out on someone else, such as a younger brother or sister? Did you say something nasty? Did you want to get even?

You have responded to criticism from people in authority since you were a child. Perhaps you have always disliked having other people tell you what to do, or perhaps you believe that everything a person in authority tells you must be right. You probably have the same attitude toward authority today as you did as a child.

Criticism can be good for you. In sports, coaches criticize. Their feedback improves the players' game and helps them develop new performance skills. Being criticized by a supervisor is somewhat like being coached. It can help you become a better employee. Suppose you are never told what you do well and where you need to improve. How would you know if you were meeting your employer's standards, if you were in trouble, or if you were progressing?

When you deal with criticism, it is important to examine your thoughts and feelings because they influence your attitude and, in turn, your behavior. When you understand your thoughts and feelings, you can learn to manage your behavior.

Your ability to get along with your supervisor depends a lot on your attitude toward criticism and authority. Your supervisor has the right and the obligation to offer constructive criticism when your work needs improvement. As a new employee, you can expect some criticism. How you handle it will influence your working relationships and future positions within the organization.

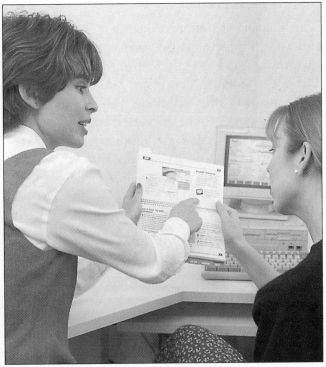

▲ *How you handle criticism will influence your future career success. How do you handle criticism from your parent(s) or guardian? your teachers? your friends?*

▲ *Successful workers view a supervisor's constructive criticism, offered in private, as a helpful learning experience.*

A considerate supervisor offers constructive criticism in private. This avoids unnecessary embarrassment and negative feelings on your part. The supervisor will clarify the work being criticized and will offer solutions. You will be given time to respond. Once criticized, you will be expected to take action to improve your performance. You can expect your supervisor to follow up to be certain that you are following the suggestions offered.

When You Don't Like the Boss

Have you ever had a teacher you did not get along with, someone you could never please? Who was at fault: the teacher, you, or both of you? Did you attempt to solve the problem?

In some situations, a boss may make unreasonable demands and may put pressure on a subordi-

CAREER TIP

Knowing how to handle criticism in a positive manner will help you grow in your career and in your personal life.

nate to do more work than he or she can handle. Perhaps the boss is being pressured by upper-level management, or perhaps he or she expected a promotion or pay raise and didn't get it. A boss with a short temper may yell whenever something goes wrong. This behavior will cause feelings of anger, fear, and inferiority among the workers. A workaholic boss may expect subordinates to work extra hours without pay for the pure pleasure of being at work. Sometimes, a boss doesn't understand the value of complimenting a worker for a job well done.

Sooner or later, you will probably encounter a boss you don't like or one who doesn't like you. Quitting the job won't solve this type of problem; it will only help you take it someplace else. It is hoped that you will not have this problem on your first full-time job. If you do, turn it into an opportunity by learning how to develop relationships with difficult people. It is in your own best interest. These guidelines will help:

1. Accept the fact that you and the boss have personal differences.
2. Become tolerant of your differences, and make adjustments.
3. Keep any resentment to yourself.

As an employee facing these situations, you can either speak up in your defense or change your behavior. Before doing either, it is best to take a close look at yourself. Could you be the one at fault? Could you be overreacting to the situation? Be objective. If you were the boss in the same situation, how would you have handled it? Criticizing your superior to co-workers won't solve the problem, and if you do decide to quit, you'll need the boss for a reference.

Section 2

GET INVOLVED

Answer the following on a separate sheet of paper, and be prepared to discuss your responses in class.

1. Interview a parent, relative, or friend who has at least five years of full-time work experience. Record his or her answers to the following questions:
   - What are three ways you must conform to the rules of your employer?
   - What are three characteristics you like in a supervisor?
   - What are three characteristics you dislike in a supervisor?
   - Describe a time when you were glad someone in authority was supervising a situation at work.

2. Walk in the other person's shoes for a moment. Imagine that you are a supervisor who has criticized an employee's performance. The employee is taking it personally and acts dejected and uninterested in doing a good job. What can you do to get this worker back on the right track?

Section 3

Getting Along with Co-Workers

Co-workers are people who work together and rely on each other to complete work assignments. They generally have the same or nearly the same job status, skills, and work load. Most full-time employees spend more of their waking hours with co-workers than with family and friends.

You have seen teachers cooperate with one another to fulfill a job obligation. Perhaps they were conducting a school assembly, supervising a student dance, or monitoring a large-group testing program. Would things have worked as well if these teachers had not had positive interpersonal relationships?

Positive interpersonal relationships with co-workers have been shown to increase personal job satisfaction, affect the manner in which workers cooperate on assignments, and lead to increased production and sales. Poor interpersonal relationships and failure to communicate effectively cause more employees to quit or lose their jobs than any

other factor. Managers regard skills related to job performance and human relations as the two most critical components of a subordinate's success or failure. On any job you have, it will be important for you to build positive interpersonal relationships with co-workers as well as managers.

How do you get along with teachers (management) and fellow students (co-workers)? If your first full-time job is working for an organization that operates as a team, getting along with co-workers will be a must. It is similar to playing a team sport, such as basketball. When team members cooperate, the team (co-workers) and the whole school (organization) benefit from the results. If one member of the team fails to do his or her share of the work and to participate in everyday practice (work life), enjoyment (job satisfaction) and winning (production) are negatively affected. As a new employee, you must be a good team player and cooperate with your co-workers to accomplish common goals.

▲ *Whether you are a white collar, blue collar, or no collar worker, lunchtime is a good time to build friendly relationships with coworkers.*

Friendly relationships with co-workers will take time. When you are a new employee, most co-workers will be polite. Some may be critical, though, or may simply ignore you. You will be expected to conform to their expectations. As members of your work team see you doing competent work and being reliable, they will begin to trust you as a worker. As you continue to be a trustworthy member of the team, personal acceptance will grow.

The Negative Side

You may not like all of your co-workers' personal habits. Some of the most annoying behaviors are these:

- Excessive and loud talking and laughing when you're trying to concentrate
- Constant throat clearing
- Constant humming, whistling, and singing
- Smoking in a nonsmoking area
- "Back-stabbing" (being nice to your face and criticizing you behind your back)
- Nervous picking at nose, ears, or skin irritations
- Unpleasant body or clothing odors

Remember that every coin has two sides. Co-workers will be equally offended or irritated if you demonstrate these types of behaviors. Can you think of additional behaviors that "turn you off?"

You may encounter some workers who are bitter and vindictive toward you or the organization. A typical comment from these people may express surprise that you joined such a "cheapskate" organization. Perhaps they wanted your job or recommended a personal friend for it. Their open rejection lets you know that they do not want a relationship with you. However, time and experience may change their negative attitude toward you.

Avoid being influenced by the negative attitudes of other workers. A negative co-worker may be prejudiced against your sex, race, religion, or ethnic (cultural) background. Whatever the cause, do not overreact. Just do your job and be prepared to communicate whenever the other person is ready. Refuse to be intimidated. It is in your favor to build a good but not close working relationship with this type of individual. He or she will probably loosen up and be receptive to your good manners after a few weeks or months. Have you ever had a relationship start off poorly but eventually

▲ *Loud talking and laughing are not appropriate when other workers are trying to concentrate. Save it for scheduled breaks and lunchtime.*

▲ *Being involved in leisure-time activities with coworkers will help you build personal relationships. Which of your leisure interests would you enjoy pursuing in an employee group?*

work out? If so, what happened to turn the relationship around?

All organizations, both large and small, have internal politics and rumor mills. Don't let these disrupt you. Rumors (unproved reports) are like stray dogs. If you don't feed them, they will probably go away. You may have a few gossips in your school. They thrive on creating and spreading rumors about fellow students and the school. Worrying over rumors and gossip that is beyond your control or might never happen takes energy away from important tasks. Can you think of a rumor that circulated through your school, had students upset, and turned out to be false?

On the job, try to avoid eating lunch or having coffee breaks with the workplace gossips. Be courteous and objective in conversations with them, but do not become so personally involved in their gossip that your feelings have a negative effect on your job performance or on relationships with others.

Building Relationships with Co-Workers

Being liked by others and belonging to groups that have a common purpose (school, church, club, or profession) are basic social needs of all people. You will begin to meet these needs on the job as you learn the names of your co-workers and enter into daily conversations with them.

In some instances, you may build personal relationships based on common interests outside the job as well as your experiences working together. You may share an interest in music, fishing, church, volunteer work, golf, or any of a number of leisure activities. With other co-workers, you may find that simple courtesies, such as talking about the weather or something to do with the job, will be the highest level of interpersonal relationship you can expect. Just as your relationships with family and friends are special, so, too, are your relationships with co-workers. They are in a position to provide you with encouragement, sympathy, and companionship on the job.

In Chapter 9, you learned to follow accepted protocol (business etiquette) to earn the respect of your supervisor. Use the same rules of etiquette to gain acceptance from co-workers. In some organizations, a new employee is expected to call co-workers by their formal names. In other organizations, first names are preferred. If you are not sure which is most acceptable, use formal names until you are asked to use first names. Showing respect for the wisdom and skill of senior co-workers will usually cause them to accept you personally and share their knowledge with you.

Effective interpersonal skills can be learned. Regular practice and experience using these skills will enhance your interpersonal relationships with family and friends as well as on the job.

Remember the Golden Rule: Do unto others as you would have others do unto you. How many words or phrases can you substitute for the word *do* in order to turn this into a golden rule for building positive interpersonal relationships? An example would be "Provide assistance unto others as you would have others provide assistance unto you."

Here are some questions you can ask yourself to find out how effective you are at getting along with others:

- Are you respectful of others? Do you allow for individual differences? Respect the experience and expertise of co-workers. Everyone is unique.
- Do you avoid starting or repeating rumors? Don't eavesdrop on private conversations or talk negatively about others. Be sure of your facts before you speak.
- Do you refuse to allow others to take advantage of you? Be assertive but not aggressive.
- Do you give credit where credit is due? When your work is praised by co-workers, acknowledge their work and praise them in return. We all like to be recognized and appreciated.

- Do you apologize when you are wrong? Co-workers will respect you more if you do.
- Are you sensitive to the problems of others? Be a good listener.
- Do you withhold your comments until the other person has finished speaking? Listen to all of the information before responding.
- Can you resolve personal conflicts between yourself and others quietly? Learn to accept other points of view, and compromise.
- Do you mind your own business? Avoid asking questions involving matters that are not related to your assignment.
- Do you mean what you say and say what you mean? Follow through with your promises as quickly as you can.
- Do you avoid making excuses? Learn to establish priorities and make time lines.
- Are you willing to do more than your share? All players on a winning team do more than their share.
- Do you have a sense of humor? Finding humor in a bad situation makes it less stressful. Co-workers always prefer laughter to complaints.
- Do you respond to others as you would like them to respond to you? Show a friendly, helpful, and sincere concern for your co-workers.

What were your responses? *If you answered "no" to any of these questions, think of ways to improve your human relations skills in those particular areas.*

CAREER TIP

Business protocol dictates that you contribute to customary coffee funds, gifts for co-workers, and flower funds. Your contribution shows others that you are part of the team and helps build positive relationships.

Resolving Conflicts

Conflicts and confrontations will always occur. These are usually nothing more than simple misunderstandings. No matter how serious the conflict, you must know how to handle yourself honorably.

Don't expect to resolve conflicts by blowing your cool and confronting your antagonist while you're angry. Angry people are more likely to say or do things they will regret at a later time. Don't embarrass the other person by making him or her look bad in front of others. Never make threats or call someone names. Try not to let differences build. If they do, repair them at the earliest possible moment. As soon as you realize that you have made a mistake, apologize. If at all possible, handle your problems with co-workers without involving your supervisor.

When you feel anger building, practice self-control. If the situation allows, say nothing and go to another area. Determine how your view of the situation may be different from the other people's by "walking in their shoes." Perhaps your expecta-

▲ *Apologizing for an honest mistake demonstrates your maturity and self-confidence.*

tions are unrealistic. Perhaps you don't understand the total situation. Don't prejudge. Tolerance and flexibility toward the individual differences of others will lessen conflict and promote harmony. Remember that no one is perfect. When you are wrong, admit it. When others are wrong, be tolerant.

Section 3 GET INVOLVED

Interview a relative or friend who has at least five years of full-time work experience. Write this person's answers to the following interview questions on a separate sheet of paper, and be prepared to discuss them in class.

1. Did you ever lose your temper with a co-worker and later regret it? Please explain.

2. Have any of your co-workers become good personal friends? If so, what do you think caused this friendship to grow? If not, why didn't your co-workers become personal friends?

3. What advice can you give to young people to help them get along with their co-workers?

Section
4

Career Advancement Through Promotion

Most Americans believe in the **work ethic**. This is the idea that America is the land of opportunity and that through hard work individuals can make their own success. For most people, this means **career advancement** (moving up in an organization) through promotions to higher level jobs. The increased income and prestige connected with career advancement can provide a great deal of personal satisfaction.

Career advances may be horizontal or vertical. In most organizations, career advancement is known as a **line of progression** (steps that employees follow from lower- to higher-level positions). Horizontal changes may result in higher pay or more personal challenge, but the jobs are considered to be on the same level.

Vertical changes result in higher pay and more authority. They are considered to be a promotion to a higher level. In terms of a management track, this is also know as the chain of command. For example, if you are hired as a grocery bagger in a supermarket, you might gain experience through a series of horizontal changes. These might include stock clerk, meat counter clerk, and cashier. After gaining a broad range of experience in the business, obtaining additional education and training, and demonstrating your ability and dependability, you might receive a vertical promotion to manager trainee.

▲ *Take a look at the photo. Where do you think the line of progression begins? ends?*

As you become familiar with a particular job and master the required skills, you can begin to look at ways to grow and achieve your next-highest career goal. Opportunities for promotion occur when

- someone is promoted and the vacant position must be filled
- someone leaves the organization
- a new position is created

In some organizations, openings are posted on a bulletin board. In others, management invites potential candidates to apply. Promotions are sometimes based on supervisor recommendations, and promotional opportunities are sometimes discovered by staying alert and networking with other employees.

In general, promotions are made from within an organization. This encourages employees to strive for high levels of performance and commitment to the job. Whether organizations promote from within or outside, they usually review all candidates for a position who apply and are qualified, not just those who are next in line for the position.

In organizations with a promotion-from-within policy, a student with a high school diploma in business/office education may begin at the entry level as an office assistant and eventually reach a supervisory or even management-level position. This person must improve his or her knowledge and skills by taking evening courses at a technical school or college, participating in relevant company-sponsored training programs, and perhaps by obtaining a two-year associate degree or even a four-year college diploma. Most promotions require a combination of continuing education and training, outstanding performance appraisals, and personal motivation.

Preparing Yourself for Promotions

The best predictor of future performance is past performance. For example, suppose that you are being considered for a promotion or more challenging career opportunity, the quality of work and attitude that you have displayed at your present job will be the main factors used to evaluate you for the new position.

In determining your readiness to compete for promotions, consider the values that large corporations frequently express. The following corporate values are listed in order, with 1 being most important. Which of these values are most like you? Which are least like you? Can you identify a time when you expressed these values?

1. Ability to take the initiative
2. Pride in performance
3. Self-confidence
4. Open-mindedness
5. Flexibility
6. Satisfaction in creating something new
7. Cooperativeness
8. Honesty
9. Coolness under stress
10. Pleasure in learning something new
11. Sense of humor
12. Loyalty to others
13. Openness and spontaneity
14. Independence
15. Friendliness
16. Attitude toward authority
17. Compassion
18. Generosity
19. Idealism

Mentoring

A **mentor** (a trusted advisor) can help you prepare for promotions and move up the chain of command. A mentor may be a boss or someone with whom you get along well. A mentor is like a special teacher. The mentor relationship is usually personal enough so that you can request feedback, ask questions, air misgivings, and get honest advice about how best to use your employment situation for personal career advancement. A mentor functions as a role model.

When the opportunity for a promotion occurs, you can expect competition. Co-workers with **seniority** (length of time spent with a company)

BUILDING SELF-ESTEEM

A Feeling of Pride

"Hector, you have earned this promotion to supervisor," Mrs. Watson Said. "Mr. Clark recommended you highly, and I have been very pleased with the progress you've made during your four years at MCS Manufacturing Systems." Mrs. Watson was the vice-president of manufacturing. Hector felt ten feet tall when she walked him to the door of her office and shook his hand again.

Hector Fermin was filled with excitement as he approached the door of the department manager, Donald Clark. He was eager to tell Don about his promotion to supervisor and to thank him for being such a great boss. Four years ago, when Hector started work as a machine operator, Mr. Clark was production supervisor. Now that was Hector's job.

The supervisor position opened up when Mr. Clark was promoted to department manager. Several employees were well qualified for the job, but only Hector had Mr. Clark's recommendation. That tipped the scales in his favor.

Although Mr. Clark was only six years older than Hector, he seemed like a combination of father and big brother on the job. Mr. Clark was one of the people who interviewed Hector for his first job with MCS. From the very beginning, Hector asked him for advice on shop problems and on what he could do to get ahead in his career. Hector always followed through on Mr. Clark's advice, and it helped him develop the skills he needed to become a senior machine operator. Hector and his wife had invited Mr. and Mrs. Clark to their house for dinner a few times, and Mr. Clark had invited them to his home. Hector and Mr. Clark went fishing together a couple of times every summer. In the privacy of Mr. Clark's office, they called each other "Don" and "Hector." In front of the other employees, though, it was always "Mr. Clark" and "Hector."

Hector planned to continue his career advancement. He knew that Mr. Clark would continue to be his mentor and friend. He also knew that if he received good performance evaluations as a supervisor and continued to learn from Mr. Clark, someday Mr. Hector Fermin would be the department manager.

Critical Thinking

1. To get a job promotion, what do you think is more important: what you know, who you know, or a combination of both? Explain your answer.
2. Why do you think Mr. Clark became a mentor to Hector rather than to some other employee?
3. If Mr. Clark had failed to train an employee for the position of supervisor, would he have been promoted? Explain your answer.

and proven loyalty to the organization are usually given first consideration. However, these qualities alone do not merit promotions. Competition will also include the evaluation of job skills, education and training, quality of work produced, personal initiative, interpersonal skills, positive attitude, proven reliability, and leadership potential.

If you apply, you will be evaluated in each of these areas in relation to the position requirements and the level of your competition. You will have to decide if you have the expertise to compete with more-experienced employees. You will also have to decide if you are ready for more responsibility and different duties.

Job Skills. Be prepared with the necessary education and training. Attend company-sponsored seminars, participate in on-the-job training programs, or take classes at a community college, a vocational school, or a four-year college or university. Decide which job skills you need to improve, and work on improving them. Join a professional or trade association.

Performance. Prepare for the job of your immediate boss. Observe your boss's leadership qualities and the methods he or she uses to inspire confidence, obtain cooperation, and make effective decisions.

The quantity and quality of your work performance are important considerations. High-quality work is critical, but it is also important to complete the work on time, especially on an assembly line or a construction site. Frequently review your job performance. Compare the quality of your work to that of your co-workers. Is it better, worse, or about the same?

Be visible to people in management positions. Make sure that they know your name, are aware of your interest in career advancement, and hear about your successes on the job. They are in positions of power and will decide who gets promoted and who doesn't.

In some jobs, levels of productivity are not easily measured. What could you do to be considered exceptional as a secretary or as a mechanic?

Human Relations Skills. Build good working relationships with co-workers and management. Reread the section in this chapter titled "Getting Along with Co-Workers."

Conformity to the Organization's Values. Make fitting in with the organization and all levels of employees a top personal priority. Learn all there is to know about the organization. Make a pact with yourself to be committed to doing your very best for the company. Carry out orders cheerfully, be honest and loyal, and put the needs of the organization ahead of personal plans that can be rescheduled. Demonstrate initiative by volunteering for new responsibilities and doing more than is expected.

▲ *The quantity and quality of Saleema's work and her working relations with co-workers and management is excellent. She is attending night school to qualify for a promotion.*

Disadvantages of Promotions

There may be some disadvantages to being promoted. If you become the team leader or supervisor of your former co-workers, personal relationships will change. Before the promotion you could overlook a co-worker who takes extra long breaks. In the role of supervisor or team leader, however, you must deal with this problem as a violation of company rules. If you are a junior (less-

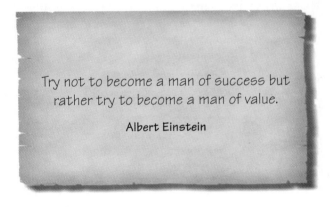

Try not to become a man of success but rather try to become a man of value.

Albert Einstein

▲ *Laura was promoted to "data control team leader" six months ago. She works about an hour beyond quitting time each evening. Her working over usually eliminates the need to take work home.*

experienced) employee, senior employees may resent you.

It may be necessary for you to spend time beyond your required working hours to complete certain jobs effectively. You will be evaluated and criticized by the employees who work for you, by those who are at your level, and by your boss. Will you be ready to accept these disadvantages?

Managing Your Time

Time is irreversible. It cannot be saved, but it can be used wisely. Have you ever heard the expression "just killing time?" For a business, killing time can mean the difference between profit and loss, growth and layoffs.

Time management is planning ahead to make the best use of your time. This requires knowing what needs to be done, setting priorities, planning the work, and completing projects in the time allotted. As an employee, you will be expected to use your time wisely.

Observe how co-workers and supervisors manage their time, schedule priorities, and handle interruptions. Use what you learn to identify how your time is wasted and how it could be better managed. Learning good time management will result in greater satisfaction and accomplishment both at work and in your personal life.

Section 4 GET INVOLVED

Answer the following on a separate sheet of paper, and be prepared to discuss your responses in class.

1. Managing time is important in both your personal life and your work life. Start now to manage time to your best advantage.

   a. Analyze your use of time over a one-day period by listing your activities in fifteen-minute intervals from the time you get up in the morning until you go to bed at night. (Do not include your sleeping time.)

   b. Review your log after a period of one day. Cross out all the activities that you now feel were unnecessary.

   c. Rank the ten most important activities you did during the day, with 1 being most important. Which activities would you like to spend more time doing? Which activities could take the place of those you crossed out as unnecessary?

   d. List the specific ways you could save time in your daily schedule.

   e. Based on the results of your log. are you a time waster or a time saver?

   f. Now that you have reviewed your first log, plan your day tomorrow. Be sure that your plan includes priorities and allows for schedule changes. Commit yourself to sticking to your new priorities and going back to them when you get sidetracked. Check your new plan at the end of the day.

Section 5

Labor Unions

At the close of the Civil War in 1865, a great change was taking place in America's world of work. Handmade products that had been produced by skilled craftsmen for hundreds of years were being produced in factories. Unable to compete with the factories, the craftsmen were forced to seek employment as factory workers. Children were frequently expected to work full-time jobs for very low wages. A working day of ten hours or more and weekly wages of ten dollars or less were common. Working conditions in factories, sweat shops, and mines were frequently unhealthy and dangerous. American workers struggled against these conditions.

During these years of struggle, numerous **labor unions** (organizations that represent workers in negotiations regarding employee rights) were formed by various segments of the American labor force. Among the goals of these unions were:

- Elimination of child labor
- Elimination of laws used to break up unions
- Acceptance of the principle of collective bargaining
- Establishment of state and federal bureaus of labor
- Passing of workman's compensation laws
- Eight-hour workday

American workers achieved a national unity during the early decades of the twentieth century when a flood of legislation from the federal government established the right of workers to negotiate with their employers for a fair wage and a safe work environment. America's labor relations and collective bargaining practices matured during labor's struggle for recognition in the Great Depression of the 1930s. They flourished in the heyday of high productivity and market suprema-

▲ *In the early 1900s, a living wage and worker safety were the major goals of most labor unions.*

Getting More Information

For information about careers in arbitration and other aspects of dispute resolution, contact

American Arbitration Association
140 West 51st St.
New York, NY 10021.

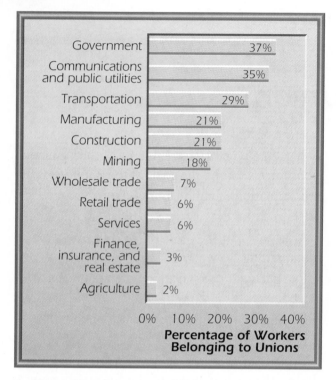

▲ *Figure 10.4 Percentage of Union Members in Various Types of Employment, 1990.*

cy that characterized the nation's dominant position in the world's economy after World War II. Membership in labor unions peaked in 1975. In that year, labor unions represented 35 percent of all American workers. By 1991, the situation had changed, and less than 17 percent of workers belonged to labor unions.

Figure 10.4 depicts union members as a percentage of all employed wage and salary workers in various groups. Why do you think such a small percentage of agricultural workers belong to unions? Why are there so many union members in transportation? Why has the percentage of union workers in manufacturing declined?

The National Labor Relations Board

The National Labor Relations Board **(NLRB)** is an independent federal agency that was established in 1935 to administer the National Labor

Relations Act (NLRA), the nation's principal labor relations law. This act generally applies to all interstate commerce except railroads and airlines. (These two industries are covered by the Railway Labor Act.)

The purpose of the NLRA is to serve the public interest by reducing interruptions in commerce caused by industrial conflict. It does this by providing orderly processes for protecting and implementing the rights of employees, employers, and unions in their relations with one another. The purpose of the National Labor Relations Board is to administer, interpret, and enforce this act.

The U.S. courts of appeals hand down some 350 decisions each year related to the enforcement and/or review of NLRB orders in unfair labor practice proceedings. Of these, about 85 percent favor the NLRB in whole or in part.

Collective Bargaining

With the exception of minimum legal standards, the employer in a nonunion organization sets the level of wages and the hours of labor and establishes production quotas for workers. When promotions or pay raises are involved, the employer can reward favorites and ignore qualified workers with longer service. If work is slow, the employer in nonunion organizations can layoff whomever he or she chooses.

GETTING MORE INFORMATION

For additional information concerning the legal rights of workers, write to:
National Labor Relations Board
1717 Pennsylvania Ave.
Washington, D.C. 20270.

▲ *Sometimes a dispute between two parties must be settled by an independent arbitrator.*

The negotiating process between labor unions and employers is called **collective bargaining**. This negotiating process generally results in a written contract between the employer and the labor union. Collective bargaining was developed over the years as a method for introducing the ways of democracy into employer-employee relations.

In an organization that allows collective bargaining, individual workers are no longer subject to arbitrary decisions. They share with the employer the responsibility for establishing orderly procedures for determining wages, hours of work, rates of production, promotion and layoff policies, and fair penalties for the violation of necessary work rules.

When collective bargaining fails, the union may call for a vote, asking its membership for authority to strike. A union-authorized strike occurs when all members stop working and leave their jobs. This causes a loss in production or a curtailment of services to the employer. You may have seen striking workers carrying picket signs that say the union is on strike. When the labor union and the employer reach an agreement, a labor contract is signed by both the employer and labor union representatives. These contracts usually last for one to three years.

There are two kinds of labor-management disputes: (1) those resulting from differences of opinion over how contract provisions should be interpreted and (2) those resulting from differences over what provisions should be included in a new contract agreement.

Grievances

When **grievances** (differences of opinion over how contract provisions should be interpreted)

CAREER TIP

Unions exist to improve the standard of living of workers, to represent their members' varied work interests in dealings with employers, and to promote equity and social justice for all workers in society.

occur, the labor-management dispute is settled through the grievance process. Grievance procedures vary, but they always involve a method by which the individual workers can process a complaint through the union. The final appeal, in most contracts, consists of the company and the union submitting the issue to an impartial arbitrator (person chosen to settle a dispute). After hearing the evidence from both sides, the arbitrator issues a decision that is binding and legally enforceable for both sides.

Cooperating for the Future

Since the early 1970s, the country's industrial base, its work force, and the strength of foreign competition have changed dramatically. The rapid advance of technology has changed many of our traditional manufacturing processes. International competition has challenged U.S. supremacy in world markets, and a better-educated, demographically changing work force has compelled employers and unions to improve the quality of life both at work and at home.

To meet these social and economic challenges, workers and their unions, management, and government have begun to forge more cooperative and productive relationships through numerous organizations. Unions are working with manage-

▲ *Unions, management, and government are forming more cooperative relationships to meet the challenges presented by foreign competition for products, services, and jobs.*

ment to improve the economic performance of American enterprises and to help firms adapt to changes in technology, market conditions, and worker values and expectations. Where management has been receptive and where workers' interests have been adequately reflected, unions have increasingly shown a willingness to work with management for the overall success of the enterprise.

Section 5 GET INVOLVED

Answer the following on a separate sheet of paper, and be prepared to discuss your responses in class.

1. Check the yellow pages of your telephone book under the heading "Labor Organizations." How many are listed? Which are craft unions? Industrial unions? Service unions? Contact one of these unions, and invite a union representative to speak to your class. Find out why some industries are heavily unionized and others are not. Find out why membership in some unions has declined while in others it has risen.

2. Discuss union membership with a friend or relative who has been working full-time for at least three years. List the ways this person feels unions help workers, and list the reasons he or she dislikes unions.

3. If you join a union, you will be expected to pay an initiation fee when you join. You will also have to pay regular dues as a condition of membership. What is the initiation fee and monthly dues for membership in the unions in your area?

Health and Safety in the Workplace

More than 3,500 workers die each year in job-related accidents. More than 6 million lose time because of injuries that happen on the job. If you are unable to earn a living because of an accident or a health problem, the outcome will be the same: Your career and your lifestyle will be disrupted. Do you know anyone who has had a job-related accident? What effect did the accident have on his or her career and lifestyle?

Many of the factors involved in personal health and safety can be controlled. For example, these guidelines apply if you are a user of a video display terminal (VDT):

1. Understand the potential hazards.

    More than 26 million people use VDTs. Many of these users are concerned about VDT-related maladies. The problems stem from electromagnetic radiation, repetitive motion, injuries, postural problems, and stress.

2. Learn safe ways to perform tasks.

    In most cases, minor adjustments can reduce or eliminate the trouble.

3. Apply what you know in hazardous situations.

    You can take responsibility for reducing workstation discomfort at work or at school by practicing the tips listed in Figure 10.5 on page 220.

Preventing Accidents on the Job

Most people are familiar with the old saying, "An ounce of prevention is worth a pound of cure." This is certainly true when you consider that the majority of accidents in the workplace are due to human, rather than work-site, causes. In particular, the factor of worker experience is involved in more job-related accidents than any other single factor. A major study by the Bureau of Labor Statistics reported that 48 percent of injured workers had been on the job less than one year.

Another study showed that employees who are injured at work often lack information to protect themselves. For example,

- Nearly one of every five workers injured while operating power saws said that no safety training had been provided.
- Of 868 workers who suffered head injuries, 71 percent said that they had no instruction concerning hard hats.
- Of 554 workers hurt while servicing equipment, 61 percent said that they were not informed about procedures to shut off electrical or mechanical components.

In nearly every type of injury studied, the same story was repeated. Workers often do not receive the safety information they need, even on jobs involving dangerous equipment.

Workers with a poor attitude toward safety are more likely to be involved in accidents. They are usually irresponsible and often quick to anger.

CAREER TIP

Be sure that you understand all necessary safety measures before you start a work task. If the explanation is unclear, ask again.

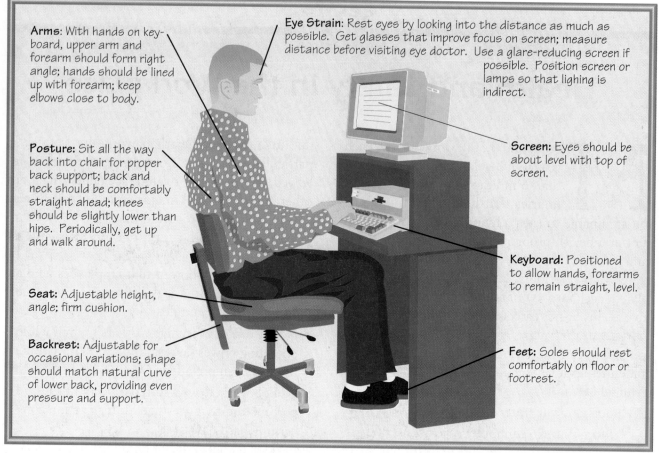

Arms: With hands on keyboard, upper arm and forearm should form right angle; hands should be lined up with forearm; keep elbows close to body.

Eye Strain: Rest eyes by looking into the distance as much as possible. Get glasses that improve focus on screen; measure distance before visiting eye doctor. Use a glare-reducing screen if possible. Position screen or lamps so that lighing is indirect.

Posture: Sit all the way back into chair for proper back support; back and neck should be comfortably straight ahead; knees should be slightly lower than hips. Periodically, get up and walk around.

Screen: Eyes should be about level with top of screen.

Seat: Adjustable height, angle; firm cushion.

Keyboard: Positioned to allow hands, forearms to remain straight, level.

Backrest: Adjustable for occasional variations; shape should match natural curve of lower back, providing even pressure and support.

Feet: Soles should rest comfortably on floor or footrest.

▲ *Figure 10.5 Video Display Terminal Health and Fitness.*

Both of these personal characteristics are dangerous in the workplace.

Worker fatigue (exhaustion) can also be a factor in accidents. Fatigue can be brought about by lack of sleep, working extra long shifts, or poor health.

Using alcohol or drugs on the job causes serious accidents. An ongoing study, the National Longitudinal Survey of Youth, has found the following:

- The incidence of drug use on the job among U.S. workers aged 19 to 27 is 7 percent.
- White men aged 19 to 23 report the highest use of drugs in the workplace.
- Blue-collar workers have higher rates of drug use than white-collar workers.

- Drug use is most common among young workers in the entertainment, recreation, and construction industries.
- Drug use is least common among young workers in professional services and public administration.
- Operatives in the transportation industry have a relatively high rate of workplace drug use. (This is notable in light of the recent tragic accidents in the transportation industry that have been attributed to drugs.)

Drug and alcohol use in the workplace is a great concern of employers and consumers. They fear that workers who engage in this type of activity on the job will be less productive, more likely to steal, and more likely to cause accidents than workers who do not use drugs or alcohol on the job.

Many firms have employee assistance programs that attempt to identify and provide treatment to workers with drug and alcohol problems before the addiction becomes a hindrance to health, family life, or the job. Parenting and marital problems, financial difficulty, work conflicts, and emotional stress are frequently related to drug and alcohol abuse. The Bureau of Labor Statistics estimates that in 1988, 30 percent of all workers had access to an employee assistance program.

The Occupational Safety and Health Act.

Congress passed the Occupational Safety and Health Act of 1970 to ensure, as far as possible, safe working conditions for the labor force. This federal law requires every American employer to provide a safe and healthful workplace. To carry out this law, the Occupational Safety and Health Administration (**OSHA**) encourages employers to work with employees to eliminate job safety and health hazards.

OSHA has approximately 1,200 federal inspectors to cover 6.5 million workplaces. The inspectors respond to complaints and conduct about 45 thousand random and scheduled inspections annually. If OSHA inspectors find health and safety violations, employers must correct those hazards within fixed time limits and may have to pay fines.

Despite this diligence, inspections sometimes don't occur often enough to save lives. A tragic fire at a food-processing plant in North Carolina killed twenty-five people and injured at least fifty-five in the early 1990s. The building had not been inspected in at least eleven years, according to union officials. Employees and witnesses said that one exit was locked and one was temporarily blocked by a truck; these were clear violations of

▲ *Do you understand the rights and responsibilities of employers and workers? Employers are required to post certain government notices regarding health, safety, and other workplace issues.*

Solving The Problem

A Healthy Choice?

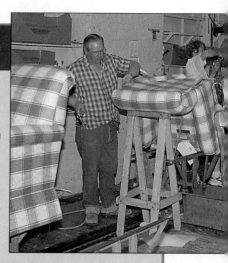

John Dent's headache is worse than usual as he steps into the hot shower after his shift. The fumes from the adhesive (glue) that he paints on the seam of each piece of fabric passing him on the production line always seem to give him a headache. Sampson Manufacturing is a very old company with outdated equipment, but the work is steady and the pay is good. John had mentioned the problem with the fumes to the foreman before but was quickly told to quit if he didn't like working there. His union representative told him that Mr. Sampson had threatened to shut down the plant the last time the workers complained about health and safety conditions.

A lot of thoughts go through John's mind as he dresses to go home. Should he report the problem to a safety agency like OSHA? The address is on the employee bulletin board. Should he bring it up at the next union meeting? Maybe they will think he is a wimp. Should he look for a new job? He can't take many more of these headaches.

Critical Thinking

1. How can John be sure that his health and safety are in jeopardy?
2. If he decides to report the problem, will Mr. Sampson really shut down the plant? Explain your answer.
3. How would you answer the questions on John's mind?

OSHA standards for building exits. Given the responsibilities of the act and considering its limited number of inspectors, what do you think OSHA should do to prevent tragedies like the one in North Carolina?

GETTING MORE INFORMATION

To register a complaint with OSHA, write to
  Occupational Safety and Health
     Administration
  U.S. Department of Labor
  Washington, DC 20210.

OSHA requires manufacturers to inform their employees about hazardous chemicals they are exposed to in the workplace. Numerous cities and states also have enacted laws that require all employers to inform their employees about any toxic substances in the workplace.

The National Labor Relations Board also has ruled that the names of chemicals and other substances that workers are exposed to in the workplace must be given to unions that request this information. One aerospace employer faced lawsuits seeking nearly one and a half billion dollars on behalf of about 250 current and former workers who claimed that they were exposed to toxic chemicals.

If you believe unsafe or unhealthful conditions exist at your workplace, you have the right to file a complaint requesting an inspection. If there is a poster about the state or federal health and safety law at your workplace, you should file your com-

▲ *In past years, workers could easily identify health and safety problems in the workplace. Exposure to invisible fumes and chemicals are a major health hazard for today's worker.*

plaint with the agency indicated. If there is no poster, file your complaint with OSHA.

OSHA will withhold the names of complainants on request. If you are discharged or otherwise discriminated against for exercising your rights under this law, you may file a discrimination complaint with OSHA within thirty days of the discriminatory action.

If you are concerned about the health effects of exposure to a particular substance or working condition, you can request a health hazard evaluation of your workplace by the National Institute for Occupational Safety and Health (NIOSH).

Violent Crime and Worker Safety

Thousands of workers are endangered each year when violent crime strikes their workplace. Gas station attendants, workers in eating and drinking establishments, and convenience store clerks are especially vulnerable. These innocent workers are sometimes injured or even killed during robberies.

Workers should not try to apprehend criminals or to defend the workplace during a robbery. This should be left to professional law enforcement officers. Criminals are often inexperienced and frightened or are using alcohol or drugs. They are quick to use a knife or gun if they feel threatened by a worker or if they suspect a worker is trying to remember what they look like. Read the following suggestions. Which would be the most difficult for you to do? Which would be the easiest?

1. Don't maintain direct eye contact with robbers. They will assume that you are trying to form a description of them for the police.

2. Do try to determine the sex, height, weight, race, and any speech accent of the robbers with very short glances and by listening.

3. Don't resist the robbers in the name of false courage.

4. Do give them what they ask for. Be cooperative.

5. Don't follow the robbers out the door.

6. Do try to identify the type, age, and color of the robbers' car, which way it is parked (could indicate where they came from), and which way they go—if you can do so without exposing yourself to danger. Any license numbers you see will help.

Stress as a Job Hazard

Stress can cause physical and emotional illness that affects work and home life. Stress puts special negative demands on the body's responses and emotions. Health problems like ulcers, emotional exhaustion, high blood pressure, headaches, alcoholism, and even heart disease may result from job stress. Stress is a severe strain on personal endurance and feelings and is unique to each individual. Nearly 66 percent of companies with 750 or more employees now have stress-control programs in effect because they realize the seriousness of the problem.

High-stress jobs are generally characterized by the following conditions:

- Chronic, unrelenting demands, such as an overbearing boss
- A pace of work controlled by something other than the workers, such as a machine
- Constant concern for safety, such as the loss of customers' lives if work tasks are not performed properly
- Conflicts with co-workers, such as harassment or opposing views on issues

The effects of job stress frequently spill over into other formerly pleasurable aspects of life, such as family and leisure time. When this happens, it is difficult to escape stress and get relief. Has anything at school ever caused you a great deal of stress? What effect did it have on you emotionally and physically?

Recognizing the early signs of stress and doing something to relieve the stress can have a dramatic impact on your personal well-being. One of the keys is to identify the situations and

▲ *The mental stress of being responsible for the safety of several aircraft and their passengers can be exhausting for an air traffic controller. During busy dining periods, a waiter is under pressure to serve customers quickly and efficiently.*

events that are causing the stress and then to work on solutions. Stress is so personal that what may be relaxing to one person may be stressful to another.

Exercise is a very effective way to deal with the problem of stress. Physical activity helps bring the body back to a normal hormone balance. It relieves pent-up tensions and stretches tight muscles. Exercise also releases special hormones, called endorphins, that promote a sense of well-being.

Sharing stress through communication, knowing your limits, managing time efficiently, being assertive, taking short rest breaks, taking care of yourself through proper diet, and making time for fun also relieve stress for most people. How does stress affect you? What do you do to reduce personal stress?

Study the list in Figure 10.6 of the ten most stressful jobs. What conditions of high stress are found in each of the jobs listed?

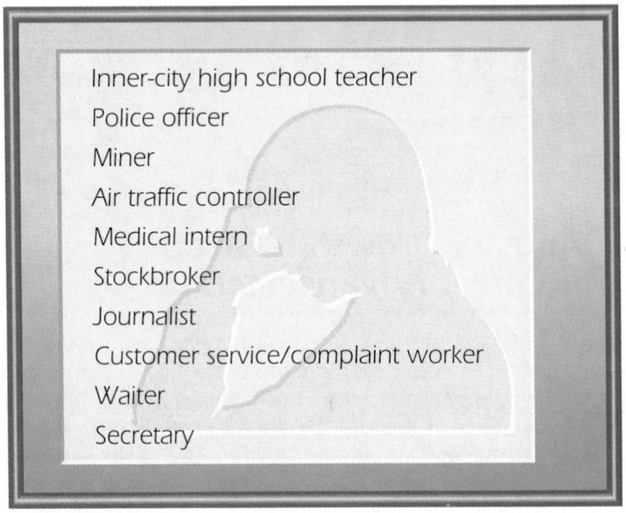

Inner-city high school teacher
Police officer
Miner
Air traffic controller
Medical intern
Stockbroker
Journalist
Customer service/complaint worker
Waiter
Secretary

▲ *Figure 10.6 The Ten Most Stressful Jobs in the United States.*

Section 6 GET INVOLVED

Answer the following on a separate sheet of paper, and be prepared to discuss your response in class.

1. More than one million workers suffer neck injuries each year, and back injuries account for one of every five workplace injuries or illnesses. Further, one-fourth of all compensation claims involve back injuries, which cost industry billions of dollars each year. Factors that can help reduce these injuries include better job design (ergonomics), training in lifting techniques, physical conditioning, and mechanical aids.

   Imagine that you are an employer and that you are starting a "safe lifting" training program for your employees. You plan to include workers from manufacturing, office, cafeteria, and warehouse areas. Employees will vary in their age, sex, body size, state of health, and general physical fitness. Write a paragraph describing the activities you would include in your program. How would you allow for the wide variety of employees enrolled in the program?

IMPORTANT FACTS

Industry Growth a Factor in Career Advancement

Career advancement can occur more quickly in expanding industries than in slow-growth or no-growth industries. New jobs in these industries mean additional staff. Once you identify a growth industry, it is important to select an organization within that industry that is successful. Listed below are the projected changes in employment for various industries from 1988 to 2000:

Service-producing Industries

Services, up 28.1 percent

Retail trade, up 19.7 percent

Finance, insurance, and real
  estate, up 16.3 percent

Wholesale trade, up 15.1 percent

Transportation and utilities, up 9.9 percent

Goods-producing Industries

Construction, up 14.8 percent

Agriculture, up 5.5 percent

Manufacturing, down 1.6 percent

Mining, down 2.2 percent

Government, up 6.6 percent

Source: U.S. Bureau of Labor Statistics, *Occupational Outlook Handbook*, 1990–91 edition.

Study Your Spelling and Grammar

In a recent study, 200 executives rated the importance of correct spelling and grammar in terms of career advancement opportunities:

Very important, 59 percent

Important, 39 percent

Unimportant, 2 percent

Source: Robert Half International.

Grievance Categories

Listed below are the matters over which employees file the most contract grievances:

- Denied sick benefits
- Discipline
- Discrimination
- Evaluation
- Excused and complimentary time
- Grievance process
- Miscellaneous
- Pay
- Performance
- Safety
- Scheduling
- Suspension
- Termination
- Training
- Transfer
- Union representation
- Vacation
- Work out of classification

Drug Testing

Drug testing was conducted by 63 percent of the firms surveyed by the American Management Association in 1991. About one-third of the companies with testing programs said that they fire workers who test positive, though often only as a last resort, and 96 percent refuse to hire applicants who test positive.

Accident Causes

Accidents resulting in personal injury or property damage normally have three cause levels: basic, indirect, and direct. An accident results when a person or object receives an amount of energy (heat, sound, hits a solid object) or hazardous material (fumes or toxic substances) that cannot be absorbed safely. This energy or hazardous material is the direct cause of the accident.

The direct cause is the result of one or more unsafe acts by a worker, unsafe working conditions, or both. These unsafe acts and conditions are the indirect causes (symptoms) of the accident.

The indirect cause is usually the result of poor management policies and decisions or personal or environmental factors. These are considered the basic causes. Most accidents can be prevented by eliminating one or more causes.

Source: U.S. Department of Labor. Safety Manual #10.

CHAPTER 10 REVIEW

ENRICH YOUR VOCABULARY

On a separate sheet of paper, number from 1 to 19, and complete the following activity. (Do not write in your textbook.) Match each statement below with the most appropriate term from the "Enrich Your Vocabulary" list at the beginning of the chapter by writing that term next to the correct statement.

1. The lowest level of experience for the job
2. The guidelines that an organization's management establishes for behavior and job performance
3. Belief that through hard work individuals make their own success
4. An employee who follows someone else's orders
5. Steps that employees follow from lower to higher positions
6. A supervisor in a team-oriented management system
7. A group of workers who identify and solve quality problems
8. People who work together as equals
9. The negotiating process between labor unions and employers
10. A person in an organization who gives orders to others
11. National Labor Relations Board
12. Differences of opinion over how contract provisions should be interpreted
13. Length of time spent with an organization
14. Moving up in an organization
15. Planning ahead to make the best use of your time
16. Occupational Safety and Health Administration
17. Organizations that represent workers in negotiations
18. A group of employees
19. A trusted advisor

CHECK YOUR KNOWLEDGE

On a separate sheet of paper, complete the following activity. (Do not write in your textbook.)

1. Why are businesses or organizations created?
2. What is the term used to describe management decisions that establish guidelines for personal behavior and job performance?
3. In a corporation, who directs the activities of other employees?
4. What are the three management levels most often found in organizations?
5. Which management system most encourages worker interdependence and group problem solving?
6. What is the purpose of constructive criticism?
7. What is the most frequent reason people quit or lose their jobs?
8. What do managers consider to be the two most critical components of a subordinate's success?
9. Would a job change from cashier to supervisor be a vertical or horizontal change?
10. If you expect to be promoted to a more important and better-paying job, what must you demonstrate to your employer?
11. What are the three most important characteristics that corporations consider when they promote employees?
12. Why were labor unions created?

DEVELOP SCANS COMPETENCIES

Government experts say that successful workers can productively use Resources, Interpersonal skills, Information, Systems, and Technology. This activity will give you practice in developing Information and System skills.

Talk with a friend or family member about the organizational structure of their place of employment. Using the information they give you, develop an organizational chart of that business. Or, you may develop an organizational chart of your school. A simple chart is given here as an example.

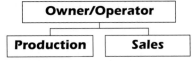

Owner/Operator	
Production	**Sales**

CHAPTER 11

Roles, Rights, and Responsibilities

Learning Objectives

After completing this chapter, you should be prepared to:

- explain the purpose and process of job performance appraisals
- list examples to demonstrate the financial, legal, and moral importance of business ethics
- discuss your legal employment rights and the federal rules and regulations that protect them
- describe various work schedule options and explain the reasons for having them
- list four major characteristics of a bureaucracy and describe its role in a complex society

Enrich Your Vocabulary

In reading this chapter and doing the exercises you will learn the following important terms:

merit rating	insider abuse
Equal Pay Act of 1963	workers' compensation laws
Civil Rights Act of 1964	Social Security Act
ethics	fringe benefits
whistle blowing	parenting leave
monopolies	credit unions
antitrust laws	contingent workers
price fixing	flextime
	workshops

What role will you play in the world of work? Who will evaluate your performance? Will you make fair and honest decisions during your career? Will you be treated with honesty and fairness?

When did you first hear about the Golden Rule? Unfortunately, the major interest of some people is to acquire personal gain at the expense of

Do unto others as you would have others do unto you.

The Golden Rule

their fellow workers and society. Their idea of the Golden Rule is "The person with the most gold rules." This unfortunate fact of human nature has caused state and federal governments to legislate (make laws) to protect your rights as a worker. State and federal laws regulate over such things as fringe benefits, compensation (payment for loss or injury), and work schedules.

Do you plan to be a leader in the world of work? If so, what philosophy will you use to make important management decisions? How should large organizations be managed? Would society be better off if we kicked out all of the bureaucrats and went back to the way organizations were managed in "the good old days"?

You have probably heard these issues being discussed at home. Perhaps you raised them yourself. As you read and discuss the information in this chapter, consider all of the different points of view.

Section
1

Employers Evaluate Performance

Employers have the right to evaluate the work performance of their employees. Most employers use a performance appraisal to measure and evaluate a worker's accomplishments over a specific period of time. The appraisal is conducted in terms of the worker's job description and the employer's goals. During your career, expect your performance appraisal to be scheduled annually and conducted by your immediate boss. As a new employee, you will probably be evaluated more often. Information contained in your performance appraisal will become part of your employer's permanent records.

Performance appraisals are not new. As far back as the third century A.D., emperors of China employed an "imperial rater" to revaluate the per-

formance of official family members. In the early 1800s, Robert Wen, owner of cotton mills in Scotland, established the first performance appraisals in industry by hanging a cube of colored wood over each employee's workstation. The color of the wood represented each worker's performance level. In the United States, performance appraisals were used as early as 1813 by General Lewis Cass of the U.S. Army. He submitted to the War Department an evaluation of each man under his command. General Cass described his men in such colorful terms as "a good natured man" or "a knave despised by all."

The Civil Rights Act of 1964 and the Equal Employment Opportunity Commission (EEOC), formed in 1966, established guidelines for the reg-

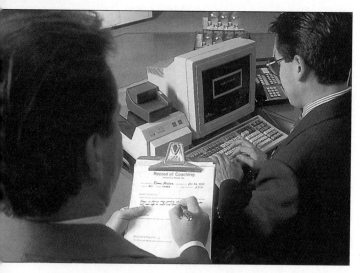

▲ *Measurement and evaluation of performance are a part of an employee's permanent record just as evaluation of academic performance is part of a student's permanent record. How high would an employer rate your student performance?*

ulation of employment selection procedures. The act and the EEOC placed strong legal pressure on employers to use performance appraisal systems that are fair to all employees.

Purpose of Evaluation

In one way or another, the degree of your career success will be measured. In a large organization, your boss might use a standard evaluation form and established procedures to evaluate your work performance. In a small organization, your evaluation might be your boss's personal observations and informal discussions with you about your job. In both cases, evaluation judgments will influence management decisions regarding your

- promotion to a better job
- salary increase
- possible discharge (firing)
- transfer to a different job or department
- admission into a training program

The amount of money you will be paid usually depends on your measured output (the quantity of work you produce) or on your **merit rating** (a formal, periodic, written evaluation of your job performance). How the information in a performance appraisal will be used is determined by the employer or, in the case of a union shop, by a contract between workers and the employer.

Evaluators must be objective (not allow personal feelings to interfere) if they are to evaluate employees accurately. If an employee is rated against others, as in the case of measured output, the rating must be put in numerical terms.

Graham Mathews' employer is very concerned that assemblers put together high-quality control boxes. The sale of defective products could result in the loss of important contracts with the aerospace industry or could be the cause of a major accident. Graham's employer uses the following rating sheet (see example below) to determine each assembler's accuracy. The rating is based on the amount of work that passes inspection the first time and doesn't require rebuilding.

Name __Graham Mathews__   Date __6-6-95__ Job Title __Electronics Assembler Dept.G__

- ☒ 95–100%   Consistently error-free
- ☐ 90–95%   High quality—seldom makes errors
- ☐ 85–90%   Satisfactory quality—meets expected standards
- ☐ 75–85%   Below average quality—must show improvement within 30 days
- ☐ Below 75% Quality is unacceptable—retrain or separate employee

Rating sheets are not appropriate for all employers. For example, the owner-operator of a small business wouldn't necessarily need a rating sheet to evaluate an employee's performance. It would probably be more efficient to use personal, daily contact to evaluate such factors as the worker's attendance and punctuality, attitude, and productivity.

In one survey, employers were asked about improvements they believed are needed in a variety of areas that prepare people for entry into full-time work. Employers were asked to base their responses on only those entry-level jobs for which education and training can normally be acquired in high school or through labor programs. Much of what employers had to say can be applied to practically any entry-level job. Employers selected the following areas as those in which improvement is most needed, in order of importance:

1. Concern for productivity
2. Pride of craftsmanship and quality work
3. Responsibility and ability to follow through on assigned tasks
4. Dependability
5. Work habits
6. Attitude toward the employer
7. Ability to write and speak effectively
8. Ability to follow instructions
9. Ability to read and apply printed information to the job
10. Ambition, motivation, and desire to get ahead

Source: Texas Advisory Council for Vocational Education

The Evaluation Meeting

After the first few months of a new job or at the completion of your probation period, your supervisor will probably schedule a meeting to discuss your work record to date. Advance scheduling will allow you time to prepare. The purpose of the meeting will be to discuss your strengths and weaknesses.

CAREER TIP

Good job performance appraisals are important. If you leave your current job for any reason, potential employers will usually check with your past employers to find out about the quality of your work.

Every job has certain critical performance areas. For example, an office clerk should expect his filing and typing skills to be evaluated. An autobody mechanic should expect the quality of her sanding skills and finish work to be evaluated. Ask your supervisor what aspects of your job performance will be appraised, how information will be collected, and how the information will be used. Make a list of what you want to learn from the evaluation meeting that will benefit you on the job. For example, you may wish to know specific ways to improve your performance.

You may be nervous about the evaluation meeting. This is normal and to be expected. At the beginning of the meeting, your supervisor will probably explain the appraisal process. This will avoid future misunderstandings. Then your supervisor will fill out a written form that lists the job criteria. Next, the two of you will discuss your evaluation. You will probably be asked to rate your own performance. Be prepared to emphasize your successes, personal strengths, and skills. (Figure 11.1 on page 233 shows a typical performance appraisal.)

Listen carefully to suggestions your supervisor makes about how you can improve your performance. Be frank and open in this discussion. If your supervisor recommends that you improve your work, don't let hurt feelings cause you to display resentment. Becoming angry or arguing with your supervisor about the conclusion he or she has reached about your performance is definitely not appropriate. If factual errors are made, such as stating that you have been absent from work seven

▲ *The supervisor and employee discuss the performance appraisal. A smart employee listens carefully to suggestions to improve in areas of weak performance, then works to improve in these areas. How is this different from a teacher's appraisal of a school subject?*

days and you are certain it has been less, make the correction tactfully.

Remember that your supervisor's role is to evaluate your performance. It is your responsibility to perform at minimum standards or above.

If your supervisor focuses on your weaknesses, try to profit from the criticism and become a better worker by improving in those areas mentioned. If your supervisor points out your weaknesses but doesn't make any recommendations to help you improve, ask for suggestions.

If you disagree with your evaluation, ask your supervisor for permission to respond to the points of disagreement. Be prepared to back up your position with supportive information. Be calm, open, and prepared to resolve differences in a mature way.

Your supervisor may schedule a follow-up meeting at which you will be asked how you are improving your weak points. Be prepared to show specific examples that demonstrate your improvement. For example, suppose a trainee in restaurant management receives a U (unsatisfactory) for her communication skills. Under comments, she is told to use less slang when speaking with customers. In the follow-up meeting, the supervisor will want to discuss her improvement or lack of improvement using verbal skills.

Plan immediately to improve the areas in which you have shown weakness. Make it your business to show improvement before the next evaluation meeting. This will demonstrate your commitment and responsibility to doing a good job.

RMJ Industrial Products, Inc.
Division of Personnel Employment
Employee Evaluation

Employee's name ___Margaret Reynolds___   Position held ___Machine Operator___

Years under my supervision ___2___   Total years of RMJ service ___2___

Column 1 to be used by the evaluator. Column 2 to be used by the employee in a self-appraisal, using this key: (O) outstanding, (VG) very good, (S) satisfactory, (NI) needs improvement, (U) unsatisfactory.

		Col 1	Col 2
1. Work performance	Demonstrates work skills needed for present assignments	O	VG
2. Communication	Communicates clearly with others using effective oral and written skills	VG	VG
3. Initiative	Sees what needs to be done and is judicious in doing it with or without direction	O	VG
4. Employee relations	Has a cooperative and open-minded attitude in working with others	O	S
5. Reliability	Is consistent, dependable, and accurate in carrying responsibilities to a successful conclusion	O	VG
6. Personality	Has a pleasant, cheerful disposition, shows enthusiasm, and has an appealing manner with co-workers	VG	S
7. Personal appearance	Grooming is neat and dress is appropriate	VG	VG
8. Stamina	Posture and bearing show evidence of energy and vitality in carrying out daily responsiblities	O	VG
9. Stability	Handles situations in a calm, objective manner	VG	S
10. Career growth	Seeks higher level skills through additional education and training	O	VG
11. Attendance pattern and punctuality	Has a good attendance record and meets responsibilities promptly	VG	S

Comments and Recommendations by Evaluator:

Margaret Reynolds started her employment with RMJ Industrial Products upon her graduation from high school. She has attended Tri-State Community College as a part-time student and has completed two years of study in accounting. She would like a permanent position in the Accounting Department. I would recommend her highly for the first available position.

Comments by Employee

I am presently attending school two evenings per week. It will take me two more years to complete my Associate degree in accounting. My present assignment has enabled me to pay for my education.

I am aware of the content of this evaluation.

Margaret Reynolds
Employee Signature

Joseph Michaels
Evaluator Signature

June 6, 1995
Date

Production Supervisor
Evaluator's Title

▲ *Figure 11.1 Sample Performance Appraisal.*

Section 2

The Matter of Ethics

A ship loaded with grain entered the harbor of a Middle Eastern nation that was suffering from a depressed economy. The grain harvest in this nation had been poor, the people needed food, and merchants were willing to pay far more than the grain was normally worth.

The businessman who owned the ship was aware that other ships would soon bring additional grain to the suffering city. Their arrival would cause the value of his grain to return to normal. Should the businessman tell the local merchants that additional grain would be available soon, or should he act quickly and sell his grain to the highest bidder? Why?

This event happened over a thousand years ago when a Greek trading ship entered the port of Rhodes. The question you have answered was presented to businessmen of ancient Rome by the philosopher Cicero. Cicero's answer—that the duty of any businessman is to make an honest and full disclosure—set ethical standards for business that are as appropriate for entrepreneurs today as they were for the Roman businessmen of Cicero's day.

The word **ethics** refers to the unwritten rules governing the code of values of a person, an organization, or a society. Ethics are the standards of conduct for what is believed to be right, the guiding morality (good) in each individual, organization, and society. Each day, you make decisions based on what you consider to be right. Your decisions are either ethical or unethical, moral or immoral. Organizations do the same.

Organizations establish ethical codes, or standards of conduct, that reflect the interests of the group they represent. For example, the ethical code of a police department might be the protec-

▲ *What responsibilities do you think the company importing these goods has to the community?*

▲ *When designing cars of the future, what should the designers be thinking about?*

tion of the people it serves. The ethical code of a major discount store might be customer satisfaction, and the ethical code of an automobile manufacturer might be public safety.

Unlike legal responsibilities, ethical responsibilities are not imposed from outside the organization, but from within. Once ethical standards are established and agreed on, all members or employees in that organization are expected to practice them. Figure 11.2 on the next page shows the policy statement of one company.

For a business to survive, its ability to earn a profit and its code of ethics must be compatible. Some automobile manufacturers have been accused, at one time or another, of concealing safety hazards. They have been required to recall millions of vehicles at great expense. Ethically, automobile manufacturers believe and state that safety is their first priority. However, safety costs must be added to manufacturing costs. If one manufacturer offers safety features, such as air bags or anti-lock brakes, and a major competitor offers the same features for a lower price, the first manufacturer must reduce prices to stay competitive. This could result in the use of less-expensive ma-

terials and manufacturing processes at the risk of reduced safety and quality.

News stories frequently report the unethical or at least questionable ethics of numerous American organizations, both public and private. The savings and loan (S&L) scandal, in which the fiscal irresponsibility exhibited by hundreds of S&L executives caused numerous institutions to go bankrupt, may be the largest financial disaster in American history. Fraud (misrepresentation of a product or service) and **insider abuse** (using knowledge obtained as a result of your position for personal gain) existed at every one of the failed savings and loan institutions.

John and Mary Lutz worked for thirty-five years for a major bakery. They retired with a small

CAREER TIP

Most employers conduct background checks before hiring new workers. Ethics, honesty, and integrity are prerequisites for positions of trust.

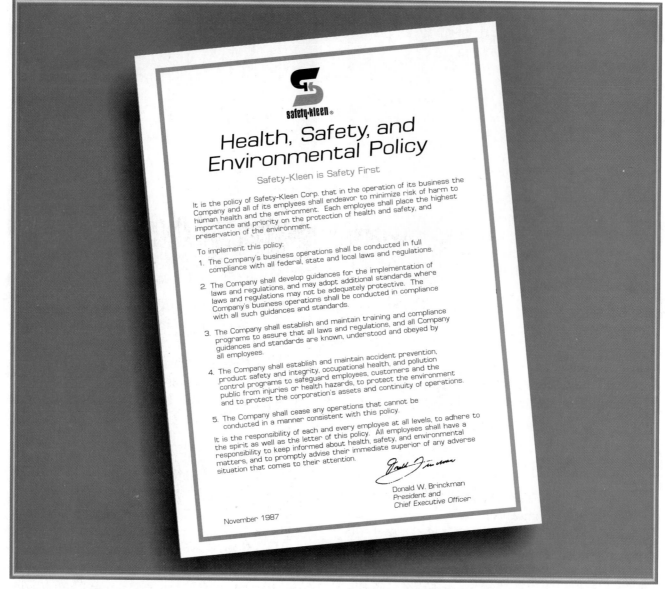

▲ 11.2 Policy Statement.

monthly pension check, Social Security benefits, and their life savings in a savings and loan association. What will the future be like for John and Mary if the savings and loan they have trusted goes out of business because of unethical top-management decisions? Could this happen to your parents or grandparents?

It would be unfair to consider all employees in an organization to be unethical because of the unethical behaviors of a few. Most employees think

of themselves as ethical, and they conduct themselves accordingly.

When employees report dishonest or wasteful company activities to a governmental authority, it is known as **whistle blowing**. This is one way to handle unethical business practices. Many states have whistle-blower laws that provide job protection for employees who report workplace hazards or wrongdoing. In 1989, President George Bush signed a bill granting additional job protection to federal employees who report their superiors' wrongdoings.

Many individuals and organizations in our society are working to promote high levels of ethical behavior. Norman Lear, a well-known television producer, is one example. He contributed a million dollars to underwrite a trust that gives national awards to companies and whistle-blowers who demonstrate courage, creativity, and social vision in the business world. The awards underscore Mr. Lear's belief that ethical behavior has always been very good business.

Can you imagine a world in which business owners were permitted to deceive you with false advertising, cheat you out of money, and sell you faulty merchandise with no fear of a penalty? As far back as the early 1900s, American businesses began policing themselves by forming watchdog groups. In 1906, Samuel Dobbs, a sales manager and later the president of Coca-Cola Company, made the public aware of dishonest practices and called for truth in advertising. His efforts resulted in the formation of vigilance committees through-

GETTING MORE INFORMATION

If you need help with a consumer question or complaint, phone your local Better Business Bureau or write to:

   Council of Better Business Bureaus, Inc.
   4200 Wilson Blvd.
   Arlington, VA 22203.

out the United States. In 1916, these committees were renamed Better Business Bureaus.

Today, the Council of Better Business Bureaus promotes ethical standards for business practices. It protects consumers through voluntary self-regulation and monitoring of business activities. The council is supported through the membership of private businesses and individual member

▲ *Organizations establish ethical codes of conduct that reflect the interests of the group they represent. What limits are placed on the behavior of professional athletes? Competition in the free enterprise system benefits consumers. What would happen to the price of soda if one company owned the entire soft-drink industry?*

Being Responsible

Unethical, Criminal, or Acceptable?

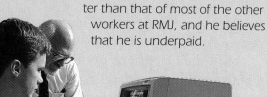

Alvin Gates attends evening classes at Tri-State Community College and works full-time in the accounting department of RMJ Industrial Products. Alvin frequently takes home about twenty-five sheets of paper or a couple of ballpoint pens. He uses his employer's paper and pens to do his school-work. Alvin considers his job performance to be better than that of most of the other workers at RMJ, and he believes that he is underpaid.

Critical Thinking

1. In your opinion, is Alvin's behavior unethical, criminal, or acceptable? Explain the logic for your answer.

2. Imagine that you are a department manager. Consider the following list of behaviors:

   - Using the company phone to make long-distance calls

   - Leaving work two hours early without permission

   - Making lengthy personal phone calls during working hours

   - Taking a laptop computer home without permission

   How would you handle each of these situations if you discovered that a worker in your department was involved? Would you discharge the employee? Would you punish him or her, and if so, how?

---

bureaus. It is not a government agency, and it is not supported by tax dollars. The nation's 172 Better Business Bureaus handled nearly 10.7 million consumer inquiries and complaints in 1990.

Government Regulation

When ethics are not defined and practiced, the results may be regulation through laws. During the late nineteenth century and the early years of the twentieth century, many businesses were **monopolies** (businesses with no competition). This practice goes against the democratic principle of free enterprise. When competition is eliminated, buyers are left without choices.

Imagine having to pay $5.00 for a twelve-ounce can of soda because one company owns the entire soft drink industry and controls the price. As a consumer, you would have two choices: pay the price, or don't enjoy a soft drink. Would you pay the price? To prevent businesses from establishing monopolies, Congress passed the Sherman Act in 1890 and the Clayton Act in 1914. Today, if a company attempts to monopolize a particular market, it is breaking the law. These laws are known as **antitrust laws**.

Another illegal business practice is **price fixing** (agreements between competitors to establish specific price ranges for their products or services). If the two largest manufactures of soft drinks agreed to fix the price for a twelve-ounce can of soda between $4.90 and $5.05, the choice for a consumer would be almost the same as a monopoly charging $5.00.

Honesty as an Ethic

Did you ever stretch the truth a little bit? Did you ever perform less than your share of the work on a project? One ethic (value) that most workers and employees agree with is honesty—the belief in truth and justice. At one time or another, you have probably heard someone say, "Do an honest day's work for an honest day's pay," or "You have my word on it." These terms frequently mean different things to different people. What do they mean to you?

Most of the ethical problems you will encounter on your job will focus on relatively small dilemmas.

Section 2 GET INVOLVED

Answer the following on a separate sheet of paper, and be prepared to discuss your responses in class.

1. If you see a co-worker stealing something, should you confront him or her directly, ignore it, or report the situation to management? Explain your answer.
2. Is a whistle-blower disloyal to the employer? Why or why not?

3. Give an example of an unethical business or professional practice for each of the following:
   a. an appliance repairperson
   b. a college coach
   c. a dentist
   d. a gas station attendant
   e. a journalist
   f. a politician

Section 3

Federal Rules and Regulations

At the beginning of the 20th century, the rapid spread of the factory system in the United States created a labor class that lived in cities and towns and depended on wages for its livelihood. Unsanitary, dangerous, and uncomfortable working conditions, combined with low wages and long working hours, caused intense dissatisfaction among the growing ranks of factory workers. The workers prompted change by forming labor unions and electing politicians who were committed to government regulation of the workplace.

In 1913, Congress created a separate executive department, the Department of Labor, to deal with the problems of workers. The Department of Labor has specific responsibilities regarding U.S. wage earners. These include

- Fostering, promoting, and developing their welfare
- Improving their working conditions
- Advancing their opportunities for profitable employment

Since the Labor Department's creation, Congress has enacted many laws that employers must follow. These federal laws protect the rights of all men and women when they are seeking a job, while they are on the job, and when they retire.

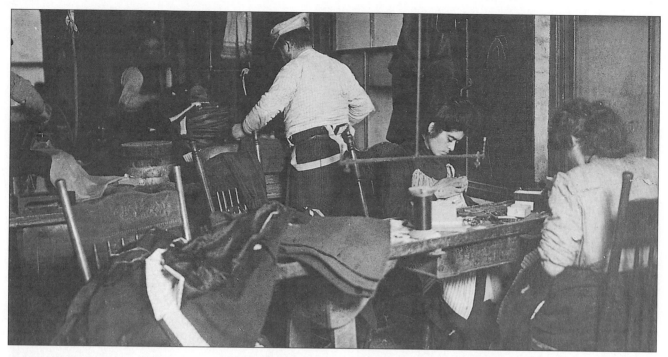

▲ *Early 20th century factory conditions were usually unsanitary, dangerous, and uncomfortable. Would you be willing to work long hours for low wages in these conditions? Changes brought about by early labor unions and government regulations still benefit today's workers.*

Many states offer similar, and sometimes broader, protection than the federal laws. Some areas of employment are governed exclusively by state law.

Asserting Your Rights

The first step in asserting your legal rights is knowing what those rights are. It is important to know the difference between employment practices that are prohibited by law and employment practices that might seem unjust but are not in violation of the law.

An employer has the right to take action against an employee for good cause. Laws that protect workers against discrimination do not prevent an employer from discharging you if you are not doing your job, nor do they require an employer to hire you if you are not qualified for the job. Job discrimination is defined as unequal treatment of workers in hiring, employment, pay, or conditions of work because of race, color, sex, national origin, religion, age, handicap, or any other characteristic not related to ability or job performance.

If you believe that you are being paid less than a legal wage or are the victim of discrimination, you are entitled to file a complaint with the agency that has responsibility for enforcing the relevant law. Procedures for making complaints vary. A telephone request is enough to set in motion an investigation into substandard wages or unequal pay, whereas a written complaint is necessary under some antidiscrimination laws.

If you feel that you are being treated unfairly, document incidents that support your complaint. Written notes on what happened, when it happened, and who was there are very useful in refreshing your memory and showing a pattern of unfair treatment.

There are time limits on filing complaints, so it is important to act promptly. If you are unsure about how the law might apply to a specific situation, call the agency that handles those complaints and ask to speak with a compliance officer.

Solving The Problem

Fair Choices or Discrimination?

Turhan Robinson arrived early for his job interview at the Casablanca. The restaurant had an opening for the job of kitchen helper. With more than a hundred employees working at the Casablanca, Turhan knew that he would have opportunities for promotion.

While waiting in the manager's outer office, Turhan noticed that the three other applicants being interviewed were white. He assumed that he was the only African American applying for the job. When the interview was over, Turhan was certain that he would be selected.

Three days later, Turhan received a letter from the manager telling him that another person had been hired for the job. The manager would keep Turhan's application on file in case of another opening. It seemed unfair to Turhan.

Critical Thinking

1. Turhan thinks that the Casablanca's manager is guilty of discrimination. He plans to contact his state's department of labor and file a complaint. If you were Turhan, what course of action would you follow? Why?

Most agencies with enforcement or administrative responsibilities for federal laws print free information pamphlets for consumers. You might obtain additional assistance and information from community-based organizations that have information and referral, counseling, or legal assistance services. Your local bar association might be able to provide information concerning the resources in your area.

Legal Rights of Employees

Workers are protected on the job by a variety of laws that prohibit discrimination and govern wages, hours, occupational safety and health, and other employment-related issues.

Minimum Wages and Overtime Pay. The Fair Labor Standards Act (FLSA) establishes and regulates the minimum wage, overtime pay, recordkeeping procedures, and child labor standards. The FLSA covers more than 73 million full-time and part-time workers in the private sector and in federal, state, and local governments. However, several million workers are still not cov-

ered by the minimum wage and overtime premium-pay provisions of the FLSA. They include

- Casual baby-sitters
- Companions for the aged and infirm
- Executive, administrative, and professional employees
- Employees of certain small, local retail or service establishments
- Outside salespeople
- Some agricultural workers

The FLSA does not limit the hours or work for employees who are sixteen years old or older.

Most covered workers are entitled to one and a half times their regular rate of pay for each hour they work in excess of forty per week. If you believe that you're not being paid the minimum wage or the required overtime pay, you may file a complaint with the Wage and Hour Division of the Department of Labor. It is listed under the heading "U.S. Government" in the white pages of most telephone directories.

On receiving notification of an FLSA violation, Wage and Hour compliance officers investigate to see whether the complaint is valid. If it is,

▲ *Casual babysitters are not covered by the minimum wage and overtime premium-pay provisions of the FLSA. Have you ever worked as a casual babysitter?*

the Wage and Hour Division attempts to persuade the employer to comply with the law. If these attempts are unsuccessful, the case is referred to the Solicitor's Office of the Department of Labor, which may decide to file suit against the employer in federal court.

In addition to the federal remedy, under FLSA you have a personal right to sue the employer for back pay, damages, attorney's fees, and court costs. However, if you begin a private suit, the Department of Labor will not pursue your case in court. To recover back pay, you must file your suit in court within two years, except in cases of willful (intentional) violations, in which case the time limit is three years.

CAREER TIP

It is unlawful to discharge or otherwise discriminate against an employee for filing a complaint or participating in a proceeding under the FLSA.

Consider the court case of *Richards v. Marriott Corporation* (549 F.2d 303 [4th Cir. 1977]). Waiters at a Marriott restaurant averaged more than the minimum wage in tips, and management paid any difference if the tips fell below the minimum wage. The U.S. Court of Appeals held that this policy violated the Fair Labor Standards Act as amended in 1974. The FLSA provided that employers must pay at least 50 percent (since January 1981, the tip credit may not exceed 40 percent) of the minimum wage regardless of the amount of tips, that employees have a right to retain their tips unless the employees are participating in a valid tip pool (one in which only those employees who customarily receive tips participate), and that the tip credit toward minimum wage was available only if employers informed employees about the provisions of the FLSA. The court ordered back wages of the full amount of the minimum wage during the period of violation because it found that the employer's failure to inform employees of the FLSA tipping provisions was in bad faith.
Source: A Working Woman's Guide to Her Job Rights, U.S. Dept. of Labor, Leaflet 55.

▲ *Unless the employees are participating in a valid tip pool, the employer pays at least 50 percent of the minimum wage to waiters and waitresses regardless of the amount of tips.*

▲ *The Equal Pay Act prohibits pay discrimination because of sex. Why is this law especially important to women?*

Equal Pay. The **Equal Pay Act of 1963** amended the FLSA to prohibit pay discrimination because of sex. It requires employers to pay equal wages within the organization to men and women doing equal work on jobs requiring equal skill, effort, and responsibility, which are performed under similar working conditions. Pay differences based on a seniority or merit system or on a system that measures earnings by quantity or quality of production are permitted. If you believe that you are not receiving equal pay for equal work, you may file a complaint with the EEOC, which enforces the Equal Pay Act.

Consider the court case of *Shults v. Wheaton Glass Co.* (432 F.2d 259 [3d Cir. 1970]). A glass manufacturing company paid male selector-packers twenty-one cents an hour more than female selector-packers. The company tried to justify the difference on the basis that men performed additional duties, such as lifting and stacking cartons and using hand trucks. The Court of Appeals ruled that under the Equal Pay Act, *equal* does not mean "identical" but rather "substantially equal" and that minor differences in duties do not justify pay differences.

Civil Rights Protection. On April 9, 1866, Congress passed the nation's first civil rights act. The act declared that "all persons born in the United States . . . are hereby declared to be citizens of the United States and such citizens of every race, creed and color shall have the same right in every State and Territory in the United States." Among the rights guaranteed were "full and equal benefits of all laws and proceedings for the security of person and property." In 1868, most of the act's provisions were incorporated into the Fourteenth Amendment to the Constitution. This act was followed by the civil rights acts of 1870, 1871, and 1875. Definitions of discrimination were expanded to include employment discrimination. For the remainder of the nineteenth century, civil rights legislation remained dormant, but it was revived during the twentieth century.

Title VII of the **Civil Rights Act of 1964** protects workers against discrimination on the basis of sex, race, color, religion, or national origin. The specific areas of employment protection include hiring, discharge, compensation, and conditions or privileges of employment. Subsequent laws and executive (presidential) orders continue to close loopholes concerning discriminatory employment practices.

In Chapter 8, you learned about your civil rights in getting hired. Almost every aspect of the workplace is subject to civil rights requirements. These include

- Employment testing
- Transfers
- Compensation
- Physical facilities
- Hiring
- Grooming
- Fringe benefits
- Layoffs
- Promotions
- Maternity leave
- Scheduling of work
- Sexual harassment

The Equal Employment Opportunity Commission has primary responsibility for enforcing Title VII. If you think that you have been treated unfairly on the job and that the basis for the unjust treatment was your sex, race, color, religion, national origin, disability, or age, you may contact the agency that enforces the law for more information about the protection provided and the enforcement process. You can also find out how to file a complaint and what your legal rights are. Remember that whistle-blower laws prohibit employers from discharging or otherwise discriminating against workers who file complaints or participate in an enforcement process.

Credit Reporting. The 1971 Fair Credit Reporting Act (FCRA) requires employers to tell rejected job applicants if they were denied a job based on credit information. Despite the FCRA, employers are increasing their use of credit reports to screen potential employees. Employers must also provide rejected applicants with the name and address of the credit bureau that supplied the report so the applicant can request a free copy of the report and check it for inaccuracies. In the early 1990s, McDonnell Douglas, Macy's, and two other companies settled charges that they failed to tell unsuccessful job applicants that credit information had figured in their rejection. The companies agreed to comply with the FCRA's dis-

▲ *Employers are required to pay workers' compensation so their employees will be compensated if they are injured on the job.*

closure requirements in dealing with future applicants. What information might appear on a job applicant's credit report that might cause potential employers to reject him or her? Why?

Compensation for Injuries. Workers who are injured on the job or who contract an occupational disease may receive compensation under state **workers' compensation laws**. These laws provide for prompt payment of benefits to injured workers. There is a minimum of red tape and no need to fix the blame for the injury. In most states, employers are required by law to cover their employees with workers' compensation protection, and heavy penalties are assessed for failure to comply with the law.

Because each state has its own law and operates its own system, the employees covered, the amount of compensation, the duration of the benefits, and the procedures for making and settling claims vary widely. Benefits can include

- Medical payments for the period of disability or for permanent disability
- Rehabilitation services
- Death benefits for a worker's family, plus burial expenses

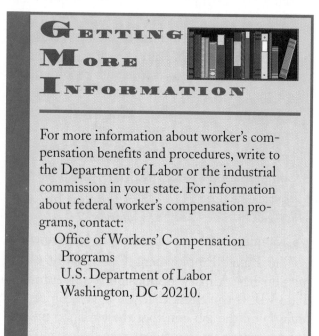

GETTING MORE INFORMATION

For more information about worker's compensation benefits and procedures, write to the Department of Labor or the industrial commission in your state. For information about federal worker's compensation programs, contact:

Office of Workers' Compensation
Programs
U.S. Department of Labor
Washington, DC 20210.

Solving The Problem

Who Pays the Bills?

Randy Browne was a telephone equipment installer for a private company. He supported a wife and a three-month-old daughter. One day, the job foreman instructed Randy to install lines through the ceiling of a new office building. The ladder provided by the employer didn't have safety feet. Randy was busy installing the lines when the ladder slipped, causing him to plunge 12 feet to the floor below. He spent six months in the hospital before the doctor told him that he will never be able to use his legs to do physical work again. He will be able to walk, but only with a severe limp.

Critical Thinking

1. How will Randy's family pay their bills while he is unable to work? Who do you think should pay Randy's medical expenses? Can Randy be compensated for a life-long injury? If so, how? If not, why not?

In some states, a person can receive workers' compensation for disability caused by work-related stress, including stress related to sexual discrimination.

Protection for the Disabled. Hailed as a landmark victory for people with disabilities, the Americans with Disabilities Act (ADA) went into effect in 1990. This law protects any "qualified individual with a disability" from employment discrimination on the basis of the disability, unless hiring the individual would impose an undue hardship on the employer. Under the act, people with "physical or mental impairment" are protected, including those with the following conditions, diseases, and infections:

- Orthopedic problems
- Cerebral palsy
- Multiple sclerosis
- HIV infection
- Visual impairment
- Epilepsy
- Alcoholism
- Cancer
- Diabetes
- Drug addiction
- Emotional illness
- Speech or hearing impairment
- Muscular dystrophy
- Mental retardation
- Heart disease
- Specific learning disabilities

Environmental Protection. The environment we work in has been threatened for many decades by human activities. Thousands of workers have died from illnesses caused by long-term exposure to toxic substances and breathing polluted air. Too many people have acted without regard for the effect on the life-sustaining, economic, and recreational value of the air, land, and water. To protect and restore the quality of these essential and irreplaceable resources, Congress enacted a series of laws. Although environmental protection laws have brought about significant environmental improvements, many challenging problems remain.

The U.S. Environmental Protection Agency (EPA) is responsible for implementing the federal laws designed to protect our working world. The agency now administers nine environmental protection laws including these:

- Clean Air Act
- Clean Water Act
- Safe Drinking Water Act
- Toxic Substances Control Act
- Uranium Mill Tailings Radiation Control Act

Social Security. The basic idea behind Social Security is a simple one. You pay taxes into the

▲ *The Clean Air Act was passed to restore the quality of the air we breathe. Can workers who drive to work daily help curb air pollution? What are the long-term effects of breathing polluted air?*

system during your working years, and you and members of your family receive monthly benefits when you retire or become disabled. Your dependent survivors collect benefits when you die. The **Social Security Act** is the federal law that established this national social insurance program. To receive full compensation benefits, you must pay the FICA tax for a stipulated length of time (ten years or forty quarters for most people).

About nine out of ten workers, including household employees and the self-employed, are covered by Social Security. Employers and employees each pay a share of the FICA tax. The employer is required to deduct FICA taxes in the amount of 6.2 percent from the wages paid to each employee. The employer adds a contribution

of 9.1 percent and remits the total payment on a weekly or quarterly basis to the Internal Revenue Service (IRS). FICA taxes are placed in trust funds from which benefits are paid to those who are eligible to receive them. FICA tax contributions are not refundable.

You have most likely had a Social Security number since you were born, and you probably know it as well as you know your own phone number. Every worker needs a Social Security card and number if the work to be done is covered by Social Security or if certain taxable income is received. When you have a bank account, insurance policy, or credit card, your Social Security card will be used for identification.

Section 3 GET INVOLVED

Answer the following on a separate sheet of paper, and be prepared to discuss your responses in class.

1. How could a worker's credit rating affect his or her job performance or honesty? Is this a fair way to screen job applicants? Why or why not?
2. Should manufacturers be required to remove pollutants from the air and water when they are proved to be health hazards for workers and the local community? What if the cost of cleaning the air or water is so high that it will drive the company out of business? What if the company is the major employer in the area?

Section
4

Fringe Benefits

Have you ever gone on a vacation or celebrated a holiday with your family? Were you ever a patient in a hospital? If you answered yes to either of these questions, the chances are good that you have profited by a family member's fringe benefits.

Fringe benefits (fringes) are forms of compensation other than salary or wages. They may be paid partially or totally by your employer. Because your fringes are not received directly as wages, they are usually not subject to taxes. As a new employee, it will be to your advantage to learn as much as possible about the fringe benefits your employer offers. There is no legal obligation requiring employers to provide most of the fringe benefits that workers receive.

Medical Insurance

When medical insurance is offered, it is available to employees and their eligible dependents. Many organizations offer employees a choice of medical plans. The amount of the employee's contribution depends on the plan selected. In addition to hospital costs, many medical plans also provide dental care, surgical benefits, prescription drug plans, and much more.

Familiarize yourself with the following terms. They will help you make the wellness (good health) choices that are most beneficial to you.

- *Hospitalization benefits* pay for hospital room and board or cash allowances toward their cost. Payments are for a certain number of days and for specific services.
- *Major medical plans* provide financial aid over and above what is normally covered by a hospitalization plan. They take effect when costly medical services are needed.
- *A second surgical opinion* occurs after a physician who is qualified to perform surgery recommends elective (optional) surgery. Most healthcare plans require a second opinion from a different surgeon before they will pay full benefits.
- *A deductible* is the amount of an expense that a beneficiary must first meet as his or her share of the cost.
- *Routine physical examinations* are physical checkups or other tests made in the absence of definite symptoms of disease or injury.
- *Outpatient care* is performed in the emergency department of a hospital, an ambulatory care center, an emergency care center, or a physician's office. Patients are expected to return home following outpatient care. Diagnostic and testing procedures and many types of surgery are routinely performed as outpatient care.

GETTING MORE INFORMATION

For information about careers in employee benefits, contact:

The International Foundation of Employee Benefit Plans
18700 W. Bluemound Rd.
Brookfield, WI 53005.

- *A health maintenance organization* (HMO) provides a full range of health coverage in exchange for a monthly fixed fee. In many organizations, an employee may elect to have his or her medical care provided by an HMO at little or no cost to the employee.

Wellness Programs

How would you like to work for an organization that offers you a longer and more enjoyable life and other free benefits? All that the employer expects in return is for you to be responsible for good health practices.

Employers have found that encouraging employees to take increased responsibility for their good health results in less absenteeism and lower insurance costs. As a result, many employers have formed wellness programs to involve their employees in health activities. Which of the following incentives would appeal to you?

- Less expensive insurance or lower deductibles for employees who exercise or quit smoking
- Free weight-loss programs, stress-management seminars, and other approved wellness programs
- An additional $354 pay each year for taking no sick days; filing no medical claims; clocking in at a normal weight, blood pressure, and cholesterol levels; and exercising at least thirteen times a month
- An additional $500 pay each year for walking up sixteen flights of stairs to your office every day
- Getting paid $10 for every pound you lose if you are overweight
- Getting paid $500 if you quit smoking
- An additional $10,000 in death benefits for your beneficiaries if you are killed in a car accident while wearing a seat belt

Vacations and Leave Time

Can you imagine phoning a travel agent to make arrangements for your first paid vacation

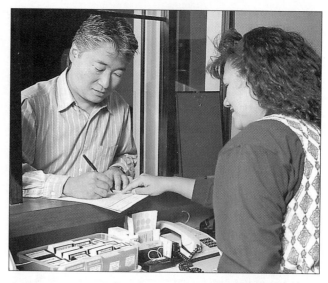

▲ *The worry about paying for the cost of medical care is relieved when medical benefits are paid for by the employer. What fringe benefits are most important to you?*

after you begin working? It is common for workers to receive one or two weeks of annual vacation time after six months to one year of continuous service. Vacation time usually increases to four or more weeks after fifteen or twenty years of service.

Leave time is excused time away from work. It may be paid or unpaid. Common reasons for using leave time include

- Personal illness
- Jury duty
- Family care
- Pregnancy
- Death in the family
- Personal reasons

Parenting leave (leave taken by mothers or fathers when a new child is born or adopted) is increasingly being granted by employers. Parenting leave days are usually subtracted from accumulated sick leave days for pay purposes. Should new parents have a right to spend time with their child? Why or why not?

Military leave from employment allows many young men and women to be active in the military reserves. Military leave for members of the U.S. Armed Forces is governed by federal laws. National Guards and other state or federal peacetime military personnel who must participate in annual training periods are usually granted a leave

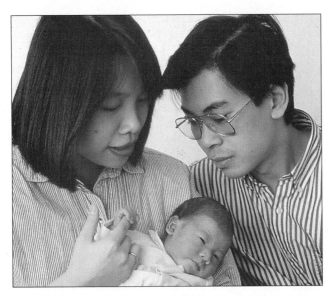

▲ *Parenting leave allows new parents time to adjust to the demands of their newborn child.*

of fifteen workdays, with pay, per year. This pay, provided by the employer, is usually the difference between the employee's regular pay and his or her military pay during the duty time. Is military leave important? Why or why not?

Sabbatical leave is an extended leave granted under certain conditions to employees who wish to acquire additional education and training or to travel extensively.

Pension Plans

Are any of your relatives or friends retired? For some workers, retirement is a time to enjoy traveling, pursue a hobby, or just take life a little easier. For others, it's a time to accomplish unfulfilled life goals. Most people have dreams for their retirement years. Financial security is needed to make those dreams come true.

The primary purpose of a pension plan is to provide regular lifetime payments to employees on retirement. Social Security was not intended to provide adequate retirement income by itself. Most workers rely on an additional pension plan obtained through their employers. Pension plans may be financed entirely by the employer, or they may require employee contributions.

Pension plans are generally classified as either defined-benefit or defined-contribution plans. Defined-benefit plans fix the amount of the benefit but not the amount of the contribution. Benefits are usually related to the worker's years of service and earnings or are a set dollar amount. Defined-contribution plans fix the amount of the worker's contributions but not the amount of the benefits. The employer's contribution, usually a percentage of profits, is divided among the employees' pension accounts. Each worker's eventual retirement benefit is determined by the total amount of his or her contributions and the investment earnings of those contributions during the years of coverage.

Accumulated pension benefits are vested (legally yours) when you have a nonforfeitable right to receive benefits at retirement, even if you leave your job before retirement age. Most pension plans require that you work five years, with a minimum of one thousand hours of service each year, before you earn pension rights.

Disability Plans

A disability is a physical or mental condition that prevents an employee from performing his or her usual occupation. If you were disabled by an accident or illness, who would pay your rent, food, and clothing expenses? What would become of your spouse or children? Employers usually sponsor an optional sickness and accident insurance plan that employees can purchase.

Most disability plans pay a percentage of the employee's regular wages or salary. Short-term disability plans usually pay about 70 percent of the disabled employee's wages or salary and last up to a full year. When this runs out, long-term disability benefits may take over, paying a smaller percentage of the employee's regular wages or salary. To be eligible for long-term disability benefits, the disability must be so severe that it prevents you from working not only in your usual occupation but in any other substantial work that is ap-

▲ *The father of a pre-school child enjoys the benefit of a child-care center at his worksite. Will this benefit be important to you some day?*

propriate for your education, training, and work experience.

Child Care

Employers lose millions of dollars annually from work-family conflicts caused when a child is sick, when day-care arrangements fall through, or when on-the-job time is spent worrying about a child's well-being. Although employer-sponsored child-care programs are not widespread, many employers are involved in finding practical solutions to the problem.

Some employers provide information about finding child care and about tax deductions for child care. Others allow parents to choose their own flexible work schedules. This helps parents maintain an effective balance between family and work obligations.

Still another solution is an employer-sponsored on-site daycare center. Employees drop off preschool children at daycare centers that are only minutes from the work site. The parents may drop in during the day to play, read, or have lunch with their children or just check up on them.

Child-care programs are costly for employers to operate. For example, the American Bankers Insurance Group sponsored an elementary school on company grounds. The startup costs were $350,000, and the annual operating costs are $60,000 plus supplies. The Dade County Public School System provides the books, desks, and teachers for eighty-four students. The curriculum is identical to that of the public schools. Is this program worth the expense? The company has found that employees with children enrolled in the Learning Center are almost never late, and their annual turnover is 10 percent lower than that of other employees.

Life Insurance

Should responsible people carry life insurance? Who should pay for a worker's life insurance? Why?

Employers carry group life insurance to provide financial support for beneficiaries (people who receive benefits from insurance policies) following an employee's death. The term *group* refers to the individuals who have a common employer, such as the employees of General Electric Corporation, which employs thousands of people, or Waterloo Transmission, Inc., which employs twenty-three.

The amount of basic life insurance provided by an employer-paid plan is usually equal to the annual base pay of the employee. Each employee in the organization does not receive the same amount. As annual wages increase through promotion or cost-of-living increases, the amount of coverage is increased to that amount.

Many employers offer their employees the option of purchasing additional life insurance at attractive rates. For example, an employee might like to have $35,000 in life insurance instead of the $20,000 amount of her annual salary. Perhaps she purchased a new car, furnished an apartment, and incurred $12,000 in debts. Not wanting her beneficiary to be responsible for these debts if something happens to her, she decides to purchase the additional $15,000 worth of insurance.

In all group life insurance policies, the employee is responsible for naming the beneficiary for the policy. The beneficiary receives the total amount of the policy soon after the employee's death. This payment is often used to pay current bills, funeral expenses, and home mortgages. The remainder is usually invested into a savings account, stocks, or bonds to produce income for the survivor.

Savings/Thrift Plans

Sooner or later, most people have a financial emergency. Perhaps the car breaks down and needs repair, a family member becomes ill, or the washing machine gasps and dies. At times like this, you appreciate having money saved, especially if your employer contributed some of it.

Employee savings, or thrift, plans are arrangements under which both the employee and the employer contribute to an investment or a savings plan in the employee's name. Employees who enroll in these plans authorize the employer to make payroll deductions from their base pay, usually between 2 and 12 percent. There are two common plans: deferred compensation (before tax) or regular (after tax). Any combination of the two is also possible. Contributions from both the employer and the employee are deposited in a trust fund. See Chapter 17 for additional information about savings, credit, and money management.

Credit unions are nonprofit banking services that employees may join. They permit members to save, borrow, and earn interest on contributions

they make through convenient payroll deductions. Credit unions only accept savings from and make loans to members. At the end of the year, an efficiently operated credit union often has a surplus of funds to distribute to its members.

Stock purchase plans are sometimes available. They enable employees to purchase stocks (shares of ownership) in the company, with or without employer contributions. The purchase terms are generally more favorable than those available in the open market. Stock option plans allow employees the privilege of purchasing company stock at a certain price and at a time of their own choosing.

Social and Recreational Programs

Some employers sponsor athletic teams that compete in organized leagues, such as softball, basketball, golf, and bowling. Other employee groups with common interests in chess, dancing, photography, fishing, biking, or other such hobbies may form clubs or meet informally. In small organizations, these activities are usually organized and administered by employee groups with assistance from the personnel or public relations department.

▲ *Credit unions provide nonprofit banking services to members.*

Figure 11.3 EMPLOYER COSTS FOR EMPLOYEE COMPENSATION PER HOUR WORKED

Compensation	Cost for All Workers in Private Industry			
	White-Collar Workers	Blue-Collar Workers	Service Workers	All Workers
Total compensation (wages and benefits)	$21.86	$17.09	$10.00	$18.43
Wage rate	15.85	11.38	$7.18	13.06
Total benefits	6.01	5.70	2.82	5.37
Paid leave benefits	1.55	1.02	.58	1.23
Vacations	.65	.52	.26	.55
Holidays	.52	.36	.18	.42
Sick leave	.28	.10	.10	.20
Other leave	.09	.05	.03	.07
Supplemental pay	.38	.57	.16	.40
Premium pay	.09	.39	.08	.17
Shift pay	.04	.07	.04	.05
Nonproduction bonuses	.25	.11	.03	.17
Insurance	1.55	1.48	.70	1.38
Retirement and savings benefits	.88	.67	.37	.73
Pensions	.76	.59	.36	.64
Savings and thrift	.13	.08	(1)	.09
Legally required benefits	1.60	1.91	1.00	1.59
Social Security	1.22	.98	.59	1.04
Federal unemployment	.02	.03	.03	.03
State unemployment	.11	.14	.08	.11
Workers' compensation	.24	.72	.30	.39
Other benefits	.04	.05	(1)	.04

— = Cost per hour worked is $0.01 or less.

Source: U.S. Department of Labor, 1994.

Employer Costs for Employee Compensation

Receiving benefits from your employer is the same as receiving cash. Sometimes, it is even better than receiving cash. You must pay taxes on cash wages, but many benefits are tax-free.

Employee benefits are very costly for the employer, however. A U.S. Department of Labor analysis in 1990s revealed some interesting facts about the costs for employee compensation, in-

cluding wages and benefits, in private industry. Take a look at Figure 11.3. The average compensation costs were higher for white-collar workers ($21.86) than for blue-collar workers ($17.09) and service workers ($10.00). The level of compensation varied by occupational group within the blue-collar and white-collar categories.

In private industry, benefits made up a larger proportion of compensation costs for blue-collar workers as a whole than for white-collar workers and service workers. Benefits made up a larger proportion of compensation cost for union workers than for nonunion workers. The proportion of compensation costs made up of benefits was similar among the Northeast, South, West, and Midwest regions of the country.

Why do you think service workers make so much less money than blue-collar or white-collar workers? Which group receives the most benefits? Which receives the least? Why?

Section 4 GET INVOLVED

Answer the following on a separate sheet of paper, and be prepared to discuss your responses in class.

1. Discuss pension plans with a retired person. Record his or her answers to the following questions.

   - If you were a young worker again, would you handle your retirement savings plan in the same way? If so, how did you handle it? If not, what would you do differently?

   - When you made career decisions, how much importance did you place on fringe benefits? Why?
   - What fringe benefits were most valuable to you during your working career? Which were least valuable?

2. If you were a working parent, would child-care benefits be important to you? If so, which benefits would be most important, and why? If not, why would they be unimportant to you?

Section 5

The Work Schedule

Some people work best in the early morning, some work best late at night, and for others it varies. Given this information, why do you suppose most employers adopt an eight-hour day and a five-day week of forty hours? Is the restriction of a fixed work schedule or a time clock necessary?

Employers have the right to establish work schedules. In doing this, their first consideration is the purpose and needs of the organization. For most office or white-collar employees, 8:00 A.M. is the normal starting time. For blue-collar employees, it's usually 7:00 or 7:30 A.M. Service businesses schedule their hours of work according to the convenience of their customers. Although most work schedules are still eight hours per day, schedules of seven and a half hours per day are not unusual. Some employers use work schedules consisting of four ten-hour shifts per week.

To understand some of the reasoning for specific work schedules, review the factors below that the owner of an automobile repair shop considered when making a work schedule for employees. Keep in mind that each of the following must take place when other businesses are open or when it is convenient for customers:

- Ordering and receiving parts and supplies
- Making money transactions

PLANNING MAKES A DIFFERENCE

A Flexible Plan

Carlin Abbott is a single parent with skills that are in high demand in the field of engineering technology. She wants to be a good mother and a good employee, and she also wants to obtain career advancements. Knowing that she must handle time conflicts between her work and family responsibilities, Carlin plans to interview with organizations that offer the option of a **flextime** work schedule. The total hours of work remain the same on a flextime schedule, but the employee is permitted to set his or her own hours of work.

On the job, Carlin uses a computer to make technical drawings. Once Carlin's job assignments are made, she requires little or no supervision. However, Carlin does need to work a few hours each day at a time when her supervisor is available to discuss her assignments. It makes little difference in the overall operation of the organization if Carlin comes in early and leaves early or comes in late and leaves late.

After several job interviews, Carlin was offered a position with a small engineering firm that uses flex-time scheduling. The personnel manager told her that the composition of the workforce, in particular the increase in the number of working mothers, has brought about a greater acceptance of flextime work schedules among many employers. In fact, 13 percent of all workers in the United States are on flextime schedules. Many single and older employees choose flextime schedules to adjust their work hours to their personal lifestyles. One survey showed that half of 521 large firms surveyed offered flextime scheduling. These companies believe that flextime scheduling has a positive effect on employee turnover, absenteeism, morale, and tardiness.

Critical Thinking

1. Carlin didn't find her flextime job by accident. How will Carlin's plan help her meet her goals as a worker? as a mother?
2. If employees could make doctor appointments, dentist appointments, or take care of family emergencies and still work an eight-hour flextime shift, how would it benefit their employers?

- Placing advertisements with radio, TV, and newspapers
- Conducting sales meetings with commercial customers
- Performing daily custodial tasks and maintenance of shop equipment
- Scheduling and providing automobile repair services

Customer demands for certain products and services can change quickly. To remain efficient and competitive in rapidly changing markets, an increasing number of employers are building their work schedules around a ring and core base. Permanent, full-time employees make up the core, and the employees whose work time can be adjusted to short-term changes make up the ring. This has led to a substantial increase in the number of part-time, temporary, contractual, and leased employees. These employees are known as **contingent workers**.

For years, retail stores and agricultural businesses have used contingent workers to meet changing seasonal as well as daily labor needs. However, the use of contingent workers across all industries is new to the American labor force. It is no longer uncommon for an employer to build a work schedule that includes part-time workers in the office for one week each month to keep up with billings or to use contractual engineers and technicians to help their full-time staff meet the demands of a specific contract.

Whatever the reason, contingent workers are available for part of a week, several weeks, or several months. Some workers prefer this type of work schedule. Others prefer the security that comes with being a permanent employee.

Work shifts make up the daily schedule of a plant and its employees. Which of the following would you prefer?

- The day shift, often called the *first shift*, occurs during daylight hours, 7:00 A.M. to 3:00 P.M., for example. The afternoon or evening shift (*second shift*) extends from midafternoon to near midnight. The third shift, often called the *night shift* or *graveyard shift* begins around midnight and runs until early the next morning, when the first shift begins its next day.

- Schedules for workers on a fixed shift remain the same week after week, while crews on a rotating shift change their hours at periodic intervals.

- A split shift is a daily work schedule divided into two or more parts.

- A swing shift is the fourth or rotating shift used on a continuous seven-day or round-the-clock operation.

Overtime is work scheduled in excess of the basic workday or workweek, as defined by law, the collective bargaining agreement, or the company. Hours of work beyond eight in one shift, or forty in one week, are usually considered to be overtime. Whether or not a company is required to pay overtime is determined by whether the employee is an exempt or nonexempt employee. Most exempt employees (those who are excused from the rule) fall into one of four classifications:

- Executive employees
- Administrative employees
- Professional employees
- Certain salespeople (outside, not retail)

▲ *A produce business schedules a "contingent" worker during the peak season. What other seasonal jobs provide opportunities for students?*

Many nonexempt employees work under a negotiated labor agreement. It is not uncommon for employers to schedule nonexempt employees at overtime rates for Saturday work, even when they are not unionized or working on a government contract. However, employers are not legally required to do so.

Sometimes, employees are scheduled for extra hours on the job and receive time off in exchange for the extra time worked. This is known as *compensatory time*. For example, if you worked forty-four hours in one week instead of the normal forty hours, you would not receive extra pay. Instead, you would be permitted to take four hours of excused time off, with pay, at a future date.

Some workers are required to use a time card to certify the time they begin working and the time they leave. A card with the employee's name is inserted into a clock that stamps the exact time on the card. A time clock enables the employer to keep an accurate record of each worker's schedule.

Section 5 — GET INVOLVED

Answer the following on a separate sheet of paper, and be prepared to discuss your responses in class.

1. What hours would you schedule your employees if you were the owner of a small bakery?

Would you schedule any particular workers at different times from others? If so, which workers, and why?

Section 6

Organizational Training and Education

Very few new employees have the necessary skills, knowledge, and experience to immediately excel in their jobs. In fact, many employers believe that employee training is more important than formal education when it comes to developing job skills. In addition, the availability of useful training fosters positive employee attitudes toward the organization.

Organizations usually encourage employees to take advanced training and education programs. They are aware that the interests of the employee and the organization are best served by developing each employee's talent. For example, Ameritech, one of the nation's leading information companies and employer of more than 75 thousand, invests about $100 million annually in employee training. The average Ameritech Bell company employee spends ten days each year in training.

Tuition reimbursement is an educational fringe benefit that some employers offer. They agree to pay part or all of the costs of the job-related training or college courses that their employees undertake. Most organizations restrict tuition reimbursement to training or education courses that

are related to the employee's current job or to another job within the organization for which the employee is preparing. Reimbursement is usually made on successful completion of the courses.

Chapter 5 described apprenticeship and on-the-job training programs within organizations as

▲ Workshops and seminars sponsored by employers usually focus on professional or personal development. Would you enjoy participating in this three-day seminar with your co-workers?

well as advanced training at colleges and universities. Unlike that type of education and training, most employee training doesn't require in-depth studies. Instead, most employers sponsor practical training in the form of workshops or seminars.

Workshops are usually one-day courses that involve a small group of employees. They provide an excellent opportunity for interaction between the presenter and the participants. Seminars are similar to workshops but often last two to five days. Most workshops and seminars focus on professional or personal development. The presenters may be employees of the organization or hired consultants. Certificates of attendance or participation are frequently awarded for completion of these programs.

Section 6 GET INVOLVED

Answer the following on a separate sheet of paper, and be prepared to discuss your responses in class.

1. Interview a friend or relative who is employed and has been involved in some form of employer-sponsored education or training. Describe the training program he or she has completed. What career skills were learned or improved as a result of the training?

IMPORTANT FACTS

Federal Rules and Regulations for Retirement and Disability

Congress enacted the Employee Retirement Income Security Act (ERISA) in 1974 to protect American workers and their beneficiaries who depend on benefits from employee pension and welfare plans. ERISA doesn't require employers to establish pension plans. However, the law does prohibit employers from discharging a worker to avoid paying a pension benefit.

Since 1981, the federal income tax laws have encouraged qualified individuals to set up personal retirement plans by allowing tax advantages for plans established according to Internal Revenue Service regulations. There are two types of personal retirement plans:

- Individual retirement accounts (IRAs), which any employed person may start

- Keogh or HR-10 plans, which are limited to self-employed people and their employees

To qualify for disability benefits from Social Security, you must have a physical or mental impairment that is expected to keep you from doing any "substantial" work for at least a year or a condition that is expected to result in your death. Social Security disability benefits are not intended for a temporary condition.

The Federal Labor Standards Act

There are a number of employment practices that the Federal Labor Standards Act does not regulate. These matters are agreements between the employer and the employees or their authorized representatives. The FLSA does not require employers to

- Provide paid vacation or holidays, severance pay, or paid sick leave

- Provide meal or rest periods, holidays off, or vacations

- Give raises or provide fringe benefits

- Provide premium pay for weekend or holiday work

- Give a discharge notice, reason for discharge, or immediate payment of final wages to terminated employees

- Limit the number of work hours for persons 16 years of age or over

Employee Benefits in Small Businesses

The first Bureau of Labor Statistics survey of employee benefits in establishments with fewer than one hundred workers revealed that

- Small establishments had less extensive benefits coverage than did establishments of one hundred workers or more

- Full-time employees were more likely to be covered by benefit plans than were part-time employees

This survey covered information on the benefit plans of 32.6 million full-time and 8.2 million part-time workers.

Sharing the Costs of Fringe Benefits

Employers are increasingly trying to contain rising health-care costs by shifting them to workers through co-payment plans or by reducing benefits. A major reason is that the costs of many employer-sponsored insurance plans are rising at three times the rate of inflation.

Family Leave for Men

Several corporations offer family-friendly benefits, ranging from parenting leave to flexible work schedules. These employers report that relatively few men take advantage of these benefits. The situation is changing, however. Surveys at Du Pont demonstrate the shift. In 1990, 64 percent of male employees indicated an interest in parenting leave to care for ill children, compared with 40 percent in 1985.

CHAPTER 11 REVIEW

ENRICH YOUR VOCABULARY

On a separate sheet of paper, number from 1 to 17, and complete the following activity. (Do not write in your textbook.) Match each statement below with the most appropriate term from the "Enrich Your Vocabulary" list at the beginning of the chapter by writing that term next to the correct statement.

1. One-day company-sponsored training sessions
2. The act that established a tax-sponsored pension and disability insurance plan
3. Using knowledge obtained as a result of your position for personal gain
4. The act that protects workers against several types of job discrimination
5. Forms of compensation other than salary or wages
6. Reporting wasteful or dishonest company activities to the government
7. Nonprofit banking services
8. A work schedule in which employees set their own hours of work
9. Agreement between competitors on the price range of products
10. Part-time, temporary, contractual, and leased employees
11. Businesses with no competition
12. The act that requires employers to pay equal wages for equal work
13. Time taken when a child is born or adopted
14. Code of values; standards for conduct
15. Formal, periodic, written evaluation of job performance
16. Laws that provide for payments to injured workers
17. Laws that make monopolies illegal

CHECK YOUR KNOWLEDGE

On a separate sheet of paper, complete the following activity. (Do not write in your textbook.)

1. When were performance appraisals first used?
2. What five major decisions do employers frequently base on their evaluation of a worker?
3. Who enforces a business organization's code of ethics?
4. Why did the American people begin to elect politicians who were committed to government regulation of the workplace?
5. What does the Fair Labor Standards Act do?
6. What was the amount of hourly compensation paid the average worker in 1994? What amount was paid as wages? as fringe benefits?
7. Why do employers prefer to use contingent workers whenever possible?
8. In the opinion of many employers, how do employees learn most of their job skills?

DEVELOP SCANS COMPETENCIES

Government experts say that successful workers can productively use Resources, Interpersonal skills, Information, Systems, and Technology. This activity will give you practice in developing Information and Interpersonal skills.

Working with classmates, develop a questionnaire to find out the environmental concerns of your students in your school. Design a comprehensive questionnaire that can be given to 100 students in your school. You might ask questions about local companies' waste disposal routines, companies that cause air or water pollution, or companies that cause noise pollution.

As a class project, duplicate the questionnaire, administer it, tally the results, and report the findings. Based on the results, write to local businesses to inform them of the students' concerns and of their legal and ethical responsibility to the community in which they are located.

CHAPTER 12

Career Change and Growth

Learning Objectives

After completing this chapter, you should be prepared to:

- explain the relationship between work, family, and friends in a successful career
- list several forms of direct compensation
- make a systematic, positive job change
- list the benefits and job-placement assistance that are available to voluntarily or involuntarily displaced workers

Enrich Your Vocabulary

In reading this chapter and doing the exercises you will learn the following important terms:

job security
direct compensation
salary
wages
net pay
base pay
incentives
premium pay
commissions
cost-of-living
  adjustments
merit increase

profit sharing
unemployed
layoff
pink slip
severance pay
outplacement
  programs
unemployment
  insurance
discharge
COBRA

The career path you select will entail numerous personal and occupational changes. Some changes will be planned (voluntary); others may be beyond your control (involuntary).

Those who study the future world of work estimate that workers will change jobs up to ten times or more before they reach retirement. This number is even greater if you count career moves in large organizations that have promotion-from-

> Success is full of promise till men get it: and then it is last year's nest, from which the bird has flown.
>
> **Henry Ward Beecher**

within policies. You may have ten or more different positions within one company if you start at the entry level and move progressively up the job ladder.

Is career growth more than being promoted? How do you know? When you answer "yes" to any of the following questions, it will be time to review your goals and redirect your career:

1. Have you grown beyond your position?
2. Are layoffs imminent?
3. Are you in danger of being fired?

Whenever you are considering a career change, reevaluate your interests, goals, and skills before making a final decision.

People, jobs, and life situations change continually, making career and life planning a lifelong process. Just as you cannot completely separate school from other parts of your life, neither can you isolate your career. Through periodic review and self-assessment, you exercise control over the direction of your life, instead of letting the forces of life direct you.

Section 1

Career Success

What will it take to make you feel successful? Accumulating great wealth? Creating something beautiful? Establishing meaningful relationships with family and friends? Being in a position of power and prestige? Your answer today probably differs from what you would have said five years ago and what you will say five years from now. Each life stage has an impact on your personal view of success.

In general, success in work
- Brings about a feeling of satisfaction with life

- Provides a satisfactory lifestyle
- Makes you feel like a valuable part of society
- Assures a means of paying essential bills and providing the necessities of life
- Can be gauged by how well it supports leisure activities

Personal Success

Family, friends, and social and professional support are all interrelated with job satisfaction in

CAREER TIP

> Building on past successes and failures helps you meet greater life challenges.

a worker's overall feeling of success. The success you feel in your future role as a worker won't exist separately from your life outside the job. Success will, in part, be determined by how well you plan a lifestyle that balances your time, energies, capabilities, and needs with the demands and rewards of your job. Margaret Hilburn and Ed Reicher are examples of workers who had to make changes to balance their work and lifestyle demands.

Margaret Hilburn is a wife, a mother, and a computer operator. Her husband developed a severe problem with arthritis, and the family was forced to move to the Southwest for his health. Margaret gave up her job as a computer operator in order to make the move. She is currently working as a word-processing specialist in Phoenix,

Arizona. Her husband is experiencing better health in the new climate. Family responsibilities changed Margaret's role as a worker.

Ed Reicher is a husband, a father, and a sales representative for a large computer manufacturer. Ed was promoted from the local office to a national sales position that requires extensive overnight travel. His salary almost doubled. Ed can no longer take care of his two small children while his wife attends evening classes at the local university, so the family has hired a baby-sitter. They have also hired someone to do many of the household repairs that Ed had been able to do previously. Ed's role as a worker changed several of his family responsibilities.

More Than a Paycheck

Do you believe that interesting and fulfilling work, job security, or considerate management can be more important than the amount of a paycheck? As you change your role from student to employee, the importance you attach to different aspects of having a job will change. After a period of time, you may find that your job is not as satisfying as it was when you began. You may decide that your paycheck is not worth the daily grind of doing a task that you dislike. You may want more than a good paycheck.

The following are indications that employees are experiencing job dissatisfaction. Watch for

▲ *Success is a personal feeling. What will it take to make you feel successful?*

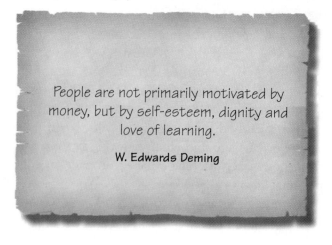

> People are not primarily motivated by money, but by self-esteem, dignity and love of learning.
>
> **W. Edwards Deming**

▲ *Laura considers her job as a "data control team leader" to be interesting and fulfilling work. What job would you consider to be interesting and fulfilling?*

these symptoms in yourself as you participate in the world of work:

- Increase in absenteeism or tardiness
- Inability to finish tasks
- Sick leave without medical causes
- Interpersonal conflicts and strained work relationships
- Low morale and productivity
- Physical complaints, such as headaches, back pain, and indigestion
- Alcohol or drug dependence

Your definition of a satisfying job may change as you gain work experience and learn how your personal characteristics and goals fit or do not fit a particular job. You may find that progress is more important than you had believed or that co-workers and managers make a bigger difference in job satisfaction than you had imagined. You may find that you still do not know what you really want to do for your career. However, every job has negative and positive factors. Expecting a job to be totally satisfying and free of frustrations is unrealistic.

Every job provides you with an opportunity to learn more about your personal likes and dislikes and to improve your skill in getting along with others. After you have been employed for a few months, you will be able to evaluate all aspects of having a job. You will realize that any job is the sum of all its parts and that the paycheck is just one of those parts.

Rewards Include the Paycheck

Without adequate pay, the importance of the work tasks, **job security** (protection against loss of employment and earnings), and good management greatly diminish. Compensation is the direct and indirect payment that employees receive for a job performed. In Chapter 11, you learned how fringe benefits become part of your paycheck in the form of indirect compensation. The part of the paycheck that provides you with a source of cash is **direct compensation**. The following terms are associated with direct compensation:

- **Salary**: Employee compensation that is calculated weekly, biweekly, monthly, or annually. The term *salary* generally refers to the pay received by clerical, technical, professional, managerial, and other employees hired on a weekly, monthly, or annual basis.
- **Wages**: Employee compensation that is calculated hourly. Wages are the price of labor. For piecework, wages are a set amount of money for each piece of work completed, and the total wages are based at how many pieces the worker completes in an hour or a shift.
- **Net pay**: The amount an employee receives after deductions.
- **Base pay**: The regular salary or wage, excluding incentive pay, bonuses, fringe benefits, overtime pay, and all other extra compensation.
- **Incentives**: Extra financial payments for production above a predetermined standard. Incentive plans depend on output rather than

BUILDING SELF-ESTEEM

Challenging Work?

Angel Brunson is a quality inspector for Hampton Controls, Inc. He works on an assembly line. Angel removes each unit from the assembly line and plugs it into his testing machine. He checks six different circuit systems and returns all satisfactory units to the line. His testing machine makes a printed report for each unit he checks.

When Angel started the job last fall, he thought it was exciting, important, and well paying. By the time summer came, he had decided that his job was monotonous and not as important as that of the technicians who build the units. He also decided that he was underpaid. The technicians earned $5.25 per hour more than he did and they were invited to training meetings with the engineers and the managers.

The department manager has called Angel into the office twice in the last six weeks to ask if there are any problems he would like to discuss. Angel's work is excellent, but he has been late to work about once a week during the past three months. He has also had a couple of arguments with the technicians who build the units he inspects. The whole situation at work gives him headaches.

Critical Thinking

1. If Angel were your friend, what advice would you give him?
2. Why do you think Angel changed his opinion about his job?
3. How does Angel demonstrate that he is dissatisfied with his job?

---

number of hours worked and may include profit sharing, commissions, bonuses, or gain sharing.

- Gain sharing: An incentive compensation program in which an employee's pay is based on productivity increases. Employees are rewarded for results they can influence.
- Shift differential pay: The additional compensation paid to employees who work shifts other than regular daytime hours.
- Straight time pay: Compensation for time worked at the regular pay rate.
- Overtime pay: Compensation for work performed in excess of the basic workday or workweek. Overtime is generally paid for hours worked beyond forty hours in one week or eight hours in one day.

- Premium pay: Compensation at greater than regular rates, such as overtime pay or shift differential pay.
- Time and a half: Premium pay of one and a half times the employee's regular rate when overtime is paid.
- Bonus plan: A wage system that includes payments in addition to regular wages for production in excess of the standard for the job, department, or plan. The term also refers to any payment in addition to the regular wage, such as a Christmas bonus, which is an extra payment given to workers during the Christmas season. Companies usually rely on spot bonuses to reward extraordinary performance.
- Commissions: Compensation to salespeople based on a predetermined percentage of the

salesperson's sales value. Commissions may be additions to a guaranteed salary rate, or they may constitute the total pay.

- **Cost-of-living adjustments** (COLAs): Changes to wages or salaries in accordance with changes in the cost-of-living index. COLAs are usually pay increases based on the amount that the cost of living has increased according to the Department of Labor's consumer price index studies.
- Hourly rate: The rate of pay, expressed in dollars and cents, for workers paid by the hour.
- **Merit increase**: An increase in a worker's pay rate, usually given on the basis of such criteria as efficiency or performance.
- **Profit sharing**: An incentive compensation in which a percentage of company profits is distributed to the employees involved in producing those profits.
- Pay packages are usually reserved for upper management. They might include salaries, bonuses, stock-option plans, and similar incentives and benefits.

Most entry-level jobs pay a straight salary or a specific hourly wage with overtime for hours worked beyond the regular schedule.

Jobs Do Not Pay the Same

Management knows that good pay attracts many people, which allows the company to pick the most highly qualified applicants. When pay packages that include salary and wage scales are set, they are determined in accordance with the prevailing rates for a particular job in the organization, the competition's prevailing rate, and economic conditions.

Jobs have numerous characteristics that make them desirable or undesirable to workers. Some jobs involve dirt, noise, high temperature, monotony, danger, hard physical labor, irregular employment, low social prestige, or other undesirable features. For such work, a higher wage may be necessary to attract workers away from the more desirable jobs that require similar skills. What jobs can you think of that fit this description?

Not all workers have identical talents, skills, and effectiveness. Thus, the supply of labor to various occupations is not the same. For example, during the 1960s through the 1980s, the demand for computer-related positions was very great because there were few candidates qualified for the numerous positions that needed to be filled. Then schools began turning out skilled programmers, operators, and analysts, and demand eventually lessened. This area of employment is still growing rapidly, but organizations can now be more selective in hiring new employees. This example demonstrates why high wages tend to go to those who possess rare talents and skills.

Geographic location also affects wage rates. Examine the data presented in Figure 12.1 on the next page. Would the differences in average weekly earnings be enough to cause you to relocate for higher wages? Some people are reluctant to leave their homes and seek employment elsewhere because they would have to leave family and friends. Does this apply to you?

Getting a Raise

The type of job you have and the policy of your company will have a lot to do with when you will receive a pay raise. You may work for a company that gives automatic pay raises or has a job classification system with a set pay scale. If you do not know your company's policy on pay increases, the personnel department is a reliable source of information. Ask about your employer's compensation policies regarding cost-of-living increases, hourly and salary levels, and merit raises.

Many people say, "If you don't ask, you won't get it." This is especially true in the working world regarding pay raises. You may hope that your boss recognizes what an outstanding contributor you are. However, waiting for a greater financial reward to be bestowed on you without asking for it

Figure 12.1 AVERAGE EARNINGS FOR SELECTED OCCUPATIONS

	Survey Area						
Occupation	Austin, TX	Baltimore, MD	Boise City, ID	Boston, MA	Chicago, IL	Fresno, CA	Orlando, FL
Average Weekly Earnings							
Secretary	$407.00	$460.00	$403.51	$476.00	$463.50	$408.50	$394.00
Computer analyst	$848.00	$775.00	$753.50	$796.00	$815.00	—	$769.00
Computer operator	$383.50	$437.50	$355.00	$458.00	$445.50	$402.00	$389.50
Electronics technician	$571.00	$608.50	—	$536.50	$660.00	$609.00	$545.50
Average Hourly Earnings							
Motor vehicle mechanic	$11.87	—	$12.87	$16.14	$18.80	$14.32	$12.50
Truck driver	$10.82	$13.48	$12.81	$15.34	$15.14	$12.60	$11.74

— = not available.

Source: U.S. Department of Labor, Bureau of Labor Statistics, Summary 90-14 (no. 2 of 3).

may take a long time.

When you decide to seek a pay raise, improve your chance of success by following these guidelines:

1. Give your boss advance notice by writing a note requesting a personal meeting or telling him or her of your intent. This is good business etiquette, and it gives your boss time to analyze the budget and consider your request before meeting with you.

2. Be prepared for the meeting. Know why you deserve a raise. You can do this by making a list of your accomplishments and contributions to the organization from the time you were hired or received your last raise. Know also the dollar amount you believe you should receive.

3. Learn the market value of your job so you know what your skills are worth. You can do this by asking co-workers and reading job advertisements in newspapers, trade journals, and government compensation reports for typical salaries or wages for positions similar to yours.

4. Time your request. There are times when the likelihood of getting a raise is better than others. Because most raises are merit raises, it is generally a very good time to ask during the

performance appraisal meeting, when you are given a promotion, or when you are asked to take on extra responsibilities. Avoid asking for raises when you know that the organization is losing money. Time your request to coincide with periods of economic prosperity.

5. Don't threaten to quit if you don't get the raise you request. If you are a valuable employee, the boss knows it. The boss also knows that you can probably sell your expertise elsewhere. Your boss may not have the final say in whether or not you get a raise. Most likely, he or she will have to sell the idea to superiors.

6. Anticipate objections. If you are told that the financial situation is such that the company cannot afford to increase your salary, try to set up a date to renegotiate during the next few months. Reiterate that you really like your job but you feel that your are worth more. If you are told you are not quite ready for a raise, ask what you can do or learn to merit a raise.

7. Don't respond to a rejection by voicing negative opinions to fellow employees or by being less productive. This type of behavior can only hurt you if you stay with the employer, and it will influence your boss's recommendation if you leave for another job. After all, the reason for the rejection could be valid.

8. Thank your boss when you do get a raise. It's good business etiquette.

▲ *Rachel is glad that she followed the eight guidelines for getting a pay raise. Being a well-qualified worker and knowing how to acquire a pay raise are important success factors.*

Section 1   GET INVOLVED

Answer the following on a separate sheet of paper, and be prepared to discuss your responses in class.

1. The following questions evaluate your feelings about *work*. If you are not employed, substitute the word *schoolwork* for *work*. After answering these questions, ask an adult worker to answer them, and then compare your answers.

Family Satisfaction

a. Is it easy for you to talk with family members about your work (schoolwork)?

b. Do family members seem interested in your work (schoolwork)?

c. Would you discuss a new job opportunity (or a new course at school) with family members before making a change?

Friendship Satisfaction

a. Do you consider any of your co-workers (fellow students) to be close friends?

b. If you had a problem, would you ask one of these friends (from a. above) for help?

Work Satisfaction

a. Are you generally satisfied with your job (school)?

b. Do you generally like your job (school) environment (surroundings)?

c. Considering your present age, are you satisfied with your success as a worker (student)?

If you answered "yes" to all eight statements, you have exceptional career or school satisfaction. If you answered "no" to more than one statement in each category, you should consider ways to improve your satisfaction in that area.

2. Ask a parent, relative, or adult friend about job rewards other than a paycheck. Report your findings to the class.

Section 2

Changing Jobs

Millions of Americans change jobs each year. Many choose to change; others have no choice.

William Jackson is only twenty-three years old, and he has already had four jobs since graduating from Pleasantview Vocational High School. William majored in welding. His first job was that of a welder's assistant for the TMC Tank Company. He took a specialized course in welding at night school while working full-time for TMC. At the end of ten months, William was promoted to welder first class.

TMC was losing money building large tanks with hand-welding techniques. To be competitive, TMC installed automatic welding equipment, and William was laid off. After three months of job searching, William was hired by a shipyard, 850 miles from home. Although the product was different from the tanks he built at TMC, the welding techniques were very similar.

Once again, William went back to school. This time he took courses to learn how to work with computerized control systems like the ones used on automatic welding machines.

Next week, William begins working for the company that builds the automatic welding machines that put him out of work at TMC. He will need to travel a lot in his new job, which involves installing and adjusting automatic welding equipment.

William's job situation is not unique. Increasingly tight and competitive economic situations cause employers to reorganize, close, and make major technological changes. In turn, workers are forced to be flexible in a competitive job market. Add to this the fact that American workers are getting more education and training after high school to prepare for jobs with higher skill requirements, and it becomes clear why you will probably change jobs several times during your working years. In fact, if you are like most workers, you will leave your first job after high school within two years.

The Right Time?

You might not make the best decision in choosing your first job, but you can gain valuable work experience and learn about yourself on that job. After several months or a year, you may discover that what you thought you wanted in a job isn't what you want at all. It may be a good time to reconsider your career path.

Don't make a hasty career decision and quit a job too quickly; that could be a mistake. If you are seeking a sizable pay increase or a promotion, you need enough time on the job to gain experience. Less than a year is rarely enough time. If possible, always make certain that there is a significant, clearly defined benefit to making a job change.

Lack of experience makes your first job difficult to obtain. When you do your second job search, you'll be able to document your experience and worth as an employee. What is worth and experience, and what improvements should you make before you change jobs?

1. Determine if you have learned all of the job skills you can on your present job.
2. Evaluate how well you get along with co-workers and managers.
3. Match your present job skills and people skills with the new job you are seeking.

▲ *William Jackson has experienced more career changes in his twenty-three years than his father and grandfather experienced in their lifetimes. Are you prepared to deal with career changes?*

This honest comparison will help you make your decision. Remember that it's not uncommon to want higher pay and a better job, but you may need to improve your human relations skills, acquire more experience, or obtain more training before you are qualified for a new opportunity.

The Process of Resigning

Don't make the mistake of being angry and creating bad feelings when you resign from a job. You could hurt yourself in terms of future references. There's also the possibility that you might wish to work for this employer later in your career.

Being a lifetime employee of one company is not as commonplace as it once was. However, a responsible employee still accepts and performs assigned work tasks until the last day of employment is completed. This means continuing to carry out all duties and responsibilities to the best of your ability and with a positive attitude. In this way, you continue to build a record of accomplishment, even though you are seeking a change or even working out a notice (the period when you are still employed but have established a date for terminating your employment).

It is good business etiquette to give a minimum of two weeks advance notice of your intent to re-

▲ *Daniel Ward is submitting his letter of resignation to accept a higher-level position with another employer. He is proud of his work and appreciates his boss and co-workers.*

sign. This should be done face-to-face with your supervisor or the personnel administrator. Don't criticize the organization, your co-workers, or the management. Don't offer unsolicited advice on how to improve the organization. Instead, mention the good things that have happened, thank your boss and co-workers for the positive things they have done, wish them good luck, and leave with a handshake. Always volunteer to train your successor and complete any unfinished work that

is urgently needed. No one will blame you for seeking a better job.

If you are asked to submit a letter of resignation, keep it positive. Simply write out the statements you plan to make when you resign.

Remember that the managers in an organization will change over a period of years, and so will the workers. Having a good record on file may help you at some future date.

Section 2 GET INVOLVED

Answer the following on a separate sheet of paper, and be prepared to discuss your responses in class.

1. From the early 1900s until the 1970s it was common for employees to stay with one employer for twenty-five or even forty years and to retire with a gold watch, a dinner honoring their loyalty and service, and a lifetime pension. People who changed jobs more than once every five to ten years were referred to as *job jumpers*. Ask your grandparents or someone who is now retired about those days. Find out

- If they feel that career opportunities were better in the past
- If they believe that they had more job security than most workers do today
- If they ever changed employers after they were thirty years old
- The longest number of years they worked for one employer
- If they were honored by their employer when they retired

Section 3

Losing Your Job

Millions of American workers are involuntarily laid off or fired from their jobs every year. These firings and layoffs have a negative, even devastating, effect on their standard of living and their self-esteem. At some time during your employment years, you may join the ranks of the unemployed (Figure 12.2 on the next page).

People are classified as **unemployed** (not employed and looking for work) regardless of their eligibility for unemployment benefits or public assistance if, while the Bureau of Labor Statistics is conducting its survey, they had no employment, were available for work, and made specific efforts to find employment. People who have been laid off from their former jobs and are awaiting recall and those who expect to report to a job within thirty days are also counted as unemployed.

Involuntary unemployment usually occurs for reasons beyond the control of the individual worker. The cause may be

- An organizational merger, such as two banks joining together to form one
- An economic downturn that results in a recession that affects the whole country (such as the one in the early 1990s that caused 7.1 percent unemployment in January 1992)
- A technological change that eliminates a whole industry, such as when the automobile industry replaced the carriage industry or when computer technology lessened the need for file clerks and bank tellers
- Seasonal work, such as agriculture and construction, that can occur only during certain months
- The movement of an organization or industry to another geographic area—for example, the manufacturing of some automobile parts moved from the Midwestern United States to nations with lower wage rates
- A labor market imbalance caused by the closing of a plant or the completion of a large construction project

Whatever the cause of unemployment, those who are most highly skilled and trained are most likely to be reemployed. Take a look at Figure 12.3 on the next page. Why do you think a worker's level of education has such a significant effect on his or her employment opportunities?

There is no general law that prohibits private employers from discharging employees without good cause. Employers have historically had the

▲ *Several years ago, this outdated factory provided paychecks for more than a thousand families. Twenty years from now, will you be willing to update your job skills and relocate?*

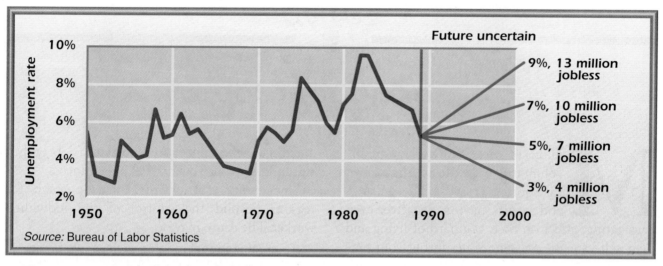

▲ *Figure 12.2 Unemployment Will Hit Millions of Workers in the 1990s.*

right to fire employees at will unless there was a written contract that protected against it. This broad right has been limited by a number of federal laws that prohibit discrimination based on sex, race, color, religion, national origin, age, physical or mental disability, union activity, wage garnishment, and filing complaints or assisting in procedures related to enforcing these laws.

In addition to these federal laws, some states and municipalities have passed laws that prohibit employers from discharging employees who serve on jury duty, file workers' compensation claims, or refuse to take lie detector tests. Other state and local laws prohibit discrimination based on marital status or sexual orientation. Employee complaint procedures and collective bargaining agreements between employers and unions also place limitations on an employer's absolute right to fire workers.

Some employees who have challenged their discharges in court have succeeded in placing additional limitations on the employer's right to discharge. Courts in some states have ruled in favor of discharged employees when the discharge was contrary to public policies. For example, an employee cannot be fired

- for refusing to commit perjury (act of swearing that something is true when one knows it to be false)
- for refusing to approve market testing of a potentially harmful drug when it is not based on good faith and fair dealing
- for refusing to date a supervisor
- to save the employer from paying a large commission
- when there was an implied promise of continued employment (such as the employee's length of service, the nature of the job, actions or communication by the employer, and industry practices)

Education	Men%	Women%
No high school degree	57.2	46.9
High school degree	75.2	64.9
Some college	73.2	65.8
College degree or more	90.8	81.8
Source: *Monthly Labor Review*, July 1991		

▲ *Figure 12.3 Percentage of Displaced Workers Who Were Reemployed.*

▲ *The "pink slip" in John's hand was in his office mailbox this morning. John is a highly skilled accountant with an excellent work record. How would you feel in this situation?*

Layoffs

A **layoff** is an involuntary separation of an employee from an employer for a temporary or indefinite period, through no fault of the employee. The term *layoff* suggests that workers will eventually be recalled to their jobs or that employers at least intend to recall workers. The term *reduction in force* usually signifies a permanent layoff. A sluggish or recessionary economy may cause employees to be laid off.

Organizations are not consistent in how they lay off or terminate employees. The methods used by some employers are almost horror stories. For example, when employees at one New England newspaper tried to log onto their desktop computers, they could not get into the system. Instead, they were directed to an editor's office, where they received an envelope containing either a new password for the computer, which meant that they still had a job, or a note to see a supervisor, which meant that they were being terminated. It had nothing to do with computer failure. It was the way workers learned which ones among

them would be getting a **pink slip** (notice of termination).

Another organization that eventually laid off one thousand workers required employees to come in for two-hour shifts and to wait by their phones for word on continuing employment from management. If the employee wasn't called, then he or she still had a job. Employees who were called were given boxes to use for packing their belongings.

Most organizations are not like this. Most make every effort to ease the pain of reducing their workforce at considerable expense to the organization. They may offer employees some of the following benefits.

Voluntary Buyouts. Voluntary buyouts include early-retirement programs and severance pay. Early-retirement programs artificially add years to an older employee's age or length of service at the company to make the worker eligible for a pension before retirement age. With the other kind of incentive, **severance pay**, employees are offered a certain number of weeks' pay for each year of service with the company. One large organization offered 30 months' pay to any employee who agreed to leave. In these programs, employees have a "window of time"—typically sixty to ninety days—in which to accept the offer. They may also be offered an extension of health insurance and other benefits.

Outplacement Programs. **Outplacement programs** provide assistance and training to help released employees find new positions. These programs are intended to help terminated employees face the shock of being unemployed, deal with personal feelings, and put the termination into perspective. Counseling helps employees reassess their interests, values, and skills and set short- and long-term goals. Occupational and organizational information is made available, and assistance with résumé writing, job searching, and interviewing techniques is provided. One major company committed more than one million dollars to assist its

BUILDING SELF-ESTEEM

Persistence Pays Off

As he cast his line into the still waters around the boat, Ken Schaum took a bite out of the cheese sandwich his mom had packed into the cooler that morning. The splash of the sinker broke the silence of the hot summer afternoon. Ken glanced at his grandfather. He hated to tell him that he was out of work and couldn't find a job. After all, Grandpa had always had a good job, and Ken didn't want to seem like a failure. Ken was thinking about how proud Grandpa had been two years ago when Ken started working at DRS Bearings, the same firm that Grandpa had retired from after forty-two years of service. Now Ken had to tell him that he had been laid off from DRS and couldn't find another job.

Ken started talking, and the story poured out. DRS planned to close the plant. Ken's interviews with six other employers had all ended in rejection. It was so embarrassing that Ken almost hated to be interviewed by another employer for fear of being turned down again.

Grandpa listened quietly, and then he reminded Ken about the vegetable garden they had planted when Ken was in the fifth grade. They worked an entire day preparing the soil and planting the seeds. Ken checked the garden every day, but nothing seemed

to be growing. He became discouraged. Then one morning, Ken and Grandpa went out to look at the garden and saw the first green sprouts coming through the ground.

They were both quiet for a while, and then Grandpa said, "I was proud of you then, and I'm proud of you now. You're not a quitter, Ken."

That evening at home, Ken thought a lot about being laid off, searching for a new job, and the garden he helped plant years ago. He sorted through several employment ads he had cut out of the newspaper but hadn't answered. He would send his résumé to those employers in the morning, and this time he would be proud of himself.

Critical Thinking

1. On a separate sheet of paper, describe something you have accomplished that makes you feel proud. List any failures you experienced before you succeeded. How did you overcome your failures? What advice would you give to someone who wanted to accomplish what you have done?

2. Ken managed to overcome his feeling of depression and increase his sense of personal confidence. Using events in the story, list as many reasons as you can for Ken's change of attitude. Can you use any of the reasons on your list to increase your sense of confidence? If so, how? If not, why not?

employees with outplacement services when economic conditions forced it to close six manufacturing plants.

Unemployment Insurance. **Unemployment insurance** is a joint federal-state program under which state-administered funds pay a weekly benefit for a limited time to eligible workers when they are involuntarily unemployed. The purpose

of the payment is to tide unemployed workers over until they find jobs for which they are reasonably suited in terms of training, past experience, and past wages. Benefits are paid in cash and are not based on need. Federal law establishes certain minimum requirements, but each state determines who is eligible, how much money each person receives, and how long benefits are paid. To be eligible, a person must be unemployed, able

▲ *Workers who are involuntarily unemployed should register at their local State Employment (Job Service) office.*

to work, available for employment, and seeking work. The employer pays the premiums for this insurance.

Termination by Discharge

Discharge of an employee means dismissal from employment. The term implies discipline for unsatisfactory performance. Virtually all courts have supported the employer's right to discharge an employee who is demonstrably unacceptable, incompetent, lazy, uncooperative, or abusive to other employees.

In most firings, the employee to be released knows in advance or at least has some suggestion that termination is coming. It may be in the form of a bad performance rating or an advance warning from the supervisor. The boss may avoid talking directly to the employee, may give fewer assignments without any explanation, or may increase the number of reviews of the employee's work performance. The employee may even hear about an impending discharge through the organization's rumor mill.

In some organizations, a series of progressively more serious warnings is required for all hourly employees before termination can be considered. The employee is formally notified of the need for improvement in performance and is given the opportunity to improve. Discharge is used only as a last resort. When some employees are forewarned, they decide to quit before the situation deteriorates into a discharge.

If you are called into your boss's office and dismissed because of some fault in your work performance, follow this advice:

1. Don't lose your temper. Accept the firing calmly, and maintain your dignity. The time to deal with your emotions is when you are away from the boss's office.

2. Ask your boss or the personnel staff for help in finding a new job. You may be eligible for severance pay, unemployment insurance, unused vacation time, and COBRA benefits.

A New Beginning

Once you are over the shock, disbelief, and anger of firing or layoff, take time to get your feelings out in the open. Find a friend, relative, religious leader, or counselor whom you trust, and talk openly about your experience and your feelings. Anger at the boss, shame, feelings of failure, fears for the future, concern over financial problems, sadness, and self-pity for being treated unfairly are all normal.

CAREER TIP

Don't quit a job until you have a new one. People who quit their jobs appear to be just that—quitters. If you look for a new job while you are still working, you'll have the additional advantage of continuing income.

▲ *When you face difficult career choices, it is important to reappraise yourself and your career path. Can you trust and talk openly with a friend, relative, religious leader, or counselor?*

Reappraise yourself and your career path once you overcome your feelings of fear and doubt. Take inventory, and make sure you understand the reasons you were discharged. If the firing was your fault, take measures to correct your failings before starting a new job.

1. Were you unqualified for the job? If so, what can you do now to become qualified?
2. Did you have enough experience for the job level? If not, what job level would be appropriate for your experience?
3. Did you get along with management and co-workers?
4. Did you follow the organization's rules and carry out your job responsibilities?
5. Were you dependable?

When you begin planning for the future and set out on a new job search, review and use the techniques you learned in Chapters 7 and 8. Keep in mind that you will probably be asked why you left your most recent job.

COBRA. In 1985, Congress passed the Consolidated Omnibus Budget Reconciliation Act **(COBRA)** to provide certain terminated employees, or those who lose insurance coverage because of reduced work, to be able to buy group insurance

GETTING MORE INFORMATION

For more information about COBRA, write to:

    U.S. Department of Labor, Pension and Welfare Benefits Administration, Division of Technical Assistance and Inquiries, 200 Constitution Ave., N.W. Washington, DC 20210.

coverage for themselves and their families for a limited period of time. Once COBRA coverage is chosen, the former employee must pay for the insurance. Employers can charge the covered person up to 102 percent of the insurance premium cost.

Group health coverage for COBRA participants is usually more expensive than health coverage for active employees because the employer usually pays a large part of the premium for employees. However, it is ordinarily less expensive than individual health coverage.

For example, if you are terminated but have participated in the group health plan maintained by your employer, you may choose to pay for a maximum of eighteen months coverage at the company's group health rate plus two percent. If your employer has fewer than twenty employees, you will not be entitled to COBRA coverage.

Section 3 GET INVOLVED

Answer the following on a separate sheet of paper, and be prepared to discuss your responses in class.

1. In the early 1900s, the average duration of unemployment was 14.2 weeks. Other than what has been mentioned in this section, what could be done to help the unemployed find new employment?

2. At one point, 76,841 individuals exhausted their unemployment benefits. If you were one of those individuals, what changes in lifestyle would you have to make?

3. Review the following reasons given to the Department of Labor as to why employees were separated from the organization. These reasons cover the causes of unemployment for 586,370 employees in forty-five states. Which reasons would most likely result in a temporary layoff? Which would result in a permanent layoff? Explain your answers.

Reason	Number Reported
Automation	11
Business ownership change	78
Contract completion	210
Import competition	69
Material shortages	20
Overseas relocation	13
Seasonal work	883
Vacation period	15
Bankruptcy	99
Contract cancellation	48
Domestic relocation	114
Labor-management dispute	18
Model changeover	15
Plant or machine repairs	27
Slack work	941
Weather-related curtailment	84

IMPORTANT FACTS

Stretch Your Dollar Earnings

How well you live has a lot to do with where you live, not just how much you earn. For example, according to one study, the cost of living in Minneapolis matches the national average. The cost of living in New York City, San Francisco, Los Angeles, and Boston is more than the national average, and in Miami, Houston, Seattle, and New Orleans, it's less.

Getting Back to Work

Nearly 7 in 10 workers who were displaced during the 1991–93 period from jobs they had held for at least 3 years were reemployed in February 1994. The reemployment rate was the highest (73 percent) for workers ages 25 to 54. Only about half of the displaced workers ages 55 to 64 and 20 percent of those 65 and older, had found new jobs.

Source: Bureau of Labor Statistics, USDL 1994.

Pay for Performance

Sibson & Company, a compensation consulting firm, predicts that by the year 2000, between 10 and 15 percent of all employees will receive performance-based pay, an increase from less than 5 percent in 1980.

Reasons for Job Loss

Between 1991 and 1993, 42 percent of displaced workers cited plant or company closings or moves as the reason for their job loss. Insufficient work and position or shift abolishment accounted for 30 and 28 percent, respectively, of the displacements.

Source: Bureau of Labor Statistics, USDL. (Current Population Survey 1994).

Causes for Termination

In a survey conducted by the Texas Advisory Council for Vocational Education, employers ranked the following as the five major causes of employee termination, with 1 being the most frequent:

1. Absenteeism
2. Lack of interest in the job
3. Continually making costly mistakes
4. Not following instructions
5. Showing an unwillingness to learn

Labor Imbalance

There are growing gaps between job demands and the skills and expectations of workers. In the early 1990s, so many people flooded Xerox Corporation's Webster, New York, facility in pursuit of 300 new copier-assembly jobs that officials "had to go to some Xerox machines to keep up with the demand" for applications. More than 3,500 prospects barely yielded enough qualified candidates. For every five hundred applicants, Xerox expected to find just 65 who could pass the battery of required tests. When its copiers were less complex, Xerox could have filled assembly jobs from a pool of candidates only one-third as large.

Involuntary Unemployment

During times of economic recession, the proportion of the involuntarily unemployed differs widely among geographical areas. In both New Jersey and New Hampshire, job losers accounted for slightly more than 60 percent of the unemployed in 1990. Rhode Island, Pennsylvania, and Massachusetts also had large proportions of job losers (56 to 59 percent). In contrast, only 32 percent of the unemployed in South Dakota and about 38 percent in Nebraska and Virginia had lost their last jobs.

Source: Bureau of Labor Statistics, USDL 91-332.

CHAPTER 12 REVIEW

ENRICH YOUR VOCABULARY

On a separate sheet of paper, number from 1 to 20, and complete the following activity. (Do not write in your textbook.) Match each statement below with the most appropriate term from the "Enrich Your Vocabulary" list at the beginning of the chapter by writing that term next to the correct statement.

1. The part of your paycheck that provides you with cash
2. Provides a weekly benefit to qualified unemployed workers
3. Employee compensation that is calculated hourly
4. Extra financial payments for production above a standard
5. Compensation to salespeople based on a percentage of sales
6. Compensation at greater than regular rates
7. Wage changes based on the consumer price index
8. Incentive compensation in which a company shares financial gains with employees
9. The amount an employee receives after deductions
10. The regular salary or wage, excluding all other compensation
11. Employee compensation that is calculated weekly, biweekly, monthly, or annually
12. Not employed and looking for work
13. Protection against loss of employment and earnings
14. An involuntary separation from a job for a temporary or indefinite time
15. A lump-sum payment in exchange for quitting or retiring from a job
16. Assistance and training to help released employees find new jobs
17. Dismissal from a job for discipline or unsatisfactory performance
18. Consolidated Omnibus Budget Reconciliation Act of 1985
19. A written notice of discharge or layoff
20. A pay raise given for efficiency or performance

CHECK YOUR KNOWLEDGE

On a separate sheet of paper, complete the following activity. (Do not write in your textbook.)

1. List at least five indicators that suggest that an employee is dissatisfied with the job.
2. What factors determine wage scales or salary for a particular job?
3. What would be a good time to ask for a pay raise?
4. What factors have increased the number of job changes that workers make?
5. What effect does a layoff or firing have on workers?
6. What has limited the employer's right to fire employees at will?
7. What are the normal feelings of a worker who is fired or laid off?

DEVELOP SCANS COMPETENCIES

Government experts say that successful workers can productively use Resources, Interpersonal skills, Information, Systems, and Technology. This activity will give you practice in developing Information and Interpersonal skills.

Conduct a telephone survey of businesses in your area to find what types of direct compensation are paid to employees. Choose a variety of different businesses such as those that hire unskilled labor, those that hire skilled labor, those that hire professional help, retail businesses, businesses that offer services, and so on. Be sure to write down the type of businesses you call and the answers you get from each business.

Ask at each place you call what type of direct compensation employees receive. You might want to give them a choice of answers such as hourly pay, salary, overtime pay, shift differential pay, bonuses, commissions, profit sharing, merit increases, and cost-of-living adjustments.

After you have accumulated all of your data, analyze the results. Try to determine whether one type of business seems to offer a better pay package than other types of businesses.

Unit Three

Understanding the World of Work

CHAPTERS

13 A Changing Workplace
14 Economics and Work
15 Entrepreneurs and Small Business Ownership
16 Researching and Understanding Career Information

A Changing Workplace

Learning Objectives

After completing this chapter, you should be prepared to:

● give examples of how the role of women in the U.S. workforce has changed in the last 100 years

● list five major issues confronting working women, minorities, and families

● plan for the process of career change

● explain the conflicts of meeting family needs and employment requirements

● compare differences between service- and manufacturing-sector opportunities

Enrich Your Vocabulary

In reading this chapter and doing the exercises you will learn the following important terms:

mergers
acquisitions
downsizing
deregulation
nontraditional
    occupations
stereotype
sex-role stereotypes
gender identity
comparable worth
glass ceiling
sexual harassment

maternity leave
goods-producing
    sector
service-producing
    sector
production flexibility
offshore
CBERA (Caribbean
    Basin Economic
    Recovery Act)
urban area

If the last 50,000 years of man's existence were divided into lifetimes of approximately sixty-two years each, there would have been about 800 such lifetimes. Of these 800, fully 650 were spent in caves.
Only during the last seventy lifetimes has it been possible to communicate effectively from one lifetime to another—as writing made it possible to do. Only during the last six lifetimes did masses of men see a printed word. Only during the last four has it been possible to measure time with any precision. Only in the last two has anyone anywhere used an electric motor. And the overwhelming majority of all material goods we use in daily life today have been developed within the present, the 800th, lifetime.

Alvin Toffler, *Future Shock*
Copyright-Random House, Inc.

	1990	2005 (Projected)
Men	54.7%	52.3%
Women	45.3%	47.7%

▲ *Figure 13.1 Percentage of Women and Men of All Races in the Labor Force.*

another), and **downsizing** (reduction in an organization's size to increase efficiency) will continue to change the personnel composition and operations of many companies.

The **deregulation** (elimination of government controls) of many industries, such as the communications, financial, and transportation industries, will continue to create new and unfamiliar business climates for employers and employees.

International competition will continue to require employers to control labor costs and ensure managerial flexibility. This will be done by developing new strategies for managing human resources.

These changes will make continuous skill development a lifelong requirement for competitive workers as new products are developed and new services are created.

As the year 2000 marks the beginning of a new century, your work life will be far different from that of your parents' or grandparents'.

Working age women will constitute 47.7 percent of the work force, and men will retain a slight majority (52.3 percent) (Figure 13.1). This increase in the number of women in the workforce will result in more two-income families and more single-parent households, creating greater diversity in the structure of American families.

Pressure on companies to be profitable will result in changes in organization and technology. **Mergers** (the joining together of organizations), **acquisitions** (purchases of one organization by

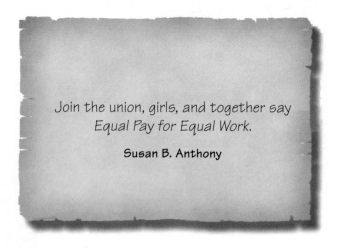

Join the union, girls, and together say
Equal Pay for Equal Work.

Susan B. Anthony

Section 1

The Changing Role of Women

The role of women in the workplace has changed significantly during the last 100 years. In the nineteenth century, economic equality between the sexes was a distant goal, far out of the reach of the average woman. Women who worked outside the home were generally young, unmarried, poor immigrants. Married middle-class women remained at home. This was a reflection of the societal view that the role of women was to perform nonpaid work in the home, while the role of men was to participate in the labor market to earn income to support their dependent wives and families.

In an 1888 study entitled "Working Women in Large Cities," the Bureau of Labor emphasized that women who worked were both honest and virtuous. During this period of U.S. history, there was an influx of foreign labor, a rapid development of factories, and a migration of workers from the farms to the cities. All of these developments increased women's participation in the labor market. Most female factory workers were extremely young, worked long hours, and had very low earnings (an average of $5.24 per week). Many lived in lodging houses that had no parlor or reception room in which to receive callers. This arrangement made it necessary for the women to receive visiting friends in their rooms. According to Bureau of Labor agents, "such a condition tends either in the direction of crushing out social [contact], especially between the sexes, or of carrying it beyond the limit of prudence."

Social values regarding the roles of men and women slowly changed. A major reason for this change was the mobilization of men to fight in World War II. The war created severe labor shortages, and women found acceptance in the labor market. Between 1940 and 1944, the number of women in the labor force increased by more than a third. Even then, most women were employed in traditional occupations and usually in lower-paying industries. Their earnings, even for full-time, year-round jobs, were less than two-thirds the average for men.

During the mid-1960s, U.S. families continued a trend toward fewer children. The rapid decline in birth rates made it more acceptable for married women to work. Women were achieving higher levels of education, the overall economy was expanding, and jobs were available for those who sought them. During this period, the feminist movement grew, and women were encouraged to seek a larger role in the labor market. Civil rights

▲ *During the late 1800s, it was common for poor women and children to work in "sweatshops" (factories in which the workers were subjected to long hours, low wages, and unpleasant working conditions).*

▲ *During the 1960s, the feminist movement grew. How do you feel about equality in the workplace? How do you think the women and children shown in the photo on page 283 would feel about equality in the workplace?*

legislation provided legal support for equal opportunities in the job market.

In 1970, less than 40 percent of wives living with their husbands and children worked outside the home, and the participation rate for those with preschool children was only 3 percent. The 1970s, a decade of inflation, changing lifestyles, and family stress, changed these patterns. Divorce became more common; by the end of the 1970s, one out of every two marriages was ending in divorce. Although many divorced women later remarried, they often found themselves faced with the sudden and unexpected need to earn money to maintain their families. In addition, a marked increase occurred in the number of never-married

women with children. Single-parent families, most of them maintained by women, became an increasingly common family type.

In past decades, most women left the labor force during their childbearing years. Today, an increasing number of women in this group are working or looking for work. As the twenty-first century approaches, U.S. women continue to make changes and overcome barriers as their numbers in the workforce approach those of men.

Women are a vital part of our nation's economy. Their multiple responsibilities to work, family, and other pursuits has changed traditional concepts about separation of work and family life. The concept of what women can do in the workplace and in society as a whole has also changed. In the past several decades, an increasing number of women have completed higher levels of education and have sought opportunities for higher salaries and long-term career progress. They have also made it very clear that their income is important and in many cases vital to their survival.

Women's Work

Women make up more than half of the workforce of nearly a dozen industries, including such

CAREER TIP

It is important for young women to prepare for job satisfaction and career success. They can expect to spend thirty or more years gainfully employed.

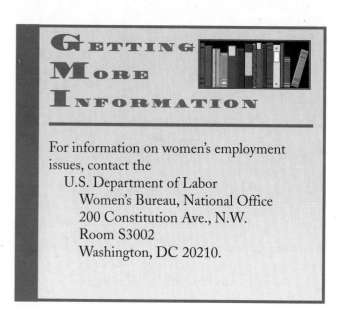

GETTING MORE INFORMATION

For information on women's employment issues, contact the
   U.S. Department of Labor
      Women's Bureau, National Office
      200 Constitution Ave., N.W.
      Room S3002
      Washington, DC 20210.

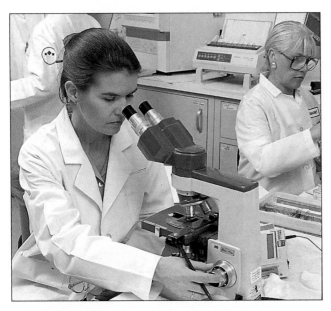

▲ *Donna is a clinical laboratory technologist. She has a bachelor's degree from State College. Medical technologists play a crucial role in the detection, diagnosis, and treatment of disease.*

fast-growing industries as health services, banking, legal services, insurance, and retail. Once clustered in only a handful of "traditional" jobs, women have branched out into such fields as accounting, law, medicine, science, computer engineering and design, banking, and finance.

Still, in many fields, sex roles have been an underlying factor in the distribution of women and men across occupations. Sex roles have also affected levels of employment and promotion within occupational fields. For example, women represented 80 percent of all administrative support (clerical) workers as recently as 1989. From 1900 through 1940, women held less than 3 percent of all skilled craft, labor, and technical jobs. By 1989, this number had only increased to about 9 percent. The opportunities or lack of opportunities for women in **nontraditional occupations** (those in which women comprise 25 percent or less of the workforce) have not changed significantly.

Review the information in Figure 13.2. Which of the careers listed are still nontraditional for women? Why do you think so many women are still cashiers, nurses, and elementary school teach-

ers? Why do so few women become electricians, carpenters, physicians, engineers, firefighters, and mechanics?

Sex-Role Stereotyping

Are the following statements true or false?

- A woman's place is in the home.
- Girls are sweet, and boys are tough.
- Men shouldn't cry.
- Men make better decisions than women.
- Boys are better in math than girls.
- Women are better clerical workers than men.
- A woman's career is not as important as a man's.
- Men are smarter than women.
- Women are more caring than men.
- Women don't make good leaders.
- Girls are better readers than boys.

If you answer "true" to any of these statements, you are expressing a sex-role stereotype of men or women. A **stereotype** is a label placed on groups of people, without regard to individual differences. It is a generalization about a group of people that is not based on reality. **Sex-role stereotypes** are based on roles assigned to people because of their sex without relation to personal skills or interests.

When did you first learn what it means to be male or female? From the time you were a baby, you were probably treated in certain ways because of your sex. If you are male, you probably weren't dressed in pink. If you are female, you probably were encouraged to play with dolls and dishes. Studies have shown that infant girls are held and spoken to more frequently than infant boys. Boys are expected to be independent earlier than girls, and boys are treated more roughly. This includes being punished more often. Do you think these findings are true?

By age three, boys and girls generally have a **gender identity** (sexual identity). They know that

Figure 13.2 EMPLOYED WOMEN LISTED BY OCCUPATIONS

Occupation	Total Number in Occupation	Women in This Occupation	Women as a Percentage of the Total Employed	Women's Earnings as a Percentage of Men's Earnings
Executive, administrative, and managerial	11,165,000	4,764,000	42.4%	65.4%
Accountants and auditors	1,186,000	636,000	53.6%	75%
Engineers, architects, and surveyors	1,866,000	158,000	8.5%	88.6%
Computer systems analysts and scientists	542,000	191,000	35.2%	82.7%
Chemists	119,000	30,000	25.2%	N/A
Physicians	266,000	68,000	25.6%	82%
Registered nurses	1,181,000	1,104,000	93.5%	98.7%
Elementary school teachers	1,311,000	1,111,000	84.7%	89.2%
Athletes	41,000	8,000	20.2%	N/A
Dental hygienists	33,000	33,000	100%	N/A
Sales workers: apparel	173,000	132,000	76.3%	N/A
Cashiers	1,081,000	850,000	78.6%	86.8%
Secretaries	3,183,000	3,154,000	99.1%	N/A
Mail carriers	306,000	65,000	21.2%	93.4%
Fire fighters and fire prevention specialists	207,000	6,000	2.9%	N/A
Automobile mechanics	649,000	3,000	.5%	N/A
Industrial machinery repairers	491,000	16,000	3.3%	N/A
Brickmasons and stonemasons	134,000	0	0%	N/A
Carpenters	861,000	11,000	1.3%	N/A
Electricians	605,000	9,000	1.5%	N/A
Oil-well drillers	27,000	0	0%	N/A
Tool and die makers	148,000	3,000	2.0%	N/A
Textile sewing machine operators	663,000	585,000	88.2%	N/A
Truck drivers	1,614,000	28,000	1.7%	N/A

N/A = Not available.

Source: U.S. Department of Labor.

BUILDING SELF-ESTEEM

What's the Message?

In many career decision-making situations, sex-role stereotypes place restrictions on both men and women.

Jamie Bachman noticed the following ad in the help-wanted section of her local newspaper.

Jamie has an associate degree from Midwestern University, where she studied sales and marketing. She is currently working for a small office supplies company but would like to make an upward career change.

Critical Thinking

1. What message does the ad send to Jamie about women? about herself?

2. How could you rewrite the ad to make it more attractive to Jamie and other women?

▲ *Gina and her mother are painting Gina's room. When she grows up, will Gina consider "painting" to be a man's job? How do you think this experience will affect Gina's self-esteem?*

▲ *Larry enjoys helping his father wash the car. He associates this work with being a male. Think back to the time when you were Larry's age. What experiences did you have that you associated with being a male or female?*

their sex is permanent and cannot be changed by merely changing clothes or deciding to be the other sex. Stereotypical roles and behaviors become part of our "growing up," and eventually we accept this part of ourself as "the way we are." Sex-role stereotypes are learned from our childhood experiences in our family, house of worship, school, and community.

Labeling jobs as "for men only" or "for women only" can discourage women and men from seeking careers that would match their true interests and abilities. As women's roles change, so do men's. The traditional values and stereotypes of previous generations should not apply in today's world of work.

Section 1 GET INVOLVED

Answer the following on a separate sheet of paper, and be prepared to discuss your responses in class.

1. Women are working longer than ever before in our nation's history. Interview three women who are at least fifteen years apart in age (ideally one who is in her twenties, one in her forties, and one in her sixties). Ask them about the following:

   - Their views on women in the work force
   - The jobs they have had outside the home since they were in high school (if any)
   - The obstacles they feel are most difficult for women to overcome in the work force
   - What they have enjoyed most and least

   about working outside the home
   - What advice they would give to high school girls to help them prepare for career success

2. Like women, men may also be discouraged from pursuing certain careers because of sex-role stereotypes about work. Review the information in Figure 13.2. Which occupations are held by women more than 75 percent of the time? What is the image of elementary school teachers and registered nurses that discourages many males from entering these careers? What obstacles would be most difficult to overcome if a male chose to become a secretary?

Section 2

Issues in a Changing Workplace

The United States is recognized around the world for political freedom and equality in the voting booth. However, equality in the workplace remains a distant goal for many workers. For many minority groups, unequal pay and limited advancement opportunities are issues that must still be resolved. For many pregnant women, maternity leave and

related benefits are not equitably provided. For most families with children, access to high-quality, reliable child care is a major issue.

Wage Discrimination

Title VII of the Civil Rights Act of 1964, as amended, prohibits wage discrimination based on

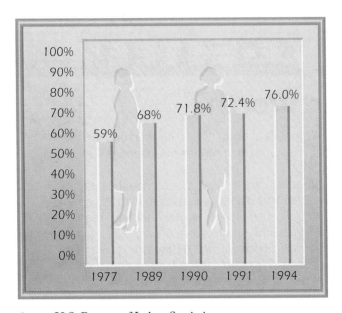

Source: U.S. Bureau of Labor Statistics.

▲ *Figure 13.3 Closing the Gap. Women's salaries as a percentage of men's salaries.*

sex, race, religion, and national origin. In 1981, the U.S. Supreme Court decided that wage discrimination is not limited to unequal pay for equal work. How many violations of this law can you find in the next two paragraphs?

The earnings gap between men and women can be seen by comparing average weekly earnings. Although the gap is narrowing, women still earn an average of 27.6 percent less than men. Figure 13.3 shows the annual earnings of full-time female workers as a percentage of the earnings of full-time male workers.

This earnings gap also exists for minority men. College-educated African American men had average weekly earnings of about 75 percent of the average for similarly educated white men.

CAREER TIP

Title VII legislation requires that leave for child care be granted on the same basis as leave for other nonmedical reasons, such as non-related travel or education.

▲ *Less than 2 percent of all corporate board officers are women. If you were the owner of this company, would you hire a highly qualified female vice-president or a less qualified male? Why or why not?*

The Glass Ceiling

Minorities and women have made significant gains at the entry level of employment and in the first levels of management. They have not experienced similar gains in the middle and senior levels of management, though, even when they possess the required experience, credentials, and general qualifications.

This artificial barrier to higher-level promotions is known as the **glass ceiling**. It is based on attitudinal or organizational bias that prevents qualified individuals from advancing into higher management positions.

In a sample of ninety-four reviews of corporate headquarters of America's 1,000 largest companies, the Department of Labor uncovered these facts:

• Of 147,179 employees at these companies, women represented 37.2 percent, and minorities represented 15.5 percent.

• Of the 147,179 employees, 31,184 were in management, from the supervisor of a clerical pool to the chief executive officer and the chairman of the board. Of this number, 5,278, or

BUILDING SELF-ESTEEM

What's Your Worth?

Some women who work in traditional jobs for women have filed complaints under Title VII, charging that their work is undervalued and underpaid in comparison with other work (generally work performed by men) that is different in content but requires the same or less educational preparation, experience, skill, and responsibility. This issue focuses on **comparable worth**. Tests of comparable worth usually compare skills, education, energy, and working conditions.

In one equal-pay lawsuit filed by a multiunion council against hundreds of New York City hotels and motels, the settlement cost the hotels and motels about ten million dollars to end a long-standing wage-discrimination pattern. The settlement meant extra pay hikes for twelve thousand female hotel maids, who are now called *room attendants*. The arguments in the case weren't complicated. The female room attendants cleaned and polished rooms. The male house attendants also cleaned and polished, but they worked in hallways and lobbies—for more money.

In other cases, nurses questioned their pay compared to that of city sanitarians (health inspectors), and clerical employees claimed discrimination in comparing their wages to those of employees working in the physical plant. This is a developing area of the law, and it is not yet clear what practices the courts will decide amount to sex-based discrimination.

Critical Thinking

1. How would the settlement with the hotels and motels build the self-esteem of the room attendants?
2. How would you rule if you had been the judge in the case of the room attendants?
3. In what ways did the case meet the usual comparable-worth tests?
4. How can you fairly compare nurses' pay and that of city sanitarians, or clerical employees' pay and that of physical plant employees?

16.9 percent, were women and 1,885, or 6.0 percent, were minorities.

- Of 4,491 managers at the executive level (assistant vice-president and higher), 6.6 percent were women and 2.6 percent were minorities.

In a separate survey, minorities and women were found to hold less than 5 percent of the top executive positions in our nation's 1,000 largest corporations. In yet another report, minority women were shown to make up only 3.3 percent of all female corporate officers, who in turn make up less than 2 percent of all corporate officers.

Sexual Harassment

Sexual harassment, a form of sex discrimination, is an unlawful employment practice. The Equal Employment Opportunity Commission's (EEOC) "Guidelines on Discrimination Because of Sex" state that unwelcome sexual advances, requests for sexual favors, and other verbal or physical conduct of a sexual nature constitute sexual harassment.

An employer may be held responsible for the acts of its workers and supervisory employees, regardless of whether the specific acts complained of were forbidden and regardless of whether the employer knew of their occurrence. An employer is responsible for sexual harassment by co-workers if the employer knew or should have known of the conduct and failed to take immediate and appropriate corrective action. An employer may also be responsible for sexual harassment by clients or customers.

Consider the following examples of sexual harassment:

- Jodi White was working on the word-processing machine when the manager walked up behind her, placed his hand on her shoulder, and said, "Jodi, if my wife was as pretty as you, I would be a happy man." Harassers frequently defend this type of behavior as simply being complimentary.
- Tricia Hoyle worked in the accounting department. Mr. Burriss, her supervisor, called her into his office at least once a week to go over the departmental budget. He kept magazines with pictures of nude women opened on the table with the budget documents. He addressed her as "honey" or "sweetheart" and never failed to ask Tricia if she ever thought about posing for nude pictures.

Tricia decided that she wouldn't take any more harassment from Mr. Burriss. She told him that he must either behave in a businesslike manner or she would find it necessary to go to his boss and explain what he was doing. Mr. Burriss warned Tricia that if she tried anything like that, it would be his word against hers, and he would see to it that she was fired.

What advice would you offer to Jodi and Tricia? What good things might happen to each of them if they follow your advice? What unpleasant things might happen?

Sexual harassment is frequently a way that insecure people attempt to exercise power over others. Although some harassers are in positions of authority (supervisor, employer, or teacher), co-workers and students can also harass one another. Sexual harassers almost always act alone and fre-

GETTING MORE INFORMATION

For further information on procedures to follow if you are sexually harassed, contact the

Equal Employment Opportunity
Commission
Office of Communications and
LegislativeAffairs
Washington, DC 20507.

quently harass several different people at the same time. Harassment is usually directed toward the victim consistently over a long period of time, and victims sometimes feel powerless to stop it.

Do any of the following facts surprise you?

- The victim of sexual harassment may be a woman or a man, and the harasser does not have to be of the opposite sex.
- The victims of sexual harassment can include anyone who is affected by the offensive conduct.
- It is not necessary for the victim to be fired or denied opportunities for advancement for a case to be considered unlawful sexual harassment.
- The victim must make it clear to the harasser that his or her conduct is unwelcome.

Women are harassed more frequently than men. Research indicates that only one out of ten men will encounter sexual harassment on the job. However, one out of two females will encounter sexual harassment during their careers. If you are a victim of sexual harassment, follow these guidelines:

1. Inform the harasser directly that the conduct is unwelcome and must stop. Refuse all invitations firmly.

▲ *To avoid legal responsibility for sexual harassment, employers must: have a policy against harassment, have a proper complaint procedure, and communicate disapproval of harassment to their employees.*

2. Write a letter to the offender, detailing the specific behaviors you want stopped and describing the action you will take if the behavior continues. Date the letter, sign it, and keep a copy. Give the letter to the offender in front of a witness.

3. Keep a written record of the dates, times, places, and details of any incidents of harassment. Be sure to record your response.

4. Keep a copy of all performance evaluations.

5. Try to find witnesses or other victims of harassment in your workplace.

6. Follow the grievance procedures (if any) in your employee's handbook to give your employer an opportunity to correct the situation. Tell a supervisor, if appropriate, or contact the employer's human resources department.

7. Promptly file a complaint with the local field office of the U.S. Equal Employment Opportunity Commission. (There are time limits on claims.) If the results of your other efforts are unsatisfactory, consider filing a lawsuit.

Pregnancy

As more women enter the labor force, the need for maternity and parenting leave for the birth or adoption of a child is increasing. Men as well as women have to combine the responsibilities of work and family life. **Maternity leave** is disability leave granted to women as a result of pregnancy or childbirth or to care for a newborn or newly adopted child. Parenting leave is time given to mothers and fathers to care for a newborn or newly adopted child.

Employers cannot legally refuse to hire a woman because of her pregnancy as long as she is able to perform the major functions of the job. They can't legally refuse to hire her because of their prejudice against pregnant workers or the prejudice of co-workers, clients, or customers.

Child Care

More than 60 percent of U.S. children have mothers who are either employed or looking for work. This factor alone makes the availability and affordability of child care an important matter of national policy. Research shows that child care is needed at all income levels, even though the type of care selected varies according to family income. When employees face difficulty in arranging for child care, the frequent results are absenteeism, tardiness, low morale, and reduced productivity.

The number of employers who provide day-care centers at the workplace is increasing, but

C AREER TIP

The Family and Medical Leave Act requires employers with fifty or more workers to provide employees with unpaid time off for the birth or adoption of a child. This law covers about 40 percent of the nation's work force and about 5 percent of all employers.

▲ *David's mother is a mechanical engineer. This will be her first day on the job and David's first day to stay at the company's daycare center. What do you suppose David is thinking? David's mother is thinking?*

these few centers do not meet the demand for day care. Continued reliance on women in the work force is expected to influence more employers to expand or adjust their personnel and benefits policies to meet the needs of working parents. Product quality, worker productivity, and competitiveness in the international market are directly related to this issue.

Contingent Employment

The high cost of overtime pay during peak periods of business, when larger-than-normal quantities of goods or services must be provided, can destroy the profitability of a company. To control labor costs and ensure production flexibility, many employers use large numbers of contingent (part-time, contracted, and temporary) workers.

In Chapter 11, you learned about the growth of contingent employment in all areas of the job market. There are both benefits and pitfalls to this type of employment. Contingent work allows many employees to pursue dual roles, such as work and family or work and special interests. Flexible work schedules, supplemental income, and the opportunity to maintain skill levels when full-time work is neither needed nor desired are beneficial aspects of this type of employment. Contingent work also serves as a stopgap when full-time employment cannot be found and it frequently leads to offers of full-time employment.

On the downside, employers rarely include contingent employees in benefit programs, such as health insurance, paid leave, or pensions. The lack of benefits requires contingent employees to purchase benefits at much higher costs than group rates or to do without. The salaries and wages of contingent workers are also generally lower than those of full-time employees, except when a contract is negotiated for a specific amount. Finally, contingent workers do not acquire seniority in an organization. As the number of contingent employees in the U.S. work force continues to increase, these issues will demand more public attention.

Section 2 GET INVOLVED

Answer the following on a separate sheet of paper, and be prepared to discuss your responses in class.

1. What is it about your gender that makes you feel most proud to be a male or female? What makes you feel the least proud of your gender?
2. Would you consider a nontraditional career? Why or why not?
3. Research the four highest-level jobs in a regional business or large institution. How many of these positions are held by women, minorities, and white men?
4. Consider the inequality in earnings between men and women. To what extent do you suppose this is due to each of the following factors:
   - Differences in the quality of education
   - The field chosen for a career
   - Local labor market factors
   - Job performance evaluations
   - The size and financial strength of employers

Give specific examples of situations that support your ideas.

Section 3

Changing Opportunities

The U.S. work force will include 147 million people by the year 2005, an increase of 20 percent from 1990. Events and trends taking place in today's economy and population will shape and characterize the workforce of the future. An understanding of these events and trends will help you prepare for career success. Compared to today's work force, the work force you enter will have these features:

- More older workers and fewer younger workers
- More women, minorities, and immigrants
- A continuing shift to service occupations
- More international competition
- Rapidly advancing technological changes
- An increasing demand for highly skilled workers

Several factors will cause changes in an industry's demand for workers in a specific occupation. These include changes in business practices, technology, and the goods or services provided. For example, changing business practices will benefit paralegals, who will perform more of the work presently done by lawyers. On the other hand, changing technology will lower the demand for gasoline service station attendants and bank tellers. They will be victims of automated gasoline pumps and banking machines.

Shifts in the kinds of products or services that consumers demand will benefit gardeners and groundskeepers. Growing numbers of two-career families have increased the demand for gardening and lawn services. In contrast, the decline in defense spending by the federal government will reduce the demand for blue-collar and technical workers in many defense-related occupations.

Figure 13.4 on the next page shows the occupations with the greatest projected changes in employment. Can you think of an occupation that will benefit or suffer because of a major event that took place in the past year?

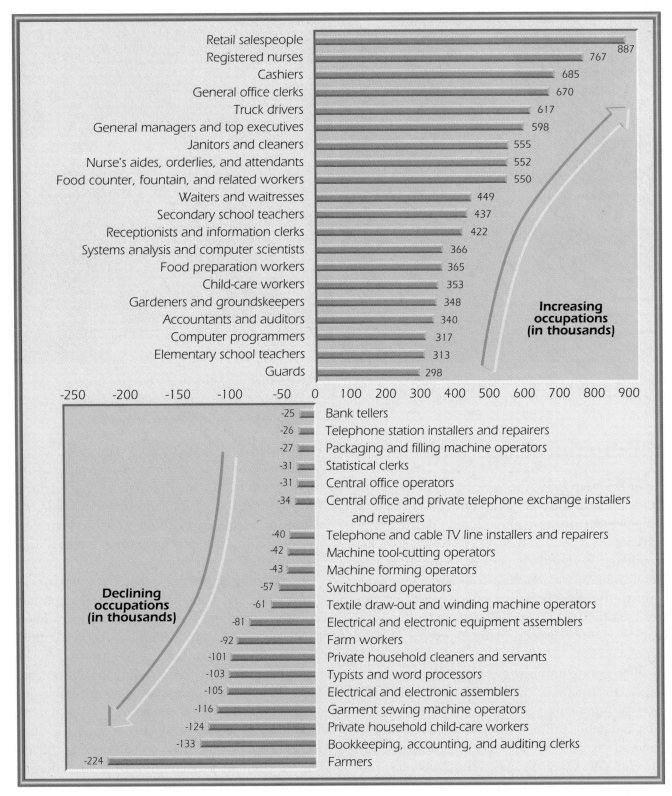

▲ *Figure 13.4 Occupations with the Greatest Projected Increases and Declines in Employment, 1990–2005.*

▲ *During your working years, manufacturing employment will decline. However, the use of automated machinery will increase the amount of goods produced.*

▲ *Ramon likes people and enjoys working in the service-producing sector. Working in a growing industry provides him with a sense of job security.*

Production to Service

In the year 1850, the agriculture sector of the economy accounted for almost 60 percent of total employment in the United States, and the non-agricultural goods and services sectors each accounted for about 20 percent. Since then, the services industry has shown almost continuous growth. By the 1920s, the service-producing sector took the lead in employment. Today, the agriculture sector represents only 3 percent of total employment.

The **goods-producing sector** includes mining, construction, and manufacturing. The **service-producing sector** includes transportation and public utilities, wholesale and retail trade, finance, insurance, real estate, other services, and government. Over the past several decades, service-producing organizations have dominated economic growth, and goods-producing organizations have declined.

Between 1990 and 2005, 75 percent of all employment growth is expected to take place in the services and retail trade industries. Health, education, business services, and restaurants will account for a large part of this growth. What does this mean for students preparing for the work force of 2005?

Identifying occupations that have a favorable growth rate and many job openings is important in career planning. It is also important to know which occupations are declining. As an example, the health-services industry is growing much faster than the average. Therefore, health occupations are among those providing favorable job prospects at all levels of education.

Within the goods-producing sector, agriculture and construction occupations will increase, offsetting a decline in manufacturing and mining employment. Construction is the only goods-producing sector expected to have job growth. Almost a million new jobs will boost employment in the construction industry to 6.1 million by the year 2005. Government spending for additions and improvements to roads, bridges, sewers, and water systems is the main reason for this projected growth.

Overall, the goods-producing sector is expected to have increasing output, but it will employ fewer workers. The number of goods-producing workers is projected to be 25.2 million.

Technology and a Change of Pace

About 90 percent of all scientific discoveries occurred during the last thirty years. During the next ten to fifteen years, this pool of knowledge will double again. The pace of technological development is so rapid that electronics products and processes become outdated in three to five years. In most other industries, product life rarely exceeds five to ten years. Changing technology will continue to alter the products we make and how we do our work.

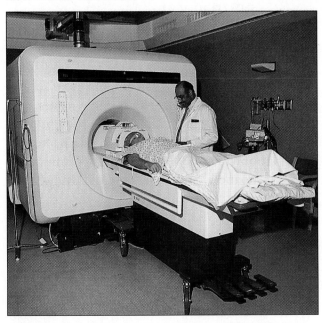

▲ *Robert is a magnetic resonance imaging (MRI) technologist. Having several years' experience as a radiographer (X-ray technician) enabled him to obtain his MRI license in one year of evening classes.*

Technology affects our personal lives, workplace, and life span. The development of the magnetic resonance imaging (MRI) scanner is one example. This complex instrument allows physicians to view the very early stages of a developing disease inside the body. Early detection of disease shows great promise for increasing the human life span. For each two-million-dollar MRI scanner a hospital or clinic buys, it must add at least two full-time technologists to its staff.

Superior technology is an important source of competitive advantage. It eliminates jobs that are no longer efficient and creates new jobs to replace them. Automated machinery has resulted in higher levels of productivity from workers in the manufacturing sector.

Technology is a driving force in determining what tasks a certain occupation will perform as well as how many or how few workers will be needed. For example, business offices have increased their use of computers and other communications technologies at a rapid pace. As a result, the demand for clerical and managerial jobs has declined, but the demand for workers with a knowledge of computers and office technology (systems analysts) has increased.

A Global World of Work

The competitiveness of U.S. products in terms of quality and cost is continually tested in the global marketplace. Countries in Europe, Asia, and other parts of the world have emerged as strong challengers in international commerce. Americans have been forced to recognize that competition from abroad is exerting as much influence on the quantity and quality of jobs as is competition from within the U.S. economy.

American employers are continually seeking ways to reduce labor costs, maintain product quality, and remain competitive in a global economy. The impact of foreign competition can be measured by the loss of domestic and foreign markets and the decline of many basic industries in the United States.

To improve their global competitiveness, U.S. industries are continually adjusting production and job requirements to reflect consumer demand. When it becomes necessary to make major changes rapidly within an industry, worker displacement (layoffs) may result.

American employers use several strategies to cut costs and maintain **production flexibility** (ability to respond quickly to production demands). As mentioned previously, contingent workers can be moved on and off the payroll as they are needed. Hiring contingent workers is less expensive than maintaining permanent workers.

Employers also lower their costs by moving production to **offshore** (not on the U.S. mainland) manufacturing and service operations. The U.S. firms that do the largest amount of offshore assembly are electrical machinery, transportation equipment, and metals companies. Their principal products include semiconductors, textiles, television sets and components, and motor vehicles.

Other examples of U.S. companies that have service operations offshore are seen in computer-

▲ *Thirty-nine steel mills located in the United States are owned by Japanese corporations. What preparation are you making to become a competitive worker in a rapidly changing international economy?*

ized data- and text-entry work. These operations may be as far away as Barbados, India, or Hong Kong. Wage rates are as little as one-tenth of U.S. rates. Workers in the offshore sites usually use American-made word processors or computer workstations. In some cases, two or more workers may key in (type) the same information, and a comparison is made to detect errors. Because wage rates are so low, this process is less costly than doing the work in the United States.

Workers who lose their jobs or whose hours or wages are reduced as a result of increased imports are eligible for trade-adjustment assistance under the Trade Act of 1974. Trade-adjustment assistance includes a variety of benefits and reemployment services to help unemployed U.S. workers prepare for and obtain suitable employment. Workers may be eligible for training, a job search allowance, a relocation allowance, and other reemployment services.

The number of Americans employed by foreign-owned companies in the United States has increased dramatically in the last decade. As an example, BP (British Petroleum) America employs almost forty thousand workers in the United States. Japanese-owned facilities located in Ohio, Illinois, Michigan, Indiana, Kentucky, and Tennessee include thirty-nine steel mills, nine rubber and tire factories, seven auto-assembly plants, and 250 auto-parts suppliers. These facilities provide U.S. workers with about 100,000 manufacturing jobs. Nationwide, more than 350,000 Americans work for Japanese companies in either the service or manufacturing sectors.

In October 1983, the Caribbean Basin Economic Recovery Act **(CBERA)** was signed into law by President Reagan. CBERA is a trade and tax law to help solve economic problems of the Caribbean Basin region. CBERA includes a provision directing the president, when designating specific Caribbean Basin countries as eligible for trade preferences, to take into account whether workers in the country are afforded "reasonable workplace conditions and enjoy the right to orga-

Solving The Problem

Made in America?

Manuel Perez worked nine years in the Great Lakes region for an American-owned automobile company. He and his co-workers assembled automobile engines. Manuel started out working on the assembly line and spent his last six years as a quality-control technician. He ran tests on a variety of parts to ensure that they were machined to specific tolerances (allowable deviations from a standard) before they were used in an engine. Many of the engine parts that Manuel checked were manufactured in foreign countries.

During a period of economic recession, the owners closed the plant where Manuel worked and replaced it with an offshore engine-assembly plant. The savings from wages and taxes enabled the company to assemble their engines at a healthy profit. The assembled engines were then shipped back to the United States, where they became part of "American-built" automobiles.

Manuel and nine hundred other workers were laid off. Workers with ten years or more of service were able to retain their pension benefits. Manuel received three months pay but no benefits. He was allowed to keep his health and life insurance if he wished to pay the premiums. Five months later, Manuel was still out of work and out of money.

It seemed like everyone in town wanted to sell their homes. The price of houses fell until most people owed more on their homes than they could recover by selling them. The engine plant was the largest taxpayer in the community. The loss of the plant's tax revenue forced the local government and the schools to reduce services and lay off employees.

After ten months of job hunting, Manuel was hired by a Japanese-owned automobile company in Tennessee. More than 95 percent of the workers in the Japanese-owned factory are American. It is a very modern factory, and Manuel is very satisfied with his wages and benefits. Manuel quickly noticed that many of the parts used in the Japanese car he helps assemble are made in the United States. The factory where Manuel works is the largest taxpayer in the region. The taxes they pay help support a fine school system and pay for services in the town where Manuel lives.

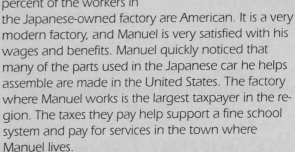

Critical Thinking

1. Slogans like "Buy American" are very popular. Which one of Manuel's employers builds an "American" car? Defend your answer.

2. Which of Manuel's employers do you consider to be the best citizen? Why? How would this question be answered by people in the Great Lakes region? in Tennessee? in Japan?

nize and bargain collectively." Countries that comply receive trade preferences, such as duty-free trade treatment for a wide range of U.S. imports from their region. They may also receive other kinds of trading incentives.

When you enter the workforce, America's economic strength in a technologically advanced and increasingly competitive global world of work will depend on you, your co-workers, and your leaders. It is impossible to predict the exact demands that the future world of work will place on U.S. workers, but it is certain that being flexible and adapting to changing workplace demands will make individual workers and employers more successful.

Answer the following on a separate sheet of paper, and be prepared to discuss your responses in class.

1. The wage gap between jobs in the service sector and jobs in the manufacturing sector is wide. In some cases, service workers earn only fifty-one cents for every dollar that manufacturing workers earn. Should service-sector jobs pay as much as manufacturing jobs? Support your viewpoint.

2. Ask a parent, friend, or neighbor to help you locate a worker who lost his or her job in the past three years because of new technology or offshore production. How is this person presently earning a livelihood? How does his or her present job compare to the previous job?

3. Is it wise to use U.S. trade laws to promote international fair labor standards with our global trading partners? How could this help or hurt U.S. workers?

Section 4

Preparing for a Changing World of Work

This quote, taken from "Building a Quality Workforce," a joint publication of the U.S. Departments of Labor, Education, and Commerce, sends a clear message to students who are preparing for career success. The constantly changing world of work will require them to be flexible and adaptable.

Stay Prepared

As you enter the changing world of work, the needs of business will require that you adapt your skills to new worker roles throughout your career. As a worker of the future, you will be more responsible for your own career development and job security. In fact, your job security will depend on your marketable skills.

Another important consideration when planning your future career is the above-average growth rate for jobs that require higher levels of education and training (Figure 13.5). In 1990, ad-

> Our jobs are changing rapidly due to reorganization and technological changes. Our workers of the future can expect at least three to four career changes requiring retraining during their careers in our companies. They will increasingly be called upon to adapt and learn ways to conduct our business. Also, the international business environment we operate in requires increased flexibility.
>
> Patricia Donald, BellSouth Corporation, Atlanta, Georgia

Occupational group	Percentage of Educational Attainment of Workers				
	Projected change, 1990-2005	Less Than High School	High School	One to Three Years of College	Four Years of College or More
All occupations	20%	15%	39%	22%	24%
Managerial	27%	4%	27%	24%	45%
Professional specialty	32%	1%	8%	16%	74%
Technicians	37%	3%	28%	37%	33%
Marketing and sales	24%	12%	39%	25%	24%
Administrative support	13%	6%	51%	31%	13%
Services	29%	28%	45%	19%	6%
Precision production	13%	21%	53%	20%	6%
Operators	4%	31%	52%	13%	3%
Agriculture-related	5%	35%	41%	14%	8%

▲ *Figure 13.5 Projected Occupational Growth, 1990–2005, and Distribution by Educational Attainment.*

ministrative, executive, and managerial workers, professional specialty occupations, and technicians and related support occupations represented slightly more than 25 percent of the U.S. work force. It is projected that these three major occupational groups will account for 41 percent of all job growth between 1990 and 2005. By contrast, blue-collar employment is predicted to decline or experience only slow growth.

Cultivating new skills will increase your job options and your employment security. Learning may include formal class instruction, on-the-job training, mentoring by someone already doing the job, or a combination of these.

Job Mobility: Moving On

Since the first settlers began moving west seeking less-expensive land and more opportunities, Americans have been a mobile society. In the past, job mobility meant moving from the farm to job opportunities in the city. Today, it means moving from one **urban area** (a community of 2,500 or more) to another. More than 50 million Americans change their address every year.

Six of the fastest-growing metropolitan areas in the early 1990s were in the West, and four were in the South (only one of them in Florida). By contrast, nine of the ten fastest-growing metropolitan areas during the 1980s were in Florida.

In past years, the average American could expect to live in one area and work for one employer for most of his or her career. Today, the job market shifts with changes in technology and global mar-

▲ *In today's world of work, finding a job or being promoted could require moving from one urban area to another. What factors will you consider before you move?*

Figure 13.6 AVERAGE ANNUAL PAY IN SELECTED STATES

State	Average Annual Pay	State	Average Annual Pay
Alabama	$19,593	Minnesota	$22,155
Arizona	20,808	Mississippi	17,047
California	24,921	Nebraska	17,694
Florida	20,072	New Jersey	26,780
Georgia	21,071	New Mexico	18,667
Idaho	18,146	New York	27,303
Illinois	24,211	North Dakota	16,932
Kentucky	19,001	Ohio	21,986
Louisiana	19,750	Tennessee	19,712
Massachusetts	25,233	Texas	21,740
Michigan	24,853	Washington, DC	32,106

Source: U.S. Bureau of Labor Statistics.

ket demands. In the future, workers will probably make several geographical moves during a working career.

Two factors that workers should consider as they make geographical moves are the differences in average earnings and the cost of living. Earnings have generally been highest on the West and East Coasts and the lowest in the South. Among industry divisions, average earnings are highest in transportation and utilities and are lowest in retail trade.

Differences in pay levels within individual geographic areas reflect a number of factors, such as the type of industry, extent of unionization, average size (number of employees) of employers, and length of service of employees in their current jobs. Figure 13.6 provides examples of the average earnings for various sections of the United States.

Area cost-of-living factors are an important consideration when relocating. These expenses generally require 70 percent of a worker's income: housing-related expenditures, state and local taxes, and transportation. The cost-of-living index

measures relative price levels for consumer goods and services in a geographic area for a middle-management standard of living. The national average equals 100. Figure 13.7 presents the cost-of-living index for several metropolitan areas. Each participant's index is read as a percentage of the national average.

Metropolitan Area	Cost-of-Living Index
Albuquerque, NM	99.1
Augusta, GA	99.3
Cleveland, OH	90.7
Dallas, TX	103.1
Jacksonville, FL	96.7
Knoxville, TN	90.9
Los Angeles, CA	127.4
Lexington, KY	100.1
Mobile, AL	95.5
Nassau-Suffolk, NY	159.3
Omaha, NE	91.2

▲ *Figure 13.7 Cost of Living Index for Selected Metropolitan Areas, First Quarter 1990.*

How do these cost-of-living figures compare with the average annual earnings shown in Figure 13.6? Are workers really earning a great deal more when they make geographic changes, or do they spend their additional income on everyday living expenses?

Section 4 GET INVOLVED

Answer the following on a separate sheet of paper, and be prepared to discuss your responses in class.

1. Interview a friend or relative who has worked for more than fifteen years. Use the following questions:
   - How has your work changed because of advances in technology?
   - How has your work remained the same?
   - Have you found it necessary to learn new skills during your career? If so, what new skills have you learned? How did you learn them?
   - What effect has learning or not learning new skills had on your career?

2. Make a brief list of your most important personal and career interests.
   a. What areas of the country would be best suited to your personal interests? Why?
   b. What areas of the country would be best suited to your career interests? Why?

3. Which geographic area would provide you with the most desirable career future? Which would provide your family with the most desirable lifestyle? Give specific reasons for each answer.

IMPORTANT FACTS

Sexual Harassment

A poll of 1,300 members of the National Association for Female Executives revealed that 53 percent had been sexually harassed by people with power over their jobs or careers. Sixty-four percent did not report the incident, and half of those who did said that the problem wasn't solved to their satisfaction.

The Cost of an Hour's Work

Manufacturers in four of the world's twelve leading industrial countries pay their workers more for an hour of labor than U.S. manufacturers do. The figures below are in U.S. dollars and include fringe benefits.

Country	Hourly Wage
Norway	$21.86
West Germany	$21.30
Sweden	$20.93
Canada	$16.02
United States	$14.77
Japan	$12.64
Spain	$11.61
Taiwan	$3.95
Korea	$3.82
Portugal	$3.69
Hong Kong	$3.20
Mexico	$1.80

Source: U.S. Bureau of Labor Statistics.

Technology: Boon or Doom

It is projected that the following manufacturing jobs will be lost by the year 2005 due to the adoption of computer-controlled machinery and other automated processes:

- Electrical and electronic assemblers (105,000)
- Forming machine operators and tenders, metal and plastic (43,000)
- Tool-cutting machine operators and tenders, metal and plastic (42,000)
- Lathe and turning machine tool setters and setup operators, metal and plastic (20,000)

African American Women in the Labor Force

Increasing numbers of African American women are entering the high-paying and career-oriented managerial and professional specialty occupations. The following list represents a sampling of the talented African American women who have been added to the payrolls during a four-year period.

Occupation	Number
Social workers	36,000
Accountants and auditors	28,000
Investigators and adjusters (except insurance)	29,000
Registered nurses	23,000
Police officers and detectives	16,000
Administrators in education and related fields	9,000
Lawyers	6,000

Pregnant Women in the Workforce

- 71 percent of all women who become pregnant are employed
- 38 percent reenter the workforce by the time their children are three months old
- 58 percent are working by the time their children reach one year of age

Source: Rand Corporation.

Top Jobs for Women—When?

"At the current rate of increase in executive women, it will take until the year 2466—or over 450 years—to reach equality with executive men."

Eleanor Smeal, head of the Feminist Majority Foundation, 1991.

CHAPTER 13 REVIEW

ENRICH YOUR VOCABULARY

On a separate sheet of paper, number from 1 to 18, and complete the following activity. (Do not write in your textbook.) Match each statement below with the most appropriate term from the "Enrich Your Vocabulary" list at the beginning of the chapter by writing that term next to the correct statement.

1. The part of the economy that includes transportation and public utilities
2. Not on the U.S. mainland
3. A community of 2,500 or more
4. The joining together of organizations
5. Being paid and valued in relation to similar work
6. Ability to respond quickly to production demands
7. Jobs in which women comprise 25 percent or less of the workforce
8. An artificial barrier to high-level promotions
9. Reduction in an organization's size to increase efficiency
10. Caribbean Basin Economic Recovery Act
11. An unlawful form of sex discrimination
12. A label placed on groups of people
13. Disability leave for pregnancy or childbirth
14. Elimination of government controls
15. Roles assigned to people because of their sex
16. Sexual identity
17. The part of the economy that includes mining, construction, and manufacturing
18. Purchases of one organization by another

CHECK YOUR KNOWLEDGE

On a separate sheet of paper, complete the following activity. (Do not write in your textbook.)

1. List three major factors that increased the number of American women in the workforce between 1940 and 1980.
2. Who is legally responsible when an act of sexual harassment takes place in the world of work?
3. List five of the events or trends that will shape the workforce of the future.
4. Where will the majority of employment growth take place between 1990 and 2005?
5. What effect has technology had on the useful life of U.S. products?
6. What two major strategies do U.S. firms use to cut costs and maintain production flexibility?
7. Why are some employers moving their production offshore?
8. In terms of job skills, which occupational groups will have the highest growth rate in the future? What responsibilities will this place on the individual worker?

DEVELOP SCANS COMPETENCIES

Government experts say that successful workers can productively use Resources, Interpersonal skills, Information, Systems, and Technology. This activity will give you practice in developing Resource, Information, and Interpersonal skills.

Form cooperative learning groups to develop a time line of the changing workplace.

Assign group members to research changes that have occurred in the workplace over the past 100 years. Changes can include such things as the number of women and minorities in the workforce and the change in the types of jobs available. Use the information from your text, and add information from your group's research.

After you have completed the historical aspect of changes in the workplace, find information that will allow you to continue your time line into the future. What types of jobs will be available in the year 2010? How will women and minorities be affected by these changes?

Illustrate your time line by drawing your own pictures or cutting out pictures from magazines.

Economics and Work

Learning Objectives

After completing this chapter, you should be prepared to:

- define and describe five major components of our economic system
- give examples of the relationship between supply and demand and the price of goods and services
- list several facts that emphasize the importance of individual workers in our economic system
- explain government's role in maintaining a balance between dollars spent for goods and services and the capacity of business to produce them
- view the world of work as "global" rather than local

Enrich Your Vocabulary

In reading this chapter and doing the exercises you will learn the following important terms:

economics
limited resources
scarcity
economic system
free enterprise system
industrial products
services
profit
market
opportunity cost

demand
supply
competition
consumer
Federal Reserve
  System
gross domestic
  product
technology
comparative

Economics is the name of the social science concerned with the way a society uses its productive resources to fulfill the needs (necessities) and wants (luxuries) of each member. The word *economics* comes from the ancient Greek word oikonomikos, meaning "the management of a household."

From ancient times to the present, societies all over the world have shared the basic need for food and shelter. From the various Native American cultures to the present time, people on our continent have used an economic process to satisfy their basic need for food and shelter.

The system for producing and distributing food has changed greatly, but it was as much a part of the Native American economic process as it is a part of our present economic process. The condominiums, apartment buildings, and houses of today are very different from the tepees, pueblos, and hogans of early societies, but all of these dwellings satisfy the same human needs. All were made available to people by the economic process of their societies.

▲ *Consider the many ways that you use forest products. How would unrestricted cutting of forests influence your lifestyle? the careers of more than 135,000 forestry and logging workers?*

Limited resources (natural resources, labor, capital, and management) prevent people from producing and consuming unlimited quantities of a good or service. For example, the early colonists considered their source of wood to be unlimited. After all, the forests stretched for thousands of miles beyond the first settlements. Today, the United States faces a shortage of available timber, and difficult decisions must be made. The unrestricted cutting of timber may result in the loss of a great natural resource. On the other hand, restrictions on the cutting of timber could result in the loss of thousands of jobs in the logging and milling industries. Finding a balance between the consumption, conservation, and recycling of natural resources and the jobs created and maintained by ever-expanding businesses is a major economic concern in the world of work.

When people have limited resources compared to their wants, a condition of **scarcity** exists. All serious economic problems can be traced to a problem of scarcity. It affects us as individuals and as a society. Each of us must make choices concerning the use of our resources to satisfy our wants.

The method a society uses to determine how it will use and distribute available resources (resource allocation) is known as its **economic system**. The major purpose of an economic system is to provide a process for the production and distribution of goods and services. The economic system of a society represents the input of private, government, and social institutions as well as laws, values, and individual priorities. Individually, these factors influence economic decision making; collectively, they determine the economic system.

The U.S. economy is a **free enterprise system**. In our system, people may own the means of production, they have the freedom to use them as they see fit, and they may freely create and operate businesses. All consumers, workers, producers, savers, and investors are involved in the decisions of our free enterprise system. Many economists refer to the U.S. economy as a capitalist, or mar-

▲ *In our free enterprise system, large corporations sell shares of their stock to investors through a stock exchange. More than 200,000 securities and financial services sales representatives are employed nationwide. Would you enjoy working at this major stock exchange?*

ket, system. For most purposes, the terms *capitalist system*, *market system*, and *free enterprise system* have the same meaning.

Freedom of choice is important in our free enterprise system, but the individual freedoms of consumers and producers are limited by social and ethical pressure and laws. These regulators of free choice occur where the freedom of one individual or group ends and the freedom of another individual or group begins.

When matters concerning the public sector are at stake, government frequently intervenes and establishes protective regulations. These regulations may limit certain areas of free choice, private ownership, competition between businesses, or the right to make unlimited margins of profit. Numerous government agencies carry out the government's role in the economy.

Government regulation of our free enterprise system

- Reduces the fluctuations (continual changes) between good times and bad times
- Promotes the growth of businesses and the number of jobs in our society
- Ensures fair competition between businesses
- Provides programs of importance to all people, such as transportation, national defense, and public education
- Takes care of the minimum basic needs of adults and children who are victims of unemployment or other unfortunate circumstances

When a private business or industry makes use of public resources or provides a service that is essential to the public good, it is usually subjected to government controls.

More than ever before in our nation's history, the American public is concerned about economic questions:

- What should be produced?
- How should it be produced?
- For whom should it be produced?

CAREER TIP

Understanding our economic system is an important part of understanding the world of work and planning for career success.

• What effect will production have on our environment?

Developing a basic understanding of our economic system will help you achieve your career goals. It will also help you make wise decisions in your role as consumer and citizen. These decisions will benefit you individually and society as a whole.

Section
1

Production and Service Systems

Satisfying the changing demand for goods and services is the goal of economic activity. Every time a new idea is turned into a product or a service and a business is formed to produce the product or provide the service, jobs are created for workers, and the opportunity to earn profits is created for employers.

The purpose of a production system is to produce goods (items that can be physically weighed or measured) to sell to others. **Industrial products** are goods that are produced for and sold to other producers. For example, a factory may only produce synthetic fibers (plastic threads such as nylon or polyester). Synthetic fibers are industrial products and are sold to companies that manufacture carpets, clothing, or tires. When products are sold to consumers and used for personal, family, or household use, they are consumer goods. What consumer goods have you used this week? What industrial products were used to manufacture those consumer goods?

The purpose of a service system is to provide **services** (tasks that other people or machines do that cannot be physically weighed or measured) to consumers or other businesses. Industrial services are used by businesses. Companies that sell these services include accounting firms, trucking companies, and architectural firms. The services of a doctor, beauty shop, or repair shop are used by individuals; these are consumer services. What services are used by both businesses and consumers?

The sector of our free enterprise system that provides services is growing at a much faster rate than the sector that produces goods. In fact, the service sector will account for about four out of every five jobs by the year 2005 (Figure 14.1).

▲ *Manuel Salerno is an architect. His company is designing an office building (providing industrial services) for a real estate development company on the site he is describing. More than 90,000 architects, 19,000 landscape architects, and 100,000 drafters work for construction-related employers.*

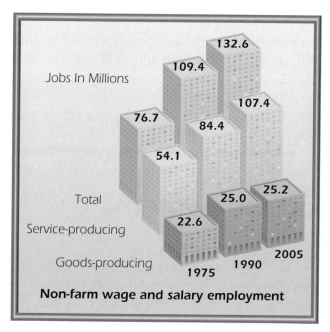

▲ *Figure 14.1 Projected Growth of Service-producing and Goods-producing Sectors.*

The Profit Motive

Profit is the major motivator of every business. The desire to make a **profit** (money that is left over after all of the expenses are paid) is found in businesses of all sizes. Profit is necessary for the creation of new jobs, the training of workers, and the cleanup of industrial pollution. Without profit, companies go out of business, jobs are lost, and office buildings and factories are left to decay. Responsible, efficient, profitable companies are the foundation of a healthy free enterprise system. Have you ever heard someone criticize a company for making a profit?

In both good times and bad times, investors purchase shares of stock in the hopes of making a profit. Depending on the type of stock, stockholders are entitled to certain shares of the profits and are permitted to vote on certain corporate matters. Most people think of stockholders (owners of stock) as wealthy, yet most stockholders are ordinary people. In fact, individuals own 54 percent of all stocks (ownership shares in a corpora-

tion). How would you like to own part of a business with the opportunity to make a profit?

Marketing Goods and Services

A **market** is a group of people or organizations that purchase a particular good or service. If you purchased a pair of shoes in the last year, you are part of the shoe market. The U.S. Army purchased several thousand pairs of shoes last year. It is probably the biggest organization in the shoe market. What other markets are you involved in?

Market research (collecting and using information to link the marketer to the marketplace) is conducted to determine the market demand (what consumers want to buy) before new companies are formed or before established companies expand their production. Market research also tells the organization which consumers are most likely to buy their product or service. These consumers make up the organization's target market. Examples of target markets are small children who watch cereal or toy commercials on TV and senior citizens who read ads for health products. What are some of the products or services that have targeted the teenage market?

In our free enterprise system, numerous companies compete for business in their market. Each company strives for a certain market share (a percentage of sales in a market). Frequently, one company is the leader in its market. Who is the current leader in the shoe market, the cereal market, and the entertainment market? What might cause a leader's market share to go up or down?

Factors of Production

As a business strives to make a profit, it must give up certain resources or benefits to produce a particular product or to provide a particular service. The resource or benefit given up is known as the business's **opportunity cost**. For example, an

Solving The Problem

Investment Creates Jobs

Fran Gomez graduated from an eighteen-month technical school in 1987 with a major in drafting technology. She received very similar job offers from the R.W. Anderson Corporation, a manufacturer of industrial machinery, and SNC Plastic Products, a manufacturer of plastic kitchen products.

Fran wanted to work for a stable, growing company that offered the opportunity for career growth. She looked forward to buying a home, having a family, and being a member of the community. Before accepting a job with either company, Fran checked the profits and growth of each company for the ten previous years. At R.W. Anderson, the number of employees had grown very little, but the company had much higher profits than SNC Plastics. The company was owned by the Anderson family and had no debts. SNC hired new employees each year, and they borrowed money from banks to expand their business.

Fran decided that R.W. Anderson would be her best choice. After all, Anderson was the town's largest employer, was owned by local people, and had no outstanding debts.

Eight years later, in April 1995, Fran's life dreams were coming true. She had been promoted to senior design technician. She and her husband had purchased a small home and were expecting their first child in August. Six weeks before the baby was born, all of Fran's dreams exploded when R.W. Anderson announced that it was closing its factory in two weeks.

Fran learned an important economic lesson the hard way. Some companies make high profits year after year, rather than investing money in new equipment and technology to keep factories and offices modernized or developing new products for growing markets. Eventually, the market for the products they have made year after year shrinks or disappears. They are unable to compete with modern factories, and they can't afford the cost of modernization.

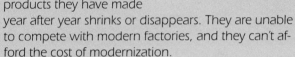

Critical Thinking

1. What should Fran have been looking for during her eight years of employment with R.W. Anderson to foresee the close of the company?
2. What criteria can employers use to figure out how much of their profits to invest each year in developing new products or services, expanding their markets, buying new equipment, updating their buildings, and training their employees?
3. Using "The Handbook of Occupational Clusters" (supplemental material) identify several industries in which Fran could use her drafting skills.
4. In what way was R.W. Anderson an irresponsible business?

automobile company may have to choose between developing and producing a new sports car or a new van if it can't afford to develop and produce both. The decision to produce a new van has the opportunity cost of not producing a new sports car. Suppose a small business must choose between hiring an additional salesperson or modernizing its office equipment. If the business chooses to modernize its office equipment, what opportunity cost will it pay? Companies must continually decide what opportunity costs they should pay.

Wants rather than needs frequently determine how resources will be used. Natural resources are limited. After a natural resource is used to produce a product, it may not be available to create

▲ *These market research analysts are employed by a market research company that is providing services to a major food processing corporation. Their group is concerned with the design, promotion, price, and distribution of a new product being developed for the Mexican-style corn chip market.*

another. Conservation and recycling of resources are important considerations for all businesses.

Distribution Systems

A production system cannot operate without a distribution system (steps involved in bringing products and services from their point of origin to the consumer). For example, every day you use toothpaste that may have been produced hundreds of miles from your home. Fortunately, drugstores are located throughout the nation to sell toothpaste. Without a transportation system, such as trucking or railroads, the toothpaste would not be available in your local drugstore. In fact, a labor force of engineers, machine operators, packaging experts, truck drivers, railroad workers, engine mechanics, construction workers, store managers, retail clerks, and hundreds of other workers are involved in making certain that you can purchase toothpaste at your local drugstore. The distribution of goods is illustrated in Figure 14.2.

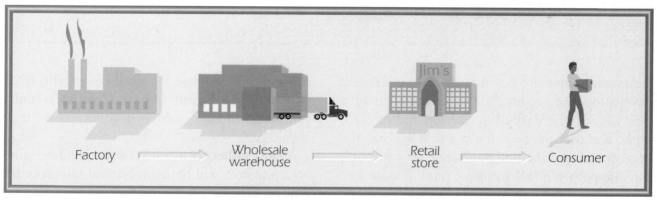

Factory ➡ Wholesale warehouse ➡ Retail store ➡ Consumer

▲ *Figure 14.2 Distribution of Goods.*

Services are usually much easier to distribute than goods. A dentist, beautician, or appliance repairperson may simply rent an office or shop and hire someone to schedule appointments. Large furniture, automobile, or appliance dealers may make repairs on their premises.

Section 1 GET INVOLVED

Answer the following on a separate sheet of paper, and be prepared to discuss your responses in class.

1. Few corporate executives have experienced the job tasks of rank-and-file workers in their organizations. How would this type of work experience help executives and managers understand the total operation of their organizations? How would it help them understand their employees and customers and the problems that their organization needs to solve?

2. One major corporation, Hyatt Hotels, developed a once-a-year training day called In-Touch Day. Corporate headquarters is closed on this training day, and everyone from top executives to office secretaries spends the day working at a rank-and-file job in one of the corporation's hotels.

   a. What message do machine operators in a factory receive when a vice-president spends the day learning and doing job tasks with them?
   b. What message does a vice-president receive when he or she is unable to effectively perform the work tasks of a rank-and-file employee?
   c. What would corporate workers and rank-and-file employees learn by talking and working together for one day as a team?
   d. What effect would this experience have on making the organization cohesive and profitable?

Section 2

Producing for Consumers

In our market economy, consumers and producers are interconnected. Consumers want to purchase as much as possible from producers at the lowest possible price. Producers want to sell their products or services and make as much profit as possible.

Consumers in a Market Economy

The real "boss" in our free enterprise system is you—the **consumer** (a person or group that buys or uses goods or services to satisfy personal needs and wants). Every time you buy a product or service, you are telling the market to supply more of that product. When you and other consumers stop buying a product or service, the merchant must sell something else or go out of business. This interaction between consumers and producers helps determine how much will be produced.

For most consumers, the share of goods and services they will consume is determined by the size of their income. What was your income last month? What goods and services did you pur-

▲ *More than 300,000 purchasers and buyers are employed by wholesaler and retail trade establishments. The buyer for this store must determine the type, amount, and quality (price) of goods the store's customers will buy in the near future. Are you good at planning and decision making?*

chase? What goods or services will you purchase next month if you win a ten-million-dollar lottery?

Figure 14.3 illustrates the importance of consumption as money flows between producers and consumers. When the personal income of the average consumer increases, his or her level of consumption also increases. When personal income decreases, the level of consumption decreases. When a great number of people are unemployed, the amount of goods and services produced will decrease, and jobs will be lost.

Consumers spend their money on different types of goods:

- Durable goods are useful for long periods of time. Automobiles, television sets, clothing, and home appliances are examples of durable goods. When times are bad, consumers can postpone replacing these items. What durable goods do you own? Which ones would you like to replace?

- Nondurable goods must be continually replaced. Toothpaste, gasoline, and food items are

examples of nondurable goods. What nondurable goods have you used this week?

- Necessity goods are essential for everyday life. Food, clothing, shelter, and medical care are ex-

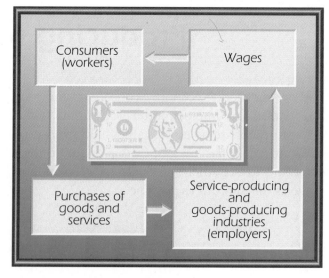

▲ *Figure 14.3 Money Flowing between Producers and Consumers.*

amples of necessity goods. What was the most expensive necessity good you used this week?

- Luxury goods are not essential for everyday life. Diamond rings, filet mignon, and compact discs are examples of luxury goods. What luxury goods would you like to have?

In Chapter 18, you will learn how to become a prudent consumer in our free enterprise system.

Supply, Demand, and Price

The willingness of consumers to buy goods or services at a certain price in the marketplace is known as **demand**. The willingness of producers to produce and sell goods or services at a certain price in the marketplace is known as **supply**. The monetary value (dollar amount) placed on goods or services in the marketplace is the price.

Changes in supply and demand influence prices in the marketplace. For example, wheat is the major raw material used to produce bread. Imagine that you are a Nebraska wheat farmer. Perfect weather conditions have resulted in a wheat crop that is twice your average annual yield. You are delighted because now you have twice as much wheat to sell (the supply). However, people don't plan to buy any more bread than usual (the demand). Also, other farmers have had a bumper crop. You suddenly have a great deal of competition for selling wheat in the marketplace (oversupply). With twice as much wheat available in the market and a demand for only half of it, what will happen to the price of your wheat? It will go down, of course. When the supply of a product or service is greater than the demand, the price goes down. What would have happened to the price of your wheat if the demand for it were greater than the quantity harvested?

Competition (striving against others to win something) plays a key role in establishing the prices of products and services. In our market economy, competition occurs when a business or service strives to win customers by offering lower prices or better quality than its competitors. Com-

GETTING MORE INFORMATION

For more information about monopolies, contact the

Federal Trade Commission
6th St. and Pennsylvania Avenue, N.W.
Washington, DC 20580.

petition exists when there are many buyers and sellers of a certain product or service. McDonald's, Wendy's, and Burger King are big competitors in the fast-food industry. Do these fast-food restaurants ever offer lower prices or better quality to attract customers?

When a business obtains complete control of the supply or demand (most often the supply) of a good or service, it becomes a monopoly. The business price of the monopoly's good or service increases to more than the real value. It represents the controlled conditions of supply and demand. Imagine a situation in which one company controls the production and supply of all the automobile tires in the United States. This single company can demand the highest possible price that consumers can afford for tires. There would be no competition to keep prices down. Consumers would have two choices: buy the tires at the market price or do not operate their automobiles.

Imagine another situation in which one company owns all of the oil refineries in the United States. Oil is of little value until it has been processed through a refinery to make oil-based products like gasoline. This single company can set the price it is willing to pay for oil because it has no competition. The numerous producers of oil would have two choices: sell oil at the price

▲ *Competition for the consumers' business exists on every busy street in America. What examples of business competition can you identify in this photo?*

being offered or go out of business. Does this seem fair in a market economy? If you were a small business owner, what would happen to your business?

The government regulates fair competition between businesses through numerous antitrust laws. These laws prohibit attempts by businesses to monopolize or dominate a particular market. Antitrust laws are necessary to ensure the growth of businesses and the number of jobs in our society. They are especially important to small and new business owners because without the assurance of fair competition between businesses, they could not survive.

Section 2 GET INVOLVED

Answer the following on a separate sheet of paper, and be prepared to discuss your responses in class.

1. Interview an automobile mechanic or car salesperson with ten years or more of experience. Ask the following questions:

   ▪ What effect did the importing of automobiles from foreign countries have on competition in the United States?

   ▪ What effect did it have on the quality of U.S. cars?

   ▪ What about the effect on size, fuel efficiency, and price? Why?

2. In our free enterprise system, consumers spend their money for goods and services. Producers try to make profits by producing and selling goods and services that consumers want. A major purpose of advertising is to increase the demand for a product or service and to get consumers to buy it.

   Choose a product or service, and find at least four ads describing it. Are the ads truthful? Do they make you want to buy the product or service? What groups of people will be attracted by the advertising? Why?

Section 3

Our Monetary System

Early settlers on the American frontier had little need for money. Instead, they exchanged goods or services for other goods or services. This system of exchange is called *bartering*. In the early 1900s, it was not uncommon for a rural physician to accept a supply of eggs, a couple of chickens, or even a pig in exchange for medical services.

In fact, money itself has little value. The value of money exists only in the value of goods and services that it represents. Its value is strengthened when producers and consumers are confident that their government has certain amounts of gold and silver to "back" the money.

As far back as 2000 B.C., gold was used as money. It was scarce, desirable, and perfectly acceptable for buying goods or services or for paying debts. During the seventeenth and eighteenth centuries A.D., wealthy people deposited their gold with local goldsmiths for safekeeping. The goldsmiths provided a paper receipt for the amount of money deposited with them. Years later, the receipts began to be traded for goods or services because of the gold that they represented. This was the beginning of paper money.

Governments eventually began to print and issue money that was backed by and could be exchanged for gold. In 1934, the U.S. government

▲ *During the 1800s, the rapid growth of American cities made "bartering" inconvenient if not impossible. The use of "money" made it easier for business owners to establish prices for their goods or services. Would you enjoy a shopping spree at this mall?*

called in all gold coins and certificates and stopped redeeming paper money in gold. Thus, the amount of money in circulation could be varied to meet both domestic and international needs.

Paper money, no longer redeemable in gold, continues to circulate as freely as ever. We have come to believe that our monetary authorities, even without the old-time discipline of gold at home, will not destroy the purchasing power of the dollar by printing and circulating too much money.

The federal government uses two methods to regulate and influence the economy to maintain a balance between the total dollar amount spent by individuals, households, businesses, and governments for goods and services and the growing capacity of business to produce goods and services.

Fiscal policy is the use of the federal government's taxing, borrowing, and spending powers to counteract ups (periods of inflation) or downs (periods of recession) in the economy. When the government acts to put more money in consumers' hands, the demand for goods and services increases, more jobs are created, and the economy moves toward an up cycle—a period of inflation. The federal government is the biggest consumer in our economy. Imagine the thousands of jobs that are created when the government buys a new fleet of airplanes, ships, or tanks; builds a new interstate highway; or gives money to state and local governments to build bridges or sewer and water systems.

The government can also increase consumers' ability to buy goods and services by reducing taxes. In addition, the government can increase the money it pays consumers in the form of Social Security checks or pensions. These are called *transfer payments*. On the other hand, when the government reduces spending on goods or services, increases taxes, or reduces the money it spends on transfer payments, the economy moves toward a down cycle—a period of recession. Balancing the economy is a lot like flying an airplane.

The pilot (the federal government) makes small adjustments to go up or down in response to changing pressures. Making large, sudden adjustments in either direction could result in a serious crash.

The second method the federal government uses to influence the economy is its monetary policy. The **Federal Reserve System**, a network of twelve regional banks, regulates banking in the United States. The Federal Reserve System increases or decreases the amount of money in our economy by printing more money or removing money from circulation. The Federal Reserve System not only regulates the amount of money flowing through the economy, but it also sets the interest rate it charges commercial banks. In turn, the commercial banks respond to the interest rates they must pay the Federal Reserve banks by lowering or raising interest rates to individual consumers or businesses. If you owned a business and wanted to buy new machinery or build a new building, would you be more likely to expand

▲ *Are you interested in a banking career? The banking industry employs more than 525,000 tellers, 100,000 loan officers, and 230,000 financial managers.*

when interest rates were high or low? What effect does business expansion have on employment?

When individuals or businesses need to borrow money, they go to a commercial (privately owned) bank. When commercial banks need money, they go to a Federal Reserve bank (owned by the federal government).

Most purchases or payments made by individuals or businesses are made with money or checks. Checks are not money, but they represent money and are widely accepted as a form of money. The banking system can increase the supply of money in our economy by making loans to individuals,

businesses, or the government. This increases spending power and the demand for goods and services. What effect would this have on employment?

When you deposit your money in most banks, it is insured by the Federal Deposit Insurance Corporation (FDIC). The FDIC is a government agency that protects small depositors against the failure of an insured bank or savings and loan institution. Before you open an account with a bank, be certain that you see the initials FDIC on its signs. The FDIC safeguards deposits up to the amount of $100,000 in each account.

Section 3 GET INVOLVED

Answer the following on a separate sheet of paper, and be prepared to discuss your responses in class.

1. If our society operated without money, what could you or your family barter to obtain food, shelter, transportation, and clothing? Why did barter work on the American frontier? What conditions have changed to make barter almost impossible in our society?

2. How would an individual or a group of people start a business if there were no banks? What effect would this have on starting or expanding a business? What effect would this have on the number and variety of jobs available in our society?

Section 4

Good Times and Bad Times

Like the pendulum on a clock, our economy swings between periods of "good times" and "bad times." These continual economic changes between prosperity and recession make up the business cycle.

During periods of good times and business peaks, economic activity reaches its highest point in the business cycle. Prosperity is evident as businesses produce goods and services at full capacity,

new businesses are started, and the number of unemployed workers is very low.

Bad times range from mild recessions (when the nation's output does not grow for at least six months) to severe depressions (when the business cycle is marked by high unemployment, numerous businesses fail, and the economy operates far below capacity), such as the Great Depression of 1929 to 1941. During bad times in the business

▲ *Experiencing the "Great Depression" influenced the career choices, and the buying and saving habits of many older Americans. How have you been influenced by good times or bad times?*

cycle, thousands of workers may be laid off from declining industries.

The business cycle affects and is affected by the production and distribution of goods and services, the earning and spending of wages by workers, the number of workers who are unemployed, the trading of goods and services with other nations, and the price of stocks, bonds, and commodities.

During the past fifty years, several safeguards have been built into our economy to help protect business owners and workers alike from large swings in the business cycle:

- Workers are protected, in part, from bad times by unemployment insurance benefits.
- Investors are protected from sharp declines in business profits by corporate policies that attempt to keep dividend payments more stable than corporate profits.
- The federal government's fiscal and monetary policies regulate the rates of interest paid by businesses or individuals when borrowing money. These policies also determine the amount and types of taxes that will be paid and the tax exemptions that will be allowed. When interest rates are lowered to encourage spending

by individuals and businesses, it is called an *easy-money policy*. During periods of easy money (low interest rates), businesses tend to invest in items like new equipment and buildings. A major result of this investment is an increase in the number of jobs available for workers. On the other hand, decreasing the amount of money in the economy and increasing the rate of interest for loans is called a *tight-money policy*. Tight money pushes the economy in the direction of less borrowing, less purchasing of goods and services, fewer jobs, and recession.

The **gross domestic product** (GDP) is the total value of goods and services that a nation produces for the marketplace during a specific time period, usually a single year (Figure 14.4).

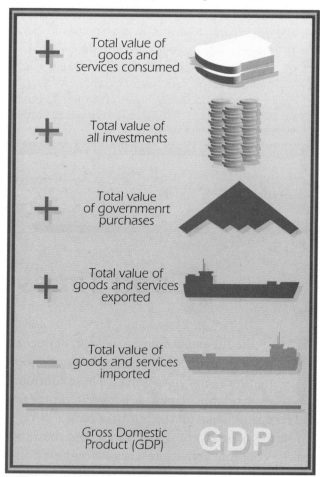

▲ *Figure 14.4 Gross Domestic Product.*

The GDP is expected to grow at a slower rate during the fifteen-year period from 1990 to 2005 than it did between 1975 and 1990. Growth in the number of workers in the work force, one of the major factors of production, is expected to slow. However, the GDP will grow faster than the labor force and employment, due to increasing worker productivity.

When the average price of goods and services increases over a prolonged period of time, the economy is in a period of inflation. During periods of inflation, the consumer demand for goods and services is greater than the quantity of goods and services available.

Remember the law of supply and demand? The increase in consumer demand plus the limited amount of goods and services available cause prices to rise. As the price of most goods and ser-vices increases, the dollar buys less. You have probably heard older people complain that the dollar isn't worth as much as it used to be. What they sometimes forget is that their labor is worth more than it used to be. As a result, they have more dollars to buy goods and services.

Statistics that forecast good times and bad times for the economy are called *leading economic indicators*. Several factors included in leading economic indicators are shown in Figure 14.5. When statistics show these factors to be declining, a recession is indicated. On the other hand, increases in these indicators predict a period of inflation. Modest upward or downward movements in a well-balanced economy indicate good times, whereas sharp prolonged increases or decreases can spell bad times for the economy.

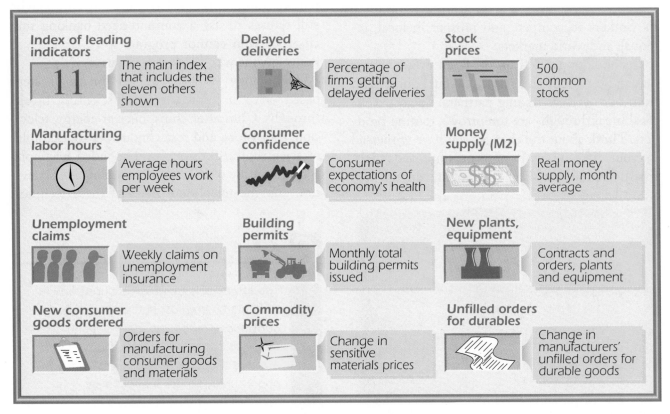

Index of leading indicators
11 — The main index that includes the eleven others shown

Delayed deliveries — Percentage of firms getting delayed deliveries

Stock prices — 500 common stocks

Manufacturing labor hours — Average hours employees work per week

Consumer confidence — Consumer expectations of economy's health

Money supply (M2) — Real money supply, month average

Unemployment claims — Weekly claims on unemployment insurance

Building permits — Monthly total building permits issued

New plants, equipment — Contracts and orders, plants and equipment

New consumer goods ordered — Orders for manufacturing consumer goods and materials

Commodity prices — Change in sensitive materials prices

Unfilled orders for durables — Change in manufacturers' unfilled orders for durable goods

▲ *Figure 14.5 Statistics Used to Forecast the Economy.*

Section 4 GET INVOLVED

Answer the following on a separate sheet of paper, and be prepared to discuss your response in class.

1. Interview a family member or friend with ten or more years of work experience. How was this person affected by periods of inflation and recession during the past ten years? What rate of inflation would he or she consider to be acceptable for our economy? Why?

Section 5

Technology and Change

Technology (the science of mechanical and industrial arts) is the foundation of change in today's world of work. It determines the ability of our nation and its workers to compete and prosper in local, regional, and world markets.

Technology is used to satisfy an ever-growing demand for goods and services in our country and from our overseas trading partners. Today's technical breakthroughs are tomorrow's routine products. Think about the changes you have witnessed in your lifetime with new or improved tools, transportation, medical treatment, energy resources, fabrics, construction materials, computer applications, and agriculture. Many of those products were very expensive ten or twenty years ago but are common today. Do you know anyone who still refuses to use a computerized banking machine or who cannot program a VCR? Do you know anyone who has had laser surgery?

Technology usually changes in small steps based on past knowledge and scientific breakthroughs. Computer chips, nuclear energy, television, transistors, and semiconductors are examples of scientific breakthroughs. The video telephone is based on the well-known technologies of television and the telephone. Each of these technical

> There is nothing permanent except change.
>
> **Heracleitus (sixth century, B.C.)**

CAREER TIP

The effect of change on occupations is difficult to predict; but as technology continues to become more sophisticated, the work force will change. Successful workers will take advantage of every opportunity to learn about new technology in their selected occupations.

▲ *How will your personal lifestyle and the career you are considering be influenced by the widespread use of video telephones?*

▲ *Ralph sells custom-colored paints and related supplies. Although most of his customers are "do-it-yourself" painters, more than 200,000 workers are employed as painters.*

developments eventually opened the door for millions of jobs worldwide.

Technological change is often thought of as a one-time breakthrough or discovery in a product. In fact, industries spend millions of dollars each year working on advances and improvements in their products. The paint industry is one example. From the 1800s until about 1950, paint was manufactured with an oil-based solvent, and lead was a common ingredient. Painting homes, factories, or offices was dangerous and required special skills. Paint fumes were highly flammable and even explosive in confined areas. Fumes were toxic and caused headaches in the short run and cancer over a period of time. Paint spills were impossible to remove from clothing, carpets, furniture, and other fabrics.

Technical change came to the paint industry about 1950, due in part to World War II. During World War II, Japan shut off America's source of natural rubber from the South Pacific. As a result, American researchers developed a synthetic latex that enabled numerous products, formerly made from natural rubber, to continue to be produced.

Without this technical change, the United States would not have been able to produce tires for its jeeps, trucks, and airplanes, life rafts for sailors, and numerous other products.

Following the war, this technology was introduced to the paint industry. Paints made from synthetic latex, using a water base rather than an oil base, were produced. Latex based paint was not explosive, the toxic fumes were gone, dangerous lead was not necessary, and spills could be cleaned up with water. Suddenly, average Americans with little patience or experience could paint everything from the outside of their homes to their living rooms, including lawn furniture and picture frames. A large industry was born, thousands of new jobs were created, and the standard of American life rose another notch. Can you think of other technical changes that have had a similar effect on American life?

Investing in advanced technology, improving current products, processes, and services, and creating entirely new ones are essential if the United States is to improve its productivity and competitiveness. Newly automated businesses must deal with worker issues that result from the use of new technology. These issues include employment security, training for new skills, changes in work organization, and a need for teamwork.

Technology has Changed the Way We Work

A quality workforce is the foundation for our nation's economic strength and international competitiveness. In today's worldwide marketplace, competition requires continual improvement by U.S. companies. They must place the most up-to-date communication and production technology in the hands of their employees. In turn, employees must maintain and develop the skills necessary to use this technology so that the maximum number of high-quality products or services is produced.

As systems of communication and production technology change at a dizzying pace, the skill requirements for jobs become more and more sophisticated. Many workers believe that they cannot keep up with the change and that they are a very unimportant part of the economy. Nothing could be farther from the truth. Labor is one of the most important factors of production. Management and labor are increasingly involved in teamwork decision making for matters related to product quality, operating procedures, and job responsibilities.

Productivity is the amount of goods or services that a worker produces in a certain period of time (usually an hour). Improving the technology of tools and machines increases worker productivity. For example, consider the improvements made in the production of corn. About three thousand years ago, Native Americans from many tribes produced corn. Numerous workers from each tribe scratched the soil with crude hand tools to clear away brush and grass. They dug holes in the soil to plant a piece of fish and a couple of corn seeds. The work was hard, the crop was small, and each meal using corn flour represented several hours of worker labor.

A hundred years ago, thousands of American farmers produced corn. A farmer with a good team of horses could plow about two acres of land

▲ *Farm operators and managers hold about 1,200,000 jobs. Most manage crop production activities while others manage livestock production. Purchasing a farm is very expensive. The trend toward fewer and larger farms is expected to continue.*

each day. Using horses to pull metal plows, disks, and seeders, each farmer could prepare, plant, cultivate, and harvest about thirty acres of land each year, producing about fifty bushels of corn per acre. A single farmer produced far more corn per year than all of the workers in the earlier Indian village.

Today, a much smaller work force of farmers, equipped with giant air-conditioned tractors, produces a much larger harvest of corn than their counterparts of 100 years ago. The difference in these three periods of corn production results from the technology available to the workers. Which farmer worked the hardest? Which had the least product to show for his or her labor? Name another area of production in which advanced technology has increased the quality and quantity of a product or service.

Just as consumers expect high-quality goods or services for the dollars they spend, employers expect high-quality production for the dollars they spend on wages. As workers have produced more goods or services per day, employers have reduced the number of hours in the workweek. For example, a sixty-hour workweek was common in 1850, but in 1950, a forty-hour week was typical. However, the average American worker's standard of living, measured in purchasing power, increased dramatically.

Occupational Specialization

One hundred and fifty years ago, more than 90 percent of the workforce was involved in agriculture. Families were largely independent, producing most of their own food and clothing and frequently building their own homes. There were few specialists in the workforce. Today, less than 4 percent of the workforce is involved in agriculture, and more than 99 percent of U.S. families are interdependent: they produce goods or provide services for others, and they use their earnings to purchase necessities and luxuries. With few exceptions, today's workers are specialists.

Occupational specialization occurs when a worker focuses on producing one particular good or providing one particular service. It is the foundation of all modern economic systems.

Through specialization, our nation is able to produce a higher volume of goods or services at a lower cost than would otherwise be possible. In turn, specialists use their wages to purchase goods and services from other specialists at a lower cost. The efficiency that results from specialization enables all members of the workforce to have a higher standard of living.

Figure 14.6 demonstrates the high degree of interdependence among workers and businesses in the U.S. economy. Notice how money flows in a cycle through our economic system.

Specialization may be regional. Regional specialization occurs when specific natural resources in a geographic region are utilized. Idaho potatoes, the wine region of California, Georgia

▲ *Keith is employed in the vineyards of a large wine producer. Ideal climate and soil conditions have helped wine production to become a regional specialization in the Napa valley of California.*

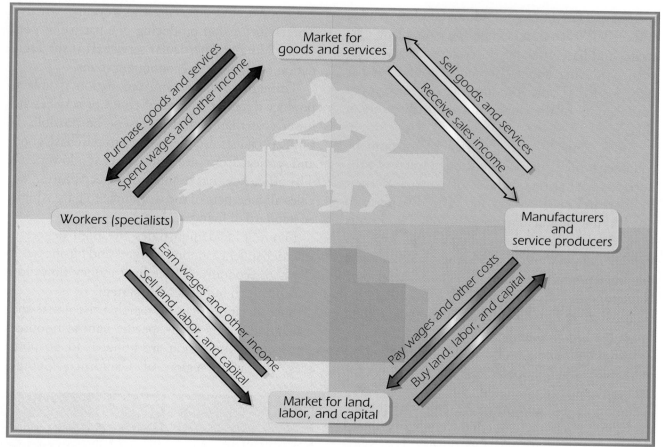

▲ *Figure 14.6 The Interdependence of Workers in a Specialized Economy.*

peaches, and the steel mills of Ohio and Pennsylvania are examples of regional specialization. What specialization takes place in your region of the country? What natural resources or other factors have influenced this specialization? What occupations are in demand because of this specialization?

When certain geographic regions or nations are able to produce more of a certain product or provide more of a certain service at a better price than others because of the efficiency they gain from specialization, they have a comparative advantage over competing regions or nations. A **comparative advantage** is the ability of a producer to provide a good or service at a lower opportunity cost than other producers. For example, the nations of Southeast Asia have a comparative advantage over most of the world in their ability to

produce natural rubber. This is largely due to the region's climate. By specializing in a product in which they have a comparative advantage, the nations of Southeast Asia are able to sell natural rubber on the world market. They use the money they receive to purchase other goods and services from other nations.

Another example of comparative advantage is our nation's real manufacturing output as a percentage of real gross national product. Our GDP has been increasing while manufacturing employment as a percentage of total payroll employment has been declining. In other words, more goods are being produced by fewer workers than in the past. What effect does this increased output have on employment opportunities in the United States? What effect does it have in your community?

Section 5

GET INVOLVED

Answer the following on a separate sheet of paper, and be prepared to discuss your responses in class.

1. Occupational specialization affects workers and nations worldwide. Workers of each nation use money earned from the sale of their specialty products to foreign nations to purchase goods that workers in other nations can produce at lower costs.

   a. List goods or services used in your region that are imported from another nation. Make another list of goods or services produced in your region and exported to other nations. Does your region export more than it imports? If so, the balance of trade is in your favor.

   b. List specific jobs gained or lost in your region due to the balance of trade with other nations.

2. Television is a major technical development of this century. How much time have you spent in the past week watching TV? How would you have used this time if television had never been invented? Without television, what jobs would be lost in the world of work? What industries would benefit? Ask older friends or relatives about industries that prospered before television.

Section

6

A Global Economy

Consider these facts:
- Census figures tell us that less than 5 percent of the world's population lives in the United States. This means that about 95 percent of the customers buying goods in the world economy live outside the United States.

- Political, economic, and social walls between nations are being removed. As a result, goods, services, information, and technology are traded in a global market.

- It is common for U.S. companies to form partnerships with companies from other nations. The combined technology and resources of these mergers enable both partners to gain a much larger share of the world market.

- The business of many companies is global. Businesses conduct production or marketing operations in several nations or through branches or subsidiaries in which they have an important interest. When a business either purchases or creates another business in another nation, it is known as *direct investment*.

- Offshore business operations developed by Americans vary widely. Many traditional high-volume, standardized production systems and low-wage, labor-intensive production systems have shifted to newly industrialized countries in Latin America, East Asia, and the Caribbean.

- This nation's competitive advantage is its sophisticated, technology-driven, precision-engineered, and custom-tailored commodities or products, which are manufactured with rapidly changing technology.

▲ *Europeans are buying Fords, Asians are drinking Coke with their Big Mac, and Americans enjoy Sony sound-systems and TVs. Ships of all nations are transporting goods around the globe. How will your career choice fit into the global economy?*

The global economy is here. The question is no longer, Will we be involved in the global economy? Rather, the question today is, What must we do to be successful in the global economy?

Government involvement, different monetary systems, and international borders pose problems that must be negotiated before nations can become trading partners. Some governments fear losing technology to other countries, and workers fear the loss of jobs to other nations. Inflation, recession, and economic growth are also international concerns because the success or failure of one world trading partner affects all of the others. For example, imagine the economic effect on

Japan if the United States had a recession and no one could afford to buy a new car. What would happen to the United States if foreign aircraft technology improved greatly and the world stopped buying U.S. aircraft?

Trade agreements like the North American Free Trade Agreement (NAFTA) and the Gener-

AREER TIP

America's economic success in the global market will affect your future career.

Solving The Problem

Changes in the Auto Industry

The U.S. automobile industry has undergone tremendous change since the late 1970s. Once the world's dominant motor vehicle producers, U.S. automakers faced increasingly fierce competition from foreign manufacturers during the 1980s. As one of the U.S. economy's largest employers, the auto industry affects the job prospects of hundreds of thousands of workers. Its lack of sustained employment growth during the 1980s had a negative impact on the U.S. economy.

Until the late 1970s, the American automobile market had remained fairly consistent throughout most of the twentieth century. The "Big Three" U.S. automakers—General Motors, Ford, and Chrysler—dominated the market.

In 1946, worldwide output of automobiles amounted to 3.9 million units, with the United States producing 3.1 million, or 80 percent of the total. Japan produced 15 thousand autos that year. By 1990, Japanese firms (both Japan- and U.S.-based) had captured 33 percent of all U.S. car sales; European firms had 5 percent and Korean firms had 2 percent. Between 1979 and 1989, America's motor vehicles and equipment industry experienced a net loss of 105,000 jobs.

Critical Thinking

1. More than 100,000 American auto-related jobs were lost in ten years due to the sale of Japanese autos. What reaction would you expect from our world trading partners if the U.S. government simply refused to allow Japanese cars to be sold in the United States?

2. How can the United States, or any other nation in the global economy, react to foreign competition without losing jobs or angering global trading partners?

3. If one industry, such as the auto industry, loses jobs because of foreign trade but other industries create new jobs, how do we transfer workers from the declining industry to the new jobs? What if they lack the necessary skills for the new jobs?

---

al Agreement of Tariffs and Trade (GATT) help trading partners resolve problems and encourage trade. Although these agreements do not resolve all trade problems, they do provide a framework for negotiation between trading partners.

Global Trading Terms

As a citizen and worker affected by the global economy, you should become familiar with terms commonly used by our trading partners.

- *Imports*: Goods and services purchased from another nation. The United States imports oil, automobiles, coffee, bananas, tea, silk, natural rubber, and electronic appliances. Many imports are essential to the welfare of a nation's citizens.

- *Exports*: Goods and services sold to another nation. The United States exports airplanes, chemicals, paper, scrap iron and steel, and electronic equipment. Shiploads of U.S. wheat and corn cross the oceans. The latest Hollywood movies, Coca Cola, and McDonald's fast-food restaurants are found around the globe. Exports provide employment opportunities for many workers.

- *Exchange rate*: The price at which a nation's currency can be bought or sold for another nation's currency. On Wednesday, September 29, 1994, one U.S. dollar could be exchanged for 1.4 Australian dollars, 7.7 Hong Kong dollars, 1,560 Italian lira, or 98.9 Japanese yen. (See a recent copy of the *Wall Street Journal* for the current rate of exchange.)

- *Trade quotas*: A limit, established by a government, on either the quantity or the value of certain goods that may be imported or exported. Nations sometimes use quotas to protect their industries from foreign competition. This policy is called *protectionism*. In other cases, nations use trade quotas to punish certain other nations for their trade policies, political behaviors, or military actions.

- *Trade surplus*: The condition that exists when a nation sells more goods and services to other nations than it buys. A nation with a trade surplus has a favorable balance of trade. A trade surplus increases the gross national product.

- *Trade deficit*: The condition that exists when a nation buys more goods and services from other countries than it sells. A nation with a trade deficit has an unfavorable balance of trade. A trade deficit decreases the gross national product.

- *Balance of payments*: The difference between the amount of money a nation's economy spends overseas and the money it receives. This is sometimes referred to as the *balance of trade*. Workers, businesses, and nations will be ruined financially if they continually spend more money than they receive.

When all is said and done, it is the capability of individual businesses that determines how competitive a nation is in the world market. It is the capability of individual workers that determines how competitive a business is in the world market. Making effective use of every employee—from the company's president to its rank-and-file workers—will keep the United States competitive in the world marketplace. This goal requires a work force with competitive skills and a positive work attitude.

Section 6 GET INVOLVED

Answer the following on a separate sheet of paper, and be prepared to discuss your responses in class.

1. High-tech communications systems make it possible for a salesperson in Chicago to sell machinery to a manufacturer in Europe without leaving the office. Using the latest computers, an automobile company in Tokyo can develop a list of potential U.S. car dealers for the company's latest marketing campaign. A customer in Paris can receive a fax from a supplier in Atlanta, Georgia (total time elapsed: two minutes). Technology has reduced the distance between world markets from days to minutes. Communications technology plays an important role in the global economy. Telephones, computers, and fax machines enable small businesses to compete in foreign countries as easily as they do in a neighboring city.

   Interview a local businessperson, a member of the chamber of commerce, or a telephone company representative, or ask one of them to speak to your class. Ask the following:

   - What are some advantages and disadvantages of selling goods and services overseas?
   - How can communications technology be helpful or troublesome for a business involved in the global economy?
   - Seventy-five years ago, very few U.S. jobs depended on foreign trade. Today, millions of U.S. jobs depend on the global economy. What has caused this change in the world of work, and what changes do you see taking place?

.IMPORTANT FACTS

Technology: Investment for the Future

In 1990, U.S. investment in information technology systems accounted for more than 40 percent of all investments in new plants and equipment, up from 20 percent in 1980 and 6 percent in 1950.

Unusual Exports

Success in exporting can occur in peculiar ways and in strange marketplaces. Consider the following:

- CalPacific exports disposable wooden chopsticks to Japan. Because the Japanese do not have a readily available supply of lumber, they "fork over" a lot of money to import some 130 million chopsticks every day.
- STP buys oil from the Middle East, processes and packages it in the United States, and exports it back to the Middle East in STP-brand containers.
- Some of the most popular leather shoes in Italy have "made in the USA" labels. Timberland Shoes adopted the attitude, "Let's give it a try and see if it works," and it has.

Source: The World Is Your Market, Washington, DC: Braddock Communications, 1990.

Productivity in the American Steel Industry

In the early 1980s, American steel companies used more than ten hours of labor to produce one ton of steel. Today, the industry average is five hours to produce one ton of steel; it is even less at some mills. American steel is now considered by many to be cost-competitive with steel made in Japan and Europe, the world's quality benchmarks. In their race to close the gap, American firms have installed computers, sophisticated gauges and sensors, automatic inspection systems, new casting plants, and improved furnaces. Yet after spending 25 billion dollars to improve its competitiveness, the U.S. steel industry still can't afford to rest. Other countries are also spending huge sums on modernization.

Source: Cleveland Plain Dealer, April 12, 1992.

Golden Opportunities

By law, the Federal Reserve cannot create paper money and bank reserves in excess of four times the value of gold held by the Treasury in Fort Knox and elsewhere. The reason for connecting the dollar to gold is to ensure that the buying power of the dollar, relative to that of other currencies, remains reasonably stable. Because all nations still desire and will accept gold, it is used as an international money. Many countries, including the United States, pay their debts to one another by transferring gold.

Source: Series for Economic Education, Federal Reserve Bank.

Giants Still Roam the Earth

- Forty-nine of the world's one hundred largest companies are headquartered in the United States.
- Twenty-three of the world's largest companies are Japanese.
- The Netherlands, Royal Dutch/Shell is the largest company in the world.
- Exxon Corporation of the United States is the second largest.
- Nippon Telegraph and Telephone of Japan is third.
- Twenty-seven of the world's one hundred largest banks are Japanese. Included in the top one hundred are thirteen German banks, ten French, eight Italian, and seven American. Seven of the top ten banks are Japanese.

Source: Wall Street Journal, September 24, 1992.

Never on Monday—or Friday

In an Accountemps survey on workplace productivity, 53 percent of the respondents said that their staff gets the most work done on Tuesday. Monday and Friday were rated as the least productive days of the week (33 percent and 59 percent, respectively).

Source: Working Woman, October 1992.

CHAPTER 14 REVIEW

ENRICH YOUR VOCABULARY

On a separate sheet of paper, number from 1 to 18, and complete the following activity. (Do not write in your textbook.) Match each statement below with the most appropriate term from the "Enrich Your Vocabulary" list at the beginning of the chapter by writing that term next to the correct statement.

1. The social science concerned with the way a society uses its productive resources to fulfill the needs and wants of each member
2. The U.S. economic system
3. A person or group that buys or uses goods or services to satisfy personal needs or wants
4. The willingness of consumers to buy goods or services at a certain price in the marketplace
5. The willingness of producers to produce and sell goods or services at a certain price in the marketplace
6. The science of mechanical and industrial arts
7. The ability of a producer to provide a good or service at a lower opportunity cost than other producers
8. A network of twelve regional banks that regulates banking in the United States
9. Natural resources, labor, capital, and management

10. The total value of goods and services that a nation produces for the marketplace during a specific time period
11. Goods produced for and sold to other producers
12. The resource or benefit that a company gives up to produce a particular product or provide a particular service
13. Money left over after all of the expenses are paid
14. Tasks that other people or machines do that cannot be physically weighed or measured
15. A group of people or organizations that purchase a particular good or service
16. Striving against others to win something
17. The method a society uses to determine how it will use and distribute available resources
18. The condition that exists when people have limited resources compared to their wants

CHECK YOUR KNOWLEDGE

On a separate sheet of paper, complete the following activity. (Do not write in your textbook.)

1. What is the major purpose of an economic system?
2. What is the role of government in the economy?
3. What is the goal of economic activity?
4. What are the two major benefits of turning new ideas into products or services and new businesses?
5. What percentage of jobs will be in the service sector by the year 2005?
6. List the five major parts of all economic systems.
7. List three reasons why profit is necessary in our free enterprise system.

8. What are the four factors of production?
9. Why has the federal government passed laws to prevent monopolies?
10. What are three safeguards that have been built into our economy to help protect both business owners and workers from large swings in the business cycle?
11. What is the major advantage of specialization?
12. What is a tight-money policy? How does it affect our economy?
13. What are the two major factors that have moved the world toward a global economy?

DEVELOP SCANS COMPETENCIES

Government experts say that successful workers can productively use Resources, Interpersonal skills, Information, Systems, and Technology. This activity will give you practice in developing Information and Interpersonal skills.

Discuss the importance of interest rates with a parent or other adult. Ask how this person's saving, borrowing, and spending decisions might change if interest rates were 2 percent higher or lower. (Do not ask about specific amounts of money.) Write a paragraph that explains the adult's answers and what they show about the importance of interest rates to consumer decisions.

Entrepreneurs and Small Business Ownership

Learning Objectives

After completing this chapter, you should be prepared to:

- describe what entrepreneurs do and how they contribute to our economic system
- evaluate the advantages and disadvantages of being an entrepreneur
- compare your personal characteristics to the characteristics commonly displayed by successful entrepreneurs
- list six major questions that you should answer before committing yourself to an enterprise
- describe the three major forms of business ownership
- describe the importance of marketing, competition, pricing, location, and assistance from experienced entrepreneurs
- estimate the cost of starting and operating a business
- be aware of required financial records, tax returns, insurance forms, and employee-related paperwork

Enrich Your Vocabulary

In reading this chapter and doing the exercises you will learn the following important terms:

entrepreneurship	venture capital
Small Business	venture capitalists
Administration	balance sheet
sole proprietorship	assets
partnership	liabilities
corporation	net worth
franchise	general ledger
target market	profit-and-loss
moonlighting	statement
start-up	cash flow
working capital	permit

333

An entrepreneur is a person who seeks a profitable opportunity and plans, organizes, finances, manages, and assumes the risks of a business to achieve his or her goal. Entrepreneurs create businesses that offer employment to millions of Americans. They value their independence and enjoy using their ideas to create products or services. Entrepreneurs thrive on the challenge of building and controlling a business. They are filled with self-confidence, and they are tenacious (persistent) in the pursuit of their goals. If they fail at one enterprise, they usually try another.

Our free enterprise economic system encourages people to become entrepreneurs. They frequently see **entrepreneurship** (small-business ownership) as the most promising path to financial success, independence, and true job satisfaction. Additional motivators include

- A strong desire to work at home
- The need to adjust a work schedule to accommodate family responsibilities
- Layoffs and the threat of unemployment

Have you ever dreamed about owning your own business? If not, learning about entrepreneurship could open a door to numerous career opportunities for you. If you have considered becoming an entrepreneur, you will need to learn as much as possible about the world of business before committing your time and money. In either case, the information presented in this chapter will help you decide

- Whether or not your personal characteristics are similar to those of most entrepreneurs
- Which legal form of business would be best for your business
- How to make a plan for your business
- How to finance your business and handle the necessary paperwork

Section

1

The American Dream: Your Own Business

In large cities, small towns, and rural communities throughout the United States, entrepreneurs work at whatever their business requires. When the enterprise is small, they handle every detail, from cleaning to buying supplies to serving customers. In addition, many entrepreneurs perform the necessary bookkeeping and paperwork themselves.

Work tasks and working conditions depend on the type of business and the entrepreneur's goal. For example, Dean Chinrock enjoys owning and operating a flower shop. Dean wants to increase his business but doesn't want to expand beyond his single location. Mary Chen also owns a flower shop, but her goal is to own a network of flower shops within her state. When Mary acquires three shops, how will her work tasks and working conditions be different from Dean's?

Career Tip

About 75 percent of all entrepreneurs obtained the training to start their businesses while working for someone else.

> Self-confidence is the first requisite to great undertakings.
>
> **Samuel Johnson**

Entrepreneurs: Who Are They?

Small business owners are involved in everything from collecting trash to providing high-technology consulting services. The unique ideas and variety of enterprises created by entrepreneurs are endless. Consider the following success stories.

In the 1970s, Debbi Fields was a twenty-year-old homemaker. She occasionally baked cookies

▲ *Most small business operations do not grow into a national chain (Mrs. Fields Cookies) or develop a value of 2.5 billion dollars (Mr. Perot). Whether or not they manufacture specialized electronic products (Apple computers) or sell the tastiest deli products in town, millions of American businesses were begun on a small scale.*

GETTING MORE INFORMATION

For more information on businesses owned by women, contact the

National Association of Women Business Owners
500 N. Michigan Ave.
Chicago, IL 60611

for her husband to take to work, and her husband's clients loved them. Armed with an idea, an entrepreneurial spirit, and a great cookie recipe, Mrs. Fields went into business. Her enterprising spirit and hard work turned her cookie recipe into a national chain of nearly 600 stores.

Ross Perot left IBM as one of its leading salesmen in 1962. IBM and most of his peers told him that his idea of full-facilities management (supplying computers and software along with the personnel to run them) didn't have a chance. By 1968, though, this idea made Mr. Perot a millionaire. In 1984, he sold his company to General Motors for two and a half billion dollars. Mr. Perot didn't have a background in computers. His expertise was selling, dealing with people effectively, understanding finance, and managing.

Entrepreneurship provides an independent career path through which individuals can pursue their strong personal interests. For example, an investment counselor left New York City to do something he really enjoyed: raising plants. He now owns and operates a small commercial nursery. An Arizona woman, limited by muscular dystrophy, valued the mobility a motorized scooter provided her. She now sells and services motorized carts and other equipment for people with physical impairments.

Where Are the Self-employed?

The U.S. Bureau of Labor Statistics surveyed self-employed workers (entrepreneurs) in 1990 to determine what type of business they operated. Figure 15.1 shows the results of that survey.

Among the entrepreneurs operating service businesses, the most common type of self-employment is as a small-scale hotelier. In 1990, lodging places (except hotels and motels) had 321,000 self-employed workers. They operate bed-and-breakfast inns, boarding houses, trailer parks, and campgrounds. Next in popularity among service ventures are beauty shops, with 292,000 self-employed workers, and car repair shops, with 281,000 self-employed workers. Among the self-employed entrepreneurs in retail trade, 253,000 operate eating and drinking establishments, and 205,000 operate various types of stores.

Advantages of Entrepreneurship

Would you enjoy being your own boss? Most entrepreneurs can live and work where they

Figure 15.1 BUSINESSES OWNED BY THE SELF-EMPLOYED

Type of Business Owned	Percentage of Entrepreneurs (%)
Service	39
Construction	15
Retail	15
Agriculture, forestry, or fisheries	14
Other	17

choose and run things their own way. Advancement depends on personal success.

Entrepreneurship frequently draws families closer together because they are working for a common goal: to make the family business successful.

Entrepreneurs have the opportunity to earn much more than people who choose to work for someone else. Most successful entrepreneurs earn better-than-average wages, and some become wealthy.

Do you take pride in accomplishing something on your own? Most entrepreneurs choose to work very long hours. They enjoy their tasks and have control over the quantity and quality of their work.

Disadvantages of Entrepreneurship

Business owners must please their customers. If customers are not satisfied with the product or service that is offered, the business will fail. According to the **Small Business Administration** (SBA), about one-quarter of all small businesses (those with fewer than 500 em-

ployees) fail within two years, and more than half fail within four years. The SBA defines a failed business as one that closes while owing money to one or more creditors.

The owner of a small business must constantly be aware of the enterprise's operating costs and profits or losses. Not having enough financing to carry a business through periods of loss or growth is a major cause of business failure. The high rate of small business failures and the lack of collateral (additional security provided by the ownership of goods, property, or savings) make it very difficult for small business owners to obtain business loans.

Most small entrepreneurs acquire business capital by taking out personal loans. If the business fails, the owner may lose his or her car, home, and just about everything else of value. Being responsible for a loan and knowing that your ability to pay depends on the success of your business can add up to many sleepless nights.

Few new enterprises offer medical insurance, paid sick leave, life insurance, paid vacation, or a pension plan. In some cases, the new entrepreneur is covered by the medical insurance of a working spouse.

▲ *Are you a risk taker? Less than half of small businesses succeed. What can an entrepreneur do to increase his or her likelihood of success?*

▲ *Jeanne Dyer is a pharmacist with six years of work experience. Jeanne is signing loan papers to obtain the capital she needs to start her own pharmacy (drugstore). If the business fails she will lose her car and furniture. Would you be willing to risk six years of savings to be an entrepreneur?*

Many small businesses are one-person shops in which the owner wears many different hats. The business consumes most of the owner's time and energy, especially during the first five years of operation. Long workdays are to be expected. In a recent survey of small business owners conducted by Mastercard, of those responding:

- 79 percent reported working more than forty hours per week
- 53 percent worked more hours since becoming a business owner
- Only 16 percent worked fewer hours as a business owner

Do You Have What It Takes to Start Your Own Business?

Imagine that you are going to start a business of your own. What business will be best for you? Do you have the personal characteristics it takes to be an entrepreneur? Are you willing to take personal risks to get the business started? These are all important questions for you to answer.

Make a list of the business courses you have completed in high school or the activities that you have helped organize and plan at school, at home, or at your place of worship. These experiences will help you be a successful entrepreneur. As a business owner you will need to:

- Establish reachable goals and develop plans
- Organize, delegate, and maintain control

GETTING MORE INFORMATION

For more information on forming a business, contact the

    U.S. Small Business Administration
      Imperial Building
      1441 L St. N.W.
      Washington, DC 20416.

• Open lines of communication and take action

Formal education, skill training, and actual work experience are all important for building a successful enterprise. Most entrepreneurs who start professional or technical businesses have an advanced college degree in an area related to their business specialty. On the other hand, entrepreneurs in nontechnical businesses may have a high school diploma and perhaps a year or two of college or technical school training. In some cases, experience and ability make up for a lack of formal education and training.

It is important for entrepreneurs to continue learning about their particular business and about business management. Staying ahead of the competition requires business owners to keep up with market trends, changing technology, and business methods.

Have you learned to be careful with money? When you go to the store, do you usually find a bargain? Entrepreneurs must find the right balance between costs, prices, and sales in order to earn a profit. Did you begin to baby-sit, deliver newspapers, take care of lawns, shovel snow, or perform similar work at an early age? If so, you started out the way that many successful entrepreneurs did.

It would seem that some people are born to create, take chances, organize, and lead. Others are more comfortable with time-proven methods, being part of a group, and following. Review the characteristics of both types in Figure 15.2. Where do you fit in?

Figure 15.2 TWO TYPES OF PEOPLE

Entrepreneurs	Other Workers
Are competitive	Are noncompetitive
Live to work	Work to live
Enjoy taking risks	Prefer security
Tolerate uncertainty	Prefer certainty
Enjoy solving problems	Give up easily
Are impatient	Are patient
Prefer work over hobbies	Prefer hobbies over work

Section 1 — GET INVOLVED

1. Review the list of personal characteristics of entrepreneurs and other workers in Figure 15.2, and answer the following on a separate sheet of paper. Be prepared to discuss your responses in class.

   a. Which of your characteristics are similar to those of the entrepreneurs? Which characteristics are similar to those of the other workers?

   b. How would each of your entrepreneurial characteristics help you to be a successful business owner? How would each of your nonentrepreneurial characteristics hinder you?

2. On a separate sheet of paper, list the specific job skills and human relations skills you possess now or expect to acquire before entering full-time employment. Next, select a small business you could start with the skills on your list. Answer the following questions in terms of that business:

   a. How would you use each of the skills on your list in the business you selected? Be specific.

   b. What would you like most about your daily work tasks? What would you dislike most?

   c. What would concern you most if you owned the business? What would concern you least?

3. Are you better suited to be an entrepreneur or to work for an established business? Why?

Section 2

Different Forms of Business Ownership

Erica Millard graduated from a two-year technical college with an associate degree in child care. After working for two years at a local day-care center, Erica decided to start her own business. She even picked out a name: The Pied Piper Day-Care Center.

Erica started her action plan by taking an evening business course at a local college. She learned that before forming a business, would-be entrepreneurs should be able to answer these six questions:

- What licensing will be required for my business?
- What are the legal restrictions?
- How much capital will I need?
- How many workers will be involved?
- What liabilities must I assume?
- What type of business organization is best?

Erica also learned that the type and size of a business are major determinants of the type of ownership and organization needed. She is carefully considering the three major types of business ownership: sole proprietorship, partnership, and corporation.

When the same person is both the owner and a worker, the type of ownership is a **sole proprietorship**. Most small gas stations, barber shops, restaurants, video stores, and campgrounds are sole proprietorships. In many cases, the sole proprietor will employ a few other workers. It is also common for this type of business to be operated by a family.

A sole proprietorship is easily formed and is not difficult to manage. However, the total financial responsibility rests on the shoulders of the owner. If the business fails, the owner may lose all of his or her personal assets as well as the business.

When two or three people own and operate a business, it is called a **partnership**. A partnership can be formed when the partners make a verbal agreement. However, this is not recommended. Most partners hire an attorney to produce a legal, written agreement (contract) that describes:

- The responsibilities of each partner
- The amount invested by each partner
- The percentage of profits each partner will receive
- How each partner's share will be disposed of in the event of his or her death

In a partnership, each partner shares in the profits, and each is liable for any losses. Having

▲ *Ed Carle started his business forty years ago as a sole proprietor. Last year, Ed changed the legal form of ownership to include both sons as partners.*

two or more people concentrating on the solution to business problems and helping with financing the business are definite advantages of a partnership.

When a number of people own and operate a business under a state-issued license or charter, it is called a **corporation**. A corporation may be owned by several million people (stockholders) or by only a few. You can become part owner of a corporation by buying one or more shares of stock.

A corporation is authorized by law to transact business and own property as a single entity. Like any individual person, a corporation must conduct business in a responsible manner. It can sue or be sued in a court of law. Most large firms (and some small firms) choose to operate as a corporation.

The corporate form of business requires more assistance from lawyers and accountants than other forms do. Although stockholders in a large business have very limited liability, this form of ownership will not necessarily protect the small business owner's property or financial assets from lawsuits. The best protection for a business owner is insurance.

Erica has decided that a sole proprietorship would probably be best for starting the Pied Piper Day-Care Center. In addition, she plans to buy liability insurance to protect herself against possible lawsuits.

Last week, Erica received information about a nationally franchised chain of day-care centers. A **franchise** is a legal contract with an established, well-recognized company. Erica would be permitted to use the organization's name, logo, and business methods in exchange for payment. Before buying into the franchise, Erica plans to determine all of the costs, the amount of initial investment required, the royalties she would be required to pay, and the amount of financing help she can expect from the franchising company. She is also concerned about any restrictions that might be placed on her future business activities if she decides to sell her franchise.

Erica's Uncle Jerome owns a successful fast-food restaurant franchise with a nationally recognized company. She made an appointment with him to discuss the advantages and disadvantages of buying into a franchise. Jerome told Erica that a good franchising company will:

- Furnish a complete training program and assist with the business start-up
- Provide on-site consultations with the owner about selling, advertising, and bookkeeping
- Guarantee exclusive rights to a specific territory
- Conduct national advertising to create widespread recognition of the company
- Continue to develop and improve the product or service

Uncle Jerome also explained that franchising is regulated by the Federal Trade Commission (FTC). The law requires all franchisors (parent companies that sell franchises) to provide a Uniform Franchise Offering Circular (UFOC). The UFOC must list twenty-two points about the franchise, including the names and telephone numbers of franchisees (people who have purchased a franchise). In addition, the UFOC must disclose any bankruptcies or lawsuits pending against the parent company.

Erica learned that franchise fees range from a few hundred dollars to over a half million dollars. In addition, advertising and royalty fees paid to the parent company could amount to half of her gross sales.

Erica likes the idea of starting a franchised day-care business with an organization that already has a record of success. However, she is concerned that she will be forced to follow so many of the parent company's rules that she will lose the independence that she is seeking.

That evening at home, Erica was reading the business ads in her newspaper when she discovered a day-care center that was offered for sale. The next morning, Erica phoned the owner to obtain more information. The owner told her that the business was seventeen years old, well known,

▲ *When you buy a franchised business, you are starting with a well-known name and a record of success. Franchised businesses are usually well known in a certain region or nationally. What are the names of some nationally known franchised businesses you are familiar with?*

and profitable. The owner wanted to retire and was willing to assist the buyer with financing.

Erica made arrangements to visit the day-care center. She found the building and equipment to be very modern and the two employees to be very competent. The owner's books revealed a business

with numerous long-term customers.

Erica now has a lot to think about. Each form of business ownership and each method of getting started has several advantages and disadvantages. Erica must review her career goals as she considers the pros and cons of her alternatives.

Section 2 GET INVOLVED

Answer the following on a separate sheet of paper, and be prepared to discuss your responses in class.

1. If you were Erica, which form of ownership would you select? Why?

2. If you were Erica, would you start your own business, buy a franchise, or buy the established business? Why?

Section 3

Planning for Success

Once you have decided on the type of business you will own, where it will be located, and the goods or services you will offer, you will need to develop a plan of action. Successful entrepreneurs develop a written plan to guide them through each step of starting and maintaining a business. A good business plan includes information about the product or service and its potential market. In addition, it describes the marketing strategy, the organization of the business, and the financial requirements for start-up and operation. The business plan should present to the reader a clear picture of the business and its operation. Financial institutions require entrepreneurs to provide them with a written business plan before they will consider making a loan.

Marketing for Success

Research the existing market for your product or service, and identify your **target market**. A target market is the group of consumers who would most likely purchase certain goods or services.

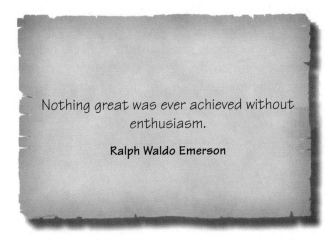

Nothing great was ever achieved without enthusiasm.

Ralph Waldo Emerson

The answers to the following questions will help you discover your target market:

- How old are they?
- Are they men, women, or both?
- What are their buying habits?
- Do they buy more during certain times of the year?

Successful entrepreneurs are not people who just got lucky. Instead, they are hard-working, energetic people who target their product or service to the right market. In addition, they find ways to make their product or service more valuable than the competition's. Consider the case of Carrie Straight on the following page.

Beginning entrepreneurs frequently make the mistake of concentrating on the product or service they are selling rather than identifying their po-

▲ *Circuit City's "target market" is the group of consumers who are most likely to buy electronic products such as computers, TV's, and sound systems.*

PLANNING MAKES A DIFFERENCE

Will Carrie Hit the Target?

Carrie Straight graduated from a vocational high school with a major in cosmetology. After three years of working in a beauty shop, she has decided to open her own business. She has selected a location that already has one beauty shop but should easily be able to support another.

Carrie noticed that the other shop opens at 9:00 A.M. and closes at 6:00 P.M. She plans to open her shop at 8:00 A.M. by appointment and to close the shop at 8:00 P.M. In the beginning, Carrie's shop will have two chairs and one employee. Carrie plans to adjust her own hours to accommodate customers who take advantage of the early opening and late closing. Carrie hopes to attract working women with her expanded schedule. This plan will mean that Carrie will work long hours in the beginning, but she plans to hire more employees as the business grows.

Critical Thinking

1. Who is Carrie's target market? Will Carrie's plan accommodate her target market? If so, how? If not, why not?

2. What advice would you offer Carrie as she plans her new business?

---

tential customers. A business usually attracts new customers through promotions and advertising. In addition, it is important to network with (obtain referrals from) current and previous customers.

Competition

Learn all you can about the products or services that your competitors offer. Pinpoint their strengths and weaknesses. How long have they been in business? Being in business a long time is a good indication of stability and profitability. When comparing your business with your competition, your target market customers will probably focus on two questions:

• Are your prices higher or lower?

• What are the benefits of using your product or service instead of your competitor's?

What Price to Charge

It is important to maintain the delicate balance between competitive prices, covering the cost of doing business, and allowing for a fair profit. You should consider four major factors when determining prices:

• The direct and indirect costs of doing business

• The amount of reasonable profit you have established as a goal

• The prices charged by major competitors

• The market demand for your goods or services

CAREER TIP

Let customers know that their business is wanted and appreciated. Always thank customers, and make certain that everyone in the organization follows this policy. Satisfied customers provide repeat business and growth.

There is rarely an exact "right" price, but rather an acceptable price range. Keep in mind that making a profit is the main purpose for starting a business. Successful entrepreneurs are just as careful when it comes to underpricing their product or service as they are about overpricing it. Market and pricing information is available from newspaper ads, trade magazines, the local chamber of commerce, the county office of economic development, business and professional organizations, and the U.S. Census Bureau.

Business Location

A good business location can mean the difference between success and failure. Successful entrepreneurs choose locations where they will have the greatest access to markets and where the business will be convenient for customers. Whether the enterprise is a neighborhood bakery or a national manufacturing facility, location is a very important consideration.

Before opening a new business, thoroughly investigate the zoning laws in the location that you are considering. Zoning laws spell out the activities that are permitted and prohibited in specific portions of a city or county. A copy of the local zoning laws can usually be obtained at the local town hall, zoning office, or library.

GETTING MORE INFORMATION

If you would like to start a business, read *The Teenage Entrepreneur's Guide* by Sarah Riehm (Chicago: Surrey Books, 1987) or *Entrepreneurship: Building the American Dream* by Sarah Riehm (St. Paul: West Publishing Company, 1993).

Seeking Help

Whether large, small, new, or well-established, sooner or later every business has problems and the owner needs help. For every current business problem, there is a book, a person, an organization, or a government agency that can help. Schools and colleges offer short courses and seminars. In addition, numerous local and national organizations serve the informational, lobbying, and networking needs of business entrepreneurs.

From time to time, a business owner must depend on the advice of a professional, such as an accountant, attorney, marketing consultant, or computer specialist. Before hiring a specialist to solve a specific problem, make sure that he or she has successfully served similar businesses with similar problems. Know beforehand what fees the specialist will charge.

▲ *Ask Joe Pappalardo to give you three reasons for his bakery's success and he will answer, "location, location, and location."*

Starting Out

Successful entrepreneurs establish a schedule to accomplish daily goals, and they stick to it. Ordering supplies, meeting with customers, paying bills, and keeping necessary records require their fair share of time.

Efficient, productive use of time is important for career success. Many entrepreneurs have identified the time wasters listed in Figure 15.3 as factors that prevent efficiency and productivity.

Demands on time, pressure to complete tasks, financial problems, and personal stress are common for beginning entrepreneurs. Use the following guidelines every day to reduce stress and increase your personal satisfaction:

1. Learn to balance the amount of time and energy you spend on your business and your personal life.

2. Build a regular fitness program into your daily schedule. Being physically fit will increase your mental alertness, productivity, and satisfaction.

3. Maintain regular communication with people. Personal contacts help build and maintain

Telephone interruptions
Visitors to the worksite
Procrastination (putting things off)
Excessive paperwork
Unclear objectives
Lack of self-discipline
Poor scheduling
Failure to delegate responsibility
Lack of skill in a needed area
Lack of standard procedures

▲ *Figure 15.3 The Top-Ten Time Wasters.*

your morale, and business contacts are essential for success in all enterprises.

Some entrepreneurs keep their regular job for a period of time while their business is getting started. This eases the financial strain. **Moonlighting** (working two jobs) has helped many entrepreneurs get started. The Bureau of Labor Statistics estimates that 244,000 women and 357,000 men moonlighted in 1991 to obtain work experience or to build up a business.

Section 3 GET INVOLVED

Answer the following on a separate sheet of paper, and be prepared to discuss your responses in class.

1. It has been said that the three major reasons for success in a business are location, location, and location. A new business could be located at the exit ramp of a large city expressway, the main street of a small town, a small business area near a large residential community, two blocks from an amusement park, and numerous other locations. Consider the following businesses: a restaurant, a tool rental shop, an auto repair garage, a small clothing store, a motel, and an apartment building.

   a. List a good location for each business. Why do you think these would be good locations?

   b. List a poor location for each business. Why would these be poor locations?

2. Review the top-ten time wasters listed in Figure 15.3. Do any of them have a negative influence on your schoolwork? What about on your job, your household responsibilities, or your personal relationships? If so, which ones? Learning to deal with the time wasters while you are a student will make it much easier for you to deal with them in your future career.

Financing a Business

Starting a business can be very expensive, and a new business is a financial risk for the owner. Entrepreneurs must carefully consider the financing for a new venture (an undertaking of chance) before making a commitment. Entrepreneurs frequently invest all of their personal savings in a venture and still need additional capital. New business owners usually turn to family members, friends, loan institutions, or investors (people who put money into an enterprise in the hopes of getting a profitable return).

It is important for a new business to begin with all of the equipment and materials required for daily operations. This usually means more-than-normal spending during the **start-up** period (when a business is beginning). Start-up expenses cause most new enterprises to lose money for several months or longer. Entrepreneurs frequently need to obtain a loan or sell a part of the ownership to operate the business until it begins to earn a profit.

Estimating Start-up Costs

Financial planning begins by estimating start-up costs. This includes all items that are paid for only once, such as licenses, permits, franchise fees, insurance, telephone deposits, tools, equipment, fixtures, installation costs, furniture, office sup-

▲ *Renting a well-located space to conduct your business is important. However, underestimating your start-up costs could put you out of business quickly.*

plies, remodeling and decorating, promotional advertising, signs, and professional fees (for an attorney, accountant, or computer programmer). In addition, entrepreneurs must consider the expense of renting or leasing space to conduct the business.

The amount of **working capital** (money required to meet the ongoing operational expenses of a business) will depend on several factors:

• The amount of money invested in the business
• The time and energy invested by the owner
• The type of business

Some business experts advise that if you expect a new enterprise to earn a profit in six months, double that time and be ready to operate without

CAREER TIP

A major reason for the failure of new businesses is a lack of financial planning.

profits for twelve months. This philosophy provides a financial cushion in case of unanticipated expenses or delays.

Projecting Operating Income and Expenses

Next, entrepreneurs should estimate the working capital needed to keep the business operating for six to twelve months. Operating expenses include salaries (including the owner's); expenses for telephone, electricity, and heat; office supplies; other supplies or materials; debt interest; advertising fees; maintenance costs; taxes; legal and accounting fees; insurance fees; business membership fees; and special service expenses (such as secretarial, copying, and delivery service).

In addition to business working capital, entrepreneurs must budget money for personal expenses. This estimate should include all normal living expenses for the entrepreneur and his or her family, such as food, household expenses, car payments, rent or mortgage, clothing, medical expenses, entertainment, and taxes.

Sources of Capital

Entrepreneurs secure needed capital in a variety of ways. Each method of financing has benefits and liabilities. Consider the following:

- Loans or gifts from family members or friends. Be certain to make businesslike, written agreements and to disclose fully the potential risk as well as the possible profit. Borrowing money has ended more than one friendship. Can you think of a time when someone borrowed something from you and didn't return it? How did it affect your relationship with that person?

- A bank loan. Banks require a comprehensive statement of the borrower's personal financial condition as well as a business plan. In addition, the loan officer will want written financial projections that include the amount to be bor-

▲ *Loretta is co-signing a business loan for her friend. If the business fails, Loretta will be responsible for the loan. Would you co-sign a loan for a friend's business?*

rowed, for what purpose, and how the loan will be repaid.

- A Small Business Administration loan guarantee. The SBA is not a bank, but it does extend guarantees and may occasionally participate in a loan when banks are unable or unwilling to provide the entire financing. The SBA loan officer will ask the same questions as bank loan officers and will require the same carefully considered data about your personal finances, start-up costs, and business projections.

- **Venture capital**. This is money invested, or earmarked for investment, in new businesses. For start-up entrepreneurs, some prior managerial or entrepreneurial track record is usually necessary to obtain venture capital. **Venture capitalists** (people who earn money by making high-risk business loans) usually require the business owner to sell them 50 to 90 percent ownership of the new business in return for the capital.

Carl's Bookstore
December 31, 1995
Balance Sheet

Cash	$3,792	Notes payable to the bank	$4,000
Accounts receivable	$2,912	Accounts payable	$4,480
Inventory	$13,644	Accruals	$1,880
Total current assets	$20,348	Total current liabilities	$10,360
Equipment and fixtures	$2,336	Total liabilities	$10,360
Prepaid expenses	$2,556	Net worth	$14,880
Total assets	$25,240	Total liabilities	$25,240

▲ *Figure 15.4 Sample Balance Sheet.*

Understanding the Balance Sheet

The **balance sheet** is a summary of **assets** (what the business owns), **liabilities** (what the business owes), and **net worth** (the difference between assets and liabilities). Reviewing the balance sheet of a business, along with the profit-and-loss statement and the cash-flow statement, helps owners, investors, and loan institutions make informed financial and business planning decisions. Figure 15.4 is a sample balance sheet for Carl's Bookstore.

A firm's balance sheet is drawn up using totals from the individual accounts kept in the **general ledger** (the principal book of accounts containing the final entries of assets and liabilities). The balance sheet shows the amount left after all creditors are paid. The assets and liabilities sections must balance, resulting in the name *balance sheet*. It can be produced quarterly, semiannually, or at the end of each calendar or fiscal year.

Current assets are anything of value (cash, inventory, or property) that the business owner can convert into cash within a year. Fixed assets are items such as land and equipment. Liabilities are debts that the business must pay. Amounts owed to suppliers are considered to be current liabilities. Numerous payments over a long period of time, such as notes owed to a bank, are considered to be long-term liabilities. Capital (also called *equity* or *net worth*) is equal to assets minus liabilities.

Understanding the Profit-and-Loss Statement

A **profit-and-loss statement** is a detailed, month-by-month record of income obtained from sales and expenses incurred to produce sales. It helps business owners evaluate the effect of business decisions on profit. Business owners use information from profit-and-loss statements to make future plans. Four types of information are included in a profit-and-loss statement:

- Sales information comprises the number of units sold and the dollar amount of sales income
- Direct expenses are the cost of labor, materials, and manufacturing overhead (fixed manufacturing costs)
- Indirect expenses are the costs the business would face even if a product were not produced or a service were not provided. They include

salaries, rent, utilities, insurance, depreciation, office supplies, taxes, and professional fees
- Income, or profit, is displayed as pre-tax and after-tax, or net, income.

A profit-and-loss statement should be prepared at least once a year, and it is a requirement for corporations. The profit-and-loss statement helps the business owner determine the economic health of the business.

Understanding the Cash-Flow Statement

Cash flow is the amount of money available in a business at a specific time. A business must have a healthy cash flow to survive. To keep track of cash flow, entrepreneurs must forecast the funds they expect to receive and pay out over a given period of time. By predicting a deficiency or surplus of cash, they can plan future business moves.

When is it time to expand the business, to hire more employees, or to use certain tax breaks? Successful entrepreneurs use the information contained in the balance sheet, profit-and-loss statement, and cash-flow statement to make these and a variety of other managerial decisions.

Section 4 GET INVOLVED

Answer the following on a separate sheet of paper, and be prepared to discuss your responses in class.

1. Imagine that a friend asks you to invest your time and money in a business partnership. List the questions you will ask before making your decision.
2. Arrange to interview the manager of the bank where your family has a checking or savings account, or invite him or her to speak to your class. What is the bank's policy on making business loans? What are the requirements? What are the interest rates? What advice can the bank manager offer to students who are interested in becoming entrepreneurs?

Section 5

Piles of Paperwork

From the time an entrepreneur registers the name of the business with local and state authorities until the enterprise is sold or closed, piles of paperwork must be completed with precision. Although you may consider keeping accurate and up-to-date business records to be a difficult, time-consuming, or even boring task, it is an essential part of business management. For some, a record-keeping course is helpful; for others, a professional accountant is the solution.

Accurate financial records are necessary for tax returns, making business decisions, and applying for loans. An accountant can help you decide on a

CAREER TIP

Never mix personal and business funds. Open a separate bank account for the business. This will ensure an accurate record of your income and expenditures.

record-keeping system that is best for your business. He or she will set up the books, organize and analyze profit-and-loss statements, and provide advice on financial decisions. In addition, an accountant can make budget forecasts, help you prepare a loan application, and handle tax matters.

Once he or she sets up a general ledger for the business, you can either record the daily transactions yourself or periodically have a bookkeeper post transactions and prepare financial statements.

Tax Obligations and Benefits

The federal government requires every new business to apply for an employer identification number. The necessary application forms are available from the Internal Revenue Service. This number will be used to complete numerous tax

▲ *Most new entrepreneurs are familiar with the daily operation of their business but unfamiliar paperwork could determine their success or failure. Are all of the restaurant's licenses up to date? Is it legal to sell certain baseball souvenirs without permission from the major-league teams? If a fire should occur, is the stock of clothing insured? Who is responsible if a child chokes on a broken piece of plastic?*

forms and other required government information forms during the life of the business.

As an entrepreneur, every business decision, purchase, or sale you make has certain tax advantages or disadvantages. Being knowledgeable about tax laws and using them to your best advantage could spell the difference between success and failure for your business.

Each type of business ownership has certain tax advantages, but all businesses must pay taxes. It is important to identify and declare as many deductions as possible. Deductions are business expenses that the government allows business owners to subtract from their gross income in order to arrive at their taxable income. Examples of business deductions include these:

- Salaries and wages paid to employees
- Rent, supplies used by the business, and utilities
- The purchase or lease of tools, machines, or equipment

Insurance

A reliable insurance agent can save your business a great deal of time and money. Entrepreneurs must select their agents with the same care they exercise in selecting an accountant, attorney, or other professional. Insurance professionals can help entrepreneurs select the right policies for their business needs. In addition, they maintain records and help settle insurance claims.

Insurance helps to safeguard businesses against loss from fire, illness, and injury. You shouldn't operate without it. Read and understand your insurance policies and reevaluate your business insurance needs with your agent about once every six months. All insurance records and policies should be kept in a safe place other than at the business. Copies should be kept at the business office for convenience. The following are some types of business insurance that you should consider:

- Product liability coverage, which protects you in the event that your product causes injury to a user
- Auto liability and "non-owned" auto liability insurance, which you should consider if a car is ever used to support the business in any way
- Medical payments insurance, which is payable if someone is injured in your place of business, whether or not it is your fault
- Worker's compensation, which is required by law
- Business interruption insurance or earnings insurance, which covers you if your business is damaged by fire or some other cause and you must totally or partially suspend operation
- Disability income protection, which is a form of health insurance in case you or an employee becomes disabled
- Business life insurance, which provides funds for transition if the owner dies
- Fire insurance, which protects the business against loss by fire

Laws and Regulations

Most localities have registration and licensing requirements that may apply to your particular business. A license is formal permission to practice a certain business activity. It is issued by the local, state, or federal government. A license may require some type of examination to certify that the recipient is qualified to run a particular business. A permit is an official certificate of permission that allows a business to operate. It is issued by local government authorities. A modest fee is usually charged for licenses and permits.

If your business has employees, you are responsible for withholding from their paychecks federal income tax, Social Security tax, and any local or state income taxes that apply. You must also pay into the worker's compensation and unemployment insurance programs. In addition, you must comply with minimum wage, child labor, and employee health laws.

CAREER TIP

Consider the liabilities of operating without proper licenses and registrations very carefully. The owner usually pays with embarrassment, time, and money when a business is not properly licensed.

If your business operations are intrastate (within a state) rather than interstate (between states), you will be concerned primarily with state and local, rather than federal, licensing. Businesses that are frequently subject to state or local control include retail food establishments, eating and drinking places, barber shops, beauty shops, plumbing firms, and taxi companies. They are primarily service businesses and are subject to regulations for the protection of public health and morals. Depending on your type of business, you may also have to comply with building and safety codes as well as Occupational Safety and Health Act requirements.

The amount of paperwork required to operate a business might seem overwhelming and overly time consuming. It is good practice to set aside a special time each day to update your records.

▲ *Street vendors frequently operate without a license, ignore tax laws, and misrepresent their merchandise. Remember the old saying, "If a deal sounds too good to be true, it probably is."*

Time spent maintaining accurate records will pay off with more tax deductions and increased efficiency.

Section 5 GET INVOLVED

Answer the following on a separate sheet of paper, and be prepared to discuss your responses in class.

1. Make an appointment to visit the owner of a small business. Make a list of the government agencies that the business must deal with in the course of a year. What licenses or permits are required? What paperwork is required each business quarter and each year? How much time is spent with paperwork? When does the owner normally do the required paperwork? What taxes must be paid? How often are taxes paid?

2. Phone or visit your local Internal Revenue Service office. Ask for a package of government information for starting a new business. After you have an opportunity to review the information packet, answer these questions:

   a. How much time would you expect to spend doing the necessary paperwork to start a new business?

   b. What additional education or training would help you become an entrepreneur?

.IMPORTANT FACTS

Entrepreneurial Opportunities in Repair Services

Did you ever consider opening a repair service? Consider the amount of money Americans spent in 1991 to maintain and repair the following:

Autos	$90.0 billion
Computers	$16.4 billion
Telecommunications hardware	$15.6 billion
Copiers	$5.4 billion
Medical electronics	$2.1 billion

Sources: Automotive Services Industry Association, *Cannata Report*, and D.F. Blumber and Associates, 1991.

The Number of Woman-Owned Businesses Is Growing

Year	Self-employed Women (Nonfarm)	Percentage of Total Self-employed Workers (%)
1990	3.1 million	35.9
1985	2.6 million	33.3
1980	2.1 million	30.0

Source: U.S. Small Business Administration.

Business Incubators

The number of business incubators (programs that offer start-ups flexible space, leases, and access to business services, financing, and expertise) has swelled to 422 in 1990 from 15 in 1980. In 1990, there were more than 6,500 tenant firms in incubators.

Types of Tenant Businesses	Percentage of Total (%)
Light manufacturing	26.5
Service	25.7
High-tech products	15.4
Research and development	8.5
Sales and marketing	7.4
Wholesale and distribution	5.5
Construction-related	3.0
Other	8.0

Source: National Business Incubation Association, 1990, 1991.

Franchising Has Appeal

The number of franchised outlets in the United States exceeds 540,000, with new units opening at a rate of one every sixteen minutes. Total sales for all franchised businesses rose to 757.8 billion dollars in 1991.

Source: International Franchise Association, 1992.

Occupations of the Unincorporated Self-employed

Sales occupations had the largest number of self-employed people in 1990: nearly 1.8 million. This number includes

- 768,000 supervisors and proprietors
- 248,000 real estate salespeople
- 145,000 street and door-to-door salespeople

Precision production, craft, and repair occupations had the next highest number of self-employed people. Most of the people in this group (over one million) worked in the construction trades, especially carpenters, painters, plumbers, and electricians. Most self-employed service workers were hairdressers, cosmetologists, and child-care workers (except private household workers). The largest increase in self-employed workers was in executive, administrative, and managerial occupations. They grew from 394,000 in 1983 to 1,606,000 in 1990.

Source: U.S. Department of Labor.

SCORE

The Service Corps of Retired Executives (SCORE) has thirteen thousand volunteer counselors throughout the United States. SCORE came into being in September 1964, when the Small Business Administration signed up more than 1,100 retired executives to help small businesses learn to achieve greater sales and profits. SCORE members provide advice and counseling to would-be entrepreneurs before they risk entering a tough, competitive marketplace.

Source: Small Business Administration.

CHAPTER 15 REVIEW

ENRICH YOUR VOCABULARY

On a separate sheet of paper, number from 1 to 20, and complete the following activity. (Do not write in your textbook.) Match each statement below with the most appropriate term from the "Enrich Your Vocabulary" list at the beginning of the chapter by writing that term next to the correct statement.

1. A form of business ownership in which the same person is both the owner and a worker
2. A legal contract with an established, well-recognized company
3. Money invested, or earmarked for investment, in new businesses
4. A group of consumers who would most likely purchase certain goods or services
5. Small-business ownership
6. A form of business ownership in which two or three people own and operate the business
7. People who earn money by making high-risk business loans
8. What the business owns
9. The difference between assets and liabilities
10. A form of business ownership in which a number of people own and operate the business under a state-issued license or charter

11. A government agency formed to assist small business entrepreneurs
12. Working two jobs
13. A summary of assets, liabilities, and net worth
14. The principal book of accounts containing the final entries of assets and liabilities
15. What the business owes
16. An official certificate of permission that allows a business to operate
17. The period of time when a business is beginning
18. A detailed monthly record of income and expenses
19. The amount of money available in a business at a specific time
20. Money required to meet the ongoing operational expenses of a business

CHECK YOUR KNOWLEDGE

On a separate sheet of paper, complete the following activity. (Do not write in your textbook.)

1. List three personal characteristics that are common to most entrepreneurs.
2. How do the wages and working hours of most entrepreneurs compare to the wages and working hours of most workers?
3. Where do most entrepreneurs obtain the training to start their own business?
4. What percentage of all self-employed people work in construction occupations? What percentage work in retail occupations?
5. What portion of all small businesses (those with fewer than 500 employees) fail within four years?

6. What six factors should a potential entrepreneur consider before starting a new business?
7. What type of business ownership is used by the owners of most small automobile service stations and video stores?
8. What information should be included in a good business plan?
9. List two of the resources that new entrepreneurs usually turn to for start-up capital.
10. List five records that an entrepreneur must maintain as an essential part of business management.

DEVELOP SCANS COMPETENCIES

Government experts say that successful workers can productively use Resources, Interpersonal skills, Information, Systems, and Technology. This activity will give you practice in developing Information and Interpersonal skills.

Talk with three entrepreneurs (people who have started their own business). Use the traits given in Figure 15.2 on page 339 (the entrepreneur list) to develop a survey for the entrepreneurs to complete. Ask them which of the traits apply to themselves, and which trait was most important in helping them to start their own business. Ask them to add any other traits they think are important to entrepreneurs. Compare your results with those of your classmates. Develop a class list of the most important traits the entrepreneurs listed.

Researching and Understanding Career Information

Learning Objectives

After completing this chapter, you should be prepared to:

- identify and use several sources of occupational information
- interview workers with questions that are related to your career concerns
- use hands-on experience when you make career decisions
- understand and use three standard methods of classifying occupational information
- relate your personal characteristics to specific occupations and broad occupational groups

Enrich Your Vocabulary

In reading this chapter and doing the exercises you will learn the following important terms:

employment outlook
Occupational Outlook Handbook
Dictionary of Occupational Titles
Guide for Occupational Exploration
computerized career information systems

transcript
classification
Standard Occupational Classification
USOE Career Clusters
Standard Industrial Classification

PLANNING MAKES A DIFFERENCE

Everyday Tasks Are Important

Latoria Lambert's understanding of her personal characteristics was very complete when she decided to become a teacher. She enjoyed helping her younger brothers and sisters understand their schoolwork. Latoria's teachers, neighbors, and relatives considered her to be friendly, helpful, and sociable.

Latoria had an image of a teacher's job, but she didn't have enough specific information about the occupation to understand its everyday tasks, problems, and rewards. For example, Latoria didn't realize that she would spend most evenings preparing lessons and grading papers. Latoria also discovered that she would be required to complete additional college courses to maintain her state teaching certificate. Latoria has learned the importance of obtaining a complete understanding of an occupation before making a choice.

After two years of employment as a fifth-grade teacher, Latoria has decided to leave teaching. She plans to spend her summer vacation looking for a different job.

Critical Thinking

1. List Latoria's personal characteristics. How do the characteristics on this list relate to the job tasks of a teacher? How do they relate to the job tasks of three occupations other than teacher? Be specific.

Students sometimes select an occupation without having enough information about it. A lack of career information can result in disappointment, dissatisfaction, and a feeling of failure. Satisfaction with your career choice depends on the extent to which it meets your personal, social, and economic needs and expectations.

Research will help you identify occupations that meet several of your personal needs. It will also help you anticipate the satisfaction that you may receive in one occupation as compared with another. Occupational information includes

- The title and specific duties of the occupation
- Its education and training requirements
- A description of the normal work site
- The range of wages
- Possible career paths and related occupations
- **Employment outlook** (present and future employment trends)

- Sources of additional information
- Organizations that hire workers in this particular occupation

Because it is impossible to remember information about the 20 to 30 thousand occupations in the world of work, classification systems have been developed to simplify the relationship of occupations to one another. In this chapter, you will become familiar with three common classification systems. You will also learn about sources

CAREER TIP

Make certain that the occupational information you are using is accurate, up-to-date, and complete.

of occupational information and methods for studying specific occupational choices.

An increased knowledge of occupations and a thorough understanding of your personal charac- teristics will help you evaluate, match, and inte- grate information about yourself and various oc- cupations into a satisfying career choice.

Reading and Research

Rita Levell plans to enter a tech-prep program (a cooperative program that links high school vocational education with two- and four-year college pro- grams) at Greenfield High next year. She is presently taking a career planning course to help her select the tech-prep program that is right for her.

Rita has already found many occupational in- formation resources in her guidance counselor's office and in the school and public libraries. She is careful to rely on recent information. Unfortu- nately, some of the information she finds is a few years old and of little value. Occupational infor- mation concerning technology, economic condi- tions, demands for certain products and services, education and training requirements, and wages can change rapidly. To get an accurate picture of an occupation, Rita uses the resources described in this chapter.

To begin your library search, look in the card catalog or the computer listings under "Vocations" or "Careers" and then under specific occupations. Also review any pamphlets the library has that de- scribe employment in different organizations. Fig- ure 16.1 on the next page shows an outline that you can use when writing a career research report.

▲ *Rita uses the library because of its extensive occupational information resources. What should she be on the lookout for if she is to get an accurate picture of the occupation?*

Occupational Outlook Handbook

The *Occupational Outlook Handbook* (OOH) is a reference book researched and published by the U.S. Department of Labor every two years. It provides detailed descriptions of about 250 occu- pations, covering about 107 million jobs, or 87 percent of all jobs in the nation. In addition, sum- mary information on eighty occupations, account- ing for another 4 percent of all jobs, is presented for occupations that are not studied in detail.

Occupations are grouped in clusters and are also found alphabetically in the index. Those

I. General information about the occupation

   A. Title of occupation

   B. Related occupations

   C. Nature of the work: What work tasks are performed? What equipment or tools are used? Is the occupation closely related to people, data, or things? What are the possible fields of specialization? How has technology changed the occupation? What future changes are expected? What are the necessary skill levels and responsibilities?

   D. Projected earnings: What is the beginning and average expected income according to geographic location and conditions? Include fringe benefits, commissions, tips, overtime, bonuses, vacations, hospitalization insurance, and retirement plans.

   E. Working conditions and surroundings: Are job tasks performed indoors or outdoors? Describe the daily and weekly time schedule, noise levels, health hazards, travel requirements, and stressful responsibilities.

II. Where are workers in this career employed?

   A. Employment: In which career cluster or industry is this occupation usually found? In what type of establishment (place of business) and in what geographic region is the work usually performed?

   B. Employment outlook (future employment trends): What trends are likely to affect employment growth or decline for this occupation during the next ten years? What is the projected number of annual openings?

III. What education and training will prepare me for this occupation?

   A. Education and training: Will I need to attend vocational school, technical school, community college, college, or professional school to prepare for this occupation? Does this occupation require one, two, three, four, or more years of education after high school? Will licensing or special certification be required? Is apprenticeship or on-the-job training possible?

   B. Career paths: What are the job titles and levels of responsibility in the usual line for advancement? What are the possibilities for transferring to related occupations through seniority and experience, on-the-job or in-service training, additional formal education, or written examinations?

IV. What type of person succeeds in the specific occupational group?

   A. Personal qualities: Are your interests, values, and aptitudes related to those of successful workers in this occupational group? Will you still consider a career path in this occupational group to be challenging in several years? If so, why? If not, why not? What have you accomplished that demonstrates your ability to be successful in this occupation?

   B. Rewards and satisfactions: What rewards and satisfactions will this occupation provide? What rewards and satisfactions won't it provide?

V. Additional information

   A. Opportunities for experience and exploration: Is summer or part-time work available in this occupational group? Are work-study college programs available?

   B. Contributions of the occupation to our social/economic system

   C. Additional sources of information about this occupation

▲ *Figure 16.1 Sample Outline for a Career Research Report.*

requiring the most education or training receive the most attention. Information about what the work is like, what education and training is needed, advancement possibilities, earnings, job outlook, related occupations to consider, and sources for additional information are provided. The DOT numbers are also listed.

- Processing
- Benchwork
- Miscellaneous

The current two-volume revision of the *DOT* includes definitions and information about occupational requirements such as interests, education and specific vocational preparation, and body strength. Each occupation is assigned a code number based on its relationship to other occupations and the relationship of its required job tasks to the worker interests of data, people, and things.

Guide for Occupational Exploration

The *Guide for Occupational Exploration* (GOE) is also published by the Department of Labor. This occupational reference book focuses on twelve clearly defined interest areas. For each interest area, work groups and subgroups are listed. For each work group, the GOE describes:

- The kind of work performed
- The skills and abilities needed
- How to determine if you would like or could learn to do this kind of work
- How to prepare for and enter the job area
- Other factors to consider about jobs in this group

Computerized Career Information Systems

Computers are used to store all types of information. In fact, some desktop computers are capable of storing as much information as a small library. Computerized career information systems are used to store large quantities of occupational information. These systems contain information about:

- Specific occupations
- Two- and four-year colleges and vocational and technical schools

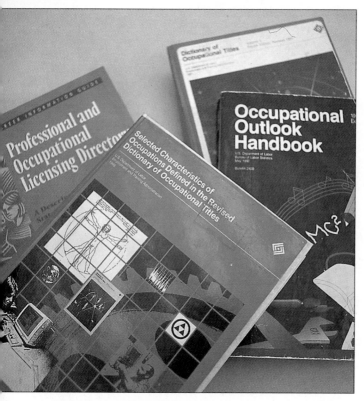

▲ *The OOH and DOT as well as other occupational reference books provide information that will help you write your career research report. What occupation are you going to research?*

Dictionary of Occupational Titles

The *Dictionary of Occupational Titles* (DOT) is another Department of Labor publication that can be used to research a specific occupation or group of occupations. It contains a definition and brief description of more than 25 thousand occupations. Related occupations are grouped together under the following titles:

- Professional, technical, and managerial
- Clerical and sales
- Farming, fishing, forestry, and related occupations
- Machine trades
- Structural work
- Computer
- Service

Types of Career Articles	Magazines
Specific career information for women	*Working Woman* and *Glamour*
Business opportunities	*Changing Times* and *Kiplinger*
Business trends	*Business Week* and *Forbes*
Personnel problems and developments	*Fortune*
Specific career information for students	*Career World*

▲ *Figure 16.2 Magazines with Information about Careers.*

• Scholarships and other forms of financial aid
• Military careers

Computerized career information systems allow students to explore occupations and educational preferences on a large database that is periodically updated. They may serve a single school, a school district, or an entire state. In addition to nationwide information, each state system usually delivers information specific to the state.

When you begin to use a computerized career information system, you will be asked to answer a series of personal questions that appear on the computer's monitor. The computer will relate your answers to information in its database. Then you will be able to use the computer's database to browse, explore, and clarify career and occupational information. Most systems allow you to obtain a printout of specific information presented on the monitor.

Periodicals and Magazines

Periodicals and magazines are worthwhile sources of information because of their timeliness. In addition, they frequently provide information about little-known career opportunities. Many daily newspapers carry special business or financial pages that feature stories about employment opportunities in new or expanding businesses. Classified newspaper advertisements can be used to acquire a realistic understanding of local employment opportunities. Annual stockholder reports published by corporations are also a good source of information about potential employers and their products or services. In addition, several magazines publish articles that focus on specific career information (Figure 16.2).

Trade and Professional Publications

Trade and professional publications provide information about specific careers. They are located in the periodicals section of the library. They can also be obtained by writing to a specific trade or professional group. Pamphlets and monographs (articles written on a particular subject) are frequently published by organizations. Keep in mind that these publications may be used to recruit workers for the publisher's particular career area and thus may minimize unfavorable aspects of the work.

▲ *A computerized career information system can help you gather information about the occupation you are researching. Is one available in your school? Have you learned how to use it?*

Films, Videos, and Audiotapes

Films, videos, and audiotapes are available in most school and public libraries. When you view a film or video or listen to a tape, keep in mind that what you observe or hear is usually general in nature and has probably been glamorized.

Section 1 GET INVOLVED

Answer the following on a separate sheet of paper, and be prepared to discuss your responses in class.

1. Using the outline presented in Figure 16.1, write a career research report about the occupation you are now considering most seriously.
2. Write to an association or company to request information about a career that interests you.
3. Read the biography of a person who is or was successful in an occupation that you are considering. Write a brief report comparing your interests, potential skills, career goals, and life goals to those of that person.

Section 2

Listen and Observe

Listening to experienced workers and visiting job sites to make observations will help you to make wise career decisions.

Guidance Services

Counselors receive special training in career planning and can help you understand the relationship between your personal characteristics and a particular occupation. Ask your guidance counselor to review your high school transcript with you. A **transcript** is a record of your academic credits earned, grades, attendance, standardized test scores, and extracurricular activities. In addition to relating your transcript information to oc-cupations that you are considering, your counselor can guide you through an assessment of your goals, values, interests, and aptitudes. Armed with this information, you can begin to consider broad career areas and specific occupations within them.

Your high school counselor is familiar with a wide range of resources to help you research occupational information. Ask him or her for information and resources concerning the job market, entry requirements for postsecondary education and training institutions, and financial aid.

In addition, contact counselors in the career planning and placement offices of colleges, private vocational or technical schools, vocational rehabilitation agencies, community service organizations, and the state job service (employment bureau).

Interviews

Interviewing a worker who is employed in the occupation you are considering is a good way to obtain realistic career information. However, it is important to research the occupation before the interview. The more information you have about the occupation before the interview, the more you will gain from the worker's answers to your questions. Use the questions suggested in Figure 16.3 to guide your interview. In addition to the worker's answers to your interview questions, record

- The worker's name
- The worker's job title and specific occupation
- A description of the work setting and general atmosphere

After you complete a worker interview, evaluate what you have learned from the experience. Ask yourself the following questions:

1. Did my expectations of the occupation differ from what I observed and learned from the interview? If so, how?
2. What job activities and benefits did I discover about this occupation that I would like as part of my future career? What would I dislike?
3. What personal qualities do I possess that could make me successful or unsuccessful in this career?

Family and Friends

Most people enjoy talking about their work. Friends, neighbors, and relatives are usually willing to share their opinions and suggestions. Lis-

▲ *Your guidance counselor is familiar with a wide range of resources that will help you relate information about yourself to occupations. Have you taken the SAT or ACT and discussed the results with your counselor?*

tening to them may help you clarify your own thinking. Don't overlook these personal contacts when you are seeking career information. They may be able to answer your questions directly or put you in touch with someone who can. This type of networking might lead to an interview with a worker who is able to answer your questions about a specific occupation. It might also give you a chance to visit an organization's work site and acquire inside information about specific career areas.

Speakers

If your school has a Career Day, take advantage of the opportunity to ask questions and discuss careers with visiting workers from different occupations. Organizations like the American Chemical Society, the American Nurses' Association, the chamber of commerce, various trade associations, labor unions, and business firms can usually put you in touch with someone who will come to your school and speak about a particular career area.

CAREER TIP

Before employing the services of a private career counselor or placement agency, be certain that the same service or information isn't available free from your high school guidance office or another public agency. Always check references.

- ❑ What organizations provide employment in this occupation?
- ❑ Why did you choose this line of work?
- ❑ In what ways do you find your work satisfying? What highlights have you experienced?
- ❑ In what ways do you find your work unsatisfactory? What were your most unpleasant work experiences?
- ❑ What skills are needed to perform your daily work tasks?
- ❑ What personal characteristics are needed to be successful on your job?
- ❑ What portion of your time is spent working with information? with people? with tools, machines, or instruments? Specifically, what are your work tasks in each of these area?
- ❑ What are some characteristics of the people with whom you work? What about the people you report to and those who report to you?
- ❑ What education, training, or certification would I need to enter this occupation?
- ❑ Compared to other jobs, what are the advantages and disadvantages of your work?
- ❑ What are the most important qualifications for success in this work?
- ❑ Will advancements in technology and changes in word economics affect this occupation? If so how? If not, why not?
- ❑ What are the career paths or areas of specialization in this occupation?
- ❑ What are the beginning earnings in this occupation? What future earnings and advancement opportunities should a successful worker anticipate?
- ❑ Does this occupation affect your family life, leisure activities, or friendships? If so, how?
- ❑ What advice would you give a young person who is considering this line of work?
- ❑ If you could do it over, would you choose this occupation? Why or why not?

▲ *Figure 16.3 Questions for Interviewing a Worker.*

▲ *Sergeant Rodreguez tells Diego that he chose this line of work because he enjoys working with people and that he believes maintaining law and order serves the public. When you interview a worker for your career research report, use the questions suggested in Figure 16.3 to guide your interview just as Diego is doing.*

Many schools have advisory committees composed of local organizations. They usually meet after school. See your counselor or principal to find out whether or not your school has an advisory committee. If so, ask if the committee would be willing to provide career speakers?

Field Experience

Visiting job sites is another good way to obtain occupational information. For example, if you are interested in learning to be a computer programmer, visit an office or plant where one is employed. Site visits may range from a few hours to a day or two.

Field experiences (sometimes called *career exploring* or *career shadowing*) can often be arranged by contacting the human resources office of an organization. People in that office have the authority to schedule an appointment to visit or observe workers in a specific occupation. Field experiences for a group are usually arranged by a teacher, counselor, or a committee of students.

Your school counselor may be able to provide information about programs that offer career field experience. Service organizations, such as the Boy Scouts and Girl Scouts of America's Explorer program, are frequently sponsors of career field experience for students.

Section 2 GET INVOLVED

Answer the following on a separate sheet of paper, and be prepared to discuss your responses in class.

1. List the family members and friends you could interview about their occupations. Use the suggested questions presented in Figure 16.3 to conduct the interviews.
2. Using your telephone book, select a business of interest to you.
   a. Phone the receptionist to obtain the name, title, and office address of the person with authority to arrange student visits.
   b. Write a letter to the appropriate person. Describe your career interest and express your desire to visit the organization. Be sure to include your telephone number and return address.
   c. If you don't receive a response to your letter within a week, make a follow-up telephone call to the appropriate person. He or she is probably very busy and on a tight schedule.

Section 3

The Real Thing

Your paid and nonpaid work experiences can be used as career rehearsals for the "real thing." For example, being on the staff of your high school newspaper or yearbook provides experiences related to the occupations of reporter, editor, word processor, layout artist, and illustrator.

Some schools have career clubs for future teachers, farmers, and business leaders. Can you think of other high school career clubs and high school experiences that are related to the "real thing"?

Throughout the United States, employers and educators are working together to create educational programs that will prepare students for the world of work. Many high schools, post-secondary technical schools, and two- and four-year colleges are cooperating with each other to prepare students with the skills needed to compete in a rapidly changing workplace.

Although the names of various high school programs and the way they are structured vary from one school district to another, the descriptions presented in this section will help you understand the basics of most career education programs. Discuss the offerings at your high school with your teachers and guidance counselor.

Co-op and Internship Programs

Co-op and internship programs provide first-hand work experience in specific occupations. These experiences help students determine their suitability for an occupation.

Many technical and skilled-trades high school programs also require practical work experience. Tech-prep and two-plus-two programs are increasingly being offered to high school students. This approach offers students a foundation in many of the job skills and academic courses that are necessary for a technical education beyond high school. Employers determine which career skills and academic competencies are needed by workers, and schools determine how they will teach those skills and competencies.

Occupational Work Experience (OWE) and co-op programs provide students with classroom instruction and on-the-job experience. In addition to the basic academic subjects of English, mathematics, science, and social studies, students receive classroom instruction in job-seeking and job-holding skills. Early release from school each day gives OWE and co-op students the time

▲ The "real thing" provides Christie with experience to edit films and decide if she is suited for an occupation in this field. What programs offer the "real thing" at your school?

to acquire and participate in part-time, paid employment.

Part-time, Volunteer, and Temporary Work

Chapter 8 provided information about part-time, volunteer, and temporary work. Actual work experience is the most direct way to explore a career area on a daily basis. It provides an opportunity for you to observe a variety of occupations and job responsibilities, the types of people employed in a specific career area, and the work environment.

Obviously, a high school student can't acquire work experience as a nurse, physical therapist, physician, or other health-care professional. However, part-time employment or volunteer service in a hospital or nursing home will enable the student to work in the same environment with these professionals, to observe them at work, and to ask questions. What other career areas can you think of where this is true?

Finding Your Place in the World of Work

As you make decisions about your career path, profit from the information you have learned about yourself. Apply it to specific occupations and work environments. For example, what amount of education and training are you willing to invest in your career? Once you have determined a specific level of education and training, narrow down your choices to a few occupations in the occupational classifications or career clusters that you find interesting. Identifying certain occupations, occupational classifications, and career clusters that you dislike will also help you narrow your occupational choices.

You may decide to change your occupational goal in a year or two. Learning to use occupational information and exploring career choices now will help you make new career decisions in the future.

C AREER TIP

Don't eliminate an occupation from consideration because of a single characteristic. A variety of characteristics and possible work settings exist for every occupation. For example, most accountants work alone, but some spend a great deal of time with clients. Most work in an office, but some travel.

Your present career goals should include learning as much as possible about yourself and about occupations. Researching and evaluating occupational information will increase your confidence in your career priorities.

Section 3 GET INVOLVED

Answer the following on a separate sheet of paper, and be prepared to discuss your responses in class.

1. Combine the experience of all the students in your class.
   a. List the part-time or volunteer jobs held by students in your class.
   b. List additional occupations they observed while they were working.
   c. How did the part-time and volunteer work experiences of your classmates affect their present career plans?

2. On a separate sheet of paper, list two or more occupations that you are considering for your future career. Then ask your school counselor
   - Whether your high school offers any type of work experience, co-op, or internship programs in the area of your career interest
   - Whether your high school cooperates with technical schools, colleges, or employers in

programs that are related to your area of career interest

3. Interview a friend, neighbor, or relative who has twenty or more years of work experience. Include the following questions in your interview:
   - How many occupations did you investigate and fully understand before you started your first full-time job? Where did you obtain your information?
   - If you could begin your career again, would you investigate fewer, more, or the same number of occupations? Why?
   - How many specific job changes have you had during your career? How many of your job changes were planned? Were any job changes forced on you?
   - How did you learn about your present occupation?

Classifying Occupational Information

Occupational information can be classified by a variety of systems. Each **classification** (grouping) system has certain advantages. These are the three major classification systems:

- The Standard Occupational Classification (SOC) system
- The fifteen U.S. Office of Education (USOE) career clusters
- The Standard Industrial Classification (SIC) system

The Standard Occupational Classification System

The *Occupational Outlook Handbook* groups occupations according to the **Standard Occupational Classification** (SOC) system. All federal agencies that collect occupational employment data use the SOC system. It divides occupations into groups, according to the type of work performed (Figure 16.4).

In the SOC system there are twelve standard occupational classifications. Occupations within these twelve classifications are labeled either as *service-producing* or *goods-producing*. Service-producing organizations are categorized into retail trade; government; finance, insurance, and real estate; wholesale trade; and transportation, communications, and public utilities. Goods-producing organizations are categorized into construction, manufacturing, mining, and agriculture.

The USOE Career Clusters

The **USOE Career Clusters** are part of a broad occupational classification system developed by the U.S. Office of Education (USOE). They comprise fifteen career groups, each of which has hundreds of job categories. The fifteen USOE clusters (Figure 16.5 on the next page) divide careers according to their relationship to one another and to society. Related occupations that require different levels of education are described in each USOE cluster.

For additional career information related to the fifteen USOE Career Clusters, see the occupational handbook that accompanies this text.

Executive, administrative, and managerial occupations
Professional specialty occupations
Technicians and related support occupations
Marketing and sales occupations
Administrative support, including clerical occupations
Service occupations
Agriculture, forestry, and fishing occupations
Mechanics, installers, and repairers
Construction traders and extractive occupations
Production occupations
Transportation and material-moving occupations
Handlers, equipment cleaners, helpers, and laborers

▲ *Figure 16.4 The Standard Occupational Classification System.*

The Standard Industrial Classification System

Where do people work? This is the question answered by the **Standard Industrial Classification** (SIC) system. The SIC system identifies the occupations in each type of organization and the number of workers employed in

Solving The Problem

Eric Faces Reality

Eric Thompson is a senior at Washington High School. He had planned to become an architect since his freshman year. However, after three attempts, Eric's highest score on the ACT college entrance test was 19, several points lower than the requirement for acceptance into an architectural school. Eric passed second-year algebra and geometry but was totally lost when he attempted precalculus. His grade point average is 2.2. Considering all of these facts, Eric realized that his ambition of becoming an architect was unrealistic in terms of his mathematics ability.

Eric reviewed all of the occupations related to architect in the USOE construction cluster, and he decided to study drafting technology at a two-year technical school. Using the cluster approach to review related occupations requiring different levels of education and training helped Eric make this major career decision.

Critical Thinking

1. Which of the USOE Career Clusters is most related to your occupational interests? (See Figure 16.5.) How is it related? Which cluster is least related?

2. Did Eric make a wise career decision? If so, why? If not, what other course of action would you have suggested?

Agribusiness and natural resources
Communications and media
Business and office
Marketing and distribution
Consumer and homemaking education
Hospitality and recreation
Fine arts and humanities
Personal service
Environment
Health
Marine science
Public service
Transportation
Construction
Manufacturing

▲ *Figure 16.5 The Fifteen USOE Career Clusters.*

these organizations. It illustrates the organizational structure in which workers with all types of training engage in all types of work activities.

The federal government developed the SIC system to make it easier to collect, present, and understand statistical data on industries. In this classification scheme, all places of employment are called *industries*. The SIC system is widely used to report all types of business information.

The SIC code consists of 9 major parts, which are divided into 91 major groups, subdivided into 519 groups of closely related industries, and further subdivided into 1,530 industries. Workplaces are grouped according to the type of product produced or the type of service provided. Figure 16.6 gives the general SIC numbers (1 to 9) for the 9 major industrial groups.

Education and Training

Occupations entail varying levels of worker skills, education and training requirements, and job responsibilities. The following displays a range of occupational levels, from professional to unskilled.

Agriculture, forestry, and fishing industry
Mining and petroleum industry
Construction industry
Manufacturing industry
Transportation, communication, and utilities industry
Wholesale and retail trade industry
Finance, insurance, and real estate industry
Services industry
Public administration industry

▲ *Figure 16.6 Standard Industrial Classification Numbers for Nine Major Industrial Groups.*

- Professional
- Managerial
- Semiprofessional
- Skilled
- Semiskilled
- Unskilled

Which occupational level do you hope to attain in your future career?

CAREER TIP

It is as important to learn **where** people in various occupations earn their living as it is to learn **how** they earn their living.

The occupational level workers attain is directly related to the education and training level they achieve. What education and training level will you need to achieve for the occupational level you hope to attain?

- High school dropout
- GED
- High school graduate
- Some post-high-school training
- Apprenticeship training
- Technical trade school
- Two-year associate degree
- Four-year bachelor degree
- Five-year (or more) college degree

Section 4 GET INVOLVED

Answer the following on a separate sheet of paper, and be prepared to discuss your responses in class.

1. Write down the title of a specific occupation you are considering for your future career. For the occupation you are considering, use the information in Figures 16.4 to 16.6 to determine
   - The Standard Occupational Classification (Figure 16.4).
   - The USOE Career Cluster (Figure 16.5).
   - The Standard Industrial Classification (Figure 16.6).

2. Considering your answers to activity 1, answer the following:

   a. Does the education and training level of the occupation match your personal education and training goals?
   b. Does the occupational level match your personal career goals?
   c. Would you be satisfied with the type of organization and work setting that is customary for this occupation?
   d. Does this occupation seem to be a good match with your personal career goals? Why or why not?

.IMPORTANT FACTS

24.6 Million New Jobs by 2005

The 24.6 million jobs that will be added to the U.S. economy by 2005 will not be evenly distributed across major industrial and occupational groups. Instead, industries that provide services will account for almost four out of five new jobs.

Where Are the Jobs?

The United States has more than six million business establishments (workplaces) with employees. Although large establishments are fewer in number, they hire more workers. In addition, they offer greater occupational mobility and advancement potential. On the other hand, small establishments offer greater interpersonal contact between workers, and they are found in almost every locality.

Workplaces that produce similar goods or provide similar services are grouped together into industries (groups of businesses with a particular concern). As you look at the figure below, note these facts:

Number of employees	Percent of establishments	Percent of workers
Total	100.0	100.0
1-4	57.8	6.3
5-9	18.2	7.8
10-19	11.3	9.9
20-49	7.7	15.1
50-99	2.8	12.3
100-249	1.6	15.8
250-499	0.4	9.8
500-999	0.2	7.9
1,000 or more	0.1	15.2

- In 1990, approximately 58 percent of all workplaces employed fewer than five workers.
- Medium-sized to large establishments employed a greater proportion of all workers.
- Establishments that employed fifty or more workers accounted for only 5 percent of all workplaces yet employed almost 61 percent of all workers.

- The large workplaces (those with more than five hundred workers) accounted for only 0.3 percent of all workplaces but employed more than 23 percent of all workers.
- The only nonmanufacturing workplace that averaged more than one hundred workers per industry was local government.

Source: Career Guide to Industries, U.S. Department of Labor, September 1992.

Some Industries Will Grow More Rapidly Than Others

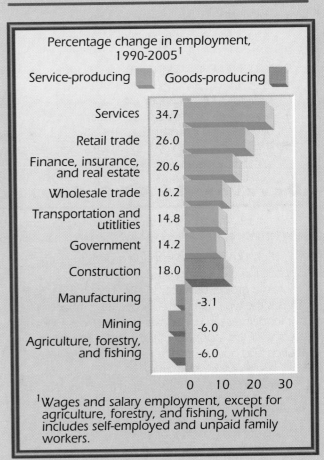

Percentage change in employment, 1990-2005[1]

Service-producing / Goods-producing

Services	34.7
Retail trade	26.0
Finance, insurance, and real estate	20.6
Wholesale trade	16.2
Transportation and utitlities	14.8
Government	14.2
Construction	18.0
Manufacturing	-3.1
Mining	-6.0
Agriculture, forestry, and fishing	-6.0

0 10 20 30

[1]Wages and salary employment, except for agriculture, forestry, and fishing, which includes self-employed and unpaid family workers.

Source: U.S. Bureau of Labor Statistics, 1992.

CHAPTER 16 REVIEW

ENRICH YOUR VOCABULARY

On a separate sheet of paper, number from 1 to 10, and complete the following activity. (Do not write in your textbook.) Match each statement below with the most appropriate term from the "Enrich Your Vocabulary" list at the beginning of the chapter by writing that term next to the correct statement.

1. A U.S. Department of Labor publication that provides detailed descriptions of about 250 occupations
2. A method for exploring occupations on an extensive database
3. A classification system for the OOH that uses twelve categories
4. A U.S. Department of Labor publication that contains brief descriptions of more than 25 thousand occupations
5. A U.S. Department of Labor publication that focuses on twelve specific career interest areas
6. A classification system, comprising fifteen groups of careers, that was developed by the U.S. Office of Education
7. A classification system that facilitates the collection and presentation of industrial data
8. Future employment trends
9. A grouping
10. A record of academic credits earned

CHECK YOUR KNOWLEDGE

On a separate sheet of paper, complete the following activity. (Do not write in your textbook.)

1. When you use the library to research careers, what is the best way to begin?
2. Where is the best place to get personal impressions about a certain career?
3. Who should a student contact to schedule a career field experience?
4. How can a high school student acquire "real" occupational experience?
5. What classification system answers the question, What type of work do people perform?
6. What classification system answers the question, Where do people work?
7. What are the six levels of employment in the world of work?
8. If you already know what career you will have, why should you research occupational information?

DEVELOP SCANS COMPETENCIES

Government experts say that successful workers can productively use Resources, Interpersonal skills, Information, Systems, and Technology. This activity will give you practice in developing Information and Interpersonal skills.

Form cooperative learning groups to research a specific job that your group decides on.

As a group, develop an information sheet that includes the type of information each member will look for in their research. For example, you may want each person to find out how many years of schooling is required and how much the job pays at entry level.

Assign each group member a different source of information to collect information from. Sources for your research should include as many of the following as possible: the *Occupational Outlook Handbook*; *Dictionary of Occupational Titles*; *Guide for Occupational Exploration*; computerized career information systems;

periodicals and magazines; trade and professional publications; films, videos, and audiotapes.

After each member has completed his or her research, compare and contrast the information collected. Make a simple chart similar to the one following to display your information for the class.

	OOH	videos	computer system
schooling			
pay			
outlook			

Unit Four

Living on Your Own

CHAPTERS

17 MANAGING YOUR INCOME

18 BEING A CONSUMER: SO MANY CHOICES

19 HEALTH: YOU CAN'T WORK WITHOUT IT!

20 WORK AND THE FAMILY

21 CIVIC RESPONSIBILITY: YOU MAKE A DIFFERENCE

22 YOUR LIFE AND YOUR CAREER

Managing Your Income

Learning Objectives

After completing this chapter, you should be prepared to:

- use sound financial management to reach your life goals and meet future financial crises
- define each category on a pay stub and check it for accuracy
- open, maintain, and use savings and checking accounts and electronic funds transfer systems
- select the most advantageous credit terms and understand the differences between various lending institutions and credit cards
- understand and make use of your consumer credit rights
- write a workable personal or household budget

Enrich Your Vocabulary

In reading this chapter and doing the exercises you will learn the following important terms:

sound financial
 management
gross earnings
endorsement
piecework
deductions
taxes
check
bank statement
canceled check
check register
bounced check
deposit slip

savings account
compounding
 interest
interest
electronic funds
 transfer system
CD (Certificate of
 Deposit)
open-ended credit
creditors
credit capacity
credit history
budget

Financial management is a key to reaching your life goals, and it is a method of meeting future financial crises. When you begin earning a paycheck, your income will probably be modest, and your financial life uncomplicated. This may tempt you to ignore long-range financial management. However, your first financial decisions will be a major factor in determining your future career success. You should

- Have a plan for spending your money
- Set aside a regular amount for savings
- Place limits on credit purchases (spending your money before you earn it)

Getting the most for your money through planned control of your earnings, savings, and spending is called **sound financial management**. There are four steps you can take to become an effective financial manager:

1. Establish your financial goals, and rank them in order of importance.
2. Develop a plan before you spend money.
3. Learn to be a wise consumer.
4. Develop a workable budget.

As you learned in Chapter 3, goals (including financial goals) are influenced by personal interests and values, and they change as a person's needs and situation change. Your present goal may

▲ *Janet and Karen moved into their new apartment today. They are sharing expenses and looking forward to "living on their own." Where are you planning to live after you graduate from high school?*

be to continue your education, buy a car, or take a vacation. When you leave home, one of your goals may be to afford an apartment with a friend. Later, you may need a house or a larger apartment in which to raise a family. The management of income and spending will remain important no matter how your goals change.

Section 1

Your Paycheck

Managing your income begins with understanding your paycheck. When you get paid, you will receive a paycheck and an attached pay stub, which is a record of your earnings. Keep all of your pay stubs for at least three years. They will enable you to verify your earnings and deductions.

The pay stub shows your **gross earnings** (total earnings before deductions). **Deductions** are those items subtracted from your earnings such as taxes, insurance, pensions, and other miscella-

Name: Roberta W. O'Day	Social Security No. 674-25-1411		Check no.: 0046271		
Pay period: 9/15/95-9/30/95					
Earnings	This Pay Period	Year to Date	Deductions	This Pay Period	Year to Date
Salary	1,154.25	26,547.75	Federal tax	142.61	3,279.92
Earnings			State tax	35.06	806.27
Hourly rate			City tax	23.09	530.96
Hours paid			FICA	106.77	4,270.80
Overtime rate			Pension		
O.T. hrs. paid			Bonds		
Sales amount			United Way		
Commission %			Health Ins.		
			Dues		175.00
			Total Deductions	307.53	
			Net pay	846.72	
Illness Unpaid	Family Illness	Jury Duty	Vacation	Sick Leave days Accum.	
				137	

▲ *Figure 17.1 Sample Pay Stub.*

neous items. The amount of pay you receive after all deductions have been subtracted is your net pay (take-home pay). Your gross earnings and your net pay will be very different in size (See Figure 17.1). A beginning worker's gross earnings of $200 per week could amount to a net pay of less than $150 because of deductions.

To cash your paycheck, you must sign the back of the check in ink. This is called your **endorsement** (the signature of a payee on the back of a check). Sign your name exactly as it appears on the front of the check.

The tax information printed on your pay stub is forwarded to the appropriate government agencies. Always check your pay stub to make sure that

it is correct. Keep accurate daily records of the hours you work. Mistakes can happen.

Earnings

Employers use a variety of methods to pay their employees, including these:

- *Salary*: Workers are paid a fixed sum of money every year. Payment is usually made once or twice a month. Wages are calculated for a year and are divided into equal pay periods.
- *Wages*: Workers are paid a fixed amount of earnings per hour, day, or week.
- **Piecework**: Workers are paid according to the amount they produce.
- *Commission*: Salespeople are paid a certain percentage of their sales.
- *Overtime pay*: Workers are paid a specified rate for work performed beyond their regular hours.

Deductions

Regardless of how you are paid, your employer is legally responsible for withholding certain deductions from your earnings. These deductions include local, state, and federal taxes. **Taxes** are payments that all citizens are required by law to make to help pay the costs of government services.

Under the law, employers must withhold tax payments from a worker's base pay and forward them to the appropriate government agency. Maintaining accurate payroll records and processing the required government forms amount to a very expensive and time-consuming process for employers. Federal income taxes are withheld on the earnings of corporations as well as individual workers.

Workers are required to pay all or a large part of their federal, state, and local income tax during the year in which they receive the income. The amount withheld depends on the amount a worker earns, his or her marital status, the number of dependents (people that the worker supports), and the percentage of tax determined by law.

All new workers are required by law to complete a W-4 tax form for their employer. The employer uses the information provided on the W-4 to calculate withholdings for each pay period. (See the sample W-4 tax form in Figure 17.2 on the next page.) The W-4 is a legal statement that gives your employer permission to deduct taxes from your paycheck and to pay them to the government for you. If the information on your W-4 is accurate, the amount withheld each year will be close to your annual tax bill.

According to the law, every taxpayer must file an income tax return by April 15 for the preceding calendar year. On the tax return, the taxpayer makes adjustments for any overpayment or underpayment of the total tax due.

By law, most workers must participate in the Federal Insurance Contributions Act (FICA) program, which is commonly referred to as *Social Security*. Social Security provides monthly income to workers who are retired or are unable to work because of sickness or injury.

Federal law requires employers to deduct 7.65 percent of each employee's pay for Social Security.

▲ *Scott Simpson and the two payroll and timekeeping clerks he supervises ensure that 857 employees' paychecks are correct and paid on time. They must understand and follow all tax and deduction laws.*

Then the employer must match the employee's FICA payment with an equal amount. Refer back to Roberta O'Day's pay stub (Figure 17.1). How much was deducted from her earnings and paid to FICA? Roberta's employer, the GMF Corporation, was required by law to match her contribution.

Employers must consider expenses for their portion of benefits like Social Security, health insurance, vacations, and sick leave as labor costs. Many employees are unaware that employers pay for these benefits.

In some cases, workers may choose whether or not to have their employers make payroll deductions for health and hospitalization plans, life insurance, company pension plans, savings programs, association or union dues, charitable contributions, or stock-buying plans.

Form W-4 (1995)

Want More Money In Your Paycheck?
If you expect to be able to take the earned income credit for 1995 and a child lives with you, you may be able to have part of the credit added to your take-home pay. For details, get Form W-5 from your employer.

Purpose. Complete Form W-4 so that your employer can withhold the correct amount of Federal income tax from your pay.

Exemption From Withholding. Read line 7 of the certificate below to see if you can claim exempt status. *If exempt, complete line 7; but do not complete lines 5 and 6.* No Federal income tax will be withheld from your pay. Your exemption is good for 1 year only. It expires February 15, 1996.

Note. *You cannot claim exemption from withholding if (1) your income exceeds $650 and includes unearned income (e.g., interest*

and dividends) and (2) another person can claim you as a dependent on their tax return.

Basic Instructions. Employees who are not exempt should complete the Personal Allowances Worksheet. Additional worksheets are provided on page 2 for employees to adjust their withholding allowances based on itemized deductions, adjustments to income, or two-earner/two-job situations. Complete all worksheets that apply to your situation. The worksheets will help you figure the number of withholding allowances you are entitled to claim. However, you may claim fewer allowances than this.

Head of Household. Generally, you may claim head of household filing status on your tax return only if you are unmarried and pay more than 50% of the costs of keeping up a home for yourself and your dependent(s) or other qualifying individuals.

Nonwage Income. If you have a large amount of nonwage income, such as interest or dividends, you should consider making

estimated tax payments using Form 1040-ES. Otherwise, you may find that you owe additional tax at the end of the year.

Two Earners/Two Jobs. If you have a working spouse or more than one job, figure the total number of allowances you are entitled to claim on all jobs using worksheets from only one Form W-4. This total should be divided among all jobs. Your withholding will usually be most accurate when all allowances are claimed on the W-4 filed for the highest paying job and zero allowances are claimed for the others.

Check Your Withholding. After your W-4 takes effect, you can use **Pub. 919,** Is My Withholding Correct for 1995?, to see how the dollar amount you are having withheld compares to your estimated total annual tax. We recommend you get Pub. 919 especially if you used the Two Earner/Two Job Worksheet and your earnings exceed $150,000 (Single) or $200,000 (Married). Call 1-800-829-3676 to order Pub. 919. Check your telephone directory for the IRS assistance number for further help.

Personal Allowances Worksheet

A   Enter "1" for **yourself** if no one else can claim you as a dependent   . . . .   **A** _____

B   Enter "1" if: • You are single and have only one job; or
              • You are married, have only one job, and your spouse does not work; or   . .   **B** _____
              • Your wages from a second job or your spouse's wages (or the total of both) are $1,000 or less.

C   Enter "1" for your **spouse.** But, you may choose to enter -0- if you are married and have either a working spouse or more than one job (this may help you avoid having too little tax withheld)   . . . .   **C** _____

D   Enter number of **dependents** (other than your spouse or yourself) you will claim on your tax return   . . . . . .   **D** _____

E   Enter "1" if you will file as **head of household** on your tax return (see conditions under **Head of Household** above)   .   **E** _____

F   Enter "1" if you have at least **$1,500** of **child or dependent care expenses** for which you plan to claim a credit   . .   **F** _____

G   Add lines A through F and enter total here. **Note:** This amount may be different from the number of exemptions you claim on your return ▶   **G** _____

For accuracy, do all worksheets that apply.
- if you plan to **itemize or claim adjustments to income** and want to reduce your withholding, see the Deductions and Adjustments Worksheet on page 2.
- If you are **single** and have **more than one job** and your combined earnings from all jobs exceed $30,000 OR if you are married and have a **working spouse or more than one job,** and the combined earnings from all jobs exceed $50,000, see the Two-Earner/Two-Job Worksheet on page 2 if you want to avoid having too little tax withheld.
- If **neither** of the above situations applies, stop here and enter the number from line G on line 5 of Form W-4 below.

.... **Cut here and give the certificate to your employer. Keep the top portion for your records.** ....

Form **W-4**
Department of the Treasury
Internal Revenue Service

Employee's Withholding Allowance Certificate

▶ **For Privacy Act and Paperwork Reduction Act Notice, see reverse.**

OMB No. 1545-0010
1995

1 Type or print your first name and middle initial Last name	2 Your social security number

Home address (number and street or rural route)

3 ☐ Single ☐ Married ☐ Married, but withhold at higher Single rate.
Note; if married, but legally separated, or spouse is a nonresident alien, check the Single box.

City or town, state, and ZIP code

4   If your last name differs from that on your social security card, check here and call 1-800-772-1213 for a new card   . . . . . ▶ ☐

5   Total number of allowances you are claiming (from line G above or from the worksheets on page 2 if they apply)   .   **5** ____

6   Additional amount, if any, you want withheld from each paycheck   . . . .   **6** $ ____

7   I claim exemption from withholding for 1995 and I certify that I meet **BOTH** of the following conditions for exemption:
- Last year I had a right to a refund of **ALL** Federal income tax withheld because I had **NO** tax liability; **AND**
- This year I expect a refund of **ALL** Federal income tax withheld because I expect to have **NO** tax liability.
If you meet both conditions, enter "EXEMPT" here   . . . . ▶   **7** ____

Under penalties of perjury, I certify that I am entitled to the number of withholding allowances claimed on this certificate or entitled to claim exempt status.

Employee's signature ▶   Date ▶   , 19 ___

8   Employer's name and address (Employer: Complete 8 and 10 only if sending to the IRS) | **9**   Office code (optional) | **10**   Employer identification number

Cat. No. 10220Q

▲ *Figure 17.2   Sample W-4 Tax Form.*

Section 1

GET INVOLVED

Answer the following on a separate sheet of paper, and be prepared to discuss your responses in class.

1. Interview workers who are paid by salary, hourly wages, piecework, and commission. Ask them about the benefits and liabilities of the way they are paid. Which method do you believe would be best in terms of managing your everyday finances? Which would be best for your long-term finances?
2. Which of the four methods of payment listed in this section would you expect if you were a
   - Cashier working in a supermarket?
   - Bricklayer working for a small, nonunion contractor?
   - Department supervisor working in a manufacturing plant?
   - Salesperson working for a real estate company?
3. Which method of wage payment would you like most? Why? Which would you like least? Why?
4. What do you suppose would happen if the Social Security number on your pay stub were wrong? What if the total hours recorded on your pay stub were less than your personal records show?

Section 2

Bank Services

The first step toward wise money management is to open a checking account and a savings account. Carefully select the financial institution that you entrust with your money. With the exception of the Federal Reserve banks described in Chapter 14, banks are businesses. Privately owned banks obtain income from various sources:

- Investments in stocks and bonds
- Interest charges on loans and credit cards
- Service charges for checking accounts
- Rental fees for safe-deposit boxes

The services and rates of interest offered by different banks are usually similar, but like all businesses, banks must compete for customers. Shop around for the best interests rates for savings accounts and loans. Check and compare the following when choosing a bank for your checking and savings accounts:

- What is the rate of interest paid on savings?
- What service fees are charged for checking accounts?
- Are your deposits insured?
- What is the rate of interest charged for consumer loans and home mortgages?
- How convenient is the bank's location and hours of service?
- Are automatic teller machines available twenty-four hours a day?

Checking Accounts

A **check** is an order written by a depositor directing the bank to pay out money (Figure 17.3).

JOHN B. BROWN
ROSALIN M. BROWN
120 LORETTA BLVD.
MICHIGAN FALLS, OHIO 45362

19 ___   **7101**

PAY TO THE
ORDER OF _____ $ [   ]

_____

G₁st **FIRST CENTRAL**
BANK
2300 CENTRAL AVE.
MICHIGAN FALLS, OHIO 45362

MEMO _____   _____

⑈1038⑈ ⑈192⑈ 036

▲ *Figure 17.3 Sample Check.*

A checking account (a bank account against which a depositor can write checks) is a safe and convenient way to make payments. It is also a useful financial-management tool. A checking account is safe because a check can be cashed only by the person or business to which the check is made payable. Writing a check for rent or other payments is convenient. It also eliminates the risk of carrying large sums of cash.

Once a check is paid by the bank, it is returned with the monthly **bank statement** (a bank report that shows the status of the depositor's account). The **canceled check** (a check that has been paid by a bank) is proof of payment. Some banks do not return canceled checks. Instead, you use a special two-layered paper to write your checks. The duplicate check is for your personal records. If you request a copy of a canceled check from the bank, it will be provided free or for a small charge.

It is important to record all of the checks you write in your check register. The **check register** is the portion of a checkbook where you can record the checks you have written (Figure 17.4). An accurate record of your expenditures and deposits will help you stay within your budget.

There are different types of checking accounts. Some pay interest; most do not. Some charge a fee for each check you write; others do not. The best choice for your checking account will depend on

• How much money you will keep in your account

• How many checks you will write each month

▲ *This retired couple keeps important documents such as their property deed, automobile title, and will in a bank safety deposit box.*

PLANNING MAKES A DIFFERENCE

Antonio's Savings Plan

Antonio Rivers started his working career five years ago. After reviewing his first budget, Antonio decided that a savings plan of $50 per month would leave him with enough money to pay his bills and maintain a reasonable lifestyle. After five years, Antonio has paid $3,000 into his savings account. With compound interest, his account is presently worth $3,601. During the next year, his account will earn $252.

Critical Thinking

1. Antonio plans to buy a new car next year. He is considering whether or not to close his savings account and use the money as a down payment. If he does, he would apply the $50 per month that he presently deposits in savings toward his monthly car payment. If you were Antonio, what would you do? Why?

• What other bank services you will use

Your first checking account will probably have unlimited checking, no interest, and a low service fee.

Before opening a checking account, ask if you are required to keep a minimum monthly balance to get free checking. How many checks are free? What is the fee for additional checks? Determine how many checks you will write each month. Is it more economical to pay a monthly service charge or a per-check fee? What fee does your bank charge for a **bounced check** (a check that is written with insufficient funds in your account)? Paying a fee for overdrawing on your account is costly and embarrassing.

When you have enough cash to meet the minimum requirements, it could be to your advantage to open an interest-bearing NOW (negotiable order of withdrawal) or Super NOW checking account. NOW accounts require larger minimum balances than regular checking accounts, but they combine the benefits of a checking and saving account. You earn interest on your account balance and there is no service charge for transactions.

RECORD ALL CHARGES OR CREDITS THAT AFFECT YOUR ACCOUNT						
Number	Date	Decribe Transaction	✓	Payment	Deposit	Balance
804	2-14	Cynthia's Flowers		25.63		604.27
	2-17	Deposit			846.72	1450.99
805	2-18	Munroe Falls Water Works		64.81		1386.18

▲ *Figure 17.4 Check Register.*

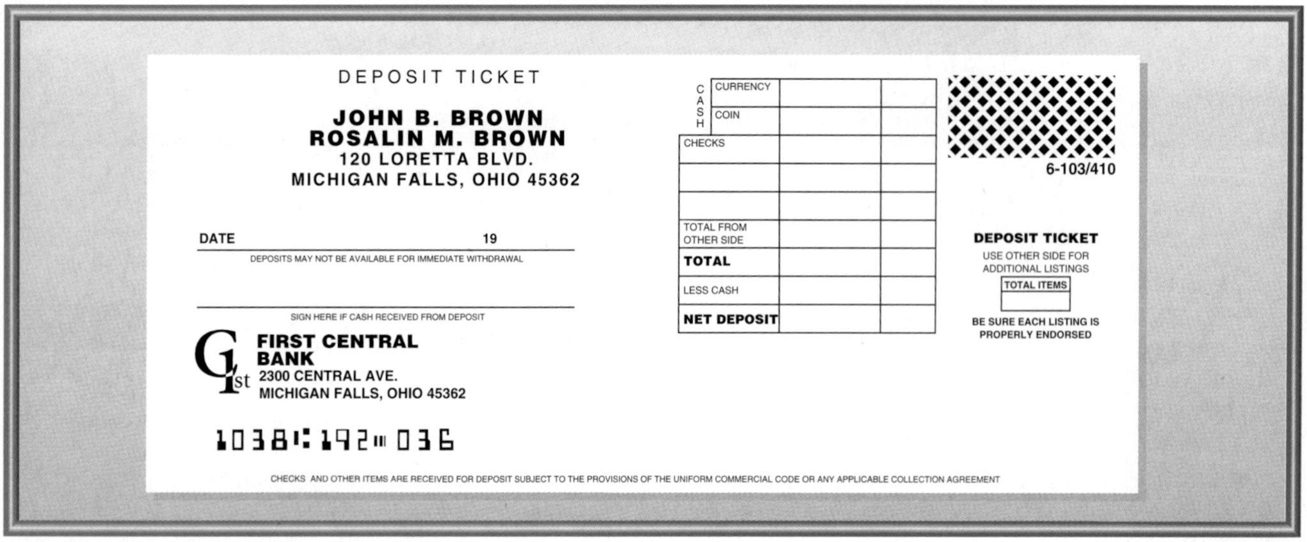
DEPOSIT TICKET

JOHN B. BROWN
ROSALIN M. BROWN
120 LORETTA BLVD.
MICHIGAN FALLS, OHIO 45362

DATE 19

DEPOSITS MAY NOT BE AVAILABLE FOR IMMEDIATE WITHDRAWAL

SIGN HERE IF CASH RECEIVED FROM DEPOSIT

FIRST CENTRAL BANK
2300 CENTRAL AVE.
MICHIGAN FALLS, OHIO 45362

1038⑆192⑈036

CASH CURRENCY		
COIN		
CHECKS		
TOTAL FROM OTHER SIDE		
TOTAL		
LESS CASH		
NET DEPOSIT		

6-103/410

DEPOSIT TICKET
USE OTHER SIDE FOR ADDITIONAL LISTINGS
TOTAL ITEMS
BE SURE EACH LISTING IS PROPERLY ENDORSED

CHECKS AND OTHER ITEMS ARE RECEIVED FOR DEPOSIT SUBJECT TO THE PROVISIONS OF THE UNIFORM COMMERCIAL CODE OR ANY APPLICABLE COLLECTION AGREEMENT

▲ *Figure 17.5 Sample Bank Deposit Slip.*

The **deposit slip** provides a record of the money put into an account (Figure 17.5). Be sure to record all of your checking account deposits in your check register.

Following the journey of a single check should help you understand that part of the banking process. Imagine that you have your car's transmission serviced and you pay the $59 bill by writing a check on your account at the First Central Bank. In other words, by writing a check you give instructions to your bank to deduct $59 from your checking account and pay it to Waterloo Transmission.

At the close of the business day, the manager of Waterloo Transmission deposits your check in the Second National Bank (Waterloo's bank). Waterloo's account is credited in the amount of $59. However, the Second National Bank doesn't collect payment directly from the First Central Bank. It would be inefficient and costly for them to pay separately for each of the thousands of checks their customers write every day. Instead, the Second National Bank sends your check to a centralized clearinghouse. Thousands of checks from several banks are added up at the clearinghouse every day. Each member bank then makes or receives one daily payment to or from other member banks.

The clearinghouse returns your check to the First Central Bank, and $59 is subtracted from your personal checking account. Your check is stamped "Paid" and will be returned to you later with your other canceled checks and your balance statement.

Savings Accounts

A **savings account** is a bank account that pays interest to customers in return for use of the customer's money. Money may not grow on trees, but it will grow if you deposit it in a savings account that pays **interest** (amounts lenders pay for use of customers' money). The amount of interest your money earns is calculated as a percentage of the amount of money in your account. For example, if you deposit $100 at an annual interest rate of 7 percent, your account will earn $7 at the end of one year (7 percent of 100 = 7). Your account will begin the second year with an amount of $107 and will earn $7.49 during the second year. This is called **compounding interest** (paying interest on the interest). The amount of interest your account earns will depend on the amount of money you deposit, the rate of interest being paid, and how often the interest is paid. Some banks compound interest on a daily basis.

Regular savings are an important part of wise money management. Savings can be used for future purchases, such as a vacation, an automobile, or education expenses. Regular deposits will add up, enabling you to pay cash for future purchases and avoid the cost of credit interest.

The process of opening a savings account is similar to that of opening a checking account. You must complete a signature card, and you will use deposit slips to deposit checks or cash in the account. The savings institution will mail you a monthly or quarterly balance statement and will issue a passbook for your use for recording savings account transactions.

You can open a savings account in a number of financial institutions, including banks, savings and loan associations, credit unions, brokerages, other financial services companies, and the federal government. These institutions offer a wide range of savings instruments, interest rates, and security.

Certificate of Deposit

A **certificate of deposit** (CD) is one widely used savings instrument. A CD is an agreement between a bank and its customer. The bank agrees to pay back the money invested, plus a specific rate of interest, on a certain date. CDs pay a higher rate of interest than ordinary passbook savings accounts do. They are usually sold in large denominations, and they require that the deposit be left for a certain period of time or there will be a penalty for early withdrawal.

Ask yourself the following questions before you choose a savings plan:

1. How much can I afford to save on a regular basis?
2. How long will I leave my deposits in the account?

▲ *Banks and other financial institutions frequently post the current rate of interest they pay for various investments. Are your dollars earning the highest possible rate of interest?*

3. In case of emergency, how quickly can I obtain my money?

A traditional passbook savings account can be opened with a small deposit and is usually the best choice for first-time savers.

Insuring Your Money

At one time, depositing money in a bank was risky business. If the bank failed, customers lost part or all of the money in their accounts. In 1933, the federal government removed this danger by establishing the Federal Depositors Insurance Corporation (FDIC). The FDIC is a government corporation, but the money for its operation is provided by member banks. The FDIC guarantees each account in an insured bank up to $100,000. All member banks of the Federal Reserve System are required to join the FDIC. State banks that are not members of the Federal Reserve System may become members of the FDIC by meeting certain requirements. Each insured bank posts signs stating that it is a member of the Federal Depositors Insurance Corporation.

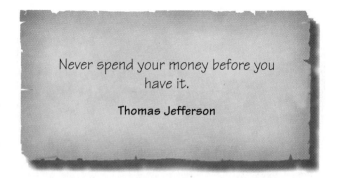

Never spend your money before you have it.

Thomas Jefferson

Savings and loan corporations are insured by a similar federal insurance program called the Federal Savings and Loan Insurance Corporation (FSLIC). As with banks, member savings and loan institutions post membership signs, and accounts are insured by the FSLIC up to $100,000. When you open a savings account, be certain that the bank or savings and loan association you select is a member of the FDIC or the FSLIC.

Remember that wise financial planners shop around. As your career progresses, you will have more financial responsibilities, and they will become more complex. Saving a part of your earnings on a regular basis and learning to be a careful spender are giant steps on the road to career success.

Electronic Funds Transfer System and ATM Cards

The **electronic funds transfer system** (EFTS) is a computer-run system that lets consumers, businesses, and governments transfer money from one account to another by electronic means. This is a fast and inexpensive method of processing money transactions. EFTS services are activated by using a personalized, plastic bank card. Each card contains the customer's identification number and is capable of accessing his or her accounts. If your bank card is lost or stolen, notify your bank immediately.

The part of the EFTS that you are probably most familiar with is the automated teller machine (ATM). ATMs are a twenty-four-hour banking convenience. With an ATM, you can:

- Withdraw cash from your checking or savings account
- Transfer funds between your accounts
- Check the balance in your accounts
- Make a deposit to your checking or savings account

Section 2 GET INVOLVED

Answer the following on a separate sheet of paper, and be prepared to discuss your responses in class.

1. Visit a local bank and speak with the manager or assistant manager. Obtain the following information and report back to the class:
   - What causes a bank to fail?
   - What happens to the customer's money if the bank goes out of business? How are deposits protected by the federal government?
   - Is it safe to work in a bank? How are the employees protected in case of a robbery?
   - What does it mean for an employee to be bonded?
   - How do electronic banking services help or hinder the operation of the bank?
   - What marketing techniques does the bank use to attract new customers and to keep old customers?
   - What happens to unclaimed savings accounts?
   - How does the bank work with the Federal Reserve?
   - Is your business a state bank or a national bank?
   - For which banking occupations would you suggest a young person prepare? What education and training are required?

Section 3

Borrowing and Credit

"Buy now, pay later" is the motto of millions of U.S. consumers, who buy goods and services worth billions of dollars on credit each year. Whether it is an automobile, a house, clothes, gasoline, or a restaurant meal, buying now and paying later is the way millions of Americans make most of their purchases.

A good credit rating is one of the most valuable financial tools you have. Good credit enables you to make major purchases and pay for them gradually. Credit can help you purchase goods or ser-

▲ *Lonzo Burdette uses his credit card to buy gasoline but he pays the full amount of his bill each month. Because of their excellent credit rating, the Fongs have no problem getting a home loan. Charles owes $3,475.00 on his credit card but he is buying a new tennis racket. What are your buying and credit habits?*

▲ *Most stores and businesses accept major credit cards such as Mastercard or Visa. Owning several "cards" makes purchasing very easy. It also makes overspending very easy. Do you know anyone who ruined his or her credit rating by overspending with credit cards?*

vices you need when money is scarce and in times of a personal emergency. By using credit wisely, you can keep your long-term savings and investments untouched and still obtain the goods and services you want or need.

Establishing Credit

There are two basic types of credit:

- Closed-ended credit is a one-time loan made for the purchase of a costly item, such as an automobile or a major appliance. The payment period, number of payments, and payment amounts are specified. Installment loans are closed-ended. A limited amount of closed-ended credit can be built into a well-planned budget.

- **Open-ended credit** is a loan made on a continuous basis for the purchase of products up to a specific dollar limit. Bills are issued monthly for a portion of the loan. Credit cards are examples of open-ended credit. Although owning a card is convenient, consumers are frequently un-

aware of the growing finance charges. Borrowing and overspending are both easy with open-ended credit.

If you plan to achieve and maintain a good credit rating, it is important that you know how **creditors** (people who lend money) determine whether or not you're a good credit risk. Your credit worthiness revolves around the three C's of credit: character, capacity, and capital.

Your character predicts how likely you are to pay off your credit in full and make each payment on time. Your past credit history and payment records will influence a lender who is deciding whether or not to approve credit for you. Missed payments or failure to pay previous debts will reduce your chance of obtaining new credit. How long have you been employed at your present job and at your previous jobs? How long have you lived at your present address and at previous addresses? Lenders will use the answers to these questions as indicators of your personal stability.

Your **credit capacity** is the amount of debt that you can afford to repay each month. Lenders weigh your current job position and income level against your living expenses, mortgage or rent payment, car payment, and other debts. Then they determine your ability to repay the credit you are seeking.

The amount of capital or collateral (possessions with cash value) that you own will influence a lender's credit decision. Collateral, such as a home, a car, bank accounts, and investments, provide an added level of assurance that you have means other than personal income to repay your credit obligation.

A spotless **credit history** (a record of how you've borrowed and repaid debts) will qualify you for the best credit terms. People with previous credit problems must usually pay higher interest rates and are usually approved for a lower purchasing limit. This policy compensates loan companies that deal with high-risk customers.

Who Are the Lenders?

When you buy on credit, a business trusts you to pay later for the product, service, or money that it gives you today. The business accepts your promise to make regular payments until you have paid all that you owe.

Banks lend money when it seems likely that the money will be repaid when due. A bank's lending requirements are usually more strict than those of other types of lending institutions. In addition, banks handle several other types of financial (related to money) business. For example, real estate loans are the main business of a savings and loan bank. On the other hand, commercial banks, ones that provide full banking services, loan money for education, automobiles, appliances, boats, and other personal needs.

Loaning money is the main way that banks earn money. This enables them to pay interest on various savings accounts and to earn a profit. Although bank loans are usually one of the least expensive means of borrowing, a wise consumer always shops around to obtain the lowest possible interest rate.

▲ *Mary Ann is applying for a revolving charge account with a local electronics store. She wants to buy an expensive sound system. What advice would you offer her?*

Consumer finance companies specialize in making small loans to borrowers with poor or no established credit. They usually lend smaller amounts of money and charge much higher interest rates than banks.

Credit unions usually charge a lower interest rate. However, you must be a member of the credit union to borrow money. (See Chapter 11.)

Retailers, such as clothing, appliance, and department stores, encourage customers to open charge accounts with them. A charge account allows you to charge up to a specific amount at the retailer's store or chain of stores. On regular charge accounts, you are expected to make full payment for goods you have purchased at the end of each monthly billing period.

Many retailers also have revolving charge accounts. Revolving accounts allow the customer to make a partial payment for the goods purchased each month. There is a limit on the total amount that can be owed at one time, and the retailer adds an interest charge to the unpaid balance. The interest rates for this type of account are usually very high.

Financial Responsibility Is Important

Robert and Tamika Perry have been married for fourteen years. They are considering the purchase of a new automobile with a monthly payment of $267 for three years. Review their Credit Analysis Worksheet (Figure 17.6 on the facing page), and imagine yourself as a loan officer considering their credit application.

Does the Perry's monthly mortgage payment exceed 28 percent of their combined gross income? Does their consumer debt (other loans and credit cards) amount to more than 10 percent of their combined take-home pay? If the answer to either question is yes, you are not permitted to approve the loan.

Critical Thinking

1. Would Robert and Tamika be better off if they purchased a used car or a less-expensive new car? Should they drive their old car for another year? Why?

2. If your income was the same as Robert and Tamika's, would you keep the same home, purchase a more-expensive home, or purchase a less-expensive home? Why?

Corporations that provide credit cards to their customers are major lenders. There are two types of credit cards:

*   Single-purpose cards. An oil company may have a single-purpose credit card for use at its service stations. A department store may have a single-purpose card for charge accounts at its store.

*   Multipurpose cards. These cards can be used at most large stores, restaurants, hotels, airlines, and service companies. Mastercard, Visa, and American Express are examples of multipurpose cards. They can be used throughout the United States and in most other nations.

Banks can join the Mastercard or Visa system and issue credit cards to earn money. When a business accepts a credit card for payment, it must pay the bank that issued the card a fee for each charge made on the card. In turn, the cardholder pays the bank interest on any charges that are not fully paid each month.

Shop around before you purchase a credit card. The interest rate charged by different banks for credit card loans may vary by as much as 10 percent. Most lending institutions charge a yearly fee for the use of the card, but other cards are free. The cost of using a credit card to make purchases is almost always greater than the cost of borrowing money from the same bank.

If you have a credit card or if you plan to obtain one, be certain to read the literature that accompanies it, especially the credit card agreement. Using the card obligates you to abide by the rules and regulations stated in the agreement. If you are unclear about the agreement, contact the card issuer to ask for an explanation.

The High Cost of Credit and Borrowing

Buying on credit is costly. The amount of interest the borrower pays depends on the amount bor-

INCOME:

Your Monthly Salary (Gross)	$1,487
Your Spouse's Monthly Salary (Gross)	$1,625
Bonuses	
Alimony	
Child Support	
Other TOTAL INCOME	$3,112

DEPTS:

Type of Dept	Outstanding Balance	Monthly Payment	% of Monthly Income (Payment /Total Income)
Mortgage	$48,000.00	$715.00	
Home Equity Loan	$2,300.00	$187.00	
Auto Loan			
Installment Loan	$840.00	$48.00	
Other			
1			
2			
3			
LOAN TOTALS	$51,140.00	$950.00	
Credit Cards			
1 United Oil	$0.00		
2 Bank Card	$1,065.00	$73.00	
3			
4			
5			
6			
CREDIT CARD TOTAL	$1,065.00	$73.00	
TOTAL DEBT	$52,205.00		

▲ *Figure 17.6 Sample Credit Analysis Worksheet.*

rowed, the length of time for which it is borrowed, and the rate of interest charged.

The Truth in Lending Act requires creditors to explain (in writing) the finance charge and the annual percentage rate charged before asking borrowers to sign an agreement. Federal law doesn't set interest rates or other credit charges, but it does require their disclosure so that consumers can compare credit costs.

The finance charge is the total dollar amount paid to use credit. It includes interest charges and other costs, such as service charges or credit-related insurance premiums. The annual percent-age rate (APR) is the percentage cost of credit on a yearly basis. When you shop for credit, the APR is the most important comparison you can make.

CAREER TIP

The more time you take to pay your loan, the larger your finance charges will be. Finance charges may cause an enormous increase in the cost of the goods or services you purchase.

PLANNING MAKES A DIFFERENCE

Rita Shops for a Loan

Rita Sampson spent several weeks shopping for a good used car. Finally, she found a car that she really wanted. The purchase price was $7,500. Rita decided to make a $1,500 down payment, and she needs to borrow $6,000.

Next, Rita started shopping for a loan. She soon discovered that small differences in credit terms can make a big difference in the total cost of a car. Rita narrowed her choices to three lending institutions. Compare their credit agreements in Figure 17.7 on the facing page.

Critical Thinking

1. Which creditor will charge Rita the highest total finance charges? Which will charge the lowest total finance charges?
2. Which creditor will charge Rita the highest monthly payment? Which will charge the lowest?
3. Which creditor's loan would Rita pay off first?
4. If you were Rita, which loan option would you accept? Why?

Suppose you buy a camera that costs $300, and you make a down payment of $200. Then you borrow the $100 balance from the camera store for one year, with a finance charge of $10. If you were allowed to keep the $100 for one year and then pay back $110, you would be paying an APR of 10 percent. If you were required to repay the $100 in twelve monthly installments, you don't have use of the $100 for the whole year. In fact, you have less use of the $100 each month. In this case, the APR actually amounts to 18 percent.

Be Alert for Signs of Trouble

When you have good credit, it's easy to buy things, do things, buy more things, and do more things, until you are unable to make your payments. Suddenly, your good credit vanishes. The ten credit commandments will help you avoid the problem of overspending:

1. Thou shall not spend more than 10 percent of your income on monthly payments.
2. Thou shall not borrow money to pay off other debts.
3. Thou shall try to make extra payments to pay off loans early.
4. Thou shall not buy things with credit cards unless you can pay for them in full on the first day of the month.
5. Thou shall not borrow from friends or relatives.
6. Thou shall ignore lenders who offer to extend the period of a debt.
7. Thou shall not charge ordinary expenses, such as groceries and lunches.
8. Thou shall not take money from your savings account to pay your bills.
9. Thou shall not borrow on insurance policies to pay your bills.
10. Thou shall always check the cost of a loan with at least three lenders before signing a credit agreement.

Illness, layoffs, and other family emergencies can create serious financial problems. Seek professional help quickly if you are unable to solve a credit problem. You may want to contact a Consumer Credit Counseling Service (CCCS). CCCS is a nonprofit organization with more than

	APR	Length of Loan	Monthly Payment	Total Finance Charge	Total of Payments
Creditor A	14%	three years	$205.07	$1,382.52	$7,382.52
Creditor B	14%	four years	$163.96	$1,870.08	$7,870.08
Creditor C	15%	four years	$166.98	$2,015.04	$8,015.04

▲ *Figure 17.7 Sample Credit Agreements.*

280 offices through the United States. CCCS counselors will try to arrange a repayment plan that is acceptable to you and your creditors. They will also help you set up a realistic budget.

Your Credit Rights

It is important for you to understand your credit rights and to know when to use them. Consumer credit rights are protected by three acts of Congress.

The Equal Credit Opportunity Act requires a lender to notify you within thirty days after you have submitted a completed loan application, regardless of whether the application has been approved. If denied, the notice of denial must be in writing. It must specify why credit was denied or must tell you how to request that information.

The Fair Credit Reporting Act requires that a credit agency show you your file, or at least discuss its contents with you, and disclose the agency's information sources if you are refused credit for a specific reason related to your credit report. You can also request information on who has received a copy of your credit report in the past six months. This information must be provided to you free of

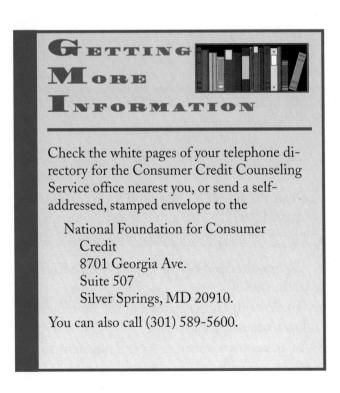

GETTING MORE INFORMATION

Check the white pages of your telephone directory for the Consumer Credit Counseling Service office nearest you, or send a self-addressed, stamped envelope to the

National Foundation for Consumer Credit
8701 Georgia Ave.
Suite 507
Silver Springs, MD 20910.

You can also call (301) 589-5600.

▲ *Pauline is paying with a credit card for the new clothing. She tries never to borrow money for items costing more than $500.00.*

FOR   FIRST NATIONAL BANK
       ANYTOWN, ANYSTATE 12345

Date Received 4/11/96	CONFIDENTIAL crediscope® REPORT
Date Mailed 4/11/96	
In File Since: April 1970	Member Associated Credit Bureaus, Inc.
Inquired As:	Joint Account

REPORT ON:	LAST NAME CONSUMER	FIRST NAME ROBERT	M. INITIAL G.	SOCIAL SECURITY NUMBER 123-45-6789	SPOUSE'S NAME BETTY R.
ADDRESS: 1234 ANY ST.	CITY ANYTOWN	STATE ANYSTATE	ZIP CODE 12333	SINCE 1983	SPOUSE'S SOCIAL SECURITY NO. 987-65-4321

COMPLETE TO HERE FOR TRADE REPORT AND SKIP TO CREDIT HISTORY

PRESENT EMPLOYER: XYZ CORPORATION	POSITION HELD: ASST. DEPT. MGR.	SINCE: 10/91	DATE EMPLOY VERIFIED 12-91	EST. MONTHLY INCME $2500

COMPLETE TO HERE FOR EMPLOYMENT AND TRADE REPORT AND SKIP TO CREDIT HISTORY

DATE OF BIRTH 5/25/60	NUMBER OF DEPENDENTS INCLUDING SELF: 4	[X] OWNS OR BUYING HOUSE	[ ] RENTS HOME	[ ] OTHER: (EXPLAIN)

FORMER ADDRESS 4321 FIRST AVE.	CITY: ANYTOWN	STATE ANYSTATE	FROM: 1980	TO: 1983
FORMER EMPLOYER: ABC & ASSOCIATES	POSITION HELD: SALES PERSON	FROM: 2/90	TO: 9/91	EST. MONTHLY INCOME $1285
SPOUSE'S EMPLOYER: BIG CITY DEPT. STORE	POSITION HELD: CASHIER	SINCE 4/91	DATE EMPLOY VERIFIED: 12/91	EST. MONTHLY INCOME $1200

CREDIT HISTORY (Complete this section for all reports)

WHOSE	KIND OF BUSINESS AND ID CODE	DATE REPORTED AND METHOD OF REPORTING	DATE OPENED	DATE OF LAST PAYMENT	HIGHEST CREDIT OR LAST CONTRACT	BALANCE OWING	PAST DUE AMOUNT	NO. OF PAYMENTS	NO. MONTHS HISTORY REVIEWED	30-59 DAYS ONLY	60-89 DAYS ONLY	90 DAYS AND OVER	TYPE & TERMS (MANNER OF PAYMENT)	REMARKS
2	CONSUMER'S BANK B 12-345	2/6/96 AUTOMTD.	12/95	1/96	1200	1100	-0-	-0-	2	-0-	-0-	-0-	INSTALLMENT	$100/MO.
3	BIG CITY DEPT. STORE D 54-321	2/10/96 MANUAL	4/91	1/96	300	100	-0-	-0-	12	-0-	-0-	-0-	REVOLVING	$25/MO.
1	SUPER CREDIT CARD N 01-1234	12/12/95 AUTOMATD.	7/92	11/95	200	100	100	1	12	1	-0-	-0-	OPEN	30-DAY

PUBLIC RECORD: SMALL CLAIMS CT. CASE #SC1001 PLAINTIFF; ANYWHERE APPLIANCES
                AMOUNT $225 PAID 4/4/92

ADDITIONAL INFORMATION: REF. SMALL CLAIMS CT. CASE #SC1001--5/30/92 SUBJECT SAYS CLAIM PAID
                        UNDER PROTEST. APPLIANCE DID NOT OPERATE PROPERLY.

▲ *Figure 17.8 Sample Credit Report.*

charge. After reviewing your credit report (Figure 17.8), ask the credit agency to reinvestigate incorrect or inaccurate information. If errors are found or if the agency cannot verify certain information, the file must be corrected. If the credit agency refuses to remove an item after the investigation, it is your right to require that your statement, limited to one hundred words, be placed in your file.

The Truth in Lending Act limits your liability for lost or stolen credit cards to fifty dollars per card if you properly and promptly notify the card issuer of the loss. Keep a record of your credit card numbers and issuer telephone numbers in a safe place.

Read the monthly statement from the issuer of your credit cards carefully. Incorrect information can be placed on your credit record if:

- An unauthorized person charges items to your credit card
- The amount on the statement for a purchase doesn't match your receipt
- An error was made in posting a payment you made

If an error is made on your statement, the following steps will help you protect your credit history.

1. Within sixty days after you receive the statement on which the error first appears, notify the issuer in writing about the nature of the billing error you believe has been made.

2. Pay any charges on the statement that you do not challenge.

3. If notified that the charges are correct, pay the bill to maintain your credit rating, and then continue to pursue a correction.

In the case of defective goods or services, you may withhold payment if:

- You have made a "good-faith effort" to solve the problem with the merchant

- The cost in dispute totals more than fifty dollars

- The item was purchased in your own state or within 100 miles of your residence.

Section 3 GET INVOLVED

Answer the following on a separate sheet of paper, and be prepared to discuss your responses in class.

1. Arrange to interview a loan officer at a local bank, or invite him or her to speak to your class. Make a list of questions you would like to ask. Your list might include these:

- How does the bank collect money from overdue accounts?
- Is there a minimum age for borrowing money or buying on credit?
- What is the best way to establish and build a credit record?
- What becomes of consumer goods that are repossessed?

2. Imagine you are a store owner. A customer has failed to make his monthly payment on a washing machine for two consecutive months because his hours of employment have been reduced. What will you do? How will your decision help your business? How might it hurt your business?

Section 4

Money Management and Budgets

A **budget** is a plan for saving and spending income. A well-planned budget will let you know where you stand financially and will prevent emergencies from causing a financial strain. By setting clear and realistic goals for the future and including a budget in your money-management plan, you can be confident that your expenses will be met and that you will always have money put aside for a rainy day.

For most people, adequate food, shelter, clothing, and financial security are common goals. The

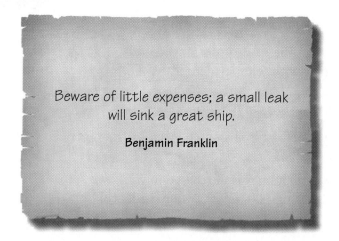

Beware of little expenses; a small leak will sink a great ship.

Benjamin Franklin

Planning a Budget

When you make a budget, you will need to estimate your available income for a specific period of time and decide how large a portion to set aside for your expenses. Doing this will help you:

- Decide what you can and cannot afford
- Avoid impulse buying
- Keep track of how you spend your income
- Make regular savings deposits
- Develop financial protection against sickness, unemployment, and accidents

Preparing a budget takes planning; following one takes determination. Good record keeping and the ability to refuse temptations to overspend are the keys to a successful day-to-day budget.

Your budget can cover any period of time (a month, three months, or a year). Most bills come due once a month. However, all bills will not be

financial goals of a young adult usually include education or training as well as personal wants and needs. As the young adult grows older, financial goals may include supporting a family, purchasing a home, or starting a business. Learning effective money-management skills now will help you achieve your present and future goals.

▲ *Carla and Albert Santiago are reviewing their monthly budget. Having the determination to follow their budget will enable them to pay cash for a great vacation this summer. How do you express your determination?*

due on the same day of the month. Insurance and taxes are generally paid quarterly (every three months) or semiannually (twice per year). Most people have some seasonal expenses (holidays, birthdays, and vacations). These special occasions should be accounted for in a budget.

Whatever time period your budget covers, it must be long enough to include most of your living expenses and income. It may be wise to plan your first budget for a short trial period to see what works and what doesn't. Continue making improvements until you are satisfied.

Most workers are paid every week or every other week. You will be able to pay your bills on time if you use each paycheck to pay your daily expenses and expenses that will be due within the next pay period. Budget a certain amount from each paycheck toward large expenses that will be due in the near future.

Getting a Budget Started

On a separate sheet of paper, estimate your income for the time period of your budget. Be sure to include in your total all of your sources of income, such as a part-time job, allowance, and gifts. If your earnings are irregular or if overtime pay is involved, it is best to use the lowest likely income for your budget. It is better to underestimate than to overestimate income. A satisfactory budget allows for unexpected expenses.

After you have estimated your income for the budget planning period, estimate your expenses. Expenses can be grouped into three categories:

- *Fixed expenses* are bills that usually remain the same each month, such as rent, house payments, and installment loans. Fixed irregular expenses are large payments due once or twice a year, such as insurance premiums or property taxes.

- *Flexible expenses* are bills that usually change from one month to the next, such as the amount spent on food, clothing, utilities, or transportation.

- *Set-asides* are amounts of money that you accumulate (collect) in your budget for special purposes, such as birthdays, holidays, vacations, emergency funds, and savings for future goals.

There is an old saying, "If you want to know what's going to happen tomorrow, look at what happened yesterday." This is especially true when making a budget. Use old records, receipts, bills, and canceled checks to estimate future expenses. Consider which expenses you can reduce and which expenses you will probably need to increase.

Carry a pocket-size notebook to record your expenses during a week or a pay period. Total your weekly or pay-period expenses for a month or two. Having an accurate record of your expenses will help you determine your average spending pattern for such things as food, housing, utilities, household operation, clothing, transportation, entertainment, and personal items. Use your spending record to estimate future expenses. In addition, plan for changing conditions that might increase or decrease your expenses.

Total your estimated expenses for a year, and divide by the number of budgeting periods you have allocated (assigned). This will help you determine the amount of money to allocate toward each expense during the budgeting period. For example:

$$\frac{\text{Total expenses per year}}{12} = \text{Monthly budget requirement}$$

$$\frac{\text{Total expenses per year}}{52} = \text{Weekly budget requirement}$$

On a separate sheet of paper, make a budgetary expense sheet similar to Figure 17.9. Using the information from your expense records, estimate each flexible and fixed budgetary expense in the space provided. Begin with the regular fixed expenses. Next, enter those fixed expenses that come due once or twice a year. Many households allo-

	January			February		
	Amount estimated	Amount spent	Difference	Amount estimated	Amount spent	Difference
Food						
At home						
Away from home						
Utilities						
Gas/fuel						
Electricity						
Telephone						
Water						
Household						
Maintenance and supplies						
Furnishings						
Decorating						
Clothing						
Household member 1						
Household member 2						
Household member 3						
Household member 4						
Health care						
Doctors						
Dentist						
Other						
Medicine and perscriptions						
Personal care						
Rent						
Mortgage						
Installments						
Credit card 1						
Credit card 2						
Credit card 3						
Automobile loan						
Personal loan						
Student loan						
Insurance						
Life						
Health						
Property						
Automobile						
Disability						
Set-asides						
Emergency fund						
Major expenses						
Goals						
Saving and investments						
Allowances						
Education						
Tuition						
Books						
Transportation						
Repairs						
Gas and taxi						
Recreation						
Gifts						
Other						
Total flexible expenses for the month						

▲ *Figure 17.9 Budgetary Expense Sheet.*

cate a specific amount each budget period toward these expenses. This practice spreads out the cost.

One way to meet major expenses is to include set-aside money in your regular budget. Keep your set-aside funds separate from other funds so you will not be tempted to spend them. If possible, keep them in an account in which they will earn interest.

Solving The Problem

Difficult Budget Decisions

Jamie Tenney balanced her budget by moving to another apartment and sharing the rent with two friends. She is living in a very nice apartment and is saving 65 percent of her former rent payment.

Alex Harper balanced his budget by selling his two-year-old car and buying a motorcycle. He uses the bus for transportation to work and uses the bike for personal transportation. Alex eliminated a car payment of $165 per month, paid cash for his bike, and has money left over to rent a car for special occasions. Instead of paying interest on a car loan, he is actually saving a small amount each month to buy a car with cash.

Critical Thinking

1. The advantage to Jamie's decision is obvious. Make a list of possible disadvantages.

2. If you were Jamie, what other budget changes would you have considered before giving up your apartment?

3. Make a list of the advantages and disadvantages of Alex's decision. If you were Alex, would you have made the same decision? Why or why not?

After you have entered your fixed expenses and your set-asides, you are ready to consider your flexible expenses. A little spending money that does not have to be accounted for gives everyone a sense of freedom and makes budgeting more interesting.

You may want to clear up debts by budgeting extra money for your installment payments. This will also reduce the amount you pay for interest charges.

Also consider budgeting a small amount of money for unexpected expenses. Did you ever have a tire go bad? A tooth start to ache? A television set quit working? Decide how much money you need to budget for these unexpected expenses. When your fund reaches the amount you have allowed, change your budget and start saving for something else. Change your budget as your spending needs change.

Compare your total expected income with your total planned expenses for the budget period you have established. Do your planned expenses equal your estimated future income? If so, you have a balanced budget. If not, you need to increase your income or decrease your spending.

If your expenses add up to more than your income, review each part of your budget plan. Where can you cut down? Where are you overspending? Next, decide which budget items are most important and which ones can wait. You may be able to trim your flexible expenses. It is sometimes necessary to reduce large fixed expenses to balance a budget.

If you reduce your expenses as much as seems reasonable and you are still unable to balance your budget, you might consider two options First, you might acquire more education or training to qualify for a better-paying job. Second, you might need to take a part-time job until you get your budget under control.

Maintaining a Budget

Maintaining a workable budget requires accurate records. By keeping track of financial records, receipts, and canceled checks, you will know exactly how much you have spent and how much your lifestyle costs. If you own or have access to a computer, you can purchase a software program to assist in budgeting and record keeping.

Whatever method you use, maintaining a successful personal or household budget requires cooperation from everyone involved. Receipts should be kept and entered at the end of each budget period in a monthly expense record (see Figure 17.9 on page 396). It is a good idea to write on the back of each receipt what the purchase was for, who made it, and the date.

Select a secure place to store your records. A file drawer with file folders or a fire-resistant box is best. However, a couple of shoe boxes containing envelopes for each category will work. The important thing is to keep everything in one place and to keep your records up to date.

Keep a separate file folder or envelope for each of your budget items. Use these folders for filing insurance policies, receipts, warranties, canceled checks, bank statements, purchase contracts, and other important financial papers. Eventually, you may need to rent a safe-deposit box from a bank for storing your most important financial papers, such as a deed, stock certificate, automobile title, or will.

After obtaining a certain amount of financial success, many people turn to financial planners for assistance with investments. These professionals include stockbrokers, insurance agents, bankers, lawyers, and income-tax preparers.

Section 4 GET INVOLVED

Answer the following on a separate sheet of paper, and be prepared to discuss your responses in class.

1. Make a list of your short-term financial goals. These may be items that you plan to purchase, savings goals, or earnings goals. What two goals do you plan to accomplish within the next six weeks? within the next six months? within a year?

2. List your long-term financial goals. What two goals do you plan to accomplish within five years? within ten years?

3. Eventually you will leave home and be responsible for all of your living expenses. How much will it cost to live on your own? One way to find out is to determine how much your family spends for food, utilities, clothing, transportation, recreation, housing, and medical and dental care.

a. Ask a parent or guardian to help you keep a detailed record of your family's income and expenses for one month. List the expenses that are fixed and those that are flexible. This experience will help you become familiar with the expenses you will have when you leave home.

b. At the end of the month, have a family meeting. Show your family any ways you have discovered to improve the family budget. Ask family members to give their opinions of your budget proposals. What are the reasons for their opinions?

IMPORTANT FACTS

One Thing You Can Count On: Income Tax

Today, nearly all American adults pay income tax. It has not always been that way, however. Over the years, the income tax has changed from a tax on the rich to a broad-based tax on most of the population. Consider the following:

- In 1861, Congress imposed a 3 percent federal tax on all incomes above 800 dollars a year to pay for the Civil War. President Lincoln signed the first income tax into law in 1862. In 1872, it was repealed.

- In 1894, Congress levied a 2 percent tax on incomes over four thousand dollars. Only one in every one hundred Americans was rich enough to pay the tax.

- In 1895, the Supreme Court struck down the federal income tax, holding that the 1894 tax was not apportioned (divided into fair shares) according to the populations of the states, as required by the Constitution.

- In 1913, Congress passed the Sixteenth Amendment to the Constitution, which authorized a federal income tax. This amendment gave Congress the power to collect taxes on all incomes.

- Following the passage of the Sixteenth Amendment, Congress enacted the Revenue Act of 1913. President Woodrow Wilson signed it into law. Less than 1 percent of the population—about 357,000 of the wealthiest people in the United States—were required to pay the new income tax. The average U.S. worker (a man, woman, or child working twelve hours a day and earning eight hundred dollars per year) was untouched by the tax. Federal judges, state officials, and the president of the United States were exempt from paying the tax on their public salaries. The 1913 income tax law took up fourteen pages in the law books.

- In 1990, the IRS used 120,000 employees to collect one trillion dollars in income taxes. The present income tax law requires about 4,100 pages in the law books, and there are an additional 5000 pages of regulations. Today, nearly half of all U.S. taxpayers seek outside help in figuring their taxes.

Where Did All the Tellers Go?

The number of bank tellers has dropped as ATM transactions rise. According to the American Bankers Association, twenty-two thousand teller positions were eliminated between 1988 and 1991.

Your Social Security Number

All workers are required to have a Social Security number. The Social Security number is the most widely recognized and most frequently used record-keeping number in America. Social Security numbers are used by workers, employers, and the government to track earnings during the working years and to track Social Security benefits after retirement.

Most workers need forty credits (ten years of work) to qualify for a retirement benefit. Younger workers need fewer credits to become eligible for disability benefits for themselves and survivors' benefits for their family members in the event of death.

Source: Social Security Administration.

Do You Need More Income?

An estimated 7.2 million people (6.2 percent of the workforce) worked at more than one job in May of 1991. About 40 percent of these dual jobholders worked at more than one job to meet regular expenses or to pay off debts. Between 1970 and 1991, the number of women holding more than one job increased nearly fivefold (from 636,000 to 3,129,000).

Banks Do Compete for Customers

Growing competition among the nation's six thousand credit card providers includes some interesting offers for customers.

One bank in North Carolina offered a fifty-dollar credit to new credit card customers at its 222 branches. The offer was coupled with an 8.9 percent interest rate on its most popular credit cards. The low-rate card had a thirty-nine-dollar annual fee. Other credit cards, including one with no annual fee, had a higher interest rate.

The message is clear. Shop for banking services just as you shop for any consumer product.

CHAPTER 17 REVIEW

ENRICH YOUR VOCABULARY

On a separate sheet of paper, number from 1 to 22, and complete the following activity. (Do not write in your textbook.) Match each statement below with the most appropriate term from the "Enrich Your Vocabulary" list at the beginning of the chapter by writing that term next to the correct statement.

1. Total earnings before deductions
2. Money subtracted from earnings
3. Earnings paid according to the amount of work produced
4. An order written by a bank depositor directing the bank to pay out money
5. The portion of a checkbook used to record the checks written
6. A bank account that pays interest to customers in return for using their money
7. People who lend money
8. Planning to get the most for your money
9. The signature of a payee on the back of a check
10. Paying interest on the interest
11. A check that has been paid by a bank
12. A record of the money put into an account
13. A limited loan made on a continuous basis for the purchase of products
14. A record of how you've borrowed and repaid debts
15. The amount paid by lenders for using customers' money
16. Payment that citizens are required to make to help pay the costs of government services
17. A bank report that shows the condition of a depositor's account
18. A check that is written with insufficient funds in the account
19. A computer-run system that lets consumers, businesses, and governments transfer money from one account to another
20. The amount of debt that you can afford to repay each month
21. A plan for saving income
22. An agreement between a bank and its customer to pay back money invested at a specific rate on a certain date.

CHECK YOUR KNOWLEDGE

On a separate sheet of paper, complete the following activity. (Do not write in your textbook.)

1. Give two reasons why financial management is important.
2. List at least three deductions that may be taken from a worker's gross earnings.
3. What is the final date in each calendar year for filing an income tax return?
4. Name four ways that privately owned banks earn their income.
5. Why is it a good idea to have a checking account? Give three reasons.
6. Why is it a good idea to keep money in a bank that is insured by the Federal Depositors Insurance Corporation or the Federal Savings and Loan Insurance Corporation?
7. List the three C's of credit worthiness.
8. How do the issuers of multipurpose credit cards, such as Mastercard and Visa, earn money?
9. Review the ten credit commandments, and write a paragraph explaining why they are important.
10. Which federal law limits your liability for lost or stolen credit cards?
11. List six ways that a budget can be an important part of sound money management.

DEVELOP SCANS COMPETENCIES

Government experts say that successful workers can productively use Resources, Interpersonal skills, Information, Systems, and Technology. This activity will give you practice in developing Resources and Systems skills.

Refer to the directions in this chapter in the section "Money Management and Budgets" to make your own budget. Make a simple budget for a period of one week. During this time, keep careful track of your income and spending. Categorize your spending as much as possible. Some categories you might use are: Food—this should include all food purchased, even soft drinks and snacks. Transportation—this will include such things as gas or bus money. Entertainment—expenses here will include such things as movies, video rentals, and baseball cards.

After you have completed your budget, analyze it. Determine where you could cut spending so that you might save more money. After you have determined where you could cut spending, try the budget for another week to find out if your new plan works better.

Being a Consumer: So Many Choices

Learning Objectives

After completing this chapter, you should be prepared to:

- compare prices, services, variety, and quality on the same or similar items and decide which is the best choice for you

- explain the value of advertising to consumers and give an example of deceptive, misleading, or illegal advertising

- list specific guidelines for selecting affordable housing, choosing a roommate, signing a lease, and furnishing an apartment or home

- name and explain the purpose of laws and groups that protect consumers

- list specific criteria that will help you make a prudent automobile purchase

- describe various types of insurance and explain why it is important to have insurance to protect yourself from certain risks

Enrich Your Vocabulary

In reading this chapter and doing the exercises you will learn the following important terms:

prudent
unit price
nutritional labeling
generic
promotional sales
warranty
fluctuating
tenant
security deposit
lease
Food and Drug
  Administration

U.S. Office of
  Consumer Affairs
fraud
Monroney sticker
invoice price
insurance
premium
liability coverage
physical coverage

As a consumer, you face endless choices and opportunities for spending your every cent. No matter how successful you are, your income will always have limits. Placing priorities on needs and wants is a crucial part of every spending plan. *Needs*, such as food, housing, clothing, transportation, and medical care, should be first. *Wants*, such as entertainment, a new automobile, or dinner at an expensive restaurant, should come last.

American consumers spend more than one and a half trillion dollars per year in our market economy. Figure 18.1 shows the average amount each American household spent on major budget items at the beginning of the 1990s. If a family had an annual income of $25,000, how much money did it spend in each category?

An important part of a successful budget is being a **prudent** (wise, shrewd, and frugal) consumer. This entails getting the most for your money, recognizing quality, avoiding waste, and realizing time costs as well as money costs when making consumer decisions.

Media advertisements, friends, and family influence your consumer choices, but you have responsibility for the final decisions. The decision-making styles and the values and goals that you learned about in Chapters 3 and 4 also apply to consumer decisions. Which decision-making style do you use as a consumer? What values and goals play an important part in your decisions? Before answering, refresh your memory with a brief review of Chapters 3 and 4.

Figure 18.1 ANNUAL EXPENDITURES OF AMERICAN FAMILIES, 1990

Budget Category	Percentage of Income %
Food, total	15.2
Food at home (8.8)	
Food away from home (6.4)	
Housing	31.3
Apparel (clothing) and services	5.7
Transportation, total	18.1
Vehicles (7.5)	
Gasoline and motor oil (3.7)	
Other transportation (6.8)	
Health care	5.2
Personal insurance and pensions, total	9.1
Life and other personal insurance (1.2)	
Pensions and Social Security (7.9)	
All other expenditures (entertainment, personal care, reading materials, education, gifts, and miscellaneous)	15.4

Source: U.S. Department of Labor.

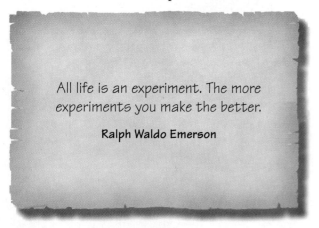

All life is an experiment. The more experiments you make the better.

Ralph Waldo Emerson

Living within your budget, being a wise consumer, and making prudent decisions are all related. Success in one causes success in another. Failure in one causes failure in another. Although the amount you spend for each budget item may differ from the percentages shown in Figure 18.1, it is important that you do a certain amount of preparation and decision making before you shop. Searching for both quality and price is worth the effort.

^{Section}
1

Necessities and Frills

As a consumer, you have almost endless opportunities for making choices among goods and services. Whatever the item, different sellers offer different prices, services, variety, and quality than their competitors. These reasons alone make prudent shopping worth the effort.

Food

Food is one of the largest and most necessary expenses in a budget. How much you spend will depend on how often you eat out, how often you cook at home, how many people you must feed, your personal tastes, and your special nutritional

▲ *The average grocery store is stocked with 20 thousand items. How many items are you familiar with? Have you compared the taste, quality, and price of specific name-brand and generic-brand products?*

Robert Discovers Comparison Shopping

Robert Long graduated last month, landed a job with the Brice Manufacturing Company, and moved into his first apartment. Our story begins as he walks up and down the aisles of the local supermarket for the first time.

Robert keeps one eye on his grocery list and one on the overhead signs describing the food and merchandise located on each aisle. He quickly discovers that the labels on containers can be very confusing. For example, three 16-ounce cans of pork and beans cost 96¢, a 34-ounce can costs 69¢, and a third company sells a 400-gram can for 39¢. The third can is quite a bit larger than the other two.

As Robert places the 400-gram can in his cart, a silver-haired woman tells him to put it back. "You're getting gypped, young man," she says while punching the numbers into her hand-held calculator. "That big can holds less than the smaller 16-ounce cans. They do that to trick you, son. You see, 453.6 grams is equal to 16 ounces, or a pound. Here, give the cashier this coupon, and get 25¢ off of two 34-ounce cans. That's a real bargain."

Later, at home, Robert vows to never again make fun of coupon cutters. He looks for his hand-held calculator and checks the register slip against the contents of his grocery bags. He decides to take his calculator along on his next shopping trip to make comparison shopping easier.

Robert is on the road to being a wise shopper. He is even planning to check the Sunday paper for coupons.

Critical Thinking

1. What did Robert learn from his conversation in the supermarket?
2. What did Robert do that indicated that he intended to be a prudent shopper even before he met the silver-haired woman?

---

requirements. If you shop carefully, you can stretch your food dollars and have tasty, healthful meals.

The average grocery store is stocked with 20 thousand items, and approximately 12 thousand new products squeeze onto the shelves each year. While you are still in high school, it is a good idea for you to learn the techniques that prudent shoppers use when purchasing groceries.

1. Plan your meals ahead, and make a shopping list before going to the grocery store. Plan some meals with foods that are inexpensive and can be used for leftovers. Divide your list into different categories of grocery items, such as fruit and vegetables, meats and fish, canned goods, dairy products, cleaning products, bread and bakery products, and snack foods.

2. Learn when and where supermarkets advertise weekly specials and offer special discount coupons. Note which meats, vegetables, and products are offered at special prices. Most fruits and vegetables are in greater supply and sell for lower prices at certain times during the year. For example, strawberries and asparagus are "in season" during the spring; tomatoes and beans are in season during the summer.

3. When stores are out of an advertised special, ask the cashier for a rain check (a receipt that

allows you to purchase the item at the advertised price by a certain date). The Federal Trade Commission requires merchants to honor your request for a rain check.

4. Use manufacturer's coupons (the kind Robert learned about). These come through the mail or in newspaper supplements. Coupons offer discounts that can add up to significant savings. Experienced coupon cutters expect to save between 5 and 10 percent on their total bill.

5. Take the time to read the weight and volume of the products you purchase. The size of a can or package can be deceiving. Whether you use the English system of weights and measures or the metric system, the price per ounce, pound, gram, kilogram, quart, or liter can point out large price differences between similar products. For example, two brands of bacon may look alike, but one package may weigh 12 ounces and another 16 ounces.

6. The **unit price** (the cost of one standard measure of a product) can help you compare the price of products that have different weights or volumes. This information is displayed on the shelves below food items.

7. Read the label. It contains useful information. The **nutritional labeling** on a product states the number of servings per container and tells how the food is packaged. For example, tuna might be packed in water or oil; pineapple slices might be packed in water or syrup. The label also lists the various nutrients in the product. It will tell you what percentages of the U.S. Recommended Daily Allowances (U.S. RDA) the product supplies. For products that can spoil, such as milk, cream, and orange juice, the date by which the product should be consumed is stamped on the package. If you wish to write to the manufacturer of a food product, you will find the address on the label.

8. Many stores sell their own "house" brand for less than nationally advertised brands. One re-

port showed that private-label goods account for 18.3 percent of all units sold in grocery stores and nearly 14 percent of the total supermarket dollar volume. House brands are frequently packaged for stores by the same companies that package the nationally advertised brands.

9. **Generic** brands (having no trademark) cost even less than house brands. They generally have the same or nearly the same nutritional value as the brand-name products, but may have a slightly inferior quality or taste.

The type of store where you shop influences the prices you pay. Supermarkets operate on a self-service basis and are able to sell food products at a lower margin of profit because of their large volume of business. On the other hand, convenience stores charge higher prices than supermarkets but are located in or near residential neighborhoods for the convenience of shoppers. They are often open from early in the morning until late at night. Their lower volume of sales and higher overhead costs require higher prices.

Clothing

Clothing is a basic necessity that reflects your personality, confidence, and lifestyle. The money you spend on a clothing item must be considered against the value you place on the product. For ex-

CAREER TIP

Whether you can return merchandise for credit or a refund depends entirely on the policy of the company with whom you do business, unless a contract provides otherwise. Returns are a privilege some stores extend to customers.

- Decide what you can afford to spend, and identify the features and options you need in the product.

- Ask friends and relatives for personal recommendations, and check your school or public library for consumer magazines, reports, and other publications that compare products and services.

- Narrow your choices to specific brands (the name of a product that distinguishes it from another) and model numbers.

- Compare the prices and service of several stores that sell the product. Do not assume that an item is a bargain just because it is advertised as one. Take advantage of sales.

- If you are uncertain about the reputation of the business, check with the Better Business Bureau to see if consumers have registered complaints against the business and how they were resolved.

- Check for extra charges, such as delivery fees, installation charges, and service costs.

- Ask the salesperson to clarify the service policy and the return or exchange policy. Request a written copy.

- Read and compare contracts and warranties. A warranty is a guarantee that the product is of a certain quality or that defective parts will be replaced. Be sure that you understand what you must do and what the manufacturer or merchant must do if you have a problem.

- Before you sign for delivered merchandise, carefully examine it to be sure that nothing is missing or damaged.

- Be sure that you read and understand the manufacturer's recommended use and care instructions before attempting to use the product.

▲ *Figure 18.2 Before You Make a Purchase.*

▲ *Have you heard the old saying, "All that glitters is not gold"? Learn to recognize the quality and value of sale items.*

ample, Tim Parker wants to buy a Nautica or a Starter jacket. He is the first to admit that they are very expensive and that a certain element of prestige is involved. Buying either brand will use up Tim's total clothing budget for three months, and Tim will need shoes and a couple of new shirts in the next few weeks. He is considering a charge account at the clothing store. What would you do if you were Tim? Why?

Conspicuous consumption (the practice of buying products and services to impress others) can be very costly if you are living on a tight budget. Being in fashion may be a high personal value of yours, but it can create serious financial problems if you consider it to be more important than necessary expenses.

Before shopping for clothing, select stores that have a range of prices and will allow you to make the most of your clothing budget. Make your money go farther by taking advantage of the three major types of sales:

- **Promotional sales**, which promote regular merchandise through temporary price reductions

> • Read all instructions and warranty provisions carefully to ensure your safety and to avoid doing anything that may void the warranty. Use the product only for the purposes outlined by the manufacturer's instructions.
>
> • File all sales receipts, warranties, and use and care information for future reference.
>
> • Provide proper maintenance, and follow the use and care recommendations from the manufacturer.
>
> • If a problem develops, report the difficulty to the merchant or manufacturer as soon as possible. Trying to repair the product yourself could cancel your rights to service under the warranty.

▲ *Figure 18.3 After You Make a Purchase.*

• Clearance sales, which feature reduced prices on goods that a retailer no longer wants

• Special-purchase sales, in which goods are bought for a special sale rather than marked down from the regular merchandise

Retail stores generally run sales at the same times year after year. For example, Presidents' Day sales, January and August white sales, anniversary sales, and end of the month and clearance sales. For considerable savings, shop for clothes at the end of a season. Buy winter clothes in the spring, and summer clothes in the fall.

Learn to read clothing labels, recognize quality, and follow care instructions. Knowing about the various qualities of certain fabrics used in the manufacture of clothing can save you a lot of money. Labels not only tell you what clothing is made of but also the care it requires.

As you enter the world of work, the environment in which you are employed will dictate your choices for appropriate clothing. Clothing expenses for employed persons usually exceed those of other family members. Workers who entertain clients will usually spend more than those who don't.

High-Ticket Items

When you leave home, will you live in a furnished or unfurnished apartment? If you move into an unfurnished apartment, you will need to purchase some high-ticket (expensive) items. You may need to purchase a microwave oven, a sofa, a refrigerator, a bedroom set, or a washer and dryer. The consumer advice listed in Figures 18.2 and 18.3 will help you make the most of your money and avoid problems related to the quality of your purchase.

Section 1 GET INVOLVED

Answer the following on a separate sheet of paper, and be prepared to discuss your responses in class.

1. Imagine that you are entertaining a group of four (including yourself) for a special dinner. Use grocery ads to write a menu for your dinner and determine the cost of each item. Compare the quality and cost of your menu with the menus that your classmates create.

2. Select two big-ticket items, such as a piano, computer, washing machine, bedroom suite, TV set, or stove. Make a list of the quality features you want in each of your two items. Visit several stores to compare brands and prices. Make your selections, and report your findings and decisions to the class.

3. Food, clothing, and entertainment expenses vary from person to person. The amount to budget will depend on family income. How much would you allot for food, clothing, and housing if you used the percentages shown in Figure 18.1 on page 402 and earned $15,000 a year? What if you earned $25,000 a year?

Section 2

Advertisements and the Media: Wanting It All

Imagine living in a world with no television, radio, signs, mail, motion pictures, newspapers, or magazines. How would you know what to buy? Who would influence your choices? In fact, media advertising provides the major source of product and service information for most consumers.

Advertising is intended to promote the sale of a product or service, advance an idea, or bring about some other effect that the advertiser desires. Prudent consumers learn to read, view, or listen to advertising carefully and to compare various features of competing products or services. Advertising offers a way to learn how to use products and services, identify their particular features, compare prices, and be aware of special sales.

▲ *Do you use advertising to compare the special features and prices of competitive products?*

Most advertising provides helpful information. However, as a wise consumer, you must be alert to deceptive, misleading, or illegal advertising. Consider the experience of Mary Sherman.

Mary wants to purchase a name-brand sweater that costs fifty dollars at a local clothing store. She has looked at it three times in the last month, hoping it might be on sale.

The store advertised a big sale in the paper yesterday, and Mary arrived this morning when the doors opened. She was delighted to see "her sweater" on a rack marked "33% off." However, she was very confused when the price tag on her sweater was marked seventy-five dollars with a red sale tag of fifty dollars.

Mary and all of the other customers in the store are victims of false pricing. The merchant simply raised the price of certain items, reticketed them with the higher price, and put red sale tags on the items at the regular price.

Mary quietly told the store manager that she was aware of the false pricing and would no longer shop at his store. She also visited the local Better Business Bureau to inform them about the false pricing. While she was at the BBB, Mary picked up a pamphlet that described several dishonest or illegal advertising practices. The following were included:

- Bait and switch: The advertisement describes a product or service that is not available when the customer offers to purchase it. The ad is the *bait*, and the salesperson attempts to *switch* the customer to a more expensive product or service.

- Referral plans: The salesperson describes a special introductory offer. For each customer you refer to the salesperson, he or she will pay you a certain amount of money. In many cases, the salesperson tries to convince you that by making easy referrals of your friends and relatives, you will end up getting the product or service free. Remember the old saying, "If it sounds too good to be true, it probably is."

- High-pressure tactics: The salesperson refuses to take "no" for an answer. He or she may call in the sales manager or another salesperson. Together, they try to convince you that the price is going up, that this is the last item, or that if you don't buy now, you will never have the opportunity again.

- Overstated sales claims: Our laundry soap will make your clothes twice as clean as any other soap on the market! Your skin will look twenty years younger if you use our lotion! Your engine will last thousands of miles longer if you use our gasoline! How many times have you come in contact with this type of advertising? Will the manufacturer back these claims with a written guarantee? If not, beware of the product or service.

Advertising is big business. The top five hundred advertising agencies in the United States earn billions of dollars annually. The advertising industry employed more than 200,000 workers in 1993, and this number is expected to increase through the year 2005. These numbers do not include the enormous fees paid to media resources or the earnings of thousands of temporary workers connected with advertising campaigns, such as actors, musicians, outside professionals, and technicians.

Why do you purchase an advertised product or service? If you are like most consumers, your decision to purchase involves these factors:

- The source of the communication. Most consumers are persuaded by people they trust and believe, or they identify with someone's background, personality, or race. Testimonials and endorsements are examples of this type of advertisement.

- The message. What is said and how it is said influence buying decisions. The purpose of the advertising message is to get the reader's, viewer's, or listener's attention and hold it. The message should then arouse the desire for the product or service. The choices people make are affected by the style, repetition, timing, and novelty of the advertisement.

When you decide to buy a certain type of automobile (a product) or use a particular long-distance telephone company (a service), your decision might be influenced by a credible authority (someone you trust and respect). The advice you receive might be based on what the authority has read in a newspaper or magazine, has heard on the radio, or has seen on television about the relative virtues of the product or service. In this case, the media has influenced your decision indirectly by influencing a person you trust and respect.

Have you ever received a personally addressed business letter, inviting you to purchase an outstanding product that is only available to a select

▲ *If you are interested in an advertising career, explore information about occupations such as graphic artist, writer, and marketing research analyst.*

group of people? Welcome to the world of direct-mail advertising (junk mail). Notice the bulk-mail postage stamp in place of a regular stamp? This tells you that thousands of letters, exactly the same, were mailed to potential consumers from a mailing list.

Direct-mail advertising is sent only to targeted groups, such as people who live in a certain area, are between certain ages, own a particular product, or work in a particular occupation. Direct mail allows an advertiser to send a message with selective appeal. The purchase of what types of products or services would place you on a direct-mail advertising list? Why?

When is the last time you enjoyed a special program on television, purchased a daily newspaper, or enjoyed a favorite magazine? It is important to remember that producers of products and services buy advertising time on television and radio to provide us with programs we enjoy. In addition, the cost of daily newspapers and magazines is kept low because of paid advertisements. All of these advertisers are spending a great deal of money to persuade you to buy their products. Therefore, you must analyze the content of the ads carefully before rushing out to buy.

Section 2 GET INVOLVED

Answer the following on a separate sheet of paper, and be prepared to discuss your responses in class.

1. Newspaper and magazine ads frequently make outrageous claims for certain products. Find one ad that you consider to be untrue, and cut it out. Write to the company that produced the product or to the agency that developed the advertising, and ask for verification of the claims made about the product. Enclose the ad with your letter.

2. Pay particular attention to television commercials for the next week. Make a list of the products and the specific advertising messages that appeal to your desire to be attractive, important, or wealthy.

3. Make a list of brand-name products that you have purchased. Include clothes, shoes, and big-ticket items like a bike or a sound system. Make a similar list of brand-name food products you have purchased. Why did you decide to buy each of the items rather than a competing brand?

Section 3

Finding a Place to Live

Whether it's an expensive house or a low-budget rental apartment, a well-managed home can provide you with a sense of security and independence. Today's housing market presents choices for every lifestyle and every budget. Housing costs will probably make up the largest part of your living expenses.

▲ *Where will you live after you graduate from high school? Have you considered the benefits and disadvantages of various types of housing?*

Each type of housing has its benefits and disadvantages. If you are seeking a low-maintenance, hassle-free lifestyle, renting an apartment or buying a condominium is probably your best choice.

> Mid pleasures and palaces, though we may roam,
> Be it ever so humble, there's no place like home.
>
> John H. Payne (1823)

On the other hand, a single-family home provides more privacy and offers the opportunity for a lawn and a garden. Whatever your goal, the perfect place may not be available or affordable when you first begin working. You may need to compromise and develop a savings plan to reach your housing goal.

The housing you choose should fit your budget and your lifestyle. A housing budget includes rent or a mortgage, utilities, homeowner's or renter's insurance, furnishings, decorating, and maintenance. A general rule is to allow no more than one-quarter of your take-home pay for housing. Remember that you must have enough money left in your budget for food, clothing, transportation, and the other essentials you will need to live on your own.

The Option of Renting

Renting is usually the most suitable choice for single people or couples who are just starting out and trying to keep expenses down. Renting is also a wise choice for workers who are required to move frequently, have **fluctuating** (irregular, unsteady) or seasonal employment, or prefer to avoid homeownership responsibilities. There are advantages to renting:

- It doesn't require a large down payment.
- The maximum long-term debt is a one-year lease agreement.
- It is usually less expensive than mortgage payments.
- It is easier to relocate for career opportunities.
- The landlord (owner who rents the property) is responsible for repairs.
- The failure to make payments will not cause loss of a major investment.
- It allows you to learn about a new community before making an investment.

Renting also presents several disadvantages. As a **tenant** (person paying rent for the temporary use of another person's building or land), you are seldom motivated to improve the property. Carpets and other decor may not be satisfactory. You must have permission of the landlord to make changes, and any improvements become the property of the landlord. However, some owners will agree to reduce your rent for certain improvements you make. This could include interior or exterior painting, replacement of carpets or drapes, or necessary maintenance.

Should You Have a Roommate?

Sharing an apartment or a house with another person can save on expenses. Rent, utilities, and grocery costs can be divided equally. In addition, a roommate can help with household tasks, such as cooking and cleaning. Roommates are frequently friends and share social experiences outside the apartment or house.

Conflicts are bound to arise when two or more people share the same living quarters. What conflicts did you have when you lived at home? Expect similar problems with your roommate. It is better to avoid conflicts and resolve potential problems before you make a commitment to live with someone for any period of time. Even good friends should set up some ground rules in writing. Discuss the following points with potential roommates:

1. How much will each of you contribute toward the rent? If one bedroom is larger or nicer than the other, should the person with that room pay more?

2. Will utility expenses be shared equally? How should the expense of long-distance telephone calls be handled?

3. How will cleaning and laundry tasks be shared? What rules can be established to help a poor housekeeper and a "clean machine" get along?

4. Will grocery shopping and cooking be shared or up to each individual? What if one of you eats out a lot or prefers to snack a lot? Buying food that will not be eaten wastes a lot of money.

5. What hours of "peace and quiet" do each of you need? What if one person works the night or evening shift?

6. Does loud music bother either of you? How will you allow for individual preferences in types of music (country, popular, classical) or selection of television programs?

7. Do you want to party on the weekends or get some rest? How many guests should be allowed to visit at one time?

8. Do either of you smoke? If so, how can you avoid any problems this might cause?

9. If one of you loses his or her job, how will expenses be met? Would you be willing to pay your roommate's share of the expense for a month or two?

10. Will having a roommate allow you to be as independent as you want to be? How are your obligations and responsibilities to a roommate similar to the obligations and responsibilities of living at home?

11. If your roommate decides to move, could you find another one in time to pay monthly expenses? A written agreement giving each other at least a thirty-day notice would provide added security for each of you.

Hunting for an Apartment

The search for an apartment should be an enjoyable experience. Decide ahead of time the amount you are willing to pay, the size you want, and the general location that suits you best. The "for-rent" ads in the Sunday newspaper are a good source of information. They will help you determine the cost and availability of rental units in your area. In addition, network with your family, friends, and co-workers for rental leads. Use the yellow pages of the phone book for real estate agencies that have listings of rental properties. Rent is usually higher through an agency as the owner must pay a fee for the service. In some cases the rental fee equals one month's rent.

It is wise to talk with other residents in a rental complex about their likes and dislikes before you make a final decision. Ask for their views on

▲ Deciding whether or not to share an apartment or house with another person is a major decision.

whether the landlord or caretaker tries to keep the complex in good condition. If neighbors from nearby properties are outside, tell them that you are considering the unit, and ask them what they like or dislike about the area. Compare several rental units before making a decision. Be certain that you are satisfied with the unit before signing any type of rental agreement.

Tenant and Landlord Rights and Responsibilities

Learn your rights and responsibilities as a tenant as well as those of the landlord. The landlord will probably have you fill out an application form if you are interested in a rental unit. He or she will probably request credit references and will want to check your past rental record. Most landlords require a **security deposit** (money you entrust with the landlord to cover any damage you cause to the rental unit) before they accept you as a tenant. In addition, most require a month's rent in advance. These are simply good business practices on the landlord's part. They do not suggest that you cannot be trusted.

▲ *All agreements and understandings between a landlord and tenant should be in writing and signed by both parties.*

The landlord returns the security deposit after a tenant vacates the unit if he or she finds no damage during the moving-out inspection. Some landlords place the security deposit in a special bank account, and the earned interest is also paid to the tenant after moving out. The advance rental payment can be used for the last month's rent or will be returned with the security deposit.

Before moving in, it is a good consumer practice to make an inventory (listing) of all items fur-

nished in the rental unit and to rate the condition of the furnishings and the overall condition of the unit. The inventory should be dated and signed by both you and the landlord. If an item is in poor condition before you move in, it will be documented, and you can't be held responsible for it later. An accurate inventory assures a responsible tenant of receiving the full security deposit when leaving and protects the landlord from damages caused by irresponsible tenants.

A rental **lease** is a contract that involves a financial commitment for a specific period of time, usually a year. It may be up to several pages in length and may contain numerous details. The responsibilities of both the tenant and the landlord are defined in the lease. Both parties are legally required to live up to a signed agreement. Once the lessor (owner) and lessee (renter) sign the lease, it's enforceable by law.

The amount of the rent and the due date should be clearly defined. Some leases permit the

CAREER TIP

Can someone legally enter your home without your permission? Many rental agreements give the landlord permission to enter the unit to make an inspection of the property. Check your rental agreement.

landlord to change the rent for certain reasons. Leases usually state how much notice the renter must give before he or she moves out.

Be sure to read a lease very carefully, and discuss each point with the landlord before signing. Make certain that you understand and are willing to meet all of the terms. Will you be expected to pay any expenses that are not covered in the lease? What are the tenant's and landlord's rights and responsibilities? What specific rules and regulations must tenants follow? What changes are tenants allowed to make to the property?

A rental agreement is somewhat different from a lease. It can usually be terminated by the tenant or the landlord with a month's notice. A landlord may be persuaded to grant a rental agreement instead of a lease, particularly if he or she is having difficulty getting long-term tenants. What advantages would a tenant have with a rental agreement? What are the disadvantages?

Water and trash collection are usually paid by the landlord. Utility costs such as gas and electric vary with rental units. Telephone installation fees and monthly charges are paid by the tenant. Charges for painting, cleaning, and repairs vary with landlords.

Some landlords will not allow pets. If you have a pet, make certain that your rental agreement or lease grants you permission for the animal.

Furnishing an Apartment

Whether you rent a furnished or unfurnished apartment, certain items are not supplied by the landlord. If this is your first rental home, you will probably need to purchase sheets, blankets, dishes, and towels. You may already have some possessions, such as a radio or television. Determine which furnishings you must have immediately. Purchase the others as you can afford them.

You can furnish a first apartment with limited funds if you are willing to shop for bargains. Goodwill and Salvation Army thrift stores, garage sales, and classified ads for used furnishings are

▲ *Is home ownership one of your major life goals? Will your earnings from the occupations you are considering enable you to purchase the home of your choice?*

good sources of inexpensive furniture, dishes, lamps, pots and pans, small appliances, and decorative items.

Refinishing used furniture is easier and less expensive than you might think. Your public library is a good source of how-to books of all types. Your local paint or hardware store can help with the needed materials.

CAREER TIP

Once you start accumulating furnishings, ask an insurance agency to explain the benefits of renter's insurance. It will protect you from loss in case of fire or theft.

Buying a Home

Although most young workers can't afford to purchase a home, they frequently establish home-ownership as a major life goal. It has been part of the American dream for generations (Figure 18.4).

Homeownership means having something that's all yours. If you want a yellow kitchen with blue carpet and pink walls, it's your choice. It is a place where you can express your own personal style. For most people, a home is the largest single expenditure they will make. When you can afford the down payment, closing costs, and mortgage payments, you will be a prime candidate for homeownership.

Before deciding to purchase a home, analyze your financial prospects and employment security. How much you can afford to spend depends on your current net income, your current nonhousing expenses, and the amount of savings you have available for a down payment. As a general rule, financial planners recommend that your mortgage payments not exceed 28 or 29 percent of your gross income (monthly income before taxes and other deductions).

How much home will you be able to afford? In Figure 18.4, locate your expected annual or monthly gross income. On the same line, locate the maximum amount (29 percent of gross in-

Annual Gross Income	Monthly Gross Income	29% of Monthly Gross Income
$15,000	$1,250	$363
$20,000	$1,667	$484
$25,000	$2,083	$604
$30,000	$2,500	$725
$35,000	$2,917	$846
$40,000	$3,333	$967
$45,000	$3,750	$1,088
$50,000	$4,167	$1,208

▲ *Figure 18.4 How Much Home Can You Afford?*

come) that you should spend for your monthly mortgage payment. Once you know how much you can afford each month, you will be on your way to finding out how much home you can afford. The interest rate of your mortgage will make a big difference in your total payment.

Don't commit yourself to larger housing payments than you can afford. Decide whether your income is stable and growing and your employment secure before taking on a large mortgage. A large mortgage with high monthly payments can become a major hardship if you experience prolonged unemployment, illness, disability, or decreased income.

Section 3 GET INVOLVED

Answer the following on a separate sheet of paper, and be prepared to discuss your responses in class.

1. Explain what is meant by "A man's home is his castle."
2. Check local classified ads to find the cost of renting an apartment in your community. Discuss your findings with the class.
3. Develop a list of your ten most important cri-

teria for selecting a roommate. Do you know of a friend or relative who meets these criteria? Would *you* be an "ideal" roommate? Explain your answer.

4. Arrange an interview with a landlord, and inquire about landlord and tenant responsibilities and relationships.

Section
4

Consumers Have Rights

In a message sent to Congress in 1962, President John F. Kennedy declared that every consumer has four basic rights:

- The right to information: The right to be given the accurate product information needed to make an informed and free choice and the right to be protected against false or misleading advertising, labeling, or sales practices
- The right to choice: The right to be able to choose from a variety of products and services and the right to be assured of the availability of competitive prices
- The right to safety: The right to expect that the buyer's health and safety are taken into account by the manufacturer and that products will perform according to the manufacturer's claims
- The right to be heard: The right to register dissatisfaction and have a complaint heard and given consideration when a buyer's interests are badly served and the right to be assured that consumer interests will be fully considered by government lawmakers and enforcement officials

In 1975, President Ford added a fifth consumer right:

- The right to consumer education, without which consumers cannot maximize their resources, become more effective in the marketplace, or gain the full benefit of the other four rights

Laws enacted and passed by Congress since then are now enforced by various agencies of the government, which have a direct responsibility to consumers. The federal agencies charged with some aspect of consumer protection include the following:

- The Consumer Product Safety Commission develops safety standards for products to protect the public against unreasonable risk. It also handles complaints and questions about manufacturers' recalls, unsafe products, and shopping for safe ones.
- The **Food and Drug Administration** (FDA) enforces laws and regulations concerning the purity, quality, and labeling of food, drugs, and cosmetics. It certifies new drugs and inspects drug- and food-processing plants. The FDA also accepts inquiries about food and food labeling, diet products, drugs, cosmetics, health, fraud, and pesticides.

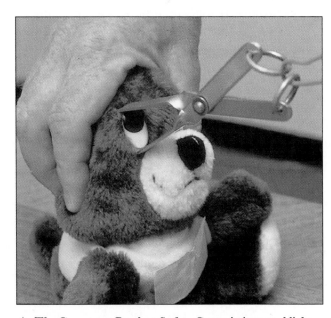

▲ *The Consumer Product Safety Commission establishes safety standards for products ranging from teddy bears to new cars.*

Being Responsible

Alan's Honest Mistake?

Alan Benson purchased a new gasoline-powered lawn mower. He saved twenty-five dollars by assembling the mower at home. Alan didn't bother to read the instruction manual. After all, he had been using lawn mowers since the age of twelve.

After he finished assembling the mower, Alan filled the tank with gasoline and started to mow the yard. Ten minutes later, the mower began to make a screeching noise, and the engine quit. Alan checked each step in the user's manual that came with the mower. When he read step 14, Alan realized that he hadn't put oil in the engine before starting it. The en-

gine on his new mower would require extensive repairs. Alan added the proper amount of oil to his mower and returned it to the dealer. He told the dealer that the mower was no good, and he demanded his money back.

Critical Thinking

1. Is Alan a responsible consumer? What did he do that supports your point of view?
2. How would you handle the situation if you were the dealer? Why?

- The Federal Trade Commission (FTC) enforces laws regarding advertising and selling. The areas of concern to the FTC include deceptive advertising, credit bureau reports and equal credit opportunity, failure to disclose lending and leasing costs, loans, and warranties.

- The Postal Inspection Service investigates mail fraud and misrepresentation, sexually oriented ads, and unsolicited merchandise sent through the mail.

- The Department of Transportation handles complaints involving delayed flights, lost luggage, and problems with ground packages (hotel and ground transportation) purchased in conjunction with flights. Individual airlines also handle consumer problems.

- The Department of Agriculture sets standards and inspects and grades meat, poultry, and canned fruits and vegetables. It follows up on reports concerning the cleanliness of food stores and restaurants and the purity of questionable drugs. It also investigates the use of

pesticides, animal health, and weights and measures. The Department of Agriculture provides numerous publications about food, clothing, and household items; these publications are often available through the local office of State Extension Services.

In addition to these federal agencies, there are many private groups that also serve as a voice for consumer rights. The Direct Marketing Association, the Insurance Information Institute, and the Major Appliance Consumer Action Panel are examples of private consumer-action groups. These organizations provide useful consumer information about various products and services.

Consumer Responsibility

Have you ever heard the warning, "Let the buyer beware"? Basic rights established by law and enforced by numerous government agencies and private consumer groups have changed the meaning of this old saying. In today's economy, it would be more accurate to say, "Let the buyer become aware." As it is with all individual rights in a democracy, consumer rights are accompanied by certain responsibilities. As a consumer, you have these responsibilities:

1. Become informed about products or services that you plan to buy by actively seeking and using consumer information.

2. Be an honest consumer by using products and services as they were meant to be used. Follow the manufacturer's or provider's recommendations.

3. Make yourself heard by being assertive (not aggressive) when your consumer rights are violated. Always report defective goods, and let businesses know when goods or services do not measure up to your expectations.

4. Report unethical business practices to protect other consumers.

As a consumer, you have the right to expect quality products and services at fair prices. If something goes wrong, your first step is to try to handle your own complaint. The following actions can help you resolve the problem:

1. Collect records and start a file about your complaint. Be sure to include copies of sales receipts, repair orders, warranties, canceled checks, and contracts to back up your complaint.

2. Go back to where you made the purchase. Contact the person who sold you the item or

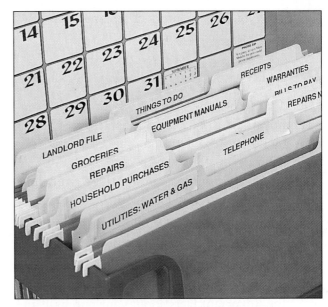

▲ *A wise consumer keeps accurate records about the products and services he or she buys.*

performed the service. Calmly and accurately explain the problem and state the action you would like. If the salesperson is not helpful, ask to speak to the supervisor or manager, and restate your case.

3. Allow a reasonable amount of time for each person you contact to resolve the problem before you contact someone else.

4. Keep a record of your efforts, and include notes about whom you spoke with and what was done about the problem. Save copies of letters you send or receive concerning the problem.

5. Don't give up. If you are not satisfied with the response at the local level, phone or write a letter to the person responsible for consumer complaints at the company's headquarters. If you are unable to name the responsible person, send your letter to the consumer office or to the president of the company.

6. When you complain to a company, be sure to describe the problem, what you have done to try to resolve it, and what you think is a fair solution. Do you want your money back?

CAREER TIP

Many companies have toll-free telephone numbers. These "800" numbers are often printed on product packaging. Check your local library for a directory of toll-free telephone numbers, or phone 1(800) 555-1212 to learn whether a company has a toll-free telephone number.

Would you like the product repaired? Do you want the product exchanged?

Writing a Complaint Letter

If talking with the salesperson or company representative fails to provide a satisfactory solution, you should write a letter to the company. The **U.S. Office of Consumer Affairs** (USOCA) suggests that consumers follow these guidelines when writing a letter of complaint:

1. Include your name, address, home and work telephone numbers, and account number (if appropriate).

2. Keep your letter brief and to the point. List all of the important facts about your purchase, including the date and place you made the purchase and any information you can give about the product, such as the model and serial numbers.

3. If you are writing to complain about a service you received, describe the service and give the name of the person who performed it.

4. State exactly what you want done about the problem and how long you are willing to wait for resolution. Be reasonable.

5. Include copies of all documents regarding the problem. Be sure to send copies, not originals.

6. Don't write an angry, sarcastic, or threatening letter. The person reading your letter probably was not responsible for your problem but may be very helpful in resolving it. Type your letter if possible.

7. Keep a copy of all correspondence.

Figure 18.5 is a sample complaint letter that follows the USOCA guidelines. If you write a letter to the Better Business Bureau, a government agency, a trade association, or another source of help, include information about what you have done so far to get your complaint resolved. Be sure to keep copies of your letter and all related documents.

Consumer Contacts and Information

There are many private and consumer-aid resources. Agencies and groups that handle consumer complaints include the following:

Better Business Bureaus. There are about 180 Better Business Bureaus (BBBs) in the United States. These bureaus are nonprofit organizations, sponsored by private, local businesses. Each BBB has its own policy about reporting information. A bureau may or may not tell you the nature of the complaint against a business, but it will tell you if a complaint has been registered.

Trade Associations. There are nearly 40 thousand trade and professional associations in the United States. They represent a variety of interests (including banks, insurance companies, and clothing manufacturers) and professionals (such as accountants, lawyers, doctors, and therapists). Trade associations have various consumer functions, which are described in the book *National Trade and Professional Associations of the United States*. Check your local library for this book and for related sources of help.

State, County, and City Government Consumer Offices. These offices are easy to contact and are familiar with local businesses and laws. They are a good source of information because many of them enforce consumer protection and fraud laws. If there is no local consumer office in your area, contact a state consumer office. Many states also have special commissions and agencies that handle consumer questions and complaints about banks, insurance companies, utilities, vocational and rehabilitation services, and weights and measures.

Federal Agencies. Many federal agencies have enforcement or complaint-handling duties for products and services used by the general public. Others act for the benefit of the public but do not resolve individual consumer problems. If you

Your address
Your City, State, and zip code
Date

Name of contact person
Title
Company name
Street address
City, State, and zip code

Dear (Name of contact person):
    On (date), I purchased (or had repaired) a (name of the product with serial or model number or service performed). I made this purchase at (location, date, and other important details of the transaction).
    Unfortuately, your product (or service) has not performed well (or the service was inadequate) because (state the problem).
    Therefore, to resolve the problem, I would appreciate (state the specific action you want). Enclosed are copies (copies, not originals) of my records (receipts, guarantees, warranties, cancelled checks, contracts, model and serial numbers, and any other documents).
    I look forward to your reply and a resolution to my problem. I will wait (set time limit) before seeking third-party assistance. Please contact me at the above address or by phone at (home and office numbers, with area codes).

Sincerely,

Your Signature

Your name
Your account number

▲ *Figure 18.5 Sample Complaint Letter.*

need help in deciding where to go with your consumer problem, call the nearest Federal Information Center, which is listed in the yellow pages under "Government."

Occupational and Professional Licensing Boards. Many state agencies license or register

CAREER TIP

Whenever you telephone a consumer contact association or agency, be certain to have on hand copies of your sales receipts, other sales documents, and all correspondence with the company.

members of various professions, including doctors, lawyers, nurses, accountants, pharmacists, funeral directors, plumbers, electricians, car repair shops, employment agencies, collection agencies, beauticians, and television and radio repair shops.

These boards also handle consumer complaints. If you have a complaint and contact a licensing agency, the agency will contact the professional on your behalf. If necessary, the agency may conduct an investigation and take disciplinary action against the professional. Check your local telephone directory or state consumer office to locate a particular licensing board.

Financial Institutions. If you are unable to resolve a complaint against a financial institution directly, you can contact the financial institution's

▲ *Are you aware of the consumer-aid agencies and groups that are available to handle your consumer complaints?*

regulatory agency for assistance. The regulatory agencies will be able to help resolve the complaint if the financial institution has violated a banking law or regulation. The Federal Trade Commission can help you contact the appropriate financial agency in your state.

Legal Help. Small-claims courts resolve disputes involving claims for small debts and accounts. Court procedures generally are simple, inexpensive, quick, and informal. Check your local telephone directory under the municipal, county, or state government heading for small-claims court offices.

Car Manufacturers. Most foreign and U.S. car manufacturers have regional offices that handle consumer complaints that are not resolved by your local car dealer. Contact the dealer to obtain the phone number and address of the regional office headquarters.

State Utility Commissions. State utility commissions regulate consumer services and rates for gas, electricity, and a variety of other services within your state. Many utility commissions han-

dle consumer complaints. Sometimes, if many complaints are received about the same matter, they will conduct investigations. If you have a question or complaint about a utility matter, write or phone the utility commission in your state.

Legal Aid Offices. Legal aid offices offer free legal services to those who qualify. There are more than one thousand of these offices around the country. They generally offer legal assistance with problems such as landlord-tenant relations, credit, utilities, family issues (such as divorce and adoption), Social Security, welfare, unemployment, and workers' compensation. Check the telephone directory, or call your local consumer protection office to find the address and telephone number of a legal aid office near you.

Consumer Fraud

The USOCA estimates that **fraud** (intentional misrepresentation of a product or service) costs consumers 10 billion dollars a year. Unsuspecting citizens become victims, just as Janet Kames did shortly after obtaining her first credit card.

Janet graduated from high school last June. Last month, Janet received an exciting phone call. The caller told Janet that she was a grand prize winner in a national sweepstakes drawing. The caller asked Janet for her address and credit card number so Janet could prove who she was. The caller told Janet that she would have a visitor from the company within two days to award the prize money.

Janet didn't receive a prize, but her next credit card bill showed several large purchases that she knew nothing about. Janet was a victim of consumer fraud.

As a consumer, watch for the following warning signs when dealing with a solicitor (person who seeks trade, business, or donations):

• Sweepstakes that require consumers to pay an entry fee

- Notices of prizes that require consumers to call a "900" number
- Mail that looks as though it is from a government agency but isn't
- Classified employment or business opportunity advertisements promising easy money for little work
- Prize awards that require consumers to give credit card or bank account numbers
- Callers who ask for your telephone calling card number or ask you to agree to accept someone else's calls as part of a phone company investigation
- Offers of easy credit despite your past credit history

Section 4: GET INVOLVED

Answer the following on a separate sheet of paper, and be prepared to discuss your responses in class.

1. Using the phone book, list the consumer agencies or organizations that are located in your area. Contact at least two agencies to find out what they do to protect consumers.
2. Locate and read two or more warranties. List the statements from each warranty that provide specific, clear information. List any statements that you find to be vague or misleading.
3. Interview the manager or owner of a local business about how he or she handles consumer complaints.
4. Write a complaint letter about a product or service that has given you a problem. Use the format for writing a complaint letter shown in Figure 18.5 on page 421.

Section 5

Purchasing Your First Automobile

Whether it was sixty days or sixty years ago, most people can still remember the excitement of purchasing their first automobile. For others, it is a rite of passage that they look forward to with great anticipation.

Consider the case of Andrea Riley. Andrea is a seventeen-year-old student who works part-time. She's saved enough for most of the down payment and insurance on her first car, and her parents have agreed to provide some financial help if she makes a reasonable choice.

Andrea wants to understand all of the costs involved so she can look for a car that will best fit her budget. She found a list in her local newspaper about the costs of owning a car. It contains such items as maintenance and repair costs, state and federal taxes, average mileage per gallon for city and highway driving, and the insurance rates for various sizes and makes of cars. Comparing all

▲ *Whether they are sixteen or sixty, buying an automobile is an exciting experience for most consumers. Have you explored which makes, models, and options you want and can afford?*

of these costs will help Andrea decide whether a new car or a used car will be her best choice.

Andrea also asked her neighbor, Mr. Norman, for financial advice because he is a loan officer at a local bank. Mr. Norman suggested that she begin by asking herself a series of seven questions. These questions apply to the purchase of a car, truck, or bike.

1. What kind of transportation do I really need?
2. For what purpose will I use the vehicle?
3. Can I afford the cost of maintaining a vehicle of the size I want?
4. What price am I willing to pay?
5. Who else will be driving the vehicle?
6. What will I have to give up to afford the vehicle?
7. Will owning the vehicle make other economic opportunities available to me?

When Andrea arrived home later that evening, she discussed the seven questions with her parents.

The next day, Mr. Norman stopped by Andrea's house on his way home from work. He gave her several pamphlets published by the Federal Trade Commission. He told Andrea that he used them when he bought his last car and kept them on hand for customers at the bank.

Andrea learned a lot from the FTC pamphlets. She was surprised to discover that buying a new car is usually the second most expensive purchase many people make (the purchase of a home is the first).

Whether you decide to purchase a new car or a used one, it is a good idea to determine what makes, models, and options you want and can afford. To help evaluate different makes and models, read magazines like *Consumer Reports* and *Car and Driver*. You'll probably find them in your school or public library. In addition, study newspaper, television, and magazine advertisements carefully.

The FTC also suggests that consumers comparison shop by visiting several dealerships. The actual price of a car can vary greatly from dealer to dealer, and wise shopping can result in considerable savings. In new cars, check the official government **Monroney sticker** (Figure 18.6 on the next page). This label, affixed to the car window, is required by federal law. It shows the base price, the manufacturer's installed options, the manufacturer's suggested retail price, the manufacturer's transportation charge, and the fuel economy. The label may not be removed by anyone other than the purchaser. It lists specific information for the benefit of the consumer.

The suggested base price (cost of the car without options, but including standard equipment, factory warranty, and freight) is printed on the Monroney sticker. The dealer price is usually found on a supplemental sticker. It equals the Monroney sticker price plus the suggested retail price of dealer-installed options, additional dealer markup (ADM) or additional dealer profit (ADP), dealer preparation, and undercoating. Dealer preparation charges are paid by the manufacturer or are covered by the new car warranty. Check the manufacturer's suggested price, and compare it with the dealer markups.

Test-drive the cars you are considering, and check for comfort and proper handling. This will help you narrow down your choices.

Andrea discovered that after deciding on a specific car, she would need to negotiate on price. She also discovered that dealers are sometimes willing to bargain on their profit margin, which is generally between 15 and 20 percent. This is usually the difference between the manufacturer's suggested retail price and the **invoice price** (manufacturer's initial charge to the dealer). The invoice price is usually higher than the dealer's actual cost because dealers often receive rebates, allowances, discounts, and incentive awards from the manufacturer.

If the price you negotiate for a car is based on the invoice price (for example, "at invoice," "one hundred dollars below invoice," or "two percent above invoice"), be sure that freight is not added to the sales contract.

Once you have made your selection—but before you give a deposit—determine whether or not the deposit is refundable. If so, find out what the terms are.

Will a Used Car Do?

After pricing several new cars, Andrea began to wonder if perhaps a used car would be a wiser choice. She talked to a friend who was an auto mechanic and had another long discussion with her parents.

Andrea learned that used car shopping can be confusing for someone who is not familiar with the mechanics of automobiles. Doing research ahead of time, asking the advice of a knowledgeable friend, and performing a full road test can be very helpful. Before buying a used car, it is wise to have it inspected by an independent mechanic or diagnostic center to be sure that there are no hidden problems. Visual concerns include uneven or mismatched paint, excessive or uneven tire wear, leaks, and nonfunctioning accessories.

Andrea also learned to look for a buyer's guide sticker on the window of each car. The buyer's

▲ *Have you investigated and compared the advantages and disadvantages of buying a new car versus buying a used car?*

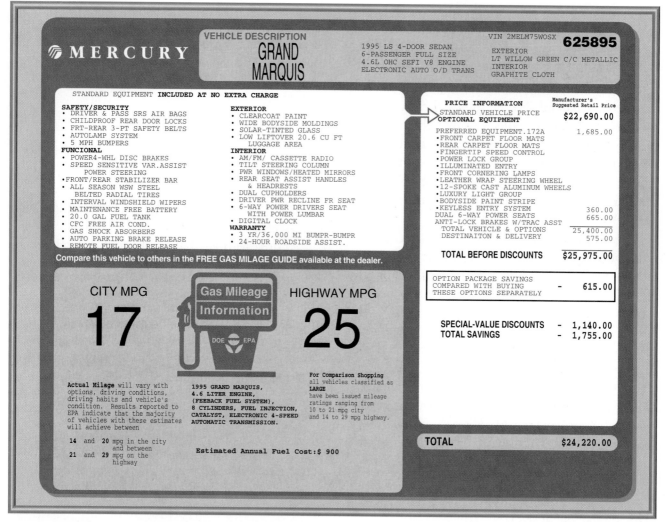

▲ *Figure 18.6 Sample Monroney Sticker.*

guide, required by the Federal Trade Commission's Used Car Rule, gives the consumer important information and suggestions to consider. It tells you

- Whether the vehicle comes with a warranty and, if so, what specific protection the dealer will provide
- Whether the vehicle comes with no warranty ("as is") or with implied warranties only
- That you should ask to have the car inspected by an independent mechanic before you buy
- That you should get all promises in writing
- What some of the major problems are that may occur with any car

Financing an Automobile

After careful consideration, Andrea decided to buy a used car in the six- to seven-thousand-dollar price range, make a 50 percent down payment, and finance the remaining 50 percent. When she considered the financing, Andrea remembered Mr. Norman's advice: "Check interest rates by shopping around for the best deal. Always compare the annual percentage rates (APR). In addition to the financing offered by the dealer, consider banks, finance companies, and credit unions. Read your purchase contract carefully before signing. Make sure you understand every-

CAREER TIP

Check the history of a used car by asking the dealer for the name and address of the previous owner. Contact the previous owner to discuss the car's mileage, service problems, and accident history. Copies of repair bills may help you verify the mileage and the car's history of mechanical breakdowns or accidents.

thing. Check all figures and draw lines through blank spaces in a contract to indicate no charge."

Maintaining a Newly Purchased Vehicle

Andrea's parents were pleased with her decision and the way she made it. They reminded her to observe proper auto maintenance suggestions to help keep her operating costs down. New cars are covered by warranties, which should promise that for a certain period of time or until a certain mileage is reached, the manufacturer will repair or replace certain parts that prove to be defective in material or workmanship. If Andrea buys a used car from a dealer, she may have a limited **warranty**, depending on the dealer's policy. She may get a lower price from an individual, but she will not receive a warranty.

Andrea's parents suggested that Andrea consider her actual driving costs (Figure 18.7). These costs include gasoline mileage and the likelihood of certain repairs or replacements, such as tires, muffler, battery, and brakes, when deciding which make and model of car to purchase. Her choice will affect the insurance rate she must pay.

When you enlist the service of an automotive technician, describe the problem and its symptoms. Let the automotive technician determine what needs fixing. For major repairs, think about getting a second opinion, even if the car must be towed to another shop. Before you leave your car for repairs, make certain that you have a written estimate and that the work order reflects what you

Cost of Owning and Operating Automobiles, Vans, and Light Trucks

Size	Depreciation	Insurance	Maintenance	Parking and tolls	Tires	Finance Charges	License, Taxes, and Registration	Fuel and Oil, Excluding Taxes	Fuel and Oil Taxes	Total Cost (cents per mile)
Subcompact	8.6*	7.1	4.0	1.3	0.7	1.6	0.8	3.5	1.3	28.9¢
Compact	8.7	7.0	3.9	1.3	0.9	1.6	0.7	4.0	1.4	29.5¢
Intermediate	10.7	7.0	4.2	1.3	1.0	2.0	0.9	4.6	1.7	33.4¢
Full-sized car	13.5	7.2	4.5	1.3	1.0	2.5	1.1	5.0	1.8	37.9¢
Compact pickup	8.7	7.2	4.0	1.3	1.0	1.8	0.9	4.2	1.5	30.6¢
Full-sized pickup	9.5	7.2	4.3	1.3	1.2	2.2	0.9	6.2	2.3	35.1¢
Minivan	11.8	7.0	4.0	1.3	1.1	2.2	0.9	5.1	1.9	35.3¢
Full-sized van	14.2	8.5	4.2	1.3	1.4	2.9	1.2	8.1	3.0	44.8¢

*All values are calculated in cents.

▲ *Figure 18.7 Costs of Owning and Operating Automobiles, Vans, and Light Trucks.*

▲ *In addition to the original purchase price, maintaining a vehicle is a major budget item. Have you compared the reliability of various makes and models?*

want done. Ask the mechanic to contact you before making repairs not covered in the work order. Keep copies of all work orders and receipts, and get all warranties in writing. Many states have "lemon" laws for new cars with recurring problems. Contact your local or state consumer office to find out if your state has these laws.

Andrea purchased a very satisfactory automobile that provided her with essential transportation when she needed it and many hours of pleasure during her leisure time. The process that Andrea followed can help you purchase a satisfactory automobile and keep it well maintained.

Driving Safely

Andrea noticed that her parents, Mr. Norman, and her auto mechanic friend all ended their advice with a message to "drive safely." A pamphlet from the Ohio Department of Highway Safety helped her understand why everyone was so concerned.

Chances are good that during your lifetime you will be injured in a traffic accident. If it happens, you will have a one-in-two chance of suffering a disabling injury. You will have a one-in-fifty chance of dying in the accident.

Andrea used the advise she received and the information in several safety pamphlets to develop her ten commandments for driving safely:

1. Thou shall "buckle up" before driving.
2. Thou shall check traffic before entering a highway.
3. Thou shall not assume what other drivers are going to do.
4. Thou shall practice defensive driving techniques. Remember, the meek shall inherit the earth.
5. Thou shall always use your side and rearview mirrors to check for traffic before changing lanes or passing.
6. Thou shall not mix driving with the use of alcohol or drugs nor ride with a driver who does.

7. Thou shall not allow music to become so loud as to distract you or prevent you from hearing sirens, horns, or trains.

8. Thou shall obey speed limits at all times.

9. Thou shall pay attention to your driving at all times.

10. Thou shall be responsible for keeping safety equipment (brakes, lights, horn, and muffler) in good working order.

Consumer Rights

We depend on our cars to operate as the manufacturers claim they will and to be serviced properly when repairs are required. If you have an auto-related problem, contact the company that advertised, sold, or repaired the vehicle. If a complaint cannot be resolved directly with the business involved, you may file a complaint with the Attorney General's Consumer Protection staff or attempt to have the problem resolved through the dealer's or manufacturer's arbitration program.

Section 5 GET INVOLVED

Answer the following on a separate sheet of paper, and be prepared to discuss your responses in class.

1. Visit a used-car lot and select a car that you would like to own. What possible problems can you detect by reading the information on the back of the Buyers Guide? List three good features of the car you selected. List three possible problems with the car you selected. How did you discover the good features? the problems?

2. Using the classified ads of your local newspaper, determine the average cost of one or more specific models of used cars from 1990 to the present. Use at least five car prices to determine the average price for each year.

3. Would it be to your financial advantage to pay cash and save on interest charges or to use credit to buy an automobile? If buying on credit, how much down payment will you be able to afford? How large a monthly payment will fit comfortably into your budget?

Section 6

Insurance Protection

According to the Insurance Information Institute, insurance companies pay more than seventy-five billion dollars each year in claims from policyholders. Those claims result from losses suffered during fires, hurricanes, tornadoes, robberies, auto accidents, dog bites, falls, and a host of other traumatic incidents.

Insurance is the act, system, or business of guaranteeing property or a person against loss or harm arising in specified occurrences, such as fire, accident, death, or loss of income, in exchange for a payment proportional to the risk involved. You can use insurance to transfer risk from yourself to the insurance company.

All insurance policies (the printed documents, issued to the policyholder by the company, that state the terms of the insurance contract) cost a **premium** (the policyholder's payment) that is determined mostly by the amount the insurance company must pay out in claims.

Purchasing Automobile Insurance

Whenever you drive an automobile, you risk having an accident. If you are ever involved in an automobile accident, the damages could be the biggest expense you'll have in owning a car.

Throughout the United States, state financial responsibility laws require people to prove that they can pay for damages that result in death, injury, or property damage. If you are responsible for an accident involving bodily injury or substantial property damage, you will be asked to present proof that you can pay damages up to the amounts required by law. In most situations, financial responsibility requirements are met through the purchase of automobile insurance.

Automobile insurance consists of two basic parts. **Liability coverage** is for bodily injuries, property damages, and medical expenses for others when you are at fault. **Physical coverage** is for damage to your vehicle caused by collision, fire, or theft.

Section 6 GET INVOLVED

Answer the following on a separate sheet of paper, and be prepared to discuss your responses in class.

1. Estimate the amount of life insurance needed by the main wage earners in your household. Consider all monthly expenses and the amount of time that the dependent family members will need to become self-sufficient. Are the wage earners in your household adequately insured, or are they underinsured?

2. A burglar's three worst enemies are light, time, and noise. Using each of these three factors, what can you do to help protect your home or apartment?

.IMPORTANT FACTS

Oh! For the Good Old Days!

How would you like to buy the following items at the prices shown? Had you lived in 1933 and had the money, this is what you would have paid:

New Pontiac Coupe	$585.00
Used 1929 Ford	29.00
Leather shoes	1.69
Man's wool suit	10.50
Gas stove	24.00
Six-bedroom house (Detroit)	2,800.00
Three-piece bedroom set	$49.50
Dental filling	1.00
Sirloin steak (lb)	.29
Quart of milk	.10

What Should You Do If You Have a Traffic Accident?

1. Notify the police, call for medical aid if needed, and warn oncoming traffic (use caution to avoid placing yourself at risk).

2. Write down the name of the other driver and his or her license plate number, vehicle type, and insurance company.

3. Don't speak with the other driver about who was at fault in the accident. Discuss the accident only with the police and your insurance representative.

4. Get the names, addresses, and telephone numbers of all witnesses.

5. Notify your insurance agent promptly. If you're traveling away from home and there are injuries, call the nearest agent or claim office.

Source: State Farm Insurance, Ohio Report.

Single Consumers

Women spend 7 percent of their total budget on apparel and services, nearly twice as much as men. Both groups spend about 20 percent of their apparel and services budget for gifts. About half of the men's gift purchases are for jewelry and watches, compared with only 10 percent for women. Single women spend a larger portion of their budgets for housing and clothing. Single men spend a larger share for food away from home, transportation, and entertainment.

Source: Monthly Labor Review, 10/91.

Warranties and Guarantees

If a product costs fifteen dollars or more, the law says that the seller must let you examine any warranty before your purchase, if you ask to see it. Use your rights to compare the terms and conditions of warranties (or guarantees) on products or services before you buy. Look for the warranty that best meets your needs.

If you forget to mail in the owner's registration card, you can still get service under the warranty if it is still valid. You can use a sales receipt or a canceled check to show the purchase date.

Source: U.S. Office of Consumer Affairs and Electronic Industries Association, Consumer Electronics Group.

Mail Fraud

If it sounds too good to be true, it almost certainly is. Fraudulent mail promotions take several forms. Here are some examples:

- Sweepstakes that require you to pay an entry fee or order a product
- Notices of prizes that require you to call a "900" number or buy a product
- Mailings that look as though they are from government agencies but are not
- Classified "employment" or "business opportunity" advertisements that promise easy money for little work
- Prize awards that ask for your credit card or bank account number

Be suspicious of notices that say you have received a prize. Usually, you have to purchase a product—for example, a lifetime supply of cosmetics or a large amount of vitamins—to become eligible to receive the prize. In fact, few of the prizes are awarded, and many are worthless.

Source: U.S. Office of Consumer Affairs.

CHAPTER 18 REVIEW

ENRICH YOUR VOCABULARY

On a separate sheet of paper, number from 1 to 19, and complete the following activity. (Do not write in your textbook.) Match each statement below with the most appropriate term from the "Enrich Your Vocabulary" list at the beginning of the chapter by writing that term next to the correct statement.

1. Having no trademark
2. Unsteady, irregular
3. A person paying rent for the temporary use of another person's building or land
4. The cost of one standard measure of a product.
5. Temporary price reductions on regular merchandise
6. A contract that involves a financial commitment
7. Money you entrust with the landlord to cover any damage you cause to the rental unit
8. Office that suggests guidelines to consumers
9. A government agency that enforces laws related to food, drugs, and cosmetics
10. Wise, shrewd, and frugal
11. Insurance for bodily injuries, property damages, and medical expenses for others when you are at fault
12. The automobile manufacturer's initial charge to the dealer
13. The policyholder's payment for an insurance policy
14. Misrepresenting a product or service
15. The act, system, or business of guaranteeing property or a person against loss or harm arising in specified occurrences
16. The label affixed to a new car's window and required by federal law
17. A guarantee that a product is of a certain quality or that defective parts will be replaced
18. Insurance for damage to your vehicle caused by collision, fire, or theft
19. A label that states the various nutrients in a product

CHECK YOUR KNOWLEDGE

On a separate sheet of paper, complete the following activity. (Do not write in your textbook.)

1. Approximately how much do Americans spend each year?
2. Food accounts for what percentage of the average American household's expenditure? What about health care?
3. Why is prudent shopping worth the effort?
4. Why is knowledge of weights and measurements important in being a prudent consumer?
5. What are the three major types of sales that stores offer to consumers?
6. Of the ten points listed in Figure 18.2 to help you stretch your dollars, which two are most important to you? Explain your answer.
7. List four dishonest or illegal advertising practices described in this chapter.
8. What is the general rule of thumb regarding how much to allow in your budget for housing expenses?
9. What percentage of American households own their homes?
10. Consumers have many rights that are protected by numerous government agencies and private consumer groups. However, consumers must also take responsibility for what they purchase. Name four responsibilities that you should accept as a consumer.
11. In addition to the make, model, and options you want, name four costs mentioned in the chapter that you should consider before deciding to buy a specific car.

DEVELOP SCANS COMPETENCIES

Government experts say that successful workers can productively use Resources, Interpersonal skills, Information, Systems, and Technology. This activity will give you practice in developing Information and Interpersonal skills.

Go computer shopping! Before you begin, decide what features the computer must have to meet the needs of your family. Features to look at include price, RAM, HD size, CPU size, CD drive, and modem. There may be other features that are important to your family.

Shop at several different stores. Record the prices and features for at least five different computers.

After you have finished shopping, analyze the information you have collected. Decide which computer would be the best buy to meet the needs of your family.

Health: You Can't Work Without It!

Learning Objectives

After completing this chapter, you should be prepared to:

- describe how your physical and mental condition affects the quality of your life
- explain how what you eat now will affect your physical condition and appearance, now and in the future
- give examples of safe-living practices on the job and away from the job
- list the specific criteria for selecting a personal physician
- explain why a workplace that is safe and free from the dangers of drug- or alcohol-induced behavior is good for both employees and employers
- explain the importance of having health insurance

Enrich Your Vocabulary

In reading this chapter and doing the exercises you will learn the following important terms:

calorie
diet
nutrients
Recommended Daily
  Allowances
Food Guide Pyramid
ATP
aerobic
cardiorespiratory
  endurance
muscular strength
muscular endurance

flexibility
hospitalization
  insurance
surgical insurance
health maintenance
  organization
drug
drug abuse
mandated

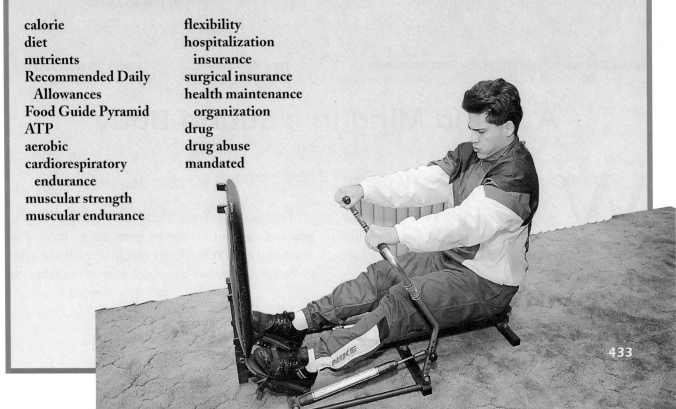

The quality of all aspects of your life is affected by your physical and mental condition. Though some of the factors that contribute to good health are beyond your control, most are simply a matter of developing good health habits. Think of what you have done today that has been good or bad for your health. How rich are you in the first wealth?

Which of the following good health habits do you consistently practice?

- Do you eat well-balanced, nutritious meals?
- Do you get at least eight hours of sleep each night?
- Do you see your doctor for regular checkups?
- Do social or school pressures only rarely get you down?
- Do you think about doing things in a safe manner?
- Do you avoid using tobacco, alcohol, and drugs of abuse?
- Do you have a positive mental attitude toward yourself and others?
- Do you participate in sports, or do you exercise on a regular basis?
- Do you make an effort to keep informed about health risks, such as infectious diseases and environmental hazards?
- Do you avoid behaviors, situations, and places that are considered to be health risks?

▲ *Regular exercise or active participation in sports are part of practicing a wellness-oriented lifestyle. Do you enjoy competitive physical activities?*

If you answered yes to all of these questions, you are practicing a wellness-oriented lifestyle. If not, take responsibility today for putting yourself on the positive health track. Take steps to turn your negative responses into positive ones.

Section

1

A Sound Mind in a Sound Body

What you eat and breathe, the genetic traits you were born with, the physical activity and mental stresses you experience, the illnesses to which you are exposed, all play a part in determining how healthy you are or will be.

You Are What You Eat

The food you eat today will determine your physical condition and appearance tomorrow. Your body is a remarkable machine with the ability to select needed chemical substances from the

▲ *Friends often enjoy eating a meal together. What nutrients are in a meal of pizza and soda pop? Where is pizza on the food guide pyramid?*

food you eat and convert them into flesh and bones and to repair and replace worn-out tissue. The food you eat provides the calories needed to stoke the "furnaces" in the cells of your body. When food is burned there, it releases the necessary energy for all of your body's activities. You owe it to yourself to "fuel it well."

With each snack or meal you eat, you consume calories. A **calorie** is the amount of heat needed to raise the temperature of one gram (453.5

The first wealth is health.

Ralph Waldo Emerson

grams = 1 pound) of water one degree centigrade. To speak of the calories that a portion of food contains is to indicate how much body heat will be produced when that food is burned. For example, the suggested calorie intake for most teenage girls is 2,200 calories per day; for teenage boys, it is 2,800 per day. If you eat more of the fuel foods than your body requires, the extra material may be changed into fat tissue, which does not promote good health.

The most important rule for a **diet** (the food and drink a person customarily consumes) is to eat sufficient food to supply the body's energy needs and to eat a varied diet to supply the **nutrients** (nourishment) for the body's growth and functioning. Unfortunately, nature packs some foods full of nutrients and shortchanges others. However, a food high in one nutrient is likely to have other healthful benefits.

Recommended Daily Allowances (RDAs) are specific nutritional standards that were established by the Food and Nutrition Board of the National Academy of Sciences. The RDAs state the precise nutrient needs for different age, sex, and weight groups. See Figure 19.1 for the RDAs for young adults.

The U.S. Department of Agriculture and the Department of Health and Human Services recommend the following guidelines for a healthful diet:

1. Eat a variety of foods to get the energy, protein, vitamins, minerals, and fiber you need for good health.

2. Maintain a healthy weight to reduce your chances of getting high blood pressure, heart disease, a stroke, certain cancers, and the most common kind of diabetes.

3. Choose a diet that is low in fat, saturated fat, and cholesterol to reduce your risk of heart attack and certain types of cancer. Because fat contains more than twice the calories of an equal amount of carbohydrates or protein, a diet low in fat can help you maintain a healthy weight.

4. Choose a diet with plenty of vegetables, fruits, and grain products, which provide needed vitamins, minerals, fiber, and complex carbohydrates and can help you lower your intake of fat.

5. Use sugar only in moderation. A diet with lots of sugar has too many calories and too few nutrients for most people and can contribute to tooth decay.

6. To help reduce your risk of high blood pressure, use salt only in moderation.

7. If you drink alcoholic beverages as an adult, do so only in moderation. Alcoholic beverages supply calories but little or no nutrients. Alcohol is also the cause of many health problems and accidents and can lead to addiction. Of course it is illegal for anyone under the age of 21 to drink alcoholic beverages.

The **Food Pyramid Guide** is an outline of what to eat each day to put the dietary guidelines into action (Figure 19.2). It's not a rigid prescription, but a general guide that lets you choose a healthful diet that is right for you. The pyramid calls for eating a variety of foods to get the nutrients you need and at the same time the right amount of calories to maintain a healthy weight. The pyramid also focuses on fat because most

Recommended Dietary Allowances (RDAs) for Young Adults

Age (Years)	Weight (Kilograms)	(Pounds)	Height (Centimeters)	(Inches)	Protein (g)	Vitamin A (g RE)	Vitamin D (g)	Vitamin E (mg ¶-TE)	Vitamin K (g)	Vitamin C (mg)	Thiamin (mg)	Riboflavin (mg)	Niacin (mg NE)	Vitamin B6 (mg)	Folate (g)	Vitamin B12 (g)	Calcium (mg)	Phosphorus (mg)	Magnesium (mg)	Iron (mg)	Zinc (mg)	Iodine (g)	Selenium (g)
Males																							
11-14	45	99	157	62	45	1,000	10	10	45	50	1.3	1.5	17	1.7	150	2.0	1,200	1,200	270	12	15	150	40
15-18	66	145	176	69	59	1,000	10	10	65	60	1.5	1.8	20	2.0	200	2.0	1,200	1,200	400	12	15	150	50
19-24	72	160	177	70	58	1,000	10	10	70	60	1.5	1.7	19	2.0	200	2.0	1,200	1,200	350	10	15	150	70
Females																							
11-14	46	101	157	62	46	800	10	8	45	50	1.1	1.3	15	1.4	150	2.0	1,200	1,200	280	15	12	150	45
15-18	55	120	163	64	44	800	10	8	55	60	1.1	1.3	15	1.5	180	2.0	1,200	1,200	300	15	12	150	50
19-24	58	128	164	65	46	800	10	8	60	60	1.1	1.3	15	1.6	180	2.0	1,200	1,200	280	15	12	150	55

▲ *Figure 19.1 Recommended Daily Allowances for Teenagers.*

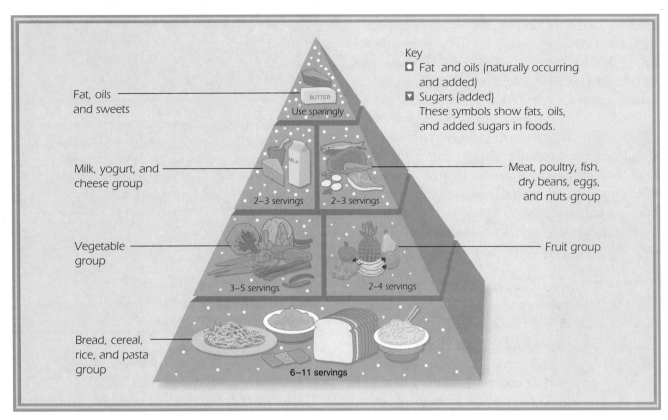

Key
☐ Fat and oils (naturally occurring and added)
▽ Sugars (added)
These symbols show fats, oils, and added sugars in foods.

Fat, oils and sweets — Use sparingly

Milk, yogurt, and cheese group — 2–3 servings

Meat, poultry, fish, dry beans, eggs, and nuts group — 2–3 servings

Vegetable group — 3–5 servings

Fruit group — 2–4 servings

Bread, cereal, rice, and pasta group — 6–11 servings

▲ *Figure 19.2 The Food Guide Pyramid.*

American diets are too high in fat, especially saturated fat.

Fitness

A wellness lifestyle is more than a well-balanced diet. Physical fitness improves your appearance, makes you stronger, and energizes your emotional well-being. Regular exercise through sports or workouts can do wonders for your energy level.

When people exercise, the number of microscopic energy factories, called *mitochondria*, in their muscle cells increases. Energy is created in these factories through a chemical reaction that begins when the body converts the carbohydrates and fat from food into a sort of chemical fuel called *adenosine triphosphate*, or **ATP**. The breakdown of ATP releases a burst of energy that serves as the power source for muscular movement.

Regular physical activity also increases both the number and the density of capillaries, which

▲ *Which of the four components of physical fitness is the Jones family getting during their afternoon of bicycling?*

transport oxygen to your cells. Oxygen is a key ingredient in the making of ATP during most activities, from running to sleeping. That's why they're called **aerobic** (with oxygen) activities. The more easily mitochondria obtain oxygen to manufacture energy, the more energetic a person feels.

Physical exercise also triggers the release of so-called fight-or-flight hormonal stimulants, such as adrenaline, into the bloodstream—the same stuff that makes your heart rev when a car swerves in front of you in fast traffic. The faster heart rate boosts the blood flow to the muscles, brain, and nervous system. When you have good circulation and plenty of oxygen being delivered, your body feels revved up.

The President's Council on Physical Fitness lists four components that are basic to physical fitness:

- **Cardiorespiratory endurance**: The ability to deliver oxygen and nutrients to tissues and to remove wastes. The ability to endure a long run or swim is a good method for measuring cardiorespiratory endurance.
- **Muscular strength**: The ability of a muscle to exert force for a brief period of time. Upper-body strength, for example, can be measured by performing various weight-lifting exercises.
- **Muscular endurance**: The ability of a muscle, or a group of muscles, to sustain repeated contractions or to continue applying force against a fixed object. Push-ups are often used to test endurance of arm and shoulder muscles.
- **Flexibility**: The ability to move joints and use muscles through their full range of motion. The

GETTING MORE INFORMATION

The American Dietetic Association and the International Food Information Council have produced a commonsense guide to good eating, titled *Ten Tips to Healthy Eating*. For a free copy, send a self-addressed, stamped envelope to

> 10 Tips
> P.O. Box 1144
> Dept. MO
> Rockville, MD 20850.

sit-and-reach exercise is a good measure of flexibility of the lower back and hamstring muscles.

You should practice a beneficial fitness program throughout the year and at least three times a week. Joining a team or group, such as a tennis, weight-lifting, or aerobics class, helps many people stick to a schedule. A fitness program can include more than one form of exercise. For example, if you live in a northern climate, you may choose to bicycle during the summer months and swim at an indoor pool during the winter. A fitness program should be enjoyable. For many people, participation in sports, such as track, basketball, or volleyball, becomes a fitness habit that they enjoy throughout their lives.

If you haven't had a physical checkup by your physician for several months, it is a good health practice to get one before beginning a strenuous fitness program. If you are really out of shape at the beginning of your fitness program, it will probably take two or three months of regular exercise to realize the benefits of your hard work and determination. Remember that the three most important parts of a successful fitness program are don't quit, don't quit, and don't quit. The benefits

CAREER TIP

Begin an exercise program gradually. Overdoing it will cause fatigue and muscle soreness. People who overdo it are more likely to quit their exercise program than those who begin gradually.

CAREER TIP

Employers know that healthy, fit employees are more productive and have better attendance than their co-workers. They also save the company money on medical insurance expenses.

to your physical health and mental well-being will be worth the effort.

Safety

Eating a healthful diet and being physically fit will be of little value to the person who works and plays in an unsafe manner. You may wish to review what you learned in Chapter 10 concerning safety habits on the job. It is important to your health to practice safe-living habits away from the job as well as on the job.

Remember the old saying, "Better safe than sorry"? Being aware of potential hazards and using safe practices can prevent accidents, injuries, and disease. Consider the following facts:

- The most common causes of traumatic brain injury are motor vehicle and bicycle accidents, violence (assault, homicide, and suicide), falls, and sports or recreational accidents. Traumatic brain injury is caused by a blow to the brain or head and may produce an altered state of consciousness.

- Despite the well-publicized menace of HIV and AIDS, teens are endangered by an unprecedented epidemic of sexually transmitted diseases (STDs).

- The number of Americans who die from diseases caused by smoking continues to increase.

- Researchers estimate that skin cancer will strike one in every ninety Americans by the year 2000. The chief villain is the sun's ultraviolet rays.

▲ *Mr. Wu's discussion with Nancy about safe driving is based on the fact that accidents are the number-one killer of children in America. What should parents do to make certain their teenage sons or daughters will drive safely?*

If you believe that safety is something other people should practice, keep in mind that the number one killer of children in America isn't drugs or disease—it's accidents.

Mental Health

Do you consider yourself to be a competent person? Are you loved by certain people and well-liked by others? Do you usually get along well with people? If you truthfully answer yes to these questions, you probably have good mental health.

People with good mental health have personal and career problems just as people with poor mental health do. In fact, they probably face more problems because they tend to be more involved in all aspects of life. However, people with good mental health find it easier to handle the everyday changes and challenges of life more effectively.

When a person loses the ability to see his or her life situations and surroundings as they really are and can no longer handle daily problems, that person is considered to have a mental illness. People of all ages can suffer from mental illness, just as they can from physical illness.

When family relationships, financial difficulties, substance abuse, or career problems reach the point where they control a person's life in a harmful way, professional help is needed. Professionals in the mental health field provide many types of assistance, ranging from personal counseling to treatment with specific drugs.

Section 1 GET INVOLVED

Answer the following on a separate sheet of paper, and be prepared to discuss your responses in class.

1. Review Figure 19.1 on page 436. For one week, keep track of the RDAs you use each day.

2. Start a fitness program for yourself by making a list of the physical activities you presently enjoy and those you think you might enjoy. Decide which activities on the list you would most likely stick to for a long time. Develop a schedule that includes physical activity at least three times a week. Follow this schedule for at least two months. Does your program include the four components of physical fitness identified by the President's Council on Physical Fitness?

3. Do you believe that some people are accident-prone because of carelessness, or is the problem beyond their control? Explain your answer.

Section 2

Medical Care and Health Insurance

Despite the human body's natural lines of defense against disease, illness still strikes. When this happens, you need the care of a physician. Sometimes your physician needs X rays and diagnostic work done by health care specialists in order to identify your health problem. When this occurs health care becomes very expensive and health insurance is needed. It is comforting to have a physician you have chosen and health insurance before you need them.

Choosing Medical Care

Choosing the right doctor is one of the most important decisions you will make for your physical well-being. Your doctor will know you as no one else does, and there may be times when your life is in your doctor's hands. Your doctor is the one who will advise and explain to you options about your medical treatment, the medicines you will use, the tests you may need, and the surgical procedures that may be necessary. Wise doctors realize their limitations and will admit to not knowing all of the answers. When you need a specialist, your doctor will be the one whose advice you will most likely follow.

Good medical care is a partnership between patient and doctor. It's very important to find a doctor whom you feel comfortable talking with about your health problems and who will take the time to explain anything you don't understand.

If you are looking for a new doctor, good sources of recommendations are family, friends, co-workers, the hospital you prefer, and the local medical society or public health department. The hospital or medical society can give you the names of local doctors, their educational backgrounds and training, the number of years they have been in practice, their specialty areas, and their office locations.

Health Insurance is Not a Frill

Rapidly rising costs for all areas of health care, a population with increasing numbers of senior citizens, and the medical know-how to save lives using very expensive technology—all of these factors have made the issue of health insurance a matter of great concern and importance to the U.S. public. In response to public pressure, the federal government has promised that the 1990s will be a time of reform in the health-care and health-insurance systems.

Young Americans, aged sixteen to twenty-four, make up just over one-third of the population. In 1993, this age group represented nearly half of the almost 14 percent of the population without health insurance coverage.

If you wish to purchase health insurance and a group plan isn't available, work out a budget that allows you to self-insure for part of your health care. For example, you may want to self-insure for routine doctor and dental visits by putting $500.00 in a savings account where it can earn interest. When you need money to pay for doctor or dental visits it would come from your savings account instead of from your insurance company. You would save the cost of premiums for routine medical care, and just buy insurance against the unexpected, high-cost health services. The amount you can afford to spend for high-cost

PLANNING MAKES A DIFFERENCE

Jackie Plans for Good Health

Jackie Blevins is twenty-two years old, employed in a small business, and not covered by health insurance. Her monthly salary is $1,200. Jackie's employer offers a shared-cost health plan that would require her to pay $96 per month. Jackie decided that it was too expensive. After all, what are the chances of a healthy twenty-two-year-old needing a hospital?

Two months ago, Jackie's best friend, Tricia, developed a serious infection that required hospital treatment. Jackie was shocked when Tricia showed her the $7,384 bill for her three-day hospital experience.

Tricia did have health insurance, but she was still responsible for hospital and doctor charges of $327. These charges were for services not covered by her health insurance. Very few policies provide 100-percent coverage.

Critical Thinking

1. Jackie is reconsidering her decision not to purchase health insurance. Would you advise her to purchase the insurance? Why or why not?

2. What possible effect could a $96-per-month health insurance bill have on Jackie's lifestyle? What about a $7,384 hospital bill?

health services will determine which coverage you purchase.

You can purchase health insurance to pay expenses for physical examinations and tests, optical and dental work, preventive care, and treatments for physical and mental illnesses. Policies can include any or all of the following coverages (for additional information, refer back to Chapter 11):

- **Hospitalization insurance** covers hospital room and board, medication, tests, and services.
- **Surgical insurance** covers specific expenses related to specific operations.
- Medical insurance covers visits to the doctor's office and diagnostic laboratory tests.
- Major medical insurance covers expenses that exceed the dollar limit of the basic coverage.
- Comprehensive coverage includes all of the above.
- Dental insurance covers most dental expenses.
- Prescriptions coverage pays for prescribed medication.

Some health insurance policies cover several health services but require large co-payments from the policy holder. Others provide less coverage but require little or no co-payment. When you shop for health insurance, compare the cost, coverage received, service provided, and business reputation of each insurer.

Don't be pressured to purchase a policy until you have read it carefully. Once you decide on a policy, complete the application carefully. Incomplete applications give the insurer a reason to deny a claim. Be certain that you understand what coverage you will receive before you sign the application. Your policy should arrive within thirty days. If not, contact your salesperson for an explanation. If sixty days go by without information, contact your state insurance department.

As an alternative to health insurance, many people choose to join a **health maintenance organization** (HMO). HMOs are a combination of an insurance company and a doctor or hospital. Like an insurance company, an HMO provides

▲ *Compare the cost of the coverage received, service provided, and business reputation of each insurer before you purchase a policy. Will dental coverage be important to you?*

GETTING MORE INFORMATION

The Medical Information Bureau (MIB) is a data base that insurance companies use. Medical and some nonmedical information about you is collected from insurers and, with your authorization, shared when you apply for individual life, health, or disability insurance. You can obtain a copy of your MIB file by writing to

Medical Information Bureau
P.O. Box 105
Essex Station
Boston, MA 02122.

coverage for your medical bills. Like a doctor or hospital, an HMO provides actual health-care services. If you join an HMO, you will be required to pay a monthly membership fee and agree to use the health-care services that the HMO provides. Compare the costs, services, coverage, and reputation of several HMOs before you join one.

Another form of health protection is disability insurance, which is sometimes referred to as *income-protection insurance*. It is designed to protect you from loss of income if you become sick or are injured. Disability insurance pays you an income until you are able to return to work or until the benefits run out. Most employers offer some form of short- or long-term disability benefits. Remember that work-related accidents are covered by workers' compensation.

The Physical Examination

If you are seeing a physician for the first time, take along information on your medical history, or make certain that your medical records from your former physician are transferred to the new one. This helps the new physician determine how frequently you should be seen.

Because some diseases are hereditary, your checkup will include questions about the medical problems of your relatives, particularly your parents, siblings, and grandparents. The doctor will also want to know about any diseases you have had, medications you are taking, problems you are experiencing, and allergies you have. This information will help the physician treat you, and it is necessary if you are to have a good partnership.

A visit to the doctor's office is not the time to be modest, to be dishonest about your lifestyle, or to hide a drug or alcohol habit. Such information can be critical, especially if you will need surgery that requires anesthesia. In addition, if you have a substance-abuse problem, your doctor might be able to point you toward a helpful rehabilitation program.

When your doctor prescribes treatment, follow his or her orders exactly, and use your medicines as directed. If the doctor asks you to phone after a few days or to return within a certain time for a checkup, do it.

Medication

Medicine can help you feel better and might even save your life. However, how you take a specific medicine makes a big difference in how effective and safe it will be for you. Timing, what you eat and when you eat, proper dosage, and many other factors can mean the difference between feeling better, staying the same, or even feeling worse. When your doctor prescribes medication, take it correctly, or you might put your health and life at risk. The most skillful physician in the world can't cure a patient who refuses to be a responsible partner in the healing process.

The following rules will help you use medicine in a responsible manner:

1. Avoid dangerous drug interactions. If your physician prescribes medication, alert him or

▲ *Mr. Huddleston always discusses the use and purpose of any new medications prescribed to Gloria by her family physician. Why is this important?*

her to any prescription or nonprescription drugs that you take on a regular basis.

2. Let your doctor know if you are allergic to any medication.

3. Discuss the purpose of any prescribed medication with your doctor.

4. Follow the prescribed schedule for your medicine. Skipping doses may prevent a drug from working.

5. Don't automatically double your dosage if you forget to take the medicine. Never adjust the dosage without first consulting your doctor.

6. Read all of the labels and package inserts included with your prescription. They provide information about possible side effects and specific warnings, such as a warning not to drive while taking a medication. If storage instructions are not included, ask the pharmacist. Some drugs should be refrigerated; others should be protected from light.

7. Make certain that you are aware of special instructions regarding food and drug interactions. Common offenders are alcohol, tobacco, caffeine, certain foods or juices, milk, and other drugs.

8. If your prescription isn't helping, check with your doctor. You may need a different dosage or a different drug.

9. Report any unexpected symptoms (such as a rash, dizziness, or a headache) to your doctor.

10. Don't stop taking prescribed medicine simply because you feel better.

11. Never take any medication without first checking the label to make absolutely certain that you're taking the correct one.

12. Never use someone else's prescription medication, and never allow another person to use yours.

13. Do not save a drug if it is no longer needed. Flush leftovers down the toilet.

Section 2 GET INVOLVED

Answer the following on a separate sheet of paper, and be prepared to discuss your responses in class.

1. Imagine that you have moved to a new town and need to visit a doctor. Write a brief medical history of yourself to give to the doctor.

2. Interview parents, aunts, uncles, and grandparents, and list the serious illnesses that they have experienced. Do any of these illnesses tend to run in families? If so, for which ones should you watch? What lifestyle changes can you make to improve your chances of not getting these illnesses?

3. Some people find it difficult or impossible to purchase insurance of any kind because of a chronic, incurable health problem. What should be done for people in this situation? What should insurers do? What should the government do?

Section 3

Substance Abuse

Earlier in this chapter, you learned about the proper use of drugs to treat or cure an ailment. The words *medicine, medication,* and *drugs* were used interchangeably. A **drug** is any chemical substance that brings about physical, emotional, or mental changes in people. This same definition may be applied to the words *medicine* and *medication.* Whether legal or illegal, when the use of a drug causes physical, mental, emotional, or social harm to the user or to others, it is considered to be **drug abuse**.

Most employers believe that employees deserve a workplace that is safe and free from the dangers of drug- or alcohol-induced behavior. Most employees feel the same way. Both groups know that chemically dependent employees can affect the morale and safety of other employees. In addition, it is illegal to use, possess, sell, or distribute drugs of abuse at the workplace.

As a result of problems associated with drug abuse in the workplace, more and more companies require employees to accept random drug and alcohol testing as a condition of employment. Several large organizations test all prospective hires for drug use. Drug testing is especially widespread in transportation companies that are **mandated** (required) by state and federal laws to test job applicants as well as employees.

CAREER TIP

Alcohol is far and away the drug most frequently involved in work-related fatalities.

In most organizations, reporting to work or working under the influence of alcohol or illegal drugs is unacceptable and generally cause for dismissal. Engaging in any off-duty, unlawful involvement with alcohol or drugs, whether or not it adversely affects work performance, is also unacceptable to most employers. In addition, concealing knowledge of another employee's illegal involvement with drugs or alcohol-related behavior is unacceptable.

In many companies, employees' lockers, desks, files, vehicles, and personal belongings on company property are subject to search, based on management's reasonable suspicion of illegal drug or alcohol activity or use. Some organizations also report suspected or known illegal drug activity to the appropriate law-enforcement agency, and any confiscated drugs are surrendered to that agency.

Recognizing an Abuser

How can I recognize a chemically dependent person? Thousands of employers, supervisors, relatives, and friends face this tough question every day. You may be one of them. Symptoms of chemical dependency at school or work include lower-than-usual productivity or grades, poor attitude, lack of motivation, disinterest, and a high rate of absenteeism and tardiness.

Physical symptoms may be as obvious as staggering and stumbling, glassy or bloodshot eyes, slurred speech, frequent physical complaints or injuries, poor hygiene, and signs of fatigue, such as sleeping on the job. The most dangerous physical symptom is a state of unconsciousness. If you discover an unconscious person, get immediate medical attention by phoning 911, an ambulance, or a physician.

▲ *As Gwynn's school counselor, Mrs. Griffin provides her with an opportunity to express her feelings and thoughts without criticism. How does this help Gwynn build the self-confidence needed to avoid substance abuse?*

Don't jump to conclusions when someone displays the symptoms of drug abuse. Keep in mind that a person suffering from a personal problem, a physical illness, or a reaction to medication might display similar symptoms. However, when people exhibit sudden, negative changes in their behavior, for whatever reason, it should be a matter of concern.

CAREER TIP

An employee's refusal to consent to an employer's request for drug or alcohol testing could result in disciplinary action, including termination.

Disciplinary problems with drug abusers in the workplace are very similar to disciplinary problems with drug abusers in high schools. Offenses include stealing, assaulting co-workers, vandalizing the facility, carrying weapons, being defiant to co-workers and management, breaking rules, failing to perform work tasks, blaming others for failure, using obscene language and gestures, cheating, and lying. In addition, it is not uncommon for a drug abuser to obtain money for his or her habit by selling drugs at work or school.

On the other hand, many drug abusers come to work or school depressed and withdrawn. When privately confronted by an employer, counselor, or principal, it is not uncommon for them to break down into crying spells and describe existing situations and future expectations in an unrealistic manner.

- Be tolerant of mistakes. Provide help and encouragement rather than criticism.
- Provide opportuniites for others to express their feelings and thoughts without criticism.
- Be certain that rules and discipline are fair and consistent.
- Offer love, affection, and attention.
- Provide opportunities for successful and exciting experiences.
- Be an honest, moral, thoughtful role model.

▲ *Figure 19.3 Six Ways to Help Others Build Self-Esteem.*

Helping Others Avoid Substance Abuse

It is generally accepted that self-confidence and a positive attitude toward other people and life situations play an important role in avoiding the temptation to abuse drugs. Unfortunately, some people are unhappy with their lives, lack confidence, and display negative attitudes. In other words, they have very low self-esteem. Building self-esteem requires assistance from other people. Figure 19.3 lists ways that you can help another person build self-esteem.

Section 3 GET INVOLVED

Answer the following on a separate sheet of paper, and be prepared to discuss your responses in class.

1. Who would be in the best position to help a person build self-esteem using each of the six tips listed in Figure 19.3: parents, friends, relatives, school personnel, employers, or co-workers? In each case, what specific help could they provide?
2. Which of the six ways to build self-esteem would you consider to be most important in preventing drug abuse? Why? Which would you consider to be least important? Why?
3. What can you do when pressured to use drugs of abuse?
4. What are the legal consequences of drug abuse in your state? What are the penalties for driving under the influence of alcohol or drugs?

IMPORTANT FACTS

An Unnecessary Waste of Life

- The smoking of tobacco products is the chief avoidable cause of death in the United States. Smokers are more likely than nonsmokers to develop heart disease. Indeed, some 170,000 people die each year from smoking-related coronary heart disease. Lung, larynx, esophageal, bladder, pancreatic, and kidney cancers also strike smokers more often than nonsmokers.

- Cigarette smoke contains some four thousand chemicals, several of which are known carcinogens (cancer-causing agents).

- Nicotine is highly addictive, making it difficult to stop smoking. Of one thousand typical smokers, fewer than 20 percent succeed in kicking the habit on the first try.

- Alcohol-related highway accidents are the principal cause of death among young people aged fifteen through twenty-four. Alcohol use is the primary cause of traffic accidents involving teenage drivers. About half of all youthful deaths in drowning, fires, suicide, and homicide are alcohol-related.

- Contrary to popular belief, a bottle of beer, a glass of wine, and a wine cooler have about the same amount of ethyl alcohol as a drink made with liquor. Those who drive "under the influence" are most likely to have been drinking beer.

- Early alcohol use is associated with subsequent alcohol dependence and related health problems. Youth who use alcohol at a younger age are also more likely to abuse other drugs, to get in trouble with the law, and, if they are girls, to become pregnant.

Source: What Works: Schools without Drugs, U.S. Department of Education.

Fit Your Feet

According to podiatrists (foot doctors), the average width of a woman's foot is two-thirds of an inch wider than the average woman's shoe. Many women try to squeeze into shoes a half size smaller than their proper size.

To ensure better-fitting shoes, measure the width of your feet. Put a ruler on the floor and stand on it, putting your full weight on one foot. Measure your other foot in the same way. Your shoe should be the same width across the sole as the larger foot measurement.

Losing Weight

An estimated fifty million Americans go on weight-loss diets every year. Some will succeed in taking off weight, but very few—perhaps 5 percent—will manage to keep all of it off over the long run.

The only proven ways to lose weight are to reduce the number of calories you eat or to increase the number of calories you burn off through exercise. Most experts recommend a combination of both.

The goal of losing about a pound a week is reasonable. A modest reduction of 500 calories per day will achieve this goal. You must burn 3,500 calories to lose one pound of fat.

Source: Federal Trade Commission and Food and Drug Administration.

Favorite Fruits

Did you know that the top banana in fruit sales in U.S. supermarkets is the banana?

Did you know that there are 2,500 varieties of apples available in the United States? The colonists introduced the apple to North America in the 1620s, and the United States is now the second largest producer of this fruit, after the former Soviet Union.

Source: U.S. Department of Health and Human Services publication no. (FDA) 88-2226.

Sniffle and Cough

Old or new, simple or sophisticated, many cold remedies will relieve some of the familiar cold symptoms, such as a stopped-up nose or a hacking cough. However, not a single one of these products—on which Americans spend an estimated $700 million a year—will prevent, cure, or even shorten the course of the common cold.

Source: U.S. Department of Health and Human Services publication no. (FDA) 77-3029.

CHAPTER 19 REVIEW

ENRICH YOUR VOCABULARY

On a separate sheet of paper, number from 1 to 17, and complete the following activity. (Do not write in your textbook.) Match each statement below with the most appropriate term from the "Enrich Your Vocabulary" list at the beginning of the chapter by writing that term next to the correct statement.

1. Insurance that covers hospital room and board, medication, tests, and services
2. Insurance that covers specific expenses related to specific operations
3. Required
4. A combination of an insurance company and a doctor or hospital
5. Any chemical substance that brings about physical, emotional, or mental changes in people
6. The amount of heat needed to raise the temperature of one gram of water one degree centigrade
7. Specific nutritional standards for different age, sex, and weight groups
8. An outline of what to eat each day to put the dietary guidelines into action
9. The ability to deliver oxygen and nutrients to tissues and to remove wastes

10. The ability of a muscle to exert force for a brief period of time
11. The ability to move joints and use muscles through their full range of motion
12. The food and drink a person customarily consumes
13. Adenosine triphosphate, a sort of chemical fuel made from carbohydrates and fat
14. The ability of a muscle, or a group of muscles, to sustain repeated contractions or to continue applying force against a fixed object
15. The use, legal or illegal, of a drug that causes physical, mental, emotional, or social harm to the user, or to others
16. Nourishment
17. With oxygen

CHECK YOUR KNOWLEDGE

On a separate sheet of paper, complete the following activity. (Do not write in your textbook.)

1. List six of the good health habits that are related to a wellness-oriented lifestyle.
2. What are the suggested calorie intakes for most teenage girls and for most teenage boys?
3. What is the most important rule for a diet?
4. State at least two reasons for choosing a diet with plenty of vegetables, fruits, and grain products.
5. List four important criteria to consider when selecting a physician.
6. Review the thirteen rules for using medicine responsibly. Select three of these rules, and explain the consequences of breaking each of them.
7. When you shop for health insurance, what four items should you compare?
8. Seven ways to build self-esteem are listed in Figure 19.3. Select one that would be easy for you to do and one that would be difficult. Explain your choices.
9. Why do more and more companies require employees to accept random drug and alcohol testing as a condition of employment?

DEVELOP SCANS COMPETENCIES

Government experts say that successful workers can productively use Resources, Interpersonal skills, Information, Systems, and Technology. This activity will give you practice in developing Information, Interpersonal, and Systems skills.

Give your home a safety inspection. Develop a chart, similar to the one shown here, which lists all rooms of your home. Then inspect each room for any potential safety hazards. You might look for such things as heavy items a younger brother or sister could pull off a shelf, dangerous chemicals or medicines that are stored where a child might get them, and steps or railings that need to be repaired.

After you have completed your inspection, try to find possible solutions. Then discuss any unsafe situations with your parents or possibly with the landlord.

	potential problem(s)	possible solution(s)
kitchen		
bedrooms		
bathroom		

Work and the Family

Learning Objectives

After completing this chapter, you should be prepared to:

- give examples that explain the difficulty of combining family expectations, lifestyles, and household circumstances with the expectations of employers

- list changes in traditional family lifestyles that have caused important changes in employer-employee relationships

- explain how and why a satisfying marriage eventually becomes the result of meeting the goals of the courtship

- compare the marriage, work, and family roles and responsibilities of each partner in today's society with those of past generations

- explain how children's needs affect parents' employment

Enrich Your Vocabulary

In reading this chapter and doing the exercises you will learn the following important terms:

dating
courtship
Pregnancy
  Discrimination Act
  of 1978
mommy track
Family and Medical
  Leave Act of 1993
accrued
exempt

love
pediatrician
Omnibus Budget
  Reconciliation Act
  of 1990
three o'clock
  syndrome
workaholics
noncustodial parent

At this point, you have probably thought about your future work and selected some tentative occupations. Have you thought about whether or not you might get married someday? If so, have you also considered the type of person you might eventually marry? Have you thought about having a family of your own? Work, marriage, and caring for a family usually occur within the same life stage. They are part of the traditional American way of life. A large part of our society expects these things.

More than any time in history, work responsibilities outside the home and family responsibilities within the home must exist together. For example, almost half of all working mothers return to their jobs before their children reach the age of one.

Relationships between work and family, employers and employees, husbands and wives, and parents and children constantly affect one another. The changing expectations, lifestyles, and household circumstances of most families have prompted important changes in employer-employee relationships.

Section 1

Dating and Courtship

Although the rules of the "mating game" have changed over the years, dating and courtship are still the traditional methods that Americans use to select a lifelong mate.

During **courtship** (the process of seeking someone's affections), couples may develop a very close (personal and private) relationship. You will probably experience **dating** (the process of having social engagements with a member of the opposite sex) and courtship several times before you develop the special relationship that will eventually lead to a satisfying and happy marriage.

Mutual trust, sharing confidences, openness about thoughts and feelings, and potential for a lasting relationship are characteristics of courtship. Think for a moment about a person you have dated. What did you learn about him or her? What did you learn about yourself?

Your lifelong mate will also be your best friend. Lasting relationships begin with people who make you feel lovable and capable. They encourage you to be the best person you can be. Think about your best friends for a moment. What personal interests and values do you share with them? What activities do you enjoy together?

Love

Giving and receiving **love** (deep affection) causes feelings of warm personal attachment and pleasure. Love is a basic need for most people. It takes on different meanings and causes new feelings at different stages in life. Family, special friends, religious faith, even our pets can provide

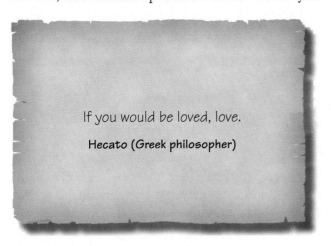

If you would be loved, love.

Hecato (Greek philosopher)

▲ *John, Donna, Phil, and Ashley attend Mohican Valley Community College. They enjoy dating and have agreed not to enter a serious relationship.*

an environment for the exchange of love. The kind of love that leads to marriage and family responsibilities affects career roles and goals.

As a child, you learned to love by being loved. Think back to your elementary school days. Did you develop a special caring or loving friendship? Has this friendship lasted into your teenage years? Following the identity stage of life, attraction for a special person frequently becomes romantic love and leads to marriage. In fact, for most individuals in our culture, marriage without love would mean no marriage at all. What effect would a love relationship have on your present career goals?

Section 1 GET INVOLVED

Answer the following on a separate sheet of paper, and be prepared to discuss your responses in class.

1. A person who has not had experiences in learning to love, who has been rejected, denied, or abused, will have a hard time learning to give and receive love. For this person, learning to love and be loved will require time, determination, and interaction with loving people. What experiences can you suggest that might help this person learn the rewards of giving and receiving love? What will be the most dif-

ficult task for this person to overcome? What positive effect can work have on this person? What difficulties will this person probably face in the workplace?

2. Make a list of newspaper or magazine articles, movies, television shows, songs, or poems that identify our society's views on the importance of marriage. Write a brief report about your findings. Locate newspaper and magazine pictures that support your position.

Section 2

Marriage

In our society, marriage is regulated by laws, rules, customs, beliefs, and attitudes that assign rights and responsibilities to each partner. Despite its complexity, more than 60

percent of all adults are married, and many unmarried adults want to be married in the future. Most survivors of failed marriages haven't rejected the idea of marriage itself. In fact, 75 percent of all

▲ *Examine this wedding photo of Albert and Leona. Do you believe they will have a successful marriage? Why, or why not?*

- Can you think of four activities you both enjoy?
- Is there less than four years' difference in your age?
- Do you have similar religious beliefs?
- Are both of you striving for similar educatiuon levels?
- Do you have similar interest in music, literature, art, and sports?
- Are you members of the same race?
- Do you agree on the role of women and men in the workplace?
- Do you want similar lifestyles?
- Do you agree on the role of women and men as spouses and parents?
- Do you have similar beliefs about politics and money?

► To evaluate your responses, see "Scoring Guide for Figure 20-1" on page 456.

▲ *Figure 20.1 Are You Ready for a Steady?*

divorced people marry again.

Two ingredients for a successful marriage are finding the right person and becoming the right person. If you are already involved or considering a serious relationship, you and your "significant other" might benefit from the quiz in Figure 20.1.

Most successful marriage partners would answer no to one or more of the questions in Figure 20.1 (see the scoring guide on page 456). However, similarity does strengthen personal attraction, and differences do provide opportunity for argument. In the case of religious or racial differences, family members and close friends frequently reduce their level of personal involvement with the couple or even reject the relationship entirely.

Entering a marriage relationship during your teens without the education and training needed to enter a rewarding career area is a good way to spell disaster. Teenage couples are likely to have difficulty supporting themselves. Money problems and increased family responsibilities, combined with a loss of personal freedom, create stress. Stress causes disagreements and marriage breakups.

Women's Changing View of Work and Marriage

Since the 1960s, the changing role of women has altered many of society's attitudes toward marriage, career, and family responsibilities. A lifetime role of full-time homemaker and mother does not exist for most young women today. In fact, most young women expect a lifelong career outside the home, interrupted only to bear and stay with small children.

Today's young women have career opportunities that did not exist for their mothers and grandmothers. Most parents have raised their daughters to believe that with the appropriate education, training, and determination, they can succeed in any career role.

Increasing occurrences of cohabitation and nonmarital childbearing have also brought about changes in women's roles and attitudes toward marriage, career, and the family. In fact, the need for this group of women to be employed is generally greater than for married women.

There are still many who hold to religious beliefs about a woman's role in the home, and when financially possible, many women choose to remain at home. Another group of well-educated and skilled women choose not to work outside of the home to avoid a collision of values and attitudes with their husbands.

Men's Changing View of Work and Marriage

As women's roles and attitudes have changed, so have men's. Not many years ago, the "man of the house" was the sole support of the family. His boss was always a man. His traditional role was as decision maker on almost all issues except routine housework. Rarely did he cook the meals or clean the house; that wasn't his job. Men did the "heavy" work on the job and at home.

Today, sharing household chores and child-rearing responsibilities is necessary when both marriage partners are employed. Some men have difficulty adjusting to shared responsibility. These men feel threatened and are uncertain of their masculine identity when they interact with a woman of equal or greater status. What problems could this cause at home and at work?

CAREER TIP

Most women who have education and training in specific career skills expect to work outside the home, even if they take time off from their careers to have children.

In one study, men, far more often than women, had arguments or felt overburdened at work if they had heavy household chores the night before or had an argument with their wife or child. Men agreed more strongly than women that one marriage partner should take a leave of absence from work to care for young children and that one spouse's career should take a higher priority than the other's. Are these findings justified and fair? Which spouse should take the leave of absence and which have the higher career priority?

Dual-Career Marriages

Almost 90 percent of young couples in the United States earn two salaries. These families have a higher standard of living and more lifestyle choices than single-income families. However, when disagreements arise over how to spend a marriage partner's income, harsh conflicts often result.

To avoid marital problems caused by financial disagreements, it is important for marriage partners to reach an early agreement about financial goals and methods to reach them. It is also important to decide who is responsible for paying routine bills, balancing the checking account, and keeping to a budget.

Many couples decide to pool their income into joint checking and savings accounts. They share all financial decisions. Others choose to maintain individual financial identities and build separate credit histories. Which method would you prefer? Should a married couple have joint ownership on everything, including a home and car?

In a dual-career marriage, it is important to divide and share household responsibilities equally or to hire outside help. This issue should be discussed before the marriage. To begin, list all of the household chores needed to keep the home operating smoothly. Next, determine the preferences of each partner. Perhaps the tasks can be easily divided. For example, some men enjoy cooking meals, and some women enjoy mowing the lawn

Solving The Problem

What's a Fair Share?

Joe and Robin Booth have been married for three years. Joe is the manager of a small restaurant and earns about $500 per week after deductions. Robin is a legal secretary, and her take-home pay is about $400 per week. Their total living expenses average $700 per week.

Joe feels that each marriage partner should do half of the work at home and contribute equally to pay the family bills. From the beginning of their marriage, Joe has reconciled their checkbook and paid the bills. In addition, he usually handles the food shopping and cooking. Robin does the cleaning, and laundry chores.

Joe takes $350 per week from Robin's check and $350 per week from his check to pay the bills. He also takes $25 from each check for their joint savings account. After the bills and savings are covered, Joe keeps his $125 per week, and Robin keeps her $25. Joe earns more, so he keeps more.

Robin would like to spend a large part of their sav-

ings on a cruise. She would also like to buy some new clothes for the trip. Joe would rather visit out-of-state relatives this summer and buy a new car for the trip. Joe and Robin had a serious argument over this question last week, and they have stopped speaking to each other.

Critical Thinking

1. Do you approve of the way Joe and Robin handle their money? What do you think of the way they divide their household responsibilities? Explain.

2. What advice would you give Joe and Robin to help them resolve their disagreement?

---

or washing the car. Consider rotating the chores that neither partner wants and the chores that both prefer. However you divide the household responsibilities, be fair.

Before you enter a dual-career marriage, anticipate potential career conflicts, and devise mutually acceptable solutions with your partner. What rewards do each of you want from a career, and what help do you expect from your partner? Will an increase in future job responsibilities reduce the time you spend together? Will it affect the time each of you spends on household responsibilities or child rearing? Try to identify various possible solutions that will enable you to meet both sets of career goals with a minimum of conflict.

If you have not decided on a specific career and you anticipate a dual-career marriage, consider occupations that are in high demand throughout

the nation. Several occupations and career areas involve transferable skills and lend themselves to relocation:

- Construction
- Education
- Word processing
- Skilled trades
- Real estate

- Truck or bus driver
- Computer programming
- Retail sales
- General office work
- Medical

Can you think of other occupations or career areas that could help you avoid relocation problems? In most cases, management-level jobs are the most difficult to relocate without a career penalty.

Staying Married

Every couple is different, and the success of a relationship depends on how the partners' unique

▲ *Betty is preparing the family breakfast while her husband, Charles, is getting ready for work. Charles will clean the kitchen and take the children to school. Betty and Charles divide the family responsibilities according to their job schedules. How would you divide family responsibilities in a dual-career marriage?*

Yes answers

9 or 10	You should have the best relationship since Romeo and Juliet.
7 or 8	You have a lot in common. Learning more about each other and finding additional areas of common interest should help you build a lasting relationship.
5 or 6	You have quite a bit in common, but you also have several areas of disagreement. You will both need to make important compromises to build your relationship.
3 or 4	The odds are against this relationship. Allow time for both of you to learn more about each other. Discuss areas of disagreement openly. It will be important for both of you to idenfify additional areas of similarity and make an effort to participate in activities that are important to the other person.
1 or 2	If this relationship works, both of you should be nominated for a Nobel Peace Prize.

Scoring Guide to "Are You Ready for a Steady?"

personalities interact. Although there is no list of proven rules for a successful marriage, several guidelines are helpful in selecting and getting along with a marriage partner.

Guidelines for Selecting a Marriage Partner:

1. Take time during the courtship to really understand each other. This will avoid unpleasant surprises after the wedding ceremony.

2. Learn the difference between sexual attraction and love.

3. Avoid getting married for selfish reasons. Getting married to escape an unhappy home life, because you believe you can change your partner, to solve personal problems, or because your friends are doing it is a poor idea.

4. Statistics show a higher failure rate for teenagers who marry than for older adults. Take time to be certain of your decision.

▲ *Richard and Jessica were married three years ago. Although they have a dual-career marriage, Richard and Jessica plan activities to enjoy and appreciate their time together. Why is this important?*

Guidelines to Follow after the Marriage:

1. Accept your partner's shortcomings. Nobody is perfect.

2. All couples experience a certain amount of conflict, hurt, disappointment, and anger. When conflicts arise, have a cooperative attitude, and be willing to give as well as take.

3. Be kind to your partner, and your love will be clear.

4. Discuss your problems. They will not go away with silence or with time; they will only grow.

5. When conflicts arise, listen, respect, and tolerate your partner's viewpoints. Don't take understanding for granted.

6. Encourage and respect your partner's individuality and uniqueness.

7. Enjoy and appreciate your time together.

Section 2 GET INVOLVED

Answer the following on a separate sheet of paper, and be prepared to discuss your responses in class.

1. Entering the work force has made wives financially less dependent on their husbands. Working women are also having fewer children. Does this mean that women today are less committed to marriage than in the past? Explain your answer.

2. Make a list of the benefits and disadvantages for the children of dual-career families. Which two benefits on your list are most important? Why? Which two disadvantages on your list concern you the most? Why?

3. How do you believe your spouse's income should be spent? What should his or her income pay for in the family budget? Should one marriage partner be in charge of handling all of the income?

Section 3

Parenting and Work

Whether your children are adopted, biological, or living with you because of family circumstances, you will be their parent. Love them, teach them the difference between right and wrong, and help them prepare for their career success.

The makeup of the American family has changed dramatically during the past fifty years. The typical family of the past included a husband supporting a nonworking wife and two children. Today, this family model represents less than 5 percent of all families. In the past, mothers rarely worked outside the home until the youngest child entered school or left home. The home situation of today's children has radically changed.

The increasing number of women in the workforce has also altered work life. Family issues, such as the availability and affordability of child care, have become front-burner questions for lawmakers and labor-management negotiators.

Preparing yourself for new responsibilities and adjusting to the role of being a parent are not easy. Parenting is a twenty-four-hour-a-day responsibility. You will be expected to provide your child with affection, security, education, social opportunities, and the basic necessities of food, clothing, shelter, and health care. How prepared are you for these responsibilities? What must you do to become better prepared?

Taking time off from a job to have a baby is a worry to many working women. They are concerned about being replaced or being demoted to a lesser position when they return to work. Despite federal and state laws barring discrimination against pregnant women, it remains a valid concern.

▲ Being a "family man" helps James Preston to be an understanding employer. When pregnancy or childbirth becomes a job issue, James uses the service of a temporary employment agency.

The **Pregnancy Discrimination Act of 1978** specifically prohibits companies with fifteen or more employees from discrimination because of pregnancy. Employers cannot

- Refuse to employ a woman because of pregnancy
- Terminate her because of pregnancy
- Force her to go on leave at an arbitrary point during her pregnancy
- Penalize her because of pregnancy in reinstatement rights, including credit for previous service, accrued retirement benefits, and accumulated seniority

This law does not require an employer to provide a specific number of weeks for maternity leave or to treat pregnant employees in any manner different from other employees with respect to hiring or promotion. It does not establish new medical leave or other benefit programs where none currently exist. The phrases "different from other employees" and "where none currently exist" have led to interpretations of this law that resulted in the loss of many pregnant women's positions.

Children Are Expensive

Whether or not to have children, whether you can afford them, and how they will affect your lifestyle are personal decisions. Children are expensive. From the maternity bill to high school graduation, the price tag for raising the average child born in 1991 is estimated to be somewhere between $89,580 and $175,380. These costs include housing, food, transportation, clothing, health care, education, child care, and miscellaneous items. As the child ages, the cost per year increases (Figure 20.2).

Working Parents

Having a child can have a dramatic effect on a couple. One partner may want to drop out of the workforce to care for the family. When this happens, more income will be needed to support the nonworking partner and the child. Neither partner may want to give up their career because both prefer working outside the home.

When you return home from work tired and wanting to relax, parenting will be difficult. However, time spent with your children may be the most valuable gift you can give them. Once this special time of life is gone, you can never get it back. Being the best possible parent could mean accepting a less orderly home.

Fatherhood

Being a father expands a man's role in life and presents him with several new priorities. In most dual-career families, the father will probably spend more time with his children and accept more direct responsibilities for their physical care than in the traditional single-income household. In today's family structure, fathers accept many responsibilities that women traditionally performed, such as bathing the baby, changing diapers, and doing the laundry.

Figure 20.2 ESTIMATED ANNUAL EXPENDITURES FOR RAISING A CHILD

Age of Child	Single-Parent Households	Husband-Wife Households
0–2	$4,030	$4,360
3–5	$5,110	$4,970
6–8	$5,520	$4,940
9–11	$5,840	$4,780
12–14	$5,690	$5,500
15–17	$6,020	$5,870
Total	$96,630	$91,260

Estimates are for the younger child in a two-child family with household income less than $32,100.

Source: U.S. Department of Agriculture, 1992.

▲ *When Luis Avila was a boy, he never dreamed that he would be responsible for babysitting his son and for the family grocery shopping. On the other hand, when Rosa Romano was a child, she didn't expect to coach her daughter's softball team. What parenting responsibilities do you expect to have in the future?*

Some employers have developed programs to help men deal with family responsibilities and expectations. For example, one organization offers fathers seminars on such topics as pregnancy education and child-care expenses. Others offer support groups for fathers, in which they can share the enjoyment and concerns of fatherhood. Why do you suppose these employers invest in parent-

ing education for fathers? Would you enjoy being in a parenting class someday?

Motherhood

Motherhood expands a woman's life role and establishes many new priorities. Despite expectations of greater male-female equality in housework, a great number of fathers still do not accept an equal responsibility for the family cooking, dish washing, house cleaning, shopping, laundry, and child care. For many women, the combination of a career and motherhood requires difficult choices about time and how it is managed.

The term **mommy track** refers to the time when a woman changes her work schedule to accommodate her young child or children. The

CAREER TIP

If you become a working parent, always have a backup babysitter in case your child becomes ill or the center you rely on can't provide service.

mommy track could mean working flexible hours at the same job or the same company, changing career paths to spend more time at home with the baby, or dropping out of the work force completely for a year or for many years.

A woman who selects the part-time track usually loses her company-paid health insurance, vacation pay, and opportunities for promotions. However, if she decides to stay employed full-time, the task of balancing her career with motherhood can become overwhelming. Some women decide to commit themselves to a family in lieu of a career, at least temporarily. When and if you become a mother, which track do you believe you will take, and why? When and if you become a father, which track would you prefer for your wife? Why?

Workplace Flexibility

As the number of working women with children has risen, the need for family-friendly organizational policies and programs has increased. Though still only a fraction of the total, some organizations are trying to help employees relieve the stress of juggling work and family responsibilities as they balance their career and family lives. The following are a few examples of employers who are sympathetic to the parents and children of this generation:

- On holidays and school breaks, John Hancock Mutual Life in Boston, Massachusetts, borrows a child-care professional from a nearby day-care center to take employees' children on field trips around the city.
- The 3M Corporation in Minneapolis, Minnesota, negotiates with the local science museum, YMCA, and Campfire groups to provide full-day activities for employees' children during the summer.
- A computer set up in Apple Computer's Cupertino, California's child-care center reports feeding, diaper change, and nap information to parents who key in their child's name.

- From January through April, Plante & Moran, an accounting firm in Southfield, Michigan, uses a conference room for day care on Saturdays because they need people to work weekends during the tax season but they don't want to keep parents from seeing their kids.

Of great importance to the growth of family-friendly organizations is the fact that work and family policies are used as a competitive tool to recruit and keep skilled workers. If you were a working parent and had the choice of working for an organization that was family-friendly and one that wasn't, what choice would you make? How far should an employer go in helping resolve employees' conflicts between work and family responsibilities?

To obtain greater workplace flexibility, many women and some men choose to work out of their homes. Some start new businesses from their homes. Others purchase a franchise from an established firm. If you decide to work out of your home when your children are small, what kinds of businesses will you consider?

Family Leave

For parents who are experiencing conflicts between family and work requirements, the **Family and Medical Leave Act of 1993** is a welcome relief. This act gives millions of employees up to twelve weeks of unpaid leave from their jobs to deal with a birth, adoption, or medical emergency in the family. Although many states already had some form of family leave law and many organizations offered family leave before this act, its passage put the importance of family needs in the national spotlight.

Here are some highlights of the Family and Medical Leave Act of 1993:

- Employers with fifty or more workers within a seventy-five-mile radius must provide unpaid time off for the birth or adoption of a child; the care of a seriously ill child, spouse, or parent; or an employee's own illness.

▲ *Should the Family and Medical Leave Act of 1993 be extended to include employers with less than fifty workers? Why, or why not?*

- The law covers nonprofit and government organizations as well as businesses.
- Employers must continue to offer health-care insurance to employees who take leave.
- Employees are guaranteed the same or comparable jobs upon their return.
- Employers may substitute an employee's **accrued** (accumulated) paid leave for any part of the twelve-week period of family leave.
- Employers may **exempt** (free from the rule) "key" employees. Key employees are defined as the highest-paid 10 percent of the workforce, whose leave would cause economic harm to the employer.
- Employers may exempt employees who haven't worked at least one year or who haven't worked at least 1,250 hours, or twenty-five hours a week, in the previous twelve months.

Although this law doesn't remove all of a worker's family worries, it signals a change in the way employers and government view the interaction of work and the family. Does this law ask too much of employers?

Financial Support and Single Parents

There is a continuing increase in the number of family households maintained by one adult with no spouse present. Most of these households are the results of divorce, separation, or children born out of wedlock.

In the late 1980s, almost one-fourth of the nation's children under 18 lived with only one parent. Based on patterns of that decade, it appears that more than half of all children today will at some time live with a single parent. Many will eventually live with a stepparent.

Almost 90 percent of all children living with a single parent live with their mothers. As a group, these mothers have below-average incomes. Many of the nation's children (almost 20 percent in 1988) live in poverty and must cope with the consequences of that poverty for many years. State and federal governments are trying to improve conditions with tougher child support laws. You will learn about additional attempts to improve the safety and well-being of these families in the next two sections.

GETTING MORE INFORMATION

For a free copy of *The Handbook on Child Support Enforcement*, write to

Handbook
    Department 628 M
    Consumer Information Center
    Pueblo, CO 81009.

Section 3 GET INVOLVED

Answer the following on a separate sheet of paper, and be prepared to discuss your responses in class.

1. Children raised in poverty are less likely to achieve in school, are more likely to be involved with the criminal system, and are more likely to have out-of-wedlock children of their own. These facts are closely related to lifetime work patterns. What effect will poverty have on tomorrow's workforce? If you were a lawmaker, what would you do to increase job opportunities for people living in poverty? to reduce the number of out-of-wedlock children? to provide a better education for children living in poverty?

2. Single fathers are one of the fastest-growing groups in the workforce. Households headed by single fathers grew to more than one million in 1992. Juggling work and family roles can be even harder for men than for women because few bosses expect men to take time away from their job duties to care for their children. Is this fair? Explain your answer.

Section 4

Raising Children

Being a successful parent requires a selfless commitment, twenty-four hours a day. It is not possible to be a perfect parent or to raise a perfect child. However, there are tried-and-true parenting skills that foster positive physical, mental, and social growth in children. Learning these skills is part of being a good parent.

Your family physician or the child's **pediatrician** (a physician who specializes in children's medical care and diseases) can suggest the most current and best-written books that describe methods for fostering growth, explain child development, give advice on discipline, and explain the importance of love and encouragement. Many communities have parenting classes that teach these skills. When you have a child of your own, it will be a good idea to keep at least one good book about parenting skills by your bedside.

Helping your child master the developmental needs of childhood are important preparation for the child's future career success. Human-development skills that are satisfied in childhood grow into adult employment skills (Figure 20.3 on the next page).

Child Care

Most parents find it difficult to leave their infant or small child in the care of others. Despite this, almost half of all preschoolers spend at least part of their day in the care of adults other than their parents.

Finding reliable child-care services is very important to working parents. Knowing their children have the best possible care lessens the worry of leaving them. Consider the following guidelines when it's time for you to select and evaluate a child-care facility:

1. Check the licensing of the facility. Licensing requirements set minimal standards, such as group size and environmental safety.

Needs of the Child	If Needs Are Satisfied, the Adult Worker. . .	If Needs Are Not Satisfied, the Adult Worker. . .
To be cared for	Will be trusting and feel secure at work	Will feel insecure with new work tasks and will have difficulty placing confidence in other workers
To be loved	Will feel wanted as a valuable contributing employee	Will feel unwanted at work
To have companionship and affection (spending time alone with parents)	Will feel he or she belongs at work	Will feel like an outsider at work
To be taught (education begins with learing to eat, walk, and talk)	Will enjoy learning new information and developing new job skills	Will have difficulty with education and training
To have positive role models (especially parents)	Will exhibit acceptable behaviors at work	Will exhibit certain behaviors that are unacceptable to the employer
To be encouraged	Will not be afraid to fail and will be open to new methods and constructive criticism	Will have a sense of being evaluated and will dislike new methods for fear of failure
To play (trying out different roles)	Will be confident of his or her present career role and will attempt new career roles	Will dislike or be confused about his or her career role but will resist any change
To socialize (learning to give and take, to get along with family members, and to be part of a group)	Will get along with co-workers and will contribute to team success	Will prefer to work alone and will resist teamwork
To develop positive vaules and attitudes (clarifying a personal values system and a positive attitude in an accepting home environment)	Will be recognized by co-workers as a positive person with a sense of integrity and honor	Will be recognized by co-workers as a negative person with questionable ethics
To make choices (parents should let children make choices in certain situations; children need to live with the results of their decisions)	Will be recognized by co-workers as a good decision maker	Will put things off at work to avoid making a decision
To have limits placed on their behavior	Will follow rules pertaining to work and safety	Will complete work tasks as he or she sees fit without following company rules or safety procedures

▲ *Figure 20.3 The Effect of Childhood Development on Adult Employment Skills.*

2. Inquire about the training of the staff members, especially in child care and development.

3. Look for a center that provides well-planned activities.

4. Find out the ratio of staff to children to be certain that supervision is well balanced. For example, one adult per five children, ages birth to 12 months, and one adult per 12 children, 3-year-olds.

5. Visit the center for observation more than once before enrolling your child.

6. Ask for the name and phone number of at least two parents whose children attend the facility, and talk with them about their opinion of the center.

7. Find out what safety precautions the facility practices.

▲ *Child-care centers can help children of working parents to fill many of the childhood needs described in Figure 20.3. Who helped you to fill these needs? Who could you help?*

8. Make certain that workers know who has your permission to pick up your child.

9. Observe the cleanliness of the center.

10. Find out the center's policy for children who are ill.

11. Make certain that nutritious meals and snacks are provided and safely prepared.

12. Obtain a written copy of all fees before enrolling your child.

13. Ask the staff and your child (if he or she is old enough to talk) what they did each day.

CAREER TIP

Children need time with their parents. Teach your child to eat, talk, play, love, trust, and develop skills. Your parenting style will be a major factor in building your child's self-esteem and future career success.

14. Ask about how child-care professionals are screened before being hired.

The care of children by working parents isn't limited to small children. By some estimates, 10 million children are on their own after school. **Three o'clock syndrome** refers to the time during the workday when parents' thoughts turn to their children who are getting out of school. Some employers report jammed phone lines as children and parents try to make contact. How would you feel about the three o'clock syndrome if you were an employer? Would your view be different if you were a parent?

Have you ever been home alone when an emergency occurred? How did you handle the situation? When you have children, make certain that they know your work telephone number and at least one other number they can call in an emergency. Children at home alone should know how to call the police and fire departments. They should be instructed to keep the doors locked and not open them to strangers under any circum-

GETTING MORE INFORMATION

For a free copy of the pamphlet *Caring about Kids: The Importance of Play*, write to

> Public Inquiries
> National Institute of Mental Health
> 5600 Fishers Lane
> Rockville, MD 20857.

stances. Well-known neighbors should be asked to be alert to any problems that arise.

The availability and affordability of child care are important concerns for most working families with children. The average working family spends about 10 percent of its income on child care. For low-income parents, the cost of child care averages more than 20 percent of income—about the same percentage as housing. Providing adequate child care for children places a very real strain on family budgets.

The **Omnibus Budget Reconciliation Act of 1990** concerns child-care policy and earned income tax credit. This legislation recognizes that the lack of affordable child care keeps many parents, especially those who are poor, from seeking employment. It includes an expansion of the earned income tax credit, a Child Care and Development Block Grant, a "wee-tots" tax credit, a child health insurance credit and a family-support grant.

What this means is that a tax credit for the actual expenses incurred for child or dependent care is available to an employed person if the money spent enables that person to be gainfully employed. The expenses may be for services provided in the taxpayer's home or for out-of-home care for dependents under age fifteen.

Section 4 GET INVOLVED

Answer the following on a separate sheet of paper, and be prepared to discuss your responses in class.

1. Choose a children's book (a short one with pictures), and read it to a child who is four or five years old. When you have finished reading, talk to the child about the story. If you don't know a small child, contact a day-care center or phone the principal of the nearest elementary school. Ask for permission, and schedule a time to read a story to a kindergarten or Head Start class. Your involvement will help a child enjoy reading. Which of the needs listed in Figure 20.3 seem to be satisfied or unsatisfied in the child or children to whom you read? What makes you think so?

2. The stress of balancing work and parenting can be exhausting. How much involvement should parents have in their children's lives? How much is too much? Should parents get away from their children occasionally? If a parent has somewhere to go alone and the child wants to go along, how should the parent handle the situation?

3. Locate a child-care center in your area. Phone for an appointment to visit and interview a staff member. During your visit, use the fourteen recommendations in this section to evaluate the quality of the center. If possible, also visit a center that is operated by an employer for employees' children. Would you recommend the day-care center you visited to a working parent? Why or why not?

Divorce

Marital relationships fail to survive when more unpleasant aspects of the relationship than pleasant ones emerge. Between the late 1960s and 1980, the divorce rate in the United States doubled, until more than 50 percent of all marriages were expected to end in divorce. During the 1990s, divorce rates may drop to 40 percent. Still, the percentage of marriages in the United States that end in divorce will continue to be among the highest in the world.

Divorce and Career

Divorce creates disruption in the workplace. It is difficult to maintain a balance between personal life and work life and not carry family problems to the job. Some newly divorced people use their work as a place to get away from personal problems. They become **workaholics** (compulsive workers who are overly involved in their jobs) to make up for their feelings of personal failure and injured self-esteem. In the process, they might become fatigued and irritable, driving their associates to distraction.

Divorced people who hide from life at the work site have no place to go if they lose their employment. Because they attach so much importance to their work, they risk greater despair and are more likely to overreact when things don't work out as they had hoped.

Other workers are so upset by a divorce that job performance declines to an unacceptable level. Talking openly to friends and seeking professional help are important. However, the boss may not be willing to accept low productivity and financial loss while the divorced worker gets his or her life together.

Divorce Is a Family Affair

Divorce creates pain for parents and children alike. More than a million children watch their fathers and mothers split up every year. They often

CAREER TIP

Divorced people who were married for more than ten years are eligible to collect Social Security benefits at age sixty-two based on their spouse's earnings if they haven't remarried.

▲ *Children of divorced parents often spend part of their time with each parent. What positive and negative feelings can this cause in a child?*

find themselves spending part of their time with each parent.

Experiencing a divorce and enduring the complications of becoming a single parent frequently lower job productivity. Instead of concentrating on work assignments, single parents are distracted with decisions ranging from day care for their children to court decisions.

Child Support

States are required to have support guidelines available to all people who set child-support amounts. Parents' employment, property, and any other sources of income or assets are used to establish payment amounts. This information is usually verified before the support order is final. The amount of child support depends on each parent's ability to pay and the needs of the child. Parents can try to have the amount of support changed if their financial situation changes. Even if the **noncustodial parent** (the parent who does not have primary custody of the child but who has a responsibility for financial support) acquires a second family, this does not eliminate his or her responsibility to the first family.

Section 5 GET INVOLVED

Answer the following on a separate sheet of paper, and be prepared to discuss your responses in class.

1. Figure a monthly budget for a divorced parent who must not only pay expenses for his or her household but also child support. Assume the parent earns $2,500 a month and that child support payments are $900 a month. Use the budget formula from Chapter 17.
2. Joint custody or visitation rights are difficult, at best. They become a major problem when one parent is transferred or accepts a job far away.

Divorced parents with careers they care about are frequently torn between living close to their children and moving to take advantage of career opportunities. If the parent moves, the risk of fading from the children's lives may result. If the parent rejects a career move to stay near the children, career objectives and opportunities for success may be sacrificed. If you were a parent and faced this choice, what would you do? Why? If your parent faced this choice, what would you want him or her to do? Why?

IMPORTANT FACTS

Times Have Changed

- Regardless of the age of their children, mothers are now more likely to work outside the home than to work solely as homemakers. In 1960, less than a third of all mothers (6.6 million) were gainfully employed. At the beginning of the 1990s, almost two-thirds (20 million) were employed outside the home.

- As the 1990s began, 16.5 percent of all family households were maintained by women, compared with 9.2 percent in 1950. In addition, 1.9 million mother-child sub-families lived in someone else's household, most often the home of the mother's parents.

- More than 93 percent of Americans are married at least once by their early forties, and on average, 60 percent of divorced people remarry.

- Kinship networks now often include former spouses and former in-laws, stepchildren, and—with increased life expectancy—more generations than was typical earlier in this century.

Source: Monthly Labor Review, March 1990.

Time Off, Please!

Juggling home life, a career, and other responsibilities leaves people starved for time. One survey asked 1,010 adults if they would give up a day's pay for free time each week. Here are the responses:

- 48 percent said yes to an extra day off.
- 17 percent would make the trade for two free days.
- 54 percent of working women wanted the free day.
- 43 percent of working men said yes.
- 70 percent of those making $30,000 a year or more said yes.
- 48 percent of those making $20,000 a year or less said yes.

Source: Hilton Hotels Corporation, 1991.

Women's Work Is Never Done

Two out of five husbands almost never do the family cooking, wash up after meals, clean the house, or shop for food. Better than three out of five rarely or never do the laundry; 86 percent almost never iron.

Seven out of ten women almost always or often pay the household bills. Almost half take out the garbage a good part of the time, and about one-fourth make arrangements for car repairs. Three out of ten do a great deal of painting and wallpapering.

On the bright side, about one-fifth of the men between twenty-five and thirty-five always or often do the laundry. This is approximately double the rate for men between fifty-five and sixty-five. Better than one-fourth of younger men are frequent house cleaners, compared with well under one in five in the older group.

Source: The Conference Board, 1991.

Federal Parent Locator Service

The Federal Parent Locator Service (FPLS) is operated by the Office of Child Support Enforcement of the U.S. Department of Health and Human Services. This service assists the states in locating "deadbeat" parents to obtain child-support payments. It is also used in cases of parental kidnapping related to custody and visitation disputes.

Source: Handbook on Child Support Enforcement, Department of Health and Human Services, 1989.

Fathers Also Raise Children

There were 1,351,000 one-parent family groups maintained by fathers in 1990. This was more than a threefold increase since 1970, when only 393,000 one-parent family groups were maintained by men.

CHAPTER 20 REVIEW

ENRICH YOUR VOCABULARY

On a separate sheet of paper, number from 1 to 13, and complete the following activity. (Do not write in your textbook.) Match each statement below with the most appropriate term from the "Enrich Your Vocabulary" list at the beginning of the chapter by writing that term next to the correct statement.

1. A physician who specializes in children's care
2. A law that concerns child-care policy and earned income tax credit
3. Free from the rule
4. Accumulated
5. A law that gives employees twelve weeks of unpaid leave for family care
6. When a woman changes her work schedule for her child
7. A law that prevents employers from discriminating against pregnant women
8. The parent who does not have primary custody of the child
9. Deep affection
10. The process of seeking someone's affections
11. The process of having social engagements with someone of the opposite sex
12. Compulsive workers who are overly involved in their jobs
13. When parents' thoughts turn to their children

CHECK YOUR KNOWLEDGE

On a separate sheet of paper, complete the following activity. (Do not write in your textbook.)

1. What percentage of all working mothers return to their jobs before their children reach the age of one?
2. What are the traditional methods that Americans use to select a lifelong mate?
3. List four characteristics of courtship.
4. What special feelings are associated with love?
5. What two facts support the statement that most adults favor marriage?
6. List five areas of similarity between two people that will strengthen a marriage relationship.
7. Approximately what percentage of young couples in the United States earn two salaries?
8. List five career areas that involve transferable skills and lend themselves to relocation.
9. What percentage of families today include a husband supporting a nonworking wife and two children?
10. How many employees must a company have before it must comply with the Pregnancy Discrimination Act of 1978?
11. How many weeks of unpaid leave from their jobs are employees entitled to receive as a result of the Family and Medical Leave Act of 1993?
12. Why are employers allowed to exempt certain employees from the Family and Medical Leave Act?
13. Based on patterns of the 1980s, how many children today will at some time live with a single parent?
14. How many households were headed by single fathers in 1992?
15. Why is it important to check for licensing at a child-care facility before enrolling a child?
16. Review Figure 20.4. What five childhood needs do you believe are the most important for career success? Explain your answer.
17. Approximately how many children watch their mothers and fathers split up every year?

DEVELOP SCANS COMPETENCIES

Government experts say that successful workers can productively use Resources, Interpersonal skills, Information, Systems, and Technology. This activity will give you practice in developing Information and Interpersonal skills.

Develop a list of questions to ask married couples about how they share household chores. Try to ask at least six couples the questions. Ask two couples who are near your own age, two couples who are near your parents' ages, and two couples who are near your grandparents' ages. Compare their answers. How are they similar? How are they different? Why do you think they are different?

Civic Responsibility: You Make a Difference

Learning Objectives

After completing this chapter, you should be prepared to:

- explain why each citizen owes allegiance to the government of the United States and is accountable to local, state, and federal laws

- explain why responsible citizenship requires a knowledge of the democratic system of government, a commitment of time, and a willingness to become involved in the affairs of government

- give examples of how, as a citizen of the world, your personal life is affected by the cooperation and conflict that take place between nations

- identify several of our nation's social problems

Enrich Your Vocabulary

In reading this chapter and doing the exercises you will learn the following important terms:

civic responsibility	U.S. Constitution	poverty thresholds
Bill of Rights	ordinances	mortality
apathy	polarization of issues	population density
charisma	Environmental	social anonymity
media	Protection Agency	detrimental
property tax		
income tax		
revenue		
laws		

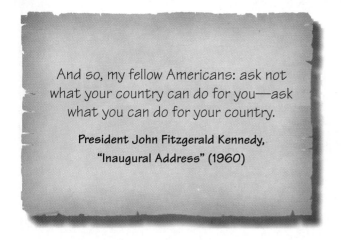

And so, my fellow Americans: ask not what your country can do for you—ask what you can do for your country.

President John Fitzgerald Kennedy, "Inaugural Address" (1960)

With this statement, President Kennedy challenged the people of the United States to accept their civic responsibility. **Civic responsibility** refers to the rights and privileges enjoyed by all citizens and their duties to the laws and policies of the community, state, and nation in which they live. Do you believe that increased civic responsibility by individuals can solve many of our nation's social problems? As you enjoy the rights and privileges of citizenship in your daily life, do you believe you have some responsibility for helping to solve the nation's problems? If citizens are indifferent to national problems and do not get involved, how will the problems get resolved? What will happen if citizens don't get involved?

Section 1

Your Civic Responsibility

Being a responsible citizen requires a knowledge of the democratic system of government, a commitment of time, and a willingness to become involved in the affairs of government. You can perform responsible acts of citizenship by completing a course in American government; volunteering to help less fortunate citizens; abiding by federal, state, and local laws; taking time to vote; serving in the armed forces; and being a productive worker.

Voting

It is an embarrassing fact that the United States has the fewest restrictions on voting of any country in the world and yet one of the smallest voter turnouts. How many of the following excuses have you heard?

- I don't like any of the candidates.

- I'm really not interested in politics.
- What's the use of voting? My vote won't make any difference

Even in presidential elections, political **apathy** (indifference) is made evident by the large percentage of eligible voters who do not go to the polls (Figure 21.1).

Voting is one of the most important civic responsibilities you will have. The right to vote allows you to protect your rights and prevent

Year	1980	1984	1988	1992
Participation	52.6%	53.1%	50.1%	53.0%

▲ *Figure 21.1 Percentage of Registered Voters Participating in Presidential Elections.*

▲ *Almost half of registered voters don't vote in presidential elections. What year will be your first to experience the excitement of voting in a presidential election?*

political abuses. Through elections, citizens can replace officials who displease the majority.

The men and women you elect will have the power to speak and act for you as they run the government. They will have the power to pass laws and regulations that will have a great influence on your life, including the world of work. They will also have the power to appoint thousands of people to government jobs each year. Did you know that the U.S. government is the largest employer and purchaser of goods and services in our economy?

How do people decide *how* to vote? The **charisma** (appealing leadership quality) of some candidates frequently sways voters. Can you think of a political candidate who demonstrated a lot of charisma in a local, state, or national election?

The **media** (newspapers, magazines, television, and radio) can have a major influence on an election. Can you think of an election in which your opinion was swayed by the media? How did the media influence your opinion?

CAREER TIP

When you reach the age of eighteen, you have the right to vote for candidates and issues of your choice. The only requirements placed on voting are minimum age, term of residence, citizenship status, and voter registration.

▲ *The quality of your public services will be influenced by your vote on tax issues.*

Have you heard the saying, "Birds of a feather, flock together"? Polls of registered voters indicate that most don't inform themselves equally about all sides of an issue or about all of the political viewpoints presented. In fact, most voters usually vote for candidates and issues supported by their political party. For example, Democrats tend to listen to speeches presented by Democrats, to read campaign literature and newspaper articles favoring Democrats, and to have friends with similar viewpoints. Republicans behave in the same manner.

A small group of independent voters frequently provides the margin of victory in elections. Independents are prone to explore all sides of an issue and to consider each candidate on the basis of ability, past performance, and position on important issues. Independents are open to change the candidates of their choice.

As a responsible citizen, follow these guidelines when deciding how to vote in an election:

1. Read information presented by people on both sides of the issue.

2. Listen to all of the candidates, and read information presented by all of the political parties.

3. Use the information you gain as you follow the steps you learned in Chapter 4 about problem solving.

Taxes

Have you ever wondered where the money for food stamps, public schools, roads, parks, police and fire protection, low-income housing, and public transportation comes from? Taxes provide money for these and other public services.

The total amount of taxes paid by citizens depends on whether or not they own property **(property tax)**, how much they earn **(federal income tax)**, where they live (local and state income tax), what they own (auto, bike, and boat license fees), and how much of certain goods and services they buy (sales tax). Customs duties on imported products and excise taxes on luxury items provide the federal government with additional **revenue** (income).

Although state and local governments use a wide variety of taxes and license fees to acquire revenue, most of the taxes you will pay during your working years will go to the federal government.

As a responsible citizen, you should be knowledgeable about what the government is doing with the money it receives in taxes. Based on your approval or disapproval, you will vote for candidates who support your beliefs about government spending.

World Citizenship

As a citizen of the world, your personal life and career are affected by the cooperation and conflict that take place between nations. Whether it is helping a famine-ravaged area of the world, defending a smaller nation against armed aggression, protecting national interests abroad, or negotiating international trade agreements, our federal government makes decisions with which each citizen must live.

Defense budgets and decisions about military conflicts are largely the responsibility of the president with the consent of Congress (a formal declaration of war must come from Congress). How willing would you have been to interrupt your education or working career to serve the United States as a member of the armed forces in Kuwait (Desert Storm), Somalia, or a similar situation?

As a responsible citizen, you should be informed about foreign affairs; how they might affect our nation's economy, security, and peace with other nations; and, in turn, how your personal life and career might be affected.

All young men must register with the selective service within a month of their eighteenth birthday. The selective service is a system under which men are called up for military service. Registration is a required citizenship responsibility for men. Do you believe that women should also be required to register for selective service?

Abiding by the Law

Laws are a body of rules or principles, prescribed by authority or established by custom, that a nation, state, or community recognizes as binding on its citizens and institutions. The **U.S. Constitution** is the highest law in the country. States also have constitutions. Cities and counties have **ordinances** (laws, edicts, or decrees enacted by a municipal government for local application).

Each level of government is responsible for certain areas of law. For example, state governments enforce and make traffic laws, regulate marriage and divorce, operate institutions of higher education, regulate public utility rates (gas, electric, and telephone), maintain state highways, license and regulate liquor dispensers, operate mental institutions, and regulate insurance companies.

Local governments enforce public health laws, operate public elementary and high schools, regu-

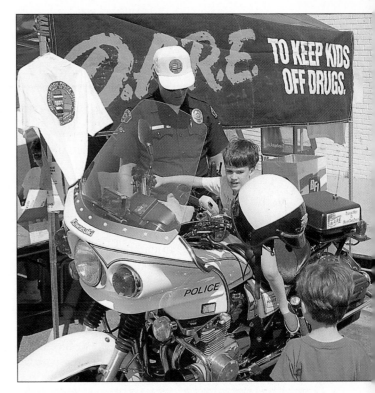

▲ *Many police officers work as hard to prevent crime as they do to enforce laws.*

late traffic, control the standards for constructing and remodeling buildings, and grant permits to bury the dead. Many operate water-purification plants and sewage-disposal systems, collect and dispose of garbage and other wastes, provide fire and police protection, and maintain local roads.

Whether at school, on the job, or while enjoying daily life, laws, established rules, and informal methods (ways of doing things) are meant to protect your rights and provide for your safety. As a responsible citizen, you must obey and respect existing laws.

Taking legitimate action through responsible group activity to change an outdated or unfair law is an act of responsible citizenship. Breaking the law or violating the rights of others to bring about change is irresponsible. When seeking a change in a law, work rule, or school policy, it is important to remember that each citizen's rights and privileges end where his or her neighbor's begin. Can you think of a situation in which one person violated another person's rights in an attempt to bring about change in a law or rule? Can you think of a case in which someone brought about a change without violating the rights of others?

Section 1 GET INVOLVED

Answer the following on a separate sheet of paper, and be prepared to discuss your responses in class.

1. The **Bill of Rights** (the first ten amendments to the U.S. Constitution) was ratified December 15, 1791. It lists and guarantees the fundamental rights and freedoms of U.S. citizenship. Select two of these amendments and explain or give an example of why you believe the privileges they extend are as important today as they were in 1791. What civic duties must you follow in order to receive the privileges cited in these amendments?

2. For a period of one week, scan one or more newspapers, and cut out articles dealing with political leaders at the local, state, or national levels. Divide the articles into two groups: those praising and those criticizing a certain leader's policies, acts, or opinions. Answer the following for each of the leaders you have selected:

   a. What positive or negative effect could the leader's policies, acts, or opinions have on your education, future career, or personal life?

   b. What responsible action could you take to influence the leader's policies, acts, or opinions?

Section 2

Solving Social Problems

The United States faces a broad range of unsolved national and international social problems during the decade of the 1990s. A list of major concerns would include the environment; educational reform; crime, law enforcement, and guns; welfare and poverty; population growth; urbanization; rights of Native Americans; and race relations and prejudice. How do these problems relate to President Eisenhower's statement on the next page? What problems would you add to the list?

Most citizens agree on what the major social problems are, but they frequently disagree on the "right" way to solve them. This can create unfa-vorable side effects, such as **polarization of issues** (seeing one side as totally right or wrong), large-scale protest demonstrations, and violence. However, most citizens agree that the resolution of our nation's social problems is beyond the control of one person or group and requires collective action from all citizens.

Consider the issues described in the remainder of this chapter. Then use the problem-solving approach to resolve them. As you resolve the issues, consider the personal, economic, and career benefits or liabilities that various solutions would have on your family, friends, neighborhood, nation, and yourself. Think about the benefits we will receive as a nation if we resolve these problems, and consider what will happen if we do not. Consider the views of family members, friends, teachers, and politicians about each issue.

The Environment

Modern industry, technology, and agriculture have improved our standard of living and the quality of our lives—but at a high cost to our environment. Many scientists have concluded that many of these improvements even threaten humanity's very existence.

The **Environmental Protection Agency** (EPA), created in 1970, is an independent government agency that is responsible for enforcing federal laws and regulations regarding the environment. This agency has done much to improve the problems facing the environment. However, the solution to environmental problems frequently comes into direct conflict with the goals of individuals and special-interest groups, such as manufacturers, farmers, labor organizations, and construction companies.

Gasoline taxes were originally passed to build and maintain streets, roads, and highways. This tax is charged at a fixed rate for each gallon of gasoline purchased. The revenue obtained from today's gasoline tax is used to defer the cost of numerous government budget items. Keeping these facts in mind, what reasons can you provide to support your position on the following issues?

1. Is the gasoline tax a fair way to pay for services used by all citizens?

2. Is it fair for a trucking, bus, or cab company to pay gasoline taxes that provide revenue for public services other than roads and highways?

3. Is it fair for the wealthy owner of a luxury car to pay the same amount of gasoline tax as an average worker?

4. How would you expect a particular political candidate to stand on this issue? Would most citizens in your classroom agree with you? Why or why not?

▲ *How do you and your family dispose of old motor oil, paint, or lawn and garden chemicals?*

An environmental alarm was sounded throughout the United States in March of 1989. The tanker Exxon Valdez ran aground and spilled an estimated 10 to 11 million gallons of oil off the coast of Alaska. Television brought scenes of oil-soaked birds struggling for life and miles of blackened beaches into millions of American homes. Volunteers, working to save the wildlife and to clean the beaches, were considered by many to be heroes.

The same Americans who were outraged by the Exxon Valdez oil spill quietly poison their im-

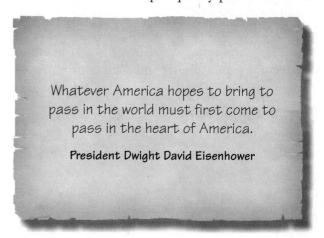

Whatever America hopes to bring to pass in the world must first come to pass in the heart of America.

President Dwight David Eisenhower

mediate environment by dumping more than one hundred million gallons of used motor oil into drains and sewers or on the ground every year.

1. What reasons might explain the general public's double standard regarding commercial oil pollution and public oil pollution?
2. What can society do to solve this problem? How can you help?

Educational Reform

The average new job (in terms of earnings) created in the United States requires a high school diploma plus an additional one and a half years of education or training. Despite this fact, two million students drop out of high school each year to join the growing ranks of unskilled workers.

While 25 percent of American students are dropping out of high school, the 75 percent who graduate are lagging behind the graduating students of several other nations in the areas of mathematics and science proficiency. In addition, the amount of money spent to support public education in the United States lags behind the amount spent in several other nations. The U.S. workforce must compete with these nations in an international economy.

1. Make a list of problems that cause students to drop out of high school. What can society do to help students solve the problems on your list and continue their education and training? How can you help?
2. What reasons might explain the general public's desire to provide youth with high-quality education and training and their continuing opposition to school levies? What can students do to help solve this national problem?

Crime, Law Enforcement, and Guns

Nationwide, reports of school violence are increasing. Deteriorating relationships in families,

schools, and houses of worship are thought to be part of the problem.

In 1991, the U.S. Justice Department reported that 100,000 students bring guns to school every day. Most experts believe that this number is rising. Students sometimes carry weapons to show off, but often they bring weapons to school because of fear.

One nationwide survey asked school administrators for the number of incidents involving guns at their school over a period of two years. Administrators reported a 20 percent increase in gun-related incidents between 1990 and 1991.

School administrators have tried several approaches to prevent students from bringing guns and other weapons to school. Some have installed metal detectors or video cameras or have hired security officers. Others have tried in-school suspension programs, strict dress codes, classes to teach nonviolent conflict resolution, and the prohibition of book bags.

1. If you were a school principal, what action would you take to prevent students from entering your school with guns? Explain the reasoning behind your ideas.
2. Should parents be held accountable for the actions of their children?
3. What could families, houses of worship, schools, and neighborhood groups do to help resolve this problem? How can you help?

Welfare and Poverty

Poverty is determined by income levels known as **poverty thresholds**, which vary by family size. In 1991, more than 35 million people, or 14.2 percent of the total U.S. population, lived below the poverty threshold. Today, families maintained solely by women make up most of those living in poverty. In 1990, the official U.S. poverty thresholds were

- $13,359 for a family of four
- $8,445 for a family of two

- $6,652 for a single adult with no children

Researchers have gathered important information about poverty and welfare. Did you know these facts?

- In 1990, federal, state, and private social welfare expenditures totaled $1.571 trillion.
- One in four of welfare recipients will remain on public assistance for eight years or longer.
- Unmarried teenage mothers are the most likely to be long-term welfare recipients.
- According to the National Center for Health Statistics, more than 25 percent of America's children were born to unmarried mothers in 1990. This percentage continues to rise.
- Most mothers receiving welfare are poorly educated and have little training, few job skills, and low earning power.

Births to unmarried mothers, increasing childhood poverty, expanding welfare rolls, and numerous other social problems are related, according to social scientists. Children growing up in poverty have different experiences, values, and attitudes from those who have never lived in poverty. In addition, poor children are ill-nourished and more likely to be exposed to crime and violence than their more-fortunate counterparts.

1. If you were a U.S. senator, what action would you take to increase future employment opportunities and to raise the living standard of children who currently live at or below the poverty level? What would you do if you were the local superintendent of schools? an unmarried mother receiving welfare? an unmarried father? a married, middle-class wage-earner with two children? Give your reasons for each situation.

Population Growth

Global population increases are on a collision course with food supplies, fresh water, and other resources necessary to sustain life. Because of overfishing, most of the world's fisheries are un-

▲ *Finding a solution to the issue of public welfare has sharply divided American voters.*

able to increase production levels, and others report declining production. Worldwide grain production has slowed to modest annual increases. Contaminated water causes the death of five million children under five every year.

The U.S. population is projected to increase from 255 million in 1993 to 383 million in 2051. That's 128 million more people to be fed, housed, educated, and employed in the next half century.

In 1970, six countries had more than 100 million inhabitants. Nine more will reach this mark by 2020. The rate of natural increase is four times as high in the developing world as in the developed world. However, in developing regions, life expectancy is lower, and infant **mortality** (death rate) is higher (Figure 21.2 on the next page).

1. What effect do you think population density has on health, education, social, and employment conditions in each of the areas mentioned in Figure 21.2 on the next page?
2. As the world population increases, how will people obtain enough safe water, food, medical

	Life Expectancy at Birth (Years)	Infant Deaths per 1,000 Live Births
World	63	65
Sub-Saharan Africa	52	104
Near East/ North Africa	66	65
Asia	62	66
Latin America/ Caribbean	68	50
North America/ Europe	74	14
Japan	79	4
Nigeria	49	—
Bangladesh	—	118

▲ *Figure 21.2 Life Expectancy and Infant Mortality around the World.*

care, and housing? What effect will a developing nation's success or failure to fill these needs have on its ability to participate in the world economy?

Urbanization

In less than a hundred years, the population of the United States has shifted from mostly rural to mostly urban. Two major reasons for this shift have been job opportunities and lifestyles. For millions of urban residents, the population shift from the country to the city hasn't helped them fulfill their dream of economic prosperity and a good life.

Several social problems have developed as a result of a growing urban population. Areas with a high **population density** (the population of an area, divided by its square miles) have problems with congestion, pollution, housing, traffic, social anonymity, and crime. Many people feel that **social anonymity** (lacking individuality) and the increased pace of urban life are **detrimental** (damaging) to good mental health. Many people consider metropolitan city living to be undesirable and unsafe.

1. If you were the mayor of a large city, what action would you take to relieve the problems of pollution, crime, homelessness, and unemployment? What groups of people and institutions would you ask for help? What could they do?

2. Many people believe that eliminating social anonymity and developing a sense of community involvement would eliminate many urban problems. What could individual urban citizens do to reduce social anonymity? How could schools, houses of worship, law-enforcement agencies, and organized neighborhood groups help? Explain the reasoning for your answers.

Rights of Native Americans

An estimated two million Native Americans are members of approximately 350 federally recognized tribes. They have a unique status with the federal government because of the recognition that they are nations within a nation. Indeed, approximately 250 treaties recognize Native Americans as special entities—sovereign nations.

Despite legal agreements with the federal government, Native Americans are underrepresented, underserved, and frequently unrecognized in the United States.

1. Imagine that you have been appointed chairperson of a government committee with responsibility for correcting the social and legal injustices suffered by Native Americans. You will have a very small budget. How will you identify the concerns of Native Americans? What types of action can your committee take with very little money?

Race Relations and Prejudice

As you learned in Chapter 3, most social attitudes are *not* based on personal experience. Instead, they are determined by particular social influences, such as family, friends, and the media.

An attitude becomes a prejudice when an individual's thoughts, feelings, and behaviors become fixed and immune to new information and experiences. A prejudice seems valid (true) in one's own mind without proof or evidence.

Racial prejudice has the best chance of being reduced in an interracial situation in which participants:

- have equal status
- will benefit from cooperation
- view members of different racial groups as individuals
- experience close personal interaction with one another

Racism is probably our most destructive urban problem. Racial attitudes reach many areas of thought, making race a very complicated, intense, and emotional subject. Racial and ethnic attitudes toward people whose skin color, language, religion, or customs are different from our own frequently bring out our strongest feelings and emotions. This problem is more complicated than it should be because of widespread misconceptions (false ideas).

1. Make a list of positive and negative racial situations that have occurred in your state, community, or school. Did racial prejudice influence the outcome of any of these situations? If so, how? Could participants of any of these situations have reduced the level of racial prejudice? If so, how?

2. Despite civil rights legislation, racial prejudice occurs in the workplace. What can employers and workers do to reduce racial prejudice on the job?

▲ *Many urban communities have several ethnic or racial neighborhoods.*

Section 2 GET INVOLVED

Answer the following on a separate sheet of paper, and be prepared to discuss your responses in class.

1. Which of the social problems described in this section have the greatest effect on your personal life? What solutions would you offer for these problems? What individuals or groups would probably support your solutions? Why? What individuals or groups would probably oppose your solutions? Why?

2. List the social problems described in this chapter. Name three occupations that are affected by each problem or involved in a possible solution. Describe how each occupation is affected or involved.

3. Have you ever changed your attitude about an issue that you felt very strongly about? Explain your answer.

.I.M.P.O.R.T.A.N.T. .F.A.C.T.S

Where Are All the Voters?

More than one-third of the U.S. voting-age population lives in only five states. Here are the top states in terms of number of voting-age people, in millions, and each state's voting-age population as a percentage of the U.S. total:

California	12.0 percent
New York	7.2 percent
Texas	6.6 percent
Florida	5.6 percent
Pennsylvania	4.8 percent

Source: U.S. Department of Commerce, Bureau of the Census, 1992.

New York City Isn't So Crowded

Among the world's seven largest cities, New York City is the least crowded. The following table shows the number of people per square mile in seven cities around the world in 1991. Cities are ranked by population size.

City		Number of People per Square Mile
Tokyo–Yokohama,	Japan	25,018
Mexico City,	Mexico	40,037
São Paulo,	Brazil	41,466
Seoul,	Korea	49,101
New York City,	United States	11,480
Osaka–Kobe–Kyoto,	Japan	28,025
Bombay,	India	127,461

Source: U.S. Department of Commerce, SB/92-9.

The Environment

- Emissions testing for motor vehicles is likely to spread as tighter Clean Air Act rules take effect. Consumers will face increased repair costs because the new test will reveal many more problems.
- Making the surfaces of buildings and homes lighter in color could save two billion dollars a year in cooling costs nationwide.
- Steel was the most widely recycled material in the United States in 1990.
- Paper and paperboard are the most recycled items typically found in municipal trash.
- A small amount of the biodegradable packaging thrown away decomposes within ten years.

Source: Environmental Protection Agency and a Roper survey.

Citizenship Defined

The Fourteenth Amendment to the Constitution of the United States, ratified July 28, 1868, states in part: All persons born or naturalized in the United States, and subject to the jurisdiction thereof, are citizens of the United States and of the State wherein they reside. No State shall make or enforce any law which shall abridge the privileges or immunities of citizens of the United States; nor shall any State deprive any person of life, liberty, or property, without due process of law; nor deny to any person within its jurisdiction the equal protection of the laws.

Sister Suffragettes, Thanks!

Until the Nineteenth Amendment to the Constitution was ratified on August 26, 1920, the right to vote was granted only to male citizens. The amendment states: "The right of citizens of the United States to vote shall not be denied or abridged by the United States or by any State on account of sex." More women than men voted in national elections in 1980, 1984, 1988, and 1992.

Is There Room for More?

It has taken only about forty years for the world's population to more than double, from under 2.6 billion in 1950 to 5.4 billion in mid-1991. By 2020, the world's population is projected to reach 8.2 billion.

Source: U.S. Bureau of the Census.

CHAPTER 21 REVIEW

ENRICH YOUR VOCABULARY

On a separate sheet of paper, number from 1 to 18, and complete the following activity. (Do not write in your textbook.) Match each statement below with the most appropriate term from the "Enrich Your Vocabulary" list at the beginning of the chapter by writing that term next to the correct statement.

1. The rights and privileges enjoyed by all citizens and their duties to the laws and policies of the community, state, and nation in which they live
2. A tax based on property owned
3. Income
4. The highest law in the United States
5. Laws, edicts, or decrees enacted by a municipal government for local application
6. The income levels that determine poverty
7. The population of an area divided by its square miles
8. The first ten amendments to the U.S. Constitution
9. Newspapers, magazines, television, and radio
10. A body of rules or principles, prescribed by authority or established by custom, that a nation, state, or community recognizes as binding on its citizens and institutions
11. A tax based on how much is earned
12. Seeing one side as totally right or wrong
13. Death rate
14. Damaging
15. Lacking individuality
16. Indifference
17. An independent government agency that is responsible for enforcing federal laws and regulations regarding the environment
18. Appealing leadership quality

CHECK YOUR KNOWLEDGE

On a separate sheet of paper, complete the following activity. (Do not write in your textbook.)

1. List at least four ways that responsible citizenship can be demonstrated.
2. What are the only requirements placed on voting in the United States?
3. List at least four services supported by tax money.
4. In 1991, approximately how many people lived below the poverty level?
5. Of the countries listed in Figure 21.2 on page 480, what is the difference in years between the country with the highest life expectancy and the one with the lowest life expectancy?
6. List five social problems associated with areas of high population density.
7. How are most social attitudes determined?
8. When does an attitude become a prejudice?

DEVELOP SCANS COMPETENCIES

Government experts say that successful workers can productively use Resources, Interpersonal skills, Information, Systems, and Technology. This activity will give you practice in developing Information and Interpersonal skills.

In a cooperative learning group, decide whether you agree or disagree with the statement: For every right we have as an American citizen, there is also a responsibility.

In your group, assign members to find and list rights we have as American citizens. Some of the rights you may want to list include freedom of speech, freedom of the press, freedom of religion, right to a trial by an impartial jury, and right to privacy.

Assign other members to list responsibilities we have as American citizens. Some of those responsibilities are voting, defending civil rights, paying taxes, attending school, defending the nation, and serving as a witness or a member of a jury.

After all members have completed their lists, combine the lists into one list that shows rights and corresponding responsibilities. (See the chart below for an example.) You may not be able to find a corresponding responsibility for each right.

Right	Responsibility
▪ Trial by an impartial jury	▪ Serving on a jury or as a witness

Your Life and Your Career

Learning Objectives

After completing this chapter, you should be prepared to:

- describe how you have been influenced by the previous stages of your life
- recognize and understand the new personal and career concerns and priorities that are likely to arise during each stage of life
- identify realistic career expectations and make necessary adjustments in your educational plan
- write your unique career philosophy

Enrich Your Vocabulary

In reading this chapter and doing the exercises you will learn the following important terms:

intimacy
generativity
ego integrity
philosophy
career philosophy
deliberate

By now, you have probably developed a career dream—the place you will fill in the world. Now you must find a way to live your dream.

You will need to spend a large part of your daily life acquiring the education and training needed for your future occupation. Talking with people who are already successful in that occupation and visiting their work sites will bring a sense of reality to your dream. Expressing important personal values, building your credentials, and developing occupational skills will elevate your feelings of self-worth.

You are preparing for career success in a rapidly changing world of work. New technology will create new occupations and will eliminate many established occupations. Throughout your career, you will need to continually develop new skills and take advantage of changing opportunities.

As you progress through your teens and into your twenties, more of your important decisions

> Every individual has a place to fill in the world, and is important in some respect, whether he chooses to be so or not.
>
> Nathaniel Hawthorne

will focus on your career, friendships, love relationships, personal values, and lifestyle. During each stage of life, new concerns and priorities will arise in your career and personal life. How you respond to them will determine the place you fill in the world.

The Stages of Life

Take a moment to think about the many physical and psychological changes you have experienced during your lifetime. Think about the changes in your interests, lifestyle, economic concerns, physical appearance, and how you deal with social relationships. This process of personal change will continue during your adult years. Being aware of likely changes will help you to prepare for them in a positive way.

As you grow older, your family, neighborhood, local community, and the greater society will continue to make certain demands regarding your personal and career behavior. How do you presently react to these demands? How does your present behavior help or hinder your preparation for career success?

Learning certain life skills at each stage of your development will help you to grow into a mature person and to be successful in your chosen career.

CAREER TIP

Whether it is fair or not, much of your career success will depend on how well others approve of your attitude and behavior.

During each stage of development, certain areas of physical or psychological growth are expected. Human development stages are not always distinct (easy to recognize) as they overlap and vary in the ages at which we normally pass from one to another.

Certain parts of each developmental stage will be dominant (most influential) at various time periods in your life. Certain behaviors and life skills must be learned before you can grow into the next stage. Can you think of a specific situation where you behave differently than you would have five years ago? How will this behavior change help you in your future career? With advancing stages of maturity, your behaviors will continue to change in positive ways. Every life skill that you learn will pave the way for further personal and career growth. Figure 22.1 on the next page illustrates examples of the stages people commonly pass through at certain ages.

Between birth and age six you learned to walk, feed yourself, talk, and relate emotionally to others, especially parents and siblings. You learned to distinguish right from wrong and started to develop a conscience. You depended on adults to care for most of your needs.

Do you remember when you learned to tie your shoes, stay in the lines as you used crayons in a coloring book, and print your name? How old were you at the time? Five? Six? Did you receive encouragement from a significant adult when you

▲ *Who appears to feel: independent? unsure? cocky? trusting? happy?*

mastered these tasks? Were you proud of what you had accomplished? Your success and mastery of these developmental tasks prepared you for the task of learning to read. Like steps on a ladder, each stage of learning prepared you for the next. Lifelong learning will be an important part of your career success.

Your childhood experiences can tell you a great deal about how you've become the person you are now. Review the stages in Figure 22.1. If you learned to do these things, you are probably a happy, self-confident person and well prepared to move ahead with your career. If you were unsuccessful in getting through certain stages, you are probably not as happy or as self-confident as you could be. Taking time to learn these important life skills will prepare you for the future stages of your life. What occupations can you think of where it would be important to:

1. trust others?

2. manipulate objects?

3. be independent?

The development of conscience (ideas and feelings within a person that give a sense of right and

The child is father to the man.

Author unknown

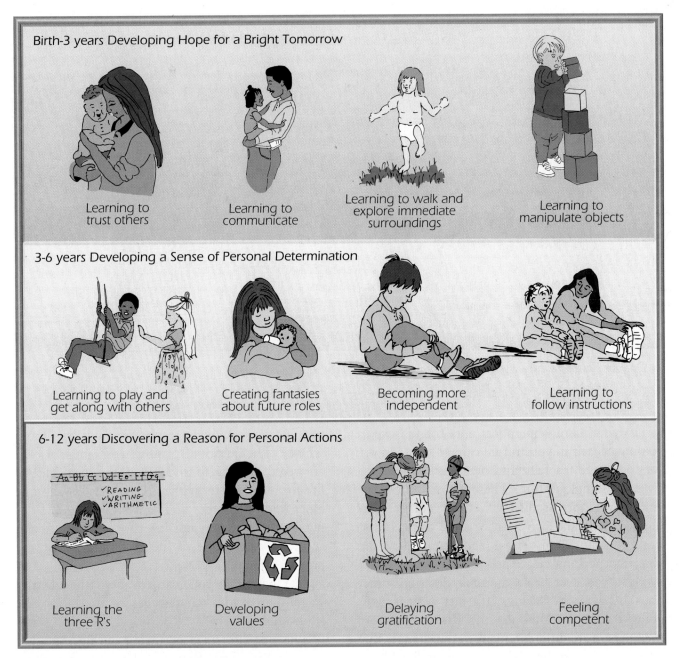

Birth-3 years Developing Hope for a Bright Tomorrow

Learning to
trust others

Learning to
communicate

Learning to walk and
explore immediate
surroundings

Learning to
manipulate objects

3-6 years Developing a Sense of Personal Determination

Learning to play and
get along with others

Creating fantasies
about future roles

Becoming more
independent

Learning to
follow instructions

6-12 years Discovering a Reason for Personal Actions

Learning the
three R's

Developing
values

Delaying
gratification

Feeling
competent

▲ *Figure 22.1 Going Through The Stages.*

wrong), a personal perception of fair play, and honesty occur in early childhood. Think back to when you were about six or seven. Did you ever cheat at a game, tell on a brother or sister so they would get in trouble, or misbehave when your teacher left the room? Sooner or later, most children get "caught" and are reprimanded for behaviors like these by a disapproving adult. Getting a reprimand instead of approval helps a child learn what is ethically and morally accepted as right or wrong. The child uses the sense of right and wrong learned in childhood situations as a foundation for his or her personal values. Is it important for all workers to have a sense of right and wrong or is it only important for workers in certain occupations? Why?

▲ *Do your classmates expect you to have a successful career? Why or why not?*

Do your family members and friends expect you to succeed in your future career? How do you suppose your teachers and neighbors would answer the same question? The most influential environmental factors that will effect your personal development and career success are the expectations of your home, school, and community, and your interpersonal relationships.

Have you ever heard an adult describe someone's behavior by saying, "It's just a stage she's going through"? Although the characteristics of each person are different, many of the changes that take place during the adult years are predictable.

You have probably noticed that some students in your class are more mature than others. In fact, they have mastered more social, physical, and psychological life skills than others. Although some people develop faster than others, young and old alike pass through a series of events, called *life stages*, at about the same age.

Imagine a stranger approaching a Chicago resident and asking, "How long does it take to drive to Chicago?" A likely response would be, "From where?" The question "from where?" must also be answered in order to understand the next stage of life for a certain individual. Like a wall, with one block laid on another and each layer of blocks depending on the previous layer for its strength and accuracy, each stage of life is influenced by the previous stages.

In Chapter 1, you learned about the identity stage. Three additional stages occur during the adult years.

The first life stage occurring during the adult years is **intimacy**. Between the ages of twenty-three and twenty-eight, most adults establish a unique sense of self that is separate from their original families. This separation is necessary in order to expand one's personal identity through friendships, love relationships, and career experiences.

Recognizing that you are an independent, responsible, productive adult should provide satisfaction for you and your parents. It is important for all of you to accept the fact that you will al-

BUILDING SELF-ESTEEM

Who Is Robert?

Robert Wilson lives with his parents and an older brother. His parents have always provided him with a stable, loving home. As far back as Robert can remember, his parents encouraged him to acquire a good education. Robert knew that he was expected to be a successful, professional person.

When Robert was a young child, his parents expected him to stay home and study when his neighborhood friends invited him to play ball or go swimming. However, when he earned high grades, they would celebrate by taking him to an amusement park or on a special vacation.

At age eleven, Robert wanted to take a part-time job and earn money for a bicycle, but his parents refused to give him permission. However, on his next birthday, they gave him a more expensive bicycle than he had ever dreamed of owning.

As Robert grew older, he received fewer and fewer invitations. Other than school activities, he was rarely involved with people his own age. Instead, he spent his time reading, watching television, and working on school assignments.

Robert graduated from college eight years ago. Although he is a very successful chemist, he still lives with his parents. He would like to marry, but meeting women and dating are very difficult for him. Robert knows many people, but most of them have families of their own, and he only sees them socially every year or so. Robert frequently feels very lonely.

Critical Thinking

1. Did Robert develop a sense of his own identity? Did Robert's parents love him? Did he love them? Use the information provided in this case study to support your answers.

2. Imagine that you are Robert's childhood friend. He has shared his feeling of social isolation with you and wants your advice. After considering the information you have learned about the life stage of intimacy, what advice would you give Robert?

---

ways be a son or a daughter, but you will never be a child again.

Maintaining a two-way bridge of love and communication provides a sense of security for parents as well as for their sons and daughters. However, each person must accept responsibility for his or her own friendships, love relationships, and career path.

Have you ever heard people refer to the broad range of time between the late twenties and the middle sixties as "the working years"? This is the life stage of **generativity**. During these years, adults who have mastered the life skills of the intimacy stage and the five stages preceding it

• Are productive in the world of work

• Develop families of their own

• Seek truth by reexamining personal beliefs and values

• Assume the role of caretaker for the knowledge and products of past generations

• Prepare the next generation for social and career roles

Like a winding brook, tumbling through a rapidly changing environment, the mature adult flows through the working years with a sense of caring, purpose, and confidence in the next generation. However, just as a stream of water can be dammed and the remaining water left to stagnate, a person who is unable to find satisfaction during

▲ *Alex and Wanda were well prepared to become parents. What could you do to prepare for the life stage called generativity?*

the working years will accept mediocrity, boredom, and self-interest.

When the working years are over, those of us who were cared for as children, and in turn cared for others, are able to accept the final years of life without fear. This last stage of life is called **ego integrity** (a sense of involvement and worth). Learning, growing, and experiencing the first seven stages of life bring a wisdom that enables us to accept the cycle of helplessness that comes at the end of our life, even as it did in the beginning.

The wisdom of ego integrity can truly make the last years of life the golden years—golden for the younger person who seeks wisdom from the older person, and golden for the older person who feels a sense of worth and involvement.

Unfortunately, many older people complete the working years without learning the important life skills. Suspicious of others, lacking in faith and confidence, without meaningful work, love, or friends, they approach the final years of life with a sense of despair and a fear of death.

Section 1 GET INVOLVED

Answer the following on a separate sheet of paper, and be prepared to discuss your responses in class.

1. Observe friends and relatives who are in the stages of intimacy, generativity, or ego integrity. What characteristics mentioned in this section can you identify in your friends and relatives?

2. Make a list of personal characteristics that you hope to display during the stages of intimacy, generativity, and ego integrity.

Section 2

Your Career Philosophy

The word **philosophy** comes from the composite Greek noun *philosophia*, which means "the pursuit of wisdom." *Sophia* suggests wide knowledge and sound judgment about the value of different things in life.

Your **career philosophy** is the **deliberate** (carefully considered) involvement of your personal beliefs and behaviors in these areas:

- Choosing an occupation
- Acquiring the necessary education and training for the occupation
- Performing day-to-day work tasks
- Planning a career that might include several occupations

Just as water must be filtered through coffee grinds to produce a unique beverage, your life ex-periences must be filtered through your inner values, interests, and attitudes to develop your unique career philosophy. At the same time, your career philosophy cannot ignore the outer pressure from the expectations and standards of family, friends, and society.

Expectations

Do you know a student who expects to attend college, have a professional career, and earn a large salary but is presently failing high school and not exploring career options? People like this are filled with great ambition, but they do not succeed in small, everyday tasks.

Being actively involved in selecting a career and exploring the necessary education and training requirements will help you establish realistic career

▲ *Every high school graduate has his or her career philosophy. What is yours?*

expectations. An exploration of the goals and requirements of high school Tech Prep, cooperative-education, vocational, work-study, and college-preparatory programs will increase your awareness of career options.

Consider your personal life expectations. Do you expect to own a car? If so, will you buy it new or used? Will it be a luxury car, a sports car, or a family car? Do you expect to rent or buy a home? Will it be very expensive, moderately priced, or inexpensive? What type of neighborhood will you live in?

Everyone has expectations from life. Some people expect a lot, and others expect very little. Some have realistic expectations, and others fantasize about the future.

Realistic expectations can be a source of motivation and personal growth. Once you have achieved a goal (satisfied an expectation), a higher-level expectation usually takes its place. On the other hand, failure to achieve your expectations can lower your self-esteem and lead to a lower level of expectations.

Each year, thousands of college diplomas are awarded to students who graduated from a high school Tech Prep, vocational, or work-study program. Many of these college graduates were not considered good students when they entered high school. Discovering a career goal and being successful in their high school programs caused them to raise the level of their expectations.

Adjustments

It is normal for people to make adjustments and change certain expectations during the span of their working years. Marriage, the birth of a child, a layoff, children going to college and leaving home, the death of a loved one, and retirement force people to adjust their life expectations. Mature adults understand what can be done, and they adjust to events that are beyond their control.

Section 2 GET INVOLVED

Answer the following on a separate sheet of paper, and be prepared to discuss your responses in class.

1. List any life experiences that have affected you so deeply that you will never forget them. They may be pleasant or unpleasant. How did each of the experiences on your list affect the way you think about careers?

2. Review what you have learned about preparing for career success, and write your own career philosophy. Be sure to include
   - Your views about work, employers, and workers
   - Your important beliefs and how they relate to work, workers, and work sites
   - A list of possible occupations on the career path you are considering
   - The education and training path you are presently considering
   - Any contributions you expect to make to your family, friends, or society through your work
   - Any rewards you expect to receive from your family, friends, or society because of your work

3. List five life expectations that you have already satisfied. Examples include learning to ride a bicycle, getting an A in English, or being selected for the basketball team. Describe any adjustments you made from your original expectations.

4. List the adjustments you have already made with certain expectations because of family problems, economics, race, or gender. Be specific.

5. List your five most important expectations for the next ten years. Of the five, which is most important to you? If you are unable to achieve your most important expectation, what adjustment will you make?

PLANNING MAKES A DIFFERENCE

Glen's Plan for Career Success

Glen Griffin is in his second year at Southview Community College. He will graduate in June with an associate degree in automotive technology. Glen presently works part-time for a major automobile dealer. He recently received three job offers at a career fair. He sometimes considers living in a different part of the country after graduation.

Knowing that his technical job skills are in demand by several potential employers provides Glen with a great deal of personal satisfaction. The career plan he made during his sophomore year of high school has really paid off.

Career choices, education and training requirements, and life goals were the last things on Glen's mind when he entered the tenth grade at Valley High School. Being selected for the varsity basketball team, keeping his grade point average high enough to remain eligible for sports, saving money for a car, and going steady with his girlfriend were Glen's most important goals.

When Glen received his class schedule, he noticed a required one-semester class on career guidance. It sounded interesting, but he didn't know what to expect. Glen was surprised to discover that the class had more than one teacher. The regular teacher, Mrs. Reynolds, was a word-processing teacher for eleventh- and twelfth-grade students. In addition, Glen's guidance counselor and several speakers from the business community helped Mrs. Reynolds. Glen found the guest speakers to be especially interesting.

When the course was over, Glen's counselor asked him if he would mind being interviewed by the school guidance committee. The committee wanted to know what the students thought about the new career course. Glen agreed to the interview. He was a little nervous that evening when he met the entire committee. Two of the community people had been speakers in his class. Glen was well prepared and presented the committee with the following list of features of the career-guidance class that he had found useful:

- Reviewing school courses he liked and disliked and taking a realistic look at his ability to succeed in various courses
- Taking a career assessment to learn more about his personal interests, aptitudes, and skills
- Relating his personal characteristics to various occupations
- Learning how to use occupational information systems (his class used the Occupational Outlook Handbook and a computerized career information system)
- Understanding the different high school programs he could take in the eleventh and twelfth grades (Valley High offered a choice of several Tech Prep programs, a college-preparatory course, and work study)
- Writing a career plan during the last three weeks of the career-guidance class; the plan included tentative choices of high school programs for grades eleven and twelve

Glen explained to the committee that he had narrowed his eleventh and twelfth grade choices to three programs: Tech Prep automotive, Tech Prep instrument repair, and college preparatory.

Critical Thinking

1. How did Glen's career expectations change during the tenth grade?
2. What adjustments did Glen make in his educational plans?

CHAPTER 22 REVIEW

ENRICH YOUR VOCABULARY

On a separate sheet of paper, number from 1 to 6, and complete the following activity. (Do not write in your textbook.) Match each statement below with the most appropriate term from the "Enrich Your Vocabulary" list at the beginning of the chapter by writing that term next to the correct statement.

1. A life stage during which adults are productive in the world of work and develop families of their own.
2. A word derived from the Greek noun meaning "the pursuit of wisdom"
3. A life stage during which adults are close and familiar

4. The deliberate involvement of personal beliefs and behaviors in planning, choosing, acquiring, and performing a career
5. A life stage that, when mastered, brings wisdom
6. Carefully considered

CHECK YOUR KNOWLEDGE

On a separate sheet of paper, complete the following activity. (Do not write in your textbook.)

1. Many, if not most, workers will need to develop new skills and take advantage of changing opportunities throughout their careers. Why?
2. What is the first life stage that occurs during the adult years?
3. Name three life situations that can expand an individual's personal identity.

4. List five tasks of the generativity stage.
5. What is ego integrity?
6. List three high school programs that will increase your awareness of career options.
7. Four components of a career philosophy are related to personal beliefs and behaviors. Name them.

DEVELOP SCANS COMPETENCIES

Government experts say that successful workers can productively use Resources, Interpersonal skills, Information, Systems, and Technology. This activity will give you practice in developing Resource and Information skills.

Develop a time line of your life. To begin, categorize at least 20 different events in your life under the following heads: physical development, intellectual development, and social and personality development. These events should show growth on your part. See the chart for some examples.

After you have categorized the events, try to determine what age you were at the time of the event. You may need to ask your parents or other family members for help.

Then, transfer the information to a time line of your life. You may add pictures to accompany the information on the time line.

Continue the time line into the future. Think about what you plan to be doing in 5, 10, or 15

years. Will you go to college or trade school? If so, where will you go? What type of job would you like to have? Will you be married? Will you have children? Add pictures to this part of the time line, also.

Physical Development	Intellectual Development	Social and Personality Development
• learning to walk • learning to ride a bike	• learning to talk • learning to read	• developing interest in opposite sex

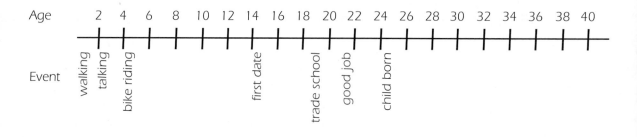

Glossary

A

ability how well a person performs a specific task

absolute earnings the amount of goods and services a person can buy with his or her income

accredited a qualification for a school stating that it has met certain minimum standards for its program of study, staff, and facilities

accrued accumulated

acquisition the purchase of one organization by another

active vocabulary words a person uses in speech or writing

aerobic with oxygen

aggressive to dominate a situation without regard to others' feelings or wishes; unfriendly, domineering, relentless

antitrust laws laws formed to prevent businesses from forming monopolies

apathy indifference; not caring about something

apprenticeship a relationship between an employer and an employee during which the beginning worker, or apprentice, learns a trade

aptitude a person's potential for success in performing a certain activity

arbitrator an objective, third-party expert used to help solve disputes

assertive the ability to express one's feelings and beliefs without being rude or ignoring the rights of others; persistent, understanding, cooperative

assets what a business owns or is owed to the business

ASVAB (Armed Services Aptitude Battery) a group of twelve tests that measure a person's aptitudes in five broad career fields

ATP a sort of chemical fuel formed when the body breaks down carbohydrates and fats

attitude the way a person thinks about things and reacts towards others

authority style of decision making when a person relies on another person to make decisions for him or her

avocation a constructive activity that provides personal satisfaction but does not provide a main source of income

B

baccalaureate degree a four-year degree in a certain subject; also called a bachelor's degree

background check an investigation to verify information, such as former employers, schools attended, and personal references, provided by a prospective employee on a job application form

balance sheet the summary of assets, liabilities, and net worth of a company

bank statement a bank report that shows the status of a depositor's account

base pay the regular salary or wage, excluding incentive pay, bonuses, fringe benefits, overtime pay, and all other extra compensation

bond a type of insurance that pays financial losses if an employee fails to perform his or her duty or is guilty of theft

bounced check a check that has been written when there are insufficient funds in a person's account

budget a plan for saving and spending income

business letter a written document sent to someone outside of a company, usually formal in style and tone

C

calorie the amount of heat needed to raise the temperature of one gram of water one degree centigrade

canceled check a check that has been paid by a bank

cardiorespiratory endurance the ability to deliver oxygen and nutrients to tissues and to remove wastes

career the paid and unpaid work a person does during his or her lifetime

career advancement moving up in an organization in relation to job responsibilities, title, and salary

career philosophy the deliberate involvement of your personal beliefs in choosing a career, acquiring necessary education and training, performing daily work tasks, and planning a career that may include several occupations

cash flow the amount of money available in a business at a specific time

CBERA a trade and tax law to help solve economic problems of the Caribbean Basin region through the granting of favored nation trade status

certificate of deposit a savings plan in which a bank agrees to pay back the money invested, plus a specific rate of interest, on a certain date

character a person's sense of morality and the ethical code by which he or she lives

charisma appealing leadership quality

check an order written by a depositor directing the bank to pay out money

check register portion of a checkbook where a person records checks that have been written and withdrawals and deposits that have been made

chronological résumé a résumé that lists the jobs a person has held in order from most recent work experience to earliest work experience

civic responsibility the rights and privileges enjoyed by all citizens and their duties to the laws and policies of the community, state, and nation in which they live

Civil Rights Act of 1964 an act passed by Congress which prohibits employers from discriminating on the basis of sex, race, color, religion, or national origin

civil service examination a pre-employment test developed by the federal government for specific government jobs

classification the groupings into which a large number of occupations is divided

co-workers people with similar job status, skills, and work load who work together and rely on each other to complete work assignments

COBRA (Consolidated Omnibus Budget Reconciliation Act) law to provide terminated employees or those who lose insurance coverage because of reduced work to be able to buy group insurance for themselves and their families for a limited amount of time

collective bargaining the negotiating process between labor unions and employers

commissions compensation to salespeople based on a predetermined percentage of the salesperson's sales volume

communication sending and receiving messages; an exchange of thoughts, ideas, and beliefs between two or more people

comparable worth deregulation when types of work, which are different in content, are found to be equal, and deserving of equal pay, because of similar education, preparation, experience, skill, and responsibility

comparative advantage the ability of a producer to provide a good or service at a lower opportunity cost than other producers

competence to be capable of performing a task correctly

competencies qualifications for a job or career

competition when a business, in a market economy, strives to win customers by offering lower prices or better quality than its competitors

components parts that make up the whole

compounding interest paying interest on interest that has already been earned

compromise when each member of a negotiation gives up some of its demands and meets the other side halfway

computerized career information systems large databases that allow people to explore and clarify career and occupational information

conciliating bringing others together; pacifying; winning over

conflict a clash or struggle that sometimes occurs when individuals or groups have different points of view

consequences the good or bad results of a decision

consumer a person or group that buys or uses goods or services to satisfy personal needs and wants

context the words that surround a particular word or passage that can shed light on the meaning of the word or passage

contingent workers part-time, temporary, contractual, and leased employees

contradictory showing an opposing point of view

corporate culture the thoughts, feelings, manners, and sense of good taste each business or organization develops

corporation a business owned by a number of people and operated under a state-issued license or charter

correspondence courses educational courses that are completed at home at the student's own pace

cost-of-living adjustments (COLAs) changes to wages or salaries in accordance with changes in the cost-of-living index

courtship the process of seeking someone's affection

cover letter a letter regarding interest in a specific job opening that accompanies the résumé, introducing the job seeker to the prospective employer

creative orientation when a person uses his or her feelings, imagination, and intuition to react to social and work situations; has good spatial perception, eye-hand coordination, musical and writing skills; introspective ability; and dislikes rigid rules of society

credit capacity the amount of debt a person can afford to repay each month

credit history a record of how a person has borrowed and repaid debts

credit unions nonprofit banking services that employees may join

creditors people who lend money

culture the way of life in the society in which you live

D

dating the process of having social engagements with members of the opposite sex

deductions money taken from an employee's gross income to pay taxes, health insurance expenses, etc.

delay gratification to postpone the acquisition of certain things or participation in certain activities to complete training or education that will result in a better future

deliberate carefully considered and acted upon

demand the willingness of consumers to buy goods or services at a certain price in the marketplace

deposit slip a record of the money put into an account

deregulation elimination of government controls

detrimental damaging

Dictionary of Occupational Titles a Department of Labor publication containing a definition and brief description of more than 25 thousand occupations that can be used to research a specific occupation or group of occupations

diet the food and drink a person customarily consumes

direct compensation the part of a paycheck that provides the worker with a source of cash

discharge dismissal from employment

downsizing reduction in an organization's size to increase efficiency

drudgery dull and tedious labor

drug any chemical substance that brings about physical, emotional, or mental changes in people

drug abuse the use of a legal or illegal drug that causes physical, mental, emotional, or social harm to the user or to others

E

economic system the method a society uses to determine how it will use and distribute available resources

economics the name of the social science concerned with the way a society uses its productive resources to fulfill the needs and wants of each member

ego integrity mastery of this 8th stage of life brings wisdom; failure results in despair

electronic funds transfer system a computer-run system that lets consumers, businesses, and governments transfer money from one account to another by electronic means

empathy the ability to understand another person's feelings and motives

empathizing sharing another's thoughts and feelings

employment eligibility verification form a document required of employers to verify a worker's eligibility to be employed in the United States

employment outlook present and future employment trends

employment service any service that helps a job seeker find employment

employment structure the types of job available in the job market

endorsement the signature of the payee on the back of a check, enabling the check to be cashed; acknowledgement of receiving the sum of money specified

entrepreneurship small-business ownership

entry level the lowest level of a job, requiring the lowest amount of experience

environment the circumstances, objects, or conditions by which a person is surrounded

environmental orientation when a person prefers physical activity in the outdoor environment; tend to be frank, open, and natural doer rather than talkers; practical and use self-control in tense situations

Environmental Protection Agency federal agency that is responsible for enforcing federal laws and regulations regarding the environment

equal pay to be paid the same amount as one's co-workers, regardless of age, sex, or race

Equal Pay Act of 1963 an act passed by Congress that requires employers to pay equal wages within the organization to men and women doing equal work on jobs requiring equal skill, effort, and responsibility, which are performed under similar working conditions

ethics the unwritten rules governing the code of values of a person, an organization, or a society; the standard of what is right and what is wrong

etiquette socially acceptable manners

exempt to be free from a rule

F

facilitate to encourage or make something easier to accomplish

fair employment program program similar to an affirmative-action program in which employers may be required to hire minorities, women, or the physically challenged

Fair Labor Standards Act important federal legislation that includes laws which protect all workers, including minors

Family and Medical Leave Act of 1993 a federal act that gives employees up to twelve weeks of unpaid leave from their jobs to deal with a birth, adoption, or medical emergency in the family

fatalistic style of decision making believing that whatever a person decides will happen anyway

federal income tax taxes paid to the federal government based on a person's earnings

Federal Reserve System a network of twelve regional banks that regulates the banking in the United States by increasing or decreasing the amount of money in our economy and by setting the interest rate charged to commercial banks

feedback a reaction or response to what is said, including verbal and nonverbal communication

felony a serious crime

flexibility the ability to move joints and use muscles through their full range of motion

flextime a plan in which an employee's total number of work hours is set, but the worker can choose when he or she works those hours

fluctuating irregular, changing, unsteady

Food and Drug Administration federal agency that enforces laws and regulations concerning the purity, quality, and labeling of food, drugs, and cosmetics

Food Guide Pyramid an outline of what to eat each day to put good dietary guidelines into action

franchise a business that has a legal contract to operate using an established name and method of production

fraud intentional misrepresentation of a product or service

free enterprise system economic system in which people may own the means of production, have the freedom to use them as they see fit, and may freely create and operate businesses

fringe benefits forms of compensation paid to an employee other than wages or salary

full potential to reach the highest level of productivity; completely efficient

full-time job a job consisting of forty hours per week that requires a major commitment of time and labor

functional résumé a résumé that highlights qualifications, skills, and accomplishments over dates and jobs held

G

GATB (General Aptitude Test Battery) a test which suggests job clusters for which a person shows strong aptitudes

GED a general equivalency diploma that states a person has passed a five-part test in the areas of writing, social studies, science, reading, and math; equal to a high school diploma

gender identity sexual identity; a person knowing that their sex is permanent and cannot be changed

general ledger the principal book of accounts containing the final entries of assets and liabilities

generativity stage of human development often referred to as the "working years"; between a person's late twenties and early sixties, when he or she is productive in the world of work, develop a family, reexamine personal beliefs and values

generic brands having no trademark

glass ceiling an artificial barrier to career advancement faced by women and minorities

goal an aim or objective to be accomplished in a certain amount of time

goods-producing sector the percentage of total employment including mining, construction, and manufacturing

grievances differences of opinion over how contract provisions should be interpreted

gross domestic product the total value of goods and services that a nation produces for the marketplace during a specific time period

gross earnings total earnings before deductions

Guide for Occupational Exploration a Department of Labor occupational reference publication that focuses on twelve clearly defined interest areas

guilds worker unions of craftsmen

H

health maintenance organization a combination of an insurance company and a doctor or hospital, providing both coverage for medical bills and actual health-care services

health certificate document that certifies that an employee is free of specific infectious diseases and certain drugs

heredity the transmission of physical and mental characteristics from parent to child

hospitalization insurance insurance that covers hospital room and board, medication, tests, and services

human relationships the personal connections people develop with others through their thoughts and behaviors

I

image consultants people who help others project a desired image through their outward appearance

impulsive style of decision making making decisions without thinking about them or their consequences

incentives extra financial payments for production above a predetermined standard; may include profit sharing, bonuses, or gain sharing

industrial products goods that are produced for and sold to other producers

inflection a change in tone or pitch of a person's voice used to convey meaning

initial screening an interview used by an employment agency to eliminate job seekers who are obviously unsuited for a particular job opening

initiative readiness and ability to take the first steps in a project

insider abuse a worker using knowledge obtained as a result of his or her position for personal gain

insurance the act, system, or business of guaranteeing property or a person against loss or harm arising in specified occurrences, such as fire, accident, death, or loss of income, in exchange for a payment proportional to the risk involved

interdependence to depend on a group that depends on you

achieving the highest level of human relationships in the world of work

interest amounts lenders pay for use of customer's or a bank's money

interest surveys tests that measure a person's interests and then match those interests with work activities or situations experienced in certain occupations

interests the preferences a person has for specific topics or activities

intimacy the first stage of life occurring in the adult years

introspective ability skill to examine one's own thoughts and feelings

intuitive style of decision making to make a decision based on the choice that feels best and seems like the right thing to do

invoice price manufacturer's initial charge to a car dealer

J

job applicant a person who applies for employment with a specific company

job application form form used by an employer used to gain the facts (personal information, education, previous employment, and references) about a prospective employee

Job Corps federally administered employment and training program serving severely disadvantaged young people, ages sixteen to twenty-one

job fair gathering attended by several potential employers who can distribute information about their organization and briefly discuss career opportunities with interested job seekers

job interview opportunity for a prospective employee to present himself or herself personally to the employer

job jargon abbreviations used in job advertisements to get as much information as possible into limited space

job lead information about an organization that is hiring new employees and the name of the person who is responsible for hiring

job market the type and number of jobs available at one specific time

job offer a specific offer of employment at a company

job orientation meetings and activities to acquaint a new employee with an employer's purpose and organization

job search the process of looking for employment

job security protection against loss of employment and earnings

journey worker a certified, experienced, skilled craftsperson who has successfully completed an apprenticeship

L

labor union an organization that represents workers in negotiations regarding employee rights

laws body of rules or principles, prescribed by authority or established by custom, that a nation, state, or community recognizes as binding on its citizens and institutions

layoff an involuntary separation of the employee from the employer for a temporary or indefinite period, through no fault of the employee

lease a contract that involves a financial commitment on a rental for a specific amount of time

legitimate absence when an employee must miss work for a reason that is acceptable to the employer

leisure time time free from every-day job responsibilities during which a person can pursue personal interests and hobbies

liabilities what a business owes

liability coverage insurance to cover bodily injuries, property damages, and medical expenses for others when the policyholder is at fault

life experiences significant events in a person's life that affects his or her actions and attitudes

lifestyle the way a person lives his or her life, including geographic location, type of home, method of transportation, and social situations

limited resources natural resources, labor, capital, and management; resources found in limited quantities

line of progression steps that employees follow from lower- to higher-level positions

love feelings of warm, personal attachment, pleasure, and deep affection

M

mandated to be required

manuals handbooks detailing the use or repair of equipment or describing procedures to be followed on a job

market a group of people or organizations that purchase a particular good or service

materialistic something that has monetary worth

maternity leave disability leave granted to women as a result of pregnancy or childbirth or to care for a newborn or newly adopted child

mechanical orientation when a person prefers work involving machines, tools, and logic; has

good spatial perception; and is practical and physical in his or her approach to problem solving

media newspapers, magazines, television, and radio

memorandum a note sent within a company used to aid the memory of the recipient, usually concerning office matters in a company

mentor a trusted advisor

mergers the joining together of organizations to form one company

merit increase an increase in a worker's pay rate, usually given on the basis of such criteria as efficiency or performance

merit rating a formal, periodic, written evaluation of a worker's job performance

minimum wage the lowest wage an employer may pay for certain types of work

mommy track the time when a woman changes her work schedule to accommodate her young child or children

monitor to supervise or check for accuracy

monopolies a situation in which only one business offers a product for sale with no competition

Monroney sticker label required to be on all new vehicles stating the base price, the manufacturer's installed options, the manufacturer's suggested retail price, the manufacturer's transportation charge, and the fuel economy

moonlighting working two jobs

mortality the death rate

muscular endurance the ability of a muscle or a group of muscles to sustain repeated contractions or to continue applying force against a fixed object

muscular strength the ability of a muscle to exert force for a brief period of time

N

negative attitude to view a job as drudgery or as a responsibility that must be filled; frequently complaining, being critical, having careless work habits, and being indifferent to the needs of others

negotiation bargaining through persuasion rather than argument to resolve disputes between two or more individuals or groups

net pay the amount of money an employee receives after deductions

net worth the difference between the value of a business's assets and liabilities

networking using personal contacts to find a job

NLRB (National Labor Relations Board) an independent federal agency that was established in 1935 to administer the National Labor Relations Act, an act created to serve the public's interest by reducing interruptions in commerce caused by industrial conflict

noncustodial parent the parent who does not have primary custody of a child but who has a responsibility for the financial support of the child

nonmaterialistic value something without monetary worth, but that provides a personal sense of satisfaction

nontraditional occupations occupations in which women comprise 25 percent or less of the work force

nonverbal communication facial expressions and body positions that relay a person's feeling

nutritional labeling labeling on a product stating the number of servings per container and how the food is packaged, the percentage of the U.S. RDA the product supplies, the date by which the product should be consumed, and the address of the manufacturer

O

Occupational Outlook Handbook a reference book researched and published every two years by the U.S. Department of Labor that provides detailed descriptions of about 250 occupations

offshore not on the U.S. mainland

Omnibus Budget Reconciliation Act of 1990 a federal act that allows employees to take a tax credit for the actual expenses incurred for child or dependent care if the money spent enables that person to be gainfully employed

on-the-job training (OJT) a wide range of education and training provided by employers for their employees, usually involving supervised work experience

open-admissions policy admission of students without regard to grade point average, test scores, or class rank

open-ended credit a loan made on a continuous basis for the purchase of products up to a specific dollar amount

opportunity cost the resource or benefit given up to produce a particular product

ordinances laws, edicts, or decrees enacted by a municipal government for local application

orientation period the first few weeks or months on a job

OSHA (Occupational Safety and Health Act) an act passed by Congress that encourages employers to work with employees to eliminate job safety and health hazards

outplacement programs programs that provide assistance and training to help released employees find new positions

P

paraphrasing a listening technique that requires the listener to repeat the speaker's ideas or thoughts in his or her own words

parenting leave leave taken by mothers or fathers when a new child is born or adopted

partnership when two or three people own and operate a business

pediatrician a physician who specializes in children's medical care and diseases

permit an official certificate of permission that allows a business to operate

personal appearance "looking the part" by wearing appropriate clothes and using appropriate grooming techniques for a job, as well as a job interview

personal characteristics qualities that make an individual unique

personal data sheet a list of accurate information about a person that employers may ask for when that person fills out a job application

personal orientation unique individual direction which is a combination of a person's abilities, interests, aptitudes, and overall personality

personality the relationship that exists between all of a person's psychological parts that determines the unique way each person influences and responds to his or her surroundings

personality trait any personality characteristic that can be measured

personnel department the department responsible for recruiting and hiring new employees, for administering employee benefit programs, and for employee relations

persuasive orientation when a person has strong personal relations, persuasion, verbal communication, organization and leadership skills; enjoys involvement with people more than information or things; make decisions on facts provided and the desired goal

philosophy the pursuit of wide knowledge and sound judgment about the value of different things in life

physical coverage insurance to cover cost of damage to the policyholder's vehicle caused by collision, fire, or theft

piecework workers being paid according to the amount they produce

pink slip notice of termination

polarization of issues seeing one side of an issue as completely right or wrong

policies and procedures rules established to serve an organization's unique needs, purpose, and management system

population density the population of an area, divided by its square miles

positive attitude to view a new job as an opportunity, a chance to learn new things, and to act interested and enthusiastic about the whole experience; courteous, cooperative and considerate with co-workers and superiors

postsecondary occurring after high school, especially referring to education

poverty thresholds the income level by which poverty is determined

preconceived beliefs opinions formed before a situation occurs

preemployment test test given before a person is hired to determine how well he or she can perform a specific job function

Pregnancy Discrimination Act of 1978 federal law prohibiting companies with fifteen or more employees from discrimination because of pregnancy

prejudice an attitude or stereotype that refuses to change, regardless of new contradictory information or experiences; thoughts, feelings, and behaviors become fixed and immune to new information and experiences

premium the insurance policy-holder's payment to the insurance company

premium pay compensation at greater than regular rates, such as overtime pay or shift differential

preprofessional programs schools that prepare students for specific professions, such as lawyer, dentist, veterinarian, and physician, through their four-year degrees

price fixing an agreement between competitors to establish specific price ranges for their products or services

probationary period a specific period of time in which a new employee is expected to prove his or her ability to perform the job

problem solving the process used to make decisions when there are two or more possible choices; often called decision making

production flexibility ability to react quickly to changes in production demand

profit money that is left over after all of the expenses are paid

profit sharing an incentive compensation in which a percentage of company profits is distributed to the employees involved in producing those profits

profit-and-loss statement a detailed, month-by-month record of income obtained from sales and expenses incurred to produce sales

promotional sales regular merchandise promoted through temporary price reductions

property tax tax paid on property owned by a person

proprietary school a school that is privately owned and is operated for profit

prudent wise, shrewd, and frugal

Q

quality circle employees from the same department who work as a group to identify and solve quality problems with the product they manufacture or the service they provide

R

rational style of decision making making decisions based on the feelings of the decision maker and the facts of the situation

realistic obtainable; within the realm of possibility

recognition vocabulary the words a person understands when he or she reads them or hears them spoken

Recommended Daily Allowances specific nutritional standards that were established by the Food and Nutrition Board of the National Academy of Sciences

reference groups groups, such as the family and clubs or organizations, that set standards of ideal behavior for their members

references people who have agreed to provide an employer with a written or verbal statement about a job applicant's character or ability

relative earnings the amount of goods and services a person can buy with his or her income compared with what his or her neighbors can buy with theirs

résumé a written summary of a job seeker's employment objectives, work experience, education and training, proven skills, and certain personal information

revenue income

S

salary usually refers to the pay received by clerical, technical, professional, managerial, and other employees hired on a weekly, monthly, or annual basis

savings account a bank account that pays interest to customers in return for use of the customers' money

scarcity when people have limited resources compared to their unlimited wants

scheduled breaks rest periods that employers provide so employees can take time out from the workday to relax, have refreshments, handle personal needs, or socialize with co-workers

scientific orientation when a person prefers to use his or her intellect more than physical or social skills to solve problems, enjoy working with their thoughts and speculating about possible solutions to problems; prefers working with information to working with people

security deposit money entrusted with a landlord to cover any damage a tenant may cause to a rental unit

self your attitude towards your personality

self-concept how people view their own skills, interests, and competence level

self-esteem a personal evaluation of one's level of competence and adequacy as a person

self-fulfilling prophesy when preconceived beliefs are held onto so tightly in a situation that the assumed outcome of the situation actually happens

seniority length of time spent with a company

service-producing sector the percentage of total employment including transportation and public utilities, wholesale and retail trade, finance, insurance, real estate, other service, and government

services tasks that other people or machines do that cannot be physically weighed or measured

severance pay when employees are offered a certain number of weeks' pay for each year of service at a company; usually occurs in a voluntary buyout situation

sex-role stereotypes stereotypes based on roles assigned to people because of their sex without relation to personal skills or interests

sexual harassment unwelcome sexual advances, requests for sexual favors, and other verbal or physical conduct of a sexual nature

Small Business Administration a government agency that helps small businesses get started

sociable orientation when a person is usually helpful to others; relies on personal concern and emotion in decision making; enjoys time spent with other people; and displays skill in speaking, teaching, empathizing, listening, and conciliating

social anonymity lacking individuality

social environment the people with whom a person is frequently in contact

Social Security Act the federal law that established a national social insurance program in which a worker pays taxes into the system during working years and

receives monthly benefits when he or she retires or becomes disabled

social self a person's involvement with other people and his or her view of what others think of him or her

sole proprietorship when the same person is both the owner and a worker of a business

sound financial management getting the most for a person's money through planned control of earnings, savings, and spending

spatial perception recognizing forms in space and the relationships of plane and solid objects

staff a group of employees who work for and with someone in charge of them

Standard Industrial Classification a system that identifies the occupations in each type of organization and the number of workers employed in these organizations

Standard Occupational Classification the system in which occupations are divided into groups according to the type of work performed

start-up the period of time when a business is beginning

stereotype a label placed on groups of people, without regard to individual differences

stress tension that can occur for a new employee as he or she deals with new procedures and people at a new job

structured orientation when a person tends to select educational and career goals approved by society; is skilled in coding, classifying, and computing information; and prefers clearly defined tasks to ones requiring imagination and adjustments

submissive to be willing to yield to the commands or wishes of others; apologetic, indifferent, passive

subordinate a member of a supervisor's staff

success a favorable result or a hoped-for ending

superior the person in charge of a group of subordinates

supply the willingness of producers to produce and sell goods or services at a certain price in the marketplace

surgical insurance insurance that covers specific expenses related to specific operations

T

tangible something that can be easily perceived, especially touched

target market a group of consumers who would most likely purchase certain goods or services

taxes payments that all citizens are required by law to make to help pay the costs of government services

team advisor the title of the supervisor in an organization that uses the team management system

Tech Prep program a type of occupational training for technical career fields that begins in high school and ends with an apprenticeship certificate or graduation from a community college program

technical school a school that focuses on training students in fields related to engineering and the physical sciences

technology the science of mechanical and industrial arts which determines the ability of our nation and its workers to compete and prosper in local, regional and world markets

temperament the way a person usually acts, feels, and thinks in certain situations

temporary service agencies that "rent out" their employees to companies for limited amounts of time

tentative not fully developed or worked out; trial

three o'clock syndrome the time during the workday when parents' thoughts turn to their children who are getting out of school

time line schedule for completion of goals; due date

time management when a person plans ahead to make the best use of his or her time

traits characteristics

transcript a record of academic credits earned, grades, attendance, standardized test scores, and extracurricular activities

U

U. S. Office of Consumer Affairs federal agency to handle complaints of the consumer

U.S. Constitution the highest law in the United States

underemployed to be overqualified for a specific job

unemployed not employed and looking for work

unemployment insurance a joint state-federal program under which state-administered funds pay a weekly benefit for a limited time to eligible workers when they are involuntarily unemployed

unit price the cost of one standard measure of a product

university the largest type of institution for higher learning composed of several undergraduate colleges and graduate schools for advanced study

urban area a community of 2,500 or more people

USOE Career Clusters a broad occupational classification system comprised of fifteen career groups divided according to their relationship to one another and to society

V

valid true and supported by facts

values cherished ideas and beliefs that affect decisions a person makes

variety a periodic change in the task, pace, or location of work

venture capital money invested, or earmarked for investment, in new businesses

venture capitalists people who earn money by making high-risk business loans

volunteer work a contribution of free labor, usually to a non-profit organization

W

wages employee compensation that is calculated hourly; the price of labor

warranty an agreement that the manufacturer, for a certain amount of time or until a certain mileage is reached, will repair or replace certain parts that prove to be defective in material or workmanship

whistle-blowing when employees report dishonest or wasteful company activities to a governmental authority

withdrawal to pull away from a volatile situation and give the other party time to cool off before attempting to resolve the conflict

work environment work settings

work ethic the idea that through hard work individuals can make their own success

work permit a special permit needed for employees under eighteen years of age that allows them to work a nonfarm job

workaholics compulsive workers who are overly involved in their jobs

Worker Trait Groups a category of occupations created by the U.S. Department of Labor into which more than 20,000 jobs have been arranged, depending on the characteristics of that job

workers' compensation laws laws to provide for prompt payments of benefits to workers injured on the job or who contract an occupational disease

working capital money required to meet the ongoing operational expenses of a business

working with data working with verbal or numeric information in a work situation

working with people working with human relationships in a work situation

working with things working with tools, instruments, or machines in a work situation

workshops one-day courses of practical work training involving a small group of employees

Index

A

Abilities, 16, 27
  aptitudes and, 39
  entrepreneurship and, 339
  performance appraisal and, 231
  Worker Trait Groups and, 28
Absences/absenteeism, 190
  common reasons for, 175, 193
  job dissatisfaction and, 263
  termination and, 278
Absolute earnings, 14
Academic achievements/performance, 9, 226
Acceptance, interpersonal relationships and, 117
Accidents (automobile), 430, 431, 448
Accidents (workplace), 219–223, 226, 258
Accountants, 41, 91
  African American women as, 304
  entrepreneurship and, 350–351
  leisure time of, 41
  projected employment of, 295
  women as, 137, 286
Accounting clerk, 79
Accredited school, 87–88, 92
Accrued paid leave, 462
Acquisitions, 282
Active vocabulary, 103
Actors, 74
Actuary, 79
ADA. *See* Americans with Disabilities Act (ADA)
Adapting, 73
Additional dealer markup (ADM), 425
Additional dealer profit (ADP), 425
Adenosine triphosphate (ATP), 437–438
Adjusters, 304
ADM. *See* Additional dealer markup (ADM)
Administrative occupations, 91
  African American women in, 304
  projected growth in, 301
  self-employment in, 354
  women in, 286
Adoption assistance/leave, 258, 292, 461

ADP. *See* Additional dealer profit (ADP)
Adult education courses, 93
Advertising
  consumer choices and, 402, 408–410
  consumer fraud and, 423
  direct-mail, 410
  entrepreneurship and, 344
  See also Help-wanted ads
Aerobic activities, 438
Affirmative action, 166
African American women, 304
African Americans, 137, 289
Age
  change in career goals with, 69
  change in interests with, 32
  leisure time and, 40–41
Aggressive people, 11–12, 208
Agriculture, Department of, 418, 435
Agriculture, job growth in, 296, 301, 325
AIDS, 439, 449
Air traffic controller, 91, 225
Aircraft electrician/mechanic, 91
Airline travel, 431
Airplane engine specialist, 38
Alcohol, 445, 448
  accidents and, 220
  job dissatisfaction and, 263
  violent crime and, 223
Ambition, 25, 492
American Bankers Insurance Group, 250
American Dream, 334–339
Americans with Disabilities Act (ADA), 245
Ameritech, 256
Analyzing alternatives, 62–63
Annual percentage rate (APR), 389, 426
Antitrust laws, 238, 316
Apathy, 472
Apologizing, 126, 208, 209
Appearance. *See* Personal appearance
Apple Computer, 188–189, 461
Apprenticeship, 9–18, 82–84, 256
  defined, 82
  Tech Prep and, 78. *See also* Tech Prep
APR. *See* Annual percentage rate (APR)

Aptitude tests, 39, 157
Aptitudes, 28
  assessment of, 493
  career goals and, 51
  counseling and, 362
  and delaying education, 35
  identifying, 36–39
  knowing your, 21–42
  spatial, 37
Arbitrator, 125
Architects, 41, 79, 286
Argument, negotiation vs., 123–124
Arithmetic, 36–37, 96. *See also* Mathematics
Armed Services Vocational Aptitude Battery (ASVAB), 39
Art, 79
Artist, 41, 79
Asian Americans, 137
Assayer, 79
Assertive people, 12, 208
Assets, 349
Astronomer, 41, 79
ASVAB. *See* Armed Services Vocational Aptitude Battery (ASVAB)
Athlete, professional, 79, 286
ATM. *See* Automated teller machine (ATM)
ATP. *See* Adenosine triphosphate (ATP)
Attendance, 190, 231
Attitudes, 22, 52–56
  career goals and, 55, 56
  career success and, 485
  communication and, 100
  defined, 52
  ethnic, 480–481
  formation of, 179–180
  job interview and, 162, 168
  job success and, 178
  performance appraisal and, 231
  positive vs. negative, 53–54
  poverty and, 479
  promotions and, 211
  racial prejudice and, 481
  toward safety, 219
  stereotypes and, 54

Auditors, 286, 295, 304

Authority style of decision making, 61

Automated teller machine (ATM), 384, 399

Automation, 174, 297

Automobile industry, 328

Automobile insurance, 352, 430

Automobile mechanics, 38, 79
  apprenticeship for, 84
  earnings for, 266
  women as, 286

Automobile purchase, 423–429

Automobile/car repair shops, 336, 354

Avocations, 40, 42

B

Baccalaureate degree, 93, 95

Bachelor of Arts, 94

Bachelor of Science, 94

Background check, 155, 235

Bagger, 35, 210

Bait and switch, 408

Balance of trade, 330

Balance sheet, 349

Bank cashier, 79

Bank statement, 380

Bank tellers, 41, 399
  projected employment of, 295
  women's jobs in, 137

Banks, 318–319, 379–384, 387
  competition among, 399
  loans from, 348

Barber shops, 353

Bartering, 317

Base pay, 263

Baseball player, 38

Basic skills, 77, 78, 127

BBB. *See* Better Business Bureau (BBB)

Beauty shops, 336, 353. *See also* Hairdressers

Bed-and-breakfast inns, 336

Beliefs
  attitudes and, 54
  career philosophy and, 491
  communication and, 100
  preconceived, 54–55
  values and, 45

Benefits, *See* Fringe benefits

Better Business Bureau (BBB), 86, 237–238, 408, 420

Biologist, 79

Biology, 79

Birth certificate, 152, 163

Board of directors, 196

Boarding houses, 336

Body language/posture, 105, 107
  job interview and, 162

Bond (insurance), 156

Bonds, business cycle and, 320

Bonus plan, 264, 265

Bookkeepers, 18, 36, 37
  leisure time of, 41
  entrepreneurship and, 351
  projected employment of, 295

Borrowing, 385–393
  cost of, 388–390
  See also Automobile purchase; Home, buying a

Bounced check, 381

Breaks, 190, 207

Bricklayer, 48, 79, 84

Brickmasons, women as, 286

British Petroleum (BP), 298

Budget, 375, 393–398
  consumer choices and, 402
  entrepreneurship and, 351
  repaying loans and, 391

Budgetary expense sheet, 395–396

Bulldozer operator, 48

Bureau of Employment Services, 137–138, 157, 362

Bureaus of labor, 215

Business cycle, 319–320

Business education, 79

Business incubators, 354

Business interruption insurance, 352

Business letter, 113–114

Business life insurance, 352

Business location, 345, 346

Business ownership, 333–335
  financing, 347–350
  forms of, 340–342
  taxes and, 351–352
  by women, 354
  See also Entrepreneurship; Small businesses

Busser (restaurant), 184

Butcher, 38

Buyer, 79

C

Cable TV installers and repairers, 295

Cafeteria plans, 258

Calories, 434, 448

CalPacific, 331

Campgrounds, 336

Canceled check, 380

Capital
  venture, 348
  working, 347–348

Capitalist system, 307–308

Car manufacturers, 422

Cardiopulmonary and EKG technician, 91

Cardiorespiratory endurance, 438

Career
  change and growth in, 8, 69, 366, 260–279
  child care and. *See* Child care
  choosing your, 6–12
  classification of, 368–370
  defined, 6
  divorce and, 467–468
  fatherhood and, 460, 469
  goals and. *See* Career goals
  health and safety and, 219. *See also* Health; Safety
  information on, 356–372, 493
  marriage and, 452–457, 469
  motherhood and, 461. *See also* Motherhood
  planning your, 8–10, 362, 493
  sacrifices for, 10
  success in. *See* Success (in career/job)
  See also Job; Occupations

Career advancement, 210–214
  industry growth, 226
  and spelling and grammar, 226

Career assessment, 493

Career clubs, 365

Career Day, 363

Career decisions, 64–68, 186

Career exploration, 7, 365

Career goals, 50, 51–52
  attitudes and, 55, 56
  change in, 69
  expectations and, 492, 493
  See also Goals

Career guidance, 362–363, 493

Career information delivery system (CIDS), 371
Career interests, 9, 10, 25
  culture and, 23
  See also Interests
Career path, 8, 10
  changes and, 261
  after discharge, 276
  and stages of life, 489
Career philosophy, 491–492
Career planning services, 362
Career shadowing, 7, 365
Career skills. *See* Skills
Cargo specialist, 91
Caribbean Basic Economic Recovery Act (CBERA), 298–299
Carpenters, 37, 79, 137
  apprenticeship for, 84
  self-employed, 354
  women as, 286
Cartographer, 79
Cash flow, 350
Cash-flow statement, 349, 350
Cashiers, 35, 38, 79, 210
  projected employment of, 295
  women as, 286
CBERA. *See* Caribbean Basic Economic Recovery Act (CBERA)
CCCS. *See* Consumer Credit Counseling Service (CCCS)
CD. *See* Certificate of deposit (CD)
Central office operators, 295
Ceramic engineer, 79
Certificate of deposit (CD), 383
Certificates, 183
Chain of command, 210
Change
  career and, 260–279
  and stages of life, 485–490
  technology and, 322–327
  women and, 283–288
  in work opportunities, 294–304
  in workplace, 281–305
Character, 26, 28
Charge accounts, 387
Charisma, 473
Check register, 380
Checking account, 379–382, 384
Checks, 379–382
Chemical engineer, 79

Chemists, 41, 79, 286
Chemistry, 79, 137
Chief executive, 196. *See also* Top management
Child care, 463–467, 492
  company-provided, 250, 258, 292–293, 461
  poverty and, 479
  and stages of life, 486
  unmarried mothers and, 479
  See also Parenting
Child labor, 215, 241, 352
Child support, 468, 469
Child-care workers
  projected employment of, 295
  self-employed, 354
Chiropractor, 79
Choices, making, 59–71
Choreographers, 74
Chronological résumé, 144–145
Chrysler, 201
Church, 24
Citizenship
  Fourteenth Amendment and, 482
  world, 474–475
  See also Civil responsibility
Civic responsibility, 471–483
  social problems and, 476–482
  voting and, 472–474
  world citizenship and, 474–475
Civil engineer, 79
Civil Rights Act of 1964, 165, 243–244
  performance appraisal and, 229
  wage discrimination and, 288–289
Civil rights protection, 243
  racial prejudice and, 481
  women and, 283–284
Civil service examination, 157
Clayton Act, 238
Cleaners, 295
Clerical perception, 38
Clerks, 295, 297
Closed groups, 120–121
Clothing expense (for consumers), 405–407
Coaches, 79
Coaching, and beginning a new job, 183
COBRA. *See* Consolidated Omnibus Budget Reconciliation Act (COBRA)

Coca-Cola Company, 237
COLAs. *See* Cost-of-living adjustments (COLAs)
Collective bargaining, 215, 216–217
  CBERA and, 299
  overtime and, 255
Colleges, 17, 92–95
  career guidance and, 365
  corporate-owned, 90
  entrepreneurship and, 339
  and on-the-job training, 183
  promotions and, 213
  specialized, 95
Color discrimination, 38
Commissions, 264–265, 376
  discharge and, 272
Commitment
  goals and, 50
  promotions and, 213
Commodities, business cycle and, 320
Communication, 96, 99–129
  conflict and, 123
  deficiencies in, 77
  defined, 100
  entrepreneurship and, 339, 346
  group relationships and, 119
  human relationships and, 15
  interpersonal relationships and, 118
  on job interview, 162–163
  job success and, 184
  nonverbal. *See* Nonverbal communication
  persuasive orientation and, 68
  process of, 100–101
  responding and, 107–108
  submissive people and, 10
  technology and, 324
  telephone, 108–110
  See also Listening; Reading; Speaking; Writing
Community colleges, 78, 90, 92–93, 213
Company image. *See* Organizational/company image
Company secrets, 193
Comparable worth, 290
Comparative advantage, 326
Comparison shopping, 404
Compassion, promotions and, 211
Compensation/pay
  average, for different states, 302

career success and, 263–265
control- vs. team-oriented
   management and, 200
in different countries, 304
direct, 263–265
employer costs for employee, 252–253
See also Earnings; Money; Paycheck
Compensatory time, 255
Competence, 16, 92
   attitudes and, 179
   job success and, 186
Competency tests, 18
Competition
   defined, 315
   entrepreneurship and, 344
   international. *See* International
     competition
   market economy and, 315
   technology and, 323, 324
Competitive advantage
   global economy and, 327
   technology and, 297, 327
Components (of attitudes), 53
Compounding interest, 382–383
Compromise, 125
Computation skills, 96
Computer analysts
   earnings for, 266
   women as, 286
Computer operators, 91, 266
Computer programmer, 91, 295
Computer repair, 354
Computer scientists, 265, 295, 304
Computerized career information
   systems, 9, 360–361, 493
Computer-related jobs, 265, 297, 304
   offshore sites and, 298
   women in, 286
Conciliating, 67
Confidence
   career planning and, 8
   entrepreneurship and, 334
   goals and, 50
   job interview and, 164
   personal appearance and, 188
   promotions and, 211
   submissive people and, 11
   success and, 87
Conflict
   defined, 123

and drug and alcohol use, 221
job dissatisfaction and, 263
personality, 193
stress and, 224
Conflict resolution, 106, 123–126, 209
   co-workers and, 208
   "I" and "you" statements in, 126
   schools and, 478
   third party assistance in, 125
Conforming (to organization), 196–198,
   213
Conscience, 486–487
Consequences, 60–61, 69
Conservation, 312
Consolidated Omnibus Budget
   Reconciliation Act (COBRA), 275,
   276–277
Construction
   business incubators and, 354
   job growth in, 296, 297
Consumer Credit Counseling Service
   (CCCS), 390–391
Consumer finance companies, 387
Consumer fraud, 422–423
Consumer price index, 265
Consumer Protection Office, 86
Consumers, 313–316, 401–432
   airline travel by, 431
   annual expenditures of American, 402
   automobile purchase by, 423–429
   clothing expense of, 405–407
   food expense of, 402–405
   high-ticket items and, 407
   housing for, 410–416
   responsibilities of, 418–419
   rights of, 417–418, 429
   being wise, 375, 402
   women vs. men as, 431
   See also Demand; Goods; Services;
     Supply
Context, 103
Contingent employees, 254–255, 293,
   298
Contradictory information, 54
Controlling leadership, 121
Cooks, 74, 84
Cooperative learning (Co-op) programs,
   90, 366
Copiers, repair shops for, 354
Corning Glass, 201

Corporate culture, 197–198, 199
Corporation, 340, 341
Correction officer, apprenticeship for, 84
Correspondence courses, 88, 183
Cosmetologist, 38, 354
Cost of living, 278, 302–303
   for different metropolitan areas, 302
Cost-of-living adjustments (COLAs),
   265
Counseling
   for career guidance, 362–363
   for credit trouble, 390–391
   outplacement and, 273
Counselor, high school, 35, 39, 79, 362
   field experience and, 365
Court clerk, 79
Courtesy, 187, 207
Courtship, 451–452
Cover letter, 145–147
Co-workers, 205–209
   and beginning a new job, 181–182
   building relationships with, 207–208
   competition among, 212–213
   courtesy to, 187
   criticizing boss to, 204
   job satisfaction and, 205, 263
   job success and, 187
   stress and, 224
Craft occupations, 83, 354
Creative orientation, 66–67
Creativity, 48
Credit, 385–393
   consumer fraud and, 423
   cost of, 388–390
   open-ended vs. close-ended, 386
   rights regarding, 391–393
   trouble with, 390–393
Credit capacity, 386–387
Credit cards, 388, 392, 399
Credit history, 387, 393
Credit insurance, 389
Credit report (sample of), 392
Credit unions, 251, 387
Creditors, 386, 389
Crime, 223–224, 478, 479
Criticism, 202–204
Culture, 23–24, 25. *See also* Corporate
   culture
Current assets, 349

Current liabilities, 349
Customer relations, 192
Customer satisfaction, 109
Customer service worker, stress and, 225
Customers, entrepreneurship and, 344
Customs engineer, 79

D

Dancers, 74, 79
Data, working with, 33–35, 96
Data-entry specialist, 91
Data-processing equipment operators, 74
Dating, 451–452
Day-care worker, 41
Decision making, 10, 60
    as consumer, 402
    group relationships and, 120
    process of, 61–64
    rational, 62–64
    technology and, 324
    See also Problem solving
Declaration of Independence, 46
Deductible, 247
Deductions
    income tax, 352, 353, 474
    on paycheck, 375–377
Delaying gratification, 18
Deliberate involvement, 491
Demand, 315, 318, 319
    entrepreneurship and, 344–345
    GDP and, 321
Democratic groups, 120, 121
Democratic party, 474
Dental hygienist/assistant, 74, 79, 91, 286
Dentist, 37, 79
Department of Agriculture, 418, 435
Department of Education, 87
Department of Health and Human Services, 435
Department of Labor, 37, 84, 96, 132
    creation of, 239
    employment eligibility and, 154
    filing a complaint with, 241
    minimum wage and, 171–172
    publications by, 358–360
Department of Transportation, 418
Deposit slip, 382
Depression, 319–320
Deregulation, 282

Designer, 41, 79
Detectives, 304
Detrimental (effect of urbanization), 480
Dictionary of Occupational Titles (DOT), 28, 34, 37–38
Diesel mechanic, 38
Diet, 434–436
Dietitian, 79
Direct compensation, 263–265
Direct investment, 327
Direct Marketing Association, 418
Directors, 74
Disabilities, people with, 148, 245. See also Americans with Disabilities Act (ADA); Physically challenged people
Disability insurance, 443
Discharge
    defined, 275
    discrimination and, 272
    FLSA and, 258
    without good cause, 271–272
    major causes of, 278
Discipline (of employees), 183, 275
Discrimination, 243
    discharge and, 272
    filing a complaint of, 240–241
    job interviews and, 166
    OSHA and, 223
    preemployment tests and, 157
    Title VII and, 243–244, 288–289
    in wages, 288–289
Dispatcher, 91
Distribution system, 312–313
    business cycle and, 320
    business incubators and, 354
Divorce, 467–468, 469
DOT, 359, 360
DOT. See Dictionary of Occupational Titles (DOT)
Downsizing, 282
Drafter, 38, 79
Dress code, 185, 187, 188–190
    in school, 478
Drudgery, 14, 16
Drug abuse, 445–447
Drug testing, 226, 445
Drugs, 439, 445–447
    accidents and, 220
    defined, 445
    generic vs. brand-name, 449

    job dissatisfaction and, 263
    prescription, 443–444, 445, 449
    violent crime and, 223
Du Pont, 258
Dual-career marriages, 454–455

E

Early retirement, 273
Earnings
    average, for different occupations, 18
    for different occupations, 266
    gross, 375
    for men vs. women, 286, 289
    of minorities, 289
    types of, 376
    in U.S. vs. other countries, 331
    See also Compensation/pay
Earnings insurance, 352
Easy-money policy, 320
Economic system, 307, 325
Economics/economy, 307–332
    business cycle and, 320
    fiscal policy and, 318
    forecasting, 321
    global, 327–330
    job skills and changes in, 174
    women and, 284
    See also Monetary system
Editor, 37, 79, 304
Education, 17, 72–97
    attitudes toward, 55
    career philosophy and, 492
    colleges and universities and, 92–95
    correspondence courses and, 88
    cost of, 96
    counseling regarding, 362
    delaying, 35
    employment opportunities and, 271, 272
    entrepreneurship and, 339
    financial aid for, 362
    government job-training and, 88–89
    high school, 77–84
    home study and, 88
    money and, 17–18
    occupational level and, 370
    organizational, 256–257
    projected job growth and, 300, 301
    promotions and, 210, 211

specialized colleges and schools and, 95

vocational. *See* Vocational training

Worker Trait Groups and, 28

Education, Department of, 87

Educational assistance, 258. *See also* Tuition reimbursement

Educational reform, 478

EEG technologists, 74

EEO rights. *See* Equal employment opportunity (EEO) rights

EEOC. *See* Equal Employment Opportunity Commission (EEOC)

EFTS. *See* Electronic funds transfer system (EFTS)

Ego integrity, 490

EKG technician, 79, 91

Electrical assemblers, 295, 304

Electrical engineer, 79

Electrician, 79, 91

apprenticeship for, 84

self-employed, 354

women as, 286

Electromagnetic radiation, 219

Electromedical and biomedical equipment repairers, 74

Electronic assemblers, 295, 304

Electronic funds transfer system (EFTS), 384

Electronics technicians, 79, 91

apprenticeship for, 84

earnings for, 266

Emergency medical care, apprenticeship for, 84

Emotions, 28

attitudes and, 53, 54

creative orientation and, 66

stress and, 185

Empathy, 67, 108, 117

Employability Skills Survey, 96

Employee assistance programs, 221

Employee Retirement Income Security Act (ERISA), 258

Employee savings/thrifts plans, 251

Employee theft, 193

Employees

cost of replacing, 148

exempt vs. nonexempt, 255

newly hired, 148. *See also* Job, beginning a new

in offshore locations, 298

rights of, 240–246

See also Workers

Employers

expectations of, 183–185

rights of, 229, 240, 253, 272

Employment

business cycle and, 320

GDP and, 326

interest rates and, 319

projected, 295–304, 309–310

Employment agencies, 362–363

Employment contract, 139

Employment eligibility verification form, 154

Employment outlook, 357

Employment projections, 371

Employment services, 135–140

Employment structure, 74–75

Encouragement, 30, 56, 201

Endorsement, 376

Engineering

jobs for minorities in, 137

jobs for women in, 137

Engineers, 37, 79, 91

African American women as, 304

apprenticeship for operating, 84

leisure time of, 41

women as, 286

English

communication skill in, 77, 101

as subject in high school, 79

varieties of, 101–102

Enjoyment, 16, 17, 31

Entertainers, 74

Entrepreneurship, 333–355

advantages of, 336–337

business location and, 345, 346

defined, 334

disadvantages of, 337–338

help in, 345

paperwork and, 350–353

success in, 343–346

Entry level, 196, 261

compensation for, 265

performance appraisal and, 231

Environment, 22–23, 25, 28

social, 47

work, 48, 65

Environmental health specialist, 91

Environmental orientation, 65–66

Environmental protection, 245, 309, 477–478, 482

Environmental Protection Agency (EPA), 245, 477

EPA. *See* Environmental Protection Agency (EPA)

Equal Credit Opportunity Act, 391

Equal Employment Opportunity Commission (EEOC)

filing a complaint with, 243, 292

performance appraisal and, 229–230

sexual harassment and, 290–292

Title VII and, 243–244

Equal employment opportunity (EEO) rights, 165–166

Equal pay, 14

Equal Pay Act of 1963, 243

Equal protection, 482

Equity, 349

ERISA. *See* Employee Retirement Income Security Act (ERISA)

Ethics, 234–239

economic system and, 308

government regulations and, 238

honesty and, 229, 239

and stages of life, 487

Ethnic attitudes, 480–481

Etiquette, 181, 267

and resigning your job, 269

in reading, 115

Evaluations, 15, 64. *See also* Performance appraisal

Exchange rate, 329–330

Executives

projected employment of, 295, 301

self-employed, 354

women as, 286, 304

Exempt employees, 255, 462

Exercise, 437–438

Expectations

career success and, 488, 491–492, 493

of employer, 183–185

life, 490–492

performance, 200

Experience, 9

career advancement and, 210

and changing jobs, 269

entrepreneurship and, 339

job satisfaction and, 263

moonlighting for, 346

part-time or volunteer work to obtain, 366

self-concept and, 28

See also Life experiences

Exports, 329, 331

Exxon Corporation, 331, 477–478

Eye-hand coordination, 38, 67

F

Facial expressions, 105, 106, 162

Facilitating, 121, 201

Facsimile (FAX) machines, 110

Factors of production, 310–311, 321, 324

Factory jobs, 40

Fair Credit Reporting Act (FCRA), 244, 391–392

Fair employment program, 166

Fair Labor Standards Act (FLSA), 152–154, 241–243

discharge and, 258

tip credit and, 175

training wage and, 172

Family (and work), 450–470, 491

Family leave, 258

Family and Medical Leave Act, 292, 461–462

Family relationships, 48

Family-friendly benefits, 258, 461

Farmers, 41, 295, 324–325

Fashion designer, 79

Fatalistic style of decision making, 61

Fatherhood, 459–460, 469

Fatigue, worker, 220

FAX machines. *See* Facsimile (FAX) machines

FCRA. *See* Fair Credit Reporting Act (FCRA)

FDA. *See* Food and Drug Administration (FDA)

FDIC. *See* Federal Depositors Insurance Corporation (FDIC)

Federal agencies, 420–421. *See also* Government

Federal bureau of labor, 215

Federal Depositors Insurance Corporation (FDIC), 319, 383–384

Federal income tax, 352, 353, 474. *See also* Taxes

Federal Information Center, 421

Federal Insurance Contribution Act (FICA), 246, 377

Federal Parent Locator Service (FPLS), 469

Federal Reserve System, 318–319, 331

Federal Savings and Loan Insurance Corporation (FSLIC), 384

Federal Trade Commission (FTC), 341, 422, 424, 418

Used Car Rule of, 426

Feedback, 106, 107

group relationships and, 119

from mentor, 211

Feelings

attitudes and, 54

creative orientation and, 66

decision making and, 61, 62

introspective ability and, 67

Felony, 156

FICA. *See* Federal Insurance Contribution Act (FICA)

Field experiences, 365

File clerk or office clerk, 38, 79

Finance charge, 389

Financial institutions, 421–422. *See also* Banks; Savings and loans

Financial management, 374–400. *See also* Consumers

Financial statements, 349–351

Financing a business, 347–350

Finger dexterity, 38

Fire insurance, 352

Firefighters, 35, 79

apprenticeship for, 84

women as, 286

Firing. *See* Discharge

First-line manager/supervisor, 196, 198, 199

Fiscal policy, 318, 320

Fish and game warden, 41

Fixed assets, 349

Fixed expenses, 395

Flexibility

contingent workers and, 293, 298

family-work issues and, 461

international competition and, 282

physical, 438

production, 298

promotions and, 211

Flexible benefit plans, 258

Flexible expenses, 395

Flexible work schedules, 40, 460–461

Flight attendant, 79

Flight engineer, 91

Floral designer, 38

FLSA. *See* Fair Labor Standards Act (FLSA)

Fluctuating employment, 412

Food

health and, 433–437, 449

expense for, 402–405

Food and Drug Administration (FDA), 417

Food and Nutrition Board, 434

Food Pyramid Guide, 435–436

Food workers, projected employment of, 295

Foreign correspondent, 79

Foreign languages, 79, 104

Foreman, 198. *See* Supervisor

Forester, 41, 48

Forklift operator, 38

Form perception, 38

Fortune-500 firms, 187–188

Fourteenth Amendment, 243, 482

FPLS. *See* Federal Parent Locator Service (FPLS)

Franchise, 341, 354

Fraud, 235, 422–423, 431

Free enterprise system, 307–308

consumers and, 313–316

entrepreneurship and, 334

market share and, 310

profit and, 310

Free time, career and, 6

Friendships, 485, 488–489

career philosophy and, 491

Fringe benefits, 247–253

cash instead of, 258

contingent workers and, 293

cost of, 258

day care and, 293

FLSA and, 258

paycheck and, 377

small businesses and, 258

tuition reimbursement as, 256

for upper management, 265

voluntary buyouts and, 273

FSLIC. *See* Federal Savings and Loan Insurance Corporation (FSLIC)

FTC. *See* Federal Trade Commission (FTC)

Fulfillment, 22

Full potential, 182

Full-time jobs, 173–174

contingent employment leading to, 293

co-workers and, 205

fringe benefits and, 258

performance appraisal and, 231

Functional résumé, 145

Furniture assembler, 38

G

Gain sharing, 264

Game warden, 41, 79

Gardeners, 295

GATB. *See* General Aptitude Test Battery (GATB)

GATT. *See* General Agreement on Tariffs and Trade (GATT)

GDP. *See* Gross domestic product (GDP)

GED. *See* General equivalency diploma (GED)

Gender identity, 285, 287

General Agreement on Tariffs and Trade (GATT), 328

General Aptitude Test Battery (GATB), 39

General Electric Corporation, 250

General equivalency diploma (GED), 86

General learning ability, 37

General ledger, 349, 351

General Motors, 336

Generativity, 489

Generic brands, 405, 449

Geographic location, 56

average pay for different, 302

comparative advantage and, 326

cost of living and, 278

future and, 302

leisure time and, 40, 41

occupational specialization and, 325–326

urbanization and, 482

voting and, 482

wage rates and, 265

Glass ceiling, 289–290

Global competition, 297–300, 301–302. *See also* International competition

Global economy, 327–330

Goals

aptitudes and, 39

career change and, 261

changing your, 366

counseling and, 362

defining, 49–52

entrepreneurship and, 338

expectations and, 492

financial, 375, 394, 395

group relationships and, 119

knowing your, 44–58

long- vs. short-term, 9–10, 49

long-term, 51

management system and, 196

materialistic vs. nonmaterialistic, 49–50

plan of action for, 50

realistic, 29, 50

short-term, 50–51

values and, 50

See also Career goals

GOE. *See Guide for Occupational Exploration (GOE)*

Gold, 317–318, 331

Goods

business cycle and, 320

comparative advantage and, 326

consumers and, 313–316

defined, 309

demand and supply of, 315, 318, 319

distribution of, 312

durable vs. nondurable, 314

entrepreneurship and, 344–345

GDP and, 321, 326

global economy and, 329–330

necessity vs. luxury, 314–315, 325

occupational specialization and, 325

Goods-producing sector, 296–297, 309, 310

SOC system and, 368

Gossip, 207

Government, 475–476

construction job growth and, 297

consumer offices of, 420

global economy and, 327

monetary system and, 317–319

projected employment for, 371

SIC system and, 369

SOC system and, 368

state and local, 475–476

taxes and, 474. *See also* Taxes

technology and, 327

See also Civic responsibility

Government job-training, 88–89

Government jobs, 157

Government regulation, 238–246

competition and, 316

deregulation and, 282

entrepreneurship and, 352–353

free enterprise system and, 308

Graduate schools, 94

Grammar, 18, 226

Graveyard shift, 255

Great Depression, 319–320

Grievances, 217–218, 226

sexual harassment and, 292

Gross domestic product (GDP), 320–321

comparative advantage and, 326

taxes as percentage of, 482

Gross earnings, 375

Gross national product, 330

Group relationships, 118–120

Groups, democratic vs. closed, 120–121

Guards, projected employment of, 295

Guide for Occupational Exploration (GOE), 360

Guilds, 82

Guns, 478

H

Hairdressers, 354. *See also* Beauty shop

Hazards, workplace, 219, 222, 224–225

Health

cold remedies and, 449

health and, 433–437, 449

public, 353, 433–449, 475

workplace, 219–225, 352

See also Department of Health and Human Services

Health certificate, 154

Health education, 79

Health insurance, 258, 440–443

contingent workers and, 293

after discharge, 276–277

entrepreneurship and, 352

motherhood and, 461

paycheck deductions and, 377

voluntary buyouts and, 273

See also Medical insurance

Health maintenance organization (HMO), 248, 442–443

Health services occupations, 74, 296

Heating and cooling mechanic, 91

Help-wanted ads, 132, 134–135, 136

   by employment agencies, 139

Heredity, 23, 25

High school, 17

   career guidance from, 362–365, 493

   competency tests and, 18

   counselor in. *See* Counselor, high school

   dropouts from, 478

   importance of, 77–84

   subjects in, related to occupations, 78, 79

   vocational training and, 86

   See also School; Student

High-pressure tactics, 409

Hispanics, 137

HIV, 439, 449

HMO. *See* Health maintenance organization (HMO)

Hobbies, 41

Holidays, 40, 258

Home, buying a, 416

Home, working at, 334

Home responsibility, 8

Home study, 88

Honesty, 229, 239

   promotions and, 211

   and stages of life, 487

Honeywell, 201

Hospitalization insurance, 247, 442

   paycheck and, 377

Hoteliers, 336

Hours

   for entrepreneurs, 338

Household workers, 295, 354

Housing, 410–416

HR-10 plans, 258

Human relations skills, 205, 208, 213, 226

Human relationships, 15

Humor, 208, 211

I

"I" and "you" statements, 126

IBM. *See* International Business Machines (IBM)

Ideal self, 29, 30

Identifying problems, 62

Identity, 7–8, 16, 488

   gender, 285, 287

Image

   consultants regarding, 188

   organizational/company, 109, 160, 188–189, 198

   self-, 28–29, 188

Immigration and Naturalization Service, 154

Immigration worker, 79

Imports, 329

Impulsive style of decision making, 61

Incentives, 263–264, 265

   for upper management, 265

Income tax, 258, 474. *See also* Taxes

Income-protection insurance, 443

Independence, 15, 48

Individual retirement accounts (IRAs), 258

Industrial arts, 79

Industrial engineer, 79

Industrial machinery repairers, women as, 286

Industrial products, 309

Industries

   list of, 131

   different pay levels and, 302

   employment projections for, 371

   See also Standard Industrial Classification (SIC)

Infant mortality, 480

Inflation, 318, 321, 327

Inflection, 106

Information, 6

   working with, 66

   career, 356–372, 493

   vocabulary and, 103

Initial screening, 139

Initiative

   job interview and, 159

   promotions and, 211, 213

Insider abuse, 235

Insurance, 429–431

   defined, 430

   entrepreneurship and, 352

   See also specific types

Insurance Information Institute, 418, 429

Intellect, 66

Intelligence, 37

Intelligence specialist, 91

Intelligence tests, 157

Interdependence, 179, 199, 325

Interest rates, 318–319, 382–383, 389

   business cycle and, 320

Interest surveys, 32

Interests, 9, 10, 16

   career change and, 261

   change in, 32, 485

   counseling and, 362

   defined, 27

   goals and, 38–39

   identifying, 31–33

   knowing your, 21–42

   Worker Trait Groups and, 28

   See also Career interests; Personal interests

Interior designer, 38

Internal Revenue Service (IRS), 246, 258, 351, 399

International Business Machines (IBM), 188–189, 336

International competition, 282, 297–300, 331

   day care and, 293

   See also Global competition; Global economy

Internship programs, 366

Interpersonal relationships, 117–122

   with co-workers, 205, 208

   groups and, 118–120

   job satisfaction and, 263

Interstate business, 352

Intimacy, 488–489

Intrastate business, 352

Introspective ability, 67

Intuitive style of decision making, 61

Inventory, 18

Investigators, 304

Invoice price, 425

Involvement, 48

IRAs. *See* Individual retirement accounts (IRAs)

IRS. *See* Internal Revenue Service (IRS)

J

Janitors, 295

Japanese companies, 201, 298, 299, 331

Job

   beginning a new, 181–185

changing your, 8, 174, 268–270

enjoyment of, 16, 17, 31

holding more than one, 399. *See also* Moonlighting

keeping your, 10, 175

losing your, 271–277, 278, 298

making progress on, 195–201

market value of, 266

overqualified for, 16

resigning your, 269–270. *See also* Quitting

rewards of, 15, 16, 263–265

success vs. failure in, 16. *See also* Success (in career/job)

summer, 175

Job applicant, defined, 130

Job application forms, 151–156

job interview and, 163

at state bureau of employment, 138

See also Personal data sheet; Résumés

Job classifications, 357, 367, 368–370

Job Corps, 88–89

Job descriptions, employment agencies and, 139

Job design, 200

Job fairs, 135, 137

Job families, 28

Job interviews, 159–175

becoming informed about company before, 159

defined, 162

evaluation of, 167–168

follow-up on, 166–167

making a good impression on, 159–161

preemployment tests and, 158

preparing for, 163–164

rights in, 165–166

successful, 161–169

thank-you letter for, 167

videotaped, 175

"W" questions in, 175

Job jargon, 135

Job leads

cards for, 140

defined, 132

finding, 132–140

following up on, 140

Job market, 17, 130–132

changes in, 174, 300–303

counseling regarding, 362

Job mobility, 301–302

Job offer, 168–169

Job orientation. *See* Orientation

Job rotation, 90

Job satisfaction, 15, 16, 39

career success and, 261–263

co-workers and, 205, 263

and increase in job skills, 173

women and, 284

Job search, 10, 129–148

cover letter and, 145–147

defined, 130

after discharge, 276

finding job leads in, 132–140

following up on job leads in, 140

networking in, 132, 133–134

outplacement programs and, 273–274

personal data sheet and, 141–142

planning your, 130–132

résumé and, 141, 143–145

Trade Act of 1974 and, 298

want ads and, 132, 134–135, 136

See also Job application

Job security, 14–15

in changing world of work, 300, 301

compensation and, 263

importance of, 263

job success and, 186

skills and, 301

technology and, 324

Job Service, 138

Job skills. *See* Skills

Job-keeping skills, 10

"Job-match" system, 138

Job-seeking skills, 10

John Hancock Mutual Life, 461

Joint Apprenticeship Committee, 84

Journalist, 225

Journeyman, 83

Junk mail, 410

Jury duty, 272

Justice Department, 478

K

Keogh plans, 258

"Key" employees, 462

Kinship networks, 469

Knowing yourself

career decisions and, 64–68

interests and aptitudes and, 21–42

values and goals and, 44–58

Knowledge, 48

L

Labor, Department of. *See* Department of Labor

Labor movement, 40

Labor unions, 40, 215–218

benefits and, 252–253

control-oriented management and, 199

different pay levels and, 302

dues for, 377

job search and, 137

as training partners, 96

Labor-management relations, 218

control- vs. team-oriented management and, 200

disputes and, 217

technology and, 324

See also Labor unions

Labor/work force

future, 294, 295

global economy and, 330

men vs. women in, 282

Laboratory technician, 79, 91

Landscape worker, 79

Language, 101–104. *See also* Body language/posture

Lathe and turning machine tool setters, 304

Law enforcement, 84, 478. *See also* Police officers

Laws, 475–476, 482

Lawyer, 79, 304

Layoffs, 217, 271, 273–275

entrepreneurship and, 334

Leadership, 48, 66, 67, 68, 213

facilitating and, 121

group relationships and, 119, 120–122

shared vs. controlling, 121

team advisor and, 201

Leading economic indicators, 321

Learning, 78, 79

entrepreneurship and, 339

job security and, 301

promotions and, 211

Lease, 414–415

Leave time, 248–249. *See also* Paid leave

Legal aid offices, 422

Legal responsibilities, ethics vs., 235

Legal rights, 241–246

Legal secretaries, 74, 79

Legitimate absence, 190

Leisure time, 40–42
   automobile purchase and, 428
   career success and, 261
   stress and, 224

Letter of resignation, 270

Liabilities, 349

Liability coverage (insurance), 430

Librarian, 79

Licensed practical nurse, 74, 79

Licenses, 183, 352, 353

Lie detector tests, 272

Life, 5–20, 484–494
   career change and, 261
   entrepreneurship and personal, 346
   expectations and, 490–492
   goals for, 50
   health and, 433. *See also* Health
   job and pattern of, 17
   stages of, 485–490
   stress and, 224
   See also Civil responsibility; Courtship;
      Dating; Family (and work);
      Marriage

Life experiences, 23–24, 25
   group relationships and, 120
   poverty and, 479
   and stages of life, 486
   See also Experience

Life insurance, 250–251, 258
   entrepreneurship and, 337, 352

Life skills, 485, 489

Lifeguard, 79

Lifestyle, 6, 8, 14, 450, 485
   career success and, 261
   change in, 485
   health and safety and, 219
   healthy, 433. *See also* Health
   job success and, 187
   occupations and, 56–57
   options for, 57
   planning a, 56–57
   See also Family (and work)

Limited resources, 307

Line of progression, 210, 261

Listening, 15, 67, 78, 105, 107
   co-workers and, 208

job success and, 184
   learning the skill of, 127
   overlapping with other communication
      skills, 104
   responding and, 107
   time spent, 101, 127

Lockheed, 201

Locksmith, 79

Logic, 66

Long-term disability programs, 250, 258,
   443

Long-term liabilities, 349

Love, 451–452, 485, 488–489

Loyalty, 8, 15, 185
   of group, 121
   promotions and, 211, 212

Lunches, 207
   liabilities, 349

M

Machine forming operators, 295, 304

Machine repairers, African American
   women as, 304

Machine tool operator, 38, 295, 304

Machinist, 37, 79, 91
   apprenticeship for, 84
   leisure time of, 41

Macy's, 244

Magazines, and career information, 361

Magnetic resonance imaging (MRI), 297

Mail carriers, 286

Mail fraud, 431

Major Appliance Consumer Action
   Panel, 418

Major medical plans, 247

Management
   control-oriented, 199, 200
   team-oriented, 199–201. *See also*
      Teamwork

Management system, 196

Managers, 15, 41, 79
   job satisfaction and, 263
   projected employment of, 295, 297,
      301
   self-employed, 354
   women as, 286
   writing and, 18
   See also Supervisor

Mandated drug testing, 445

Manual dexterity, 38

Manuals, 183, 192

Manufacturers, offshore, 298, 327

Manufacturing jobs, 73, 77
   automation and, 297
   business incubators and, 354
   decline in, 296, 304

Marital problems, 221

Market, 310, 311
   defined, 310
   demand and supply in, 315, 318, 319
   global economy and, 327–330
   target. *See* Target market

Market economy system, 307–311
   consumers and, 313–316

Market price, 315

Market research, 310, 343

Market value of job, 266

Marketing
   business incubators and, 354
   entrepreneurship and, 343–344
   projected employment in, 301

Marriage, 452–457, 469, 492
   divorce and, 467–468, 469
   dual-career, 454–455

Master craftsman, 83

Materialistic goal, 49

Maternity leave, 292

Mathematics, 18, 77, 79, 478. *See also*
   Arithmetic

McDonald's Hamburger University, 89

McDonnell Douglas, 244

Mechanical engineer, 37

Mechanical orientation, 65, 66

Mechanics, 35, 38, 91
   African American women as, 304
   apprenticeship for maintenance, 84
   leisure time of, 41

Media, 473

Medical assistants, 74

Medical care, 440–444

Medical electronics, 354

Medical insurance, 247
   entrepreneurship and, 337, 352
   See also Health insurance

Medical intern, stress and, 225

Medical records technicians, 74

Memorandum, 112, 113

Mental health, 439–440

Mentoring, 211–212, 301

Mergers, 282, 327

Merit increases/raises, 265, 266

Merit rating, 230

Merit system, 243

Metallurgist, 79

Meterologist, 79

Middle management, 196, 199, 289

Military leave, 248

Military on-the-job training, 90–91

Military service, 475

Millwright, 84

Miners

  decline in employment for, 296

  stress and, 225

Minimum age, 154

Minimum wage, 24, 171–172, 241

  entrepreneurship and, 352

  tips and, 175

Minorities

  earnings of, 289

  fair employment program and, 166

  glass ceiling and, 289–290

Minors, employment of, 152–154

Missionary, 79

Mitochondria, 437

Mommy tract, 460–461

Monetary policy, business cycle and, 320

Monetary system, 317–319, 331

Money, 48

  career and, 6, 14, 56

  education and, 17–18

  entrepreneurship and, 339

  managing, 374–400. *See also* Consumers

  See also Compensation/pay; Earnings; Paycheck

Monitoring, in reading, 114

Monopolies, 238, 315

Monroney sticker, 425

Moonlighting, 346. *See also* Job, holding more than one

Morale, 187

  entrepreneurship and, 346

  job dissatisfaction and, 263

  personality conflicts and, 193

Mortality (infant), 480

Motherhood, 460–461, 462, 469

  teenage, 479

  unmarried, 479

  See also Single parents

Motivation

  job success and, 186

  performance appraisal and, 231

  promotions and, 211

  team advisor and, 201

Motor coordination, 38

Mrs. Fields Incorporated, 336

Muscular endurance, 438

Muscular strength, 438

Music industry, 137

Musical skills, 67

N

NAFTA. *See* North American Free Trade Agreement (NAFTA)

National Association of Manufacturers, 77

National Guards, 248

National Institute for Occupational Safety and Health (NIOSH), 223

National Labor Relations Act (NLRA), 214

National Labor Relations Board (NLRB), 214, 222

National Technological University, 90

Native Americans, 137, 307, 324, 480

Natural resources, 311–312

Negative attitude, 53–54, 179

Negotiable order of withdrawal (NOW), 381

Negotiation, 119, 123–124

  collective bargaining and, 217

  defined, 123

Neighborhood, 23, 24

Net pay, 263, 376

Net worth, 349

Networking, 132, 133–134

Newly hired employees, 148. *See also* Job, beginning a new

Night shift, 255

Nineteenth Amendment, 482

NIOSH. *See* National Institute for Occupational Safety and Health (NIOSH)

Nippon Telegraph, 331

NLRA. *See* National Labor Relations Act (NLRA)

NLRB. *See* National Labor Relations Board (NLRB)

Noncustodial parent, 468

Nonexempt employees, 255

Nonmaterialistic goal, 50

Nontraditional occupations, 285

Nonverbal communication, 105–107

  job interview and, 162

  personal appearance as form of, 188

North American Free Trade Agreement (NAFTA), 327–328

Northrop, 201

NOW. *See* Negotiable order of withdrawal (NOW)

Nuclear medical technologists, 74

Numerical aptitude, 37

Nurse's aides, 295

Nursery worker, 79

Nurses, 35, 37, 74, 79, 91

Nursing technician, 91

Nutrients, 434–435

Nutritional labeling, 405

O

Occupational Health and Safety Act, 221

Occupational Health and Safety Administration (OSHA), 221–223, 353

Occupational Outlook Handbook (OOH), 358–359, 493

Occupational specialization, 325–326

Occupational therapy assistants and aides, 74

Occupational training, 78

Occupational Work Experience (OWE), 366

Occupations

  African American women and, 304

  average earnings for different, 18

  change from production to service, 296–297

  classifications of, 368–370

  computerized information about, 9, 10

  high school subjects related to different, 78, 79

  and identifying interests, 31–33

  information about, 356–372, 493

  leisure time and, 41

  lifestyle and, 56–57

  number of women in different, 286

  personality and, 41

  postsecondary education for, 74

  projected employment in different, 295, 296, 300–301, 304

  projections for employment in, 371

  technology and, 322

work values and, 48

See also specific ones; Career; Job

Oceanographer, 41, 79

Office clerks, 295

Office manager, 79

Offshore operations, 298, 327

Oil-well drillers, 286

OJT. *See* On-the-job training (OJT)

Omnibus Reconciliation Act, 466

On-the-job training (OJT), 89–91, 256

and beginning a new job, 183

job security and, 301

promotions and, 213

OOH. See Occupational Outlook Handbook (OOH)

Open-admissions policy, 92

Open-ended credit, 386

Open-mindedness, promotions and, 211

Operating engineer, 84

Opportunity cost, 310–311

Opticians, 74

Orderlies, 295

Ordinances, 475

Organization

conforming to, 196–198, 213

investment by, 311

Organizational/company image, 109, 160, 188–189, 198

Orientation

personal, 65–68

job, 181–182, 183, 187

OSHA. *See* Occupational Health and Safety Administration (OSHA)

Outdoors, working in, 48, 65

Outpatient care, 247

Outplacement programs, 273–274

Overstated sales claims, 409

Overtime pay, 241, 255, 264

contingent workers and, 293

defined, 376

for entry-level job, 265

OWE. *See* Occupational Work Experience (OWE)

P

Packaging and filling machine operators, 295

Paid leave

accrued, 462

contingent workers and, 293

entrepreneurship and, 337

Family and Medical Leave Act and, 462

See also Sick leave

Painters, 84, 354

Paper industry, 137

Paperhanger, 38

Paraphrasing, 108

Parenting (and work), 458–463

child care and, 463–467

noncustodial, 468

single, 462–463, 468, 469

Parenting leave, 248, 258

Park ranger, 79

Partnership, 340–341

Part-time employment, 7, 41, 170–172

time management and, 8

Part-time job, 366

fringe benefits and, 258

motherhood and, 461

Paternalism, 121

Pay for performance, 278

Pay packages, 265

Paycheck, 14

career success and, 262–265

understanding your, 374–379

See also Compensation/pay; Money; Raises

Payroll specialist, 91

Pediatrician, 463

Pensions, 258

contingent workers and, 293

entrepreneurship and, 337

monetary system and, 318

paycheck and, 377

voluntary buyouts and, 273

People, working with, 33–35, 48, 67, 96

Performance

expectations of, 200

promotions and, 213

success and, 226

Performance-based pay, 278

Performance appraisal, 229–234

asking for a raise during, 267

promotions and, 211

purpose of, 230–231

sample, 233

Performance evaluations, 12

Periodicals, and career information, 361

Perjury, 272

Permit, 352. *See also* Work permit

Perseverance, 78

Personal appearance

job interview and, 160–161, 168, 175

job success and, 185, 187–190, 226

Personal characteristics, 68

defined, 64–65

entrepreneurship and, 339

job satisfaction and, 263

lifestyle options and, 56–57

occupation choice and, 493

See also Orientation, personal

Personal data sheet, 141–142, 163

and beginning a new job, 181

job application form and, 151

Personal fulfillment, 22

Personal hygiene, 185

Personal interests, 9, 33

assessment of, 493

career goals and, 51

See also Career interests; Interests

Personal orientation, 65–68

Personal telephone calls, 185

Personal values, 485. *See also* Values

Personality, 26–31

examining, 27–28

leisure activity according to, 41

perception of, 27

Personality trait, 27–28. *See also* Traits

Personnel department, 162

Personnel specialists, 15, 91

Persuasion, 123–124

Persuasive orientation, 67–68

Pharmacist, 79

Philosophy, 491–492

Photographer, 79

Physical and corrective therapy assistants, 74

Physical characteristics, 23, 27, 28. *See also* Personal appearance

Physical coverage (insurance), 430

Physical demands (of job), 28

Physical education, 79

Physical examination, 247, 443

Physical fitness, 346, 437–439

Physical skills, 65, 66

Physically challenged persons, 148, 166

Physicians, 34, 37, 79, 91, 286

Physics, 79

Picketing, 217

Piecework, 376

Pilot, 91

Pink slip, 273

Pipe fitter, 84

Placement services, 362, 363

Plan of action, 50

Plante & Moran, 461

Plumbers, 79, 84, 353

apprenticeship for, 84

self-employed, 354

Polarization of issues, 476

Police officers

African American women as, 304

stress and, 225

See also Law enforcement

Policies and procedures, 191–192, 200

Political scientist, 79

Politician, 41, 79

Population density, 480

Population growth, 479–480, 482

Positive attitude, 53–54, 56

global economy and, 330

job success and, 178–179, 184

and resigning your job, 269

Postal Inspection Service, 418

Postsecondary education, 73, 74, 75

career guidance and, 366

Potential, 36–39, 182

Poverty thresholds, 478–479

Powerhouse mechanic, 91

Precision instrument repairer, 91

Precision production, 354

Preconceived beliefs, 54–55

Preemployment tests, 156–158

Pregnancy, 292, 304, 449

Pregnancy Discrimination Act, 458–459

Prejudice, 54, 480–481

Premium (insurance), 430

Premium pay, 264

Prepaid legal services, 258

Preprofessional programs, 95

President's Council on Physical Fitness, 438

Price fixing, 238

Private employment agencies, 138–140

Probationary period, 182–183

Problem solving, 59–71

deficiencies in, 77

defined, 60

group relationships and, 119

team advisor and, 201

See also Decision making

Producers, 74

Product liability insurance, 352

Production

business cycle and, 320

consumers and, 313–316

distribution system and, 312–313

factors of, 310–311, 321, 324

free enterprise system and, 308–309

service systems and, 309–313

Production flexibility, 298

Production schedules, 18–19

Productivity

in American steel industry, 331

day care and, 293

days of week and, 331

divorce and, 468

GDP and, 321

job dissatisfaction and, 263

performance appraisal and, 231

technology and, 297, 323, 324

Professional associations

promotions and, 213

publications by, 137, 361

Professional occupations, projected growth in, 301

Professional schools, 94–95

Proficiency tests, 157

Profit

defined, 310

entrepreneurship and, 344, 347

Profit motive, 310

Profit sharing, 265

Profitability, contingent workers and, 293

Profit-and-loss statement, 349–350, 351

Promotional sales, 406–407

Promotions, 11, 12

asking for a raise at time of, 267

career growth and, 261

collective bargaining and, 217

disadvantages of, 213–214

job success and, 186

line of progression and, 210–211

motherhood and, 461

personal appearance and, 187–188

preparing for, 211

seniority and, 211–212

from within, 211, 261

Proofreader, 38, 79

Proofreading (your writing), 111–112

Property tax, 474

Proprietary school, 85

Protectionism, 330

Protocol, 181

Prudent consumer, 402

Psychological characteristics, 27, 28

Psychological tests, 157

Psychologists, 15, 79

Public health, 353

Public service occupations, 84

Punctuality, 185, 190–191

performance appraisal and, 231

See also Tardiness

Q

Quality

day care and product, 293

pay and, 243

promotions and, 213

technology and product, 324, 325

wages and, 325

Quality circles, 105, 106, 201–202

Quantity (of work), 213, 243

Quartermaster, 91

Quitting, 275. *See also* Resigning

R

Racism, 480–481

Radiologic technologists or technicians, 74, 79

Railway Labor Act, 216

Raises, 12, 258, 265–267

job success and, 186

Rancher, 79

Rational style of decision making, 62–64

RDA. *See* U.S. Recommended Daily Allowances (U.S. RDA)

Reading, 15, 18, 96

deficiencies in, 77, 127

grade level of, in workplace, 127

overlapping with other communication skills, 104

skimming and, 116

time spent, 101, 127

See also Grammar; Spelling

Real estate salespeople, 304, 354

Realistic goals, 29, 50

Reasoning skills, 96

Receptionists, 295

Recession, 318, 319, 327

Recognition, 15, 186

Recognition vocabulary, 102–103

Recommendations, 12

Recordkeeping, 241
  budget and, 398
  entrepreneurship and, 350–353

Recreation, 40, 79, 251

Recycling, 312

Reduction in force, 273

Reemployment, 272, 278, 298

Reference groups, 30

References, 143, 269

Referral plans, 409

Registered nurses, 35, 37, 74, 79
  African American women as, 304
  projected employment of, 295
  women as, 286

Registration
  of business, 352, 353
  owner's (of product), 431

Relative earnings, 14

Reliability, 78, 185

Religion, 48

Relocation allowance, 298

Renting, 412–415

Repair services, 354

Repetitive motion, 219

Reporter, 79, 304

Republicans, 474

Resigning, 269–270

Resources, 307, 311–312
  global economy and, 327

Respect, 22, 78
  co-workers and, 208
  interpersonal relationships and, 117
  supervisor and, 184, 187

Respiratory therapists, 74, 79

Responding, 107–108

Responsibility, 78
  assigned, on job, 183
  career planning and, 8, 13
  with equipment, 184
  performance appraisal and, 231
  raises and added, 267
  team-oriented management and, 199
  technology and, 324

Rest periods, 40, 190, 258

Résumés, 141, 143–145, 146
  job interview and, 163
  outplacement programs and, 273

Retail food establishments, 353

Retail trade industry, 296, 336

Retirement, 492
  early, 273
  See also Employee Retirement Income
    Security Act (ERISA)

Revenue, defined, 474

Revenue Act of 1913, 399

Rewards, 15, 16, 263–265

Role models, 47

Roofer, 84

Royal/Dutch Shell, 331

Rules (of employer), 181, 183, 185. See
  also Policies and procedures

Rumors, 207, 208, 275

S

Safety
  driving, 428–429
  personal, 439
  product, 431
  public, 475
  standards, 182, 192
  workplace, 219–225, 353

Salary, 263, 265, 376
  commissions and, 265
  contingent workers and, 293
  for upper management, 265

Salespeople, 15, 37, 67, 79
  African American women as, 304
  entrepreneurship and, 354
  projected employment of, 295, 301
  women as, 286

Satellite universities, 90

Savings account, 382–383, 384

Savings and loan companies, 235, 387

Savings programs, paycheck and, 377

SBA. See Small Business Administration
  (SBA)

SCANS. See Secretary of Labor's
  Commission on Achieving
  Necessary Skills (SCANS)

Scarcity, 307

Scheduled breaks, 190

School
  crime in, 478, 479
  management system of, 196

nonviolent conflict resolution taught
  in, 478
  work compared with, 193
  See also High school

Science, 478

Scientific orientation, 66

Scientist, 79

SCORE. See Service Corps of Retired
  Executives (SCORE)

Second surgical opinion, 247

Secretaries, 74, 79
  earnings for, 266
  reading and, 18
  stress and, 225
  women as, 286

Secretary of Labor's Commission on
  Achieving Necessary Skills
  (SCANS), 96

Security, 48

Security deposit, 413–414

Selective service, 475

Self, 28, 29, 30

Self-acceptance, 28–29

Self-appraisal, 39

Self-concept, 16, 28–31

Self-confidence. See Confidence

Self-control, 65

Self-discipline, 68, 78

Self-employed, 336, 354. See also
  Business ownership;
  Entrepreneurship

Self-esteem, 8, 16, 30–31
  criticism and, 202
  expectations and, 492
  goals and, 50
  substance abuse and, 447
  success and, 87
  values and, 46

Self-expression, 15, 22, 99–128

Self-fulfilling prophecy, 55

Self-image, 28–29, 188

Self-respect, 11, 28–29

Self-understanding, 25, 46

Seminars, 212, 257

Senior managers, 289–290. See also Top
  management

Seniority, 211–212, 243
  contingent workers and, 293

Service charge, 389

Service Corps of Retired Executives
  (SCORE), 354

Service-producing sector, 296–297, 309, 310
  offshore operations in, 298
  SOC system and, 368
Services
  business cycle and, 320
  comparative advantage and, 326
  consumers and, 313–316
  defined, 309
  demand and supply of, 315, 318, 319
  distribution of, 313
  entrepreneurship and, 344–345, 354
  GDP and, 321
  global economy and, 329–330
  occupational specialization and, 325
  public health and, 353
Set-asides, 395
Setup operators, 304
Severance pay, 258, 273, 275
Sex discrimination, 243
Sex-role stereotypes, 285, 287–288
Sexual harassment, 290–292, 304
Sexually transmitted diseases (STDs), 439
Shared leadership, 121
Sheet-metal worker, 79, 84
Sherman Act, 238
Shift differential pay, 264
Shifts, 255
Shipping/receiving specialist, 91
Shults v. Wheaton Glass Co., 243
Sibson & Company, 278
SIC. *See* Standard Industrial Classification (SIC)
Sick leave, 258
  entrepreneurship and, 337
  job dissatisfaction and, 263
  See also Paid leave
Sickness insurance, 258. *See also* Medical insurance
Single parents, 462, 463, 468, 469. *See also* Motherhood, unmarried
Skills, 6
  abilities and, 27
  aptitudes and, 39
  assessment of, 493
  career change and, 261
  career philosophy and, 491
  career planning and, 8, 9
  and changes in economy, 174

  and changes in technology, 174
  communication. *See* Communication
  continuous development of, 282
  deficiencies in, 77, 127
  developing career, 17–19
  entrepreneurship and, 339
  gap between job demands and, 278
  global economy and, 330
  in human relations, 205
  increase in, and job satisfaction, 173
  job interview and, 162
  job security and, 301
  lack of, 18–19
  life, 485, 489
  life experiences and, 25
  market value of, 266
  promotions and, 212–213
  success and, 226
  technology and, 324
  training and, 256
  wages and, 265
  welfare mothers and, 478
Skimming, 116
Skin cancer, 439
Small Business Administration (SBA), 337, 348, 354
Small businesses, 333–355
  antitrust laws and, 316
  fringe benefits and, 258
  opportunity costs and, 311
  See also Business ownership; Entrepreneurship
Small-claims courts, 422
Smoking, 439, 448
SOC. *See* Standard Occupational Classification (SOC)
Sociable orientation, 67
Social anonymity, 480
Social environment, 47
Social programs, 251
Social relationships, 48
Social Security, 245–246
  disability and, 250, 258
  entrepreneurship and, 352
  monetary system and, 318
  paycheck and, 377
Social Security Act, 246
Social Security card/number, 152, 163, 399
Social self, 28–29

Social studies, 79
Social worker, 41, 79, 304
Society
  career philosophy and, 491
  career success and, 261
  problems of, 476–482
Socioeconomic background, 226
Sole proprietorship, 340, 354
Sound financial management, 375
Spatial aptitude, 37
Spatial perception, 66, 67
Speaking, 15, 67, 104–106
  group relationships and, 120
  "I" and "you" statements in, 126
  job success and, 184
  responding and, 107
  time spent, 101, 127
  See also Grammar; Spelling
Spelling, 111, 226
Sportswriter, 79
Staff, 198
Standard Industrial Classification (SIC), 368–369
Standard Occupational Classification (SOC), 368
Standard of living, 14
  leisure time and, 40
  occupational specialization and, 325
  technology and, 325
Start-up (of new business), 347–348
State bureau of labor, 215
State employment agencies, 137–138, 362
State utility commissions, 422
STDs. *See* Sexually transmitted diseases (STDs)
Steel industry, 331
Stenographer, 79, 79
Stereotypes, 54, 285, 287–288
Stock purchase plans, 251
Stockbroker, stress and, 225
Stockholders, 196, 310, 341
Stock-option plans, 265
Stocks
  business cycle and, 320
  paycheck deductions and, 377
Stonemasons, 286
STP, 331
Straight time pay, 264, 265
Strategy, 125

Stress, 181, 185
  and drug and alcohol use, 221
  entrepreneurship and, 346
  as job hazard, 224–225
  promotions and, 211
Strikes, 217
Structural-steel worker, 84
Structured orientation, 68
Submissive people, 10–11
Subordinate, 198, 199, 204, 205
  success of, 226
Success (as student), 80–81
Success (in career/job), 16, 39, 177–193,
    261–268
  confidence and, 87
  defined, 186
  economic system and, 308
  encouragement and, 56
  as entrepreneur, 343–346
  expectations and, 488, 491–492, 493
  factors in, 187–189
  global economy and, 327
  laying groundwork for, 186–192
  life skills and, 485
  policies and procedures and, 192
  preparing for, in changing world of
    work, 300–303
  short- vs. long-term goals and, 51
  of subordinates, 226
  women and, 284
Summarizing (in reading), 115
Summer job, 175
Superior, 198, 237
Supervisor, 41, 196, 198–205
  and beginning a new job, 182–183
  cooperation and, 184
  courtesy to, 187
  criticism from, 204
  dating a, 272
  job success and, 187
  performance appraisal and, 232
  problems with, 204
  promotions and, 211, 213
  recommendation of, 211, 226
  respect and, 184, 187
  self-employed, 354
  writing and, 18
Supply, 315, 318, 319
  GDP and, 321

Surgeon, 38
Surgical insurance, 442
Surgical technologists, 74
Surveyors, 286
Swimming instructor, 79
Switchboard operators, 295
Systems analysts
  African American women as, 304
  increase in employment for, 295, 297

T
Take-home pay, 376
Talents, 23
  career planning and, 10
  wages and, 265
Tangible item, 49–50
Tardiness
  cost of, 193
  job dissatisfaction and, 263
  See also Punctuality
Target markets, 310, 343, 344
Taxes, 258, 399, 474
  business cycle and, 320
  deductions in, 352, 353
  defined, 377
  entrepreneurship and, 350, 351–352
  monetary system and, 318
  paycheck and, 377–378, 399
  as percentage of GDP, 482
  profit-and-loss statement and, 350
Taxi companies, 353
Teachers, 15, 37, 79
  African American women as, 304
  leisure time of, 41
  projected employment of, 295
  stress and, 225
  women as, 286
Teaching skills, 67
Team advisor, 201
Teamwork, 96
  deficiencies in, 77
  interpersonal relationships and, 119
  technology and, 324
Tech Prep, 78, 366, 492, 493
Technical school/training, 17, 85, 362
Technicians, projected job growth for,
    301
Technology, 96, 297, 301–302, 331
  business incubators and, 354
  change and, 322–327

  defined, 322
  entrepreneurship and, 339
  global economy and, 327
  government and, 327
  job skills and changes in, 174
  projected employment and, 304
  women's jobs in, 137
Telecommunications, 354
Telephone communication, 108–110
Telephone installers and repairers, 295
Temperament, 26–27, 28
Temporary employment services,
    139–140, 170
Temporary work, 175, 366
Tenant, 412
Tentative occupations, 47–48
Termination
  coping with, 278
  by discharge. See Discharge
  by layoff. See Layoffs
  major causes of, 278
  by resignation, 269–270
Textile designer, 38
Textile sewing machine operators, 286,
    295
Three o'clock syndrome, 465
3M Corporation, 461
Thrifts plans, 251
Tight-money policy, 320
Timberland Shoes, 331
Time card, 255
Time line, 50–51
Time management, 8, 214
Tips, 175
Title VII, 243–244, 288–289
Tool and die makers, 84, 286
Top management, 196, 199
  projected employment of, 295
  See also Chief executive; Senior
    managers
Trade Act of 1974, 298
Trade associations, 137, 420
  publications by, 361
  promotions and, 213
Trade deficit, 330
Trade journals and magazines, 137
Trade quotas, 330
Trade surplus, 330
Trailer parks, 336

Training, 17–18, 72–97, 256–257
and beginning a new job, 183
career philosophy and, 492
cost of, 96, 193
counseling regarding, 362
entrepreneurship and, 339
occupational level and, 370
partners in, 96
projected job growth and, 300
promotions and, 210, 211
technology and, 324
Trade Act of 1974 and, 298
Training time (for job), 28
Traits, 28
Transcript, 362
Transfer payments, 318
Transportation, Department of, 418
Transportation industry, 220, 445
Travel agent, 79
Truck drivers, 38
earnings for, 266
projected employment of, 295
women as, 286
Trust, 117, 118, 206
Truth in Lending Act, 389, 392
Tuition reimbursement, 256. See also Educational assistance
Tutorial program, 24
Two-plus-two programs, 366
Typist, 35, 79, 295

U

U.S. Armed Forces, 91, 229, 248, 310, 475
U.S. Constitution, 243, 475
U.S. Department of Labor. See Department of Labor
U.S. Employment Service (USES), 137–138
U.S. Office of Consumer Affairs (USOCA), 420, 422
U.S. Office of Education (USOE), 368
U.S. Recommended Daily Allowances (U.S. RDA), 405, 434–435
UFOC. See Uniform Franchise Offering Circular (UFOC)
Umpire, 79
Underemployment, 16
Understanding
interpersonal relationships and, 117, 118

language and, 101–104
See also Knowing yourself
Unemployment, 96, 271–278
business cycle and, 320
education and, 271, 272
entrepreneurship and threat of, 334
reemployment after, 272, 278, 298
Unemployment insurance, 274–275
business cycle and, 320
entrepreneurship and, 352
Uniform Franchise Offering Circular (UFOC), 341
Union Bank of Switzerland, 331
Unions. See Labor unions
Unit price, 405
Universities, 90, 93–95
community colleges and transfer to, 92
defined, 93
promotions and, 213
Upholsterer, 38
Urban area, 301–302
Urban planner, 79
Urbanization, 480, 482
USES. See U.S. Employment Service (USES)
USOCA. See U.S. Office of Consumer Affairs (USOCA)
USOE Career Clusters, 368, 369
USOE. See U.S. Office of Education (USOE)

V

Vacation, 40, 248, 258
entrepreneurship and, 337
motherhood and, 461
unused, and discharge, 275
Valid (preemployment test), 157
Values, 485
career planning and, 8, 9, 10
clarifying, 45–49
communication and, 100
counseling and, 362
decision making and, 61, 62
in Declaration of Independence, 46
defined, 45
goals and, 39, 50
job success and, 186
knowing your, 44–58
life experiences and, 25
poverty and, 479

promotions and, 211
work, 47–48, 186
VDT. See Video display terminal (VDT)
Venture capital, 348
Venture capitalists, 348
Verbal aptitude, 37
Verbal communication, 105. See also Speaking
Verbal skills, 65, 68
Veterinarian, 79
Video display terminal (VDT), 219
Violent crime, 223–224. See also Crime
Vocabulary
job-related, 78
recognition vs. active, 102–103
Vocational training, 17, 28, 85–89
counseling and, 362
promotions and, 213
Voice inflection, 106
Voluntary buyouts, 273
Volunteer work, 7, 24, 41, 172, 366
Voting, 472–474, 482

W

W-4 tax form, 377, 378
Wage and hour laws, 241–242
FLSA and, 258
See also Minimum wage; Workday
Wages, 263, 265, 376
business cycle and, 320
contingent workers and, 293
discrimination in, 288–289
offshore sites and, 298
reduction in, 298
See also Earnings; Paycheck
Waiters, 34, 295
Waitresses, 295
Wall Street Journal, 330
Warranty, 427–428, 431
Waterloo Transmission, Inc., 250
Weight loss, 499
Welfare system, 479
Wellness lifestyle, 437
Wellness programs, 248
Whistle blowing, 236–237, 244
Withdrawal, 126
Women
African American, 304
business ownership by, 354
changing role of, 283–288

as consumers, 431

earnings of men vs., 286, 289

Equal Pay Act and, 243

fair employment program and, 166

foot problems of, 449

glass ceiling and, 289–290

holding more than one job, 399

journals on jobs for, 137

marriage and, 453–455, 469

Nineteenth Amendment and, 482

occupations and, 286, 304

in work force, 282

Word-processing operator, 38, 79, 295

Words

communication and, 100, 101–103

listening and, 107

vague, 105

Work

attitude toward, 56

changing opportunities in, 294–304

child care and. *See* Child care

economics and, 307–332

family and, 450–470. *See also* Family; Marriage

ideas about, 13–14

lifestyle and. *See* Life; Lifestyle

meaningful, 39

reasons for, 12–13

school compared with, 193

self-expression in, 15

technology and, 324–325. *See also* Technology

variety in, 16

Work environment, 48, 65

Work ethic, 210

Work permit, 152, 163

Work schedule, 253–256

entrepreneurship and, 334

motherhood and, 460–461

See also Flexible work schedules

Work task, 15–16

Work values, 47–48, 186. *See also* Values

Workaholics, 467

Workday, eight-hour, 215

Worker Trait Groups, 28

Worker's compensation, 215, 244–245, 272, 443

entrepreneurship and, 352

Workers, entrepreneurs compared with other, 339

Working capital, 347–348

Working outdoors, 48

Working with data, 33–35

Working with (your) hands, 48, 65

Working with information, 66

Working with machines, 48

Working with people, 33–35, 48, 67

Working with things, 33–35

"Working years," 489

Workplace

changes in, 281–305

changing role of women in, 283–288

projections regarding, 371

SIC system and, 369

statistics regarding, 371

See also Health, workplace; Safety, workplace

Workplace flexibility, 461. *See also* Flexibility

Workshops, 257

Workweek, average, 40

productivity and, 331

technology and, 325

Writer, professional (author), 79

Writing, 15, 18, 67, 96, 110–114

business, 112–114

group relationships and, 120

job success and, 184

overlapping with other communication skills, 104

time spent, 101, 127

vocabulary and, 103

See also Grammar; Spelling

X

Xerox Corporation, 278

Xerox Learning Center, 89

Y

Yellow pages, 133

Z

Zoning laws, 345

Credits